The Homeowner's Complete
Tree & Shrub Handbook

The Homeowner's Complete TREE & SHRUB Handbook

The Essential Guide to Choosing, Planting, and Maintaining Perfect Landscape Plants

Penelope O'Sullivan

PHOTOGRAPHY BY **KAREN BUSSOLINI**

Storey Publishing

part 1

A Practical Plan for Landscape Beauty

WE BEGIN OUR JOURNEY by tackling garden planning, including how to select healthy trees for your particular landscape. Finding the right plants for your site is crucial to your plan's success. As you look in depth at the landscape function of trees and shrubs, you will begin to understand how to use them to fulfill your family's unique needs. In addition to their practical attributes, of course, woody plants offer beauty. Study the various plant lists in these chapters to help you make informed decisions, both practical and aesthetic, at the nursery or garden center.

CHAPTER 1

A MATTER OF DESIGN

BEFORE YOU START BUYING AND PLANTING trees and shrubs, you need to decide what you want them to do for you. Whether you live in a brand new house or want to improve an established landscape, planning clarifies your goals and keeps you from making costly mistakes. You'll dodge planting trees and shrubs that are out of place in your garden, expensive to buy, and time consuming to install.

Getting Personal Is Okay

MANY FACTORS go into landscaping your house. Childhood memories often figure prominently in grownup desires. The crooked branches and waxy fragrant blossoms of saucer magnolias, for example, make me long for family and friends in St. Louis, where I was born. In my New Hampshire garden, therefore, I grow not one, but a collection of magnolias that link me to my past. You may feel the same way about roses, cherry blossoms, or the messy fruit of a mulberry tree. Take time to remember your past and focus on what makes you happy today. Even if particular beloved trees or shrubs can't grow in your present climate or conditions, you can use them to inspire a color scheme or uncover a yearning for shade or fragrance, which you can satisfy with other, more suitable plants.

Understanding your desires, family needs, and the physical advantages and disadvantages of your property helps you decide what to do. It's also the best way to make your yard useful, comfortable, attractive, and easy to maintain. For example, if you want to install a swimming pool in a few years, plan to phase it in when you can afford it without neglecting the rest of your landscape. With a solid plan, you can arrange plants and garden structures to enhance your house, please your family, and simplify your life.

Keeping Up with the Times

Remember that landscapes are in constant flux. Trees and shrubs grow, change, and eventually die. A sunny, new landscape may become partly or fully shaded after 20 or 25 years. Life spans of different plants vary. While the natural garden life of a southern magnolia (*Magnolia grandiflora*) is about 80 years, a Sargent cherry (*Prunus sargentii*) lives only about 20 years. Modify your landscape for its changing needs. When choosing plants, keep in mind their mature size and shape, so they can grow *into* their space rather than outgrow their location. New landscapes may look sparse, especially when you stage the installation over several years. If bare space bothers you, fill it with ferns, flowers, or ornamental grasses that are easy to remove. Trees and shrubs will grow, and lushness will return to the garden.

▲ **The nostalgia effect.** The scents and colors of certain trees, like this saucer magnolia (*Magnolia* x *soulangeana*), can evoke vivid memories of other times and places.

Principles of Design

THE PRINCIPLES of design work, whether you're designing a room in your home or your garden. They are not inviolable laws. Once you master them, you may break them if you like and enjoy the consequences.

Disparate Parts Equal a Convincing Whole

Unity is the basic element of landscape design. In a unified landscape, the disparate parts fit together to create a convincing whole that meets your family's needs and expresses coherence through harmonious plant choices and construction materials that suit the site. Making curvilinear beds around randomly planted mature trees and shrubs in close proximity highlights their visual relationship.

Repetition of specific plants, shapes, textures, colors, or combinations throughout the garden can bring it together. You can build a path and a patio from the same construction material, or use a planting pattern or a particular curve more than once.

Sequence unifies the garden by connecting one area to the next in an orderly and consistent way. In other words, a sequence joins objects through space.

◀ **Repetition.** Repeating the dense, light-absorbing texture of dark green conifer foliage helps unify the collection of woodland plants on either side of this garden path. The repetition ends where the cultivated path starts to merge into the wild.

Getting the Right Balance

Balance deals with the relative stability of what you see. Your viewpoint — where you are when you are observing something — affects how you perceive the visual weight of plants and objects around you. Balanced views feel permanent and secure. Two kinds of balance exist: formal and informal. In the landscape, formal balance is symmetrical, meaning the design on one side of a central axis mirrors that on the other. Symmetry looks manmade and suggests that humans can control nature.

Asymmetrical balance, on the other hand, is more elusive. It looks informal, curving, and naturalistic. Asymmetry balances different masses on either side of an imaginary vertical line. In other words, what you see on either side of the axis appears equal but not identical.

▲ **Balance and symmetry.** *Near* symmetry is more dynamic than *pure* symmetry and thus perfect for gardens, which change over time. Here, the centerline divides two almost identical halves, which vary by the presence of a few different plants and garden furniture versus an array of terracotta urns.

TREE OR SHRUB?

According to Alex L. Shigo, former chief scientist at the United States Forest Service, both trees and shrubs are woody perennials. The former, such as this maple (*Acer griseum*) is usually single stemmed and more than 9 feet tall; the latter, like the pieris (*Pieris* 'Brouwer's Beauty') that surrounds the tree, is multi-stemmed and less than 9 feet high. Woody plants compartmentalize their wounds by forming boundaries around their injuries. These boundaries save the plant's vital systems, walling off and resisting the spread of infections. Woody plants produce new cells in new places, in contrast with animals, which replace dead cells.

▲ **Scale.** Choose plants that are in proportion to the size of your home.

Everything Is Relative

Scale defines relationships. It's the size of landscape elements relative to you, your house, neighboring homes, and the sky. Trees and shrubs should be big enough to make you feel enclosed and secure, but not so big that they overwhelm you with their size. Huge old trees near a cottage engulf the building, whereas tiny trees and shrubs around a large suburban home look silly and make the house appear to float.

Spicing Things Up

Accents add zest to your design. You can create accents in many ways. Just as changing the slope of the land adds variety to a design, a tall, spiky shrub brings pause to a border of low, rounded ones. You can also create year-round color emphasis by including a gold-needled conifer in a dark green evergreen screen.

A **focal point** is stronger than an accent. Focal points break up a visual sequence by drawing your attention to a standout plant or object and giving you a place to rest your gaze. A striking flower-filled container framed by an arbor and set at the end of a path can lure a garden visitor along a walkway from start to finish. Likewise, a well-placed bench can also highlight particular garden areas. If you paint the bench bold scarlet or turquoise, flank it with potted plants, and set it at the far end of the main garden axis running from your deck to a distant sitting area, the bench becomes the focal point of the entire design. While one focal point per view can work wonders in a garden plan, multiple focal points per view create overload and confusion.

◀ **Focal point.** An armillary sundial serves as a focal point, drawing you down a path flanked by upright junipers (*Juniperus scopulorum* 'Wichita Blue') and pleached seckel pears (*Pyrus*) through an open gate.

The Big Four: Line, Form, Texture, and Color

Line, form, texture, and color are design characteristics that flesh out the essentials and help unify your plan. They are also an important part of your garden-making toolbox. Along with the mature height, width, and growth cycles of chosen plants, each plays a role in planning agreeable gardens. When used without understanding, however, they lead to garden chaos.

Line. I think of line as the muscle of design because of the movement it creates. Line directs the gaze forward on a path or moves it around a corner to the next bend. Line can also stop the gaze at a focal point. Line determines speed. You can fly down the straight center path of a beech allée or spend time wandering and exploring the curved paths in a naturalistic woodland.

Form defines mass within an outline, whereas line determines shape. For example,

▲ **Line and movement.** Walking along this twisting woodland path ensures you'll take time to admire the flowering azaleas and rhododendrons on either side.

Fraser fir *(Abies fraseri)* has a conelike form. Grouping trees and shrubs with similar or varied forms helps balance landscape masses seen from specific points of view.

◄ **Form.** From this viewpoint, the arrangement of masses on either side of the border creates a pleasing asymmetry.

▲ **Texture.** The juxtaposition of fine-textured trees at left and medium-textured conifers on the right brings drama to this visually rich garden, dominated by varying contrasts of light and shade.

Texture, which ranges from fine to coarse, gives your garden personality. The texture of deciduous plants often changes from summer to winter with the presence or absence of leaves, while the texture of evergreens remains the same year round. For instance, bald cypress *(Taxodium distichum)* has a fine texture in leaf and a medium to medium-fine texture after leaf drop. Little-leaf box-wood *(Buxus microphylla)* has fine-textured foliage, while the leaves of golden catalpa *(Catalpa bignonioides* 'Aurea') are coarse.

Consider two side-by-side shrubs of the same shape, size, and color. One is fine-textured and the other coarse. The shrub with fine-texture tends to recede into the background, whereas the coarse-textured shrub jumps forward. The play of light and shade is much more active and evident on coarse-textured plants than on plants where fine foliage evenly disperses light.

Inserting a coarse-textured plant in a group of fine- or medium-textured plants makes a visual accent or pause. You can use texture to alter perspective. By placing bold-leafed shrubs such as rosebay rhododendron in the foreground of a garden scene and fine-textured shrubs like yew in the back, you can make a garden look longer, because the background appears to recede. If fine-foliaged shrubs are in front and coarse ones in back, the garden will shrink. *Note:* Bold textures look best when used sparingly, since their overuse creates restlessness and visual exhaustion.

Color sums up a garden's emotional content. It also has an effect on garden perspective. Cool colors like blue, blue-green, and violet-blue recede and feel restful, while warm colors — red, orange, yellow, for instance — come forward with excitement and pizzazz.

Most of us care more about color in the garden than anything else. Why? The previous example shows that it has a powerful psychological effect. People who use color to its best advantage in the landscape know how to create a pleasing experience. They avoid the tedium that comes from using one identical plant throughout. They also dodge the bedlam that occurs when disparate forms, colors, and textures appear willy-nilly without an underlying sense of balance. They use color to bring order and beauty to the landscape.

◀ **Color.** Yellow Tiger Eyes sumac (*Rhus typhina* 'Bailtiger') is the focal point of this vivid berm planting, which screens a small backyard from the street. The glowing yellow foliage pops in contrast with the blackish red coleus below, which acts like a deep shadowy foil.

COLOR THEORY 101

To understand color relationships, you can refer to a color wheel based on red, yellow, and blue. A basic color circle contains these three primary hues, from which all other colors are mixed. More complicated diagrams show many colors with their accompanying shades and tints. A *shade* is a color mixed with black, while a *tint* is a color mixed with white.

Analogous colors. A simple way to create a harmonious color scheme is to use two or three colors that are side by side on the color wheel (analogous), such as 2 and 3. Limiting yourself to two or three hues also makes planning easier. For example, a bed of witch hazels with brick red, coppery orange, and butter yellow blooms looks stunning in the late winter or early spring landscape. Opposite colors like red and green or violet and yellow have maximum contrast but also look stable because they carry equal visual impact. Think of holly with its vivid red berries set against a leafy backdrop of rich deep green.

Color triads. Triangles of three colors equally spaced on a color wheel (color triads) are also attractive and harmonious. Red, blue, and yellow, the primary colors, form the best-known color triad, while orange, green, and violet make a secondary triad (for example, 2, 4, and 6 on the color wheel). Depending upon the number of colors depicted, the choice of color triads is wide. Remember that color changes throughout the seasons. Leaves, fruits, and flowers all come into play when choosing plants for color in your garden.

What a Difference a Climate Makes

▲ **Pacific Northwest.** Foggy vapors envelop the mountains, seen from sub-alpine meadows on Hurricane Ridge in Washington's Olympic National Park.

A New Plant Palette

Jason, a college student and summer gardener, moved from New Hampshire to Arizona two years ago. When he left, he took with him an impressive array of gardening skills learned in the northern New England climate. While Jason was glad that his gardening skills would serve him well anywhere in the country, he realized that he'd have to learn a new palette of plants and construction materials. To grasp the wild beauty of the Southwest, he hiked in the desert and explored the region's natural and cultural resources to acclimate himself to his totally new environment.

IN THE UNITED STATES, various climates affect soil composition, creating regional differences in growing conditions. I live in New Hampshire, where winters are long and cold with abundant precipitation in the form of rain, snow, and ice. Summers are warm and humid, and the growing season is about four months long. Woodland and forests of oak, maple, hemlock, and pine prevail, and the soil is acid and rocky. With some variation, this climate occurs across northern New England and around the Great Lakes.

Southern New England, the Mid-Atlantic, and the midwestern Corn Belt also have cold winters but extremely humid and hot summers. Precipitation is usually plentiful. Soils contain abundant clay, which hangs onto soil nutrients and makes soils fertile. Originally comprised of hardwood forests and tall grass prairies, the region is now full of farms and cities. Gardens tend to be lush because of ample moisture, fertile soil, and a long growing season.

Winters in the Southeast are mild and summers are long, hot, and humid. The plentiful rain, especially in summer, can wash away soil nutrients, so you may have to feed your garden to keep it healthy. Southern gardens may experience rapid plant growth due to abundant moisture and a long growing season. Native habitats include southern pine forests, bald cypress groves in swamplands, and the subtropical broadleaf-evergreen forest with its array of shrubs, little palms, herbaceous plants, and ferns on the forest floor.

Alkaline soils, light precipitation, and variable temperatures characterize the semi-arid climate of the Great Plains, which separates the desert of the Southwest from more humid areas to the east. With adequate irrigation, organic matter, and fertilization, you can garden on this land.

The Southwest has long hot summers and mild short winters. The region receives little rain, and what it gets evaporates quickly in the heat. Soils are alkaline with elevated levels of salts and little organic matter. The plants that grow best are succulents like cactus, with its thick leaves that store water, and shrubs like tap-rooted sagebrush, which has hairy, gray-green leaves that prevent excessive water loss from heat and wind.

California's coastal and central climates recall the Mediterranean region, with long arid summers and temperate winters when much of the rainfall occurs. Low shrubs and small trees native to the area grow mostly in winter and endure the hot, dry summer because of their stout bark, long taproots, and moisture-retentive rubbery leaves.

▲ **South.** Live oak (*Quercus virginiana*), with its gnarly, moss-draped limbs and leathery, evergreen leaves, is abundant on the sandy coasts and moist, rich woodlands of the lower Coastal Plain.

The Pacific Northwest runs along the mountainous western coast of northern California, Oregon, and Washington. This temperate marine climate has relatively cool summers and mild, wet, foggy winters. Huge conifer forests are native to the region. Soils are acid, but because of copious rainfall and, where necessary, applications of lime and fertilizer, gardens can experience lavish growth.

◄ **Northeast.** Spring produces a show of flowers and tender young leaves on red maple, sugar maple, and ash in the Eastern hardwood forest.

Habitat as Part of Design

▼ **In touch with nature.** A row of young white pines *(Pinus strobus)* forms a backdrop for a small fountain and a shade-tolerant border of ferns, bugbane *(Actaea simplex),* and lamb's ear *(Stachys byzantina).* The planting eases the transition from manicured lawn to uncultivated woods.

IN THE WILD, plants occur in particular habitats (natural environments) and on specific terrains. Although your land may not be pristine, you can begin to understand the kinds of trees and shrubs that will thrive on it if you observe carefully. No matter how big or small your lot, get to know it well by walking from end to end and corner to corner in all kinds of weather and every season. Are there low-lying areas or wet spots where the lawn squishes beneath your feet after spring thaw or heavy rain? Is your house in sheltering shady woodland with deep humus-rich soil, or does it stand exposed on a sunny bluff?

Is your gardening space on a rooftop, where trees and shrubs have to grow in soil-filled containers? Each place is individual and may contain areas with different soil conditions, wind exposure, and amounts of moisture and sunlight, which you can exploit in your garden design. Thus, if your manmade garden resembles natural woodland, it will likely draw wildlife that thrives in similar woodland areas.

Observing how trees and shrubs grow in nature can help you choose the right plants for your garden. In the wild, groups of plants with similar growth requirements form vari-

ous plant communities. Like neighborhoods, these communities change over time as the area in which they grow matures and develops. After a succession of plant associations, a climax community forms when the plants are in balance with the environment. Depending upon where you live, some common American habitats include forest, woodland, edge or transitional, meadow, and wetlands.

Forested land has more than 60 percent tree canopy, referring to the top layer of large trees shading the plants beneath them and thus affecting the microclimate on the ground. The understory (the plant layer between the tallest forest trees and the ground-level plants) comprises the leafy branches of shrubs, small trees, and young canopy trees. Herbaceous plants such as ferns, mosses, grasses, sedges, and wildflowers make up the ground layer, along with low shrubby plants. The forest floor contains topsoil, decomposing organic debris, and tiny creatures key to forest growth.

Woodland, on the other hand, has 20 to 60 percent tree canopy. Beneath this lies a rich understory of small trees and bushes, below which are wildflowers, woody ground covers, decaying logs, and heaved rocks under which tiny organisms thrive. Many beautiful gardens originate in woodland and flow into the manmade landscape.

Edges, the transitional area between two different communities, often link forests or woodlands to home landscapes. Much wildlife lives along these edges, including the very species that disrupt our gardens. Squirrels and white-tailed deer aren't picky about food and thrive in edgy environments, along with crows, robins, and sparrows. You may see them foraging in your yard, especially if your lot borders a park or strip of woods, or if your landscape includes wide shrub borders and beds of ornamental grasses.

Wetlands. If your property has low spots and areas with poor drainage, you may have a type of wetlands. Periodic flooding, underground springs, surface water, or a shallow water table may result in the development of small ponds, swamps, and marshes. *Swamps* are wooded places with trees and shrubs growing in muck. Swamp vegetation varies from red maples and swamp azaleas in the northern United States to bald cypress with kneelike roots above the water in the South. *Marshes*, on the other hand, tend to be treeless and exposed with reeds, cattails, and rushes thriving partly submerged in water.

WHEN IT'S GOOD TO MICROMANAGE

In addition to macroclimates, you also need to consider microclimates — those variations from the surrounding areas that are unique to your land. Do you have an area enclosed by a south-facing wall, where you can grow plants from a warmer region; an exposed shady bed on the north side of your house, perfect for shade- and wind-tolerant bayberry and high-bush blueberry; or a soil depression where frost settles and only the hardiest plants can survive? These spots need special attention because their climate (their *microclimate*) differs from other garden areas.

A Sense of Place

When you assess your property for a sense of place, consider how you can accent its local character. Study the world of nature around you. Understanding your region's soil, climate, growing conditions, and native materials helps inform your choices when you landscape your particular site.

If boulders emerge from the rocky soil around your home, turn the ledge into a rock garden studded with dwarf conifers. Perhaps you have a drystone wall that has survived a century of neglect. Restoring it could mature a country home and join it to the site. Besides arming yourself with books and taking courses, discover your area's distinct character by hiking or riding through undeveloped land, since development often wipes out natural variations in favor of conformity.

Look critically at landscapes you admire. Chances are, the best ones have this sense of place because they relate to their surroundings and look like they belong there. In Santa Fe, New Mexico, an adobe-walled garden would be a studied response to local materials and precedents. Conversely, this same garden would look odd in northern New Hampshire, where granite rules. In addition to using and repeating some plants and materials native to your area, you can also increase the sense of place by enhancing a distant natural view.

◀ **Natural by design.** Careful observation of nature inspired this lavish, spring-blooming rock garden, where rhododendrons *keiskei* (yellow) (**A**) and 'Mary Fleming' (two-toned peachy flowers) (**B**) grow with 'Avalanche' birch (*Betula*) (**C**) and pink-flowered Chinese redbud (*Cercis chinensis*) (**D**) in the distance.

▲ **A layered look.** This woodland garden mimics nature's design, with layers of vegetation under a canopy of tall trees. Shrubs and small trees form the middle tier, while shade-loving perennials hug the ground. Rhododendrons 'Boule de Neige' (**A**) and 'Ken Janeck' (**B**), underplanted with barrenworts (*Epimedium*) (**C**) and primula (*Primula sieboldii*) (**D**), edge the garden and join it with the sunnier landscape near the house.

DOING YOUR HOMEWORK

- Explore wild areas near your home and think about the plants and landforms you see. In many states, nature centers sponsor guided walks or hikes.
- Visit local gardens to observe plants and materials.
- Ask neighbors about the trees and shrubs that do best in their gardens.
- Research plants and building materials native to your region.
- Search out sources for local building materials.
- Ask nursery staff about the best trees and shrubs for your region. Many regions have award programs for the best-performing local plants.

▲ **A complementary theme.** An informal rock garden with small-scale plants welcomes visitors to this clapboard house, bordered by woods and water in southern Maine.

BEFORE SITING and choosing trees and shrubs, look at your home's style, size, and orientation on the lot. Some shrubs, for example, like boxwood *(Buxus)* and yew *(Taxus)* lend themselves to formal treatment. They're often used near a house, where the landscape continues the geometry and architecture of the building. Other shrubs, particularly deciduous suckering plants like forsythia, kerria, and arrowwood viburnum *(V. dentatum),* suit naturalistic plantings and look better viewed from afar.

Be objective. How does your home relate to your neighbor's property? Perhaps the view from your front porch is the parking area for your neighbors' boat or the place they store old cars. If so, you can block the view with evergreens or distract your attention to the neighbors by planting a border of evergreen and deciduous shrubs and trees. If you live in a detached house on a narrow urban lot, it may feel like your neighbors live on top of you. The best privacy solution for your yard may be fastigiate (columnar) trees or a tall fence planted with woody vines.

If your landscape is overgrown, you can remove old plants and start from scratch or renew the landscape slowly over a period of years. You can reduce the size of rhododen-drons, for instance, by cutting the whole plant back at once or by pruning it over a period of three to four years so the effect won't be drastic and noticeable.

◄ **Privacy — naturally.** Closely planted columnar conifers serve a dual purpose: they give swimmers some privacy and screen off ugly pool utilities from view.

Making a Plan

A GARDEN PLAN shows you the ups and downs of your property. It puts your ideas on paper, so you can see if they work. Planning clarifies what to highlight and what you should improve. You don't need to make a professional-quality plan. Even a series of simple sketches can help you realize the garden of your dreams.

1. Start with a base plan, showing some fundamental data about your lot and your home. Outline the lot on graph paper. Label known dimensions. Using a compass, mark North, South, East, and West. If you can copy the information from a boundary survey or construction plan of your property, it will save you measuring and drawing time.

2. If there's no survey, measure the lot's perimeter with a distance roller, landscaper's tape measure, or laser-measuring device, all available at a hardware store. Note measurements on your sketch. Write distances to the nearest whole number.

3. Mark location of utility lines, well, and septic system, since these affect the placement of landscape features.

4. Observe the views from key rooms inside the house and mark their range on the plan.

5. Indicate with arrows the direction of prevailing winds and the angle of the sun at different times of year.

Make several copies of your plan so you can test different ideas later in the process. On one plan, show existing gardens, trees, large shrubs, outdoor spigots, swing sets, and the like. As you study your site, note on the sketch anything that concerns you or that you may want to change. For instance, if the view of your neighbor's garage bothers you, write that down on the site survey, so you can improve that when making your final plan.

As you progress on your garden-making journey, jot ideas on fresh copies of the basic plan. For example, do you need privacy? A windbreak? Summer shade? Outline areas where these conditions are desirable, noting what you need. Would you like to let more light onto your property? You may want to move small trees and shrubs, limb some up, take out others, and set out new plants where necessary. Keep in mind the principles of design as you begin to plan.

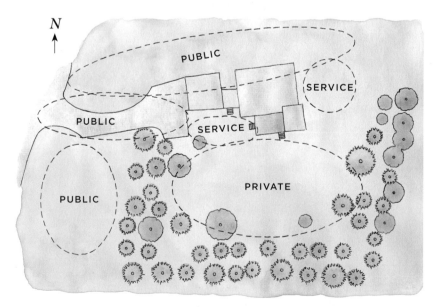

▲ **Split your landscape** into three main areas — public area (usually the front yard), private area (typically the backyard), and service area (usually at the back or side of the house) — by circling and labeling them on the plan.

Dividing the Landscape

The public area is the façade that you show to the world. It includes the house, the entry path, the front door or area visible from the street, the driveway, lampposts, lawn, and foundation or other plantings. Your house is the key element, and any landscaping should enhance it. To show off your house to advantage, look at the house as a series of geometrical shapes (probably squares and rectangles) and balance those masses with trees and shrubs in your plan.

Depending upon the style and shape of your house, the balance can be symmetrical or asymmetrical. In symmetrical balance, objects on one side of a centerline mirror those on the other. Symmetry, used extensively in historical landscapes, gives your property a formal look. Asymmetrical balance looks informal and is harder to achieve. When done successfully, however, it can produce a pleasing, naturalistic effect.

Plan to make the hardscape (the non-plant landscape) elements big enough for comfort. Instead of building a skinny 3-foot-wide entry path, make a 5-foot-wide walkway that accommodates two average-size people walking shoulder to shoulder to the front door. A 3-foot-wide path meandering through a woodland garden behind the house is fine.

In the public area, devise plantings that will blend your house into its surroundings, keeping plants in proportion to the size of the house. In general, trees and shrubs off the corner of the house should stay below two-thirds of the height from the eaves to the ground; while plants near the entrance maintain a lower profile, with a mature height no more than one-quarter of the height from the eaves to the ground. Plants with rounded shapes make a more effective transition from house to surrounding environment than plants with columnar or pyramidal shapes.

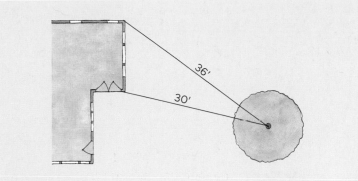

That's not to say you can't use a tall skinny accent shrub in an entry garden, but rounded plants should predominate. (See chapter 2 and part 3 for specific plants.)

The private area is where you live when you're outdoors. It's usually, but not always, in the backyard and includes decks, patios, swimming pools, gazebos, swing sets, sandboxes, and whatever else suits the leisure needs of your family. Your private area extends the inside of your house outdoors and may incorporate hedges, fences, walls, and shrub borders that make your living space more private. A privacy planting doesn't have to be tall. It just needs to distract your attention from the space beyond it and give a psychological feeling of enclosure.

The service area contains the utilitarian aspects of your landscape. Items like sheds, garbage cans, and compost bins belong there. Shrubs with edible fruit not integrated into the ornamental landscape belong in the service area, where you can plant them in rows for easy harvesting.

Path of the sun. Watch the sun travel in your yard through the seasons. On June 21, the summer solstice and longest day of the year, the sun's path is at its highest in the northern sky. The shortest day is December 21, the winter solstice, when the sun's path is lowest in the southern sky. Twelve-hour days occur when the sun moves exactly east to west on the spring and fall equinoxes.

To Start You Thinking

Changing your landscape with trees and shrubs works best when you know exactly what you'd like them to do for you. The best way to find that out is to analyze your family's needs and interests and think about what makes your property unique. By asking yourself and your family some easy questions, you can determine what will work best for you. Repeat this procedure when your needs change. For example, after your children have gone to college or moved away from home, you may want to change play areas into shady beds or places to entertain.

YOUR FEELINGS

What surroundings made you feel happy as a child? Answer using all your senses!

How do you feel about your present home?

What pleases you about the land you own?

Are there aspects of your house or lot you'd like to emphasize — or hide? Why?

Does something about your setting bother you?

What would you like to do about it?

YOUR ENVIRONMENT

What is the sun's path across your lot during different times of the year?

Where do you have shade and how deep is it in different areas and at different times of the year?

Do you have clay, silt, or sandy soil? (See page 34.)

Is your soil moist, wet, or dry? (If your soil is poorly drained, you may also have areas of standing water on your land or a wet basement.)

What is the prevailing direction of summer breezes? Where does the winter wind come from? Look at your weathervane for a week in winter, or make your own by attaching a cloth strip to a stick and seeing what direction the cloth blows.

Which parts of your lot are exposed to winter gales? To glaring sun?

Are there any high spots, steep slopes, or depressions on your land?

THE RELATIONSHIP OF YOUR HOUSE TO THE LAND

Are there natural beauty spots in your landscape, such as striking trees, unusual boulders, or a pond? How can you draw attention to them?

Do you have a borrowed view? (A borrowed view is an attractive scene visible but distant from your property.) How can you frame it?

Where are the best views from inside to outside your house?

How are the views from your front door, picture window, sliding glass doors, French doors, deck, and/or kitchen window? Can you improve them?

Do you have ugly views (for example, your neighbor's garbage cans, a junkyard, or a nearby apartment complex)?

Do you have privacy where you want it, or would some screening plants help?

How functional is your landscape?

How do public, private, and service areas flow into each other?

Is the entry to your house defined, inviting, and well lit?

Is your house landscaped for safety? Are there overgrown shrubs near the front door? Is the front path flat, wide, and easily shoveled, if necessary?

Is there visual separation between the service and private areas? (Services include trash storage, pet areas, and a tool shed or shelf.)

Would you like your private area set off from the rest of the yard?

Do you have enough parking near the service area?

Do you want to watch your children playing in the yard while you stand in the kitchen?

Is your landscape easy to maintain?

Are there problems with snow removal, ice buildup, or flooding?

How do you remove snow from your walks and driveway? Shovel? Blower? Plough?

Do you have decaying trees or dead branches on your land?

Do your trees need thinning to allow in more sunlight? Pruning for shape?

Are there any problems with existing lawns, shrubs, or gardens?

▲ **Kids' play areas.** This sugar maple makes a sturdy support for a treehouse, as would strong-branched beech, oak, fir, or hemlock.

▲ **Privacy.** Oak-leaf hydrangea's big leaves partly screen this eating nook from the house for a sense of psychological seclusion.

▲ **Architectural style**. A heavy mass of juniper, dwarf Alberta spruce, false cypress, and heather on the left balances a covered doorway on the right façade of this traditional clapboard house.

YOUR NEEDS AND PREFERENCES

How long do you plan to live in this house?

How great is your interest in plants and gardening?

Will you maintain the garden yourself or will you need outside help?

How great is your tolerance for wildness?

Are you interested in plantings to attract songbirds and hummingbirds?

What are your other interests (for instance, attracting butterflies)?

Do you have outdoor hobbies, such as croquet, badminton, and vegetable gardening, to consider in planning?

If you have pets, what do they need (for instance, a perimeter wall, a fence, an electric fence, winter weather protection)?

Do you need to consider children's interests (swing set, children's garden, goalie net, baseball field)?

What is the architectural style of your house (for instance, colonial, Japanese, prairie, Georgian, Federal, Victorian)?

Would you like your landscape to harmonize with the architectural style of your house?

What landscape style do you prefer (for instance, colonial, romantic, Japanese, naturalistic, contemporary, whimsical, pastoral)?

When are you most likely to enjoy the garden? Think about times of day, days of the week, and weeks of the year.

What times of the year are you typically out of town (holidays, vacation home, time share)?

What sort of paving surfaces do you prefer (brick, concrete, gravel, stone, or imitation brick and stone)?

What are your favorite flowers and flower colors?

Do you have a favorite type of tree? Is it deciduous or evergreen?

List particular trees, shrubs, flowers, and ground covers that you admire.

WHICH OF THE FOLLOWING WOULD YOU LIKE TO DESIGN OR REDESIGN?

- ☐ Car access, turnaround, driveway
- ☐ Garage
- ☐ Parking area (number of cars)
- ☐ Front walk, entryway, handicap access
- ☐ Foundation plantings
- ☐ Terraces
- ☐ Pergola, arbor, or other sun shade
- ☐ Deck and/or patio
- ☐ Screened porch
- ☐ Tool shed, woodshed, or other small building
- ☐ Barn
- ☐ Dog run
- ☐ Orchard
- ☐ Greenhouse
- ☐ Wood storage
- ☐ Boat storage
- ☐ Solar installation
- ☐ Swimming pool
- ☐ Hot tub

- ☐ Fountain, waterfall, or other water feature
- ☐ Tennis court
- ☐ Fire pit or outdoor kitchen
- ☐ Council ring
- ☐ Lawn
- ☐ Paths
- ☐ Prairie
- ☐ Meadow
- ☐ Windbreak
- ☐ Hedges
- ☐ Ornamental shrubs, such as roses, hydrangeas, dwarf conifers, etc.
- ☐ Perennial garden
- ☐ Cutting garden
- ☐ Vegetable garden
- ☐ Cold frame
- ☐ Herb garden
- ☐ Rock garden
- ☐ Wildflower garden

After you've thought about these questions and taken some notes, go back to your plan. See how you can incorporate plants and ideas that matter to you in your design. The following chapters will help you accomplish your aims.

▶ **Development creativity.** Who says big lawns are a must in the suburbs? Most of this sloping front yard contains tough woody groundcovers, including *Microbiota decussata* and *Cotoneaster* 'Little Gem'. Redbud (*Cercis*) shades the porch.

2

THE
CHOICE
IS YOURS

IF YOU KEEP THE ESSENCE OF YOUR SITE IN mind when choosing plants, your garden will thrive. This chapter suggests some dos and don'ts of picking plants for your specific landscape conditions. Before making a final choice, however, check the encyclopedia of trees and shrubs in part 3 of the book to make sure they will suit your climate and your site.

Criteria for Choosing Trees and Shrubs

MANY FACTORS go into deciding which plant is right for your garden, including hardiness, size, growth rate, seasonal interest, plant use, light and soil, the time you have to give your plants, pest- and disease-resistance, and personal preferences.

Plant hardiness is probably the first consideration. Who wants to waste money on trees and shrubs that can't withstand average temperatures in your region?

Height and width are also crucial. Buying plants that are too big for the allotted space means you'll spend a lot of time pruning them to keep them little. When plants are too small for a given area, they upset the design's scale, making the landscape feel exposed and open to view. Until your trees and shrubs reach maturity, you can intersperse them with flowers, ground covers, or ornamental grasses to fill any unattractive gaps.

Growth rate. Knowing a plant's growth rate helps determine the speed at which a planting will mature and thus fill its allotted space. Fast-growing plants may need frequent pruning to keep their growth in check, but a slow-growing plant may never need to be pruned. If you need quick shade near the house, for example, you can plant a fast-growing shade tree near a slow-growing, but choice, specimen. Later, when the fast grower declines and the slower-growing tree casts adequate shade, you can cut down the former and give the latter room to expand. Giving plants less than ideal conditions may slow their growth rate. A tree that likes partial shade and rich, moist soil suffers when jammed into a dry, sunny spot, where it vies for water and nutrients with others.

▲ **Right plant, right place.** Skinny Italian cypress suit the design and the fast drainage on a steep, Seattle hillside path.

► **Interest over the long haul.** This planting of evergreen *Chamaecyparis obtusa* 'Nana Gracilis' and white-barked *Betula utilis* var. *jacquemontii,* seen here in late November, looks good in every season.

Take a Second Look

A newly married couple had a tree planted by the previous owners off the southwest corner of their deck. The deck is about 15 feet from the ground, while the tree, planted on the downward slope away from the deck, also stands about 15 feet high. The owners saw no benefit to the tree, which was too small to shade their hot, sunny deck. When they asked me to get rid of it, however, I pointed out that it was a tulip tree *(Liriodendron tulipifera),* a fast-growing specimen native to most of the eastern United States but uncommon in southeastern New Hampshire. It has big, lobed leaves; yellow fall color; a powerful, upright habit; and lovely, large, orange-and-chartreuse flowers carried high in the tree in late spring. Because their tree was too young to bloom and to shade their hot, sunny deck, the couple found it easy to pass by the tree, unaware that their patience would soon pay off in welcome shade and tuliplike blooms seen from the deck. Although this tree, which grows to more than 100 feet tall, may one day be too big for the scale of their house, it can function on the site for decades.

Seasonal interest refers to fragrance and form as well as color and texture. Evergreen or deciduous foliage; colorful or textured bark; and fragrant, edible, and attractive fruits or flowers can enhance woody ornamentals at different times of year. Bloom time matters when you are coordinating plants in beds and borders. For a lavish display, plant trees and shrubs that bloom at the same time or extend flowering for months by choosing plants with successive periods of bloom.

Garden usage affects the plants you choose. For example, to screen an ugly view from the family room, you can make an impenetrable visual barrier with dense, tall conifers branched from top to bottom. Or mix evergreen and deciduous shrubs that grow about six feet high for a less imposing, friendlier screen that creates a psychological, not physical, wall.

Light is a condition of growth crucial to a plant's well being. Some trees and shrubs prefer full sun, while others like dappled or deep shade. Many sun-loving plants tolerate a little shade, but given too much, they grow feeble stretching toward the sunlight in an attempt to survive. Shade-lovers can withstand some gentle morning sun but not the glare of strong afternoon sunlight, which causes withering.

Soil, too, determines whether a plant lives or dies. While many plants thrive in moist, well-drained garden soil, others need special conditions such as a high or low pH; swampy conditions or fast-draining sandy or rocky soils; or lean soils or soils with high fertility.

Time. Easy-to-grow plants suit busy people with packed schedules. These folks don't have time for constant pruning, spraying, or babying of any kind. They want maximum beauty for minimum effort. Trees and shrubs requiring higher maintenance may still be worth growing for foliage, flowers, or fruits. Unless you have the time to care for them or the money to pay someone else to do the job, however, include only a few of these in your landscape.

Pest and disease resistance add to a plant's desirability. Tougher plants require less maintenance and need less frequent replacing. However, some gardeners consider some problem-prone plants like flowering cherries worth the trouble, just for their lush spring floral display.

Personal preference plays an important part in gardening. My husband and I are plant collectors. He goes gaga for beeches, while I crave viburnums and magnolias.

Doing the Numbers

The number of trees and shrubs in a garden plan depends on many factors, such as the size of your lot, the plants you choose and their mature sizes, the size and style of your house, and your individual gardens. It's best to keep your design simple, unifying it by keeping the number of different species to a minimum, especially if your lot is small. If you're designing in a naturalistic style, remember that odd-numbered groups (3, 5, 7, or more) of similar plants look more natural than even numbers.

▼ **The numbers game.** In this suburban driveway garden, grouped perennials balance bigger, bolder woody plants like *Hydrangea anomala* ssp. *petiolaris* (**A**); *Deutzia gracilis* 'Nikko' (**B**) at the intersection of driveway and path; and *Syringa reticulata* 'Ivory Silk' (**C**) by the back deck.

Sizing Things Up

How long you expect to live in your house may influence how much time and money you're willing to spend on landscaping. And both time and money come into play when considering the size of the plants you choose. Young, inexpensive trees may look like sticks for years before filling out and

coming into their own. On the other hand, hefty plants that look good when you plant them may turn out over time to be quite a bit bigger than you bargained for. Don't purchase jumbo plants to fill an immediate gap unless money's no object and you're buying big in March to prepare for an outdoor fete in July. For most of us, patience pays. Choose the right plant for the site. Selecting a small young plant that will grow into a space saves future time spent pruning a giant or money for its replacement.

Although it's easy for me to say, "Choose plants that complement the scale of your property" and "Don't plant big shade trees too close to your house," the reality is that people choose big trees and shrubs because they like them, they grew up with them, or they don't want to remove them from their property when building or buying a house. I love a particular pair of "marriage trees" (sugar maples) that are planted side by side in front of a late eighteenth-century farmhouse on an Exeter, New Hampshire, back road. By my standards, the farmer planted the huge-trunk trees too close to the house and too close together, yet they look fine, an authentic reminder of the day they were planted and the bond between the folks who planted them. If you plant trees too big for your site, enjoy them for all the reasons you planted them, but know that you or your descendents may have to deal with them some day. Still, plant growth rate is important to consider when planning a garden. If you have a tiny garden, small or slow-growing trees and shrubs may work best for you, and big trees may quickly look out of place.

◄ **Old friends.** Large, old trees close to a house provide welcome shade, but they may need to be removed if they become diseased or encroach too much on the roof or siding.

Landscaping for the Long Haul

Whether you create your own plan or hire a landscape designer, you can phase in a design installation over several years. Phasing spreads out your costs, making high-quality results achievable at a reasonable annual price. Have a plan, however, before you start buying plants. Even if you want to landscape the front yard this year and the backyard five years down the road, having a comprehensive plan ensures unity, so that different areas work together to accomplish your landscape goals.

A simple way to do a landscape in stages is to begin the first year with the overall plan. Study your property, decide what you need, and how you'll go about achieving your landscape goals. In the first or second year, concentrate on the public area, moving or removing existing plants that are sick, overgrown, or in the wrong place. Continue working on the entry, installing hardscape elements such as a front walk and any secondary paths. Do this early in the process, since you may need to adjust your plans to accommodate glitches like a buried oil tank that you hadn't known about when sketching your design. (Yup, it once happened to me.) Then, put in front-yard trees and shrubs to complete the skeleton of your entry. If time and money allow, put in decorative beds and borders and perennial ground covers. Over the next few years, construct walls, walks, a deck, and a patio around the rest of the house. Then add trees, shrubs, and finally herbaceous perennials to those spots. When we moved into our home, I drew up a rough plan for the property and we're still putting ideas from that plan into effect.

▶ **First things first.** Begin your landscaping by establishing the hardscape and plantings at your front entry.

TREES AS CELEBRATIONS

In eighteenth century America, a husband and wife sometimes planted a pair of trees side by side in front of their house to mark the occasion of their marriage. Marriage trees embodied the promise of married life, two individuals made one in a loving, productive partnership. Trees symbolized eternity — the Biblical tree of life — connecting past and future generations. Couples also planted trees to honor the birth of a child.

Right Plant, Right Place

Nature's Classroom

Neil Jorgensen, a landscape designer specializing in woodland design, became my friend and mentor when he was teaching a Radcliffe Seminars landscape design course in Cambridge, Massachusetts. Every week we hiked the woods, fields, and mountains of Massachusetts, looking at native ecosystems and seeing which plants grow together in forests, mountainsides, bogs, and meadows. Neil showed us shady residential landscapes where nature had been selectively preserved and how, with careful attention to natural features, to draw out and expand the mysterious beauty of shade.

He pointed out the vertical structure of forests, in which sunlight decreases from top to bottom, and how the reduced light affects what grows in each layer, from the tallest oak or pine to low bunchberry (*Cornus canadensis*) and tiny pipsissewa (*Chimaphila umbellata*). The fairly open pine and oak woods created a dry, warm environment flecked with sunlight. The heavier shade of sugar maples made the air below cool and moist. The northern exposure of a small glacial hollow was so dark that nothing grew beneath the hemlock canopy.

Garden magic happens when nature and design unite in a harmonious marriage. Nature alone can be splendid beyond words but may not suit your needs for outdoor living. Design alone is pragmatic, a way to make a useful, attractive setting for your home. When the two conjoin, however, the result is enchanting. A happy arrangement of trees, shrubs, and herbaceous plants casts a spell on a mundane design and brings it to life.

Combining nature and design makes good sense. There's no better way to give your landscape a sense of place than by working in the trees, shrubs, and building materials native to your region. That doesn't mean that all your plants need to be natives. Far from it. But your garden plants can take a cue from nature and look like they belong where they grow. For example, though hostas originate in Asia, they make a striking shade-tolerant ground cover under woodland garden trees. Likewise, Japanese maples lend refinement to a woodsy setting when grown as an understory tree. On the following pages, I offer trees and shrubs to suit your environment, to meet your special needs, and to surround you with beauty all year long.

A Shady Deal

If you're lucky enough to own a home on a wooded lot, the first thing to do is look around you, as we did in our landscape seminar (see Nature's Classroom at left). Identify the trees, shrubs, and herbaceous plants on the site. Really study your trees. Look at the outlines of their trunks and examine them for healthy growth. In the woods, you may find straight trees, fallen trees serving as wildlife habitat, multi-trunk trees arising from old stumps, and trees growing at acute angles to the ground. In the area closest to the house or along a woodland path, remove trees if they are unsafe or their silhouettes do not please you.

Here's an example of what you might be dealing with: At a suburban home surrounded by hemlocks in southern New Hampshire, we tidied up the entry for a tamer, but still naturalized, woodsy look. Arborists removed brush and dead, rotting, and unattractive trees in front of the house, plus some of the wild deciduous trees that had sprung up along the woods' edge. Over the years, branches had broken on the hemlock trunks, making perches for birds, but giving the entry an unkempt look. The arborists removed these dead and dying limbs from the remaining trees.

Now, the hemlocks' black trunks, straight and tall like cathedral pillars, look impressive from the front windows of the house. Although the front of the lot is still shady, enough light penetrates the landscape for an informal, naturalistic entry garden to thrive near the house. The new plantings include star magnolia *(Magnolia stellata)*, an upright Japanese maple *(Acer palmatum)* with brilliant red-orange fall color, existing red-vein enkianthus *(E. campanulatus)*, existing rhododendron, and Taunton yew *(Taxus × media* 'Tauntonii'). Long-leafed Bethlehem sage *(Pulmonaria longifolia)* underplants the yews and edges the main path.

A Cautionary Tale

Some of your discoveries may not be pleasant ones. A family I know bought a rundown but architecturally significant house, extensively landscaped in the mid-twentieth century. Among the plantings were masses of burning bush *(Euonymus alata)*, a rounded shrub with a two-week explosion of red fall color. By the time I saw the landscape in the twenty-first century, burning bush had seeded into the surrounding two or three acres of woodland, forming an ugly understory of woody trunks and branches straggling toward the light. If you live in the East, perhaps this plant has overrun your woods. If you don't recognize the shrub by its leaves, look for its ridged stems. If you think you have it, clip a branch and take it to a nearby Cooperative Extension for identification. Note on your site plan to remove unwanted plants when you clean up the brush and tie colorful plastic tape on any trees and shrubs you want to remove.

Euonymus alatus

A Matter of Degree

Degrees of shade exist in nature. Factors affecting shade patterns include the presence or absence of leaves on deciduous trees and the sun's position in the sky at various times of day and diverse times of year. Determine how much light and shade your property receives by observing each area at different times of day throughout the year. Jot your observations in a notebook and, if you like, on your plan.

Are there any spots between the house and garage or under a tall, dense tree that stay shady all day? Is the sunny lot you bought 30 years ago now shaded not just by trees on your land but by those of your neighbors? If those trees are mostly deciduous, what's shady in summer may be sunny in winter.

SHADES OF DARKNESS

Deep or full shade: 0–2 hours of direct sun. The floor of a dense hemlock woods on a north-facing slope is in deep shade, with little to nothing growing beneath the trees.

Partial shade: 2–6 hours of direct sunlight. Most plants for partial shade prefer gentle morning sunlight. The hot, intense sunlight of afternoon can scorch shade-loving plants.

Dappled or light shade: sometimes all day. This type of partial shade occurs under open trees such as birch and honey locust that create moving patterns of light and shade on the ground, and is ideal for many plants. Plants such as dogwood, witch hazel, and spicebush thrive in these conditions and are useful to bridge the gap between sunny open areas and woods.

▲ **Partial shade.** A canopy of limbed-up white pines (*Pinus strobus*) lets in enough light for Japanese andromeda (*Pieris japonica*) to thrive along this woodland walk.

Trees and Shrubs for Shady Places

FULL SHADE

Variegated five-leaf aralia[1]	*Eleutherococcus sieboldianus* 'Variegatus'
Japanese holly	*Ilex crenata*
Mountain laurel[2]	*Kalmia latifolia*
Leucothoe[3]	*Leucothoe* species
Rosebay rhododendron[3]	*Rhododendron maximum*
Catawba rhododendron[3]	*Rhododendron catawbiense*
Fragrant sarcococca	*Sarcococca hookeriana* var. *humilis*
Hemlock[3]	*Tsuga* species
Low-bush blueberry[4]	*Vaccinium angustifolium*
Maple-leaf viburnum	*Viburnum acerifolium*
Wayfaring tree	*Viburnum alnifolium*
Yellowroot	*Xanthorhiza simplicissima*

PARTIAL SHADE

Japanese maple	*Acer palmatum*
Serviceberry	*Amelanchier* species
Sweet azalea	*Azalea arborescens*
Boxwood[5]	*Buxus* species
Redbud	*Cercis canadensis*
Hinoki false cypress	*Chamaecyparis obtusa*
Fothergilla	*Fothergilla* species
Smooth hydrangea	*Hydrangea arborescens*
Sweet bay	*Magnolia virginiana*
Firethorn[4]	*Pyracantha coccinea*
Korean rhododendron	*Rhododendron mucronulatum*
Royal azalea	*Rhododendron schlippenbachii*

DAPPLED OR LIGHT SHADE

Red chokeberry[4]	*Aronia arbutifolia*
Summersweet[5]	*Clethra alnifolia*
Dogwood	*Cornus* species
Enkianthus	*Enkianthus* species
Witch hazel	*Hamamelis* species
Inkberry	*Ilex glabra*
American holly	*Ilex opaca*
Spicebush	*Lindera benzoin*
Mahonia[5]	*Mahonia* species
Andromeda	*Pieris* species
Yew[5]	*Taxus* species
Arborvitae[5]	*Thuja* species

[1]Partial to full shade [2]Better flowering with more light [3]Light to full shade
[4]More fruit with more light [5]Light to partial shade

Cornus controversa 'Variegata'

Fothergilla major

Enkianthus perulatus

▲ **Cypresses for swampy areas.** Bald cypress (*Taxodium distichum* var. *distichum,* center) and pond cypress (*T. distichum* 'Nutans', right) flourish in swamps and ponds.

Planting in Wet Soils

When faced with heavy clay soils that drain poorly, you have choices. In wet, low-lying places, you can truck in enough soil to make a berm (a mound of soil), which you can use for planting. Near the berm, you can excavate the lowest spot for a pond to capture the runoff with an overflow pipe or channel it into a nearby stream, drain, or moving body of water. To tackle this big a project, you should probably ask a landscaper or professional designer for help. In small areas, on the other hand, you may be able to improve soil aeration by spreading compost or organic mulch on the soil. By improving drainage, you can boost root growth and cultivate a wider variety of trees.

The most efficient approach, however, is to plant trees that suit the site. Many ornamental trees and shrubs, from fragrant sweetbay magnolia and graceful weeping willow to peeling river birch and giant dawn redwood, thrive with wet feet. By planting these in wet areas, you increase your chance for success.

▲ **A tolerant choice.** Black tupelo (*Nyssa sylvatica*) grows best in moist, deep, well-drained soil but can adjust to wet conditions.

ESTIMATING DRAINAGE: THE HOLE TEST

To test how well your soil drains, dig a hole roughly 1 foot deep, then fill with water. If the water level decreases by an inch an hour, the soil is well drained. A faster rate means the soil is dry and sandy, while a slower rate means the soil is damp and likely full of clay.

Deciduous Trees for Wet Soils

Red maple	*Acer rubrum*
Downy serviceberry	*Amelanchier arborea*
Shadblow serviceberry	*Amelanchier canadensis*
River birch	*Betula nigra*
American hornbeam	*Carpinus caroliniana*
Hackberry	*Celtis occidentalis*
Thornless honey locust	*Gleditsia triacanthos* f. *inermis*
Tamarack	*Larix laricina*
Sweet gum	*Liquidambar styraciflua*
Dawn redwood	*Metasequoia glyptostroboides*
Sour gum	*Nyssa sylvatica*
Swamp white oak	*Quercus bicolor*
Pin oak	*Quercus palustris*
Willow oak	*Quercus phellos*
Coral bark willow	*Salix alba*
Weeping willow	*Salix babylonica*
Bald cypress	*Taxodium distichum*

Evergreen Trees for Wet Soils

American holly	*Ilex opaca*
Southern magnolia	*Magnolia grandiflora*
Sweetbay magnolia (deciduous to evergreen)	*Magnolia virginiana*
Live oak	*Quercus virginiana*
Eastern arborvitae	*Thuja occidentalis*

Deciduous Shrubs for Wet Soils

Chokeberry	*Aronia* species
Carolina allspice	*Calycanthus floridus*
Buttonbush	*Cephalanthus occidentalis*
Summersweet	*Clethra alnifolia*
Tatarian dogwood	*Cornus alba*
Red osier dogwood	*Cornus sericea*
Winterberry	*Ilex verticillata*
Sweetspire	*Itea virginica*
Spicebush	*Lindera benzoin*
Bayberry	*Myrica pensylvanica*
Swamp azalea	*Rhododendron viscosum*
Elderberry	*Sambucus* species
High-bush blueberry	*Vaccinium corymbosum*
Arrowwood viburnum	*Viburnum dentatum*
American cranberry bush viburnum	*Viburnum trilobum*

Evergreen Shrubs for Wet Soils

Bog rosemary	*Andromeda polifolia*
Inkberry	*Ilex glabra*
Sheep laurel	*Kalmia angustifolia*
Bog laurel	*Kalmia polifolia*
Rosebay rhododendron	*Rhododendron maximum*
Eastern arborvitae	*Thuja occidentalis*

Aronia arbutifolia　　**Ilex verticillata** 'Winter Gold'　　**Calycanthus floridus** 'Athens'

Planting in Dry Soils

You can't beat a sunny site in moist, well-drained soil for planting a specimen tree or shrub. Given enough space and soil nutrients, most trees and shrubs will reach their full glory in these conditions. If, however, you have plenty of sun but lack abundant moisture, you can plant trees that tolerate dry conditions. Because water is scarce in some parts of the country, the latter approach is often the best. Trees with extra-deep or extra-wide root systems are able to absorb more moisture from the soil. Other adaptations occur with the leaves of trees and shrubs. Look for leaves that are fuzzy silver or gray-green, fat succulent leaves, and leaves with waxy coatings giving them a dull blue or frosty cast. All these variations increase the leaf's ability to obtain and hold moisture in the plant.

▲ **Not choosy.** *Ginkgo biloba* 'Princeton Sentry', which turns yellow in fall, grows on both dry, rocky slopes and in moist, well-drained soil.

Deciduous Trees for Dry Soils

Siberian pea shrub	*Caragana arborescens*
Hackberry	*Celtis occidentalis*
Maidenhair tree	*Ginkgo biloba*
Thornless honey locust	*Gleditsia triacanthos* f. *inermis*
Golden raintree	*Koelreuteria paniculata*
Sweet gum	*Liquidambar styraciflua*
London plane tree	*Platanus* × *hispanica*
Hardy orange	*Poncirus trifoliata*
Flowering plum	*Prunus cerasifera*
Northern red oak	*Quercus rubra*
Chinese scholar tree	*Sophora japonica*
Little-leaf linden	*Tilia cordata*
Chinese elm	*Ulmus parvifolia*
Japanese zelkova	*Zelkova serrata*

Evergreen Trees for Dry Soils

Spotted laurel	*Aucuba japonica*
Atlas cedar	*Cedrus libani* subsp. *atlantica*
Deodar cedar	*Cedrus deodora*
Chinese holly	*Ilex cornuta*
Chinese juniper	*Juniperus chinensis*
Eastern red cedar	*Juniperus virginiana*
Scotch pine	*Pinus sylvestris*
Japanese black pine	*Pinus thunbergii*
Live oak	*Quercus virginiana*

Deciduous & Evergreen Shrubs for Dry Soils

Sweetfern	*Comptonia peregrina*
Beautybush	*Kolkwitzia amabilis*
Bayberry	*Myrica pensylvanica*
Oriental photinia	*Photinia villosa*
Ninebark	*Physocarpus opulifolius*
Shrubby cinquefoil	*Potentilla fruticosa*
Sumac	*Rhus* species
Spirea	*Spiraea* species
Low-bush blueberry	*Vaccinium angustifolium*
Arrowwood viburnum	*Viburnum dentatum*
Blackhaw	*Viburnum prunifolium*
Juniper	*Juniperus* species

Rhus aromatica 'Grow-Low'

Platanus x hispanica 'Columbia'

Aucuba japonica 'Gold Dust'

Koelreuteria paniculata

Physocarpus opulifolius 'Monlo' (Diabolo)

Ilex cornuta 'Burfordii Nana'

Caragana arborescens 'Walker'

Plants with Salt Tolerance

Salt tolerance brings to mind different situations. Some soils, particularly those west of the Mississippi River, are alkaline and high in salts. Salty mist also penetrates the foliage and soil of coastal gardens. When salt spray comes into contact with evergreens, it can turn the foliage brown. It can also kill the twigs and buds of deciduous trees and shrubs. In northern and mountainous areas, where salting streets is a common winter practice, splashing salt may also damage the leaves and root zone of nearby trees and shrubs. No matter what the source, super-salty conditions can keep essential elements out of the reach of the plants that need them.

Other conditions exacerbate the damage salt can do. For instance, in low spots with compacted heavy soils, water cannot drain the soluble salts from the soil below the root zones of plants. The salt accumulates on the soil surface like a white scab. Too much fertilizer or manure products also increase soil salts. The way to successfully remove them is by leaching them out with a deep watering. Six inches of water leaches about 50 percent of the salt from the soil, unless the soil is particularly heavy or compacted and the water cannot drain. Improving drainage with organic mulches or by tilling in non-manure-based organic compost improves your ability to decrease the soil's salt content.

Evergreen Salt-Tolerant Shrubs

Wintergreen barberry	*Berberis julianae*
Bearberry cotoneaster	*Cotoneaster dammeri*
Little-leaf cotoneaster	*Cotoneaster microphyllus*
Inkberry	*Ilex glabra*
Shore juniper	*Juniperus conferta*
Creeping juniper	*Juniperus horizontalis*
Oleander	*Nerium oleander*
Colorado spruce	*Picea pungens*
Swiss mountain pine	*Pinus mugo*
Japanese mock orange	*Pittosporum tobira*
Firethorn	*Pyracantha coccinea*
Yucca	*Yucca* species

Deciduous Salt-Tolerant Shrubs

Bearberry	*Arctostaphylos uva-ursi*
Red chokeberry	*Aronia arbutifolia*
Groundsel bush	*Baccharis halimifolia*
Siberian pea shrub	*Caragana arborescens*
California lilac	*Ceanothus* hybrids
Buttonbush	*Cephalanthus occidentalis*
Rock rose	*Cistus* hybrids
Summersweet	*Clethra alnifolia*
Sweetfern	*Comptonia peregrina*
Cotoneaster	*Cotoneaster* species
Forsythia	*Forsythia* species
Rose of Sharon	*Hibiscus syriacus*
Sea buckthorn	*Hippophae rhamnoides*
Hydrangea	*Hydrangea* species
Winterberry	*Ilex verticillata*
Sweetspire	*Itea virginica*
Beautybush	*Kolkwitzia amabilis*
Bayberry	*Myrica pensylvanica*
Sweet mock orange	*Philadelphus coronarius*
Shrubby cinquefoil	*Potentilla fruticosa*
Beach plum	*Prunus maritima*
Royal azalea	*Rhododendron schlippenbachii*
Staghorn sumac	*Rhus typhina*
Alpine currant	*Ribes alpinum*
Beach rose	*Rosa rugosa*
Virginia rose	*Rosa virginiana*
Rosemary	*Rosmarinus* species
Spirea	*Spiraea* species
Lilac	*Syringa* species
Wall germander	*Teucrium chamaedrys*
High-bush blueberry	*Vaccinium corymbosum*
Arrowwood viburnum	*Viburnum dentatum*
Blackhaw	*Viburnum prunifolium*
Chaste tree	*Vitex agnus-castus*

Deciduous Salt-Tolerant Trees

Trident maple	*Acer buergerianum*
Hedge maple	*Acer campestre*
Amur maple	*Acer tataricum* subsp. *ginnala*
Horse chestnut	*Aesculus hippocastanum*
Yellow birch	*Betula allegh

eniensis* |
Northern catalpa	*Catalpa speciosa*
Hackberry	*Celtis* species
Persimmon	*Diospyros virginiana*
White ash	*Fraxinus americana*
Maidenhair tree	*Ginkgo biloba*
Thornless honey locust	*Gleditsia triacanthos* f. *inermis*
Black walnut	*Juglans nigra*
Golden raintree	*Koelreuteria paniculata*
Sweet gum	*Liquidambar styraciflua*
Mulberry	*Morus* species
Sour gum, tupelo	*Nyssa sylvatica*
London plane tree	*Platanus* × *hispanica*
Poplar	*Populus* species
Sargent cherry	*Prunus sargentii*
White oak	*Quercus alba*
Red oak	*Quercus rubra*
Black locust	*Robinia pseudoacacia*
Chinese scholar tree	*Sophora japonica*
Japanese tree lilac	*Syringa reticulata*
Bald cypress	*Taxodium distichum*

Evergreen Salt-Tolerant Trees

Chinese juniper	*Juniperus chinensis*
Eastern red cedar	*Juniperus virginiana*
Southern magnolia	*Magnolia grandiflora*
Live oak	*Quercus virginiana*
White spruce	*Picea glauca*
Colorado spruce	*Picea pungens*
Swiss mountain pine	*Pinus mugo*
Japanese black pine	*Pinus thunbergii*
Arborvitae	*Thuja* species

Thuja occidentalis 'Sunkist'

Magnolia grandiflora

Robinia pseudoacacia 'Frisia'

Made to Order

Trees and shrubs fill many roles in landscape design. In addition to forming the skeleton of the landscape and giving it structure and mass, they alter climate, promote a feeling of security and seclusion, create mood and character, direct foot traffic, and draw you outdoors. Two of their main roles are to create privacy and screen out ugliness. While walls and fences can also fulfill the latter functions, living barriers reduce noise, protect from wind, make habitat for birds and other wildlife, and add richness and color to the landscape.

Creating a Living Windbreak

Modifying climate can be especially useful if your house is in an exposed location with cold winter winds. A well-sited windbreak of trees and shrubs filters the wind, slows the wind's speed, and deflects it from the house, thus reducing your heating bill by as much as 25 percent. The taller your windbreak, the greater the area it can shield. In the Midwest, a windbreak to the north and west of a house redirects the prevailing winds of winter.

Spruce *(Picea)*, yew *(Taxus)*, Douglas fir *(Abies),* and other dense-needled evergreen conifers branched to the ground impede wind flow all year. Arborvitae and Eastern red cedar are also useful for windbreaks. Place tall trees toward the area to be protected and progressively shorter layers of trees and

◀ **Energy-savers.** Dense, low-branched evergreens can deflect wind, thus lowering energy bills when grown on the windward side of your house.

shrubs on the windward side to ensure maximum wind protection and the multitude of branches necessary at ground level to break up wind force. In leaf, deciduous trees and shrubs make good summer windbreaks. Bare branches can also deflect some winter wind.

The National Renewable Energy Laboratory advises planting windbreaks at a distance from your house of two to five times the planting's mature height. On the sheltered side, a windbreak alters wind strength for a distance of at least ten times its height, while on the other side it reduces the wind's intensity two to five times the barrier's height.

A cautionary note: Cold air may collect near the windward base of a windbreak and result in frost damage unless you grow suitably hardy plants on that side. Leave about 15 feet between trees and shrub layers and 20 feet or more between tree rows. If you plant closely, the windbreak will start to be effective at a younger age, but you will have to thin the plants as it matures and individuals need more space. Where space is limited and winds whip, stick to a couple of densely planted rows of arborvitae or Eastern red cedar, depending upon your site requirements.

If you have to have a gate in your windbreak, line it with shrubs on either side or angle it about 45 degrees to the wind. If you don't, you may create a wind tunnel allowing wind to speed through the opening.

AN INSULATION FACTOR

Planting low evergreen shrubs that mature about 12 to 18 inches away from your foundation may also help you save on your heating bill because the shrubs insulate the base of your house. They block icy winds and drifting snow from blowing around the foundation and trap warmer air on the sheltered side. Evergreen shrubs or a combination of evergreen and deciduous shrubs can also create a year-round, insulating air cushion that helps regulate the loss of cooled indoor air in summer. Keep side branches at least a foot from your home and top branches below your windows, particularly on the south side, where they could prevent low winter sun from streaming into your house.

▼ **Four-row windbreak.** Place your windbreak at a distance from your house of two to five times the planting's mature height.

It's Too Darn Hot

Well-placed deciduous trees and shrubs can also influence climate by providing a house with cooling shade in summer and bright sun in winter.

In summer, the sun is high in the sky and days are long because the sun's path across the sky is at its longest. By planting a large deciduous shade tree or group of trees southwest of the house, you can reduce the heat of glaring afternoon summer sun in your house. Tall, leafy canopies absorb sunlight, thus cooling your roof and protecting your house from the heat of a sunny summer afternoon.

Days are short in winter, on the other hand, because the sun is lower in the sky, shortening its path across the sky. In winter, the bare trees allow warming sunlight to stream into the house through the windows. Just as deciduous trees can cool and shade a deck in summer, they can also reduce energy costs by cooling your home in summer and keeping it warm in winter.

In winter, sun penetrates the branches of the leafless trees and warms the inside of the house. To amplify winter sunlight in cool climates, plant trees on the west side of your house, not the south. Keeping the south side tree-free allows maximum light to reach indoors, since even bare branches can obstruct the sun. In the Northeast, useful shade trees include red or sugar maple, American or European beech, and pin, red, or white oak; in the Southeast, tulip tree, bald cypress, Japanese zelkova, red maple, and sawtooth or willow oak are possibilities; in the West, try gingko, lacebark elm, zelkova, 'Autumn Blaze' maple, and little-leaf linden.

◀ **Just what you need.** Deciduous trees shade and cool the house in summer, but allow welcome light into the house in winter.

If you can't use your deck because the sun is too hot for your comfort and safety, think about adding deciduous shade trees for their cooling effect. They can shield you from the strong rays of the midday and late afternoon summer sun. In winter, the leaves are off the trees and the sunlight can once again warm and brighten your house. If you need summer shade, the first step is to track the movement of the sun across your property to see where trees will be most effective. Planting a group of trees such as dogwoods, birches, or mid-sized maples ensures that the canopies will intermingle as the trees develop, thus making more shade.

▲ **Relaxing shade.** Small flowering trees like the Japanese tree lilac (*Syringa reticulata*) at the left are perfect to plant near low decks and patios. Fragrant flowers, an attractive form, and deciduous leaves bring shade and seasonal interest but keep the tree from obstructing winter light.

A Shady Deck

My friends Debbie and Neil have a deck overlooking the backyard on the hot, sunny south side of their house. When their kids were small and needed kicking space, the empty yard suited their needs. The children, however, grew up. Deb and Neil wanted the deck for entertaining, but the intense sunlight made it too hot to use. They asked me for ideas about making the area more usable. We came up with a plan that added shade trees to the south and west sides of the house, including a bed of fast-growing, closely planted river birches on a slope near the deck. Behind the bed at the top of the slope, we planted a slow-growing, large-canopied yellowwood for dense future shade.

GROWING TREES, SHRUBS, AND WOODY VINES IN CONTAINERS

Sometimes the best way to cool a wall or shade a deck or patio is to grow a shrub, tree, or woody vine in a pot. As the sun moves around the deck, you can move the pot to accommodate your need for shade. Similarly, you can keep a trellised vine or espaliered tree in a container near an exposed wall to absorb sunlight and cool the house. Make sure you allow some air space between the wall and the trellised plant to avoid harm to the house and encourage good air circulation and thus plant health. To keep potted shrubs and trees attractive, inspect regularly for pests and diseases and prune out-of-scale stems when necessary. After flowering, trim back dead blooms. (For more on growing trees and shrubs in containers, see Container-Grown Plants, page 92.)

It's a Private Matter

Sometimes shade plantings, as well as windbreaks, do double duty as privacy plantings or screening. Privacy plantings conceal you from the your neighbors' sight, whereas screening hinders your view of an objectionable scene, be it your neighbors' house, yard, or a distant vista. Many Northeasterners plant green privacy walls of arborvitae along their property lines. Although such plantings may also deflect the wind, these tall, narrow evergreens may split under the weight of snow and ice and eventually need to be replaced, especially in their northernmost range. When a tree in a hedge splits, it creates a gap large enough to destroy the wind protection. Even if you replace a mature tree the following spring, it can take years for a young tree to reach a significant height. Thus, if you have room, plant a mixed conifer screen for privacy or combine deciduous and evergreen trees and shrubs for an attractive informal alternative to these evergreens alone. (For more on hedges, see page 115.)

Designing for Direction and Movement

BY THEIR SIZE AND PLACEMENT, trees and shrubs can create direction and movement in the garden. Depending on how you place them, they can literally cause you to slow down or speed up as you move around. A large, round rhododendron, for example, can block the view around a curve, forcing to keep walking to discover what's around the next turn. Widespread twiggy branches invade your sight line, and you slow down as you move forward, because your next step is unclear. On the other hand, a straight, tree-lined driveway moves you along faster than a winding lane edged with wide-branched shrubs.

Allées for a Purpose

An allée is a straight walk or driveway lined on both sides with trees or tall shrubs of the same species, age, and height. An allée creates direction and movement through space. Many stately homes have grand allées, but you don't need a mansion to create this attractive feature on your property. Planting a double row of trees or tall hedging on axis with an entry to your house or garden focal point can give a similar effect even on a small residential scale. Depending upon your soil, climate, and lot size, many trees and shrubs may suit your allée. When planting, make sure you look up the mature size so that you can estimate proper planting distance.

◀ **Giving direction.** Maples lining a long drive-way focus a driver's attention on his or her destination, be it the house or, conversely, the main road.

▲ **Purposeful allée.** A garden bench under a white birch is the focal point of a flowering crabapple allée underplanted with spring bulbs. The straight lines of trees and flower-beds zoom your gaze to the bench and convey a sense of intention.

CHANGING SPACES

If your lot is long and narrow and you want to create the illusion of more width, use trees and shrubs to break the tunnel-like space into separate garden areas. Or plant an allée that is wide at the far end and narrower at the near end. Conversely, you can make a short space look longer by narrowing an allée as it recedes.

Texture and color also affect perspective. Bold-textured plants with big, long-stemmed mobile leaves shrink space when planted at the sides or far end of a garden, while similarly placed, fine-textured plants make an area look bigger.

Likewise, planting shrubs with warm leaf hues like gold or orangey red at a distance moves the background closer. Cool colors like dark blackish green or blue-green recede. To make the garden longer, use warm-hued leafy or flowering plants close up and silver-leafed or blue-flowered plants at a distance.

Good Trees for a Garden Allée

River birch	*Betula nigra*
Paper birch	*Betula papyrifera*
European hornbeam	*Carpinus betulus*
European beech	*Fagus sylvatica*
Golden raintree	*Koelreuteria paniculata*
Southern magnolia	*Magnolia grandiflora*
Crabapple	*Malus* species
London plane tree	*Platanus × hispanica*
Live oak	*Quercus virginiana*
Yew	*Taxus* species
Japanese zelkova	*Zelkova serrata*

▲ **Don't touch!** Sharp spines on the stems of showy scarlet firethorn (*Pyracantha coccinea*) make it a natural choice for a barrier hedge.

◄ **Eyecatcher.** A simple arrangement of white Adirondack chairs, set against shadowed woods and framed by yellow 'Frisia' black locust (*Robinia pseudoacia* 'Frisia'), is the focal point of a large lawn.

Working with a Corner Lot

If you live on a big corner lot and are tired of walkers cutting through your property, consider planting barrier shrubs to deter them. A large, mixed corner bed with one or two small flowering trees underplanted with shrubs and ground covers is the low-maintenance way to foil trespassers and beautify your neighborhood. If that sounds too complicated, you can line the edge of your lot with dense shrubs and make an informal green fence. The more serious you are about keeping people out, the more intimidating those shrubs can be. Barberry, firethorn, and beach rose are all shrubs with unpleasant thorns that can pierce tender skin.

Creating Focal Points in Your Landscape

A focal point is an attention grabber, something that makes you take a closer look at the garden. Although you can have several focal points in your overall landscape, it's a good idea to limit your focal points to one per viewing area. Seeing one focal point at a time helps you order and make sense of your surroundings. A successful focal point adds to the garden's unity but contrasts sharply with other garden elements in form, color, or texture. You can use focal points to move people through space. Focal points at each end of an allée bring a sense of destination to the experience of moving from one end to the other. Focal points range from well-placed boulders, fountains, sculptures, benches, or urns planted with colorful flowers, shrubs, or grasses to an ornamental gate under a vine-covered arbor leading to another point.

Accentuate the Positive

In contrast to a focal point, a garden accent carries less visual weight or importance in the garden design. Accents keep your garden interesting. For example, the young scarlet stems of a stripe-bark maple (*Acer pensylvanicum* 'Erythrocladum') bring beauty and interest to a winter border against a muted backdrop of snow-covered granite walls.

Borrowing a View

Sometimes the best views from your house or garden are on your neighbor's lot. If you're lucky enough to live next to a golf course, park, or pasture, or if you can see ponds, rivers, oceans, or mountains from your land, then take advantage of the view. Frame it with trees and make it the focal point of a path or allée. Borrowed views make your garden seem bigger.

◄ **A pause for refreshment.** Garden accents like this concrete sculpture silhouetted against a dark green conifer give your gaze a place to pause when traveling around the yard.

▼ **Taking advantage of views.** When clearing trees from a wooded property, keep those that frame borrowed views, such as distant rivers and lakes.

Growing in Containers

Place trees and shrubs in pots where they'll direct traffic by blocking access to a door, edge, or railing, or provide privacy by screening adjacent areas. You can increase a wall's height by capping it with a row of small potted shrubs. A collection of potted shrubs and trees can also ease the transition from an architectural space like a deck to the greater landscape.

Growing shrubs and trees in pots lets you cultivate a wider range of plants than those hardy in your climate. Moreover, shrubs that require different growing conditions from those on your land can thrive in containers. To protect these tender species, simply move them to an unheated garage in fall. You can keep your hardier woodies near a warm outdoor wall with mulch, leaves, compost, or hay piled around them for insulation. Slow-growers and dwarf plants tend to grow better in pots than fast growers, thanks to the slow-growers' more compact root systems. If you have to move the container, lift it or roll it on its side. Do not move the pot by lifting the tree by its trunk.

The Pot of Your Choice

The type of pot you choose is a matter of personal preference. Ceramic and terra cotta pots are handsome but crack in winter. Resin pots don't fracture from frost, weigh little, and look as handsome as the terra cotta or limestone containers they resemble. Heavy cement containers can survive winter but will

◄ **Container-grown shrubs.** Bring the garden to your doorstep by growing it in pots. Here, potted chokeberry (*Aronia arbutifolia* 'Brilliant') flanks a slider, along with a bevy of other container-grown plants.

eventually show the wear and tear of aging, which some people consider appealing.

The key to your plant's survival is a pot with good drainage and proper size. A 2-foot shrub, for example, needs a container with a 12-inch diameter; a 10-foot tree requires a 24-inch wide pot; and a 20- to 24-foot tree may need a container 4 to 5 feet wide.

Give Them the Soil Mix They Need

When potting shrubs and trees, use a high-quality, soilless potting mix. Avoid mixes with chunky material more than ¼-inch wide. Buy potting mix containing plant food or plan on fertilizing regularly, since potted ornamentals use more fertilizer than those planted in the ground. Mix slow-release plant food into the potting mix according to the package directions. (See Potting Up below.)

Along with slow-release fertilizer, add water-absorbent crystals or gel to the potting mix. Because these polymers hold up to 400 times their weight in water, you won't have to water your pots as often. Follow the package directions when adding gel to the soilless mix and water when soil feels dry.

▲ **A movable feast.** At times of peak appeal, display potted shrubs such as this boxwood and the blue *Hydrangea macrophylla* 'Blue Danube', setting them on a low wall or on feet for best drainage. Move containers out of sight when interest fades.

POTTING UP

1. Before planting, clean the pot and make sure it has open drainage holes about 1½-inch wide. Buy a bag of lightweight soilless potting mix, pour some in a wheelbarrow or bucket, and, if needed, dampen with water. Add slow-release fertilizer to the mix if it's not part of the potting medium.

2. Spread a paper towel or piece of newspaper on the bottom of the pot to keep the soil inside while allowing it to drain. Add enough potting medium to the container to put the plant's rootball 2 to 3 inches below the rim when potted. (See at right.)

3. Remove the plant from the original container by laying it on its side and lightly tapping the pot. Don't lift it by the trunk. Set the plant in the new container and fill the space around the rootball with potting medium. Keep the top of the rootball free from excess soil.

Beyond the Practical: Beauty Rules

W E'VE LOOKED at trees and shrubs that suit your site and those that do a job. Now's the time to look at them for fun. Just as a fine painting or sculpture can bring you unexpected thrills, so you can also take pleasure in trees and shrubs for their seductive charms.

The Beauty of Bark

I'm a sucker for bark. I go wobbly at the sight of a mature paperbark maple, a shagbark hickory makes me drool, and my jaw drops when I see a Pacific madrone. What is it about bark that excites me? Bark is always there, hiding just below the leaves, ready to reveal its sensual beauty if I just take time to look.

Bark is a tree's protective coat. Some barks look decorative year round. You can always see the arced plates of shagbark hickory, the ginger curls of paperbark maple, and the peely white skin of paper birch. But other barks reveal themselves best when trees or shrubs are bare. An example, the yellow-twig ash (*Fraxinus excelsior* 'Aurea'). Once those fabulous lemon-yellow autumn leaves fall to the ground, you can see the butter-yellow young stems contrasting with the round, black velvet leaf buds.

My favorite trees with colorful bark, however, are the stripe-bark maples — brilliant, coral-stemmed moosewood (*Acer pensylvanicum* 'Erythrocladum') and red snake-bark

◀ **Show-off bark.** Plant paperbark maple singly or in groups to show off its curly, peeling, ginger-colored bark, which looks great year-round. For extra impact, remove low branches to see more trunk.

maple *(A. capillipes)*. Moosewood's gleaming red-and-white-striped stems glow in a snowy winter landscape, while the bark of red snake-bark maple has vertical stripes in white and olive gray-green with red shoots.

Red willow *(Salix alba* 'Britzensis') and shrubby dogwoods also come into their own after leaf drop. Native red-osier dogwood *(Cornus sericea)* has dark red young stems in winter. The cultivar 'Cardinal' has brighter stems and more disease resistance than other popular varieties. Yellow-twig dogwood *(Cornus alba* 'Bud's Yellow') produces disease-resistant, school-bus-yellow stems. *Cornus sanguinea* 'Midwinter Fire' has flamelike stems of red, orange, and yellow. Remember that new stem growth is the most colorful, so cut these shrubs to the base each spring, or you'll end up with dull-barked plants.

Just as landscape texture refers to a tree's visual nature, it may also pertain to the sense of touch. Smooth, muscled beech bark thus differs by sight and touch from the rough, plated bark of old sugar maples.

Lagerstroemia indica **'Muskogee'**

Bark Standouts

Snakebark	*Acer capillipes*		American beech	*Fagus grandifolia*
Paperbark maple	*Acer griseum*		European beech	*Fagus sylvatica*
Moosewood	*Acer pensylvanicum* 'Erythrocladum'		Golden European ash	*Fraxinus excelsior* 'Aurea'
Madrone	*Arbutus menziesii*		Seven-son flower	*Heptacodium miconioides*
River birch	*Betula nigra*		Crape myrtle	*Lagerstroemia indica*
Paper birch	*Betula papyrifera*		Persian parrotia	*Parrotia persica*
Shagbark hickory	*Carya ovata*		Lacebark pine	*Pinus bungeana*
Tatarian yellow-twig dogwood	*Cornus sericea* 'Budd's Yellow'		Red pine	*Pinus resinosa*
Kousa dogwood	*Cornus kousa*		Japanese flowering cherry	*Prunus serrulata*
Red osier dogwood	*Cornus sericea*		Japanese stewartia	*Stewartia pseudocamellia*

Betula nigra **'Heritage'**

Phellodendron amurense

Arbutus menziesii

Carya ovata

Cornus sericea 'Flaviramea' (yellow) and 'Baileyi' (red)

Stewartia pseudocamellia

Fabulous Colorful Foliage

Each spring when our golden locust (*Robinia pseudoacacia* 'Frisia') leafs out, I marvel at how it transforms the landscape. Rather lopsided, this 30-foot-by-20-foot tree is not pretty in a structural sense, but its golden chartreuse leaves glow against a backdrop of dark evergreen trees and contrast admirably with the clear cerulean sky of a warm New Hampshire day.

Near the locust grows Rivers purple beech (*Fagus sylvatica* 'Riversii'), a tree my husband adores. This tree has a dense canopy of blackish purple leaves on ground-skimming branches. Handsome up close, it looks like a gaping black hole in the landscape when viewed from a distance.

Color is a powerful landscape tool and it takes some skill to use it wisely. The leaf color of a deciduous tree can change three times a year, with each change having a different effect on the scenery. Weeping katsura (*Cercidiphyllum japonicum* 'Pendulum'), for example, has showy copper-bronze leaves in spring. As the heart-shaped leaves mature, they change to light bluish green. In fall, they

Robinia pseudoacacia 'Frisia'

Salix integra 'Hakuro-nishiki'

Fagus sylvatica 'Tricolor'

Cotinus coggygria 'Royal Purple'

For Summer Color

SHRUBS

'Royal Purple' smokebush	*Cotinus coggygria* 'Royal Purple'	Purple
Coppertina ninebark	*Physocarpus opulifolious* 'Mindia' (Coppertina)	Orange copper to red
Tiger Eyes sumac	*Rhus typhina* 'Bailtiger' (Tiger Eyes)	Bright yellow
Dappled willow	*Salix integra* 'Hakuro-nishiki'	Pink-and-white variegation
Black Lace elderberry	*Sambucus nigra* 'Eva' (Black Lace)	Near black

TREES

'Bloodgood' Japanese maple	*Acer palmatum* 'Bloodgood'	Deep red
Rivers European beech	*Fagus sylvatica* 'Riversii'	Blackish maroon
'Tricolor' European beech	*Fagus sylvatica* 'Tricolor'	Rosy pink, cream, green
'Concordia' English oak	*Quercus robur* 'Concordia'	Yellow
'Frisia' black locust	*Robinia pseudoacacia* 'Frisia'	Yellow

turn golden apricot, giving the tree three seasons of interest because of its foliage alone.

Yellow, red, purple, blue, silver, and variegated deciduous leaves make fine accents for gardens that are mostly green in summer. Dark colors like purple work best when contrasted with lighter-colored plants in front of them. Variegated foliage lightens a dark corner, while yellow, red, and copper foliage highlights masses of green-leafed plants. Red and yellow leaves look harmonious in small doses, while blue, silver, and blue-green foliage also create an appealing harmony. Warm yellow and cool silvery blue leaves, on the other hand, are difficult to pair. The combination tends to make the yellow leaves look harsh or brassy.

Autumn leaves add another dimension to a color garden. Fall gardens are rich in red, gold, orange, yellow, and purple hues, and trees and shrubs are ideal ways to bring those colors into the garden. When planning autumn color, think not only about the plants close at hand, but also about the native trees surrounding your property. Fall color reaches its glory when your private garden merges with the natural landscape in a hot-hued blaze.

Disanthus cercidifolius   *Fothergilla gardenii* 'Mount Airy'   *Ginkgo biloba* 'Princeton Sentry'

For Fall Color

SHRUBS

'Heptalobum' Japanese maple	*Acer palmatum* 'Heptalobum'	Brilliant orange-red
'Brilliant' red chokeberry	*Aronia arbutifolia* 'Brilliant'	Red
Carolina allspice	*Calycanthus floridus*	Yellow
Disanthus	*Disanthus cercidifolius*	Red
Dwarf fothergilla	*Fothergilla gardenii*	Yellow/orange/scarlet
High-bush blueberry	*Vaccinium corymbosum*	Red

TREES

'Hogyoku' Japanese maple	*Acer palmatum* 'Hogyoku'	Pumpkin orange
Red maple	*Acer rubrum*	Intense red
Sugar maple	*Acer saccharum*	Golden orange to scarlet
Golden European ash	*Fraxinus excelsior* 'Aurea'	Bright yellow
Maidenhair tree	*Ginkgo biloba*	Yellow
Korean mountain ash	*Sorbus alnifolia*	Golden orange

Aronia arbutifolia 'Brilliant'

The Surprising Colors of Evergreen Foliage

Evergreen trees and shrubs bring year-round mass, color, and structure to the garden. If you need absolute year-round screening, then evergreens are the plants of choice. Hedges of bright to dark green evergreens, such as yew or holly, also make ideal backdrops for perennial gardens, sculptures, and other garden ornaments.

The term *evergreen* is a bit of a misnomer, as needled and broad-leaf evergreens are also available in a wide range of colors, including silvery blue, yellow, copper, blue-green, gray-green, gold, chartreuse, and green and white or yellow-variegated evergreens. Most brightly colored evergreens work better as garden accents rather than massed. A small bright blue or gold conifer can bring winter interest to a perennial bed, especially when contrasted with grasses, showy sedum's dark seedheads, and all-green conifers.

Massing ground cover junipers or Russian arborvitae, which turns purplish bronze in winter, is common practice. Before you invest in them, however, check their winter appearance to make sure you appreciate the hue. I find the bronzy purple cast can look unappealing when used on a large scale or in a prominent location, for instance, facing down scarlet winterberries in an entry garden. If you agree, choose a juniper cultivar that keeps its summer color year round. Those include *Juniperus sabina* 'Broadmoor', *J. sabina* 'Buffalo', *J. chinensis* var. *sargentii*, and *J. chinensis* 'Sea Green', which has deep green foliage that darkens in winter.

Colorful Evergreens

GREEN OR BLUE-GREEN SHIFTING TO RED, PURPLE, OR BRONZE IN FALL

Elegans Japanese cedar	*Cryptomeria japonica* 'Pygmaea'	Plum
'Bar Harbor' creeping juniper	*Juniperus horizontalis* 'Bar Harbor'	Plum
'Burkii' Eastern red cedar	*Juniperus virginiana* 'Burkii'	Purple
Siberian cypress	*Microbiota decussata*	Bronze
'PJM' rhododenron	*Rhododendron* 'PJM'	Dark burgundy-purple

BLUE

Weeping blue Atlas cedar	*Cedrus libani* subsp. *atlantica* 'Glauca Pendula'	Light gray blue
'Blue Forest' juniper	*Juniperus sabina* 'Blue Forest'	Blue
'Wichita Blue' juniper	*Juniperus scopulorum* 'Wichita Blue'	Silvery blue
'Blue Carpet' juniper	*Juniperus squamata* 'Blue Carpet'	Bright blue
'Hoopsii' blue spruce	*Picea pungens* 'Hoopsii'	Silver-blue

VARIEGATED

Horstman's 'Silberlocke' Korean fir	*Abies koreana* 'Silberlocke'	Curved needles show white undersides
'Snow Sprite' deodar cedar	*Cedrus deodara* 'Snow Sprite'	Ivory to creamy yellow new growth
'Carol Mackie' daphne	*Daphne × burkwoodii* 'Carol Mackie'	Cream-edged green
'Goshiki' false-holly	*Osmanthus heterophyllus* 'Goshiki'	Gold to cream variegation on green
'Moon Frost' hemlock	*Tsuga canadensis* 'Moon Frost'	Whitish in winter

YELLOW, GOLD, AND CHARTREUSE

'Golden Mop' false cypress	*Chamaecyparis pisifera* 'Golden Mop'	Bright yellow
'Sunrise' winter creeper	*Euonymus fortunei* 'Sunrise'	Yellow to yellow-green leaves
Gold Star juniper	*Juniperus chinensis* 'Bakaurea' (Gold Star)	Light green with gold tips
'Skylands' oriental spruce	*Picea orientalis* 'Skylands'	Yellow with dark green interior
Techny Gold arborvitae	*Thuja occidentalis* 'Walter Brown' Techny Gold	Bright gold and green

Abies koreana 'Silberlocke'

Microbiota decussata

Osmanthus heterophyllus 'Goshiki'

Picea orientalis 'Skylands'

Microbiota decussata

Juniperus horizontalis 'Wiltonii'

Picea abies 'Elegans'

Rich Evergreen Textures

Texture affects two senses: vision *and* touch. Coarse-textured shrubs and trees have large leaves that create bold patterns of light and shade on the plant's surface. Coarse plants leap forward in a landscape. On the other hand, trees and shrubs with fine-textured foliage have little contrast between light and dark. Their even surface more easily fades into the background. Planting bold textured shrubs such as Oregon grape holly (*Mahonia aquifolium*) at the back of the garden, therefore, makes it feel smaller, while planting fine-textured plants like yew or pine enlarges the space.

Repeating plants of similar texture throughout a garden unifies it. However, a garden with plants all of the same texture grows boring. To break the boredom, grow a contrasting tree or shrub as an accent or focal point. For example, a garden screened by fine-textured yews would benefit from one or more groups of coarse-textured spotted laurel to bring visual rhythm and balance to the scene.

Texture is not just how something looks but also how it feels. Leaf surfaces that are rough to the touch with hairs or big veins tend to look dull and absorb light. Broad, smooth surfaces look shiny and reflect light. Because evergreens don't drop their leaves in the manner of deciduous trees, they bring a consistent year-round texture to the landscape.

The needled foliage of conifers is usually fine-textured compared with the bigger leaves and coarser texture of many broadleaf evergreens. You can use both coarse and fine-textured evergreens for garden screening and privacy, because they maintain their foliage and thus their visual density all year. In shady landscapes, for example, rosebay rhododendrons make a stunning backdrop for a varied summer garden of gold, green, blue, or variegated hostas, as well as other shade-loving plants.

Cryptomeria japonica 'Yoshino'

Ilex x meserveae 'Blue Princess'

Taxus cuspidata 'Dwarf Bright Gold'

Viburnum x rhytidophylloides 'Alleghany'

Evergreens with Superior Texture

Spotted laurel	*Aucuba japonica*	Bold
Blue holly	*Ilex × meserveae*	Medium
Southern magnolia	*Magnolia grandiflora*	Bold
Eastern white pine	*Pinus strobus*	Fine
Rosebay rhododendron	*Rhododendron maximum*	Bold
Yak rhododendron	*Rhododendron yakushimanum*	Medium-bold: thick brown "wool" under leaves; white-felted new growth
'Winter Green' umbrella pine	*Sciadopitys verticillata* 'Winter Green'	Medium: long plasticlike shiny needles
Yew	*Taxus* species	Fine: dense dark green needles
Leather-leaf viburnum	*Viburnum rhytidophyllum*	Bold

Aralia elata 'Variegata'   *Styrax japonicus*

Textures of Decidous Foliage

The texture of deciduous trees and shrubs may change with the season and the presence or absence of leaves. The trick is to use these textural changes to your advantage when laying out your garden, using some of the tips suggested on the previous page.

Textural changes in deciduous plants can be extreme. My Chicago Luster viburnum (*Viburnum dentatum* 'Synnestvedt'), for example, turns from an 8-foot-by-8-foot leafy mound in summer to a jumble of delicate brown twigs in winter. During the growing season, its glossy, deep green leaves, which are about 2 to 4 inches long and wide, grow abundantly, giving the plant a medium texture. Winter exposes its abundant twigs, and in my shrub border the overall texture is fine.

On the other hand, shagbark hickory looks bold year round. Its jumbo compound leaves, made up of five to seven 5-inch leaflets, can be more than a foot long. The canopy is not round and smooth but coarse and broken into contrasting leafy light and dark shady green segments with big areas of sky showing through. In winter, the silhouette is coarse, and the bark plates look warped and showy with both ends lifting off the trunk.

The texture of weeping trees can also change with the seasons. Trees with contorted trunks or branches take on a bolder look once they lose their leaves. A weeping katsura that is medium textured in leaf looks coarser without leaves, due to its twisted structure and exfoliating bark, which are covered by foliage during the growing season.

Aesculus parviflora

Trees and Shrubs with Unusual Textures

Bottlebrush buckeye	*Aesculus parviflora*	Bold in summer, medium-bold in winter
Variegated Japanese angelica	*Aralia elata* 'Variegata'	Fine in summer; bold in winter
Catalpa	*Catalpa* species	Bold in summer and winter
Bush clover	*Lespedeza thunbergii*	Fine in summer; cut to ground in late fall
Star magnolia	*Magnolia stellata*	Medium all year
Empress tree	*Paulownia tomentosa*	Bold all year; coppiced trees have particularly bold tropical-looking foliage all summer
Ninebark	*Physocarpus opulifolius*	Medium in summer; bold in winter
Japanese snowbell	*Styrax japonicus*	Fine all year
Common lilac	*Syringa vulgaris*	Medium in summer; bold in winter

Fleeting, but Memorable

Robert Herrick, a seventeenth-century English poet, summed up the brief sweetness of youth by comparing it to a shrub in bloom: "Gather ye rosebuds while ye may/Old Time is still a-flying;/And this same flower that smiles today/Tomorrow will be dying."

Herrick understood well that flowers, though beautiful, don't last much more than a week or two. We understand that, too, but it doesn't keep us from growing common lilac (*Syringa vulgaris*), which blooms briefly in spring before powdery mildew wrecks its lovely heart-shaped leaves. Likewise, after its electrifying spring bloom, forsythia *(Forsythia × intermedia)* offers little except for long, leafy suckering stems. Still, we love these shrubs for their flowers, buy them non-stop from box stores and garden centers, and give them key spots in the landscape.

Don't get me wrong. I love flowering shrubs with a passion, but I try to use ones with multi-season appeal where they'll have maximum impact and keep those with short season interest where I can appreciate them in bloom, then make them disappear into a mixed border as the season progresses.

There's another way that I deal with shrubs that have great flowers and little else going for them. I look for cultivars or different species of the same plant that work harder for me in the garden. For example, I grow 'Miss Kim' lilac (*Syringa patula* 'Miss Kim') along the path to my front door. It not only offers masses of perfumed pale lilac blooms in late spring, but it also has a neat round to oval habit, especially when compared with common lilac's suckering ways. This cultivar has attractive green leaves all summer — no powdery mildew — and lovely burgundy fall color.

Similarly, I find Gold Tide forsythia (*Forsythia* × 'Courtasol') more pleasing than regular border forsythia because of the cultivar's dense, dwarf, spreading habit, 2 feet high and 4 feet wide. Its form makes it suitable as a tall ground cover for banks and open spaces. Gold Tide produces lemon-yellow flowers in April, attractive light green leaves in summer, and purple foliage in fall.

Hydrangea paniculata 'Tardiva'

Spiraea thunbergii 'Ogon'

Top-Choice Flowering Shrubs

White forsythia	*Abeliophyllum distichum*	White
Sweetshrub	*Calycanthus* species	Burgundy red, greenish white
Camellia	*Camellia* species	White, pink, red, variegated
Blue mist	*Caryopteris × clandonensis*	Blue, purple
Flowering quince	*Chaenomeles speciosa*	White, pink, red, orange, variegated
Deutzia	*Deutzia gracilis*	White
Fothergilla	*Fothergilla* species	White
Rose of Sharon	*Hibiscus syriacus* cultivars	White, pink, red, purple, blue, violet, lavender, and bicolor
Smooth hydrangea	*Hydrangea arborescens* cultivars	White
Big-leaf hydrangea	*Hydrangea macrophylla* cultivars	Blue, pink, purple[1], pastel-tinted white, and bicolor
Panicle hydrangea	*Hydrangea paniculata* cultivars	White, greenish white, maturing to dusky pink
Mountain laurel	*Kalmia latifolia*	White, pink, some with red variegation
Japanese kerria	*Kerria japonica*	Yellow
Oregon grape	*Mahonia* species	Yellow
Tree peony	*Paeonia suffruticosa*	Every color but blue, including white, lemon, green, pink, red, deep purple, and bicolor
Mock orange	*Philadelphus coronarius*	White
Rhododendron, azalea	*Rhododendron* species	White, pink, red, yellow, orange, purple
Spirea	*Spiraea* species	White, pink
Lilac	*Syringa vulgaris*	White, lilac blue, purple, maroon
Viburnum	*Viburnum* species	White, creamy white, light pink
Chaste tree	*Vitex agnus-castus*	Lilac blue
Weigela	*Weigela florida*	Pink, rose
Adam's needle	*Yucca filamentosa*	White

[1] Depending upon the soil's pH and cultivar

Hibiscus syriacus **cultivar**

Hydrangea arborescens **'Annabelle'**

Malus 'Donald Wyman'

The Magnificence of Flowering Trees

Who can resist a southern magnolia blossom's lemony sweet fragrance and outrageous beauty? Not I, who quiver at the thought of its baby-smooth petals and sublime scent. A backdrop of large, leathery evergreen leaves heightens the creamy blooms' sensual appeal.

Flowers are reproductive organs that attract what they need for pollination. A pollinated flower matures into a fruit containing the seeds of the species' next generation. If you grow trees for their flowers, be aware that flowering can be fast, a few days for most; if the tree has bracts, the period of color may last for several weeks.

Flowers come at different times of year for different plants. Red maple's red flowers blush the crown in spring before the leaves appear. A mass of female trees on a hill or along a drive transforms the view into a subtle, yet rich red haze. Even as red maples come into leaf, reddish fruits appear in clusters, prolonging the ruddy glow. (In a garden, some folks gripe that once those pretty spring flowers become abundant fruits they result in messy seedlings that need plucking one by one.) Stewartia's lovely white flowers occur in summer when most other trees have finished blooming, and franklinia's delightful flowers appear in fall, just before frost where I live.

When you grow a tree for flowers, the blooms should be visible among the leaves and branches. Tulip tree (*Liriodendron tulipifera*) produces large, cupped, chartreuse and orange blossoms. The tuliplike flowers are striking, but the giant tree grows so fast that, unless your house is near the height of the tree's canopy, you can hardly see the blooms. I know, because I had one that towered over my house when I lived in Delaware. Quite honestly, tulip trees (also known as tulip poplars) are too big for most residential lots, but we liked ours and kept it for its straight towering trunk, handsome light green leaves and yellow fall color.

Another tree grown for its flower clusters is fragrant styrax (*Styrax obassia*). This small flowering tree is quite pretty near a patio, but its droopy white bloom clusters sometimes seem hidden amid the leaves, which grow to 8 inches long and 6 inches wide. Even if you can't always see the scented flowers, however, you can smell them and appreciate the tree's smooth, ruddy bark and exfoliating young stems.

Gardeners grow some trees for flowers alone, including a few ornamental plums and cherries. Be careful which trees you choose, as many cherries and plums, which belong to the Rose Family, are prone to diseases of that group. Even disease-resistant varieties may attract tent caterpillars or Japanese beetles in areas where they are pests, and the trees thus require regular picking or spraying. *Prunus* 'Hally Jolivette', my favorite cherry for its lush, tiny pink-on-pink flowers, yellow fall color, and delicate airy habit, still gets Japanese beetles every July, but I grow it with a group of other shrubs that the beetles do not bother.

What appear to be flowers may in fact be showy bracts, big petal-like leaves that attract animals to the small flower cluster they surround. A wonderful ornamental known for its bracts is Kousa dogwood (*Cornus kousa*). It produces four pointed white bracts that turn pinkish with age surrounding a little greenish flower cluster at their center.

Laburnum x watereri 'Vossii'

Prunus 'Accolade'

Chionanthus virginicus

Prunus 'Okame'

Trees with Great Flowers

Red maple	*Acer rubrum*	Red
Redbud	*Cercis canadensis*	Pink, white
White fringe tree	*Chionanthus virginicus*	White
Yellowwood	*Cladastris kentukea*	White
Flowering dogwood	*Cornus florida*	White, pink bracts
Kousa dogwood	*Cornus kousa*	White, pink bracts
Dove tree	*Davidia involucrata*	White bracts
Franklinia	*Franklinia alatamaha*	White
Carolina silverbell	*Halesia carolina*	White, pinkish white
Golden raintree	*Koelreuteria paniculata*	Yellow
Golden chain tree	*Laburnum × watereri* 'Vossii'	Yellow
Magnolias	*Magnolia* species	White, pink, purple, cream, yellow
Apple and crabapple	*Malus* species	White, pink, deep pink
Sourwood	*Oxydendrum arboreum*	White
Ornamental cherry	*Prunus* species	Pink, white
Japanese stewartia	*Stewartia pseudocamellia*	White
Snowbell	*Styrax* species	White
Japanese tree lilac	*Syringa reticulata*	Creamy white

Davidia involucrata

Callicarpa bodinieri var. giraldii

Rosa glauca

Fruiting Trees and Shrubs

In addition to fabulous flowers and awesome autumn hues, shrubs and trees can produce showy fruit that magnifies your garden's charm. Technically, fruiting is the part of a plant's reproductive process that occurs after flowering. Fruit comes from the female part of a seed-bearing plant. It holds the fertilized seed or seeds of that plant's next generation. Some plants have showy fruits to attract wildlife that eat the fruit and disperse its seeds. People, of course, also eat fruit, so shrubs with edible fruit may serve a dual purpose of enjoyment in our gardens. In fact, the word *fruit* derives from the Latin root, *fructus,* or enjoyment.

Shrubs that are nondescript for most of the year take on a new look when they fruit. Purple beautyberry's *(Callicarpa dichotoma)* tight clusters of bright purple fruit appear on a rather plain twiggy shrub in my shrub border, where I don't pay it much attention until handsome purple berries appear in fall. Wow! The fruit quantity changes from year to year, but the color always delights me.

Likewise, driving a marshy stretch of highway near my home becomes a new experience in fall, when winterberry's *(Ilex verticillata)* branches, naked of leaves but lush with bright red berries, transform the muck into a cloud of brilliant red. That inspired me to plant 'Winter Red' winterberry, the berries of which may last all winter in my backyard. Imagine my surprise on one very cold Thanksgiving Day when I watched a flock of wild turkeys consume them. Besides red, you can also find winterberry in orange (*Ilex verticillata* f. *aurantiaca*) and yellow ('Winter Gold') cultivars.

The fruit of some evergreen hollies stands out against the foliage, providing fall to winter interest. 'Ivory Queen' inkberry (*Ilex glabra* 'Ivory Queen') has white fruit and evergreen leaves on a short plant suitable for a foundation planting. Blue holly cultivars worth growing for abundant fruit include 'Blue Princess' and 'Mesog' China Girl. These fairly small hollies look great grouped in borders or used as an informal hedge. 'Nellie R. Stevens' holly is not as hardy as blue holly, but this popular cultivar has a good fruit set. Although Meserve hybrids and most other hollies require a male plant for lavish fruiting, Nellie can fruit on its own, though it fruits better with a male, particularly 'Edward J. Stevens', participating in the process.

Planted alone, holly can make an outstanding garden specimen, particularly in winter, when there's little color to hold your attention. James G. Esson altaclera holly grows 25 feet or more. From October to January it displays large, clear red berries against its shiny, dark green leaves. 'Miss Helen', 'Comet', 'Prancer', and fast-growing 'Carnival' with orangey red fruit, are showy American hollies that can also stand on their own. 'East Palatka' and 'Foster's #2' holly make attractive fruiting screens, hedges, or specimens. Make sure you plant a male for fruiting and find the best varieties for your climate.

Excellent Fruiting Plants

TREES

Apple serviceberry	*Amelanchier × grandiflora*
Magnolias	*Magnolia* species
Apples and crabapples	*Malus* species
Sourwood	*Oxydendrum arboreum*
Korean mountain ash	*Sorbus alnifolia*

SHRUBS

Beautyberry	*Callicarpa* species
Flowering quince	*Chaenomeles speciosa*
Blue holly	*Ilex × meserveae*
Red-leaf rose	*Rosa glauca*
Sapphire berry	*Symplocos paniculata*
Low-bush blueberry	*Vaccinium corymbosum*
Shasta doublefile viburnum	*Viburnum plicatum* 'Shasta'

Sorbus decora

Malus **'Snowdrift'**

Acer palmatum 'Ornatum'

Acer palmatum 'Ornatum'

Fagus sylvatica 'Pendula'

The Year-Round Architecture of Deciduous Silhouettes

When I write of architectural trees and shrubs, I mean those with such unified exceptional form that they order and influence the space around them. Just as light, shadow, texture, pattern, and other characteristics contribute to effective sculpture, the interplay of those traits also enhances architectural plants. I do not refer to the science of tree architecture, which studies how trees change and adjust their form over time, but to trees and shrubs as outstanding live shapes that transform gardens from plain to distinctive.

Gardens are architectural manmade spaces, and trees and shrubs may serve as the framework for everything that happens in them. Earlier, we examined how to use them to create structure, stability, and balance. Here, we look at trees and shrubs used as accents and focal points, chosen for mass and silhouette. You can use these ornamentals as garden specimens that stand on their own, perhaps in a bed of ground cover or underplanted with masses of perennials. You can also integrate them into beds and borders, but only where you can appreciate and not hide their unique form.

Trees grown as pampered lawn specimens in ideal soil and climate conditions can develop extraordinary trunks and vast branch networks. I've seen magnificent beeches (*Fagus* species) growing on estates in Newport, Rhode Island, in open lawns and full sun, where no expense has been spared to maintain them. Their brawny trunks are smooth, yet rippled like well-developed quadriceps supporting the crown's great weight. Similarly, evergreen live oaks throughout the South produce magnificent buttressed trunks to bear their huge spreading limbs. Because of their open structure, the tree casts medium to dappled shade on the ground beneath it. Lining drives or standing alone on a moist sandy lawn, these trees can be stunning assets to warm-climate landscapes.

On a small scale, a shrub like Harry Lauder's walking stick (*Corylus avellana* 'Contorta') which looks silly and contrived in its summer green, becomes a twisted sculpture when its branches are bare. Rock cotoneaster (*Cotoneaster horizontalis*) is also remarkable for its branches, which form a herringbone pattern that is evident all year,

▲ **Aging splendor.** The upright trunk and irregular branches of a solitary white oak (*Quercus alba*) bring character to a bare March landscape in Connecticut. The tree's architecture, shaped by weather and the human hand, is most evident after leaf drop.

thanks to its tiny leaves. As an added bonus, in fall its foliage turns red and in winter it bears bright red berries, which draw continual attention to the plant.

Striking Silhouettes

DECIDUOUS

Japanese maple	*Acer palmatum*
Pagoda dogwood	*Cornus alternifolia*
Harry Lauder's walking stick	*Corylus avellana* 'Contorta'
Rock cotoneaster	*Cotoneaster horizontalis*
European beech	*Fagus sylvatica* cultivars
Weeping willow	*Salix babylonica*
Bald cypress	*Taxodium distichum*

▶ **Sculptural evergreens.** An upright yet droopy conifer that resembles a lanky scarecrow in silhouette draws your gaze to the entry of this tall stucco house. The form stands out from the array of conifers in the opposite bed, which range from mounded and spreading to columnar and pyramidal.

▲ **Architectural record.** If trunks could talk, the gnarly bole of this old cherry tree would tell stories of gains, losses, and constant transformation.

Sculpted by Nature

Sometimes a tree's striking looks result from the hardships of weather and location it has survived. Think of the bristlecone pines of California's White Mountains, where there's a tree more than 4,600 years old. Its gnarled trunk and warped stubby limbs express the damage it endures 10,000 feet above the sea level. Even though we can't own these ancient trees, many gardeners simulate their architecture by training conifers as bonsai. Evergreen foliage gives the strong distorted silhouettes of weeping conifers year-round substance and mass. Weeping Norway spruce, for example, which can both grow upward and spread along the ground, depending upon how it is trained, stands out for its bent and draping shape. Hollywood juniper is similarly dramatic, with its twisted upright branches, giving it an arty, irregular form. Evergreen shrubs such as spiky yucca and skinny Sky Pencil holly also boast strong silhouettes for added garden excitement.

Garden wit. A clipped sphere (known as a topiary standard) adds contrast, height, and humor to a low, loose planting by seeming to hover above the flowers.

Echoing shapes. An evergreen pyramid accents the formal geometry of the pool area and balances the peaked roof of the cabana-like entry to the poolhouse.

Unnatural Attractions: Topiary

Trees and shrubs don't always end up as nature intended. Some folks can turn plants into topiaries by shearing or pruning. Topiaries are shrubs, trees, or hedges clipped to resemble objects, animals, and abstract or geometric shapes, such as cubes, cones, clouds, waves, spheres, spirals, and obelisks. You can train some woodies into standards with straight bare trunks and crowns trimmed into a ball or other geometric form. Topiary looks good in both formal and informal gardens. In formal beds, it often marks the corners or center and can be used to create a rhythm or pattern of its own. In a cottage garden, it adds a whimsical accent to borders. A topiary hedge can be a freestanding sculpture or a functional divider. You can grow topiaries in the ground or cultivate them in pots. Traditional materials for topiary include shrubs like common yew (*Taxus baccata*) and English boxwood (*Buxus sempervirens* 'Suffruticosa'), a broad-leaf evergreen, but you can also use plants native to your climate, such as white pine or arborvitae in New England.

Good Candidates for Evergreen Topiary

Boxwood	*Buxus* species
'Boulevard' false cypress	*Chamaecyparis pisifera* 'Boulevard'
Burford holly	*Ilex cornuta* 'Burfordii'
Japanese holly	*Ilex crenata*
Yaupon	*Ilex vomitoria*
Juniper	*Juniperus* species
Sweet bay	*Laurus nobilis*
Olive	*Olea europaea*
Japanese yew pine	*Podocarpus chinensis*
Rosemary	*Rosmarinus officinalis*
Yew	*Taxus* species

▲ *Clethra barbinervis* offers interest from both bark and flowers.
▼ *Fothergilla gardenii* bears lovely spring flowers and brilliant fall foliage.

Show-Offs: Plants for More Than One Season

Trees and shrubs with multi-season interest don't have to be evergreens. Some deciduous trees have so much appeal that they look good every season of the year. Both paper birch and river birch fit that description. Paper birch has yellow fall color and white peeling bark, which shines against dark evergreens in the northern landscape. River birch has fine yellow fall color and cream-hued bark that peels in big curls. Planted in close groups with sedums and low- to medium-size ornamental grasses, these birches bring year-round beauty to a residential lot.

The bark of Kousa dogwood exfoliates with age, often developing a tan, cream, and gray mottling. Leaves are rich green. Four ornate white to pink bracts surround the nondescript flowers and last for six weeks starting in June. The blooms are especially showy, since they occur on stems held above the leaves. The fruits, which mature from August through October, are big, red edible balls resembling space capsules or raspberries and are held at the end of long stems. In fall, the leaves turn long-lasting purple-red before dropping.

Because of their smaller size, shrubs with extended appeal are particularly useful in home gardens. High-bush blueberry (a good substitute for burning bush where the latter is a pest) has four seasons of interest. In spring, white urnlike blooms occur in groups along the stem, followed in summer by attractive, blue edible fruit that attracts people and animals. At home, our corgi, Ivy, eats every blueberry on her level, which (if you know corgis) isn't very high. With the onset of cold weather, blueberry's leaves turn anywhere from a brilliant red to reddish purple. Although old wood is dark, smooth young stems range from deep crimson to yellowy green when bare. Planted in a group or massed in borders, the stems make a colorful impact through the winter.

Likewise, Japanese clethra *(Clethra barbinervis)* has elongated droopy clusters of fragrant white flowers, followed by similar fruits. These remain visible against the red fall leaves. Dr. Richard Iversen limbed up a mature specimen in a shady nook of the display garden at the State University of New York at Farmingdale, so that visitors can appreciate its marvelous mottled bark.

You can't beat crape myrtle *(Lagerstroemia* hybrids) for exfoliating bark, showy flowers, and excellent fall color. Hybrids (hardy to Zone 7A) from the U.S. National Arboretum, have flowers ranging from white to pinks, purple, red, coral, and lavender. Crape myrtles are multi-stemmed shrubs or small trees that are usually pruned up to show off the smooth grayish bark that peels away to display mottled green, brown, and red-brown bark. Fall color can be red, orange, or yellow. Use crape myrtle as a small patio tree or a specimen in an entry garden where you can enjoy the handsome bark.

Plants with Many Seasons of Interest

SHRUBS

Japanese clethra	*Clethra barbinervis*
Fothergilla	*Fothergilla* species
Seven-son flower	*Heptacodium miconioides*
Crape myrtle	*Lagerstroemia* hybrids
Blueberry	*Vaccinium* species

TREES

River birch	*Betula nigra*
Katsura tree	*Cercidiphyllum japonicum*
Kousa dogwood	*Cornus kousa*
'Winter King' hawthorn	*Crataegus viridis* 'Winter King'
Franklinia	*Franklinia alatamaha*
Japanese stewartia	*Stewartia pseudocamellia*
China Snow Peking lilac	*Syringa pekinensis* 'Morton'

▲ ***Cercidiphyllum japonicum*** (above) bears lovely spring flowers and colorful fall foliage.

▼ ***Stewartia pseudocamellia*** (below) flowers in summer and features vivid fall foliage.

Vaccinium corymbosum

Viburnum 'Oneida'

Sambucus canadensis 'Laciniata'

Attracting Birds and Other Wildlife

Birds flock to the gray dogwoods *(Cornus racemosa)* in my backyard. Chirping loudly, they perch on the fine branches, take cover in the thicket of stems, and feed on the white fruits from late summer to fall. Native to the Eastern United States, these shrubby trees already lived on our lot when we built our house. We saved them not just for the birds, but also for their showy white-clustered flowers in late spring, purple fall foliage, and pretty fruits on vivid red stems that stay showy after the fruits have disappeared. Depending upon their location, gray dogwoods may draw Eastern bluebirds, Northern cardinals, Northern flickers, Northern bobwhites, and ring-necked pheasants.

Watching birds, butterflies, bees, and other benign wildlife interact with nature is one of life's joys. Hearing birds sing and bees buzz lifts you above stressful thoughts to contemplation of life's essential order. There's magic in nature, but there's nothing magical about how to bring these creatures into your life.

Birds, bees, and butterflies will find your garden if you give them what they need to survive — food, cover, water, and breeding spots. This kind of gardening gives back to wildlife the habitat that strip malls, industry, and tract housing take away. Depending upon the conditions in our yards, we can create little woodlands, bogs, or meadows on our lots.

The best way to provide for wildlife is with various native trees, shrubs, and flowers that bloom and fruit at different times throughout the growing season. Plants native to your locale are suited to your environment. Use the straight species when possible, rather than fancy cultivars. Single-flowered shrub species are better than those with decorative double blooms, because the single flower form makes it easier for birds and insects to retrieve the nectar. A combination of deciduous and evergreen trees and shrubs adds welcome variety. Evergreens like American holly and Eastern red cedar provide food, shelter, and winter warmth.

Think of your wildlife garden as a small woods with a canopy of tall trees, some understory trees, and below them twiggy fruiting shrubs such as arrowwood (*Viburnum dentatum*) and blackhaw (*V. prunifolium*). If your garden has messy places, take heart: that's what wildlife prefer. Postpone garden cleanup until spring. Worms and insects hide under rocks and fallen leaves or branches, potential snacks for hungry birds. Fallen leaves and little branchlets, however, may also harbor infectious disease spores, like anthracnose and tar spot on maples and black spot on roses. Weed the garden by hand and suppress further unwanted growth with mulch rather than synthetic herbicides. Go for organic pest control if possible, and avoid broad-spectrum insecticides.

To provide the birds with water, set a birdbath in the sunlight near some shrubs and keep the water fresh. Butterflies prefer puddles. A low spot that turns muddy after rain will do the trick. Butterflies also need sunshine for basking and shelter from the wind. A flat-topped boulder in an open garden behind a windbreak of shrubs and trees protects them so they can expose themselves to the sun's warmth.

Native Plants that Attract Wildlife

SHRUBS

Red chokeberry	*Aronia arbutifolia*
Winterberry	*Ilex verticillata*
Chokecherry	*Prunus virginiana*
Elderberry	*Sambucus canadensis*
Blueberry	*Vaccinium* species
Viburnum	*Viburnum* species

TREES

Serviceberry	*Amelanchier* species
Dogwood	*Cornus* species
Hawthorn	*Crataegus* species
Persimmon	*Diospyros virginiana*
American hollly	*Ilex opaca*
Eastern red cedar	*Juniperus virginiana*

▲ **Natural home.** This standing stump is riddled with cracks and crevices that offer shelter to birds and other small creatures.

Crataegus viridis 'Winter King'

Aronia arbutifolia

Cornus kousa 'Milky Way'

SUMMER   LATE FALL   WINTER

2 part

Landscape Plants from the Ground Up

AFTER READING THE FIRST PART of the book, you have a pretty good idea of which plants to grow for a special effect. But picking the right plant species is only half of the garden equation. You also need to know how to keep your woodies alive and healthy. Part 2 shows specific techniques for choosing the best trees and shrubs at the nursery. Then you'll learn what to do with them when you get home — how to plant them, plus techniques for pruning woody plants for best growth and to accomplish your decorative goals.

3

BUYING AND PLANTING YOUR LANDSCAPE PLANTS

DEVELOPING CHECKLISTS, personal preferences, and landscape plans is not only creative and stimulating, it's also basic to the design process. In this chapter, however, we begin to discover how to put your ideas into action. A better landscape is almost yours. Now let's go shopping.

Visiting Nurseries and Garden Centers

BUYING TREES AND SHRUBS at local nurseries and garden centers has advantages. You see what you're getting. This is important if you're choosing trees and shrubs for their leaf or flower color, decorative fruits, ornamental bark, or succession of bloom. Nurseries stock heavily in spring when most people do their planting, and also in fall, another common planting time. Pay attention to ideal planting times in your locale so you can find the freshest, healthiest stock.

You can buy trees and shrubs at independent nurseries, big-box stores, and even supermarkets. While it's hard to beat the prices at big-box stores and supermarket chains, nurseries usually offer more tree and shrub varieties and individual trees in a range of sizes. While expensive large specimens over 4 feet high fill more garden space at first, younger, cheaper trees shorter than 4 feet (particularly *whips* or tree shoots with minimal or no branching) adapt readily to their new surroundings. Once established, early growth of a whip is often fast. In fact, the growth rate of whips can outstrip that of newly planted big trees after several years.

Some nurseries guarantee the trees and shrubs you buy for one year (be sure to save the receipt). Others replace material that dies after a year if their employees did the original planting. To avoid future surprises or disappointments, be sure to ask about a nursery's return or replacement policy before you purchase the plants.

▲ **Shoppers' delight.** Many well-stocked nurseries not only offer a wide selection of plants at different prices and sizes, but also have plant lovers on staff to advise you on your purchase.

Buying Mail-Order Plants

YOU CAN ALSO BUY PLANTS over the Internet or from mail-order catalogs. I delight in skimming plant catalogs on snowy nights, a cup of cocoa in hand. Mail-order plant shopping is convenient. Even people who hate shopping can do it undisturbed from home, and the plant selection is vast. Moreover, you can sometimes find uncommon plants not available nearby. The disadvantages range from not being able to see what you're buying to shipping damage and relatively small plant sizes.

One way to avoid disappointment is by recognizing that all nurseries are in business to sell and therefore the gorgeous plant photos and descriptions you see in the catalogs may give you an overly optimistic view when it comes to growing the same plants in your garden. Discipline yourself to buy only plants that fit your hardiness zone and soil and light conditions. When in doubt, phone your Cooperative Extension Service and ask an extension specialist or a master gardener help-line for advice.

Deal with mail-order nurseries recommended to you by knowledgeable gardeners. If you're looking for rare plants, you may have to deal with an unfamiliar specialized nursery and take more of a chance. Mail-order nurseries should ship to your house at the correct time for planting and practice shipping methods that protect the plants from mishandling and shipping damage. Many mail-order nurseries also have online catalogs. These listings sometimes include more plants than do printed catalogs, since the nurseries can offer plants available in smaller numbers online.

As soon as mail-order plants arrive, open the box. Check your order to make sure that you received the right trees and shrubs and that they arrived in good condition. If plants arrive damaged, contact the nursery immediately for a refund or replacement. If the plants are in good shape, plant them right away. Soak plants shipped bare-root for several hours or overnight in a bucket of clear water before planting. If your plants arrive in soil-filled containers, water them straight away. Where it's too cold to plant, shelter them outdoors for several days, until it's safe to plant them. However you obtain your plants, keep them shaded and moist until planting or they may not survive the process.

YOU GET WHAT YOU PAY FOR

A bargain is not always a bargain, whether you're shopping at a nursery, garden center, or box store. Although it's true that there are great sales in late October and November, it may also be true that, depending upon the severity of your winter, the plant you buy on sale at that time of year may not survive until spring.

Limited selection is another disadvantage of buying what's on hand. Although nurseries and garden centers stock tree and shrub species hardy in your area, they cannot carry every cultivar. Therefore, if you see a rare shrub in a gardening magazine, you may not be able to acquire it locally, even if it is hardy near you. Some nurseries can order particular plants for you with advance notice. As time goes by, identify local plant sellers whom you trust and develop positive business relationships with them.

Tree and Shrub Buyer's Checklist

Choose trees with the following characteristics:

- Sound and sturdy rather than tall and leggy, which may signal weakness.
- Wraps not hiding the physical condition of the lower stem. (Look beneath trunk or stem wraps that protect trees during transport.)
- Single trunks well-developed and straight, tapering to a slight flare at the base.
- Multi-stemmed plants full and attractive from all angles.
- Evenly spaced limbs along and around the trunk.
- Strong branch unions with trunk. (Limbs that seem squeezed to the trunk because of the narrow angle they form with it are weakly attached; tight multiple trunks are also weak. Vertical cracks may form below the union of trunk and limb, leading to breaks after storms.)
- Clean, healthy, well-shaped leaves.
- Enlarged buds with substance.
- A big rootball with sufficient roots for healthy development.
- Moist, fibrous (not woody) roots.

If your tree or shrub shows any of the following characteristics, reject it:

- Injured limbs.
- Dead branches or brown, dried-up buds.
- Trunks harmed by mowing or incorrect pruning.
- Bark splits.
- Spindly appearance.
- Insect infestation on leaves, bark, or soil. (Look for evidence like cocoons and galls.)
- Wilting leaves and stems.
- Curled leaves, discolored margins, or foliage marked black, brown, or yellow.
- Two leaders.
- Weak, narrow branch crotches. (Often branches formed at a narrow angle to the trunk develop *included bark* at the top of the crotch. Included bark grows down into the crotch, detaching part of the limb from the tree and making it susceptible to weather damage.)
- Dry or damaged rootballs.
- Potbound, with circling or girdled roots.

Choosing the Right Site

Before buying a house, you look for an agreeable community where you can raise a family, put down roots, and thrive. Similarly, before planting trees and shrubs, you consider where they'll do best in the garden. Understanding where your trees and shrubs grow in the wild can help you determine the best places to grow them on your lot. Supplying their preferred conditions and appropriate amounts of sun and moisture ensures that they will grow strong.

Plenty of Elbow Room

Think about the mature size that a tree or shrub may achieve. If you plant it too close to the house, you may need to prune it excessively or even cut it down while it's still healthy and relatively young. Check with your town office for information about requirements for how close you're allowed to plant to roads, sidewalks, and property lines (setbacks). If you violate these setbacks, you may have to remove a healthy mature tree. Investigate the location of underground utilities to avoid cutting cables or power lines. In addition to considering what's underground, look up. If you see power lines overhead, avoid planting tall trees that will interfere with them in the future. The power company may come along and prune or remove the trees altogether.

▼ **An overwhelming problem.** Mature evergreen and deciduous plants overwhelm this house and the bed in which they're planted. By replacing overgrown trees and shrubs, the owners can restore scale and balance to the facade.

Good Plant Neighbors

If you live on a wooded property and want to plant a shade garden under a canopy of wild trees, decide which existing trees to keep. There's nothing wrong with reducing the number of trees on a lot, especially when you intend to grow plants underneath. Start by removing dead or extensively damaged trees, trees leaning close to the house, and trees with unattractive forms. Keep strong trees with single vertical trunks and well-branched crowns. You may also want to preserve natural groves of birches or masses of small trees or shrubs with striking characteristics such as showy fruit, flowers, bark, or stunning fall color. Remove enough material to provide adequate light and space for the new plants you want to grow.

In general, new understory plantings of trees and shrubs work best under large deep- or tap-rooted trees such as oak, hickory, pecan, sour gum, and bald cypress — all North American natives — and exotics like little-leaf linden (*Tilia cordata*) and scholar tree (*Sophora japonica*). Plant small, young specimens, choosing a spot between big

IF THE TREE FITS, BUY IT

When buying conifers, the following guidelines from the American Conifer Society may help you choose the right size for your site:

Miniature. Growth per year less than 1"; approximate size at 10 years (referring to growth in any direction) less than 1'

Dwarf. 1"–6" growth per year; 1'–6' at 10 years

Intermediate. 6"–12" growth per year; 6'–15' at 10 years

Large. More than 12" growth per year; more than 15' at 10 years

▶ **Artful layers.** A lavish border including purple chasteberry (**A**), purple-leaf sand cherry (**B**), glossy abelia (**C**), and 'Mariesii Perfecta' big-leaf hydrangea (**D**) grows under a white pine with low and crowding branches removed.

▲ **Mulched beds.** Spring bulbs, groundcovers, summer perennials, and deciduous shrubs lend seasonal interest to the mulched beds under a Heritage birch allée.

roots near the soil surface. Dig the planting hole carefully and by hand to avoid hurting these established trees. Most of the roots that take up essential elements are within a foot of the soil surface. The deeper roots of these trees are more important for water uptake and structural stability.

Trees and turf don't mix, so site new plantings in mulched beds separate from the lawn. A healthy lawn's dense roots are ravenous and compete for nutrients with hungry shallow-rooted trees like beech, birch, and maple, which are feeding in the top 12 to 18 inches of soil. Landscape trees and shrubs do best in beds planted singly or, even better, grouped as in the wild. Beds and borders also protect new trees and shrubs from mower damage and prevent soil compaction and oxygen loss from foot traffic over the network of surface roots.

"Packaging" Trees and Shrubs

Nursery trees and shrubs come in three forms: container-grown, balled-and-burlapped, and bare-root. Let's look at the containerized plant first.

It's All in the Container

Containerized trees and shrubs are raised in pots that hold their entire root system. Buying potted plants has some advantages. A healthy potted plant experiences less stress than other plants when planted out in the garden because its roots are intact. Also, a container-grown plant cultivated in soil-free potting mix weighs less than a typical field-grown plant of similar size, making it convenient if you're planting trees and shrubs by yourself. As long as potted plants receive proper aftercare, you have much more leeway when you plant them. Typical pot sizes range from 2 to 20 gallons.

Potted trees and shrubs should have a sturdy, fibrous root system that fills the pot without being potbound. (The roots of potbound trees and shrubs grow woody, encircle the rootball, and sometimes emerge from the drainage holes.) The size of the plant should be in proportion to the pot. If a trunk looks too big for its pot, ask the nursery staff to remove it from the pot so you can see if the roots are white and finely meshed. If the trunk looks too small, it may have recently been stepped up to a larger container and is not ready to sell, because the roots have not yet established themselves. The soil around a new transplant may crumble, exposing the rootball from the original pot. For advice about how to plant a container-grown tree, see page 92.

▲ **A good start.** Nursery-grown trees and shrubs raised in containers are easily transplanted into the garden because their root systems are intact.

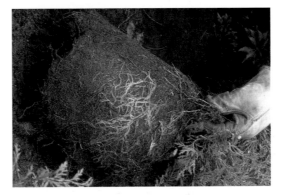

▲ **At the root of the matter.** The roots of this shrub are light, not woody, forming a fibrous network that binds the soil.

Balled-and-Burlapped Plants

Although smaller plants establish more efficiently than larger ones, you may want to plant big trees and shrubs to fill space in public areas fast. The traditional way to buy large landscape material is balled-and-burlapped, often called "b&b." Most nurseries offer b&b deciduous trees and evergreen trees and shrubs. These plants are field-grown in rows, then dug up with a ball of soil around the roots. The grower wraps the rootball in natural or synthetic burlap and binds it together with twine or straps, or sets it into a wire shipping basket. When b&b plants are harvested, much of the root system is cut off, making these plants more difficult to establish than a well-grown container or bare-root specimen.

When you plant b&b plants, remove as much of the protective materials as you can without damaging the ball. Do not buy the plant if the trunk feels loose, the rootball is dry, split, or broken, or the roots look woody. Instead, look for a plant with a fibrous root system in a firm, moist rootball. At the nursery, make sure the staff carries b&b plants by the rootball, not the trunk. When buying balled-and-burlapped plants, ask to see the top of the rootball. Ideally, the trunk flare should be visible above the soil. Sometimes, however, the digging and bagging process causes soil to bunch up on the trunk, making the soil level appear higher than it was in the field. Before planting, you may have to look for the root collar by scraping away the top of the rootball so you can determine the proper planting level. If you see tiny feeder roots growing above the flare, wait until the tree is established in the ground before removing all the soil above the root collar. If there are no feeder roots growing from the trunk, then you can brush away the excess soil and expose the flare of the trunk when you plant. (For step-by-step b&b planting information, see page 86.)

If you find planting b&b material heavy and cumbersome, hire the nursery supplying your trees to plant them. You may save money in the end, since many nurseries guarantee the material if they plant it.

Trees and shrubs purchased as b&b establish best if you plant them in very early spring or early fall. They release little water vapor through their leaves at these times. Moreover, these are the times of year when the soil tends to be moist and cool, providing excellent conditions for root growth.

▶ **Probing for the root collar.** When needed, gently rub off some soil at the trunk's base to find the root collar, a key factor in digging the planting hole to the correct depth.

In too deep. This dove tree is dying from the top down because its feeder roots lack the air needed to survive.

Like children, if treated well, trees stay healthy and reward you with years of robust growth. That means starting out with good stock that suits your climate and planting it in a way that benefits its growth. If you remember only one thing about planting trees and shrubs, let it be this: Successful tree planting means keeping the trunk flare visible and setting the rootball high enough for air to reach and circulate around the root system. This means that you should plant the root collar (where the trunk meets the roots) at ground level. If your tree has a high rootball, then plant the top of the rootball above soil level. Most root activity occurs in the top foot of soil. Planting high lets the roots breathe.

Look at trees in the wild or grand old specimens growing in a park. Do you see how trunks spread out at the base? That's no accident. Flares mark the transition between trunk and roots. Planting trees low in the ground stresses them, because they lack the oxygen necessary for healthy growth, making them susceptible to disease. A diseased tree is a weakened tree, at risk for insect and weather damage and ultimately death.

A Matter of Timing

The best time to plant either a container-grown or balled-and-burlapped tree depends upon your climate. In cool climates, plant trees in early spring and early fall when it typically rains more and soils and temperatures are cool. Mulch root zones with a 3-inch layer of shredded leaf litter or bark after planting. Because mulched soil stays warmer than bare soil, trees continue their underground root development for weeks or months after air temperatures have dropped below freezing. Planting after mid-October, however, may not leave time for newly planted trees to produce enough root growth to support their survival. If you live in a very cold climate, trees may not have enough time to establish before the soil freezes. Spring is the best time to plant in that situation. In Zone 7 and warmer, you can plant potted trees year-round. Balled-and-burlapped trees are usually planted in fall after leaf drop.

Sassafras albidum

DIG IT?

Some gardeners acquire plants by collecting them from the wild, a questionable practice that's best to avoid. Removing plants, especially rare ones, from the wild endangers the natural environment where they grow. With an owner's permission, however, you can dig a common seedling from private property and transplant it into your yard. My husband, Bob, and I did that after years of frustration trying to grow sassafras purchased from nurseries. Our neighbor owns a wild sassafras grove with many seedlings and gave us permission to dig one. We did, but it didn't survive. Eventually we found sassafras raised from seed and grown in a container at a specialty nursery. It's thriving.

DIGGING IN

Many of the techniques for planting a tree or shrub are the same, whether it's been put up in a container, balled and burlapped, or shipped bare-root. Let's start with a step-by-step look at planting a balled-and-burlapped tree, in this case, a Japanese stewartia (*Stewartia pseudocamellia*).

Using colored chalk, spray paint, or a garden hose, mark a circle at least two or preferably three times the diameter of the rootball, container, or bare-root system. If you want your circle to be absolutely symmetrical, put a bamboo stake at the center, tie a piece of string the length of the radius to it, and measure your circle by moving the string around the stake. Lift the sod inside the circle with a flat-edged spade or sod lifter and use it to patch bare spots in your lawn.

1 **Measure the depth** of the rootball with a yardstick or tool handle. Use a shovel to dig a hole almost as deep as the rootball, setting the soil you remove on a mat at the side of the hole. As a safeguard against planting the rootball too deep, check the root collar and the actual depth of the rootball. (See also photographs on page 84.)

2 **Rough up the sides** and base of the hole with a hand rake so roots can penetrate native soil more easily. The shovel, pushed against surrounding soil, may have glazed the hole, slowing the root system's expansion. In heavy clay soil, add a *little* compost or peat moss — no more than 10 to 15 percent of total backfill. Plants establish better in well-drained, amendment-free, native soil.

3 **Put the plant in a wheelbarrow** to bring it to the planting hole. If you don't have a wheelbarrow, support the rootball from below when you carry it: Do *not* carry the plant by its trunk. Take the tree or shrub to firm ground at the edge of the planting hole, then carefully set the plant in the center of the hole.

4 **Open the burlap** and remove it before backfilling the hole. If a crumbly or damaged rootball makes that impossible, cut away the burlap from the top and sides of the rootball once you've situated it in the hole. Equally important, if there's a wire cage, use wire cutters to remove as much of it as possible before backfilling.

5 **Lay a yardstick** or handle across the hole to check that you are not planting too deep. The trunk flare should be at or just above ground level. There should be no space between the handle and the top of the rootball. Never bury the flare. Carefully adjust the soil level in the hole, supporting the rootball as you add (or remove) soil, if needed.

6 **Trim** any ragged roots that are exposed. Roots may have been torn in the original digging process at the nursery. Clip off the ends of frayed roots that are exposed, because roots with fresh, smooth cuts will close up better than rough breaks once planted.

7 **Add the soil back** into the hole until it is half full. Take care to keep the trunk flare and top of the rootball above ground level. Tamp the soil gently with your foot, then water it in. The soil will settle. Add enough soil to fill the hole, tamping as you go.

8 **Make a ridge** of soil around the periphery of the hole. This creates a bowl that will retain both rainfall and irrigation water, so they can nurture the new tree. Water the plant thoroughly, adding a little more topsoil if the soil settles noticeably around the rootball after watering. Slow watering is better than strong hosing. Too much water too fast can ruin the soil's minute air pockets, from which roots absorb the air they need. Staking is rarely necessary, except on windy or exposed sites, and should be removed after one year. Here, a flat, flexible band loops the trunk at the lowest branch so the treetop can still move. The band attaches to a 2" × 2" wooden stake angled and pounded 18" deep into virgin soil in line with the prevailing wind. Flag the stake and band to prevent tripping.

It's Never Too Early to Start Training

Eliminate crossing or rubbing branches.

Pruning your new tree at planting time will help it get established more quickly and also maximize its chances of attaining an attractive shape when it matures. Here are some potential problems you can correct.

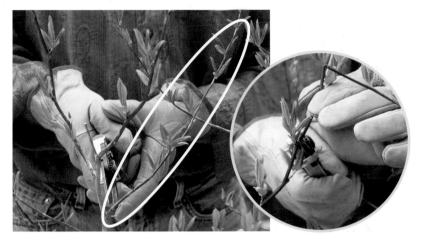

Take out inward-growing branches.

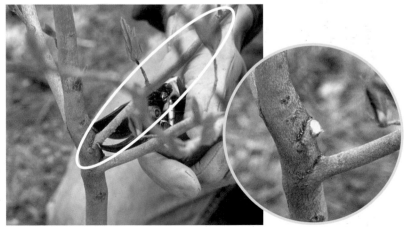

Prune off branches that are too close together.

Prune overall to shape.

BARE-ROOT PLANTS

Sometimes roses and mail-order trees and shrubs are sold bare-root. Bare-root means that roots are free of soil. The original soil was washed off, so the plants are light to ship. Bare-root plants usually sell for less than half the cost of their containerized counterparts. They are packed in slightly moist spaghnum moss or wood shavings. When shipped and planted, bare-root plants should be dormant, meaning that the plant should not be in active growth. Both the plant and the root system should be well formed and balanced in appearance. Roots should be moist and fibrous, not damaged or woody. Here's how to a plant bare-root rose.

1 **Soak plant** for several hours or overnight in a bucket of water before planting.

2 **Partially backfill hole** to create a mound of soil up to surrounding ground level. Make sure the hole is deep enough for the roots to spread down and out over the mound of soil in the center.

3 **Arrange roots** over mound. If join between stem and roots is not at or just above ground level, adjust mound by pressing on or taking off some soil. Trim torn, injured, or too-long roots with clean, sharp pruners before backfilling. Don't curl overly long roots around circumference of hole. Roses should be planted with the swollen graft at or above soil level (or about 2" below ground in the north, to prevent freezing.)

4 **Backfill hole** about halfway, pressing soil down gently but firmly. Work the soil among the roots of the plant to keep large air pockets from forming and to stabilize the plant. If you're planting new roses where other roses have grown, you'll have to remove and discard all old roots and soil from the hole and substitute a planting mix made for roses.

5 **Water well** after you have backfilled the hole half full of soil. Let the water drain fully to eliminate air pockets at the bottom of the hole. Continue filling the hole with soil, tamping it with your hands and then watering it in.

6 **Complete planting** as for balled-and-burlapped planting (page 86). Create a raised ring of soil around edge of planting hole to form a shallow basin, making it easier to keep water around the planting hole, until plant is established.

CONTAINER-GROWN PLANTS

For the most part, planting a container-grown specimen is similar to planting balled-and-burlapped trees. Prepare the site following steps 1 and 2 on page 86. Right before planting, take the plant to the edge of the hole. Then tip the container gently with one hand while tapping the pot to release the plant with the other. If you find that the plant has compacted or girdling roots, carefully loosen them by teasing them apart with your fingers or a hand rake. Proceed with steps 5–8 on pages 87–88.

When you bring container-grown plants home from the nursery, you can try them out in different sites before digging and getting them into the ground. Don't forget that they're standing higher in their pots than they will once you've settled them into their permanent spots.

Water: Elixir of Life

ADEQUATE WATER helps newly planted trees and shrubs recover from transplant shock so their roots can establish in the soil, a process that may take up to three years. If a tree is large at planting time, it will take longer to become established than a small tree does. Unless you plant drought-tolerant varieties, it's especially important to water established plants in stressful times to help them maintain their vigor. Keeping them hydrated and healthy reduces the chances of stress-related pests and diseases.

Transplants need water on a regular basis when the top couple of inches of soil feel dry but before the deeper planting soil completely dries out. Water trees deeply at least once or twice a week with an irrigation bag (such as a TreeGator, a low-cost plastic bag that dispenses water automatically out of holes in the bottom) or a soaker hose, or leave a dribbling garden hose at the base of the plant. Continue watering long and deeply throughout the growing season and repeat the following year until the plant is well established and growing at a relatively consistent rate. Establishing a newly planted tree depends upon both climate and planting conditions.

WATER EFFICIENCY

Planting the right plant in the right place is the first step to water efficiency. If you group plants requiring little water in one area and plants that need lots of water in another space, then wasting this precious natural resource is less likely. Once trees and shrubs are established, they usually survive without extra moisture.

Soak It to Them!

My preference for economically and efficiently delivering moisture to transplanted trees and shrubs is a soaker hose. Water seeps through tiny pores along the hose, penetrating the soil around the roots where the plant needs it most. Soaker hose reduces the likelihood of transmitting disease by water splashing from one plant onto another. Moreover, you can hide soaker hose under a thin layer of mulch or topsoil, although clogs are less likely above ground.

A well-made hose resists cracking, clogging, decay, and frost damage, though you may want to check for clogs if you move the hose frequently. A high-quality, 60-foot black soaker hose with a ⅝-inch diameter sells for as little as $13. If your plant is at a distance from the source of water, attach a garden hose to your faucet and a soaker hose at the end of the garden hose. For large areas, you can attach a second soaker hose to the first, but make sure that water reaches the end of the second line. Fitting a Y-joint to your faucet lets you install a second hose close to the water's source.

In our garden, we automated sprinklers and soaker hoses by installing an irrigation system. Before my husband and I figured out the flow rate of the soaker hoses in one large raised mixed bed, we drowned a lovely franklinia and a young Japanese maple by watering too long. Now we know that we can deep-water this particular bed on a hot, droughty day in five minutes. A second franklinia planted 10 feet from the first in a mixed border and never irrigated survives to this day as a small multi-stemmed shrub.

RULES OF THUMB FOR WATERING

- Newly planted trees need more watering than established trees and shrubs.
- Water moisture-hungry trees more than drought-tolerant species.
- Water more in mid- and late summer when temperatures are high.
- Water more during times of drought.
- If you dig in a root zone and injure some roots, water more until new roots grow.

How Long to Water? It Depends . . .

The duration of watering also varies with root depth and soil composition. A tree planted in porous sandy soil may need more frequent watering than the same tree planted in slow-draining heavy clay where water pools on the soil surface. Gauge how much water your plants need by digging a small hole with a narrow trowel in the watering zone and checking after 15 minutes to see if water has reached the deeper roots. Note that most tree roots occur in the top 12 inches of soil. Check every few minutes to see if you need to keep watering for full saturation. Determine how long it takes for moisture to reach the entire root zone, then water your garden for that amount of time or set your automatic timer to run for the duration. Depending upon your region and the weather, you may want to water established trees as much as twice a week or as little as once every two weeks. Once established, trees planted in a moist open environment probably don't need watering except during dry spells.

Mulch: More than Just Decorative

Just as clothes make the man, organic mulch brings refinement to a garden. I like to use dark brown conifer mulches, such as shredded hemlock or pine bark nuggets, around trees. In areas with many pines, fine-textured tan pine needles look attractive, especially under massed evergreens. Aged compost, chopped leaves, and humus are other choices that work well. When used properly, however, these mulches do far more for trees and shrubs than make them look pretty. Here are just a few additional benefits.

- **Enhances overall design.** Mulching unifies a garden. Mulch colors and defines garden beds and borders. Avoid red or

◄ **A pleasing whole.** A natural mulch unifies this mixed planting of trees, shrubs, and perennials.

yellow dyed mulches, however; instead of adding natural beauty to your garden, they make it look sick and unappealing. Shape the tree and shrub beds in any way that enhances your garden layout and design.

- **Keeps plants clean.** When water from rain or irrigation hits hard bare soil, it splashes dirt on the trunk and leaves. Because mulch absorbs this splatter, it helps keep plants clean.

- **Helps protect against injury.** Lawn mower nicks and scratches on tree trunks open the door to pests and diseases. When you mulch around trees and shrubs, you don't have to get up close to the plants when you're mowing, and you thus avoid the risk of injury from trimmers or heavy equipment.

- **Suffocates weeds.** Mulch robs weeds of the light and air they need to grow.

- **Helps retain moisture.** A 2- to 3-inch-thick layer of mulch prevents the speedy evaporation of water from the soil.

- **Moderates soil temperature.** Mulch blankets and warms the earth in cold weather and shades and cools the soil in the heat.

- **Improves soil.** Organic mulches nourish the soil when they decompose.

- **Provides beneficial, natural growing conditions.** Mulching groups of trees and shrubs in discrete beds and borders ensures they have their own growing territory, apart from the surrounding grass. Both lawns and trees need food, light, and water, and compete for those essentials when they share the same area. Healthy turf has a dense system of feeder roots in the top foot of soil, just like trees. By mulching groups of trees and keeping them separate from the lawn, you create more natural, forestlike growing conditions where they can thrive.

- **Protects against chemicals.** If you use herbicides on your lawn, growing plants in a mulched bed away from grass can shield them from possible damage.

If brown bores you, plant a shade-tolerant groundcover that suits your climate around your trees and shrubs. Some options include hosta, barrenwort, 'Green Sheen' Japanese pachysandra, or native Allegheny pachysandra.

▶ **Groundcovers** add richness of color and texture to the ground plane: bigroot geranium *(Geranium macrorrhizum)* (**A**), barrenwort *(Epimedium* species) (**B**), bigroot geranium (**C**). They also soften the appearance of hard materials and straight lines: spotted deadnettle *(Lamium maculatum* cultivar) (**D**).

Applying Mulches

Mulching trees and shrubs for health and beauty is simple and satisfying when you follow these few simple rules:

- **Depth.** Apply organic mulch 2 to 3 inches deep, replenishing it each year, or more often as it decomposes.
- **Air space.** Ring mulch around plants. Keep it 1 to 2 inches away from the trunk of an established tree or the ground-level branches of a shrub to defend against bark decay. Hilling mulch against bark creates the warm damp conditions that can lead to pest infestations and disease outbreaks. Avoid those mulch volcanoes you see hugging young trees in industrial parks and corporate headquarters around the country.
- **Newly planted trees.** Apply the mulch at least as far as the spread of the canopy and preferably several inches beyond.
- **Old established trees.** Mulch an area a minimum of 10 feet beyond the trunk, though the tree's root system extends even farther than the diameter of the crown.
- **Renewal.** When you need to add more mulch, first rake the existing mulch to break up any crust, then add just enough new material to create a 2- to 3-inch layer. Before adding the new mulch, pull any weeds growing through the old layer.
- **Spring mulching.** In mixed flower and shrub borders, apply mulch in spring after the soil has warmed up.
- **Fall mulching.** If you want to moderate freezing winter temperatures for shrubs with borderline hardiness, then apply mulch in fall after the ground has frozen. We used to mulch earlier in the fall until one spring when we discovered that voles had nested in leafy mulch under a low shrub. Now we clean out the border and later mulch with chopped leaves to give the rodents time to find a different home.

▲ **Finishing touches.** Mulch extends several inches beyond the canopy of this newly planted stewartia.

HOW MUCH MULCH SHOULD I BUY?

1. Calculate the area in square feet by multiplying the length by the width of the bed. Square off circular and irregular beds to estimate length and width.
2. Multiply the square footage of the bed by the depth of the mulch in inches.
3. Divide the resulting number by 324 for the cubic yardage you need to cover the bed.

A Bracing Subject

BUY HEALTHY PLANTS and don't stake a tree unless absolutely necessary. Unstaked tree trunks grow fatter more quickly than staked ones, and unstabilized trees produce farther-reaching root systems. You may occasionally need to steady a newly planted tree in the ground, however, if you discover that the rootball is not as sturdy as it looked at the nursery. When you unwrap the burlap, for instance, you may find a crumbly or damaged rootball that cannot support the tree. Another tree may be sturdy, but the planting site slopes or is exposed to strong winds that affect the tree's early stability and establishment. Trees with small diameter trunks (less than 2 inches) typically need no staking. When proper planting and mulching are not enough to keep a tree upright, you'll need to stake it in the ground.

▲ **Placing a brace.** Straps loop around the trunk at the lowest branch juncture to allow a bit of movement in the canopy.

▶ **Setting stakes.** Drive three notched equidistant stakes outside the perimeter of the planting hole to anchor the straps.

Sound Staking Procedures

Sink metal or wooden stakes about 24 inches into the soil, several inches beyond the circumference of the rootball but still within the mulched bed or groundcover area. Small trees need one stake, while larger ones need two or three. For a tree up to 12 feet tall to stay upright in strong winds, set two stakes at 90-degree angles to the wind.

The best materials for bracing are wide, flat, and stretchy. Bike tubes, webbed straps, and canvas bands all work. Wire or hose-wrapped wire can grind and injure the bark when the tree sways in the wind.

Trees need wiggle room. It's natural for a healthy tree to sway in the wind. Trunks held rigid may break when staked or perhaps after you remove the stakes. When you stake a trunk, make sure the top of the tree can sway and keep braces as low as practical on the trunk. Make sure you keep the cord or cable attaching the brace to the stake loose enough so that the tree can sway in the wind. Trunks grow weak above a too-tight brace.

Be sure to remove the brace once the tree is established. Trees may establish in a few months or a couple of years, depending upon the climate and growing conditions. In warm moist conditions, establishment may be fast, whereas in cold dry prairie conditions, it can take considerably longer. Failure to remove the brace may result in wood growing around the support, which then girdles or strangles the trunk. If you forget to remove the support and the trunk starts to envelop it, remove only the bracing material that is exposed and leave the rest of the support alone.

◄ **Choosing your style.** Ideas vary on bracing styles and the right number of stakes. Here, flat bands, which cause less damage to trees than wire fed through rubber hose, give the tree some sway but are neither too loose nor too taut to harm the bark. When staking a tree where people walk or play, flag the straps and stakes, or erect a circle of temporary fencing high enough to prevent tripping.

CHAPTER 4

CARING FOR YOUR LANDSCAPE PLANTS

TREES AND SHRUBS GROW EVERYWHERE, from suburban landscapes to natural swamps, so why should those on our properties need special care? Our home landscapes extend indoor living space. Because we're asking that plants in those landscapes fulfill various functions, their planting sites lack some of the safeguards that nature provides in a natural forest. If we can provide conditions in our home landscapes that imitate those that trees and shrubs experience in the wild, however, we can better ensure their health. In this chapter, we'll take a look at how to do this.

Working with Professionals

ALTHOUGH YOU CAN DO much of the care and maintenance of your trees yourself, certain tasks are best left to professionals. Always get professional help from a certified arborist when your safety is involved or when you're just not sure what to do. Whether it's climbing a mature oak to prune sprouts along the trunk or applying a specialized (or even toxic treatment, if that's your choice), I think that trained arborists should do the job. Yes, the cost is more than doing it yourself, but it's cheap compared with your family's ultimate well-being.

Finding a Certified Arborist

The International Society of Arboriculture (ISA), headquartered in Champaign, Illinois, offers an internationally recognized certification program in tree care. ISA supports shade and ornamental tree research around the world. For information and a list of ISA certified arborists, check your phone book (look for the logo) or refer to the Resources in the Appendix for the website. Other certification programs exist. For example, the Massachusetts Arborists Association has a certification program, renewable on an annual basis. Professional organizations include the American Society of Consulting Arborists (ASCA) and the Tree Care Industry Association (TCIA).

▶ **Don't do this at home.** Caution! Leave pruning high in the tree canopy and other dangerous jobs to a professional arborist.

Contracting with Professionals

Before you engage a tree-care specialist, don't be afraid to ask for and check references, and to require proof of insurance and a thorough written estimate. The proposal and "Terms and Conditions" shown here are approved by the Tree Care Industry Association (TCIA) and used with permission.

Your Favorite Tree Care Co. Inc.
123 Public Street
Anytown, AB, 12345
Phone: 1-800-111-1111
Info@YourFavoriteTreeCareCoInc.com

TCIA
VOICE OF TREE CARE

Proposal

Performed according to ANSI A300 industry standards for tree care.
unless noted otherwise.

Requested by:
JANE AND JOE HOMEOWNER
123 CALL-A-PRO DRIVE
YOUR TOWN, USA   (555) 555-5555

Type of Work	Clean	Thin	Raise	Reduce	Other	Objectives and Specifications *See back for definitions, terms, and conditions.*	Amount
Pruning 20" DIAMETER OAK IN BACKYARD	✓	✓				OBJECTIVES: IMPROVE AESTHETICS AND ALLOW GREATER LIGHT PENETRATION FOR POOL AREA.	
Pruning						PRUNING: REMOVE DEAD, DISEASED AND BROKEN BRANCHES 1-INCH DIAMETER OR GREATER. REDUCE THE LENGTH OF TWO LARGE	
Pruning						BRANCHES OVERHAN... 8 TO 10 FEET. T... PORTION OF THE T... BY REMOVING APPR...	
Pruning						LATERALS OF 1-IN...	

Arborist: Date: This prop...

"Professional tree care done right"

Work auth...

Signature:

Terms and Conditions

It is agreed by and between [Company] and [Authorizing Party (customer and/or customer's agent)] that the following provisions are made as part of this contract:

Insurance by Contractor: [Company] warrants that it is insured for liability resulting from injury to person(s) or property and that all employees are covered by Workers' Compensation as required by law. Certificates of coverage are available upon request.

Cancellation Fee: [Company] kindly requests that [Authorizing Party] provide at least 24 hours advance notice of any full or partial work cancellation. If a crew has been dispatched to the job site, the customer will be assessed a mobilization fee of $00.00 for incurred expenses.

Completion of Contract: [Company] agrees to do its best to meet any agreed upon performance dates, but shall not be liable in damages or otherwise for delays because of inclement weather, labor, or any other cause beyond its control; nor shall the customer be relieved of completion for delays.

Tree Ownership: [Authorizing Party] warrants that all trees listed are located on the customer's property, and, if not, that the authorizing party as received full permission from the owner to allow [Company] to perform the specified work. Should any tree be mistakenly identified as to ownership, the customer agrees to indemnify [Company] for any damages or costs incurred from the result thereof.

Safety: [Company] warrants that all arboricultural operations will follow the latest version of the ANSI Z133.1 industry safety standards. The authorizing party agrees to not enter the work area during arboricultural operations unless authorized by the crew leader on-site.

ANSI A300 Tree Care Standard Definitions: The following definitions apply to specifications detailed in this proposal.

clean: Selective pruning to remove one or more of the following parts: dead, diseased, and/or broken branches. Unless noted otherwise on this proposal, all cleaning will be of branches 1 inch diameter or greater throughout the entire crown.

crown: The leaves and branches of a tree measured from the lowest branch on the trunk to the top of the tree.

leader: A dominant or co-dominant, upright stem.

raise: Selective pruning to provide vertical clearance.

reduce: Selective pruning to decrease height and/or spread by removing specified branches.

restore: Selective pruning to improve the structure, form, and appearnce of trees that have been severely headed, vandalized, or damaged.

thin: Selective pruning to reduce density of live branches, usually by removing entire branches.

vista pruning: Selective pruning to allow a specific view, usually by creating view "windows" through the tree's crown.

Stump Removal: Unless specified in the proposal, stump removal is not included in the price quoted. Grindings from stump removal are not hauled unless specified in this proposal. Surface and subsurface roots beyond the stump are not removed unless specified in this proposal.

Concealed Contingencies: Any additional work or equipment required to complete the work, caused by the authorizing party's failure to make known or caused by previously unknown foreign material in the trunk, the branches, underground or any other condition not apparent in estimating the work specified, shall be paid for by the customer on a time and material basis. [Company] is not responsible for damages to underground sprinklers, drain lines, invisible fences or underground cables unless the system(s) are adequately and accurately mapped by [Authorizing Party] and a copy is presented before or at the time the work is performed.

Clean-up: Clean-up shall include removing wood, brush, and clippings, and raking of the entire area affected by the specified work, unless noted otherwise in this proposal.

Lawn Repair: [Company] will attempt to minimize all disturbances to the customer's lawn. Lawn repairs are not included in the contract price, unless noted otherwise on the proposal.

Terms of Payment: Unless otherwise noted in this proposal, the customer agrees to pay the account in full within 30 days of work completion. Failure to remit full payment within the payment term will result in a finance charge of [00.00%] per month.

Returned Check Fee: There will be a [$00.00] fee charged for all checks returned to our office for non-sufficient funds.

Pruning Demystified

Until you understand its simple logic, pruning can be one of gardening's great mysteries. Pruning plants for the right reasons with the right tools at the right time and in the right places on the plant can make both your plants and the landscape that surrounds them more refined and more beautiful. There are many reasons to prune, and all of them make good sense.

Healthier, more vital plants. Cut off dead or diseased branches not only to improve a plant's appearance, but also to prevent the spread of disease. Remove crossed and rubbing branches, a condition that can wear away protective bark, compromising the plant's health. Prune back limbs damaged by ice, heavy wet snow, strong winds, or mechanical damage. In some cases, you may have to remove whole plants, while in others only damaged areas need cutting.

Beauty. Good pruning can show off or even improve the basic form or structure of the plant.

Safety. If a low branch extends over a path, you may need to remove it to prevent tripping. Phone the power company if high limbs interfere with power lines. Prune back bushy plants growing near a road or at corners where the plants may block a driver's line of vision on the road or emerging from a driveway.

▶ **Pruning with purpose.** A plant's natural shape offers clues about pruning it and directing new growth. With roses (shown here) pruning goals include shaping for beauty, improving air circulation, and promoting new blooms.

Tender-Loving Tool Care

Whatever tools you choose, keep them clean, since dirty blades can spread pests and infections from plant to plant. Disinfect cutting surfaces with rubbing alcohol applied to a clean rag or paper towel. Tuck a fresh rag in your belt for wiping dirt and sap from the blades before each cut.

When necessary, follow the manufacturer's directions for taking apart pruners and saws. Remove rust from blades with fine sandpaper or a wire brush. Oil joints and springs regularly, and use a sharpening stone to hone the outer beveled edge of dull blades. Taking good care of saws and pruners ensures clean healthy cuts that benefit rather than damage the tree.

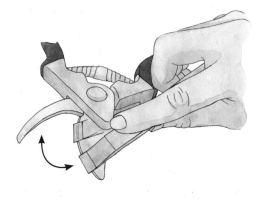

▶ **Sharp and clean.** For clean, safe pruning cuts, keep the slanting outer edge of your pruner blades sharp, and wipe them with a fresh rag or paper towel after each use.

PRUNING TOOLS
THAT ARE A CUT ABOVE

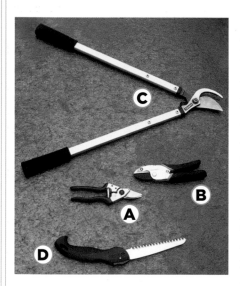

Hand pruners. Use hand pruners for stems up to ½-inch wide that are easy to reach. You'll find two kinds of hand pruners, each of which has specific uses. Bypass pruners (A) have two blades and cut like scissors. The upper blade curves past the lower blade, making it easy to cut cleanly into live green wood. Anvil pruners (B) on the other hand, make rough cuts with a knifelike action. They are best for thinning brush and removing hard or dead wood because their upper cutting edge squeezes the stem against an anvil or metal cutting block. Keep your cutting blade sharp, because a dull cutting edge can mash the stem. If you want one pair of hand pruners, then splurge on the best bypass pruners that you can afford. They give you more flexibility and do less damage to live wood. Some companies make hand pruners for lefties like me.

Loppers. Similar to hand pruners in the way they work, loppers (C) usually have longer handles and blades that let you cut branches up to 2 inches across. They come with either bypass or anvil-style blades. Loppers are good for reaching deep into a shrub and thinning excess growth, for cutting thorny branches, and for more forceful cuts because of the extra leverage the long handles provide.

Pruning saw. A folding pruning (D) saw is another useful item. I use my saw, which has a blade about 6½ inches long, to make clean cuts in stems less than 4 inches across. The pullback action required for cutting makes pruning the fat stems of my dieback paulownia fast and easy each fall.

Pruning a Branch

Dr. Alex Shigo, former chief scientist in the U.S. Forest Service, discusses natural target pruning in his book *Modern Arboriculture*. He recommends that proper pruning cuts be made close to the *branch collar* (the bulge under a branch where branch and stem tissues intersect) not flush with the trunk. Unlike humans, who heal by renewing injured tissue, trees compartmentalize, or close off, an injury from the rest of the tree by forming new wood over the damaged spot. Flush cuts that take off the branch collar enlarge the wound and spread more decay within the tree.

Let pruning wounds heal naturally. Don't paint them with wound dressing; dressings slow the healing process and keep the healthy new wood from forming.

Trees look their best when natural growth patterns guide your pruning efforts. Don't top trees. Topping is the practice of cutting back, or "heading," a tree's large branches, leaving long, ugly stubs from which many weak sprouts will grow. Topping destroys a tree's looks and makes it prone to disease and decay. It's better to remove a too-big tree, replacing it with one that suits the site, than to take this drastic and mistaken measure to control tree growth.

The drawings below (The Three-Part Cut) illustrate the technique for pruning off any branches that are at least 1½ inches in diameter.

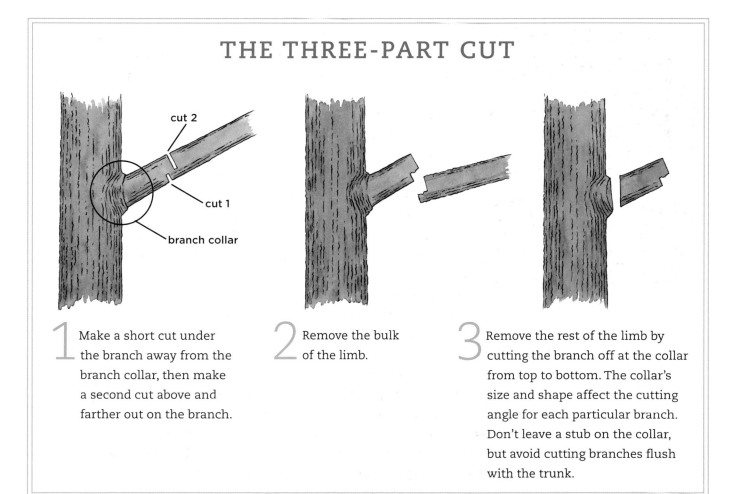

THE THREE-PART CUT

1 Make a short cut under the branch away from the branch collar, then make a second cut above and farther out on the branch.

2 Remove the bulk of the limb.

3 Remove the rest of the limb by cutting the branch off at the collar from top to bottom. The collar's size and shape affect the cutting angle for each particular branch. Don't leave a stub on the collar, but avoid cutting branches flush with the trunk.

Deutzia gracilis 'Nikko'

Kerria japonica 'Golden Guinea'

WHEN? IT'S THE BIG QUESTION

When to prune woodies depends upon your intention. For their health, remove dead or injured branches any time. Shape deciduous plants when bare. In general, for more flowers trim summer and fall bloomers when dormant, and spring-bloomers after flowering before new buds form.

PRUNE WHEN DORMANT

Nandina domestica 'Fire Power'

Symphoricarpos species

Timing Your Pruning

Among the factors that determine the best time to prune woodies are why you're growing them and when they bloom. Did you plant them for lush leaves, lavish flowers, or luscious fruits? Do they bloom in winter, spring, summer, or fall? And when do they form flower buds on their branches?

Basic pruning guidelines. Pruning deciduous trees and shrubs during late fall and winter dormancy helps limit contact with insects or fungi, which tend to be more active in warm weather. Dormant-pruning plants in the rose family helps prevent fireblight but may affect that year's flowers. Pruning when the trees are bare also allows you to see the shape of the tree.

Flowering trees and shrubs. The general rule is to prune flowering shrubs and trees that bloom on new wood (the current growth) in late winter or early spring before the start of this season's growth. Prune those that bloom on old wood (stems developed before the current growing season) soon after flowering to avoid removing this year's blossoms.

Problematic branches. You can remove dead, damaged, or diseased branches any time. It's best to remove crossed or rubbing branches when dormant, especially if they ruin the plant's structural appeal by making it look congested. Many shrubs need little pruning beyond that.

If you're busy, you may not have much choice about when to prune: you just prune when you have free time. That's okay even for flowering trees and shrubs, if you don't mind sacrificing one season's flowers. By selectively pruning shrubs blooming on old wood soon before they bloom, you'll give up some flowers. But if, for example, you clip a lilac hedge in late summer after it has set buds for the following spring you may be cutting off all the flowers.

Flowering Plants to Prune After Blooming

Prune plants that bloom on old wood as soon as possible after flowering, preferably within a month.

White forsythia	*Abeliophyllum distichum*
Serviceberry	*Amelanchier* species
Chokeberry	*Aronia* species
Alternate-leaf butterfly bush	*Buddleja alternifolia*
Sweetshrub	*Calycanthus* species
Camellia	*Camellia japonica*
Redbud	*Cercis* species
Flowering quince	*Chaenomeles speciosa*
Fringetree	*Chionanthus virginicus*
Flowering dogwood	*Cornus florida*
Kousa dogwood	*Cornus kousa*
Cornelian cherry	*Cornus mas*
Winter hazel	*Corylopsis pauciflora*
Daphne	*Daphne* species
Deutzia	*Deutzia gracilis*
Pearl bush	*Exochorda* × *macrantha*
Forsythia	*Forsythia* hybrids
Gardenia	*Gardenia jasminoides*
Witch-hazel	*Hamamelis* species
Big-leaf hydrangea	*Hydrangea macrophylla*
Oak-leaf hydrangea	*Hydrangea quercifolia*
Japanese kerria	*Kerria japonica*
Beautybush	*Kolkwitzia amabilis*
Magnolia	*Magnolia* species
Apple, Crabapple	*Malus* species
Sweet mockorange	*Philadelphus coronarius*
Almond, apricot, cherry, peach, plum	*Prunus* species
Ornamental pear	*Pyrus calleryana*
Azalea and rhododendron	*Rhododendron* species
Flowering currant	*Ribes sanguineum*
Rose (once bloomers)	*Rosa* species
Bridalwreath spiraea	*Spiraea prunifolia*
Thunberg spirea	*Spiraea thunbergii*
Japanese tree lilac	*Syringa reticulata*
Common lilac	*Syringa vulgaris*
Korean spice viburnum	*Viburnum carlesii*
European cranberry bush	*Viburnum opulus*
Doublefile viburnum	*Viburnum plicatum* f. *tomentosum*
Weigela	*Weigela florida*

Cornus kousa

Viburnum carlesii 'Aurora'

Rhododendron periclymenoides

Hamamelis virginiana

Flowering Plants to Prune When Dormant

Prune shrubs and trees that flower on the current season's growth (new wood) in late winter or early spring before they start growing and before bloom. Depending upon how large you want the shrub to grow, you can cut them back as far as the first pair of buds above the soil. For taller shrubs, prune plants higher above the ground.

Oxydendrum arboreum

Vitex agnus-castus

Glossy abelia	Abelia × grandiflora
Groundsel bush	Baccharis halimifolia
Barberry (deciduous)	Berberis species
Butterfly bush	Buddleja davidii
Beautyberry	Callicarpa species
Sasanqua camellia	Camellia sasanqua
Blue mist	Caryopteris × clandonensis
Summersweet	Clethra alnifolia
Smokebush	Cotinus coggygria [1]
Rose of Sharon	Hibiscus syriacus
Smooth hydrangea	Hydrangea arborescens
Panicle hydrangea	Hydrangea paniculata
Golden raintree	Koelreuteria paniculata
Crape myrtle	Lagerstroemia indica
Bush clover	Lespedeza thunbergii
Heavenly bamboo	Nandina domestica
Sourwood	Oxydendrum arboreum
Hybrid tea	Rosa cultivars
Elderberry	Sambucus species
Japanese spirea	Spiraea japonica
Snowberry	Symphoricarpos species
Blackhaw	Viburnum prunifolium
American cranberry bush	Viburnum trilobum
Chaste tree	Vitex agnus-castus

[1] When grown for foliage

Callicarpa bodinieri var. giraldii

Sambucus canadensis 'Laciniata'

Rhododendron 'Koromo-shikibu' | *Kalmia latifolia* 'Shooting Star'

Pruning Broad-Leaf Evergreens

In general, broad-leaf evergreens need little pruning. When necessary, prune them just before spring growth begins or immediately after flowering. If you choose the former, you'll give up some blooms this year, but you'll take advantage of their spring growth spurt for rejuvenation. Cut off dead, sick, injured, crossing, or rubbing stems, as well as stray stems for better shaping. Some broad-leaf evergreens may need more extreme pruning, particularly if you've put shrubs like jumbo rosebay rhododendrons (*Rhododendron maximum*) in foundation plantings without taking account of their mature size.

DEADHEADING RHODODENDERONS

Deadhead faded flowers of broad-leaf evergreens, such as rhododendrons, andromeda, and mountain laurel, just as you would the deciduous common lilac. Detaching faded flowers before seeds develop encourages these shrubs to direct their energy into next year's buds. As a result, plants look neater and will flower more next year. To deadhead rhodos, grasp a branch in one hand and a flower truss or cluster in the other, then carefully snap it off at its base with a quick twist of the wrist.

PRUNING OVERGROWN RHODODENDRONS

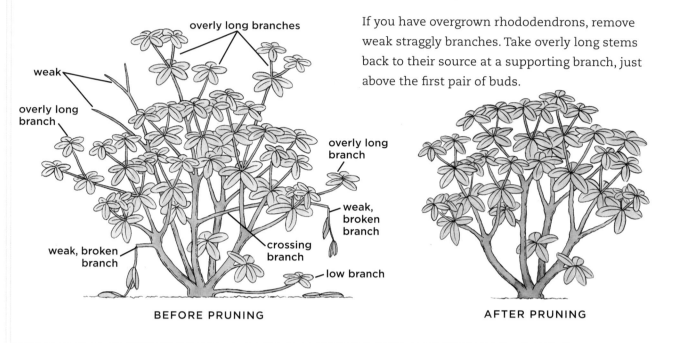

If you have overgrown rhododendrons, remove weak straggly branches. Take overly long stems back to their source at a supporting branch, just above the first pair of buds.

overly long branches

weak

overly long branch

overly long branch

weak, broken branch

weak, broken branch

crossing branch

low branch

BEFORE PRUNING

AFTER PRUNING

PRUNING CUTS

Check your handiwork frequently. Think about the shrub's natural shape and cut stems to inward or outward facing buds or branches to enhance the form. When in doubt about whether or not to prune a particular branch, be conservative: skip it and move on.

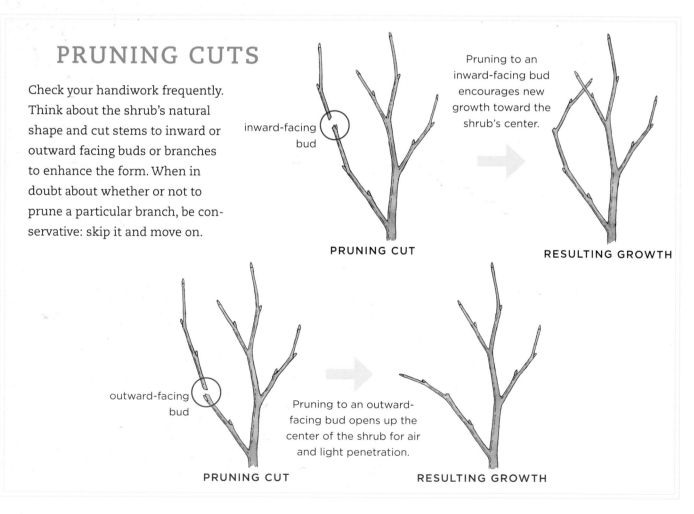

inward-facing bud

PRUNING CUT

Pruning to an inward-facing bud encourages new growth toward the shrub's center.

RESULTING GROWTH

outward-facing bud

PRUNING CUT

Pruning to an outward-facing bud opens up the center of the shrub for air and light penetration.

RESULTING GROWTH

Pruning Deciduous Trees

Some deciduous trees produce excessive sap in late winter and early spring, just before and when new growth begins. If you prune these trees, known as bleeders, during that time, sap runs from the fresh wounds. Because we love our trees, we project our feelings onto them and assume that "bleeding" hurts. It doesn't. Nor does it injure the tree. Prune the following bleeders during dormancy. If flowing sap bothers you and you don't like pruning in late winter or early spring, make cuts after the leaves have unfurled, around July. Do not prune when the tree just starts leafing out, however, or from late summer to midfall, when new weak growth can occur and the presence of pests and diseases is high.

Deciduous Trees to Prune When Dormant

Maple	*Acer* species
Horse chestnut	*Aesculus hippocastanum*
Birch	*Betula* species
Hornbeam	*Carpinus* species
Hickory/pecan	*Carya* species
Yellowwood	*Cladrastis kentukea*
Beech	*Fagus* species
Walnut	*Juglans* species
Osage orange	*Maclura pomifera*
Mulberry	*Morus* species
Poplar	*Populus* (some species)
Oak	*Quercus* species
Willow	*Salix* species
Chinese scholar tree	*Sophora japonica*
Linden	*Tilia* species
Elm	*Ulmus* species

Prunus x subhirtella 'Scott Early'

Rejuvenating Shrubs

TWO OPTIONS

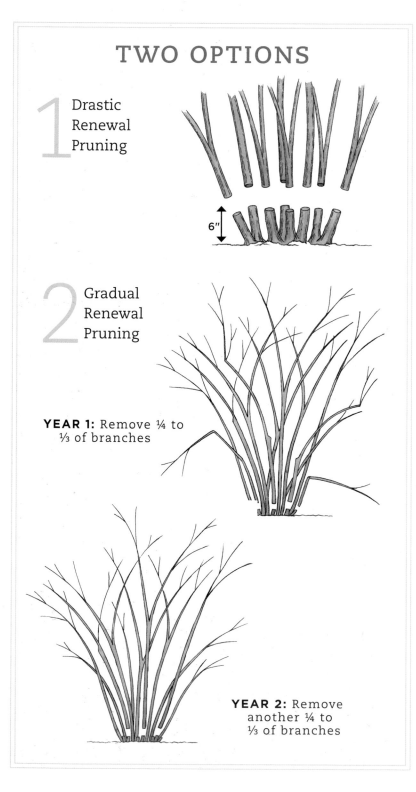

1 Drastic Renewal Pruning

6"

2 Gradual Renewal Pruning

YEAR 1: Remove ¼ to ⅓ of branches

YEAR 2: Remove another ¼ to ⅓ of branches

WHEN YOU HAVE an upright shrub that doesn't flower or color up as it did in the past, or one that looks overgrown, weak, congested, or straggly, it may be a candidate for renewal pruning. Drastic renewal is easy, but not suitable for every shrub. Simply cut down the whole shrub, leaving about 6 inches of stem at the base.

If you worry that whacking back a shrub in this way will cause a big hole in your view, you don't have to be quite this extreme. Spread the rejuvenation over three or four years, cutting back one quarter to one third of the branches each year. Start in early spring before new growth begins, clipping the oldest, biggest branches first, then the weak and ugly stems.

Repeat the process each year until the shrub has been renewed.

Depending upon the shrub, you may not want to stop pruning it after four years. For example, pruning a quarter of your forsythia stems down each year could keep blooms abundant and excessive growth under control.

Weigela florida 'Variegata'

Deciduous Shrubs
You Can Cut to the Ground

Glossy abelia	*Abelia × grandiflora*
Barberry	*Berberis* species
Beautyberry	*Callicarpa* species
Bluebeard	*Caryopteris × clandonensis*
Buttonbush	*Cephalanthus occidentalis*
Wintersweet	*Chimonanthus praecox*
Harlequin glorybower	*Clerodendrum trichotomum*
Forsythia	*Forsythia* hybrids
Bush clover	*Lespedeza thunbergii*
Honeysuckle	*Lonicera fragrantissima*
Ninebark	*Physocarpus opulifolius*
Shrubby cinquefoil	*Potentilla fruticosa*
Common lilac	*Syringa vulgaris*
Spirea	*Spiraea* species
Chaste tree	*Vitex agnus-castus*
Weigela	*Weigela* species

Chimonanthus praecox 'Luteus'

Caryopteris x *clandonensis*

Coppicing

Coppicing is a simple pruning technique that stimulates robust new growth by cutting trees and shrubs to the ground in late winter or early spring before new growth begins. Some folks coppice shrubby dogwoods and willows to promote brilliant stem colors. Because doing that removes flowers and fruits, you may want to coppice these shrubs every other year. You can coppice big trees like catalpa and paulownia annually to create bushy plants with giant leaves.

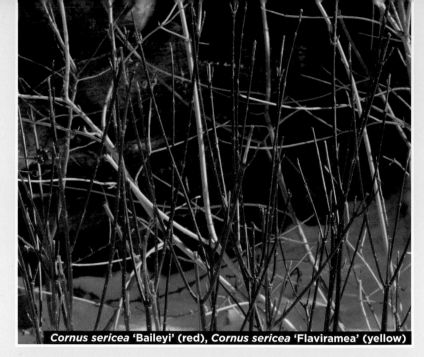
Cornus sericea 'Baileyi' (red), Cornus sericea 'Flaviramea' (yellow)

Plants That Can Be Coppiced
Cut down these ornamentals before growth begins in spring.

Butterfly bush	Buddleja davidii	To control size and increase blooms
Catalpa	Catalpa species	For huge tropical-style leaves on a multi-stem shrub
Tatarian dogwood	Cornus alba	To promote bright red stem color
Blood-twig dogwood	Cornus sanguinea	To promote red or yellow stems
Red osier dogwood	Cornus sericea	To promote bright red or yellow stems
Smooth hydrangea	Hydrangea arborescens 'Annabelle' and 'Grandiflora'	To encourage bigger flower heads on a more compact shrub
Bush clover	Lespedeza thunbergii	For arching, floriferous stems
Empress tree	Paulownia tomentosa	For huge tropical-style leaves on a multi-stem shrub
Coral bark willow	Salix alba 'Chermesina'	To promote bright orangey-red stems

▲ In spring, a pollarded 'Royal Purple' smokebush (*Cotinus coggygria* 'Royal Purple') develops numerous sprouts full of large, garnet-colored leaves, making it an attractive background shrub for a rose garden or mixed border.

Pollarding

Pollarding is another pruning technique to limit tree size and increase the dimensions of the leaves. Cutting stems back to the same spot on a trunk or major branches each year creates shrubby growth with larger leaves on the knobby fists that form at the ends of the branches. We pollarded a purple smokebush to keep it shrubby and to emphasize its gorgeous purple leaves. Instead of growing into a small flowering tree, it remained forever leafy and purple. Peegee hydrangeas are another plant that gardeners sometimes pollard to keep small and tidy. In general, however, you'll find many more coppiced than pollarded plants in American gardens.

Hedging Your Bets

I KNOW A NEWLY MARRIED COUPLE who bought a house surrounded by homes with young families. All the backyards abut, forming one fairly open swath of green where children run and shout at dusk. That's not what the newlyweds want to hear. They seek peace, privacy, and birdsong after busy days at work. Sure, they could install a fence, but that would be mighty unfriendly. A kinder gentler way to achieve the visual and psychological privacy they desire is to plant a fast-growing informal hedge or perhaps a mixed border of shrubs and trees.

Hedges create privacy and keep out ugly or unwanted views. They can be formal and geometric or loose and informal, depending upon the plants you use and the way you treat them. High or low, formal hedges make elegant backdrops for flowerbeds and borders.

You can create garden rooms, almost like the rooms in your house, if you plant a rectangle of four formal hedges with an opening. Some gardeners prune doors and windows into tall formal hedges, but these take considerable upkeep if you want them to resemble smooth green walls.

Informal hedges are easier to maintain, because the plants look more natural, though they may need thinning or renewal from time to time. Like formal hedges, informal hedges can also be short or tall. Typically, gardeners use one kind of plant per hedge, though I've seen amazing formal hedges comprised of interplanted green and purple-leafed European beech. Hedgerows marking property boundaries often include a variety of fruit-bearing shrubs and trees that attract wildlife.

▲ **Snaking forms.** Low, round hedges of 'Wintergreen' boxwood (*Buxus sinica* 'Wintergreen') call attention to the columnar emerald arborvitae (*Thuja occidentales*) growing within their curves.

▲ **Hedging for definition.** A low, rectangular hedge defines this little yard and joins the tiered geometry of the house with the space outdoors.

For Formal Hedges

EVERGREEN

Boxwood	*Buxus* species
Holly	*Ilex* species
Sweet bay	*Laurus nobilis*
Privet	*Ligustrum* species
Box honeysuckle	*Lonicera nitida*
False holly	*Osmanthus heterophyllus*
Yew	*Taxus* species
Arborvitae	*Thuja* species

DECIDUOUS

European hornbeam	*Carpinus betulus*
European beech	*Fagus sylvatica*

AND ONE TO SPARE

When you put in a new hedge, buy one more shrub than you need. Grow the extra plant elsewhere on your property. Then, if you have to remove a damaged plant from the hedge, you'll have a similar-sized shrub all ready to substitute in its place.

For Informal Hedges

EVERGREEN

Spotted laurel	*Aucuba japonica*
California lilac	*Ceanothus* species
Gardenia	*Gardenia jasminoides*
English holly	*Ilex aquifolium*
Chinese holly	*Ilex cornuta*
Japanese holly	*Ilex crenata*
Inkberry	*Ilex glabra*
American holly	*Ilex opaca*
Chinese juniper	*Juniperus chinensis*
Eastern red cedar	*Juniperus virginiana*
Mountain laurel	*Kalmia latifolia*
Oregon grape holly	*Mahonia aquifolium*
Sweet olive	*Osmanthus fragrans*
Photinia, redtip	*Photinia* species
Cherry laurel	*Prunus laurocerasus*
Azalea, rhododendron	*Rhododendron* species and hybrids
Yew	*Taxus* species

DECIDUOUS

Glossy abelia	*Abelia × grandiflora*
Many-flowered cotoneaster	*Cotoneaster multiflorus*
Willow-leaf cotoneaster	*Cotoneaster salicifolius*
Slender deutzia	*Deutzia gracilis*
Fothergilla	*Fothergilla* species
Hydrangea	*Hydrangea* species
Shrubby cinquefoil	*Potentilla fruticosa*
Bridal wreath spirea	*Spiraea prunifolia*
Lilac	*Syringa* species
Viburnum	*Viburnum* species

Viburnum dilatatum 'Michael Dodge'

Fothergilla major

For Barriers

Flowering quince	*Chaenomeles speciosa*
Hawthorn	*Crataegus* species
Osage apple	*Maclura pomifera*
Leather-leaf mahonia	*Mahonia bealei*
Firethorn	*Pyracantha coccinea*
Beach rose	*Rosa rugosa*

For Hedgerows or Boundaries

Hedge maple	*Acer campestre*
Spreading cotoneaster	*Cotoneaster divaricatus*
'Winter King' hawthorn	*Crataegus viridis* 'Winter King'
Sea buckthorn	*Hippophae rhamnoides*
Big-leaf hydrangea	*Hydrangea macrophylla*
Juniper	*Juniperus* species
Sweet bay	*Laurus nobilis*
Eastern red cedar	*Juniperus virginiana*
Osage orange	*Maclura pomifera*
Bayberry	*Myrica pensylvanica*
Currant	*Ribes* species
Dog rose	*Rosa canina*
High-bush blueberry	*Vaccinium corymbosum*
American cranberry bush	*Viburnum trilobum*

For Shade

Boxwood	*Buxus* species
False cypress	*Chamaecyparis* species
Oak-leaf hydrangea	*Hydrangea quercifolia*
Inkberry	*Ilex glabra*
California privet	*Ligustrum ovalifolium*
Cherry laurel	*Prunus laurocerasus*
Nanking cherry	*Prunus tomentosa*
Yew	*Taxus* species

For Sunny Sites

Little-leaf boxwood	*Buxus microphylla*
Lavender	*Lavandula angustifolia*
Rosemary	*Rosmarinus officinalis*
Lavender cotton	*Santolina chamaecyparissus*
Wall germander	*Teucrium chamaedrys*

For Wet Sites

Summersweet	*Clethra alnifolia*
Tatarian dogwood	*Cornus alba*
Blood-twig dogwood	*Cornus sanguinea*
Inkberry	*Ilex glabra*
Winterberry	*Ilex verticillata*
Arborvitae	*Thuja* species
Arrowwood viburnum	*Viburnum dentatum*

Thuja occidentalis 'Yellow Ribbon'   **Clethra alnifolia 'Ruby Spice'**   **Cornus alba 'Elegantissima'**

Planting a Formal Hedge

Dig individual holes or a trench and plant as usual. Set plants an equal distance apart, about 1 to 2 feet in single-row hedges and roughly 3 feet apart in double-row staggered hedges. If you're planting a mini-hedge in a formal parterre, however, planting distances would be closer, about 4 to 6 inches. Stimulate branching by pruning newly planted 1- to 2-year-old shrubs to about 8 inches tall. Remove the top third of more mature shrubs. Avoid setting lines of shrubs under the eaves of your house where they can be damaged by snow sliding off the roof.

The sides of formal hedges should taper inwards, or batter, from bottom to top. Slanting from a wide bottom to a narrow top lets sunlight reach the entire hedge and generates maximum new growth. If your hedge has sides at right angles to the top, on the other hand, sunlight cannot reach the base and the lower branches will eventually die out. If you have a 4-foot-tall hedge, for instance, it should be about 3 feet wide at the bottom and 1½ feet wide at the top. To help you maintain the proper batter when you shear the hedge, make a plywood pattern of the planned silhouette, then place it over the hedge and move it along as you cut. For old, well-maintained hedges, you can often use the shape beneath the straggly young shoots as a shearing guide. Choose rounded or pointed tops for hedges in snow country. A heavy snow load can crush and spoil a flat-topped hedge with its weight.

▲ **Batter up.** Trim formal hedges to the proper slant with a simple plywood guide that you can move along the top.

PRUNING EVERGREENS

For most evergreens, do hard pruning in spring. Shape white pines in late spring or early summer when you can see the new growth or candles at the branch tips. Remove up to two-thirds of each candle to control growth. If you cut into the shrub beyond the candle, the whole branch may die out.

Prune an informal hedge as you would an individual plant, thinning the oldest wood and clipping stray stems that interrupt the hedge's pleasing shape.

Timing Your Hedge Clipping

Clipping times vary for hedges, depending upon the plant material. Trim hedge shrubs that flower on last year's growth soon after blooming. Shrubs that flower on this year's growth should be clipped in late winter or just before new growth begins in spring. Avoid pruning deciduous and evergreen hedges in late summer and fall, since that could stimulate new growth. This tender growth may not harden before winter and come to harm. If you have to do a severe pruning, wait until deciduous plants are dormant.

TURNING A SHRUB INTO A SMALL TREE

With a little pruning, some big shrubs make small, single- or multi-trunk trees, ideal for tight spots and tiny gardens. This method can be helpful when you want to grow bulbs or ground covers underneath the canopy of the new tree. (See page 120 for suitable shrubs.)

Single-Trunk Tree

Year One. Plant a multi-stemmed shrub, and prune it to one upright stem.

Year Two. Remove suckers and low branches.

Later. Keep clipping suckers from the base and the lowest branches until the tree looks as you wish.

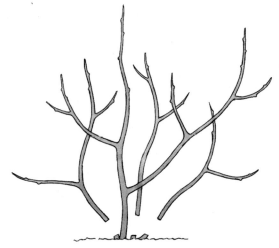

Multi-Trunk Tree

Year One. Plant a multi-stemmed shrub or prune an existing overgrown shrub. Choose three or more vigorous open stems that do not cross or rub and remove other stems

Year Two. Remove suckers and low branches.

Later. Clip low branching shoots and any suckers growing up from the base. Keep the interior of the plant fairly open for good air circulation.

Aralia elata 'Variegata'

Shrubs that Make Great Small Trees

Shadblow	*Amelancher canadensis*
Variegated Japanese angelica	*Aralia elata* 'Variegata'
Groundsel bush	*Baccharis halimifolia*
'Little King' birch	*Betula nigra* 'Little King'
Alternate-leaf butterfly bush	*Buddleja alternifolia*
Cornelian cherry dogwood	*Cornus mas*
Franklinia	*Franklinia alatamaha*
Seven-son flower	*Heptacodium miconioides*
Panicle hydrangea cultivars	*Hydrangea paniculata* 'Grandiflora', 'Tardiva', 'Praecox', 'Unique'
Star magnolia	*Magnolia stellata*
'Hally Jolivette' flowering cherry	*Prunus* 'Hally Jolivette'
Oriental photinia	*Photinia villosa*
Cut-leaf staghorn sumac	*Rhus typhina* 'Laciniata'
Blackhaw	*Viburnum prunifolium*

Heptacodium miconioides

Hydrangea paniculata 'Grandiflora'

Franklinia alatamaha

Magnolia stellata

Limbing Up

A YOUNG 10-FOOT-TALL Japanese stewartia grows in our front yard. We chose it about seven years ago for its yellow-centered white flowers, yellow to purple fall color, and flaking gray, tan, and orangey bark. Trouble was, we couldn't see any of that bark because the tree was branched almost to the ground. We decided to limb it up while it was small, since we expect it to grow about 25 feet tall. We did the work ourselves with hand pruners when the branches were less than 1½ inches in diameter.

We also have a shade border with a sugar maple, a red maple, a pin oak, and some shade-tolerant shrubs and perennials. I had a problem with those trees some years ago, however. When I weeded newly planted primulas and barrenworts under the trees, I'd whack my head on the lowest branches. The trees were not fully mature but they were already big — about 25 feet tall for the 13-year-old sugar maple. For a big tree-pruning job like that, we turned to certified arborists rather than do it ourselves. Over a few winters, they removed some branches and made my shade garden a joy to maintain. The trees are still full and beautiful, but I no longer have to worry about banging my head.

Limbing up, also known as raising the crown, frees space for people, other plants, and buildings. It can open a distant view and provide more sunlight to plants growing underneath the canopy. It also increases air circulation under the branches.

If you have aged conifers like the white pines I see from my office window, give them a second look. Sometimes the tops of old

▲ **Opening things up.** Limbed up trees in the foreground frame a handsome woodland scene, adding depth, diversity, and a unique sense of place to the home landscape

conifers shade out lower branches, which then die and break off in storms. Although birds like to perch on those snagged limbs, you can achieve a more refined look if you remove the low dead growth.

Not every tree needs limbing up. While my pin oak, with its droopy lower branches, kept me from gardening successfully, there are other trees I wouldn't touch. For example, the low twisted branches of our Tortuosa European beech create variety and visual interest in the landscape. Similarly, our sourwood is so perfect in its pattern of growth, beautiful droopy flower clusters, and long-lasting burgundy fall color that I wouldn't change a thing about it.

Raise a tree's canopy in late winter or early spring before new growth starts. Beware of removing too many branches at any one time. Foliage collects energy necessary for healthy roots. A big reduction in leaves may stress a tree, making it prone to damage from disease or insects. Prolong the process of limbing up over several years if necessary, so that you can leave at least three-quarters of the crown intact with each pruning.

Limbing up trees increases the amount of light that reaches the ground. Do you grow dense-canopied trees in your lawn, surrounded by individual rings of mulch instead of grouping them in larger beds? Raising the crowns may help the turf below them to survive.

◄ **Limbing up.**
Raising the crown of this 'Heritage' river birch (*Betula nigra* 'Heritage') displays its showy, peeling bark to folks on the porch and in the garden.

The Intrigue of Espalier

VISITING A PRIVATE ESTATE on the southern coast of Maine, I came across a glorious sight. Against the brick walls of the main house were old espaliered apple trees reaching the second floor bedroom windows. Imagine being able to open your bedroom window and sniff the fragrance of apple blossoms in spring and, later in the summer, pick fresh apples.

An espalier is a shrub or tree trained in a formal branching pattern on a fence, trellis, wall, or even on freestanding posts and wires.

You can use espalier to soften walls, enhance fences, grow fruits in small gardens, and create live dividers (known as Belgian fences) for narrow spaces. Espalier is an art form that anyone can learn.

If you live in a cold climate, grow your espalier against a south-facing, dark wall (like brick), which draws heat from the sun and enhances the plant's growth. In warm regions, avoid planting against dark walls in full sun. A reflective white-painted wall or fence out of direct sunlight is a better bet.

▼ **Wall art.** An espaliered apple tree framed by a portal is the focal point of a lattice-covered garage wall.

CREATING AN ESPALIER

Choose a pattern that suits the size of your wall, your taste, and your desire to prune. Shapes range from fans, palmettes, and candelabras to tiers, fountains, triangles, and diamonds. Or, instead of a predictable design, you can let whimsy be your guide and create a shape all your own. I've seen freeform wavy shapes, as well as Boulevard cypress pruned into heart-shaped espaliers. The key to successful espalier is having fun and doing a design you like. Here's how to create a simple tiered cordon on a wall, a good beginner's project:

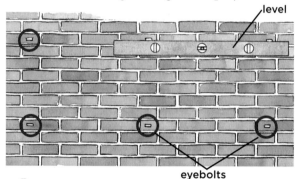

1 On a brick wall, mark with chalk where you want to drill for the eyebolts that will support the espalier wires. Work with a level to keep each tier horizontal. Make your first mark 18 inches from soil level. Sketch in marks at the same height every 2 to 3 feet to the ends of the wall. Add another line of marks 18 inches above the first. Repeat until you reach the top of the wall or the desired height of your espalier.

VARIATION ON THE THEME

If you prefer a more complicated pattern, bend the branches as they develop. Tie them with landscape twine to the wire in the pattern of your choice.

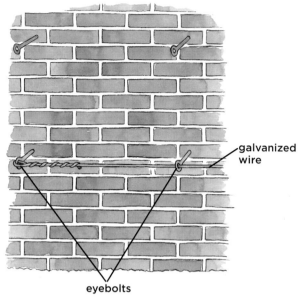

2 Using a masonry drill, drill holes at every mark, then insert 5- to 7-inch eyebolts with expanding lead anchors into the prepared holes. Thread 14-gauge galvanized wire through one eyebolt, winding the tail around the longer side 5 or 6 times to fix it in place. Stretch the long wire horizontally to the next eyebolt, threading it through the second hole, drawing it taut, and securing it as before. There should be 4 to 6 inches between the wire and the wall for air circulation.

3 For one tree or shrub, pound a vertical 4-foot stake in the ground at the planting site. Then plant a bareroot whip (a young, typically unbranched shoot) next to it, about 6 inches in front of the wall and at the center of the wires. If the tree is grafted onto rootstock, set the bulge or bud union about 2 inches above ground to keep the graft from growing roots (see illustration

of a bud union on page 146). Keep the trunk straight by loosely tying it to the upright stake with a piece of twine looped around it in a figure-8. Slacken the twine as the trunk grows. Remove the stake when the pattern of growth is established.

bud union ——

4 With sharp pruners, snip off the top of the tree right below the bottom wire. Be sure to make your cut at a spot above where two buds show on either side of the stem.

5 When new shoots develop, select one to train upright and two to train to either side. Attach side shoots to the wire. Avoid

making the ties so tight that the trunk and branches don't have room to grow. Never use wire to attach branches to the horizontal wires. Rub all other developing shoots off the trunk until the plant reaches the second wire, and shorten shoots on the limbs by pinching.

6 When the main stem reaches the second wire, trim it just below the wire as in step 4, then train the main stem and two side branches as in step 5. Repeat this process for each level.

7 When growth reaches the top wire, cut off the top of the trunk but keep two branches on the sides. Take out the stake, and secure the trunk to the horizontal wires. Check each year to see if ties need replacing. If you see dead, diseased, or damaged branches during the growing season, remove them. Also take off wayward shoots that spoil the lines of the espalier.

Popular Trees and Shrubs for Espalier

Camellia	*Camellia* species
Flowering quince	*Chaenomeles speciosa*
Lemon, lime, orange	*Citrus* species
Cotoneaster	*Cotoneaster* species
Dwarf apple, crabapple	*Malus* species
Mock orange	*Philadelphus coronarius*
Firethorn	*Pyracantha coccinea*
Yew	*Taxus* species
Viburnum	*Viburnum* species

Viburnum carlesii

Pyrus 'Korean Giant'

Fertilizing Trees and Shrubs

TREES IN THE WOODS grow in humus that has developed over years from soil and fallen leaves. The give-and-take between tree roots and fungi — known scientifically as mycorrhizae — helps the roots stay robust under attack from a multitude of pests and diseases. In this relationship the plant contributes food (sugars) to the fungus and the fungus improves the plant's ability to absorb minerals from the soil. In home landscapes, this important relationship may be compromised, but we can inoculate tree roots with mycorrhizae, mulch trees with shredded leaf compost, and avoid compacting soil at the base of trees to give our plants an environment more similar to that found in nature. Let me give you examples.

Our Tortuosa beech, the focal point in a swath of lawn, looked sick. I examined it and found an insect, which we couldn't identify, in a small area of bark damage on the southern exposure. A phone call to the arborist brought a diagnosis and help. He removed the injured bark, revealing more widespread damage than first seen and said the tree had probably suffered sunscald when it was a young transplant. Insects had come later, taking advantage of the tree's weakened condition. He treated the tree's root zone with an injection of a biostimulant composed of beneficial fungi and bacteria. He also told us to gather rotting leaves from the woods behind our house and spread a 2- to 3-inch layer at least as wide as the tree's canopy. Although we used pine nuggets instead of leaves, the results amazed us. The beech recovered, growing fuller, leafier, and more beautiful than ever.

The fungal spores he applied are mycorrhizae (my-ko-RY-zee), a Greek word meaning *fungus roots*. It refers to the mutually beneficial relationship between certain branched fungi and the roots of the trees where they live. Through the tree roots, these special fungi gain access to sugars produced in the leaves. At the same time, the fungi's rootlike vegetative branching increases the surface area of the tree's root system, enabling the tree to take up more moisture and minerals from the soil.

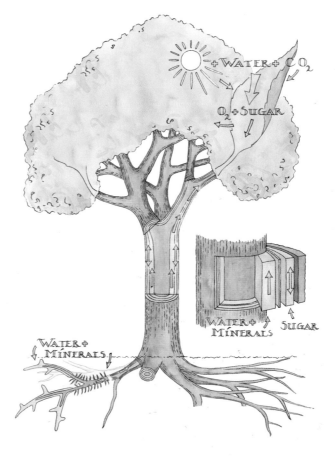

▲ **Fueling a tree.** Trees are nourished through their leaves and roots.

There are several kinds of mycorrhizae, classified by anatomy and the type of tree and fungus. These beneficial plant and fungus partnerships may be inhibited in compacted urban and suburban soils damaged by construction equipment, run over by cars and lawnmowers, or overtreated with fungicides and fertilizers. Even gardening practices like extensive hoeing and digging in a tree's root zone can alter this symbiotic association. Soil injection with beneficial fungal spores can benefit your plants by promoting their root development and ability to withstand drought and other environmental stresses. Best of all, mycorrhizal fungi are harmless to you, your family, and your pets.

Under a microscope, ectomycorrhizae are marvelous to behold. They look like succulent white to orangey rootlike structures emerging from or sheathing the tree roots. Injecting the spores into the root zone of new or established landscape trees helps those trees mimic growing conditions they would experience if they were growing in the woods near other plants, instead of in the compacted soil of the typical suburban lot. Ironically, the more traditional fertilizers and lawn and garden chemicals you use around your trees, the less mycorrhizae can do for them.

Some companies make granular products with beneficial fungi and bacteria to apply to the planting holes of trees and shrubs, applications you can probably do yourself. Just make sure the product suits the particular type of plant you're trying to grow. According to ISA-certified arborist Jeff Ott of Portsmouth, New Hampshire, microspores need to be dormant to be effective, and products containing the word "propagules" on the label have a short shelf life and may not work.

Once the fungi colonize your tree and shrub roots, you shouldn't have to reapply them. But environmental trauma or stress factors like soil compaction, road salt, and continuous lawn maintenance including heavy mowers and treatments with fungicide and high nitrogen fertilizer may affect the roots' future health. If homeowners request tree fertilization after a spore treatment to enhance root growth, Jeff may use an organic treatment with sea kelp, humic acid, and beneficial soil bacteria or a slow-release N-K-P product (see below) that takes two years to break down fully and is not soluble in water, depending upon his assessment of the tree and the property.

Choosing a Fertilizer

Fertilizer is not plant food. Trees, like all green plants, make their own food. Unlike mycorrhizal products, fertilizers contain elements essential for tree growth that may be missing from depleted soils. For the first year after planting, trees and shrubs need no additional fertilizers, and those treated with mycorrhizae can probably fend for themselves. Likewise, mature established trees need no extra nutrients when grown in healthy undisturbed soil. Most gardens, however, contain trees and shrubs planted for the gardener's pleasure and not because that's where they would naturally grow. That's why they need the occasional nutrient boost that a fertilizer gives. Fertilizers vary in their mix of the basic nutrients: nitrogen (N), phosphorus (P), and potassium (K). Nitrogen promotes leaf and stem growth;

phosphorus and potassium (potash) support flowering and root development. Whenever you read a fertilizer label, the numbers representing the percentages of each nutrient always appear on the label in that order. This is true whether the fertilizer is granular, liquid, or a soluble powder.

The organic approach. Instead of using fertilizers, organic gardeners keep their soils healthy with compost, a jumble of decaying organic matter such as leaves, clipped grass, and worm castings, that enhances soil structure and supplies nutrients to plants. An excellent nitrogen-rich organic soil additive is the rotted manure of bats, cows, chickens, and horses. Sometimes you can find dehydrated, pelletized, composted manure packaged as an easy-to-use organic fertilizer. Other organic fertilizers range from liquids made from fish and seaweed to bonemeal, blood meal, cottonseed meal, and alfalfa meal. Organic fertilizers not only supply necessary nutrients, they usually condition the soil, adding organic matter and improving the soil's moisture and nutrient retention. Follow the package directions to establish the necessary amount for your plants.

Synthetic fertilizers. If you prefer using synthetic fertilizer blends, then it's even more important to understand how much of each nutrient you need. You can discover that information from a soil test.

Dry granular synthetic fertilizers are cheap and easy to apply but they must be watered in to release their nutrients. The ideal ratio of NPK for trees and shrubs is about 3:1:1. Thus, if you see a product labeled 27-9-9 or 30-10-7, it would fall into this range. If you broadcast fertilizer, keep it off your driveway, patio, and walkways, because rain or sprinklers can wash it from your property and into drains and culverts, eventually spilling into nearby bodies of water. Also, make sure you

▲ **Peaceful coexistence.** Trees growing in a regularly fertilized lawn take up nutrients from the turf application and will likely need no extra fertilizer.

apply fertilizer at the correct rate and in the right location, because a tree's root zone may expand in any direction two to three times the radius of the crown. For instance, if the crown of the tree is 15 feet wide, skip the area closest to the trunk and apply the granules under the canopy starting 5 feet from the edge of the crown to about 15 feet beyond it.

You may want a tree service to inject a liquid product into the root zones. Most tree roots that take up nutrients exist in the top 6 to 8 inches of soil, so deeper injections are unnecessary and not as useful to the plant. If a tree grows in lawn, an arborist will feed it just below the turf roots.

TIMING FERTILIZATION

Certified arborist Jeff Ott reminds us, "Millions of years ago trees and grass decided to live apart, but the arborist has accomplished a reconciliation of sorts through proper fertilization."

Fertilize in late fall after active growth stops or early spring before new growth begins. Overfertilizing injures plants and squanders the product and your money. Moreover, surplus nitrogen from fertilizers leaches into ground water, and excess phosphorus eventually drains into lakes and bays, where it can damage plants and wildlife.

Pieris japonica

Rhododendron prunifolium

Picea orientalis 'Skylands'

Leucothoe fontanesiana 'Rainbow'

Oxydendrum arboreum

The Acid Test

Some shrubs and trees prefer acidic soils. When they grow in alkaline or sweet soils, certain important mineral nutrients can't dissolve. They're "locked up," unavailable to the roots for absorption. If your plants start to decline, it may be a sign that they're not getting the nutrients they need because the soil's not acid enough. Yellow or whitish leaves, foliage with blotchy yellow edges, small dark dead-tipped leaves, and shrunken light green leaves can all be attributed to nutrient deficiencies. For more flowers and more vigorous growth, apply an organic fertilizer formulated for acid-loving plants.

Organic fertilizers release nutrients gradually and may require fewer applications than a synthetic fertizer, unless you use a slow-release product. Try mixing an organic fertilizer with compost to build up the quality of the soil around these shrubs and trees.

Acid-Loving Shrubs and Trees

Heather	*Calluna vulgaris*
Camellia	*Camellia* species
Atlantic white cedar	*Chamaecyparis thyoides*
Flowering dogwood	*Cornus florida*
Kousa dogwood	*Cornus kousa*
Heath	*Erica* species
Fothergilla	*Fothergilla* species
Gardenia	*Gardenia jasminoides*
Winterberry	*Ilex verticillata*
Mountain laurel	*Kalmia latifolia*
Leucothoe	*Leucothoe* species
Sour gum	*Nyssa sylvatica*
Sourwood	*Oxydendrum arboreum*
Spruce	*Picea* species
Pieris	*Pieris* species
Loblolly pine	*Pinus taeda*
Pin oak	*Quercus palustris*
Willow oak	*Quercus phellos*
Azalea, rhododendron	*Rhododendron* species
Hemlock	*Tsuga* species
Blueberry	*Vaccinium* species

Clean and Healthy Shrubs and Trees

PREVENTING DISEASE and insect infestation is easier than curing it. Healthy trees and shrubs growing in good conditions resist pests and disease better than plants whose vigor is already compromised by environmental stress or poor sanitation. Trees stressed by disease are more likely to succumb to an insect invasion. The following tips may keep your plants strong and make your life as a gardener easier and more enjoyable.

Pest- and disease-resistant varieties. Choose pest- and disease-resistant trees and shrubs when available. Do your research before buying and planting, and discover which species and cultivars of particular plants are the healthiest. Winter King hawthorn, for example, resists fungal rusts better than other hawthorns. Likewise, Kousa dogwoods and the hybrid Stellar series of dogwoods withstand the anthracnose plaguing our native flowering and Pacific dogwoods.

Healthy plants. Start with healthy plant material. That means inspecting plants for diseases and insect infestations before buying them. Although many insects are benign, some eat by sucking, chewing, or boring into plants, while others transmit disease. Check for damage on leaves and stems, and see my recommendations on buying trees and shrubs (page 79). Deal with reputable stores and nurseries that carry plants well suited to your locale.

Right plant, right place. The old adage, "Choose the right plant for the right place" couldn't be truer when it comes to disease prevention. The best planting location is

Nyssa sylvatica

▼ Successful pairings. Group plants with similar growing needs for best results, and give them enough room to grow.

where your plant will experience the least stress. Find the place that most closely meets your tree or shrub's growing requirements for light, soil type, moisture, and fertility.

Optimal planting conditions. A lack of air circulation may promote fungal diseases like powdery mildew. Pay attention to how far apart you plant your material to maintain proper airflow. Consider a shrub's or tree's mature size rather than its present size when planting. Help trees and shrubs become

established by keeping them well watered for at least the first year after planting. Make sure you remove the burlap around the root ball and the ties that hold balled-and-burlapped plants together. (See page 87.)

Avoid stress. Once established, keep plants as stress-free as possible. Water them deeply when the soil dries out, and water them well during times of drought. If you live where water is scarce, plant only trees and shrubs that tolerate long periods of drought. If you irrigate with automatic sprinklers, use them from late at night until early in the morning, say 8 or 9 A.M. at the latest, because there is less evaporation than in full daylight.

Pay attention. Walk the garden and stay on top of changes to your plants. A daily tour of the garden has a dual benefit. First, you enjoy the fruits of your efforts. Second, you get to know your plants well and immediately recognize when they show early symptoms of disease or signs of insect infestation. By catching problems early, you can deal with them quickly and often save the plant. Delays jeopardize not only the affected plant but also the plants around it, since harmful fungi, bacteria, viruses, and insects sometimes spread from plant to plant.

Keep your garden clean. If leaves from a diseased plant fall to the ground, pick them up and remove them from the garden. Prune sick leaves and branches off your plants. Throw the fallen debris and prunings into a closed bag or trashcan and not onto the compost pile.

Clean gardening tools. Wipe dirt off trowels, pruners, and other implements. Before trimming healthy branches, clean pruners that have cut through diseased wood. If you've been dealing with diseased plant material, clean pruners with alcohol or diluted bleach.

Common Tree and Plant Diseases

EVEN THE BEST GARDENS and the most doting gardeners have an occasional bout of mildew or pest infestation on a tree. Don't let it get you down. We'll tell you how to spot and deal with a few common pests and diseases. When in doubt, phone a certified arborist or your Cooperative Extension Service for advice.

CANKER

Description: Cankers are long, dark, sometimes sunken lesions with defined edges on limbs and trunks of woody plants. The lesions sometimes may ooze tacky, tawny sap. Canker can destroy leaves, twigs, and branches. Trunk cankers can kill your trees. The rim of bark around the canker may turn inside, giving the lesion a rolled edge.

Canker

Cause: Canker-causing fungi and bacteria attack weak trees and shrubs, which may have been harmed by environmental stresses such as sunscald, flooding, or frost damage, or human error such as driving a lawn mower into a tree trunk.

Preventive measures: Mulch around trees and shrubs to avoid damaging them with landscape equipment.

Treatment: Treat your woodies well. Maintain the health of established trees and shrubs by fertilizing when necessary and watering them during prolonged dryspells. Prune off severely damaged limbs.

LEAF SPOT

Leaf spot

Description: Foliage of numerous trees and shrubs develops spots that vary in shape, size, and color. Sometimes leaf spots grow bigger until they slow the tree's or shrub's development. Other kinds of leaf spots may develop holes in the middle.

Cause: Different fungi and bacteria cause leaf spots. Some infections occur during rainy springs when spattering water carries bacteria from twigs to shoots.

Preventive measures: After fall leaf drop, rake up and discard diseased leaves and twigs. Weed under evergreens for good air circulation. Plant disease-resistant cultivars.

Treatment: For bacterial leaf spot, which often starts out pale green and becomes brown with clear borders, spray with Bordeaux mix (copper sulfate) as buds begin to expand in wet weather. If it's dry when buds expand, although the plant will look bad, it will not be as weakened by the disease.

AT THE HEART OF IT ALL

According to Alex L. Shigo, there is no such fungal disease as heart rot. The most damaging wood decay diseases are canker rots. In canker rots, the disease-causing fungus alternates between attacking the wood and attacking the bark, thus avoiding some of the tree defenses. Although the bark may cover the canker rot for some years, decay occurs in wood beneath the bark. Other wood decay fungi can also take advantage of canker rot injury and cause further infections. You may see a mushroom or conk on the surface of the decaying stem or branch. Unfortunately removing the mushroom does not stop the decay infection.

MILDEWS

Description: Mildews are parasitic fungal diseases that affect live trees and shrubs. *Downy mildews* show up mostly on the foliage of plants, including redbud *(Cercis canadensis),* hackberry *(Celtis species), Viburnum* species, brambles *(Rubus* species), currants *(Ribes* species), and roses *(Rosa* species). If your woodies have downy mildew, you'll see on leaf tops some spotty discoloration that eventually turns brown. Grayish white fuzz appears on the underside of the patches. The diseased spots can spread so much that early leaf drop occurs. If you see splotchy, pale gray areas on leaf and stem surfaces, this is most likely a layer of white, powdery spores known as *powdery mildew.* A few of the many, many woodies affected by powdery mildew are common lilac *(Syringa vulgaris),* apples and crabapples *(Malus* species), roses *(Rosa* species), ornamental cherries and other stone fruit trees *(Prunus* species), redtip *(Photinia* species),

Downy mildew

Powdery mildew

hydrangea *(Hydrangea* species), crape myrtle *(Lagerstroemia indica),* and gardenia *(Gardenia jasminoides).* Both mildews may warp the buds and developing foliage, though powdery mildew rarely causes permanent harm.

Cause: Downy mildews occur in cool to warm humid weather. Water splashing from dead sick leaves on the ground to the plant's lower leaves replays the cycle of mildew infection year after year. Powdery mildews come about with warm days and cool nights in dry or humid, but not rainy, weather. Where I live, the warm days, cool nights, and dry conditions of the typical summer frequently lead to powdery mildew on susceptible plants.

▲ **Good air circulation.** An understory of dainty, open-branched Japanese maples allows air to circulate freely through this woodland garden.

Preventive measures: Pick up infected leaves and dispose of them in the trash. Choose mildew-resistant varieties of susceptible plants when available. Prune trees and shrubs to allow maximum air circulation so foliage can dry out quickly from dew, rain (downy mildew only; rain actually impedes the spread of powdery mildew), or watering. A sunny breezy site not too closely planted also helps air circulate.

Treatment: Improve air circulation. Remove infected leaves, plant parts, or when necessary, the entire plant. Spray plants with 1 tablespoon of baking soda dissolved in 3 quarts of water for powdery mildew. For downy mildew, spray with fungicide derived from copper.

PHYTOPTHORA ROOT ROT

Description: This soil-borne organism causes root rot in many trees and shrubs and eventually kills them. You may notice wilting, yellowing, and the preservation of dried leaves due to the roots' inability to take up water. You first notice root rot in summer when plants are more water stressed. Some of the fungal spores stay active even after the plant has died.

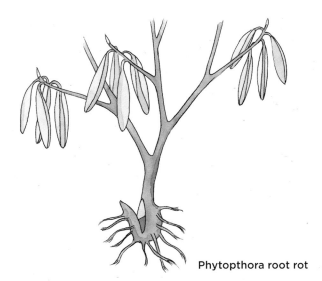

Phytopthora root rot

Cause: Moist warm soils are necessary for this fungus to thrive and spread from plant to plant. The disease disperses downhill.

Preventive measures: Use good plant hygiene as described on pages 131–132.

Treatment: Fungicide in the affected soil may keep the disease from spreading to other plants. An increase in the amount of organic matter in the soil may further reduce fungal activity.

SOOTY MOLD

Description: If you see black mold growing on twigs and foliage, your plant may be infected with sooty molds or dark fungi. These develop on honeydew (a sugary juice) produced by sapsucking insects such as scales, aphids, whiteflies, and mealybugs.

Cause: A fungus that grows on secretions of sapsucking insects. The presence of sooty molds may be rising due to global warming and the stress of hotter, drier weather, which can increase the number of certain sapsucking insects.

Sooty mold

Preventive measures: Identify the insect by referring to pictures and descriptions, then reduce the specific insect population by methods mentioned in this book. You can also consult your local Cooperative Extension Service for help identifying and dealing with insect problems.

Treatment: Sooty mold rubs easily off leaves and can rinse off in the rain. By decreasing the number of sapsucking insects on your plant, you can control the spread of sooty mold.

VERTICILLIUM WILT

Description: A common fungal disease among landscape plants, verticillium wilt clogs the vascular system, depriving the plant of water and nutrients and causing leaves to wilt and branches to die back either one by one or on one side of the plant. Verticillium wilt

Verticillium wilt

can kill plants quickly or slowly over many years, depending upon how far the disease progresses through the root system. Many woody plants are vulnerable to this disease, including maple (*Acer* species), weigela, magnolias, viburnums, rhododendrons, and tulip-tree (*Liriodendron tulipifera*).

Cause: Caused by soil-borne fungi, especially in cool areas of North America, the disease is also spread by contaminated garden tools and by the wind.

Preventive measures: Plant resistant trees such as hawthorn (*Crataegus* species), London planetree (*Platanus × acerifolia*), holly (*Ilex* species), katsura (*Cercidiphyllum japonicum*), oak (*Quercus* species), and thornless honey locust (*Gleditsia triacanthos finermis*). You can also grow plants with exposed seed, such as conifers and ginkgo, which are not prone to the disease.

Treatment: None.

APHID

Description: Aphids are sapsucking insects that come in many colors and textures from red, yellow, green, purple, brown, and black to whitish because of a light all-over secretion.

Aphid

Some have wings and some don't, and many prefer congregating on the lower surface of leaves. What they have in common is their tiny size, pear-shaped bodies, long legs, and long antennae. They tend to be group feeders on leaves and stems, but you'll occasionally see a loner. Aphids probably won't destroy your trees and shrubs, but sooty mold can turn the sticky honeydew they release black. You may also notice the foliage wilt, yellow, or distort.

Cause: Regular infestations.

Preventive measures: You can't escape them: an aphid species is linked with almost every tree and shrub.

Treatment: Tree and shrub damage is usually more visual than life threatening. Live and let live, unless they really bother you or the infestation is severe. Hose foliage and stems with a powerful stream of water to displace them. If you want something more, spray your plant with insecticidal soap or horticultural oil. Many beneficial insects such as ants, lady beetles, and parasitic wasps will destroy aphids if you don't destroy them first. Skip heavy-duty insecticides because they kill not just the bad guys but also the good.

GALL

Description: Galls are abnormal growths of plant tissue on leaves, twigs, and bark of trees. Oaks host most galls, but they also appear on other trees and shrubs.

Cause: Mites, wasps, aphids, and midge flies can all bring about galls. The insects that make galls are most active when trees leaf out in spring.

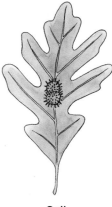

Gall

Preventive measures: Keep trees healthy. Galls are not pretty but they don't do permanent damage to your woody plants. You don't know your trees have galls until you see them, and spraying them won't help because the gall shields the larvae.

Treatment: Hold off on chemical sprays. Sometimes tolerating a pest is the best thing to do. If the infestation is severe, you can prune out ugly twigs.

LACEBUG

Description: Lacebugs get their name from their decorative wings and hood adorned with a lacy pattern of veins. These sapsucking pests about ⅛ inch long come

Lacebug

in many species that affect a multitude of woody plants. They live on leaf bottoms, where they excrete spots of dark crud as they eat. Minor lacebug damage looks like yellowy white dots on the upper leaf surface. Heavier damage is unsightly and leads to blistered yellow leaves and eventually early leaf drop. Repeated severe infestations can kill a plant. Different species attack evergreen and deciduous plants, but damage is most common on evergreens.

Cause: Incorrect planting sites encourage some infestations of lace bug.

Preventive measures: Lace bugs thrive in sun. Set vulnerable plants such as azalea and andromeda in shade.

Treatment: In early spring, start checking under the leaves for eggs, newly hatched nymphs, and adults. Keep checking every couple of weeks, since several generations may hatch in a year. Dealing promptly with infestations prevents ugly damage from occurring. As with aphids, you can set upon lacebugs with a hose and give them a hard spray to displace and kill nymphs (immature insects) in spring. Encourage beneficial insects that prey on lace bugs by avoiding the use of chemical insecticides. Instead, drench leaves (especially the bottoms) with insecticidal soaps or horticultural oils to control the nymphs when they hatch.

Rhododendron 'Babylon'

▲ **Shady lady.** Rhododendrons are prime targets of lacebugs, so these plants are best sited in shade.

EARTH-FRIENDLY REMEDIES

Bordeaux mix can kill some disease-causing bacteria and fungi that affect both woody ornamentals and trees and shrubs grown for fruits or nuts. Bordeaux is good to use full strength as a long-lasting fungicide in fall, winter, and spring before a plant breaks dormancy; you can also use it at reduced strength after spring growth begins. You need proper safety gear (goggles and protective clothing) to apply this mixture, which you can buy prepackaged or make fresh. One gallon of Bordeaux mix requires blending 3⅓ tablespoons of copper sulfate and 10 tablespoons of hydrated lime with 1 gallon of water. It should be used right after mixing. Bordeaux mix can control some mildews, fireblight, and apple scab.

Fixed copper fungicides, which are different copper compounds mixed with water, are safer to apply and safer to use on tender plants. You can also buy these ready made.

Insecticidal soaps kill vulnerable soft-bodied insects on contact. For efficacy, you have to ensure thorough coverage of affected plants, including stems and upper and lower leaf surfaces. The application may work better if you spray early in the morning or in the evening to prevent quick evaporation. These soaps are people-safe when you follow the package directions. As with any insecticide, use only when absolutely necessary.

Horticultural oils, which are made of refined petroleum or plant oils mixed with water, control many pesky insects on plants but tend to have limited effects on beneficial insects. Oils can kill aphids, mites, caterpillars, and scales on woody ornamentals as well as help prevent powdery mildew and rust. *Dormant oil* is horticultural oil used on trees and shrubs during their dormant season. *Summer oil* is safe to use on mature leaves during the growing season. Sometimes oils can injure sensitive species, such as juniper, hickory, black walnut, redbud, smoketree, some azaleas, spruce, Douglas fir, and Japanese cedar or cryptomeria, and Japanese, sugar, and red maples. Always follow package directions when spraying these products.

LEAF MINER

Description: Leaf miners are similar to borers except that the latter go deeper into the plant. The larvae of leaf miners live inside leaves and their damage is visible as an irregular narrow whitish trail on the leaf surface. Most

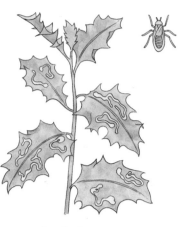

Leaf miners

attacks are visible at the beginning and end of summer in mature foliage. Most woody plant families are susceptible to their raids.

Cause: Adult beetles and moths looking for suitable host for their larvae to develop.

Preventive measures: Avoid stressing trees and shrubs with too much or too little water, and provide desirable conditions for their growth.

Treatment: Chemicals don't work because the larvae are inside the plant. Anyway, leaf miners usually don't cause permanent damage to most trees and shrubs.

SCALE

Description: Scale insects feed on the sap of both evergreen and deciduous trees and shrubs with mouth parts up to 8 times longer than their bodies. Scales hug their bodies tight to their food source and can be found on leaves, twigs, branches, and trunks. They can weaken and eventually kill the plant

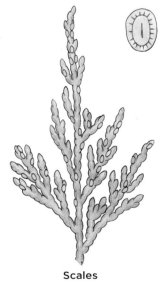

Scales

they infest, though that is not typical. Two kinds of scales exist, hard and soft. The latter makes honeydew while the former does not.

Cause: Scales occur on trees and shrubs that are stressed.

Preventive measures: Maintain healthy trees and shrubs that can survive an attack. Give your plants adequate water and nutrition, especially when stressed by injury or drought. Avoid chemicals that harm lady beetles and parasitic wasps, their natural predators.

Treatment: Rub them off by hand or prune off severely infested branches. Because adults have a waxy coating that shields them from insecticides, you have to control them when they are overwintering or immature crawlers. Dormant oils work in early spring before trees and shrubs leaf out.

SPIDER MITE

Description: Mites are in the spider family. These teeny red, brown, or spotted sapsuckers damage leaf tissues. Fine webbing will appear on deciduous trees with large infestations. Leaves become spotty, yellow, and then brown before dropping. Common

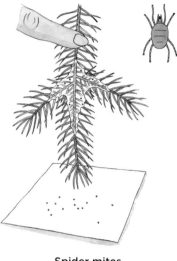

Spider mites

hosts include spruces, arborvitaes, raspberries, roses, crabapples, and shrubby cinquefoils. To see if you have mites, tap a branch while holding a sheet of white paper under it. If you see moving dots, you have spider mites.

Cause: Hot, dry, and dusty conditions grow their populations, while wet or humid weather lowers them.

Preventive measures: Keep trees and shrubs healthy, because spider mites thrive on stressed plants.

Treatment: While infestations are light, you can control them by spraying plants with hard jets of water. Do this whenever mite damage is apparent and repeat it weekly for at least 3 weeks. Use repeated applications of insecticidal soap or horticultural oil to further lower mite populations.

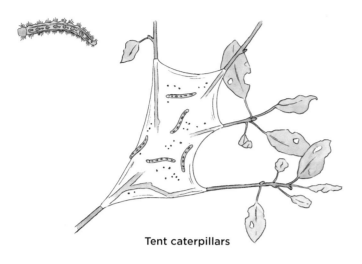

Tent caterpillars

TENT CATERPILLAR

Description: You know them — those ugly, white, larvae-holding, silken webs or tents hung up in tree branches. The caterpillars eat the leaves of deciduous trees. They attack many kinds of trees but like rose, alder, birch, willow, ash, and apple more than most. Although they don't kill trees, they can weaken them and make them vulnerable to other problems. Vigorous trees withstand an attack and releaf quickly.

Cause: Periodic infestations.

Preventive measures: Keeping trees healthy helps them survive an infestation.

Treatment: Eliminate egg cases from trees. They are made of a foamy-looking gray to brown hard substance and are about 1½ inches long. Remove the cases with pruners or by hand. Get rid of hatched caterpillars by eliminating their nests from the limbs.

WOOD BORER

Wood borers

Description: These insects, typically moths and beetles, grow under the bark of trees and shrubs, mining the inner bark in an immature, larval state. Most borers are drawn to dead, stressed, or dying trees. The beetles are dark brown, black, or red with tiny hard bodies. Many species attack conifers but the European elm bark beetle is a transmitting agent for the Dutch elm disease fungus that decimated the American elm (*Ulmus americana*) population in North America. Other examples of borers are longhorned beetles and carpenterworms, which become moths. Sawdust on the ground and sap mixed with sawdust oozing from little holes are signs that bark beetles have emerged from the trunk of conifers.

Cause: Trees stressed by drought, disease, and physical damage are more prone to wood borers than robust trees and shrubs.

Preventive measures: Keep shrubs and trees in tiptop health. Plant pest-resistant species and take good care of landscape shrubs and trees. Don't over- or underwater them, and make sure their growing conditions are conducive to maximum vigor. Baby new transplants.

Treatment: Cut off and get rid of infested branches to prevent the spread of the beetles. If the trunk shows lots of beetle damage, you may have to dispense with whole trees to save nearby trees. A certified arborist will know the right time to prune diseased branches from different types of trees.

You can't control weather, but you may be able to manage other environmental risks to the trees and shrubs on your property. Construction damage is the biggest and perhaps most destructive trauma trees can endure. Soil compaction on residential lots, trenching in root zones, grade changes, and bad pruning are some of the ways that people harm their trees. Ozone pollution, energy-sapping suckers or root shoots (see page 146), and chemical damage from maintaining a perfect lawn may all contribute to the deterioration of your trees. The good news is that you can preserve trees from most human damage and find trees that remain vigorous and beautiful in stressful environments. In this section, you'll read about challenges faced by trees and learn how to keep them safe from harm.

DEATH BY DIGGER

Although the homeowners clearly wanted the birches in their front yard, a backhoe crushing the root zones and excavating root-filled soil doomed the trees to an early end. To prevent such tree damage, erect fences around pleasing trees before construction begins, giving them as much room as possible. At a minimum, the protective barrier for a tree with a 6-inch caliper should be at least 6 feet away from the trunk on each side, and no one should walk on or throw trash into the fenced space.

Construction Damage

Building a house may be thrilling for you but traumatic for your trees. Construction equipment rolls over root zones, squeezing air from the soil and slowing water drainage. Rainfall on the bare soil increases compaction, as do the human footfalls across the root zone. Because compacted soil is denser than well-aerated soil, it's harder for roots to penetrate. Root growth and spread is hindered, making it harder for trees and shrubs to absorb water and nutrients. Drought stunts trees growing in compacted soils, while flooding lessens the amount of air that gets to their roots. Disturbed, compacted, urban and suburban soils may lack mycorrhizae and essential elements, making it hard for trees to establish. In neighborhoods with underground utilities, laying electrical cable from the electrical box to the house often cuts through the precious top foot of soil where most tree roots lie, wrecking the network of roots the trench encounters. There also may be trenches for gas, telephone, sewer, water, and cable television. Remember, even if a trench seems far from the tree, the root zone may be double or triple the diameter of the crown.

New construction may necessitate grade changes to improve drainage on the property. Roots that were formerly in the top few inches of soil may be buried alive under loads of sand and topsoil to ultimately suffocate and die. To preserve existing trees, avoid raising or lowering the soil level under the canopy of the tree.

Building a tree well is one way to maintain air circulation and drainage in the root

Pollution-Tolerant Landscape Trees and Shrubs

Hedge maple	*Acer campestre*
European hornbeam	*Carpinus betulus*
Hackberry	*Celtis occidentalis*
White fringe tree	*Chionanthus virgi*...
Hawthorn	*Crataegus* species
Ginkgo	*Ginkgo biloba*
Thornless honey locust	*Gleditsia triacanth*... f. *inermis*
Longstalk holly	*Ilex pedunculosa*
Golden raintree	*Koelreuteria panic*...
Crape myrtle	*Lagerstroemia ind*...
Magnolia	*Magnolia* species
'Donald Wyman' crabapple	*Malus* 'Donald W'...
Amur corktree	*Phellodendron am*...
White spruce	*Picea glauca*
Japanese black pine	*Pinus thunbergii*
Yoshino flowering cherry	*Prunus* × *yedoensi*...
Douglas fir	*Pseudotsuga menz*...
English oak	*Quercus robur*
Red oak	*Quercus rubra*
Sumac	*Rhus* species
Chinese scholar tree	*Sophora japonica*
Arborvitae	*Thuja* species
Little-leaf linden	*Tilia cordata*

Landscape Trees Intolerant to Air Pollution

Sugar maple	*Acer saccharum*
Red maple	*Acer rubrum*
Serviceberry	*Amelanchier* speci...
Catalpa	*Catalpa* species
Larch	*Larix* species
Black tupelo	*Nyssa sylvatica*
White pine	*Pinus strobus*
Lombardy poplar	*Populus nigra* 'Ital...
Quaking aspen	*Populus tremuloi*...
Flowering plum	*Prunus cerasifera*
Willow	*Salix* species
American elm	*Ulmus americana*

zone. Tree wells are walled shafts to the original soil grade in landscapes where soil levels have been artificially increased. Digging old-fashioned tree wells dug near a trunk doesn't work. Dr. Edward Gilman, a professor and tree specialist at the University of Florida, notes that if you're trying to save a tree with a tree well, you must build it beyond the tree's dripline, then grade the soil outside the well to keep runoff from flowing into the well. There's no guarantee that the tree will survive construction, but you improve its chances by leaving undisturbed the trunk and as wide an area as possible around it.

Another common practice that actually harms, rather than helps, is removing part of a tree's canopy to balance roots killed during construction. The fact is that to survive root disturbance, trees *need* their leaves to provide nutrients. Removing part of the crown reduces the number of leaves that are processing nutrients. If some limbs ultimately die from root damage, you can ask your arborist to remove them.

Chemical Damage

Trees and shrubs can also sustain damage from herbicides formulated to destroy unwanted plants or stop their growth. Even

▲ **Well done!** To preserve an established tree in a changing landscape, build a tree well beyond the tree's dripline to avoid grade changes in the tree's root zone.

those herbicides considered safe around people and pets may not be safe for your trees. My husband and I learned that lesson the hard way. On a muggy Delaware day with hardly any wind, Bob sprayed herbicide on some persistent weeds near a weeping Japanese maple. A breeze moved the air while he was spraying. We didn't realize that any herbicide had migrated to the tree until we noticed the decline and death of a small branch near the area where he had been.

OUT OF HARM'S WAY

Heavy construction equipment isn't the only thing that can damage a tree trunk. Dinging the trunk with a lawnmower, string trimmer, or any other machine can kill the tree. Even a small bark hit may hurt the part of a tree that carries food and water to and from the leaves and roots and the cell band from which the tree grows. The tree declines, becoming vulnerable to disease-causing organisms. Very young trees with thin bark are particularly at risk from these injuries.

The best way to protect your trees from mechanical harm is to mulch the area beneath them with wood chips, bark nuggets, or shredded bark. A 2- to 3-inch layer is plenty. Keep the mulch away from the trunk flare. You'll save mowing time and won't have to buy new trees. (See page 97.)

Many tre…
a sturdy …
and vigor…
from thes…
grow fron…
swelling …
usually n…
of their v…
or shrub,…
(grafted p…
a red rose…
Similarly,…
stick (Cor…
into its st…
C. avellan…
before the…

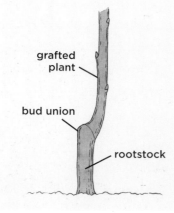

REMOVE SUCKERS

grafted plant

bud union

rootstock

When Storms Come Your Way

When a weather disaster occurs, landscape trees can't evacuate. Rooted to the spot, they rely instead on certain inborn characteristics to survive. If weather-related damage to your trees creates hazardous conditions for you, your pets, or your neighbors, call an arborist immediately. An arborist may be able to save your tree and, if not, will remove it safely from your property.

Snow and ice look magical on trees but they can destroy them. The weight of snow can crush evergreens, breaking them apart. It can weigh down deciduous tree limbs until they also break. Sometimes it weighs so heavily on a treetop that it lifts the root mass right out of the soil. Ice-coated trunks and branches bend low and sometimes snap. When a coastal ice storm hit Maine and New Hampshire one year, every young paper birch along I-95 bowed to the ground. Some broke apart, but many still survive, stooped testaments to the storm. You can help avoid permanent damage by gently brushing snow off branches you can reach. An arborist may need to stake or cable trees vulnerable to folding under the weight of ice. Whether cabled or not, let the ice melt naturally. Prune any damage so the tree will not create a hazard. Well-pruned trees and shrubs stand up better to snow and ice than trees with weak branch crotches or more than one leader (main stem). Tying up boxwood or erect evergreens like red cedar and arborvitae may help prevent injury. Crisscross the entire crown with nylon cord or fishing line, removing it promptly in spring. Protect smaller shrubs with a teepee made from two leaning boards or pieces of plywood.

▲ **Snow country help.** These homeowners protect a mountain laurel from snow sliding off the roof by covering it with a hinged wooden teepee.

▲ **Now you see it . . .** Mesh wrapped around a cone-shaped yew offers almost invisible protection from deer and heavy snowfall.

Wind. Healthy trunks and branches bend to some extent with the wind. The branches most susceptible to breaking are heavy ones that join with the trunk at an acute angle. Choosing healthy, well-formed trees can prevent this damage. If it's too late for that, you can have an arborist help you shape the tree for added strength. Wind protection is particularly important for evergreens, which keep losing water through their leaves during the winter. Making sure these trees and shrubs are well watered before the ground freezes helps prevent the foliage from turning brown. Although you should cut back the volume of water you give your trees in early fall so they can harden off for winter, keep watering them until the ground freezes.

You can also avoid damage to evergreens through proper planting. Never plant evergreens susceptible to wind damage, like arborvitae and yew, on the south or southwest sides of your house. In most of the United States and southern Canada, the westerlies or prevailing winds move from the west or southwest toward the east or northeast. Local geography, including large bodies of water and tall buildings, may affect wind speed and direction in a particular place. West-to-east airflow snakes in ridges or crests and troughs or depressions going north and south. Winds on the west side of a ridge are from the southwest (warm) and those on the east side travel from the northwest (cold). If you must, build a two- or three-sided wind fence out of stakes and burlap to block the prevailing winter wind and the southern and the southwestern exposure of the evergreens.

Lightning. If a lightning strike hits a tree on your property, you may not see the injuries, but they can range from burnt roots to systemic damage inside the tree. External damage takes many forms. Long strips of bark may hang loosely from the tree, a branch

may explode, or pests may overwhelm the injured tree, which dies. Popular landscape trees like pine, oak, and maple are among the more susceptible trees to lightning damage. Although you can't prevent a calamity, you can plant trees less vulnerable to strikes such as birch and beech. If lightning strikes a tree without doing too much damage, you can help it bounce back by first cutting off hanging bark, then fertilizing the plant, keeping its root zone mulched, and watering it during dry spells.

▼ **Lightning attractors.** Tall, exposed trees and trees with opposite branching patterns, like this maple, are susceptible to lightning injury.

Flood. Unless you plant trees and shrubs that tolerate wet feet for long periods of time, flooding can have disastrous effects on your landscape. Flooding may wear away topsoil or dump silt and debris over the root zones of your trees, either of which harms them. Flooded soil deprives tree roots of the oxygen they need for nourishment. Most tree roots are in the top foot of soil because that's where most of the oxygen is, and tree roots breathe like we do. When water fills the air pockets in the soil, it leaves no room for oxygen. Wet roots are susceptible to rot. As they give out, leaves sag, yellow, and even drop; and limbs die back. Before pruning branches, wait a year and see if limbs show signs of recovery. Fertilizer or a mycorrhizal product applied to the root zone may help restore the plant's vigor. If areas of your land flood regularly, you may be able to improve the drainage in those spots by incorporating compost or other organic material into the soil. You can also consult a landscape contractor or architect about installing a drainage system of connecting pipes to carry off excess water to a pond or drainage culvert.

Drought. A lack of water in the soil affects trees and shrubs by decreasing their vigor and even killing them. Drought destroys feeder roots and root hairs, which provide the avenue for most water absorption. Because these are mostly in the top foot of soil, they are quickly affected by moisture loss. The tree suffers stress, and leaves may wilt, scorch, or drop. Spider mites, leaf-eating insects, or wood borers are active in hot dry weather and invade the drought-stressed tree.

If you live in an area known for dry soils and you lack access to irrigation water, plant only drought-tolerant species such as hawthorn, green ash, Kentucky coffeetree, juniper, American plum, and limber and mugo pines. If you live where drought is infrequent, keep trees and shrubs well watered during dry spells and remember that it's better to water deeply and less frequently instead of briefly watering the soil surface every few days. During a drought, water newly planted trees weekly, evergreens and transplants up to five years old every two weeks, and established shrubs every four to six weeks. To water a tree deeply, set up a trickling hose around the drip line (below the crown's outer edge) and leave it in place for 30 minutes. Move the hose one-third the way around the tree and water again for the same amount of time. Repeat one more time. If the tree is very big, you'll need to move the hose to more spots around the drip line. Recently transplanted material needs special care and plenty of water to help it become established. Newly planted balled-and-burlapped trees and shrubs are particularly vulnerable to damage, since many of their feeder roots were cut in the harvesting process.

Sunscald. In winter, the sun is lower in the sky and warms the south and southwest sides of tree trunks, killing the inner bark on the south or southwest side of young deciduous tree trunks, especially thin-barked species such as maple, ash, honey locust, linden, and willow. Sunscald is particularly likely when winter days are warm and sunny and nights are below freezing. The hot sunlight activates dormant cells, which freezing nighttime temperatures destroy. Trees are less affected in places where cloudy skies and consistently cold temperatures are the norm and when planted on the east and north sides of buildings. Sunscald happens frequently in parts of the Southwest. In New England, you may see these conditions during the typical January thaw, when temperatures warm up and skies are sunny. Using commercial tree wrap to prevent sunscald on a newly planted tree is usually not necessary and can hurt the trunk, especially when wrapped too tightly. When making a decision to wrap or not, consider the kind of tree you're planting, its location on your property, and whether you've seen sunscald on other young trees in the same area. If you decide to wrap, keep the material on a newly planted tree from November to March and then remove it promptly.

Leaf scorch. When you notice that the edges of leaves turn yellow and then brown, you may be observing leaf scorch. It usually occurs as a result of dry soils, dry winds, and hot weather. Leaf scorch reduces the vigor of woody ornamentals and can lead to pest and disease problems. Similarly, woes that weaken a tree can lead to leaf scorch. Ash, oak, linden, and maple are among the trees that develop leaf scorch. To help prevent leaf scorch during hot dry periods, water trees deeply and mulch them to conserve moisture.

Conifers, like pine and spruce, and broad-leaf evergreens, like andromeda, mountain laurel, and rhododendron, are susceptible to leaf scorch in both summer and winter. Conifers and broad-leaf evergreens are particularly vulnerable on sunny or windy winter days, when the damage is known as winter burn. To prevent winter burn, keep these plants well watered throughout the growing season and water them deeply if there is a dry spell in late fall. Be aware of what you plant in the path of prevailing winter winds. You can make

▲ **Avoiding winter burn.** Broad-leaf evergreens are particularly vulnerable to winter burn, which can be prevented by keeping them well watered throughout the growing season and protecting them from prevailing winter winds.

a wooden structure to protect evergreens or wrap them with burlap. Spraying broad-leaf evergreens with an antidessicant is another possibility for late fall and midwinter. You may have to tolerate occasional winter burn on your evergreens if you don't have time for these precautions.

Plant names. The pronunciations of scientific names given here are mostly my own. Don't be afraid to use these names at a nursery. If you don't want to say them aloud, write them down before your nursery trip, then show the sales staff your list. Each tree and shrub has one scientific name but may have several common names, and many common names refer to more than one plant. Using scientific names when buying plants should ensure that you get the plants you want.

Trees and shrubs belong to plant families that offer clues about good growing conditions and possible health challenges. For example, Rose Family trees and shrubs, including hawthorn, crabapple, shrubby cinquefoil, cherry, pear, and raspberry, usually have five-petal flowers. Most thrive in full sun and slightly acid, well-drained soil. Rose Family members also share certain problems, such as fireblight (a bacterial disease), scab and rust (fungal diseases), and damage from rodents.

Shapes. These symbols (◯ △ ○ ▽ ◠ ⌂ ⌂) represent a plant's general outline as it may look from a distance. It is not exact. In nature, factors, such as health, weather, and location affect a plant's form, which changes over time and may develop irregularities with age. The same icon represents trees, and shrubs, though shrubs are usually multi-stemmed and trees, single-stemmed. Forms also may change from youth to maturity, indicated here and in the chart (pages 370–381) by an arrow pointing from the youthful to the mature shape.

Easy does it. If a plant thrives with little interference from you, the gardener, we note that with this icon: ✳ Some plants with this icon grow so easily that they are deemed invasive. Read the entry to determine if that's the case in your area.

Plant type. Here you find whether a plant is a tree or a shrub, or can be grown either way. You also learn if the foliage drops in fall (deciduous) or stays on the plant year round (evergreen). Some plants are semi-evergreen and maintain some green leaves into winter. Some semi-evergreen plants act like evergreens in mild climates, but shed their leaves in cold zones.

ABELIA

Abelia × grandiflora ○ ✳
a-BEEL-ya gran-di-FLOH-ra

Glossy abelia

Honeysuckle Family (Caprifoliaceae)
Deciduous shrub
3'–10' h x 3'–12' w

For long-lived garden color, it's hard to beat glossy abelia. With its ruddy, young stems and evergreen to semi-evergreen, opposite leaves, which are lustrous and dark green in summer and tinged a bronzy purple in fall, this shrub looks good even when it's not in flower . . .

LANDSCAPE USE
Southerners may choose glossy abelia for a handsome informal hedge . . .

ORIGIN   Garden origin

HARDINESS ZONES   6–9

LIGHT   To enhance the redness of its stems and sepals, grow glossy abelia in full sun . . .

SOIL   Well-drained, moist, acid soil.

GROWING   Relatively problem free, this fast-growing shrub is easy to maintain though powdery mildew, leaf spots, and root rot may affect it. When necessary, cut out dead stems in spring . . .

DESIGNER'S CHOICE
Abelia × grandiflora 'Compacta' Pink-tinged white flower clusters from May to frost; hardy and small. 3' h and w. Zone 6.

A. × grandiflora 'Edward Goucher' Lavender-purple, fragrant flower trumpets from May to frost. 3'–5' h and w. Zone 6 . . .

Size. The mature garden heights and widths of plants are key to your landscape design. Mature height affects a plant's visibility in the landscape, while width helps determine its siting distance from other plants. Plants often grow larger in the wild than in the garden; likewise, plants grown in ideal conditions grow bigger than their counterparts on the edge.

Plant description focuses on "Why grow this plant?" You'll find out here why I think it's worth having this particular tree or shrub in your garden.

Landscape use. A plant's usefulness is at the heart of each entry. What good's a great plant if you don't know how to use it? Look here for some ideas.

Origin. Knowing a tree's home ground or habitat helps you understand the climate and conditions that spawned it and what it needs to survive. When a tree's or shrub's origin says "Garden," it came from a planned cross between two species and did not start in the wild.

Hardiness zone. The plant's hardiness zone signifies its ability to survive winter in distinct geographical areas of the United States, Canada, and Mexico. Check the USDA Hardiness Zone map on page 382 to find your zone.

Growing conditions. In addition to the right climate, adequate light, suitable soil texture, and moisture are necessary for plant health. Though light, shade, and moisture tolerance varies, most trees and shrubs in this book grow well in moist, well-drained, loamy soils. Some trees and shrubs suffer root rot and die in heavy, wet clay soils with poor drainage, while others thrive in these conditions. Similarly, some woody plants are robust in sandy, fast-draining soils, but others experience death by drought unless given extra water and nutrients.

The final section on growing contains pruning tips, possible pests and diseases, and other pertinent information.

A few trees and shrubs include a cautionary note, which indicates that the plant or some part of it may cause you or your surroundings harm. Trees and shrubs with toxic fruits, leaves, or stems, and those with big thorns may land here. I've also used this element to flag plants considered invasive. Some plants that began as ornamentals have escaped gardens and are now invading natural areas. I discuss likely results of planting them so we can think twice before using them in our gardens. Burning bush *(Euonymus alatus),* for example, is banned from sale in New Hampshire; some other states put suspect plants on watch lists. The National Park Service publishes a U.S. weed database of these plants (see the Appendix for website information). Find alternatives to invasives by referring to the chart that begins on page 370 and noting plants that suit your desires and conditions.

Designer's choice. I list garden-worthy trees and shrubs for standout traits. These may include special flower or foliage colors, different sizes or growth rates from the main plant, distinctive forms, improved disease and pest resistance, and/or related species.

Abelia × grandiflora ○ ✳

a-BEEL-ya gran-di-FLOH-ra

Glossy abelia

Honeysuckle Family (Caprifoliaceae)
Deciduous shrub
3'–10' h x 3'–12' w

For long-lived garden color, it's hard to beat glossy abelia. With its ruddy, young stems and evergreen to semi-evergreen, opposite leaves, which are lustrous and dark green in summer and tinged a bronzy purple in fall, this shrub looks good even when it's not in flower. The scented blooms, shaped like funnels, are white flushed with pink. Blooming starts in late spring and continues through summer. Blossoms attract swallowtail butterflies. The purple sepals keep the shrub colorful after the blossoms are past. In the North, winter dieback can alter the shrub's shape.

LANDSCAPE USE
Southerners may choose glossy abelia for a handsome informal hedge. Grow glossy abelia in butterfly gardens to attract swallowtails, mass it on banks, and plant it in shrub or mixed borders where it makes a handsome backdrop for flowers. Other uses include privacy, patio, and pool plantings.

ORIGIN   Garden origin

HARDINESS ZONES   6–9

LIGHT   To enhance the redness of its stems and sepals, grow glossy abelia in full sun. It can also thrive in partial shade, as long as you grow it in well-drained, acid soil. In shady sites, however, the shrub has a more open habit and the flowers will be whiter.

SOIL   Well-drained, moist, acid soil.

GROWING   Relatively problem free, this fast-growing shrub is easy to maintain though powdery mildew, leaf spots, and root rot may affect it. When necessary,

Abelia x grandiflora

cut out dead stems in spring. If winterkill leaves the shrub unbalanced or if it overgrows its space, cut glossy abelia to the ground. When it grows back, it will be tidier and more compact. Because it blooms on new wood, plants pruned hard in late winter or early spring will flower the same year. Plant 4' on center for hedges and massing.

DESIGNER'S CHOICE
Abelia × grandiflora 'Compacta' Pink-tinged white flower clusters from May to frost; hardy and small. 3' h and w. Zone 6.

A. × grandiflora 'Edward Goucher' Lavender-purple, fragrant flower trumpets from May to frost. 3'–5' h and w. Zone 6.

A. × grandiflora 'Sunrise' Yellow variegation; yellow and green in spring; cream and green in summer. 2'–3' h and w. Zone 6.

A. mosanensis (fragrant abelia) Larger and coarser than *A. × grandiflora*; produces very fragrant, pink, white-centered blooms from May to June on buds formed the previous summer and fall; rounded habit with dense arching stems; glossy, deep green, deciduous foliage with excellent orange and red fall color. 5'–6' h and w. Zones 5–9.

Abeliophyllum distichum ○ ✳

a-bee-lee-oh-FIL-lum DIS-ti-kum

White forsythia, Korean abelialeaf

Olive Family (Oleaceae)
Deciduous shrub
5' h and w or more

Like yellow forsythia, *Abeliophyllum* doesn't look like much in summer, fall, or winter. In early spring, however, white, fragrant, forsythia-like flowers cover its branches before foliage appears. These soft white blooms look their best set against a contrasting backdrop of evergreens or a red brick wall. The shrub has a spreading habit with many arching stems that develop roots where they contact the soil. Because of this characteristic, it's easy to make more shrubs by layering (see page 358).

LANDSCAPE USE
Near a path or entry where you can enjoy its perfumed blooms.

ORIGIN   Korea

HARDINESS ZONES   (4) 5–9

LIGHT   Full sun.

SOIL   Moist, well-drained, acid soil.

GROWING   Prune right after blooming to keep in bounds and for more flowers.

Abeliophyllum distichum

Abies balsamea 'Nana' ○

AY-beez bal-SAM-ee-a

Dwarf balsam fir

Pine Family (Pinaceae)
Evergreen conifer
2' h x 3' w

Grown for its short, dense, deep green leaves, this flat-topped shrub gives cold-climate gardeners little difficulty on a sunny, moist, well-drained site.

LANDSCAPE USE
Looks great in rock gardens, mixed borders, and foundation plantings.

ORIGIN Canada

HARDINESS ZONES 3–6

LIGHT Full sun to part shade.

SOIL Well-drained soil.

GROWING Prune candles (new spring shoots) to control size.

Abies concolor △

AY-beez kon-KO-lor

White fir, Colorado fir

Pine Family (Pinaceae)
Evergreen conifer
30'–50' h x 20'–30' w

Thanks to its upright, narrow, pyramidal shape with slightly bulging sides, white fir makes a great Christmas tree. It's probably the most adaptable fir species because it tolerates cold, heat, drought, salt, and some pollution. Unlike spruce, you can squeeze the stems without yelping in pain because fir has soft, flat, upturned needles with dull tips. It has waxy, bluish-green needles, roughly 2½" long, that have a citrus scent when broken. Its bark is a smooth gray when young, growing rough and ridged over time. It maintains its dense pyramidal form longer than tall spruces, which lose their symmetry with age. Attractive chartreuse to purple cones up to 5½" long rise above the leaves. It thrives in the East, Midwest, and Northwest. Once established, this tree is hard to move.

LANDSCAPE USE
Windbreaks, hedges, privacy plantings, and conifer borders; parts provide food for deer, porcupines, small mammals, and songbirds.

ORIGIN Mountainsides in western U.S.

HARDINESS ZONES 3–7

LIGHT Full sun to light shade.

SOIL Prefers moist, well-drained, acid soil but tolerates a wide range of well drained soils; avoid clay soil.

GROWING Watch out for wooly adelgids and scales.

DESIGNER'S CHOICE
Abies concolor 'Argentea' Pale, silvery bluish-green foliage on a narrow tree. 40' h × 15' w

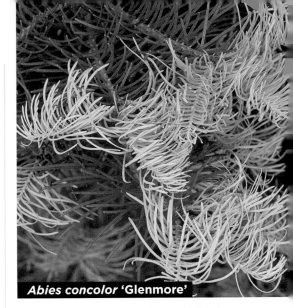
Abies concolor 'Glenmore'

A. concolor 'Compacta' Grown for its silvery blue foliage, this dwarf, asymmetrical, mounded shrub has 1½" needles on crowded branches; slow growing. 2'–10' h × 3½'–10' w.

Abies fraseri △

AY-beez FRAY-zer-i

Fraser fir

Pine Family (Pinaceae)
Evergreen conifer
30' h x 20' w

Fraser fir makes an excellent cut tree for Christmas because fresh, cone-shaped, young specimens hold their needles when well watered.

LANDSCAPE USE
Landscape specimen; charming adorned with outdoor fairy lights; good cut Christmas tree; large hedges; provides wildlife habitat.

ORIGIN High altitudes in the southeastern U.S.

HARDINESS ZONES 4–7

LIGHT Full sun.

SOIL Moist, acid, well-drained loam.

GROWING Intolerant of heat, drought, and high pH (alkaline) soils. Shield it from deer.

ALL ABOUT ABIES

These evergreen conifers are members of the Pine Family (Pinaceae). Growing to 30'–200' h x 10'–25' w, firs are not for city dwellers. For the most part, these slow-growing trees need clean air and cool summers to survive. Typically a northern or mountaintop genus, they have shallow root systems. New growth, or candles, are lighter green than old growth and appear at stem ends. Plants in this genus provide year-round color and structure for the garden. They prefer full sun, and moist, well-drained, acid soil, and good air circulation. You can control the size and shape of firs by twisting off no more than half the new growth, a technique known as candling. Watch out for rust, root rots, conifer aphids, woolly adelgid, and bark beetles.

Abies koreana △

AY-beez ko-ree-AH-na

Korean fir

Pine Family (Pinaceae)
Evergreen conifer
25' h x 10' w

Enjoy this fir's rich, dark-needled leaves, which make a handsome backdrop in a mixed conifer border; the leaves have notched tips with deep, glossy green tops and white bottoms. The bark is grayish brown. Its erect, narrow form looks striking and sculptural on its own or in a windbreak with evergreen and deciduous plants. But best of all are the showy, upright, 2"–3", dark violet cones that appear in late spring, then tan with age, even on young trees. It has an attractive tall and narrow conical habit branched to the ground that looks good year round. It has more heat tolerance than most firs. Correct siting is crucial for the plant's health.

LANDSCAPE USE
Windbreak, screening, borders, and specimen in large lawn.

ORIGIN South Korean mountains.

HARDINESS ZONES 5–6 (7)

LIGHT Full sun.

SOIL Moist, cool, well-drained, acid soil.

Abies koreana **'Silberlocke'**

GROWING Needs cool, moist soils. Intolerant of heat, drought, and high pH (alkaline) soils. Shield it from deer.

DESIGNER'S CHOICE
Abies koreana 'Goldener Traum' (Golden Dream) Yellow to lime needles with some both yellow and lime, on little conical shrub; grow in part shade for superior color, which is best in winter. 12'–15' h × 15'–20' w.

A. koreana 'Prostrate Beauty' Spreading and vigorous with long, green needles; remove any developing leader to keep the spreading form. 5'–10' h and w at 10 years.

A. koreana 'Silberlocke' Short, blue-green needles curl up so bright white undersides are visible; purple cones stand upright on the stems. Good bonsai plant. 20' h × 5' w.

Abies lasiocarpa 'Arizonica Compacta' △

AY-beez lay-zee-o-KAR-pa

Dwarf corkbark fir, Dwarf Rocky Mountain fir

Pine Family (Pinaceae)
Evergreen conifer
10'–16' h x 6'–10' w

The dwarf corkbark fir is grown for its handsome, tawny-white stems and silvery blue needles. This wide, cone-shaped, slow-growing shrub produces soft leaves radiating from dense stems.

LANDSCAPE USE
Ornamental conifer beds, shrub borders, small gardens.

ORIGIN The mountains of northwestern North America.

HARDINESS ZONES (4) 5–6

LIGHT Full sun to partial shade.

SOIL Consistently moist, well-drained, acid soil.

GROWING Grows best in the Pacific Northwest. Grown at sea level, shield from full sun. Watch out for balsam woolly adelgids.

DESIGNER'S CHOICE
Abies lasiocarpa 'Green Globe' Squat, dwarf, green ball. 2'–4' h × 2'–3' w.

Abies nordmanniana 'Golden Spreader' ◯ › △

AY-beez nord-man-nee-AN-a

Caucasian fir

Pine Family (Pinaceae)
Evergreen conifer
3' h x 5' w

This spreading, yellow conifer abounds in winter interest. Cultivate in partial shade to help maintain the bright hue.

LANDSCAPE USE
Plant near dark green conifers and purple-leafed, deciduous plants for contrast. Great for small gardens and conifer beds.

ORIGIN Caucasus

HARDINESS ZONES 4–7

LIGHT Partial shade to full sun.

SOIL Moist, well-drained, acid soil enriched with organic matter.

GROWING Intolerant of drought, wet feet, and hot dry summers. Protect from deer. Insect pests usually cause little harm.

ACER

Acer buergerianum ◑ › ◯ ✳

AY-ser ber-jer-ee-AY-num

Trident maple

Maple Family (Aceraceae)
Small deciduous tree
25'–30' h x 25' w (at 30 years old)

Grown for its compact size, attractive platy winter bark, and good fall color, trident maple can shade a patio or small lawn without overwhelming it. The canopy is broad with a rounded to oval shape. Unless trained to a single stem, trees grow bushy and low branched with multiple trunks. The three-lobed leaves are reddish to yellowish bronze in spring; rich,

ALL ABOUT ACER

Most landscape maples originated as woodland plants. Including both deciduous and evergreen species, they range from large trees to little shrubs, usually with lobed leaves. Depending upon the variety, landscape maples can be extremely ornamental with fabulous red, orange, and yellow fall color; yellow, red, deep purple or variegated spring and summer leaves; colorful twigs; decorative peeling bark; and occasionally bright red flowers and winged fruits known as samaras. Train large maples to a single trunk. Leaf scorch and verticillium wilt are common maple diseases.

shiny green in summer; and shades of yellow, orange, and red in fall. Like other maples, trident maple has opposite deciduous leaves and winged fruits, or samaras, which float to earth like little propellers. When the tree's caliper is 2" to 3", the bark begins to shed in orangey brown plates that are visible in winter. Neither the flowers nor the samaras are showy. Once established, trident maples are drought and pollution tolerant. In severe winter storms, however, branches can break under ice and snow.

LANDSCAPE USE
Small yards and patios, as street trees or under utility wires, in large containers, and as bonsai.

ORIGIN   Mountainous woods of Japan and China.

HARDINESS ZONES   5–8

LIGHT   Sun to partial shade; maintains some fall color in shade.

SOIL   Well-drained, acid soil. In alkaline soils, this tree may show signs of iron chlorosis.

GROWING   Mulch roots in dry areas. No serious pests. In exposed areas, young trident maples may be vulnerable to winter sunscald on the south side of their trunks.

DESIGNER'S CHOICE
Acer buergerianum 'Abtir' (Streetwise) Oval crown; red/purple new growth; claret red fall color; good under power lines and next to patios. 20' h × 30' w.

Acer campestre ○ ✳

AY-ser cam-PES-tre

Hedge maple, Field maple

Maple Family (Aceraceae)
Small deciduous tree
25'–35' h x 25'–35' w

As their name implies, slow-growing hedge maples take well to severe pruning and make handsome deciduous hedges. Unpruned, their dense canopies can shade out grass beneath them. They tolerate urban stresses, including drought, compaction, and air pollution, and they transplant readily.

LANDSCAPE USE
Excellent pruned hedge.

ORIGIN   Woods and hedgerows of Africa, Asia, and Europe.

HARDINESS ZONES   (4) 5–8

LIGHT   Full sun to light shade.

SOIL   Moist, fertile, well-drained soil; tolerates both acid and alkaline soils.

GROWING   Watch out for root rot, verticillium wilt, and aphids. Low tolerance to salt spray.

DESIGNER'S CHOICE
Acer campestre 'Queen Elizabeth' An upright tree with an oval crown and yellow fall color. Zones 6–8.

A. campestre 'Stgrezam' (St. Gregory) Prized for uniform, upright crown, vigorous growth, red-tinged new growth, and yellow fall color. 30' h × 25' w. Zones 5–8

Acer capillipes ○

AY-ser ka-PILL-i-peez

Snakebark, Japanese striped-bark maple, Red stripebark maple

Maple Family (Aceraceae)
Small deciduous tree
30' h and w

Leaves open reddish with reddish petioles, turn dark green in summer, then yellow to red in fall. Like a colorful thin snakeskin, bark on the red, young stems has light stripes, aging to bright white lines on greenish bark, then gray streaked by shallow, snaky, vertical fissures with age. The oxblood hue of the new stems stands out against the

Acer capillipes

Acer capillipes

muted hues of a wintry landscape. Snakebark bears clusters of greenish flowers on long, droopy stalks and attractive wide-winged samaras. It has better heat tolerance than other stripebarks.

LANDSCAPE USE
Grouped in the understory of woodland gardens, multi-trunk specimen, limbed up to show off bark pattern.

ORIGIN Moist mountain woods of Japan.

HARDINESS ZONES 5–7

LIGHT Sun to partial shade.

SOIL Moist, well-drained, fertile, cool, acid to slightly alkaline soil.

GROWING Watch out for aphids, scales, borers, tar spot, and canker and verticillium wilt.

Acer circinatum ○ › ⬱ ✳

AY-ser ser-si-NAY-tum
Vine maple

Maple Family (Aceraceae)
Small deciduous tree
15' h x 20' w

Site this bushy, finely branched, deciduous tree near your house where you can appreciate its graceful form. It has year-round interest and a spreading, multi-stemmed growth habit and grows slowly. Its up to 5"-wide foliage is reddish in spring, then has clusters of little red flowers in late spring. It may begin to get its red and orange fall color as early as August, especially when planted in drier soils. Its red samaras contrast with the green leaves. It has thin, smooth, brownish-gray-green bark; fine winter structure; and a graceful habit. Avoid planting in exposed areas and harsh climates. It earns its "easy" label when grown in its native U.S. Northwest.

LANDSCAPE USE
Equally valuable used as an informal screen, as a specimen, or as an espalier on a north wall where it shows off its vining structure in shade. It is also lovely as an understory tree in a woodland shade garden, along with camellias and conifers. Attracts wildlife.

ORIGIN Moist evergreen forests of western North America.

HARDINESS ZONES 6–9; needs a fairly mild climate to thrive.

LIGHT Full shade to full sun.

SOIL Moist, cool, and acid; can also grow in drier soil and clay soil.

GROWING Water vine maple regularly until established. Give it general-purpose fertilizer in early spring before growth begins.

DESIGNER'S CHOICE
Acer circinatum 'Little Gem' Small-leafed dwarf shrub; rare. 3' h and w.
A. circinatum 'Monroe' Dissected leaves with 7 lobes, yellow fall color, purplish stems; rare. 12' h and w.

Acer griseum ○ › ▽ ✳

AY-ser GRISS-ee-um
Paperbark maple

Maple Family (Aceraceae)
Small deciduous tree
25' h x 20' w

Paperbark maple takes its name from the outstanding, red-brown bark that peels off its stems and trunk. It always looks its best, whether silhouetted against a snowy landscape or grouped in a lawn. Even though the peeling lessens with age, the tree retains its harmonious habit and warm reddish hue. Its trifoliate, bluish-green leaves turn russet to red in fall. Autumnal leaf hues can vary from place to place and year to year. And not all paperbarks are created equal. Choose nursery trees with plentiful peeling, since flakiness doesn't improve over time.

Acer griseum

It pairs well with other deciduous small trees and shrubs, such as early blooming 'Diane' witch hazel (*Hamamelis × intermedia* 'Diane'), with its deep red flowers, or copper-flowered 'Jelena' *(H. intermedia* 'Jelena'). Underplant it with masses of spring bulbs and ferns or a groundcover such as goldenstar (*Chrysogonum virginianum). It is compact in size, with an attractive oval to vase-shaped, well-branched, erect growth habit. It grows slowly and may be expensive because of high production costs.

LANDSCAPE USE
Works well as a specimen tree, in the mixed border for fall and winter display, massed, or used as a transitional plant at the woodland's edge.

ORIGIN Wooded mountains of central China.

HARDINESS ZONES 5–7

LIGHT Full sun to partial shade.

SOIL Thrives in well-drained, moist soil but tolerates heavy soils with a wide range of pH.

GROWING Plant potted maples and balled-and-burlapped specimens in early spring to give the roots plenty of time to become established. Place it away from foot traffic, which can compact the soil around the base, a potential problem for a tree harmed by drought, compaction, and pollution.

DESIGNER'S CHOICE
Acer griseum 'Cinnamon Flake' A hybrid with Nikko maple (*A. maximowiczianum);* stems sometimes ridged; bark peels in narrower pieces than species. 15'–30' h × 20' w.

A. griseum 'Ginzam' (Gingerbread) A hybrid with Nikko maple with cinnamon exfoliating bark and orange and red fall color. More heat tolerant and faster growing than *A. griseum.* 30' h × 20' w.

Acer japonicum 'Aconitifolium'

Acer japonicum ○ › ◠
AY-ser ja-PAH-ni-kum
Full moon maple

Maple Family (Aceraceae)
Small deciduous tree
20'–30' h and w

Full moon maple is a great alternative to Japanese maple (*A. palmatum*) in Zone 5 (refer to the latter for site, use, and growing). This multi-stemmed shrub or small tree features a rounded crown and beautiful, rounded leaves with 7 to 11 toothed, pointed lobes. It bears attractive, reddish-purple flowers in spring and brilliant yellow, orange, and red foliage in fall. It is vigorous and adaptable to many soils.

LANDSCAPE USE
See *A. palmatum.*

ORIGIN Wooded mountains of Japan.

HARDINESS ZONES 5–7

LIGHT See *A. palmatum.*

SOIL See *A. palmatum.*

GROWING See *A. palmatum.*

DESIGNER'S CHOICE
Acer japonicum 'Aconitifolium' In spring, new leaves are edged in red with cherry red stalks; in fall, ferny leaves turn scarlet and purplish-red samaras give a long-lasting display. Shrubby habit up to 15' h × 20' w.

A. japonicum × 'Vitifolium' A sturdy tree with grapelike, thick, shiny leaves are less divided than those of the species, up to 10" wide and deep red to purple fall color. 20' h and w.

Acer mandschuricum ▽ › ◠ ✳
AY-ser mand-CHU-ri-kum
Manchurian maple

Maple Family (Aceraceae)
Small deciduous tree
30' h × 20'–25' w

This handsome little tree is worth growing for its bright red new stems and foliage in spring, rosy red autumn leaves, small size, and tidy habit. In early October, it kicks off the fall maple season in my garden, dropping its red leaves long before the rest. My tree grows slowly.

LANDSCAPE USE
Like paperbark maple, Manchurian maple makes a good specimen in small gardens, along a property line, or in a mixed border of trees and shrubs.

ORIGIN Manchuria, Korea

HARDINESS ZONES 4–7

LIGHT Sun to partial shade.

SOIL Moist, well drained, acid.

GROWING No serious pests and diseases.

Acer negundo ○ ✳

AY-ser ne-GUN-doh

Box elder

Maple Family (Aceraceae)
Deciduous tree
45' h x 30' w

Unless nothing else will grow in your site, don't plant box elder. This short-lived, common tree is both adaptable and weedy. Although it grows fast and tolerates drought and urban pollution, it attracts box elder bugs, and it suckers and fruits prolifically. Cultivars grow more slowly, have attractive leaves, often don't set seed, and appeal less to box elder bugs.

LANDSCAPE USE
Grow only cultivars for color or screening.

ORIGIN Moist North American riverbanks.

HARDNESS ZONES 3–8 (cultivars, 5–8).

LIGHT Full sun to partial shade.

SOIL Prefers moist soil but survives anywhere.

GROWING Prune cultivars in late winter or early spring to intensify stem color and maintain variegation. Prune species to a single trunk.

CAUTION Species considered invasive in the Northeast.

DESIGNER'S CHOICE
Acer negundo 'Flamingo' Variegated form with pink-tinted new leaflets that turn green with white edges over time; good garden accent; a male clone with no seeds. 20' h × 15' w.

A. negundo 'Kelly's Gold' Slower grow-ing than the species, this cultivar has soft yellow leaves all summer when planted in filtered sun. 30' h and w.

A. negundo 'Sensation' A pest-resistant male with soft, coppery-red leaves in spring, turning green with a reddish tint in summer, then bright red in fall. 30' h × 25' w.

Acer palmatum 'Sangokaku'

Acer palmatum ○ › ⌂

AY-ser pahl-MAY-tum

Japanese maple

Maple Family (Aceraceae)
Deciduous tree
25' h x 30' w

With Japanese maples, it's often a case of love at first sight. Who can resist the mounded branches and fluid, green foliage of *A. palmatum* 'Waterfall', the delicate architecture and pale, variegated leaves of 'Butterfly', or the cascade of purple-red, lacy leaves of *A. palmatum* 'Inaba-shidare'?

Japanese maples have a refined habit. Bark is a smooth, grayish brown. Leaf hues range from gold to red and green with variegation in pink and white; fall color can be an outstanding red, orange, or yellow. Lobed, pointed leaves vary from handlike in shape to deeply dissected. Stems can also be ornamental. While 'Sangokaku' has coral stems, many other green-leaved Japanese maples have green or reddish stems, while leaves in shades of red tend to appear on red to purple stems. You have hundreds of cultivars from which to choose the right one for you.

LANDSCAPE USE
Japanese maples make outstanding garden specimens or patio trees, and many are perfectly sized for the shrub border. Grow them with other acid-lovers, such as dwarf conifers, rhododendrons, camellias, and mountain laurel, or surround them with perennial groundcovers and low, spreading bulbs. A small weeping tree can function like a piece of living sculpture in a garden bed. Larger Japanese maples make excellent lawn specimens. Use upright forms as understory plantings in woodland gardens. Japanese maples grow well in containers and lend themselves to bonsai. With proper siting and adequate organic matter, these plants can bring elegant form and fine textures to the garden.

ORIGIN Woods and thickets of China, Japan, and Korea.

HARDNESS ZONES 6–8 (some cultivars to Zone 5).

LIGHT *Green cultivars:* Full sun to partial shade, although dissectums should be protected from hot afternoon sun. *Variegated-leaf cultivars:* Need protection from hot afternoon sun, since they are prone to sun scorch. *Red-leaf cultivars:* Need intense morning sun and some afternoon shade for best coloring.

SOIL Acid soils with a medium amount of organic matter.

GROWING Make sure you site your dissectums away from windy areas and give them shelter from afternoon heat and sun. Limited stress, such as cutting off supplemental watering in late summer, may intensify fall color. To enhance the trunk and branch architecture and keep the tree free from pests and diseases, cut out scraggly interior twigs, particularly from the dissectums, and leave structural branches intact. Do heavy pruning before bud break. Make small training or corrective cuts any time. Mulch the roots and protect potted Japanese maples when temperatures fall below 15°F.

DESIGNER'S CHOICE

Acer palmatum 'Bloodgood' Easy to find in nurseries and garden centers, these vigorous, upright trees have palmate leaves, which open crimson and darken to deep red, with prolific, showy, bright red samaras. 15'–25' h × 15' w.

A. palmatum 'Butterfly' Upright tree with small, variegated, bluish-green foliage. White margins open pink in spring, change to deep purplish red in fall. 10' h × 5' w.

A. palmatum 'Garnet' Fast-growing with wine-red leaves in summer, glossy red fall color; a good container plant. 10' h × 14' w.

A. palmatum 'Orangeola' A sturdy dissectum, this cultivar bears orange foliage in spring that turns to green-tinged orange in summer and supposedly red-orange in fall. Although compact and hardy, I find this cultivar disappointing in my garden for its dull coloration. 6' h × 10' w.

A. palmatum 'Sangokaku' (Coral Tower) This vigorous tree has coral-red bark in winter, chartreuse leaves in spring, and orange and gold fall color. 20' h × 15' w.

A. palmatum 'Seiryû' This upright dissectum bears delicate green leaves in spring and summer that turn to yellow and crimson in fall. 12' h × 10' w.

A. palmatum 'Sharp's Pygmy' Dwarf with rounded form; green leaves turning dark red in autumn. 3' h and w.

A. palmatum 'Waterfall' Deeply dissected green leaves on weeping branches turn red-tinged gold in autumn; draping stems give a ground-cover effect on a slope. 6' h × 10' w.

Acer pensylvanicum ○

AY-ser pen-sil-VAN-i-kum

Moosewood, Striped maple, Goosefoot maple

Maple Family (Aceraceae)
Small deciduous tree
25' h × 15' w

In the right situation, moosewood makes a pretty and naturalistic garden tree, especially when underplanted with ferns and woodland flowers. I grow it near a farmer's wall of piled granite rocks that separates my suburban property from adjacent woods. Grow this low-branched, deciduous, understory tree for its bright yellow fall color and attractive bark. New stems are reddish; when mature, the smooth, green to green-brown bark has vertical white stripes that give the tree winter interest. Moosewood has an irregular open silhouette. It is not a plant to choose in hot climates, as it is intolerant of heat. It is also hard to transplant and grow.

LANDSCAPE USE

Plant at the forest's edge as a transition from wild to cultivated areas. Use in naturalized woodland gardens or informal shade gardens as a border plant or in dappled shade along the edge.

ORIGIN Wooded mountain slopes of eastern North America.

HARDINESS ZONES 3–7

LIGHT Partial shade.

SOIL Moist, cool, well-drained, and somewhat acid soil.

GROWING Avoid salt spray and, if possible, provide early morning sun and afternoon shade.

DESIGNER'S CHOICE

Acer pensylvanicum 'Erythrocladum' Features outstanding winter bark with crimson shoots that turn white-striped orangey red with age. In my garden, snow intensifies the effect of 'Erythrocladum's' luminous red bark. Because it can be challenging to propagate and grow in a garden setting, the examples I've seen have been small, ranging from 5'–8' h × 3'–4' w.

Acer pensylvanicum

Acer platanoides ○ › ◌ ✳

AY-ser pla-ta-NOY-deez

Norway maple

Maple Family (Aceraceae)
Large deciduous tree
75' h × 50' w

The advantages of Norway maple may also be its faults. Grown for its vigor, adaptability, and the cool, deep shade it provides under its wide crown, this tree can overpower your yard! Along with its dense, spreading canopy comes a vast network of surface roots that out-compete other garden plants, including lawn grass, for water and nutrients. Then there are the prolific seedlings, which not only pop up in your lawn and flowerbeds, but also overrun wild areas where they crowd out native species. These trees are ubiquitous in the gardened landscape, having been overplanted by gardeners wanting a majestic, easy-to-grow tree. If you must grow this tree, plant one of the cultivars, instead of the species.

Norway maple has yellow fall color and plain, gray bark. It tolerates drought, compaction, bad drainage, and pollution and casts cooling shade. However, leaf scorch, rot, tar spot, and verticillium wilt are all potential problems.

LANDSCAPE USE
Use less invasive cultivars with narrow root spread, such as 'Columnare', for screening, street planting, and shade in the home landscape.

ORIGIN   Mountainous woods of Europe and Asia.

HARDINESS ZONES   3–7

LIGHT   Full sun to partial shade.

SOIL   Well-drained soil.

GROWING   Easy to transplant, fast growing.

CAUTION   Overused and invasive in the Northeast and parts of the Midwest, Southeast, and Northwest.

DESIGNER'S CHOICE

Acer platanoides 'Columnare' A good choice for home gardeners because of its narrow crown, which has a spread of only 15'–20'. It is less invasive than the species, and its narrower canopy and less-widespread surface roots mean that you can grow lawn underneath it. Prune off spreading branches to keep the form. 60' h × 15'–20' w.

A. platanoides 'Crimson King' Although this cultivar is smaller than the species, it exhibits similar troubles and is possibly even more prone to disease and insect problems. Use it with caution as an accent, because its blackish-red foliage is so drab that it reads like a dark hole on the horizon. Overused in large areas of the country, it is not as vigorous in climates with hot summers. 35'–45' h × 25'–35' w.

A. platanoides 'Drummondii' With its bold, variegated leaves with green centers and wide yellow to creamy white borders, this makes a great accent plant. Remove any branches that revert to all green leaves. 30'–40' h and w.

Acer pseudoplatanus ○ › ◌

AY-ser su-doh-PLA-ta-nus

Sycamore maple, Plane tree maple

Maple Family (Aceraceae)
Deciduous tree
40'–60' h and w

Sycamore maple can grow on difficult sites, since it tolerates wind, salt, and both acid and alkaline soils, although it has no tolerance for heat. Showy, flaky gray and orange bark is an additional benefit. This tree can be weedy and disease prone. Instead of the species, grow cultivars, or better yet, plant a different large shade tree instead.

LANDSCAPE USE
Shade tree for large open lawns in cool coastal states.

ORIGIN   Deciduous mountain woods of Europe and southwest Asia.

HARDINESS ZONES   4–7

LIGHT   Full sun to light shade.

SOIL   Any well-drained soil.

GROWING   Easy to grow, hard to maintain. Prone to aphids, sooty mold, cankers, and borers.

CAUTION   Considered invasive in parts of the Northeast and Midwest.

DESIGNER'S CHOICE

Acer pseudoplatanus 'Brilliantissimum' Foliage opens bright pink and yellow, then turns green in summer. Slow growing, it suits small gardens, patio plantings, or mixed beds. Best in part shade. 20' h × 25' w.

Acer pseudosieboldianum ○

AY-ser su-doh-see-bol-dee-AY-num

Purple bloom maple, Korean maple

Maple Family (Aceraceae)
Small deciduous tree
20' h and w

Grown for its compact size, fall color, and excellent cold hardiness, purple bloom maple has rounded leaves with about 9 pointed and toothed lobes. Cream and purple blooms open in early spring before the tree leafs out. In autumn, leaves take on bright red, orange, and purplish hues. For folks in Zone 4, this thin-barked Korean maple may be a practical alternative for Japanese maple (*A. palmatum*).

LANDSCAPE USE
See *Acer palmatum*.

ORIGIN   Manchuria, Korea

HARDINESS ZONES   4–7

LIGHT   Full sun to partial shade.

SOIL   Moist, well drained, acid soil.

GROWING   Watch out for winter sunscald and cankers entering trunk injuries.

Acer rubrum △ › ○ ✳

AY-ser ROO-brum

Red maple, Swamp maple

Maple Family (Aceraceae)
Medium to large deciduous tree
40′–70′ h x 30′–50′ w

Where I live in New Hampshire, red maples and sugar maples are key components of the gaudy spectacle known as *fall!* Tourists and natives clog the roads, marveling at the transformation of these common New England trees into beacons of red and gold. So it's no surprise that American gardeners want a red maple — the most common maple in North America — in their home landscapes. Different cultivars of this tree, grown for its brilliant red fall color, suit various climates. It makes an excellent shade tree because its leafy canopy is not too dense. It is perfect for parks and large lawns, since its spreading shallow root system would be a detriment in a small yard. Note that female trees often have brighter red fall color than males, but both produce red flowers in early spring before the leaves emerge.

Red maple bears ornamental, bright red, clustered flowers in spring, mostly before leaves. Its bark is thin, gray, and vulnerable to damage. It is moisture tolerant. The foliage is flushed with red when opening, then it turns medium green, and finally a stunning red or yellow in fall. Not all red maples turn red in fall, however. Some are yellow, while others have a greenish tinge. For red fall color, choose a cultivar known for its red hue. Make sure you select a variety of red maple adapted to your part of the country. Better yet, buy the tree in fall from a local nursery so you can see for yourself how it colors up in your area.

LANDSCAPE USE
Excellent shade tree, good in groups, especially on moist or swampy land

ORIGIN   Moist soils of eastern North America.

HARDINESS ZONES   3–9

LIGHT   Full sun to partial shade.

SOIL   Adaptable to wet or dry growing conditions; needs acid soil for good health and best color.

GROWING   Where possible, buy cultivars grown on their own roots rather than grafts. Leaf hoppers can be a problem for this species.

DESIGNER'S CHOICE

A. rubrum 'Autumn Flame' Early, intense red fall color on a round tree. 55′ h × 45′ w. Zones 4–8.

A. rubrum 'Franksred' (Red Sunset) Luminous orange to red leaves in early autumn. This fast-growing female also has showy red flowers and fruit in early spring and tolerates heat and drought. 60′ h × 50′ w. Zones 4–8.

A. rubrum 'Northwood' The most cold-hardy cultivar, but fall color lacks brilliance of some other cultivars; a male with red-orange fall color. 40′ h × 35′ w. Zones 3–8.

Acer rubrum 'October Brilliance' Compact crown, radiant red leaves in autumn; leafs out slowly in spring, providing frost resistance. 40′ h × 30′ w. Zones 5–7.

A. rubrum 'October Glory' This well-known cultivar holds its brilliant red to orange-red fall foliage longer than most maples. Tall, spreading, and fast growing, it makes a good specimen in a large lawn or parkland. Good choice for the Southeast, where it has a long colorful fall

Acer freemanii 'Armstrong'

season in spite of the climate, but may be a bad selection for northern New England. Because of its fame, my husband and I planted our 20-foot-tall 'October Glory' in our New Hampshire yard 10 years ago. It took an unusually warm lingering autumn (a recent trend) for me to understand its colorful reputation. In the first half of October, leaves had a ruddy tinge. By late October, the leaves were coppery red, turning fiery in sunlight. The red leaves stayed on the tree through wind and rain, finally dropping in November. 50' h and w. Zones (4) 5–8.

A. rubrum 'Scanlon' Columnar, with yellow to orange to red-orange fall color, 'Scanlon' is not appropriate for humid climates where it loses its leaves early. 50' h × 15' w.

A. freemanii 'Jeffersred' (Autumn Blaze) This hybrid represents the best features of its parents, *A. rubrum* and *A. saccharinum,* without their drawbacks. It has the brilliant scarlet fall color and sturdiness of *A. rubrum* but, unlike the latter, thrives in alkaline soils. 50' h × 40' w. Zones 4–7.

A. freemanii 'Celzam' (Celebration) Compact symmetrical form; medium-size tree; strong branch crotches; fast growing when young; red and gold fall color. Seedless, disease resistant, tolerates urban pollution. Not suitable for most small gardens or under power lines because of its size. 45' h × 30' w. Zones 4–8.

Acer saccharinum ○ › ○ ✳

AY-ser sak-ka-RYE-num

Silver maple, White maple

Maple Family (Aceraceae)
Large deciduous tree
60'– 80' h x 35'–50' w

Silver maple may be a short-term answer to the long-term problem of providing shade on a treeless property. Because of silver maple's vigorous growth and adaptability, it is a useful tree where soil is meager and nothing else will grow or where there is seasonal flooding. From a distance, you can recognize silver maple by its spreading branches with droopy branchlets that turn up at the tips. Most cultivars grow too large for urban or suburban gardens, so avoid planting them in limited spaces and where surface roots can heave driveways and sidewalks. For attractive alternatives, check cultivars of *A. freemanii,* of which silver maple is a parent.

The foliage is light green on top and silvery below; the bark is gray and smooth when young, peeling with age. A weak-wooded tree, silver maple may lose branches or split down a narrow crotch after exposure to ice and winds. It is prone to insect and disease, including anthracnose, verticillium wilt, cottony maple scale (very susceptible), and various borers, mites, and aphids.

LANDSCAPE USE

Use as a temporary solution for a difficult site that needs quick shade, but grow a strong-wooded, healthier, more attractive tree nearby. Remove the silver maple when the slower-growing tree is well established.

ORIGIN Moist flood planes of eastern North America.

HARDINESS ZONES 3–9

LIGHT Full sun.

SOIL Moist, acid soil; tolerates dry, wet, clay, compacted, and alkaline soils.

GROWING Keep this scrappy maple away from septic tanks, leach fields, and drains.

DESIGNER'S CHOICE

Acer saccharinum 'Northline' Spreading habit; hardier, slower growing, and stronger wooded than the species. 60'–80' h × 40'–45' w. Zones 3–7.

A. saccharinum 'Silver Queen' Erect tree with rounded crown; leaves vivid green, turning yellow in fall. Few seeds. 50' h × 40' w.

Acer saccharum ○ › ○

AY-ser sak-KAR-um

Sugar maple, Hard maple

Maple Family (Aceraceae)
Large deciduous tree
70' h x 40' w

In autumn, a mountainside of sugar maples is a sight to behold. Electrifying foliage of yellow, orange, and red shimmers whether the day is sunny or overcast. Their bark is smooth and gray when young; grooved and platy with age. The price for this natural beauty is a somewhat fussy tree unsuited for the rigors of city life. Many do not withstand extreme heat, bark may split after severe pruning, and they are susceptible to leaf scorch and verticillium wilt. They suffer in areas with drought, flooding, or

Acer saccharum

exposure to road salt. Sugar maples are unsuitable for curbside plantings or other narrow spaces, such as small parking-lot islands, because pollution and compacted soil also weakens them.

On the other hand, the slow-growing sugar maple is a deciduous hardwood that tolerates a wide range of soil pH. Delicious maple syrup is made by boiling down the sap.

LANDSCAPE USE

Too big for many urban and suburban yards, sugar maples look beautiful planted as shade trees, single specimens in a large lawn or parkland, or in groups where their stunning fall color has maximum impact. Large surface roots make them impractical for lining streets and driveways.

ORIGIN Rich woods of eastern North America.

HARDINESS ZONES 3–8

LIGHT Full to partial sun.

SOIL Loose, rich, moist, well-drained, slightly acidic soil.

GROWING Pruning from midwinter to midspring causes sap to "bleed" from the cuts but does not harm the tree.

DESIGNER'S CHOICE

Acer saccharum 'Astis' (Steeple) Oval habit; tolerates heat and drought; displays yellow-orange autumn leaves. 45' h × 25' w.

A. saccharum 'Barrett Cole' (Apollo) Columnar; yellow-orange to red fall color. 25' h × 20' w at 30 years. Zones 4–7.

A. saccharum 'Commemoration' Vigorous growth; spreading branches; tatter-resistant leaves turn orange to red in early fall. 50' h × 30' w at 30 years. Zones 5–8.

A. saccharum 'Goldspire' Features a tall, narrow crown and glossy, thick, green leaves that turn orange-yellow in fall. 40' h × 13' w at 30 years. Zones 4–8.

A. saccharum subsp. *grandidentatum* 'Schmidt' (Rocky Mountain Glow) Commonly called canyon maple, this cultivar is smaller than sugar maple and also more tolerant of drought and alkaline soils. 25' h × 15' w. Zones 4–6.

A. saccharum 'Legacy' Grows vigorously; displays widespread, dense branches; features thick, shiny, dark green leaves. Sometimes lasting through November, fall color ranges from red and orange to salmon and pink. An excellent choice for both North and South. 50' h × 30' w.

Acer shirasawanum 'Aureum' ○ › ◖
(syn. *A. japonicum* 'Aureum')
AY-ser shee-ra-sa-WAH-num
Golden full moon maple

Maple Family (Aceraceae)
Small deciduous tree
20' h × 15' w

Golden full moon maple is decorative throughout the growing season. Showy, 3"–4", rounded leaves with 11 lobes open pale chartreuse in spring, greening with time; foliage turns bright orange and red in fall. This small tree or large shrub is susceptible to leaf scorch in full sun in hot climates but grows better in Zone 5 than *A. palmatum*.

LANDSCAPE USE

See *A. palmatum*.

ORIGIN Japanese mountainsides and valleys.

HARDINESS ZONES 5–7

LIGHT See *A. palmatum*.

SOIL See *A. palmatum*.

GROWING Prune this slow-growing tree during dormancy and water it deeply during drought.

Acer shirasawanum 'Aureum'

Acer tataricum subsp. *ginnala* ○ ✳
(syn. *A. ginnala*)
AY-ser tar-TA-ri-kum ji-NAL-la
Amur maple

Maple Family (Aceraceae)
Deciduous small tree or shrub
20'–30' h × 15'–25' w

Cold-climate gardeners appreciate Amur maple for its terrific orange-red fall color near patios and low decks. Because of its vigor, however, this understory tree can seed itself into woods and open spaces, ousting native species. It features clusters of fragrant, pale green or yellow flowers in spring; abundant, showy, red-winged samaras in summer; and vibrant orange-red color in fall. Its smooth bark is deep grayish brown.

LANDSCAPE USE

Because of its density, full rounded silhouette, and natural low-branched form, it makes a nice informal screen, or you can prune it into a hedge. Use it as a patio tree, border accent, informal screen, pruned hedge, or planting under utility wires.

ORIGIN   River banks and mountain valleys in China and Japan.

HARDINESS ZONES   3–7

LIGHT   Full sun to partial shade.

SOIL   Well-drained, moist, acid soil, though it tolerates some dryness, wind, and heavy or alkaline soils.

GROWING   Plant potted trees from spring to early summer. Balled-and-burlapped specimens may be planted in early spring in all regions or in early fall everywhere but in the coldest range where roots would not have time to establish before deep frosts.

CAUTION   Invasive potential, especially in New England and the upper Midwest.

DESIGNER'S CHOICE

Acer tataricum subsp. *ginnala* 'Betzam' (Beethoven) Symmetrical, columnar shape; bright red samaras; glossy, dark green leaves that turn brilliant yellow to red in fall. 25' h × 15' w.

A. tataricum 'Durand Dwarf' A bushy cultivar with fall color in shades of red. 5' h × 6' w.

A. tataricum 'Embers' Creamy, fragrant spring flowers; red summer fruits; glossy scarlet fall color. Use for screening, hedge, border plant, or small specimen tree. 15'–20' h × 10'–20' w.

A. tataricum 'Emerald Elf' A great container tree with year-round interest; red/purple spring growth; shiny, dark green summer leaves; bright burgundy fall color; peeling bark. 5' h and w.

A. tataricum 'Flame' A shrub or small tree with abundant red fruits in summer and intense red fall color. 15'–25' h and w.

A. tataricum 'Mondy' (Red Rhapsody) Exceptional red fall color on a small, shrubby, fast-growing tree; 15'–20' h and w.

Acer triflorum ○ › ○

AY-ser try-FLOH-rum

Three-flower maple

Maple Family (Aceraceae)
Small deciduous tree
30' h x 25' w

Three-flower maple is a four-season tree. Lighter in color than that of the ruddy paperbark maple, its attractive golden bark exfoliates in elongated vertical pieces and looks great year round. Yellow spring flowers grouped in threes appear with bronzy new leaves. The foliage is brilliant orange to red in fall. It may be hard to find at your local nursery; check mail-order nurseries in this book for sources.

LANDSCAPE USE

This sturdy little maple suits small gardens and can grow comfortably under utility wires as well as under some larger trees. Plant near patios and decks for shade and as an accent, singly or massed in borders.

ORIGIN   Mountainous woods of northeastern Asia.

HARDINESS ZONES   (4) 5–7

LIGHT   Full sun to partial shade.

Acer triflorum

SOIL   Moist, well-drained, acid soil. Fertilize and water regularly until established.

GROWING   Needs acid soil and protection from harsh winds.

Acer 'White Tigress' ○

AY-ser

'White Tigress' striped maple

Maple Family (Aceraceae)
Small deciduous tree
20' h x 30' w

'White Tigress' striped maple boasts bold, silvery-white, vertical stripes on greenish-brown bark; its fine-textured leaves turn pale yellow in fall. Late spring frosts may harm tender new leaves.

LANDSCAPE USE

Its open form suits woodland gardens, dappled edges, partly shaded patio beds, and containers.

ORIGIN   Manchuria, Korea

HARDINESS ZONES   4–7

LIGHT   Partial shade to full sun.

SOIL   Moist, well drained, humusy, acid soil for best fall color.

GROWING   Shield young plants from harsh winds and late frosts until established. In the beginning, cover trees on freezing nights once leaves start to grow.

AESCULUS

Aesculus × *carnea* 'Briotii' ○

ES-ku-lus KAR-nee-a

Ruby red horse chestnut

Horse Chestnut Family (Hippocastanaceae)
Small deciduous tree
30' h and w

Grown for vivid red, nearly foot-high bloom clusters and improved drought tolerance, this spring-blooming tree is a hybrid between common horse chestnut (*A. hippocastanum*) and *A. pavia*. The flowers of this cultivar are a deeper red and larger than those of the species. It looks delightful and fresh in late spring when it's in bloom. The flowers are above the leaves, making them easy to see. Bark is attractive and platy, but that's not enough to make this tree a sure thing for your garden. Later in the season, leaf scorch, pests, and diseases can turn it ugly. (I saw some ruby reds on a posh Swarthmore, Pennsylvania, street one late June day after a hot dry spring and wondered why the owners would want such nasty looking trees marking their driveways.)

LANDSCAPE USE
In the right conditions, a pretty shade tree for lawns, specimen, groups.

ORIGIN Garden origin

HARDINESS ZONES (4) 5–7 (8)

LIGHT Full sun to partial shade.

SOIL Deep, rich, moist, well drained.

GROWING Litter from leaves, twigs, and nuts makes this a messy tree. Transplant when small because of deep taproot.

CAUTION Nuts are toxic.

Aesculus x carnea 'Briotii'

ALL ABOUT AESCULUS

In general, buckeyes have big, hand-shaped, opposite leaves and decorative white, red, or yellow flowers arranged in erect bunches from late spring to early summer. The trees, many of which are too big for city or suburban yards, litter the ground with dead flowers and foliage in summer and fall. Most chestnut trees found in the U.S. are really buckeyes or horse chestnuts. A widespread fungal blight destroyed most mature American chestnuts (*Castanea dentata*) from 1900 to 1940. Unlike edible chestnuts from the American chestnut tree, horse chestnuts or buckeyes are poisonous and must not be consumed.

Aesculus pavia var. splendens

Aesculus parviflora 🗠

ES-ku-lus par-vi-FLO-ra

Bottlebrush buckeye

Horse Chestnut Family
(Hippocastanaceae)
Medium to large multi-stemmed shrub
5'–10' h x 10'–20' w

Bottlebrush buckeye's name derives from its 12" h × 4" w, upright, white flower clusters, which are shaped like narrow cones and resemble bottlebrushes; they bloom in midsummer. The long, protruding stamens give the flowers an airy, spidery look. The flowers attract hummingbirds. Unlike its feathery blooms, however, the foliage is bold, coarse textured, and lacks the sheen that characterizes some buckeye species. Rough, green leaves with 5 to 7 leaflets up to 9" long are arranged like fingers on a hand; yellow fall leaves drop rapidly. The bark is smooth. The shrub's informal suckering habit makes it good for understory planting at a woodland edge. It is hard to establish.

LANDSCAPE USE
Understory planting beneath big trees, rounded landscape mass for distant viewing, and tall groundcover.

ORIGIN Woods and riverbanks in southeastern U.S.

HARDINESS ZONES 4–8

LIGHT Sun to partial shade.

SOIL Moist soil, rich in organic matter; tolerates wet soil and can even grow in mud, but prolonged drought can do it in.

GROWING Slow to establish and slow growing; prune when necessary by cutting to the ground in early spring.

Aesculus parviflora

Aesculus parviflora var. *serotina* 'Rogers' Mounded shrub; blooms later than species; drooping inflorescences up to 30" long. 8'–12' h × 8'–15' w

Aesculus pavia ○ ✳

ES-ku-lus PAY-vee-a

Red buckeye

Horse Chestnut Family
(Hippocasta naceae)
Small single- or multi-stemmed tree
10'–30' h × 10'–20' w

In spring, red buckeye bears spikes of showy, red, tubular blooms at the branch tips with slightly protruding stamens. The flowers attract hummingbirds, bees, and butterflies. Foliage is purplish bronze when young, turning dark green; before summer's end the leaves are falling to the ground, though foliage persists longer on plants grown in shade. It blooms in sun or shade, tucking nicely under a beech. Grown in sun, red buckeye has a low-branched, rounded form, but in the shade the habit is looser and more open. The furrowed bark is brownish gray.

Aesculus pavia var. *splendens*

Underplant this lovely tree with large-flowered trillium (*Trillium grandiflorum*) and massed Christmas fern (*Polystichum acrostichoides*), coralbells (*Heuchera* spp.), or foamflower (*Tiarella cordifolia*).

LANDSCAPE USE
Use as a fast-growing understory tree at the woodland's edge or as a specimen in a spring-blooming woodland border.

ORIGIN   Moist woods, ravines, and wooded streamsides in southeastern and central U.S.

HARDINESS ZONES   4–8 (9)

LIGHT   Blooms more in full sun but does best in partial shade where it retains its foliage until mid fall.

SOIL   Prefers moist loam with plenty of organic matter and neutral to basic soil. Apply lime to sweeten acid soil. Red buckeye can tolerate wet for short periods and survives short bouts of drought, though the latter may cause summer leaf drop.

GROWING   Red buckeye has better mildew resistance than other chestnuts, but it is susceptible to leaf blotch, a fungal disease. To prevent the disease from overwintering, immediately rake up and destroy dropped leaves.

CAUTION   The attractive glossy fruits are poisonous.

DOES DEFOLIATION MATTER?

Leaf diseases of deciduous trees look ugly but usually don't kill their hosts. However, trees affected several years in a row may be weakened and vulnerable to other pest and disease problems. Defoliation can cause critical damage to evergreens in a single growing season.

Aesculus pavia 'Atrosanguinea' Deep red blooms. 10'–30' h × 10'–20' w

A. pavia var. *flavescens*   Yellow flowers pollinated by bumble bees. 10'–30' h × 10'–20' w

A. pavia 'Humilis'   Squat shrub with smaller clusters of red blooms.

AMELANCHIER

Amelanchier species ○ › ○

a-muh-LAN-kee-er

Serviceberry, Saskatoon, Shadblow, Shadbush, Juneberry, Servicetree

Rose Family (Rosaceae)
Large shrub or small flowering tree
10–25' h × 6–20' w

My friend Martha Petersen adores native serviceberries. Marty, a Kittery, Maine, landscape designer, appreciates serviceberry's airy look in the landscape; its clusters of large, showy, white flowers; the delicious, edible, bluish black fruit; and its bright reddish purple fall color. Marty isn't the only one to appreciate this plant. Birds flock to the fruit and butterflies feed from the nectar-laden blossoms.

This tree looks lovely in spring, when its white-tinted pink blossoms make it stand out in the landscape; flowers age to all white. Its bluish black fruits ripen in early summer (the source of another of its common names, Juneberry); collect the fruit for jam or jelly (if you can beat the birds to it). New foliage is tinged purple; it ages to deep green and in fall turns yellow to orange and red. The smooth bark is light gray and very appealing; it furrows with age. Even in winter, the tree's fine texture and erect, oval shape are lovely to behold.

If you live in an area of poor air quality, consider a different tree, since serviceberry won't thrive in pollution, drought, and soil compacted by machinery and foot traffic or contaminated with road salt. It's best to buy named cultivars, which may come with as many as 7 trunks or as few as one.

LANDSCAPE USE

I think *Amelanchier* looks best in naturalistic settings. The prettiest serviceberries I've ever seen edged a small forest on a rolling green hillside. This mass of white-blooming trees, seen from a distant garden, lit up the landscape, giving it texture and depth. Serviceberries also work well under utility wires, in woodland borders, in groups, and as specimens in light shade. I used the multi-stem form along a woodland path shaded by oaks. Underplanted with massed coralbells, it makes a delicate accent in summer as well as when its smooth silvery gray bark is exposed in winter.

Amelanchier x grandiflora

ORIGIN   Moist woodlands of North America, Europe, and Asia.

HARDINESS ZONES   (3) 4–8 (9), depending upon species.

LIGHT   Full sun to shade.

SOIL   Tolerates many soils but prefers moist, well-drained, acid soil, preferably with plenty of organic matter.

GROWING   Given the proper cultural conditions, this tree is easy to grow. You can limb it up to enhance the shape of the crown and to make more space beneath its branches. Like other members of the rose family, serviceberry is susceptible to leaf damage by Japanese beetles, fireblight, lace bugs, and cedar apple rust.

DESIGNER'S CHOICE

Amelanchier alnifolia 'Regent' Shrubby dwarf with white blooms, vivid yellow and orange fall color; good for naturalizing; withstands alkaline soils and severe climates; edible fruits loved by birds. 4'–6' h × 4'–6' w. Zone 2.

A. 'Autumn Brilliance' Grow for plentiful white flowers, red leaves in autumn, and robust growth. Resists leaf spot and fireblight. 20' h × 15' w.

A. canadensis 'Glenform' (Rainbow Pillar) White spring blooms and mildew-resistant leaves with bright red fall color; narrow upright habit for hedging and screening. 15'–20' h × 8'–10' w.

A. × grandiflora 'Forest Prince' Copious white blooms along branches instead of just at the tips; disease-resistant leathery leaves with orangey-red fall color. 20' h × 12' w.

A. × grandiflora 'Strata' White blooms with pinkish tint; horizontal pattern of branches looks layered. 15'–20' h × 15' w.

A. laevis 'Cumulus' White flowers, red to purple fruit, and bright orange to red fall foliage on tough erect small tree; possibly susceptible to fire blight. 25' h × 15' w.

Amelanchier laevis 'Cumulus'

A. 'Princess Diana' Plant for red fall color that starts early and ends late; pretty habit; disease resistance. 20' h × 15' w.

ANDROMEDA

Andromeda polifolia ○ › ⌂

an-DRO-me-da pol-i-FOL-i-a

Bog rosemary

Heath Family (Ericaceae)
Tiny mounding shrub
Up to 16" h × 24" w

Bog rosemary is a native groundcover with narrow, pointed, evergreen leaves about 1" long and dangling clusters of 2 to 5 bell-like white or light pink blooms in spring. The bluish green leaves look like rosemary, thus its common name.

LANDSCAPE USE

Perfect for acidic bog gardens, moist woodland gardens, and for edging in damp beds and borders. Bog laurel (*Kalmia polifolia*), cranberry (*Vaccinium* species), tamarack (*Larix laricina*), purple pitcher plant (*Sarracenia purpurea*), and

Andromeda polifolia

sphagnum moss (*Sphagnum* species) are suitabable companions.

ORIGIN Peat bogs of northern North America, Europe, and Asia.

HARDINESS ZONES 2–6

LIGHT Full sun to partial shade.

SOIL Cool, consistently moist, peaty, sandy, acid soil with a pH of 4.5 to 5.

GROWING Intolerant of heat, humidity, and drought.

DESIGNER'S CHOICE

Andromeda polifolia 'Alba' White flowers with dark gray-green leaves on low-lying shrub with spreading habit. 6"–8" h × 12"–18" w.

A. polifolia 'Blue Ice' Blue leaves and pink-tinged white flowers from May to July. 12" h × 24" w.

A. polifolia 'Compacta' Pink flowers and dull green leaves on a mounded twiggy shrub. 8" h × 12" w.

A. polifolia 'Macrophylla' Rounded pink flowers age white; broad, dark green leaves. 12" h × 24" w.

ARALIA

Aralia elata ◌ › ☁ ✳

a-RAY-lee-a e-LA-ta

Japanese angelica tree

Aralia Family (Araliaceae)
Deciduous tree
Up to 40' h x 30' w

This Japanese native is one crazy little tree for a cold climate. Bold, tropical, and dramatic, Japanese angelica produces leaves 3'–4' long and cream-colored flowers in groups half the size of the massive leaves. Birds gobble the dark purple fruits that follow the flowers in late summer. Fall color is copper to ruddy purple. Better yet, grow the showy variegated cultivars. These can produce all-green suckers, which must be removed as soon as they appear.

LANDSCAPE USE

Japanese angelica tree makes a striking accent in a border. In woodland gardens it looks strange and mysterious, especially when grown near plants with contrasting texture such as giant butterbur (*Petasites japonicus* 'Giganteus').

Aralia elata

Cloaked in heavy bristles, both single and multi-stemmed Japanese angelica make excellent barrier plants.

ORIGIN Eastern Asia

HARDINESS ZONES (3) 4–8

LIGHT Full sun to partial shade.

SOIL Moist, well-drained soil.

GROWING To keep Japanese angelica under control, remove excess suckers.

CAUTION Stems have big, sharp spines. Avoid planting Japanese angelica near the house if you have young children, since the spines can scratch if they fall against them.

DESIGNER'S CHOICE

Aralia elata 'Aureovariegata' Uneven leaf margins start out yellow but lighten over the growing season. 15' h and w.

A. elata 'Variegata' Edges of leaves are creamy white. 15' h and w.

A. elata 'Silver Umbrella' smaller and more finely textured than 'Variegata' 10' h × 6' w.

A. spinosa (devil's walking stick) This native of the eastern U.S. is coarser textured, more invasive, and harder to control than *A. elata*. The compound leaves can grow up to 5' long. Use this plant carefully. My friend Neil Jorgensen took advantage of this plant's tropical feel by growing it in a Massachusetts woodland garden shaded by maples and oaks. 10'–20' h × 5'–15' w.

ARBUTUS

Arbutus menziesii ◌

ar-BU-tus men-ZEE-zee-i

Madrone, Strawberry tree

Heath Family (Ericaceae)
Evergreen tree
30'–50' h and w

Gardeners appreciate the madrone for its striking bark. Cinnamon and peeling on top, the fresh bark below appears smooth and greenish; it becomes creviced and dark over

Arbutus 'Marina'

time. Pointy, oval, evergreen leaves, which stay on trees up to 14 months, are shiny green on top and smooth, bluish white below. In late spring, erect 6"–9" clusters of white to pinkish urn-shaped blooms that attract hummingbirds open at the stem ends. Edible, red berries follow the flowers and last into winter.

LANDSCAPE USE
Madrone makes a fine garden specimen and a valuable addition to the shrub and tree border; usually only found on the West Coast.

ORIGIN Forested damp slopes of western North America.

HARDINESS ZONES (5) 7–9

LIGHT Full sun.

SOIL Well-drained soil.

GROWING Hard to transplant. Deer may eat the flowers.

DESIGNER'S CHOICE
Arbutus 'Marina' This tree, an effective plant for firescaping, has evergreen foliage larger than that of the species. Deep pink flowers bloom while red and yellow strawberry-shaped fruit are developing from the previous season. 20'–30' h and w. Zones 7–9.

A. unedo 'Compacta' This shrub or multi-trunk tree has peeling ruddy bark, dense upright branches, and profuse white autumn blooms often at the same time as the attractive red fruit from year-old flowers. Use this plant, which can grow in poor soil, alone as a focal point or massed for screening and informal hedges. 6'–8' h × 5'–6' w.

ARCTOSTAPHYLOS

Arctostaphylos uva-ursi

ark-toh-STA-fi-los U-va UR-si

Bearberry, Kinnikinick

Heath Family (Ericaceae)
Evergreen groundcover
4"–12" h x 20"–48" w

The flowers, berries, and evergreen foliage of this deer-resistant plant offer year-round interest. A slow-spreading groundcover, bearberry forms a dense, erosion-stopping mat. Its ½"–1"-long simple leaves are glossy and leathery and turn purplish to red-brown in winter. Its smooth bark is dark reddish brown, exfoliating on older stems. Its white to pink, urn-shaped spring flowers, about ¼" high, hang in clusters, attracting hummingbirds and other wildlife; the flowers are followed by shiny, red, summer berries. It is susceptible to leaf spot, galls, and mildew.

The plant's common name (bearberry) and scientific name (*A. uva-ursi*) refer to its fruit and northerly location. *Arctos* means *bear* in Greek and refers to the ancient northern hemisphere bear constellations (Ursa Major and Minor, or big and little dippers, known since the Ice Age); *staphyle* is Greek for grape cluster, referring to the plant's red fruit. Similarly *uva-ursi* is Latin for bear's grape.

LANDSCAPE USE
Erosion control on dunes and slopes, attractive groundcover on hillsides, rock garden specimen, low-water landscaping. Cut for evergreen Christmas decorations.

ORIGIN Native to sandy dunes, open mountain hillsides, and dry canyon slopes of Earth's northern regions.

HARDINESS ZONES 2–6

LIGHT Full sun to partial shade.

SOIL Thrives in acid, sandy poor soils under a hot sun. Tolerates infertile alkaline conditions.

GROWING Container-grown material is easiest to transplant. Initially, water regularly for deep spreading roots. Until plants cover an area, spread mulch among the plants to manage weeds. Do not fertilize.

DESIGNER'S CHOICE
Arctostaphylos uva-ursi 'Massachusetts' In late spring, this mat-forming northeastern U.S. bog plant produces pale pink, 2-inch bell-shaped blooms; in late summer it bears persistent red berries. Fall color has red-gold tint. Plant 5' apart or set them closer for quick coverage. 6"–12" h × 10'–15' w. Zones 3–5.

A. uva-ursi 'Vancouver Jade' Ideal groundcover for bare slopes because it spreads faster than other cultivars. Pinkish white flowers and red fruit. Foliage resists leaf spot. In full sun to partial shade it will grow from 6"–20" h × 8' w.

A. uva-ursi 'Wood's Compacta' White urn-shaped blooms flushed deep

Arctostaphylos uva-ursi 'Massachusetts'

pink in late spring give way to late summer's clear red fruit, which stays on the evergreen plant into winter. Leaves turn red in winter. 3" h × 4' w. Zones 2–8.

ARONIA

Aronia arbutifolia 🌿 ✳

a-RO-ni-a ar-bu-ti-FO-li-a

Red chokeberry

Rose Family (Rosaceae)
Deciduous shrub
5'–10' h × 3'–4' w

I recommended this terrific shrub to my friend Lynne Barnes, a lovely lady with a vernal pond in her 2-acre, Zone 5 backyard. It's become one of her favorites, thanks to its attractive clusters of white fragrant flowers in late spring, showy red summer fruit, and brilliant red fall color. It is truly showy from summer to winter.

The deciduous, shiny, green leaves of red chokeberry turn bright purplish red in fall. The smooth bark is ruddy grayish brown and blistered. The clustered, white flowers are fragrant in mid-spring as leaves open; blooms can have pink or purplish

Aronia arbutifolia

tint. The edible, shiny, red, round fruits (about ¼"–⅓" in diameter) attract birds and mammals, but they are a bird's last resort because of their tartness. Use the fruits in jams, preserves, and sauces.

Because the leaves grow toward the top of the plant, the shrub looks bare-legged unless you face it with perennials, grasses, or short shrubs. In damp soil, plant moisture-loving bulbs and perennials such as quamash (*Camassia leichtlinii),* cardinal flower (*Lobelia cardinalis),* meadow rue (*Thalictrum aquilegiifolium),* and queen-of-the-prairie (*Filipendula rubra)* around its base.

LANDSCAPE USE
Use mass plantings for an informal screen.

ORIGIN   Swamps and lowlands of the eastern U.S.

HARDINESS ZONES   4–9

LIGHT   Full sun to partial shade.

SOIL   Many soils, including wet ones, but prefers moist, well-drained soil.

GROWING   Easily transplanted and grown.

DESIGNER'S CHOICE
Aronia arbutifolia 'Brilliantissima'
   More flowers and bright red, shiny fruit than the species; spectacular red fall color. 6'–8' h × 3'–4' w.

A. melanocarpa (black chokeberry)
   Black edible fruit. 4'–5' h and w. Zones 3–8.

A. melanocarpa 'Autumn Magic'   More compact and shiny leaves; many fruits slightly larger than the species; bright autumn leaves. 3'–4' h and w. Zones 3–8.

A. melanocarpa 'Morton' (Iroquois Beauty)   Dwarf cultivar with flowers and fruits similar to species; rare. 3' h and w. Zones 3–8.

A. × *prunifolia* 'Viking' (purple-fruited chokeberry)   This cultivar has early, fragrant flowers; big, black fruits high in vitamins that stay on the

plant until spring; and lustrous, dark green leaves with outstanding red fall color. 3'–6' h and w. Zones 4–8 (9).

ASIMINA

Asimina triloba ○ › 🌿

a-SI-mi-na tri-LO-ba

Pawpaw, Custard apple

Custard-Apple Family (Annonaceae)
Small deciduous tree
20'–40' h × 20' w

Given a little time, one pawpaw can become a colony of small, droopy-leaved trees. These suckering native plants, either multi-stemmed shrubs or little trees, usually grow in groups on river banks, bottomlands, and wet woods. Grown singly in sun, pawpaw has a low-branched, pyramidal shape. Its simple, large (5"–12" long × 2"–6" wide), hanging, coarse-textured leaves are green in summer and bright to greenish yellow in fall; the leaves host zebra swallowtail caterpillars and give the plant a tropical look. This is no surprise, since pawpaw is the Custard-Apple family's only temperate tree. The warty bark is patchy light gray and brown. The nodding, open, light green flowers turn dark red-brown in spring. The edible fruits, reminiscent of short, fat bananas with a banana-like taste and custardy texture, are pollinated by insects; you need more than one cultivar for cross pollination. The 2"–5" fruits change from green to yellow to ripe dark brown in fall. Pawpaw's seeds can be toxic if eaten. Both seeds and leaves are insecticidal when compressed.

LANDSCAPE USE
Best in woodland or wild gardens, where it forms interesting airy colonies in light shade

ORIGIN   River banks, bottomlands, and wet woods of the eastern U.S.

Asimina triloba

HARDINESS ZONES 5–9

LIGHT   Full sun to partial shade.

SOIL   Moist, well-drained soil rich in organic matter.

GROWING   Foliage is susceptible to fungal diseases, but overall pawpaw tends to be a healthy plant.

AUCUBA

Aucuba japonica ○

a-KU-ba ja-PAH-ni-ka

Spotted laurel, Japanese laurel, Japanese aucuba, Gold dust plant

Dogwood Family (Aucubaceae)
Broad-leaf evergreen shrub
Up to 10′ h x 10′ w

The handsome, thick, glossy, 6"–8" evergreen leaves of spotted laurel are deep green with lighter green underside. Bark of the current season's growth is green. Spotted laurel is an attractive, slow-growing shrub with an upright, oval habit for shady gardens. Grown for its foliage, it comes in male and female forms. Females produce tiny, dark, purplish-red blossoms in summer, followed

in fall by showy, ½", shiny, red, oval berries that nestle among the leaves; the berries last through winter. If you want abundant berries, plant a male nearby for pollination. Grow with shade-loving hydrangeas, ferns, and other broad-leaf evergreens. Stems add long-lasting interest to flower arrangements. Cultivars have colorful variegated leaves year round; females produce showy, red berries.

LANDSCAPE USE

Excellent hedging or foundation plant for shade. Variegated *aucuba* make attractive specimens and accents, bringing light to dark spots in the garden. Use them for massing as well as in containers.

ORIGIN   Multiple Asian habitats.

HARDINESS ZONES   7–10

LIGHT   Prefers partial shade to full shade but can tolerate more sun in its coolest range.

SOIL   Prefers moist, well-drained, acid soil, rich in organic matter; tolerates most soils except wet.

GROWING   Shape after blooming. Needs protection from winter winds. Avoid crown rot and other fungal diseases by

Aucuba japonica 'Variegata'

planting in raised beds or other well-drained soils. Give plants adequate air circulation to avoid a buildup of humidity. Keep mulch away from the stems. Use an acid-based fertilizer in early spring, but stop fertilizing after midsummer. Remove plant debris around the base of the plant. Pay full attention to cultural practices to avoid dieback, disease, and pests such as mites, nematodes, and mealybugs.

CAUTION   Leaves and berries can be poisonous if eaten.

DESIGNER'S CHOICE

Aucuba japonica 'Mr Goldstrike' Male with bright gold variegation on the leaves; gives a glowing chartreuse effect. 5′ h and w.

A. japonica 'Serratifolia' (sawtoothed Japanese laurel) Female with scarlet berries and dark green shiny leaves with serrated edges on upright stems. 4′–6′ h and w.

A. japonica 'Variegata' (Gold Dust Japanese aucuba) Female with big, long leaves marked by bold yellow spots. Needs male pollinator for good fruiting. 3′–5′ h and w.

BACCHARIS

Baccharis halimifolia ▽ ✳

BA-ka-ris ha-li-mi-FOH-lee-a

Groundsel bush, Salt marsh elder, Sea myrtle

Daisy Family (Asteraceae)
Multi-stemmed semi-evergreen to deciduous shrub
5′–15′ h and w

Unless you live on poor soil or by a sunny tidal marsh, you probably won't grow tough, salt-tolerant groundsel bush. Usually flat gray-green, groundsel bush takes on a different look in fall. Silver-plumed, tufted fruit at the branch tips obscure the plant with billows of fine-textured white fluff. *Baccharis* has male and

Baccharis halimifolia

female forms, but only the females bear decorative fruit.

LANDSCAPE USE
Especially where salt and erosion are issues, I'd use this shrub massed for a distant screen or an informal hedge, or filler on edges of natural areas. Closer to the house, however, I'd use more interesting salt-tolerant shrubs such as bayberry (*Myrica pensylvanica*), rosemary (*Rosmarinus officinalis*), chokeberry (*Aronia*), or arrowwood (*Viburnum dentatum*), depending upon your hardiness zone.

ORIGIN U.S. coastal plain.

HARDINESS ZONES 5–9

LIGHT Full sun to partial shade.

SOIL Well drained soil.

GROWING Tolerates wet, dry, acid, alkaline, saline, infertile soils and heat, drought, and salt spray; also tolerates drastic renewal pruning, which may be needed as it tends to be leggy.

BERBERIS

Berberis × gladwynensis 'William Penn' ○ ✳

BER-ber-is glad-wi-NEN-sis

'William Penn' barberry

Barberry Family (Berberidaceae)
Evergreen shrub
4' h and w

A few years ago, I saw this shrub massed in a bed outside a bank in Hockessin, Delaware. Its glossy leaves, arched stems, and dense, mounded habit made a positive impression, while its evident spines and stiffness kept me from wanting to touch it or take the short way to the bank through the bed. Its 2"–4", dark, evergreen leaves are edged with sharp teeth arranged in rosettes; its fall effect is brilliant bronze with its winter hue a glossy bronze. The bark is brownish. It bears showy clusters of ½", cup-shaped, yellow blooms in spring and ½" purplish fruit in autumn.

William Penn barberry looks good year round, is generally healthy, is deer resistant, and shows some drought tolerance once established. It may experience some winter dieback if exposed to harsh winds and severe winter conditions, and so it is best if not planted in this environment. Because of its prickly leaves and dense, thorny stems, leaf litter and windswept trash may accumulate around the base.

LANDSCAPE USE
Thanks to its spreading mounded form, small size, and year-round interest, William Penn barberry makes a good foundation plant or low informal hedge. It works equally well massed in a shrub border or as a single specimen in a rock garden. Spiny stems make it an effective barrier between properties, under windows, and near doors.

ORIGIN Hybrid of garden origin.

HARDINESS ZONES 5–7 (8)

LIGHT Full sun for best leaf color, but tolerates partial shade.

SOIL Moist, somewhat acid, well-drained soil, but also withstands poor soils.

GROWING Fall planting increases drought survival. Water regularly until established. If desired, lightly prune to shape after blooming.

CAUTION Spiny to touch and toxic to eat.

Berberis julianae ○

BER-ber-is ju-lee-AN-i

Wintergreen barberry

Barberry Family (Berberidaceae)
Evergreen shrub
8' h and w

In the right circumstances, this barberry makes a handsome garden plant, with its glossy, dark, evergreen leaves that turn bronze to deep red in fall and its yellow flowers set in decorative groups. Flowering in spring, wintergreen barberry bears clusters of black oval fruit, frosted powdery white, in fall.

Berberis julianae 'Spring Glory'

LANDSCAPE USE

This deer-resistant barberry creates serious barriers and security or informal privacy hedges because of its dense spiny leaves and triple thorns at the base of each node.

ORIGIN   Central China

HARDINESS ZONES   (5) 6–8

LIGHT   See B. × gladwynensis.

SOIL   See B. × gladwynensis.

GROWING   See B. × gladwynensis, but best left unpruned to assume its rounded shape; tolerates drastic renewal pruning.

CAUTION   Spiny to touch and toxic to eat

DESIGNER'S CHOICE

Berberis julianae 'Spring Glory'   Mound-shaped plant with reddish new growth. 6' h and w.

Berberis koreana ○ ✳

BER-ber-is ko-ree-AH-na
Korean barberry

Barberry Family (Berberidaceae)
Deciduous shrub
6' h x 4' w

The suckering habit of this hardy barberry makes it hard to control, but its ornamental characteristics make it worth the effort. Korean barberry produces 2"–4" hanging clusters of yellow flowers in May, followed in fall by hanging bunches of red berries that can last into winter. Fall color is a rich, long-lasting, deep purplish red, especially when grown in full sun in any soil but wet.

LANDSCAPE USE

Attractive, very hardy, informal hedge, grouping, or border plant.

ORIGIN   Korea

HARDINESS ZONES   3–7

LIGHT   Full sun.

SOIL   Tolerates any soil condition except wet.

GROWING   Prune annually as described above to maintain an attractive shape.

CAUTION   Spiny to touch and toxic to eat.

DESIGNER'S CHOICE

Berberis 'Red Tears' (syn. *B. koreana* 'Red Tears')   Red-tinged foliage and 4" pendant clusters of shiny, red fruits.

Berberis × mentorensis ○

BER-ber-is men-toh-REN-sis
Mentor barberry

Barberry Family (Berberidaceae)
Semi-evergreen shrub
5' h and w

Grown for its long-lasting yellow to scarlet fall color, fast growth, and neat size, Mentor barberry features hanging clusters of yellow flowers in spring. Red fruits, however, rarely follow the flowers.

ALL ABOUT BERBERIS

Barberries range from desirable to controversial. Many species are garden favorites around the country because of their attractive leaves, flowers, or fall fruits. Small barberries make good rock garden plants, while big, spiny ones make effective barrier hedges when planted in rows.

Two barberries are considered by many horticulturists to be invasive. The highly decorative Japanese barberry (B. thunbergii) has seeded itself throughout 20 states in the Northeast and parts of the South and Midwest. It forms thick stands in natural habitats ranging from woodlands (see photo below) to wetlands and meadows, dislodges native plants, and shrinks the food supply for wildlife. Common barberry (B. vulgaris) is in the northern half of the United States and parts of southern Canada, south to North Carolina, Missouri, and Colorado. Most states have banned its sale because it is an alternate host for wheat rust.

Barberries are used for borders and as hedges or specimen plants; yellow-leafed cultivars make fine accents. They prefer well-drained soils and full sun to partial shade.

Prune evergreen barberries to remove stray shoots that ruin the natural shape after blooming. To shape deciduous shrubs, prune shoots that have flowered back to another shoot or to the base for renewal. Watch out for mites, scales, rusts, cankers, leaf spots, powdery mildew, and verticillium wilt. Barberry spines can irritate affected skin.

LANDSCAPE USE

Because of its hardiness, vigor, and size, it makes an effective spiny hedge or barrier. Good for corner plantings when you want to keep passersby from cutting across your lawn.

ORIGIN   Garden origin

HARDINESS ZONES   5–7

LIGHT   Sun to partial shade.

SOIL   Tolerates a variety of soils, as long as they are well drained.

GROWING   With its naturally broad, round form, it needs no shearing to maintain a pleasing shape.

CAUTION   Spiny to touch and toxic to eat.

Berberis thunbergii ○ ✳

BER-ber-is thun-BER-gee-i

Japanese barberry

Barberry Family (Berberidaceae)
Thorny deciduous shrub
4' h x 5' w

Beware of this exotic species, which has taken North American gardens by storm. Japanese barberry, originally promoted as an alternative to the banned common barberry, has a rounded, twiggy habit with deciduous, green leaves that turn orangey to purplish red in fall. Small, yellow spring flowers turn into prolific, red fruits in fall. Because of its adaptability, Japanese barberry seeds itself into disturbed sites and natural habitats, where it replaces native species. You can find this much-used garden plant in a variety of hues and forms, including the ubiquitous, 2' h × 2.5' w, carmine-colored 'Atropurpurea Nana' (syn. 'Crimson Pygmy'). Other cultivars range from red, purple, and pink to cream and yellow, while habits vary from slim 5' pillars to small

**Berberis thunbergii
'Atropurpurea Nana'**

1' mounds. You may do better to avoid planting these shrubs at all in affected states rather than to risk further spreading the species.

LANDSCAPE USE
Hedging, massing, and accents.

ORIGIN   Japan

HARDINESS ZONES   4–7

LIGHT   Full sun to partial shade.

SOIL   Tolerates most soils except wet ones.

GROWING   Japanese barberry loses its dense, rounded shape in excessive shade.

CAUTION   Invasive potential; listed as noxious weed in 42 U.S. states; sales banned in Canada because of threat to native species. Instead of Japanese barberry, substitute spicebush (*Lindera benzoin*), 'Little Lamb' hydrangea (*Hydrangea paniculata* 'Little Lamb'), or 'Sikes Dwarf' oakleaf hydrangea (*H. quercifolia* 'Sikes Dwarf').

DESIGNER'S CHOICE
Longwood Gardens trialed 41 barberries to determine levels of invasiveness. Their findings, published in *The American Nurseryman,* December 1, 2004, showed that those with low fruit production and thus a low invasive potential include the following:
Berberis thunbergii 'Cocorde' Rounded, seedless dwarf with red-purple leaves that maintain their color. 18"–24" h × 24"–36" w.

B. thunbergii 'Bogozam' (Bonanza Gold) Uniform mounded dwarf with bright yellow leaves and an orange fall tint; use in masses, borders, low hedges, foundation plantings. 18" h × 36" w.

B. thunbergii 'Kobold' Dwarf, green, uniform mound; orange fall color; no pruning necessary. 18"–24" h × 24"–36" w.

B. thunbergii 'Monlers' (Golden Nugget) Dense dwarf with yellow-gold leaves turning red in fall. 12" h × 18" w.

Berberis verruculosa ○

BER-ber-is ver-ru-cu-LOH-sa

Warty barberry

Barberry Family (Berberidaceae)
Evergreen shrub
3'–4' h and w

This slow-growing little barberry is grown for its dark, shiny, evergreen leaves that turn brownish red in fall and winter. Yellow flowers occur singly in late spring. The Longwood barberry study found that the warty barberry set no fruit, making it unlikely to become invasive.

LANDSCAPE USE
On banks, for informal low hedges and barriers, and as edging for shrub beds and borders.

ORIGIN   Western China

HARDINESS ZONES   6–9

LIGHT   See *B. × gladwynensis.*

SOIL   See *B. × gladwynensis.*

GROWING   See *B. × gladwynensis.*

BETULA

Betula lenta △ › ○ ✳

BET-u-la LEN-ta

Black birch, Sweet birch, Cherry birch

Birch Family (Betulaceae)
Medium-size deciduous tree
45' h × 35' w

Wander through lush woodlands of the eastern U.S. and you'll probably notice the gleaming, ruddy brown to black bark of young sweet birch. The bark, which turns a rough, scaly, charcoal gray with age, contains oil with a wintergreen scent. (Scratch and sniff a skinny twig to see for yourself.) Historically, the fragrant bark was used to flavor beer and to relieve ailments ranging from colds to cancer, while crafters built furniture from the wood. Black birch bears 2"–5", simple leaves with gold

ALL ABOUT BETULA

Birches are versatile landscape trees often valued for their bark, their fall color, and the dappled shade that younger trees produce. Most have fine yellow fall color, though some species may be yellow-brown, reddish, or orange in autumn. The beauty of birch bark includes the peeling white bark of paper birch, the creamy exfoliating (peeling) bark of river birch, and the deep red, non-peeling bark of cherry birch. The yellow to yellowish brown male catkins or flowers grow in long, dangling, decorative clusters in spring. Birches are excellent either grouped in borders or used as a specimen in a bed underplanted with groundcovers or perennials for sun to partial shade.

Betula papyrifera

fall color. In spring it produces 3"–4", dark tan male catkins.

LANDSCAPE USE
Wild and woodland gardens.

ORIGIN   Eastern U.S.

HARDINESS ZONES   3–8

LIGHT   Full sun to partial shade.

SOIL   Thrives in moist, well-drained soil, but tolerates a variety of conditions from sandy and dry to heavy clay.

GROWING   Sweet birch grows best in protected shady areas. Resistant to bronze birch borer.

Betula nigra △

BET-u-la NI-gra

River birch, Red birch, Black birch

Birch Family (Betulaceae)
Medium-sized shade tree
60' h x 40' w

This is one of my favorite informal landscape trees for year-round interest. I like using it as a specimen or in small groups because of its irresistible cream to orange-and-cinnamon bark, which sheds in dramatic curls; its yellow fall color; the 3" tan male spring catkins; and the dappled shade the tree casts when young. The foliage of river birch is simple, green, and up to 3" long with doubly serrated edges. The attractive bark is odorless. River birches come with 1 to 5 trunks. Multi-stemmed clumps look particularly handsome when limbed up to expose the bark.

As river birch ages, it changes in striking ways. Older trees cast medium shade and have a vaguely pyramidal habit. More important, however, the attractive, peeling bark stops. My single-stemmed Heritage river birch is about 20 years old with bark changing at the base from flaking salmon to uneven, blackish-brown, ridged and furrowed plates. Higher up the trunk, the bark is darkening and stiffening like the mythological Daphne, who turned from nubile nymph into a laurel tree to help her avoid amorous Apollo's advances. If you want to see peeling bark, you may have to replace these fast-growing trees with younger examples.

LANDSCAPE USE
This tree is excellent planted in groups of uneven number; it also makes a fine specimen tree or focal point in a lawn or bed. Many decorative plants can thrive in its dappled to medium shade. It is a good choice for wet sites, disturbed land, and compacted soil.

Betula nigra 'Heritage'

Martha Petersen, a Kittery, Maine, landscape designer, created a striking Heritage birch allée that frames the view from her deck to Spruce Creek, an inlet of the Atlantic Ocean, at her property's edge.

ORIGIN Forest openings, hills, floodplains, and disturbed sites in the eastern half of the U.S.

HARDINESS ZONES 4–9

LIGHT Full sun to light shade.

SOIL Most adaptable birch. Prefers deep, moist, somewhat acid to neutral, silty soils but also does well in damp, boggy conditions and dry, gravely sites. Yellowed leaves may result from alkaline soils.

GROWING Like maples, birches have ample sap during spring and early summer. Prune trees in dormancy or in midsummer to avert dripping wounds. It is an effective alternative to white-barked birches, because it is resistant to bronze birch borer, which plagues those species. It is also deer resistant, but it may sustain ice damage.

Betula nigra

DESIGNER'S CHOICE
Betula nigra 'Duraheat' Whiter bark than the species exfoliates at an early age; shiny dark green leaves with soft yellow fall color; resistant to leaf spot, bronze birch borers, leaf miners, and aphids; cold hardy (possibly to Zone 3) and heat tolerant; dense oval leaf canopy. 25'–50' h and w.

B. nigra 'Little King' (Fox Valley) Slow-growing dwarf with great bark; perfect for small spaces and groups; tolerates cold, heat, and high humidity; resists bronze birch borer and leaf spot. Neat, rounded form. 10'–15' h × 12' w.

B. nigra 'Cully' (Heritage) Salmon to cinnamon bark exfoliates at an early age; shiny, big, green leaves turn yellow in fall; resistant to bronze birch borer, leaf spot. Much improved over the species and the most commonly grown selection. 30'–60' h × 25'–40' w. Hardy to Zone 3.

Betula papyrifera △ ✳

BET-u-la pap-y-RI-fer-a

Paper birch, Canoe birch

Birch Family (Betulaceae)
Deciduous tree
60' h x 35' w

This low-branched native birch is no fan of the city life. Intolerant of pollution, heat, and drought, it has a delicate habit with a fairly open crown that casts dappled to light shade. During severe winters, the short-lived paper birch, which grows up to 2' per year, can snap in ice and wind. In spite of its drawbacks, it's valued for the effect of the white bark, which glows when planted against a dark green coniferous background or in a sunny opening in deciduous woods. In the East, paper birch grows well with groundcovers such as bearberry (*Arctostaphylos*

Betula papyrifera

uva-ursi), wintergreen (*Gaultheria procumbens*), and low-bush blueberry (*Vaccinium angustifolium*). Frequently seen along highways and roadsides in the North, paper birch has a narrow, oval to pyramidal crown.

The glossy, green, simple leaves are up to 4" long and turn brilliant yellow in autumn. Thin, smooth, white bark exfoliates in papery bands with black, streaky lenticels to expose pinkish orange inner bark; the bark is ridged and blackish brown at the base. It bears droopy clusters of male catkins up to 4" long in spring. It is a larval host for luna moths. According to the Fletcher Wildlife Garden in Ottawa, Ontario, paper birch also attracts birds, including yellow-bellied sapsuckers, black-capped chickadees, fox and American tree sparrows, common redpolls, and pine siskins.

Group it in moist beds and borders; nice transitional plant from woods to open ground; lawn specimen. It confers light shade.

ORIGIN   Native to moist stream banks and lakesides in Canada and the northern U.S. from coast to coast; often seen along northern highways in disturbed soils. Paper birch thrives where winters are long and summers are short and cool.

HARDINESS ZONES   2–6

LIGHT   Full sun.

SOIL   Prefers moist, well-drained, porous soil but adapts to many different soils, as long as they are cool in summer.

GROWING   Somewhat susceptible to bronze birch borers and leaf miners, which can enter through bark wounds. Keeping the tree healthy, watered, and fertilized and the surrounding area lightly mulched may help prevent insect damage. Susceptible to ice damage and may need replanting if growing in a site heavily exposed to the elements; deer and moose may browse the low twigs.

DESIGNER'S CHOICE

Betula papyrifera 'Snowy' Very white-barked birch; resistant to bronze birch borer.

B. papyrifera 'Varen' (Prairie Dream) Bred in North Dakota to be stress tolerant and to resist bronze birch borer; good white bark and dark green leaves.

B. papyrifera 'Renci' (Renaissance Reflection) Bred in Wisconsin for resistance to heat and bronze birch borers; bright white bark; yellow fall color. Zones 3–7. 60' h × 25' w.

Betula pendula △ › 🌀

BET-u-la PEN-du-la

European white birch, Silver birch

Birch Family (Betulaceae)
Deciduous tree
45' h × 30' w

Distinguished from paper birch by droopy, or pendulous, branches, silver birch has lustrous, green leaves with yellowish fall color and a narrow, oval form when mature. Its white bark with prominent lenticels doesn't peel but over time forms blackish crevices at the base. Yet the interesting looks of *B. pendula* don't necessarily mean this tree is right for American gardens. Bronze birch borers ravage this native of northern Asia and Europe's sandy soils. For best results, this birch needs cool summers and cold winters. Several people in my neighborhood grow this tree. One neighbor uses the species as an attractive focal point in a driveway planting bed. Another used *B. pendula* 'Youngii', the weeping form grafted on upright standards, to mark either side of a driveway entrance.

Betula pendula 'Youngii'

They died after a record cold winter, perhaps because of excessive road salt. In particular, *B. pendula* fares badly in the Midwest, where hot summer temperatures weaken the trees and make them susceptible to problems. If you're not sure which birch to grow, try one with better insect and disease resistance instead of this problematical tree. Many cultivars available; purple-leaved ones may be even less vigorous and more prone to borers.

LANDSCAPE USE

Accent in beds and borders; specimen.

ORIGIN   Northern Asia and Europe.

HARDINESS ZONES   4–7

LIGHT   Full sun.

SOIL   Acidic, well-drained, moist soils.

GROWING   High maintenance. Keep mulched and treat problems promptly.

Betula populifolia △

BET-u-la pop-u-li-FOH-lee-a

Gray birch, Old field birch

Birch Family (Betulaceae)
Deciduous tree
30' h × 15' w

Gray birch has thin, white bark that does not peel. Fast growing, short lived, and relatively small, this tree often appears in stands in forest openings. It has even less shade tolerance than *B. papyrifera* and must grow in full sun. The tree's form is narrow and low branched with pronounced black triangles at the branch bases. A few single- and multi-stemmed gray birches grow wild on our land, once an abandoned field, and we kept them when we built our house. In addition to their ornamental, chalk-white bark and yellow fall color, I like the regional feel they bring to the landscapes in the East.

Group it in informal borders; nice transitional plant from woods to open ground; good for naturalizing. It provides light shade.

ORIGIN A native white-barked birch found in and near the mountains of eastern North America.

HARDINESS ZONES 3–7

LIGHT Full sun.

SOIL Grows well in wet, dry, rocky, sandy, heavy, and acid soils, but alkaline soils may cause chlorosis.

GROWING Leaf miners are a problem with this species, but bronze birch borer doesn't trouble it much.

DESIGNER'S CHOICE

Betula populifolia 'Whitespire Senior' ('Whitespire Senior' gray birch) May sometimes be incorrectly listed as *B. platyphylla* var. *japonica* 'Whitespire' ('Whitespire' Asian white birch); fast-growing, non-peeling, white-barked birch with single or multiple trunks; has a reputation for

Betula populifolia

borer resistance, but that characteristic depends on the source of the material under propagation (seedlings from this cultivar may not have the borer resistance of tissue-cultured plants; good substitute for *B. papyrifera* in parts of the Midwest as it survives the cold winters and long, hot, humid summers of that region; may not do well in extreme heat, as marketed; may not keep white bark with age. Group it in beds and borders or use as a lawn specimen; nice transitional plant from woods to open ground; confers light shade; grow in full sun and moist, well-drained soil; intolerant of poor drainage and soils with high pH. 35' h × 30' w. Zones 4–6.

B. 'Fargo' An upright cultivar from North Dakota; may be resistant to heat and drought. 30' h × 10' w.

Betula utilis var. *jacquemontii* △

BET-u-la U-ti-lis jak-MON-tee-i

White-barked Himalayan birch

Birch Family (Betulaceae)
Deciduous tree
40' h × 30' w

My experience with this short-lived tree is not a happy one. Although you can't beat it for beautiful, snow-white bark, fine yellow fall color, and vigorous growth, it's a magnet for Japanese beetles. At least that's how I've seen it behave on New Hampshire's seacoast, where nurseries are chockablock with these pretty trees. Of course, if you live west of the Mississippi where Japanese beetles are not rampant, these tan-streaked, white-barked trees could be more desirable. Other varieties of Himalayan birch, which have bark ranging in color from

Betula utilis var. *jacquemontii*

yellow-brown to rich red-brown, grow best in full sun to light shade and cool, moist, slightly acidic soil. The USDA Forest Service says white-barked Himalayan birch is susceptible to birch leaf miner and highly prone to bronze birch borer and does not recommend it as a landscape tree. Zones 4–7.

BUDDLEJA

Buddleja alternifolia ○ › ⌂ ✳

BUD-lee-a all-ter-ni-FOH-lee-a

Alternate-leaf butterfly bush, Fountain butterfly bush, Buddleia

Butterfly Bush Family (Buddlejaceae)
Deciduous shrub
12' h × 10' w

Longwood Gardens in Pennsylvania grows fountain butterfly bushes as flowering standards around the circular pond on their Flower Garden Walk. After the plants bloom in early June, gardeners transform these standards into small weeping trees by cutting back all the old stems so that fresh shoots will emerge. When not trained to a single trunk, *B. alternifolia* has a wide, rounded form with long, loose stems that move in the wind. Its common names refer to its habit (fountainlike) and leaves (alternating on the stem instead of opposite like other *Buddleja* species). Hardier than *B. davidii*, *B. alternifolia* is the first butterfly bush of the season to bloom.

This fast-growing, pretty bush has long, graceful, arching stems, covered with fine bark. The fragrant, lilac flowers, which are clustered in leaf axils, bloom for about 2 weeks in late spring and attract butterflies. Leaves are lancelike and measure up to 4" long; they're dull green on top and hairy gray underneath and unfurl around the same time the flowers appear.

LANDSCAPE USE
Great for butterfly gardens. Use as an informal hedge or screen or as a striking specimen in a mixed border with shrubs and perennials. It has a short bloom period, so it needs proper siting and shaping to keep it attractive for the rest of the season. After flowering, it makes a handsome backdrop for later-blooming perennials.

ORIGIN Cold plains of northwest China.

HARDINESS ZONES 5–9

LIGHT Full sun to partial shade.

SOIL Prefers friable, moist, well-drained soil rich in organic matter but tolerates many conditions including dry, but not wet, soils.

GROWING Unlike the more familiar *B. davidii,* this buddleia sets its buds after blooming. Thus, to avoid sacrificing next year's flowers, prune it right after flowering. Cut away one-third of the oldest stems to shape it as a shrub or stake one stem and train it as a standard. Spider moths may cause problems.

CAUTION Invasive potential.

DESIGNER'S CHOICE
Buddleja alternifolia 'Argentea' Far more silvery leaves than the species. 8' h and w.

Buddleja davidii ○ ✳
BUD-lee-a da-VID-ee-i
Butterfly bush, Buddleia

Butterfly Bush Family (Buddlejaceae)
Deciduous shrub
5'–12' h x 5'–14' w

Butterfly bush used to be one of my favorite summer-blooming shrubs until it started seeding itself into different garden beds. Lovely, big,

flower panicles up to 28" long at the branch tips cause the arching supple stems to bend further, adding substance to this rather open shrub. The fragrant, tubular flowers come in varying colors from bright white to pinks, purples, and purplish blues, often with orange or yellow throats; yellow-flowered species and hybrids also exist, offering buddleia enthusiasts even more choices and forms. Many cultivars exude a potent fragrance. Bloom time depends on location. In southeastern New Hampshire, butterfly bush usually starts blooming in August and may continue into October. In warm regions, flowering begins as early as late spring and can continue for months if faded flowers are removed. Butterflies swarm to the lavish flowers, giving the bush a lively, fluttery surface.

Some cultivars with well-formed seedheads add winter interest to the garden. (But see below for how this can be a problem.) Dried stems and prunings make good pea stakes for floppy perennials like baby's breath or annuals like China aster. (Pea stakes are slender, branched twigs set in the ground shorter than the height of the plants they support; as the plants grow, the twiggy pea stake disappears.) Butterfly bush flowers fare best and last longest in the garden. Brought indoors, they hardly survive and the tiny, dead flowers make a mess when they drop. The gray-green, lancelike leaves, which are arranged opposite each other on the stem, are often silver underneath. The greenish stems are slender and hairy.

Butterfly bush is semi-evergreen where the climate is mild. In its northernmost reaches, this multi-stemmed shrub is deciduous, dying

Buddleja alternifolia 'Argentea'

Buddleja davidii 'Peakeep'

to the ground in winter. Other butterfly-attracting shrubs to use with or instead of *Buddleja davidii* include *B. alternifolia,* native sweet pepperbush *(Clethra alnifolia)* and Virginia sweetspire *(Itea virginica).*

LANDSCAPE USE
Great for butterfly gardens; a striking specimen in a mixed border with shrubs and perennials; a floriferous medium to tall screen. For gardeners who cut this plant to the ground each spring, you'll probably want to intersperse this plant with shrubs or early blooming perennials, since the pruned plant will leave a hole in your garden design until new stems grow up.

ORIGIN Japan and northwest China.

HARDINESS ZONES 5–10

LIGHT Full sun.

SOIL Average garden soil with good drainage. They prefer regular watering until established, after which they can tolerate some drought.

GROWING Without pruning, this plant can look like a twiggy mess. In the north, buddleia dies to the ground in winter. Since *Buddleja* blooms on new wood, treat it like a perennial in cold climates

by cutting it 6"–12" high before new growth begins. You can also do this in warmer regions to control the size of the plant and ensure larger flowers. Remove old flowers before they set seed to control the plant's tendency to self-sow. Prevent harming butterflies and other visiting insects by steering clear of pesticides near this plant. Spider mites may cause problems.

CAUTION Invasive potential. If you don't remove spent flowers, it can seed itself near and far. I've seen *B. davidii* growing in gutters, railways, and cracks in the stonework of ancient cathedrals. In my own garden, where I kept 'Pink Delight' and 'Nanho Purple' shrubs intact for winter interest, seeds ripened and *Buddleia* became a weed growing where I never planted it. Three years ago, I removed butterfly bushes from my mixed border, but I still find seedlings in my big perennial bed.

DESIGNER'S CHOICE
Buddleja davidii 'Black Knight' Dark purple; slightly more cold hardy than the species.

B. davidii 'Dartmoor' Big-branched, magenta-purple flower spikes. 5'–10' h and w.

B. davidii 'Ellen's Blue' Lavender blue, fragrant flowers with orange throats in short panicles on shrubs with compact form and handsome seed heads. Highly rated in Longwood Trials. 6' h and w, pruned.

B. davidii 'Fascinating' (often listed as 'Fascination') In shrub trials, Longwood Gardens (Zone 6) scored this cultivar high for its long, pointy, light pink to lavender flower panicles, full rounded habit, silvery new growth, and attractive weeping seed heads. 7' h and w, after pruning to 12".

B. davidii 'Harlequin' This cultivar has variegated leaves with yellow edges that fade to cream. Flowers are deep reddish purple. 'White Harlequin' is a white-flowered, cream-edged selection. In my garden, its habit was spindly compared with the non-variegated cultivars.

B. davidii 'Nanho Purple' Deep purple-hued blooms with orange throats on a compact shrub with a dense, upright, rounded form. Highly rated in Longwood Trials. 6' h and w, pruned.

Other popular *B. davidii* include bluish 'Nanho Blue', 'Pink Delight', 'Royal Red', and 'White Profusion', which has shorter panicles.

B. × weyeriana Globose clusters of yellow flowers arranged in 4" panicles on vigorous shrub with erect habit and arching green stems. Highly rated in Longwood Trials. 8' h × 6' w.

B. × weyeriana 'Honeycomb' Clusters of fragrant golden flowers; robust growth with refined arching habit; a top performer in University of Georgia trials. 6'–10' h × 6'–8' w.

Buxus microphylla ○

BUCK-sus my-kro-FIL-la

Little-leaf boxwood

Boxwood Family (Buxaceae)
Evergreen shrub
2'–3' h × 4'–5' w

Grown for its evergreen leaves, fine texture, and dense habit, little-leaf boxwood is an ideal shrub for formal gardens. It makes tidy, small hedges and can outline both knot gardens and parterres. With some imagination, you can form boxwood into geometric or sculptural shapes, using them as accents and focal points. Unimaginative gardeners can turn little-leaf boxwood into those dreaded meatballs bouncing across the foundations of many suburban homes. Naturally small, rounded, and shapely, it withstands both regular trimming and occasional hard rejuvenation pruning. Consider buying a cultivar or variety for increased hardiness and the appropriate mature height for your purpose.

Buxus microphylla

The glossy deep green, ¾" leaves have a bronzy winter color until well established. The flattened, angular stems are not ornamental. The small, whitish flowers in the leaf axils are valued for sweet odor but not their appearance. The black fruit is not ornamental either.

LANDSCAPE USE

Hedge, decorative edging, foundation planting, background for perennial garden, billowy ground cover, knot gardens, parterres, mazes, topiary, bonsai.

ORIGIN   Probably of Asian garden origin.

HARDINESS ZONES   5–9

LIGHT   Preference ranges from full sun to partial shade in colder climates and partial shade with protection from harsh winter sun in warmer climates.

SOIL   Moist, well-drained soil.

GROWING   Clip hedges in summer but reserve hard pruning for late spring. Fertilize before new growth begins, water regularly, and mulch to retain moisture and protect the shallow root system. Do not disturb the planting soil once growing. Little-leaf boxwood can experience winterburn in cold regions.

CAUTION   Leaf sap may inflame skin.

DESIGNER'S CHOICE

Buxus 'Green Gem' Globe-shaped, needing little pruning; slow growing; maintains green leaves through winter. 2' h and w.

B. 'Green Mountain' Upright pyramidal oval; small dark green leaves. 5' h × 3' w. Zones 4–9.

B. 'Green Velvet' Tight, rounded form; full sun to full shade. 2'–3' h and w. Zones 4–9.

B. 'Glencoe' (Chicagoland Green) Similar to but faster growing than 'Green Velvet'; compact spreading habit in sun to shade; excellent dark green winter color. 2'–3' h and w. Zones 4–9.

B. microphylla 'Faulkner' Maintains bright green hue all winter; slow growing; tolerates full sun to full shade and needs almost no pruning; very dense leaves. Excellent container plant. 4' h × 3' w. Zones 6–9.

B. microphylla 'Green Beauty' Leaves stay dark green year round. 4' h × 6' w. Zones (5) 6–9.

B. microphylla 'Winter Gem' (syn. *B. sinica* 'Winter Gem') Very hardy, keeps deep green leaves all year; full to partial sun; moderate growing; similar to 'Winter Beauty' and 'Wintergreen'. 4'–6' h and w. Zones 4–9.

B. sinica 'Wintergreen' (syn. *B. microphylla* 'Wintergreen') Bronzy copper fall leaves; slow growing. 2' h × 2'–3' w. Zones 4–9.

Buxus sempervirens ○

BUCK-sus sem-per-VY-rens

Common boxwood

Boxwood Family (Buxaceae)
Evergreen shrub or small tree
15' h and w

The classic boxwood of English formal gardens, *Buxus sempervirens* forms a small, twisted, multi-stemmed tree with a dense crown of shiny, dark green leaves. Its natural form is narrower at the top than the bottom. Like little-leaf boxwood, it's easily shaped into topiary, geometric

Buxus sempervirens 'Variegata'

and individual shapes. Glossy ... '–1" evergreen leaves of fine to medium texture have a bronzy winter color due to cold. Some people dislike the leaf scent. New stems are angular and greenish; mature stems are brown and not ornamental. Little, whitish blooms in April and May are valued for their sweet odor, not their appearance. The blackish fruits are not ornamental.

LANDSCAPE USE

Use as a hedge, decorative edging, foundation planting, billowy ground cover, knot garden designs, massed planting, and topiary.

ORIGIN   Southern Europe, Northern Africa, Western Asia. Native to limey soils in southern England.

HARDINESS ZONES   6–8

LIGHT   Full sun to partial shade with protection from afternoon and winter sun, wind, and cold.

SOIL   Moist, well-drained, alkaline soils; intolerant of extreme heat and cold.

GROWING   This well-proportioned shrub is easy to shear and shape. Clip hedges in summer but reserve hard pruning for late spring. Fertilize to promote fresh growth, water regularly, and mulch to retain moisture and protect the shallow root system. Do not disturb the planting soil once growing. Susceptible to boxwood leaf miner, boxwood mite, nematodes, and phytopthora. Prone to winterburn in exposed or harsh conditions.

CAUTION   Leaf sap may inflame skin.

DESIGNER'S CHOICE

Buxus sempervirens 'Graham Blandy' Columnar form; dark green color; good specimen plant. 9' h × 1½' w.

B. sempervirens 'Monrue' (Green Tower) Columnar; dark, shiny leaves, lighter underneath; heat tolerant; prefers alkaline soils; full sun; moderate to fast growth. Excellent screen or hedge. 9' h × 2' w.

B. sempervirens 'Suffruticosa' Rounded dwarf; resistant to leaf miner and deer browsing; good for edging. Grows just 1" per year. 1'–2' h and w. Zones 5–8.

B. sempervirens 'Vardar Valley' Popular and widely available; mounded; slow growing. 2'–3' h × 4'–5' w. Zones 5–8.

B. sempervirens 'Variegata' Dark green foliage with creamy edges; tolerates slightly alkaline soils; soft yellow new growth. 5'–8' h and w. Zones 5–9.

Buxus sempervirens 'Graham Blandy'

CALLICARPA

Callicarpa dichotoma ○ ✳

kal-lee-KAR-pa dye-KOT-i-ma

Purple beautyberry

Verbena Family (Verbenaceae)
Deciduous shrub
3'–4' h × 3'–5' w

Purple beautyberry's fabulous fall fruits attract birds, but the plant isn't just for birds — it's also for gardeners who can appreciate the gloriously abundant, lilac-violet berries crowding its stems. A great deciduous shrub for large gardens, it looks best planted in masses that increase the

purple effect. Although the pink, summer flowers are rather pretty, this medium green shrub, with long branches that bend to the ground and a refined rounded to drooping habit, mostly blends into the background. But when the leaves yellow and drop to expose the fruits in September and October, purple beautyberry is in its glory. Beautyberry thrives in summer heat, grows moderately, and has a medium landscape texture.

It bears 1"–3", simple, medium green leaves with pointed tips and partly serrated edges; the leaves turn yellow in fall. They occur on a single plane, so the long, arching branches have a layered, weeping effect. The thin, new stems have a ruddy cast, but the bark is not ornamental. Clusters of small, light pink flowers appear above the leaves up and down the stem from June through August. The ⅛", lilac-violet fruits appear in tight bunches along the stems in September and October, sometimes lasting into winter. This species differs from others with smaller leaves and overall habit.

LANDSCAPE USE

For maximum effect and superior fruiting, grow beautyberry in masses or small groups in beds, borders, or the understory of lightly wooded areas. If you have less room, grow it in a container or as a border accent. Beautybush can make an unusual informal hedge that attracts birds to your garden. Fruit-laden stems make striking accents in fall flower arrangements.

ORIGIN   Tropics to subtropics of China and Japan.

HARDINESS ZONES   (5) 6–8

LIGHT   Full sun to partial shade.

SOIL   Moist, well-drained, neutral soils; tolerates loam, clay, and sandy soils.

GROWING   Plant this low-maintenance

Callicarpa dichotoma 'Issai'

shrub any time during the growing season. To restore bushiness, cut back to 1' in late winter or early spring when necessary. In Zone 5, trim it to 1' every spring, since the top of the plant may not be winter hardy. Over time, plants may start looking scraggly, but that's easily remedied by cutting them back to 1' tall in late winter. Black mold, leaf spot, and stem problems may also affect plants from time to time.

DESIGNER'S CHOICE

Callicarpa dichotoma 'Early Amethyst' Profuse, lilac-purple fruits on a small arching shrub. 3'–4' h and w.

C. dichotoma 'Issai' Young plants produce abundant bright purple fruits earlier than the species. Attractive habit. 4'–6' h and w. Zones 4–8.

C. bodinieri var. *giraldii* 'Profusion' Big clusters of violet fruits in fall; new foliage is bronzy purple; more upright habit, turning green in summer and orange to purple in fall; 8' h × 5' w. Zones 5–8.

C. japonica 'Heavy Berry' Prolific fruits. 4'–6' h and w. Zones 5–8.

C. japonica 'Leucocarpa' White fruits. 4'–6' h and w. Zones 5–8.

CALLUNA

Calluna vulgaris 🌿

kal-LU-na vul-GAR-is

Heather, Scotch heather

Heath Family (Ericaceae)
Low evergreen flowering shrub
Up to 6"–24" h and to 3' w

Erect branches of heather form dense compact mats of white, pink, purple, or lavender blooms (species is rose-pink). Depending on the cultivar, heather has an extended period of interest because the leaves take on a yellow, bronze, silver, or red cast in winter. Arranged in four ranks or rows, heather's simple, opposite, scalelike leaves in green, gray, or yellow are less than $1/10$" long. The bark is dark orangey red and not decorative. Four separate petals make up the late-season flowers, unlike spring-blooming heaths (*Erica*), which have fused petals. Flowers occur in spikes in late summer and early fall; the individual blooms are bell-shaped. The fruits, which are yellow-orange capsules, are not decorative. Over 1000 selections available.

LANDSCAPE USE

This handsome, mounding ground-cover can be used on banks, slopes, and terraces, as an edging or accent in a perennial border, and for fresh or dried cut flowers.

ORIGIN   Heaths, bogs, woodlands, and moist dunes of Europe.

HARDINESS ZONES   4–6

LIGHT   Full sun is best but can take a bit of shade.

SOIL   Thrives in lean, moist, acidic soils high in organic matter and with sharp drainage. Prefers growing in a humid atmosphere away from strong drying winds. Tolerates some salt.

GROWING   Prune branches that died back over winter, as well as when necessary to maintain the tight habit. Some growers prune plants to within a few inches of the ground each spring. To protect from drying out in winter, especially if no snow cover, shield plants with evergreen boughs. Mulch to maintain moisture. Water regularly in a drought. Heather is particular about siting: it can't take strong winds, nor wet or fertile soils.

DESIGNER'S CHOICE

Calluna vulgaris 'Aurea' Pink flowers August through October; yellow leaves. 18" h and w.

C. vulgaris 'Flamingo' Red growth tips against dark green leaves; purple flowers in August and September. 12" h × 20" w.

C. vulgaris 'H. E. Beale' Silvery pink blooms from August to October. 24" h and w.

C. vulgaris 'J. H. Hamilton' Excellent, double, pink flowers. 6" h and w.

C. vulgaris 'Mrs Ronald Gray' Reddish flowers from July to September. 4" h × 18" w.

C. vulgaris 'October White' White flowers against dark green leaves on erect stems in October are good for cutting. 16" h × 18" w.

Calluna vulgaris 'Silver Knight' and 'Multicolor'

C. vulgaris 'Silver Knight' Silvery gray leaves year round with lavender blooms in late summer. 15" h × 24" w.

C. vulgaris 'Sister Anne' Blooms with pink flowers against grayish green leaves from July to September; a dense, mounding groundcover. 6" h × 18" w.

CALOCEDRUS

Calocedrus decurrens ○

ka-loh-SED-rus de-KUR-renz

California incense cedar

Cypress Family (Cupressaceae)
Mid-sized evergreen
50' h x 10' w

California incense cedar has a refined, narrow, columnar shape that complements most garden settings. Because its polished, green leaves hold their color through winter, it offers gardeners four seasons of interest. Wildlife use *Calocedrus*, a slow to moderate grower, for cover. The wood resists rot, making it useful for building jobs indoors and out. The USDA Forest Service cites the oldest California incense cedar as 542 years old.

Calocedrus decurrens

The glossy, green, scented scales of the foliage are ¼"–½" long and arranged in flat sprays. Young trees have thin, scaly, purple-red bark; old trees have thick, fibrous, fire-resistant, brownish red bark with large exfoliating scales, which make it quite attractive. Little, yellow-green female cones and yellow male cones occur on same tree. Striking 1½" brownish yellow cones with 6 semi-woody scales appear at the branch tips.

LANDSCAPE USE
This attractive landscape tree can help control erosion and tolerates some pollution. Use singly or in groups of three as an accent in large gardens. Good for tall hedges and screening.

ORIGIN   Mostly dry southwestern slopes in California and Oregon.

HARDINESS ZONES   5–8

LIGHT   Full sun to light shade.

SOIL   Thrives on deep, rich, well-drained clay or sandy loams with neutral to acidic pH but tolerates soils from coarse sand to fine clay and hot dry infertile sites.

GROWING   Site in a protected location away from the drying winds of winter. In the wild, fungal diseases enter the trees through fire scars or roots. Pests cause little damage, with beetles being the worst offender.

DESIGNER'S CHOICE
Calocedrus decurrens 'Compacta' Slow-growing dwarf with rounded habit. 6' h and w.

CALYCANTHUS

Calycanthus floridus ○ › ⚘ ✳

ka-lee-KAN-thus FLO-ri-dus

Carolina allspice

Strawberry Shrub Family
(Calycanthaceae)
Deciduous shrub
8' h x 10' w

Grown for its fragrant, late spring flowers, Carolina allspice has a dense,

Calycanthus floridus

suckering habit that looks leggy in the wild. In the garden, where you can trim it to stay in shape, it forms a big, medium-textured, green, rounded mound that makes an effective backdrop for other plantings.

The simple, oval, 4"–6", dark green leaves have smooth edges, some with pointy tips, arranged in opposite pairs at the leaf nodes. Leaf bottoms are whitish and hairy. Fall color ranges from a good, bright yellow to dull, greenish yellow. The scented, brown bark has raised lenticels (blisterlike breaks on the surface). Dark reddish brown, 2" blooms with straplike petals and fruity, strawberry-scented odor appear in late spring. Fruits look like 1"–1½" bells on long stalks and ripen from green to woody brown in late summer through early fall. Old fruits rattle when shaken.

LANDSCAPE USE

In woodland edges and gardens, as screens, under a window, or next to a door where you can appreciate the fragrance.

ORIGIN   Southeastern U.S.

HARDINESS ZONES   5–9

LIGHT   Full sun to partial shade.

SOIL   Prefers moist, rich, well-drained soil but tolerates some dryness.

GROWING   To control the plant's size and shape, cut about one-third of the oldest stems to the ground each year after flowering.

DESIGNER'S CHOICE

Calycanthus floridus 'Athens' Yellow blooms over a long period in spring (often with rebloom) with potent, fruity fragrance on bare branches; yellow fall color. 6'–8' h and w.

C. floridus 'Michael Lindsey' Potent, fruit-scented, maroon flowers; thick, shiny leaves; golden fall color; compact. 6'–8' h and w.

Sinocalycanthus chinensis (Chinese sweetshrub) This rounded shrub blossoms in late spring, when droopy, cupped, 3", unscented, pinky-white flowers with yellow centers bloom against shiny, bright green, oval leaves. Out of curiosity, I bought this shrub, supposedly hardy to Zone 6 or 7, at Avant Gardens in Massachusetts and grow it in my Zone 5 garden for its pretty blooms. It gets plenty of moisture, good drainage, partial shade, and a little wind protection and has survived −15°F with no dieback. The point is, you can play with plants just to see what happens. Sometimes luck, microclimate, and variable winters have as much to do with successful gardening as knowledge or skill. About 5'–10' h and w. Zones (5) 6–8.

CAMELLIA

Camellia japonica △

ka-MEEL-lee-a ja-PON-i-ka

Camellia, Japanese camellia

Tea Family (Theaceae)
Evergreen shrub or small tree
10'–20' h x 6'–10' w

Japanese camellia has red flowers from late winter to early spring; cultivars, available in pink, white, red, and bicolor, may flower any time between November and May. Flowers are 3"–5" wide and take forms ranging from single (with 5–7 petals) to semi-double and double, often resembling the blooms of roses, anemones, or peonies. Hundreds of cultivars are available.

LANDSCAPE USE

The dense, bushy form gives camellia year-round garden interest. Use it for hedges, borders, specimens, accents, screens, woodland understory, foundations, and evergreen background.

ORIGIN   China, Japan, and Korea.

HARDINESS ZONES   (6) 7–9

LIGHT   Partial shade with a bit more sun the farther North you live.

SOIL   Moist, acid, fertile soil high in organic matter but tolerates average garden soils.

Camellia japonica 'Rudy's Magnoliiflora'

GROWING   Plant high for good drainage. Shape after blooming in spring and mulch lightly around plants to shield shallow roots. Where possible, protect buds and blooms from harsh winds and frost. May be afflicted with leaf spot, leaf galls, canker, blight, root rot and black mold, scales, mites, or mealy bugs, among other insects.

DESIGNER'S CHOICE

Camellia japonica 'Alba Plena' Pure white, double, 3½" rosettes. 6'–8' h and w. Zones 8–10.

C. japonica 'April Remembered' Creamy pink. semi-double blooms November to April. 6'–8' h and w. Zones 6–9.

C. japonica 'Betty Sette' Rose-red rosettes with yellow centers. 6'–8' h × 4'–6' w. Zones 6–9.

ALL ABOUT CAMELLIA

To a northerner like me, camellias evoke southern belles and debutante balls. The dense, pyramidal form of these broad-leaf evergreen shrubs and small trees suggests formality and stiffness, making them effective screens, evergreen backgrounds, and woodland understory plants. Popular in the Southeast, these slow growers bloom sometime between late fall and spring, often bringing color and life to the garden when many plants nap. For 20 years, my father-in-law in Newark, Delaware, has grown 2 camellias by the brick wall at the back of his house. Though protected, they suffer dieback during harsh winters yet continue to bring him lovely roselike blooms.

C. japonica 'Elegans' (syn. *Camellia japonica chandleri elegans*) Rosy pink anemone-form flowers. 6'–8' h and w and larger.

C. japonica 'Jacks' Deep red, formal double blossoms. 6'–8' or larger h × 6'–8' w. Zones 8–10.

C. japonica 'Magnoliiflora' Semi-double, light pink rosettes with erect, curved, back petals. 6'–8' or larger h × 6'–8' w.

C. japonica × 'Mason Farm' White rosettes tinted pink with bright gold stamens. Fast growing, ultimately 25' h. 6'–8' h × 4'–6' w. Hardy to –10°F.

C. japonica 'Nuccio's Bella Rossa' Formal, crimson, 4" blooms from fall to spring from a young age. 6'–8' or larger h × 6'–8' w. Zones 8–10.

C. japonica 'Spring's Promise' Rosy red, 2½", single blooms with a central boss of tall gold stamens. 6'–8' h and w.

C. 'Polar Ice' Fragrant, white, anemone-type blooms from early November to mid-December. 6'–8' h and w. Zones 6–9.

C. 'Tom Knudsen' Dark red, formal or rose form. 6'–8' or larger h × 6'–8' w. Zones 8–10.

Camellia sasanqua △ › ◌

ka-MEEL-lee-a sa-SANK-wa

Sasanqua camellia

Tea Family (Theaceae)
Evergreen shrub or small tree
6'–12' h and w

Sasanqua camellias are smaller and less hardy than Japanese camellias but their form is more elegant. Fragrant white flowers on the species are single, cupped, and scented, while foliage is a lovely, shiny, deep green on top and light green below. The short, alternate evergreen leaves are simple, leathery ovals with pointed tips and serrated edges. The non-showy bark is brown with darker lenticels. Fall fruits are woody capsules, not showy. Twigs are slightly hairy.

LANDSCAPE USE
Some have long, thin branches that weep over sides of containers, while shorter ones are suitable for groundcovers or facing down tall, leggy shrubs at the border front. Also as screens, borders, specimens.

ORIGIN Japan

HARDINESS ZONES (6) 7–9

LIGHT See *C. japonica.*

SOIL See *C. japonica.*

GROWING See *C. japonica.*

DESIGNER'S CHOICE
Camellia sasanqua 'Chansonette' Formal, double rosette in deep pink with cascading spreading habit; 2'–3' h and w.

C. sasanqua 'Fukuzutsumi' (syn. *C. sasanqua* 'Apple Blossom') Cup-shaped flower with white petals edged in pinkish red with central yellow stamens; 10' h and w.

C. sasanqua 'Shishi-gashira' Vivid, rosy red, semi-double flowers. 4'–5' h × 6'–8' w.

C. sasanqua 'Setsugekka' Cup-shaped, semi-double, white flowers with big, ruffled petals and gold stamens. 8'–10' h and w.

C. sasanqua 'Winter Charm' Columnar form with lavender-pink, peony-like flowers in October and November. 7' h × 4'–5' w. Zones 6–9.

C. sasanqua 'Winter's Snowman' Robust columnar growth makes it a good choice for a narrow hedge. White, semi-double to anemone-type blooms from mid-November through December. 12' h × 5' w. Zones 6–9.

C. × *vernalis* 'Yuletide' Single, red, cup-shaped flowers with bright yellow stamens; 8'–10' h and w.

C. × *williamsii* 'Debbie' Rosy pink peony, rosette, and anemone-shaped blooms on same plant. 6'–8' or more h × 6'–8' w.

Camellia sinensis ◌

ka-MEEL-ee-a sye-NEN-sis

Tea

Tea Family (Theaceae)
Evergreen shrub or tree
4'–6' h and w

The beverage tea comes from the young leaves of this rounded evergreen shrub, which grows in the wild to a treelike plant 50' tall. In fall, tea bears 1½", scented blooms with white, ruffled petals and a central cluster of yellow stamens.

LANDSCAPE USE
Typically planted to harvest the leaves, tea also works in shady groups, borders, or next to the blank wall of a building for visual warmth

ORIGIN Southeast Asia

HARDINESS ZONES 6–9

LIGHT Partial shade.

SOIL Prefers rich, moist, well-drained, acid soils high in organic matter but withstands periods of drought once established.

GROWING Cannot tolerate wet feet; especially good for shady sites.

CARAGANA

Caragana arborescens ◌ ✳

ka-ra-GA-na ar-boh-RES-senz

Siberian pea shrub, Siberian pea tree

Legume Family (Fabaceae)
Deciduous shrub or small tree
15'–20' h × 15' w

If winter shivers your bones, then Siberian pea shrub is the plant for you. No beauty by most standards, this extra-hardy, deciduous shrub or small tree has its uses in the cold-climate garden. At its best, this fast-growing shrub has an oval form with erect branches, but it may need pruning to stay in shape. A healthy, low-maintenance shrub with no

Caragana arborescens 'Walker'

serious pests or diseases, it casts light shade.

Siberian pea shrub's light green, alternate leaves are 3" long and feather-like, with 8–12 elliptical, 1" leaflets; in fall, they are yellow green. In leaf, it appears medium to fine-textured in the landscape. When young, it has green stems with ridges the length of the stem. Some plants have pairs of spiny outgrowths, or stipules, at the base of the leaf stalks, particularly in the wild. It bears bright yellow, 1", pea-shaped blooms in May on old wood, but these are not showy because they're partly hidden by the leaves. In summer, skinny, 2", green pods ripen to brown. Pods are abundant and easy to harvest; each has 3–6 seeds.

LANDSCAPE USE

Because it tolerates wind, it makes a suitable screen. Wind resistance, as well as its tolerance to pruning, also makes it a good choice for deciduous hedging. It works for erosion control because its widespread roots enrich the soil and hold it in place. Reford Gardens near Rimouski, Quebec, makes the most of this cold-climate shrub by densely underplanting gnarly old standards with low-growing perennials for a charming effect.

ORIGIN Mongolia and Siberia.

HARDINESS ZONES 2–7

LIGHT Full sun.

SOIL Not fussy, as long as the soil drains well and conditions are fairly dry. Tolerates salt and acid, alkaline, and poor soils. Plant fixes atmospheric nitrogen that both it and other nearby plants can use for growth.

GROWING Avoid planting in wet soils and humid climates. *Caragana* tolerates severe pruning. Grows leggy with age. Leaf miners can yellow the leaves, and spider mites may appear in a drought.

CAUTION Considered to have invasive potential in far northern regions like Alaska and parts of Canada.

DESIGNER'S CHOICE

Caragana arborescens 'Lorbergii' Threadlike leaflets and arching stems. 5' h × 3' w.

C. arborescens 'Pendula' Weeping gnarly branches; at nurseries, it is usually found grafted on a standard; makes an attractive cold-climate specimen for the garden. 4'–5' h × 3' w.

C. arborescens 'Walker' (Dwarf fernleaf weeping Siberian pea shrub) Threadlike leaves on small weeping tree. 4' h × 3' w.

CARPINUS

Carpinus betulus ○ ✳

kar-PYE-nus BET-u-lus

European hornbeam

Birch Family (Corylaceae)
Deciduous tree
40'–60' h × 30'–40' w

For the eleven years since we planted a European hornbeam in our front yard, I've marveled at the perfection of this tree, which now stands about 16' h × 14' w. It requires no trimming to maintain its full rounded shape, with branches starting low on the trunk. Its dense, dark green leaves cast deep shade before yellowing in late fall. After the leaves die, they stay on the tree into spring, giving it a strong yet subtle winter presence, then dropping all at once, in time for new leaves to unfold. This tree's clean, simple geometry gives a garden class and structure. Europeans use it for dense formal hedging, arches, and pleaching, in which they interlace the branches to create arbors and allées.

The alternate, simple, rich green leaves are 3"–5" × 1½" with serrated edges and variable late fall color ranging from fine yellow to

Carpinus betulus 'Frans Fontaine'

undistinguished yellow green. They stay on the tree until spring. The bark is smooth, gray, and "muscled" especially on older trees, leading to another common name, musclewood. Even my relatively young tree's trunk has a fluted flare; it makes you think of a well-toned person's smooth skin over rippling muscle. Neither the catkins nor the tiny, brown nutlets are showy.

LANDSCAPE USE
Because this formal-looking, symmetrical tree tolerates severe pruning, it is ideal for clipped geometrical hedges, pleached arbors, and allées. It is also useful as a specimen, in tree and shrub borders, and as a screen.

ORIGIN   Deciduous forests and hedgerows of Europe and Asia Minor.

HARDINESS ZONES   (4) 5–7

LIGHT   Full sun to light shade.

SOIL   Prefers moist, somewhat fertile, well-drained soils. Tolerates heat, drought, acid, and alkaline soils.

GROWING   Full sun, plentiful water, well-drained soil, and periodic feeding support the health and best growth of this relatively slow-growing tree. If needed, prune stray shoots in late winter or early spring, or limb it up when young to grow shade-loving groundcovers below the canopy. A healthy beautiful tree.

DESIGNER'S CHOICE
Carpinus betulus 'Fastigiata' Columnar in youth with no central leader, becoming more rounded or pyramidal with age; good for deciduous screening because of dense, upright branching. May be easier to find than the species. 35' h × 25' w. Zones 5–7.

C. betulus 'Frans Fontaine' Similar to 'Fastigiata', but slower growing and more dense; good for specimen or hedging in small spaces. 30'–45' h × 15'–18' w.

Carpinus caroliniana ○

kar-PYE-nus kay-roh-li-nee-AY-na

American hornbeam, Blue beech, Musclewood, Ironwood

Birch Family (Corylaceae)
Deciduous tree
30' h and w

American hornbeam's smooth, blue-gray bark and muscled trunk make it attractive year round, and variable red, orange, and yellow fall color gives it added appeal. Similar to but smaller than European hornbeam, American hornbeam tolerates pruning but also suits naturalized situations and woodland gardens, where it can display its handsome, rounded winter shape.

LANDSCAPE USE
An understory tree, American hornbeam is a good choice for damp sunny to shady areas on your property.

Carpinus caroliniana

ORIGIN   Moist woods and swamps of eastern North America.

HARDINESS ZONES   3–9

LIGHT   Full sun to heavy shade.

SOIL   Moist, deep, somewhat acid soil.

GROWING   Transplant in early spring; hard to transplant.

CARYA

Carya ovata ○

KA-ree-a o-VA-ta

Shagbark hickory

Walnut Family (Juglandaceae)
Deciduous tree
60'–90' h × 30'–50' w

Though the scale of mature shagbark hickory is too big for most home landscapes, if I had one on my property, I'd keep it. This slow-growing eastern native has plenty going for it. Long, bowed bark strips cover the trunk, giving it a wild, bad-hair-day look. Needless to say, this captivating bark gives the tree year-round appeal. The habit is straight and tall with an open, oblong crown; the canopy offers medium shade.

The alternate, compound, 14" leaves feature 5–7, 4"–6" × 1½"–2" leaflets. Leaflets near the leaf base are about half the size of those at the leaf tips. In summer, the leaflets are green with yellow veins; in fall, they turn a handsome gold to golden brown. Mature bark is coarse, gray, and shaggy. Long bark plates turn up and away from the trunk at the ends but stay fixed to the tree in the middle. The catkins are not showy; the 1½", thick-shelled nuts that ripen in fall are sweet and edible for people and squirrels alike.

ORIGIN   Although one hickory species comes from China, the rest (including *Carya illinoinensis*, pecan, which is cultivated commercially for its delicious nuts) are native to rich, well-drained,

Carya ovata

hardwood forests and valleys of the eastern U.S.

HARDINESS ZONES (4) 5–8

LIGHT Full sun to partial shade.

SOIL Prefers rich, moist, well-drained loam but tolerates many soil types.

GROWING This tree is worth saving if you find one on your land. You may, however, have difficulty transplanting a shagbark hickory to your property since seedlings may have a 3' taproot after one year's growth.

CARYOPTERIS

Caryopteris × clandonensis ○

ka-ree-OP-te-ris klan-doh-NEN-sis

Bluebeard, Blue mist

Vervain Family (Verbenaceae)
Deciduous shrub and perennial
2'–4' h and w

Bluebeard, or blue mist, takes its common names from the blue to violet, terminal flower clusters that adorn the plant from late summer to fall. In Zone 5, I grow this shrub as an herbaceous perennial since cold winters kill the top growth. The shrub

blooms on new shoots, however, whether or not the winter is cold. After we built our New Hampshire house, I planted several cultivars in a sunny bed near a young red maple. As the tree grew, so did the shade, but the bluebeards kept blooming. Eventually, however, I moved the mists to a sunny lamppost perennial bed because they looked odd in the midst of what was becoming a woodland garden. The fine stems with small, lance-shaped leaves form an open, rounded habit and create a fine to medium texture in the garden.

Opposite, simple, deciduous leaves are 1½"–2" long, lancelike, hairy, and grayish green. Although the foliage has no fall color, it is fragrant when rubbed. The fuzzy, greenish stems are not showy. The flattish, scented, blue flower clusters grow in the space between the stems and the topmost leaves, typically blooming in August. The fruit is not ornamental.

LANDSCAPE USE

Bluebeard adds flower power to the garden in late summer, so plant it in perennial borders, in front of tall

Caryopteris x clandonensis 'Blue Mist'

or leggy shrubs, in dry gardens, and as a low hedge along sunny paths. It attracts bees and butterflies.

ORIGIN Garden origin

HARDINESS ZONES 6–9; variably hardy in Zone 5.

LIGHT Full sun to partial shade.

SOIL Loose, well-drained soils; intolerant of wet clay soils; drought tolerant once established.

GROWING Transplants easily; cut back hard in late winter or early spring. Dead-heading in late August may augment current season's flowering. This plant is low maintenance and drought tolerant. *Note:* Stems die back in winter in Zones 5 and 6.

DESIGNER'S CHOICE

Caryopteris × *clandonensis* 'Blue Mist' Powder-blue flowers. 2½' h × 2' w.

C. × *clandonensis* 'Dark Knight' Deep bluish-purple flowers from August to frost. 2'–3' h × 3' w.

C. × *clandonensis* 'First Choice' Dark blue buds open to deep purplish blue flowers; early flowering. 2'–3' h × 2' w.

C. × *clandonensis* 'Inoveris' (Grand Bleu) Deep blue flowers from July-September; shiny, dark green leaves on a compact shrub. 1½'–2½' h × 1½'–2½' w.

C. x clandonensis 'Dark Knight'

C. × clandonensis 'Longwood Blue'
Violet-blue flowers in August and
September contrast nicely with silvery gray leaves; one of the best
cultivars. 3'–4' h and w.

C. × clandonensis 'Worcester Gold'
Deep blue blooms in August; yellow
leaves all summer hold up well in
summer heat, then fade to green in
fall. 2'–3' h and w.

**Caryopteris x clandonensis
'Longwood Blue'**

**Caryopteris x clandonensis
'Worcester Gold'**

CASTANEA

Castanea mollissima ○

kas-TAY-nee-a mol-LIS-si-ma

Chinese chestnut

Beech Family (Fagaceae)
Deciduous tree
40'–60' h and w

Chinese chestnut, considered an
alternative to our blighted American
chestnut, grows at a moderate rate
into a medium-sized, rounded,
spreading shade tree with deeply
ridged bark. Leaves up to 8" long
are alternate and simple with spine-
tipped serrations at the edges. The
stinky flowers give way in autumn
to tasty, edible nuts surrounded by
barbed hulls.

LANDSCAPE USE
Shade tree in large lawns. Plant more
than one cultivar for edible nuts.

ORIGIN   Northern China

HARDINESS ZONES   4–8

LIGHT   Full sun.

SOIL   Deep, well-drained, slightly acidic
soil.

GROWING   Give Chinese chestnut plenty
of room to grow. It can withstand
drought but may be hard to transplant
because of its taproot. Although resistant
to chestnut blight, it is not blight-free
and is susceptible to other diseases of
American chestnut.

CAUTION   Keep the tree away from
places with heavy foot traffic, such as
your driveway, front path, or sidewalk,
where immature nuts — shielded by
prickly coats 2"–3" across — could trip
passersby.

DESIGNER'S CHOICE
Castanea mollissima 'Abundance'
Grown for copious crops of large nuts,
this is one of the original chestnut
strains introduced from China to the
U.S. 40' h and w.

Castanea mollissima

CATALPA

Catalpa bignonioides ○

ka-TAL-pa big-no-nyo-EE-dez

Southern catalpa, Indian bean
tree, Indian cigar

Trumpet Creeper or Catalpa Family
(Bignoniaceae)
Deciduous tree
25'–40' h and w

Huge, heart-shaped leaves give
this irregular tree a coarse texture
that's easy to spot in the landscape.
Although some folks grow catalpa for
its glitzy flowers, its extreme boldness
along with weak wood and messy
leaves and fruits make catalpa a poor
choice for many private gardens. If
you like catalpa, consider growing
'Aurea' for its bright yellow spring
color or 'Nana' for its small scale and
interesting shape.

Catalpa's heart-shaped, deciduous,
green leaves are 6"–12" long, arranged
in an opposite or whorled pattern.
They may turn yellow in fall right

before dropping, but fall color is not especially ornamental. The bark is grayish to reddish brown and scaly. Showy, frilled, white, bell-shaped flowers with purple and yellow markings appear in erect, branched clusters about 10" long in late May or June. In fall, clusters of brown, cigarlike, seed-containing fruits up to 15" long appear and persist through winter. The wood is rot resistant.

LANDSCAPE USE
This fast-growing tree reads better from a distance than from up close. If you're building a home on plenty of land, avoid growing catalpas near the house, but if you like the tree's bold texture and irregularity, place one or two at your property's edge.

ORIGIN Moist soils in the southeastern U.S.

HARDINESS ZONES 5–9

LIGHT Full sun to partial shade.

SOIL Prefers rich, deep, moist, well-drained soils but tolerates limey soils and both extreme drought and wetness.

GROWING Although subject to insects and diseases such as powdery mildew and leaf spots, these tough trees tend to survive permanent damage. Brittle wood means that branches can break in wind and ice. Trees are messy in fall when the big leaves drop and again when the fruits fall to the ground.

DESIGNER'S CHOICE
Catalpa bignonioides 'Aurea' Leaves open brilliant yellow, then turn green by midsummer. 25'–40' h and w.

C. bignonioides 'Nana' Globose, shrubby dwarf with 4"–8" heart-shaped leaves and few to no flowers. 20' h × 15' w.

C. speciosa (Northern or Western catalpa) Similar to but larger and hardier than *C. bignonioides*. May have invasive tendencies outside its native Midwest. 40'–60' h × 20'–30' w.

Catalpa speciosa

CEANOTHUS

Ceanothus species ◯

see-a-NO-thus

California lilac

Buckthorn Family (Rhamnaceae)
Deciduous and evergreen shrub or small tree
1'–20' h and 3'–12' w, depending upon the species or cultivar

Plant California lilac to attract butterflies to your garden. The shrub, bearing long lilac-like clusters of blue, pink, or white flowers, thrives in hot, dry summers and damp winters. Many of the approximately 50 western species are drought-tolerant evergreens with dark green foliage, hardy in Zones 8–10.

LANDSCAPE USE
Shrub border, small garden beds; use low-spreading cultivars for groundcover.

ORIGIN U.S. West Coast.

HARDINESS ZONES 8–10; some popular cultivars are hardy in zones 7–10.

LIGHT Sunny, sheltered spot.

SOIL Fast-draining soil (not alkaline).

GROWING It needs little pruning, resents transplanting, and declines in hot humid weather and extremely alkaline soils. Seldom grown outside Western gardens.

DESIGNER'S CHOICE
Ceanothus americanus (New Jersey tea) White flowers; naturalized in the East; massive root system makes it very adaptable to poor soils and harsh sites; hardiest of the genus. 3'–4' h × 3'–5' w. Zones 4–8.

Ceanothus × delilianus 'Gloire de Versailles' A popular hybrid with light blue flowers, blooms from July to September and produces small, toothed, deciduous, dark green leaves. You can prune deciduous varieties in early spring to 4" on the previous year's growth. 7' h × 5' w. Zones 7–10.

C. gloriosus (Point Reyes creeper) Dense, shiny, evergreen leaves and 2" lavender flowers. 2' h × about 10' w. Zones 7–9.

C. impressus 'Victoria' (syn. *C.* 'Victoria) Deep blue flowers in late spring; shiny green leaves; back of the border. 9' h × 10'–12' w.

C. 'Italian Skies' Deep blue flowers in late spring; border or specimen. 5' h and w.

Ceanothus 'Ray Hartman'

Cedrus deodara △

SED-rus de-oh-DA-ra

Deodar cedar, Deodara

Pine Family (Pinaceae)
Evergreen conifer
35'–60' h x 25'–40' w; up to 200' h
in the wild

Deodar cedar is a graceful, sun-loving conifer. Grown as a specimen in a large lawn, it cuts a dramatic, blue-green silhouette with dangling branchlets and droopy, lower limbs that sometimes turn up at the ends. When young, it grows quickly to about 30' in 10 years. After that, this wide pyramid of a tree, a popular evergreen in the West, grows at a moderate pace.

The blue-green, rigid, 2"-needled, evergreen foliage is arranged in thick whorls of about 20 leaves. Deodar cedar has blackish brown bark, which is smooth when young, then cracking and scaling with age. It produces male catkins on the lower canopy; the fruits are sturdy, 4" × 3", egg-shaped, upright cones on the upper limbs. Trees have both sexes, but one sex typically predominates.

Cedrus deodara 'Well's Golden'

LANDSCAPE USE
Space-hungry specimen; good tree for the property edge so you can take it all in at once.

ORIGIN   High in the Himalayas.

HARDINESS ZONES   7–9

LIGHT   Full sun.

SOIL   Prefers moist, well-drained, deep, acid soils. Established trees tolerate drought, heat, and humidity. Soil must be well drained or root rot can occur.

GROWING   Needs wind protection and moderate watering for best growth. Remove dead wood as it occurs. No significant health problems.

DESIGNER'S CHOICE
Cedrus deodara 'Aurea' Yellow new foliage turns gold-green with time. 15'–35' h × 15' w.

C. deodara 'Shalimar' Blue-green leaves, hardiest cultivar. 50' h × 30' w. Zone 6.

C. deodara 'Twisted Growth' Dwarf with twisted, down-turned branches and bluish green leaves. 5'–6' h × 5' w.

C. deodara 'White Imp' Mostly white needles on mounded dwarf. Outstanding specimen. 4'–5' h and w.

Cedrus libani △

SED-rus LEE-bah-nee

Cedar of Lebanon

Pine Family (Pinaceae)
Evergreen conifer
40'–60' h x 30'–50' w

This striking, slow-growing evergreen conifer changes from rigid and pyramidal when young to picturesque, flat-topped, and widespread when mature. The limbs look layered, especially toward the base of the tree. Silver stripes on the dark green needles give the tree a bluish tint.

LANDSCAPE USE
Broad tiered branches make this grand tree a perfect specimen for a large lawn.

Cedrus libani subsp. *atlantica* 'Glauca Pendula'

Cedrus libani

ORIGIN   Lebanon, Turkey

HARDINESS ZONES   (5) 6–9

LIGHT   Sunny open site.

SOIL   Well-drained, moist to dry soils.

GROWING   Cultivating cedar of Lebanon may be a challenge because it's hard to transplant and withstands neither shade nor urban pollution.

DESIGNER'S CHOICE
Cedrus libani subsp. *atlantica* 'Glauca' (syn. *C. atlantica* 'Glauca') (blue Atlas cedar) Gray-blue needles on pyramidal evergreen conifer; drought tolerant. Native to the Atlas Mountains of North Africa. 40'–60' h × 20'–30' w. Zones 6–9.

C. libani 'Green Prince' Dwarf with small, deep green needles; irregular habit; good for bonsai and rock gardens; rare. 2'–4' h and w.

CELTIS

Celtis occidentalis ⊂ ✳

SEL-tis ok-si-den-TA-lis

Hackberry

Elm Family (Ulmaceae)
Mid-sized deciduous tree
40'–70' h x 35'–50' w

Valued for its adaptability to extremes of climate and growing conditions, this fast-growing, tough shade tree with attractive bark occurs throughout most of the U.S. but does particularly well in the Midwest, where it withstands intense heat, cold, and winds. From a distance, hackberry has an uneven, rounded form with big, spreading limbs and a wide-flared trunk. Many birds consume hackberry's edible fruits and use the tree for nesting and cover.

Hackberry has elmlike, alternate, simple, 2"–5" leaves with serrated edges. Fall color is not ornamental. The gray-ridged, pebbled bark grows scaly and more decorative with age. The green spring flowers are not ornamental. It produces edible, scarlet fruit about ⅓" wide.

LANDSCAPE USE

Large, fast-growing shade tree for difficult areas, such as large yards in polluted cities and suburbs and along busy streets. The species looks better in naturalized boundary plantings. Its wind tolerance makes it good for mixed deciduous and evergreen windbreaks. When possible, plant cultivars chosen for their handsome appearance, not the species, in the home landscape.

Celtis occidentalis

ORIGIN   Bottomlands around the Black Hills, Great Plains, eastern U.S., and southern Canada.

HARDINESS ZONES   3–9

LIGHT   Full sun.

SOIL   Prefers moist, rich, alkaline soils but tolerates heat and drought, periodic flooding, low pH, compacted soils, wind, and pollution.

GROWING   It is medium to fast growing and requires no extraordinary care. Although this member of the Elm Family is not prone to Dutch elm disease, many other pests and diseases plague it, though none are fatal. Aesthetic problems include yellowing of the leaves, leaf spots, nipple gall, scale, and witches' broom (a thick broom-shaped cluster of weak twigs on a branch bud or growing tip).

DESIGNER'S CHOICE

Celtis occidentalis 'Chicagoland' Broad pyramidal shape with a single, straight trunk. 40' h × 50' w.

C. occidentalis 'Prairie Pride' Compact oval shape, no witches' broom, fewer larger fruits, and glossy green, substantial leaves. 60' h × 50' w.

C. occidentalis 'Windy City' Erect, spreading form with fast growth rate and improved foliage. 40' h × 45' w.

CEPHALANTHUS

Cephalanthus occidentalis ○

se-fa-LAN-thuss ok-si-den-TA-lis

Buttonbush, Button willow

Madder Family (Rubiaceae)
Deciduous shrub
4'–10' h and w

If you have wet, low spots on your land and want to attract wildlife, grow native buttonbush. In summer, bees and butterflies such as painted ladies, monarchs, and eastern black swallowtails drink nectar from round, creamy flower clusters, which resemble ping-pong balls; wood ducks, Canada geese, and mallards eat seeds from the round, brown fruits of fall. Songbirds nest among the stems while frogs and insects seek cover among its branches.

LANDSCAPE USE

Grow buttonbush in marshes and ditches, or on the banks of streams, lakes and ponds, since it tolerates flooding, grows in low standing water, and can help with erosion control.

ORIGIN   North America

HARDINESS ZONES   5–9

LIGHT   Full sun to partial shade.

SOIL   Prefers moist soil high in organic matter but grows in any soil but dry.

GROWING   Renew unkempt shrubs by cutting to the ground in early spring.

Cephalanthus occidentalis

CEPHALOTAXUS

Cephalotaxus harringtonii ○

se-fa-lo-TAX-us hayr-ring-TON-ee-i

Japanese plum yew, Cow's tail pine

Plum Yew Family (Cephalotaxaceae)
Evergreen conifer
4'–10' h and w

If you own shady property in a warm climate, you won't find a better evergreen shrub than Japanese plum yew. Very slow growing and deer resistant, this handsome plant has a nice show of green to the ground. It thrives in the South where yews (*Taxus*) may fail. You can also buy Japanese plum yew as a small tree that will eventually grow to 20' h and w, but most nurseries sell the spreading, shrubby forms. May be hard to find; great potential for more use in the South.

Japanese plum yew has shiny, dark evergreen leaves, flat and needled, with 2 light bands below and pointed tips. Needles are about 1"–2" long and arranged in 2 ranks, or rows, set at an angle to each other. With age, the bark becomes flaky and ruddy brown. The flowers are not ornamental. The female plants bear fleshy, olive to reddish-brown, edible seeds. Females will not fruit without a male plant nearby for pollination.

LANDSCAPE USE
Hedge, accent, specimen, masses foundation plantings.

ORIGIN Moist woods of China, Japan, and Korea.

HARDINESS ZONES 6–9

LIGHT Prefers shade but withstands full sun, particularly in cool spots.

SOIL Prefers moist, but very well-drained, somewhat acid soils; tolerates drought once established.

GROWING Give plants wind protection. It withstands heavy pruning, so renew leggy shrubs planted in heavy shade by cutting to about 4" high in mid spring. New growth will sprout on even the oldest wood. It is deer resistant; its heat tolerance makes it useful in the South. Late spring frosts can damage the needles.

DESIGNER'S CHOICE

Cephalotaxus harringtonii 'Fastigiata' Columnar habit makes it a good accent or focal point; leaves in spiral whorls. 10' h × 6'–8' w.

C. harringtonii 'Prostrata' Low, wide spreading form. 2'–4' h and w or more.

CERCIDIPHYLLUM

Cercidiphyllum japonicum
△ › ○

ser-si-di-PHIL-lum ja-PAH-ni-kum

Katsura tree

Katsura Family (Cercidiphyllaceae)
Deciduous tree
40'–60' h × 20'–60' w

One October, I stepped outdoors to the powerful aroma of freshly baked muffins. At first I thought Mary, my next-door neighbor, was baking, but then I remembered she was in Florida for the week. The scent made my mouth water, but I couldn't figure out the source. Then it hit me: my weeping katsura tree. I'd read about the fall leaf fragrance but had never experienced it. When sunlight warmed the autumn leaves, both those that had fallen and those still on the tree, they emitted an aroma like caramelized brown sugar. I already loved the weeping katsura for its four seasons of visual interest. The fall fragrance just added to its long list of benefits.

In the landscape, this medium- to fast-growing species is dense and pyramidal, then rounded with age. Weeping cultivars have handsome winter branch architecture, and all have grayish brown flaky bark full of character and teeny red blooms before the leaves (male and female flowers are on separate trees). The foliage is lovely to behold spring, summer, and fall. Similar to redbud (Cercis), the leaves are simple, opposite, and heart-shaped, about 3" × 3". Bronzy purple when young, they turn bluish green in summer and warm yellow flushed with apricot and red in fall.

LANDSCAPE USE
Large lawn specimen, spreading shade tree.

ORIGIN Woods of China and Japan.

HARDINESS ZONES 4–8

LIGHT Full sun.

SOIL Moist, well-drained, fertile soils; pH adaptable.

GROWING Although it may be hard to transplant, once established, katsura is easy to grow. Water it deeply during its first season and during times of drought.

Cephalotaxus harringtonii 'Prostrata'

Cercidiphyllum japonicum

Cercidiphyllum japonicum 'Herons-wood Globe' Small tree with dense, spherical crown. 15'–20' h and w.

C. japonicum 'Pendulum' I grow 'Pendulum' and neighbors and people walking through the neighborhood often stop to ask what the beautiful, architectural tree is. At 11 years old, it's about 20' h × 15' w. The branches droop with grace, retaining a dominant landscape presence. (Not the same as 'Pendula'.) Other weeping forms are 'Tidal Wave' and 'Amazing Grace'. 25' h × 20' w.

C. japonicum 'Raspberry' Raspberry-red fall color; new growth flushed red with red leaf stems. 40'–60' h × 20'–40' w.

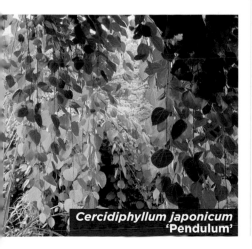
Cercidiphyllum japonicum 'Pendulum'

CERCIS

Cercis canadensis ▽ › ○

SER-sis ka-na-DEN-sis

Eastern redbud

Senna Family (Caesalpiniaceae; also seen as Fabaceae)
Small flowering tree
25' h x 30' w

The charm of this small, flowering tree lies in its pretty pink, spring flowers and lovely, summer leaves. Planted as a specimen in full sun, redbud develops rising branches and a full, rounded crown. In its native, partly shaded habitat at the woodland's edge, its rather symmetrical vase shape becomes more open and irregular with limbs that seek the sun. The tree, which can be low-branched on a single trunk or have multiple trunks, grows fast when young, slowing down after its first 10 years.

The foliage is heart-shaped in the form of 4"–5" × 4"–5" simple alternate leaves that emerge with the flowers. Spring foliage is bright green with a bronzy purple tinge, followed by clear green, summer color; fall color can be yellowy and is not ornamental. The bark is dark brown to black,

sometimes flaking with age. Clusters of rosy purple buds open to pink, pealike blooms in spring before and during the advent of leaves. Flowering lasts up to 3 weeks and occurs mostly on 2-year-old wood and the limbs and trunk. The fruit, in the form of clusters of green to brown seedpods, is not ornamental.

LANDSCAPE USE
Lovely understory tree for spring-blooming woodland gardens, lawn specimen, border accent, or grouped at the edge of the woods.

ORIGIN At the edge or in the understory of moist woodlands in the eastern and midwestern U.S.

HARDINESS ZONES 5–9

LIGHT Full sun to partial shade.

SOIL Moist, well-drained, fertile soils; adaptable to varying pH and other landscape conditions except wetness.

GROWING Plant the tree away from standing water, which can lead to rot. This tree is not long lived in manmade situations, where it tends to lean. Scales are possible pests, while potential disease problems include verticillium wilt, canker, and heartwood rot.

Cercis canadensis 'Forest Pansy'

Cercis canadensis

DESIGNER'S CHOICE

Cercis canadensis 'Alba' White flowers, chartreuse new growth. 25' h × 30' w.

C. canadensis 'Forest Pansy' Leaves open dark purple, then turn green with a reddish tinge by summer; purplish-pink flowers. Site this lovely, rounded accent tree carefully, growing it in partial shade where hot. Sometimes listed as Zone 5, but if this tree isn't well situated and established, it won't make it through the coldest winters. 20' h and 25 ft w. Zones 6–9.

C. canadensis 'Royal White' Possibly the hardiest redbud with big, white, early, plentiful blooms and young leaves without reddish tints. 25' h × 30' w.

Chaenomeles speciosa

○ › ○

ke-NAH-me-leez spee-see-O-sa

Flowering quince

Rose Family (Rosaceae)
Shrub
6'–10' h and w

Not pretty except in bloom, this ungainly, deciduous shrub brings little to most home landscapes. It rambles, spreads, or stands upright and rounded, depending upon the cultivar, and its thorny stems gather blown debris. Still, if you have an old house and are looking for an old-fashioned shrub for a barrier or border, this may be the one for you.

It produces simple, alternate leaves up to 3½" long with stipules, or tiny pairs of leaves, at the base of the leaf stalks. Leaves are shiny, green ovals with lighter undersides. The bark is brown, not showy. Single or double flowers up to 1½" wide in red, pink, or white occur alone or in small clusters before the leaves unfurl. It blooms on old wood in late winter in the South; farther north, where extreme cold may kill the buds, it blooms in spring. The flowering period is short, however. The edible, 2½", sour, red-tinged chartreuse, applelike fruits make tasty jams and jellies; these fruits ripen in mid-fall. Many cultivars may be hybrids between this species and *C. japonica*.

LANDSCAPE USE
Informal barrier hedges, kitchen gardens, massed, or part of a shrub border where its ungainly appearance won't stand out.

ORIGIN China

HARDINESS ZONES 4–8

LIGHT Full sun to partial shade.

SOIL This drought-tolerant shrub thrives in heavy soils but can grow anywhere.

GROWING Prune after the flowers fade, before next year's buds develop. Renew scraggly shrubs by cutting back almost to the ground or by removing oldest stems.

DESIGNER'S CHOICE

Chaenomeles speciosa 'Cameo' Peach-pink, double flowers; stems almost thorn-free; leaves generally disease-resistant. 4'–5' h and w.

C. speciosa 'Jet Trail' Plentiful white flowers; stems almost thorn-free. 3' h × 3'–4' w.

C. speciosa 'Moerloosei' (syn. *C. speciosa* 'Apple Blossom') 2" white blooms tinted pink. 6'–10' h and w.

C. speciosa 'Nivalis' Clean, white flowers on erect, sturdy shrub. 6'–10' h and w.

C. speciosa 'Rubra' (red flowering quince) Red flowers appear before leaves unfurl on this spreading, thorny shrub. 5'–7' h × 4'–6' w. Zones 5–8.

C. speciosa 'Texas Scarlet' Abundant scarlet blooms; stems almost thorn-free. 3' h × 3'–4' w.

Chaenomeles speciosa

Chaenomeles speciosa 'Jet Trail'

Chamaecyparis lawsoniana ◬

ka-mee-SI-pa-ris law-so-ni-A-na

Lawson false cypress, Lawson cypress, Port Orford cedar

Cypress or Redwood Family
(Cupressaceae)
Evergreen conifer
50'–60' h x 6'–10' w

Lawson cypress is a tall, thin, evergreen conifer with a wide trunk and a pyramidal shape. In the wild, this tree can be up to 200 feet tall, but it's shorter in landscape conditions. It has a widespread root system. The Japanese use Lawson cypress wood as a substitute for Hinoki cypress. Foliage occurs on small, erect branches with the blue-green, scaly leaves pressed tight to their stems. The ⅛" leaves, marked with white x's on the bottom, appear in flat, ferny, medium-textured sprays with pendant tips. The brown to grayish brown bark is up to 10" thick with long, flaky plates. The fruits and flowers are not particularly ornamental. This conifer has many cultivars, which are frequently used as specimens. Perhaps best grown in the Pacific Northwest with ample atmospheric moisture in summer and winter.

LANDSCAPE USE
For screening, in flower arrangements, and in decorative shrub borders.

ORIGIN   Siskiyou Mountains of Oregon and California.

HARDINESS ZONES   (5) 6–7

LIGHT   Full sun to partial shade.

SOIL   Prefers moist, well-drained, neutral to slightly acidic soils.

GROWING   Good drainage helps this tree avoid its biggest disease problem, root rot, which may happen in wet soils. Give Lawson cypress some wind protection since it can blow over in strong winds.

ALL ABOUT CHAMAECYPARIS

These evergreen conifers tolerate some shade. That fact alone makes them worth growing, especially for people living where hemlocks are in decline. Foliage is particularly attractive. Most cultivars have tiny scale-like adult leaves arranged in flattened sprays, but young leaves are like little needles. In the landscape, false cypress stands out for rich-hued cultivars and sensual texture, which ranges from very fine to coarse with strong contrasts of light and dark, depending upon the species. You can shear false cypress for hedges and screens but do not cut into the old wood when trimming. Be on the lookout for bagworms, and if you see their brown conelike egg sacs, destroy them right away.

Chamaecyparis nootkatensis ◬

ka-mee-SI-pa-ris noot-ka-TEN-sis

Nootka false cypress, Alaska cedar

Cypress or Redwood Family
(Cupressaceae)
Evergreen conifer
30'–45' h x 15'–20' w

The natural elegance of Nootka false cypress comes from its gracefully drooping, irregular silhouette, a trait magnified in the weeping cultivar 'Pendula'. Nootka false cypress can grow 100' tall in the wild and lives up to 3,500 years, according to the USDA Forest Service. Shaped like a narrow cone, this slow-growing tree has an upright leader and scaly, dark green leaves arranged in flat, dangling, scented sprays. The bark is shaggy and brownish gray, while the cones are small but not ornamental. 'Pendula' is smaller, growing 25'–40' h × 10'–15' w.

LANDSCAPE USE
With its saggy leader, wide-set drooping branches, and limp branchlets, 'Pendula' brings drama to the home landscape as a sculptural lawn specimen.

ORIGIN   Pacific Coast mountains from Oregon to Alaska.

HARDINESS ZONES   (4) 5–7

LIGHT   Tolerates wind and shade but prefers full sun.

SOIL   Deep, moist, well-drained soils.

GROWING   Watch out for bagworms.

Chamaecyparis nootkatensis **'Pendula'**

Chamaecyparis obtusa △

ka-mee-SI-pa-ris ob-TU-sa

Hinoki false cypress, Hinoki cypress

Cypress or Redwood Family (Cupressaceae)
Evergreen conifer
50'–75' h x 10'–20' w

Hinoki false cypress comes in a variety of shapes, colors, and sizes, making it one of the most useful evergreens for year-round garden interest. The slender, cone-shaped tree grows at a medium pace, and in its native Japan, it can reach 120' tall.

The tiny, blunt-tipped, rich green, scaly leaves are arranged in flat, fragrant, lacy sprays. The reddish-brown bark exfoliates in strips. Neither the flowers nor the rounded ½" cones are ornamental.

LANDSCAPE USE
Gorgeous deep green foliage on a dense pyramidal tree makes this a superb alternative to hemlock. Because cultivars range from tiny buns to spreading shrubs and broad, tall pyramids, Hinoki false cypress fits many landscape applications including foundation plant, specimen, rock garden shrub, accent, tall screens and hedges, and groundcover. Grow dwarfs in shrub, rock, and perennial gardens, or as sculptural specimens.

ORIGIN   Mountainsides of Japan.

HARDINESS ZONES   5–8

LIGHT   Full sun to partial shade.

SOIL   Moist, fertile, well-drained, neutral to acidic soils; can't tolerate alkaline soils.

GROWING   Prefers to grow in somewhat sheltered, humid, uncrowded surroundings. Let light reach the whole plant, which is full and branched to the ground. Containerized material transplants better than balled-and-burlapped items. There are many diverse cultivars to suit many different landscapes.

DESIGNER'S CHOICE

Chamaecyparis obtusa 'Crippsii' Long, airy sprays of yellow foliage on a wide pyramidal plant. 15'–30' h × 10'–20' w.

C. obtusa 'Elf' Tight, dark green leaves on rounded cone; good for rock gardens. 12" h and w.

C. obtusa 'Gracilis' Wide and conical in old age. 4'–8' h × 3'–4' w.

C. obtusa 'Kosteri' Dwarf, irregular pyramid with bright green, layered foliage. 3' h × 2' w.

C. obtusa 'Nana Gracilis' Erect irregular dwarf; a beauty. 30" h × 20" w.

C. obtusa 'Nana Lutea' Golden dwarf Hinoki cypress grown for its brilliant gold foliage. 2'–4' h and w.

C. obtusa 'Reis Dwarf' Tight, twisted branchlets give this bright green cultivar an upright but uneven, layered shape. 3'–5' h × 2'–3' w.

C. obtusa 'Repens' Green, cupped, soft leaves in lacy fronds. 16" h × 36" w.

C. obtusa 'Wells Special' Dark green, semi-dwarf, upright plant. 8'–10' h × 4'–5' w.

Chamaecyparis obtusa 'Kosteri'

Chamaecyparis pisifera △

ka-mee-SI-pa-ris pi-SI-fe-ra

Sawara false cypress

Cypress Family or Redwood (Cupressaceae)
Evergreen conifer
60' h x 20' w

Although you probably won't see the plain species at your local nursery, you'll surely find some shrubby cultivars. Sawara false cypress comes in different colors and textures. Yellow, blue-green, silver, dark green, and variegated green-and-cream or green-and-gold are some of your options. Some gold-leafed plants may turn greenish as summer progresses, however. Textures range from threadlike *(filifera)* to open and ferny *(plumosa)*, or needled and feathery *(squarrosa)* to plain, like the species. An excellent landscape plant, Sawara false cypress has an aromatic scent.

The foliage is dark green on top with white marks on bottom; leaves are pressed to the stem in flat, fragrant sprays. The reddish brown bark exfoliates in skinny strips. Let light reach the whole plant, which is full and branched to the ground. Containerized material transplants better than balled-and-burlapped items. Neither flowers nor ¼" cones are ornamental.

LANDSCAPE USE
Rock gardens, accents, lawn specimens, and groupings.

ORIGIN   Near mountain streams in Japan.

HARDINESS ZONES   (4) 5–8

LIGHT   Full sun.

SOIL   Moist, well-drained, acid soils.

GROWING   Likes high humidity but may brown-out in the middle.

DESIGNER'S CHOICE

Chamaecyparis pisifera 'Boulevard' Semi-dwarf pyramid with short, gray-blue needles in feathery clusters. 12' h × 5' w.

C. pisifera 'Cream Ball' Very hardy, tight, slow-growing dwarf globe with creamy foliage that won't burn in sun. About 2' h and w. Zone 4.

C. pisifera 'Filifera' Handsome, semi-weeping habit, with scaly green leaves on skinny, drooping stems. 6' h × 8' w.

C. pisifera 'Golden Mop' Slow-growing, bright gold, thread-leaf cultivar holds its color all summer long; less brassy that 'Filifera Aurea'. 6' h × 8' w at 10 years.

C. pisifera 'White Pygmy' White-tipped leaves on a dwarf bun (a mound of congested branches) often originating from a witches broom; prefers to grow in partial shade. 2' h and w.

Chamaecyparis thyoides 0 ⟩ △

ka-mee-SI-pa-ris thi-OY-deez

Atlantic white cedar, White false cypress

Redwood or Cypress Family (Cupressaceae)
Tree or shrub
40'–50' h × 10'–20' w

Atlantic white cedar is columnar when young, but with age it changes to a short, slender crown above a long, bare trunk. This eastern native prefers to grow in swamps and bogs, but most cultivars can also grow on drier soils, maintaining a medium growth rate. There are a variety of interesting cultivars in blue, yellow, green, and variegated green-and-white from which to choose.

Very small green to blue-green leaves with sharp points turn brown after one year and stay on the tree for years. The ornamental, brownish red, furrowed bark peels in long strips. Neither the flowers nor the fruit is ornamental.

LANDSCAPE USE
Swamp or bog gardens, specimen for damp spot in the yard.

***Chamaecyparis thyoides* 'Glauca Pendula'**

ORIGIN Swampy land in the eastern U.S.

HARDINESS ZONES 4–8

LIGHT Full sun.

SOIL Moist, sandy, well-drained, acid soils.

GROWING Appreciates some protection but needs enough growing space for light and air to reach all parts of it. Leaves may change to brown or yellow brown in winter. Dead foliage remains on tree.

DESIGNER'S CHOICE
Chamaecyparis thyoides 'Ericoides' Blue-green, needled young leaves with bronzy purple winter hue; compact conical form. 4'–6' h × about 4' w.

C. thyoides 'Heatherbun' Dense, rounded form with bluish green leaves that turn bronze in winter. 8'–10' h × 6'–8' w.

C. thyoides 'Hopkinton' Fast growing with blue-gray leaves and an open habit; silvery cones may remain on the tree in winter. 40' h × 20' w.

C. thyoides 'Little Jamie' Yellow leaves turn purplish bronze in winter; grows slowy to a small, narrow, pointy cone or column. 4'–5' h × 2'–3' w.

C. thyoides 'Rubicon' (Red Star Atlantic cedar) Dense column with bluish green leaves that turn purplish in winter. 15'–25' h × about 5' w.

Chimonanthus praecox ⌒

ki-mo-NAN-thus PRE-koks

Wintersweet

Strawberry Shrub Family (Calycanthaceae)
Deciduous shrub
10' h × 8' w

Grow wintersweet not for its looks but for its powerfully fragrant flowers that appear in winter when little else blooms. Small, waxy, creamy blossoms with purple petals in the center appear on leafless stems from December to early March in the South, later in the North. The dark green leaves are up to 6" long with pointed tips and yellowish green fall color.

LANDSCAPE USE
Plant this shrub near a path or door you use frequently to take advantage of the scent. Use it as a specimen, in a shrub border, against a sunny wall, or behind shrubs or perennials that bloom after wintersweet's flowers fade. Cut stems in a vase can perfume an entire room.

ORIGIN China

HARDINESS ZONES 7–9

LIGHT Full sun; tolerates partial shade.

SOIL Well-drained, average garden soil.

***Chimonanthus praecox* 'Luteus'**

GROWING Growing this shrub requires patience, since best bloom occurs on mature plants, while young bushes hardly flower. Caring for wintersweet is easy, because the less you prune it, the more it flowers. It may become leggy over time, however, and need renewal by pruning stems a foot from the ground. If an old branch declines, cut it to the basal buds right after flowering in late winter.

CHIONANTHUS

Chionanthus virginicus ○ › ◌ ✳

ki-oh-NAN-thus ver-JI-ni-cus

White fringe tree, Fringe tree, Old man's beard

Olive Family (Oleaceae)
Deciduous small flowering tree
15'–20' h and w

The first place I saw a mature, blooming fringe tree was near Hamden, Connecticut, at the crest of a sunny rock garden. The tree looked fluffy and delicate, thanks to the fine, shaggy flowers that hung in big, soft clusters from the branches. Needless to say, within a month I'd planted a little fringe tree of my own.

The rich green, oval leaves with pointed tips are slow to leaf out in spring; in fall, they are yellow to bronze. The smooth, gray to brown bark develops furrows over time. In April and May, fringe tree bears fragrant, clustered, 1", white blooms consisting of 4–6 long, skinny petals resembling fringe. Clusters of olive-shaped, green fruits ripen to blue-black in late summer on female trees.

LANDSCAPE USE
Specimen, groups, borders, or woodland's edge.

ORIGIN Bogs, rock outcrops, moist forests, and stream banks in the eastern U.S.

HARDINESS ZONES (4) 5–9

LIGHT Full sun to partial shade.

SOIL Likes moist, fertile, acid soil but adapts to many situations including heavy, wet and sandy, dry soils.

GROWING Needs little pruning. It is generally healthy but may have some leaf

Chionanthus retusus

spots, powdery mildew, scales, or borers.

DESIGNER'S CHOICE
Chionanthus retusus (Chinese fringe tree) A lovely, slow-growing shrub or tree. Unlike *C. virginicus,* it has dark, gleaming, leathery leaves with yellow fall color and flowers that occur at the ends of new shoots. It blooms later than *C. virginicus* with bright white, fragrant flowers on male and female trees and showy, ½", deep blue fruits on females. The attractive bark forms ridges and sometimes peels with age. 15' h and w. Zones (5) 6–8.

CLADRASTIS

Cladrastis kentukea ▽ › ○

cla-DRAS-tis ken-TUK-ee-a

Yellowwood

Pea Family (Fabaceae)
Deciduous tree
30'–45' h x 30'–35' w

Yellowwood, which takes its name from the yellow heartwood, is a midsized, upright, vase-shaped to rounded tree with four-season appeal: In spring, 1'-long clusters of 1"-long, white, fragrant flowers dangle from the branches; the tree's

Chionanthus virginicus

cheery, bright green leaves turn attractive yellow in fall; and in winter, the smooth, gray, beechlike bark is easy to see. The abundant, pea-type blooms that hang in wisteria-like clusters appear only every 2 or 3 years; lighter flowering occurs in other years. The compound, alternate leaves are 8" to 12" long, with 7–9 leaflets. Brown 4" pods ripen in fall.

LANDSCAPE USE
A lawn tree used alone or in groups; allées; a good size for shading small lots.

ORIGIN Southern and midwestern U.S. along stream banks and river valleys.

HARDINESS ZONES 4–8

LIGHT Full sun.

SOIL Moist, fertile, well-drained soils; pH adaptable.

GROWING Plant young trees in their permanent site. Prune in midsummer to avoid the bleeding that occurs in spring. The wood is brittle; heavy limbs at narrow angles to trunk may split at

Cladrastis kentukea

the crotch in high winds. Late spring frost may harm shoots on young trees.

DESIGNER'S CHOICE
Cladrastis kentukea 'Perkin's Pink' (syn. *C.* 'Rosea') Light pink, fragrant flower clusters up to 15" long; rare. 30'–45' h × 30'–35' w.

C. kentukea 'Sweetshade' More vigorous than the species; resistant to leafhoppers. 35'–45' h × 30'–35' w.

CLERODENDRUM

Clerodendrum trichotomum 🝙

klay-roh-DEN-dron tri-KOT-oh-mum

Harlequin glorybower

Vervain Family (Verbenaceae)
Large deciduous shrub or small tree
10'–15' h and w

Grown for its pinkish flower buds; sweetly scented, white, late summer to early fall flowers; and early fall, turquoise or metallic blue berries framed by crimson calyx; this is a popular, easy plant in warm climates. Its Japanese name means "smelly tree," presumably referring to the fragrant, clustered flowers. Its glossy, dark green, opposite leaves are 4"–8" long. The plant's typical habit is multi-stemmed and suckering, and has been politely described as "unkempt."

LANDSCAPE USE
In a shrub border or as a specimen or container plant near a low deck or patio where you can enjoy its scent and the red, white and blue effect of the blooms and fruits.

ORIGIN China and Japan.

HARDINESS ZONES (6) 7–10

LIGHT Full sun.

SOIL Light, fertile, well-drained soil in a warm, protected location.

GROWING Prune to the ground in spring, especially in cool areas with lots of dieback.

Clerodendrum trichotomum

CAUTION Invasive potential through seeds and suckering in hot climates.

CLETHRA

Clethra alnifolia O › 🝙 ✳

KLETH-ra al-ni-FOH-li-a

Summersweet

White Alder or Clethra Family (Clethraceae)
Deciduous shrub
4'–8' h and w

This deciduous shrub attracts butterflies and other pollinators. It has an informal, suckering habit that makes it perfect for partly shaded, naturalized places. Plant it in groups for best effect and be patient, because it may take more than one season to become well established. I find even established plants are relatively slow to leaf out in spring, and one winter when temperatures on New Hampshire's seacoast dropped to –15°F, newly planted shrubs survived but were even slower to green up. The popular cultivar 'Hummingbird' stays more compact. One that I've had in a partly shaded foundation planting for 5 years measures about 2' h × 3' w.

Alternate, simple, deciduous, bright green leaves are 2"–4" × 1"–2" with serrated edges; they turn yellow

Clethra alnifolia 'Ruby Spice'

Clethra alnifolia 'Hummingbird'

to golden brown in fall. The gray bark is not ornamental. Tiny, white, fragrant flowers arranged in dense, 6", upright spikes have a long bloom time in July and August. Decorative, tubular spikes made of tan capsules typically last until cut back in early spring.

LANDSCAPE USE
Woodland or native gardens, shrub borders, perennial borders, groups, masses, or partly shaded pond edges; grows well near the ocean.

ORIGIN Moist spots in eastern North America.

HARDINESS ZONES 4–9

LIGHT Full sun to partial shade.

SOIL Moist, acid, wet, or well-drained soils high in organic matter.

GROWING To maintain an attractive shape, cut some of the oldest and weakest stems to the ground before new growth begins in spring. *Clethra* has no serious insect or disease problems unless grown in droughty conditions where spider mites may be a problem.

DESIGNER'S CHOICE
Clethra alnifolia 'Hummingbird' Profuse, early, 4"–7" flowers and glossy, dark leaves with yellow to golden brown fall color on a dwarf plant; tan fruit capsules give winter interest; a fine, easy choice. 2'–3½' h × 2'–4' w.

C. alnifolia 'Ruby Spice' Deep rosy pink, persistent flower spikes with spicy fragrance. 4'–8' h and w.

C. alnifolia 'September Beauty' Upright, white, 4"–5" spikes in late September. Extends flowering season when grown with other *Clethra*. 5'–8' h × 4'–7' w.

C. alnifolia 'Sixteen Candles' Erect, white, 6", fragrant flower spikes on a compact shrub with deep green, leathery leaves. A selection from 'Hummingbird' seedlings. 2½" h × 3½" w.

Clethra barbinervis ○

KLETH-ra bar-bi-NER-vus

Japanese clethra

Clethra Family (Clethraceae)
Deciduous shrub or small tree
10'–20' h x 10'–15' w

The first time I saw this handsome four-season plant was at Longwood Gardens in a shady part of the Hillside Garden; the second was five years ago at Broken Arrow Nursery in Hamden, Connecticut, where I

purchased one for my own garden. Although mine barely survived a winter when the temperature fell to −15°F, it is still an elegant shrub with gray-brown exfoliating bark, deep green leaves near the branch tips, and light-scented white flowers in long dangling S-shaped clusters at the ends of shoots.

LANDSCAPE USE
Consider siting *C. barbinervis* by a shady stream bank or next to a pond where soils are moist. It adds an exotic presence to a woodland garden.

ORIGIN Japan

HARDINESS ZONES (5) 6–8

LIGHT Partial shade.

SOIL Moist soil high in organic matter.

GROWING Japanese clethra can grow in full sun but looks more graceful and open in the shade. Watch out for mites in hot or dry seasons and sites.

Clethra barbinervis

Comptonia peregrina ○ › ⌂

comp-TOH-ni-a pe-ri-GREE-na

Sweetfern

Bayberry Family (Myricaceae)
Deciduous shrub
2'–4' h x 4'–8' w

My favorite planting of this East Coast native is at St. Paul's School in Concord, New Hampshire, where it fills partly shaded beds around a parking lot and forms a transition into the taller woods. Sweetfern, aromatic when crushed, has narrow, oblong leaves with ferny lobes. It grows wild throughout the New Hampshire seacoast region and elsewhere in New England, spreading by stolons and forming big colonies by roadside ditches and the edges of woods. Because its roots fix (absorb) nitrogen from the air, it's useful for poor, infertile, gravelly soils.

ORIGIN   Eastern North America.

HARDINESS ZONES   2–5 (6)

LIGHT   Full sun to partial shade.

SOIL   Acid, gravelly, poor soil. It adapts to either moist or dry conditions but is hard to transplant unless raised in a container.

GROWING   No pruning and no major problems.

Comptonia peregrina

Cornus alba ○ › ⌂ ✳

KOR-nus AL-ba

Tatarian dogwood, Red-twig dogwood

Dogwood Family (Cornaceae)
Shrub
6'–10' h x 5'–6' w

An impressive planting around a pond at the Royal Horticultural Society garden, Wisley, in Surrey, England, captured my attention in January 2004. Red-twig dogwood and other shrubs with colorful winter stems grew in large masses, creating a rich fabric of red, pink, white, and yellow. This planting depended on a big, open, sunny space that you could see both from a distance and close up. The species in particular is not suited to a small garden, since its suckering habit will encroach upon other desirable plants.

The leaves are opposite, simple, and oval with a pointed tip and rounded base; they sometimes show a reddish purple color in fall. In winter, the stems are bright to dark red; color typically develops when leaves drop and cool weather begins. The yellow-tinted white flowers are occasionally decorative. Clusters of white to bluish, berrylike fruits can look decorative against the red stems after leaf drop.

LANDSCAPE USE
Masses; groups in naturalized areas around ponds and other water bodies.

ORIGIN   Siberia and northern China and Korea.

HARDINESS ZONES   3–7

LIGHT   Full sun to partial shade.

SOIL   Prefers moist, well-drained soil but tolerates many soil conditions.

GROWING   Since best color occurs on new growth, cut back shrubs to 1' in late winter or early spring before new growth begins. If you prefer, cut back one third of the oldest stems before the growing season begins. Plants are prone to severe canker in Zone 7.

DESIGNER'S CHOICE

Cornus alba 'Bailhalo' (Ivory Halo) White-edged leaves with green centers, red winter stems, rounded form. 5'–6' h and w.

C. alba 'Cream Cracker' Green-centered new leaves have gold edges, turning cream with age. Winter stems are purple-red; reports vary from leaf-spot resistant to scorch prone. Sport of *C. alba* 'Gouchaultii'. 5'–6' h × 4'–5' w.

ALL ABOUT CORNUS

Dogwood is a versatile genus, giving gardens an ornamental four-season tree, a shrub notable for its refined form, and other shrubs with spreading habits fit for short or tall groundcovers and attracting wildlife. Grow different types of dogwood for flashy pink or white flowers (which are actually four petal-like bracts); fine fall color; attractive red fruits or white berry clusters; and decorative flaky to colorful bark. Look out for diseases like anthracnose, powdery mildew, and canker.

**Cornus alba
'Elegantissima'**

C. alba 'Elegantissima' (syn. *C. alba* 'Argenteo-marginata') Variegated leaves with cream edges and gray-green centers. Maintains red stems year round. 6'–10' h × 5'–8' w.

C. alba 'Gouchaultii' Decorative leaves have jumbled rose, green, and yellow centers edged in yellow and white; dark red winter stems. Looks like *C. alba* 'Spaethii'. 6'–8' h × 5'–8' w.

C. alba 'Sibirica' Blue fruit; red fall color; bright red, young stems in winter; doesn't spread; plants can be variable. 5'–6' h and w.

Cornus alternifolia ○

KOR-nus al-ter-ni-FOH-lee-a

Pagoda dogwood

Dogwood Family (Cornaceae)
Deciduous shrub or small tree
15'–20' h × 20'–25' w

This plant's key attribute is its elegant, layered, horizontal branching that resembles a pagoda in its multiple layers. Overall, this native looks rounded, but upon inspection, you can appreciate its tiered effect. Its small, yellow, fragrant flowers grow in flat clusters that look appealing for about a week in late spring; later, it bears blue-black fruits. Although

the leaves may redden in fall, pagoda dogwood isn't grown for fall color.

LANDSCAPE USE
Naturalistic gardens and moist shady wooded areas, where its layered form can balance strong verticals like tree trunks.

ORIGIN Eastern and midwestern U.S. and Canada.

HARDINESS ZONES (3) 4–7

LIGHT Transplant this shrub when young to a site in full sun or partial shade.

SOIL Moist, well-drained, acid soil.

GROWING Blight, canker, and leaf spot may affect pagoda dogwood, which is otherwise fairly trouble free. It performs best in cool climates.

DESIGNER'S CHOICE
Cornus controversa (giant dogwood) Giant dogwood resembles a big pagoda dogwood with alternate leaves, a symmetrical layered canopy with wide-spreading horizontal branches, and similar growing requirements; showy white spring flowers, dark purplish fruit that attracts birds, and red fall color are added benefits. 25'–45' h × 20'–30' w. Zones 5–8. The cultivar 'Variegata' is elegant. It is smaller and more

delicate, with leaves edged creamy white; it prefers to grow in partial shade. 15' h × 20' w.

Cornus canadensis ☙

KOR-nus kan-a-DEN-sis

Bunchberry, Creeping dogwood

Dogwood Family (Cornaceae)
Deciduous groundcover shrub or subshrub
6–10" h × indefinite spread

This North American native always surprises me when I see it growing in a woodland garden or in the wild. Its harmonious parts strike me as large for its diminutive height, but this very contrast makes the plant a standout wherever it grows. You wouldn't notice the greenish flowers in May, June, and July if it weren't for the four, big, white, pointed bracts surrounding them. The flowers sit neatly atop what looks like a star-shaped group of 4–6 bright green leaves, which are actually simple and opposite in arrangement. By August, clusters of bright red, edible berries begin to appear. In fall, the deciduous

**Cornus controversa
'Variegata'**

leaves turn a brilliant to deep red. In some climates, leaves may remain evergreen.

LANDSCAPE USE
Shady borders, woodland gardens, naturalized areas with other acid- and moisture-loving plants.

ORIGIN   Northern North America.

HARDINESS ZONES   3–6

LIGHT   Partial to full shade.

SOIL   Moist to wet, acid soils, rich in organic matter, or acid sand-and-gravel drifts in its native northern range.

GROWING   Mulch the plant with pine needles to help the soil stay moist and cool. May be difficult to grow outside its native habitats, or where soils get above 65°F.

Cornus florida ○ › ◠

KOR-nus FLO-ri-da

Flowering dogwood

Dogwood Family (Cornaceae)
Deciduous small flowering tree
15'–30' h x 15'–20' w

Native dogwoods are admired for their blooms (really four petal-like bracts), their bright red fruits, and their outstanding fall color. Healthy trees grown in sun have a rounded form with a low trunk and horizontal, layered branches; trees in shady conditions still have tiered branching but the form is light, graceful, and more refined.

When I lived in Delaware, we bought a house with three sick flowering dogwoods in the backyard. Dying branches distorted the plant's harmonious layered shape. This dogwood species is waning in the Northeast because of susceptibility to anthracnose, a fungal disease. On the west coast a similar native, Pacific dogwood, *C. nuttali* (25 ft h), is equally vulnerable. In my experience, it's better to choose a hybrid

dogwood bred for disease resistance than to watch the decline of these beautiful native trees in your garden.

Simple, opposite, medium green, 3"–6" leaves unfurl when the tree comes into bloom; they show excellent red to purple fall color. The brown bark becomes plated with age. Hemispherical clusters of greenish or yellow, fertile flowers are surrounded by four showy, 1"–2", white, petal-like bracts, notched at the tip. Flowers appear March through June, depending upon the region. Birds and small mammals devour the clusters of bright red, beanlike fruits.

Cornus florida

Cornus florida f. rubra

LANDSCAPE USE
In nature, dogwoods usually occur in the forest understory and at the woodland's edge, where they exhibit an appealing delicacy of form because of the restricted light. They also look lovely grouped in a large lawn or as specimen trees in both large and small sunny landscapes, where they are low branched, full, and spreading.

ORIGIN   Forests of eastern North America.

HARDINESS ZONES   5–9

LIGHT   Full sun to partial shade. In its northern range, dogwood likes more sun, but in the South, it grows better when shaded.

SOIL   Moist, acid, well-drained soils rich in organic matter.

GROWING   Water during drought, because stressed dogwoods are the most disease-prone. Anthracnose is the worst dogwood disease. This fungus first appears as purple-edged spots on the leaves in cool, damp, foggy springs and autumns. Wounding or drought aggravates the effect. Woodland understory trees are more affected by anthracnose than trees planted in the open. Other problems include scale, cankers, powdery mildew, and phytopthora blight. Borers may attack sick trees.

DESIGNER'S CHOICE
Many lovely cultivars exist, but so far, just white-flowered *C. florida* 'Appalachian Spring' (20' h in 10 years) shows some anthracnose resistance.

Depending upon your climate and location, you may want to plant disease-resistant hybrids with *C. kousa* rather than trees with pure *C. florida* parentage. Examples include 'Aurora', 'Celestial', 'Ruth Ellen', 'Star Dust', and 'Stellar Pink'.

Cornus kousa ▽ › ◠ ✳

KOR-nus KOO-sa

Kousa dogwood

Dogwood Family (Cornaceae)
Deciduous small flowering tree
20'–30' h and w

You won't find finer examples of this four-season tree than at Longwood Gardens, in Kennett Square, Pennsylvania, where extraordinary specimens grow on the main lawn along the walk to the cafeteria. Rounded, spreading, and wider than tall, these trees always look good. Although you may lack Longwood's resources, you can still grow a mighty nice kousa at home.

Young kousa dogwoods start out vase shaped, developing a rounded habit with horizontal branching over time. They bloom later than native flowering dogwoods, and their showy bracts last longer. In addition to having edible, bright red fruits; handsome, dark green leaves; excellent red to purple fall color, and gorgeous, flaking bark, these slow-growing deciduous trees resist the anthracnose fungus that decimates our native species.

The simple, opposite, 2"–4", dark green leaves turn red to purple in fall. Mature bark exfoliates (peels), creating a patchwork of gray, beige, and reddish brown. Tiny green to yellowish flowers packed into a tight, round cluster are surrounded by 4 showy, 2", white or pink-tinged bracts. Edible ornamental red fruit resembles a long-stalked, 1"-round strawberry dangling above the leaves. Birds eat the fruits, which ripen from August to October. The fruit I've eaten is mealy but rather sweet — not bad at all.

LANDSCAPE USE
Specimen, groves, or patio tree that looks good year round.

ORIGIN Mountain forests of Japan, Korea, China.

HARDINESS ZONES 5–8

LIGHT Full sun to partial shade.

SOIL Moist, acid, well-drained, fertile soil rich in organic matter.

GROWING Consider pruning off low branches so you can display the bark.

Cornus kousa 'Gold Star'

DESIGNER'S CHOICE

Cornus kousa var. *chinensis* Larger bracts and fruits than species, supposedly hardier than the species. 'Milky Way' is a *chinensis* cultivar that has more flowers. 20'–30' h and w.

C. kousa 'Elizabeth Lustgarten' Elegant weeping form with rounded crown. 5'–7' h × 5' w.

C. kousa 'Satomi' (syn. *C. kousa* 'Rosabella', 'Heart Throb') Rosy pink bracts; robust, pretty, and popular. 15'–20' h and w.

C. kousa 'Square Dance' White, overlapping bracts form a square, persisting into summer; burgundy purple fall color. 15'–20' h and w. Zones 6–8.

C. kousa 'Summer Stars' Holds bracts for so long that fruit may form with bracts still on the tree; burgundy fall color. 15'–25' h × 15'–20' w.

C. 'Rutdan' (Celestial; Galaxy) One of the Rutgers hybrids, which are crosses between our native *C. florida* and *C. kousa.* Vigorous and resistant to anthracnose and borers. Floral bracts touch but do not overlap, occurring midway between bloom cycles of native and kousa dogwoods; fruit is not ornamental; fall color is purplish burgundy. 15'–20' h and w.

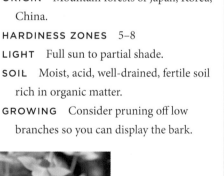

Cornus kousa

Cornus mas ◐ › ◯ ✳

KOR-nus MAS

Cornelian cherry dogwood, Cornelian cherry

Dogwood Family (Cornaceae)
Deciduous small flowering tree
20'–25' h x 10'–15' w

This big, suckering, multi-stemmed shrub or small tree is a cold-climate delight when it blooms in March and other flowering plants are scarce. The modest clusters of yellow flowers look best growing against a contrasting background so they stand out. In one North Hampton, New Hampshire, garden, we transplanted this deciduous tree, trained to a single stem, from a sunny spot in the middle of a backyard to a partly shaded border that forms a transition between hemlocks and a lawn. When it bloomed against snow or a dead bluegrass lawn, this tree looked lost; set against its new dark background, however, the flowers glow for weeks. Although Cornelian cherry dogwood has year-round interest, it's not as showy as a kousa dogwood. It does have edible, crimson fruit,

purplish red fall color, and flaky bark, however.

ORIGIN Europe and Asia.

HARDINESS ZONES 5–7

LIGHT Sun to partial shade.

SOIL Fertile, well-drained soil with either acid or alkaline pH.

GROWING Mostly pest-free and disease resistant. Use for hedging, since it withstands severe pruning.

DESIGNER'S CHOICE

Cornus mas 'Golden Glory' Small upright tree with mounded form and shiny, dark green leaves; profuse, clear yellow flowers in early spring; ⅝", red, cherrylike, summer fruits. Best in warmer climates. 20'–25' h × 10'–15' w.

Cornus mas 'Golden Glory'

Cornus sericea ◯ › ⬱ ✳

KOR-nus se-RI-see-a

Red-osier dogwood

Dogwood Family (Cornaceae)
Deciduous shrub
7'–9' h x 8'–10' w

This deciduous shrub is easy to cultivate but overall not that attractive in a small home landscape. Its suckering habit lends itself to mass plantings in large, naturalized areas. Grown for its red, winter stem color and attractive, though variable, purplish red fall foliage color, red-osier dogwood is a good choice if you need a fast-growing filler or screen in a wet spot on your property, although other shrubs, such as winterberry, red chokeberry, or red-twig dogwood have more multi-season ornamental value.

The medium to dark green, 2"–5" leaves are simple and opposite, with pointed tips; they turn purplish red in fall. The bark is red in fall and winter, and green in spring and summer. Tiny, whitish flowers appear in flat, 2" clusters in late spring.

Cornus sericea 'Baileyi'

Attractive round, white fruits show up against the green leaves and deep red stems; birds eat the fruit. The plant is somewhat deer resistant.

LANDSCAPE USE

Massed, red winter stems look dramatic against snow, evergreens, or the tan foliage of tall ornamental grasses. Similarly, the reddish purple fall color shows well against both evergreens and ornamental grasses. In addition to growing in naturalized shrub beds and borders, *C. sericea* looks attractive around a pond or next to a stream where its far-reaching roots help to stabilize the banks.

ORIGIN Throughout the U.S. and Canada.

HARDINESS ZONES 3–7

LIGHT Full sun to partial shade.

SOIL Prefers moist to wet soils but tolerates most soils and conditions, including drought.

GROWING Cut back old stems in spring in favor of fresh, brightly colored shoots. It tends to have various problems, including scale, bagworms, canker, and leaf spot.

C. sericea 'Budd's Yellow' Yellow stems; yellow fall color; more disease resistant than yellow-stemmed *C. sericea* 'Flaviramea'; 6'–8' h × 5'–7' w.

Cornus sericea 'Cardinal' Bright red stems; less vibrant or more yellowish in warmer climates. 8'–10' h and w.

C. sericea 'Isanti' Smaller habit with intense red stems; may get leaf spots. 5'–6' h × 8'–10' w.

C. sericea 'Kelseyi' Compact, red-stemmed groundcover lacks the deep stem and fall leaf color of species. 2'–3' h and w.

C. sericea 'Silver and Gold' Variegated leaves with green centers and irregular creamy margins. 6'–8' h × 8'–10' w.

CORYLOPSIS

Corylopsis pauciflora ○

ko-ri-LOP-sis paw-si-FLO-ra

Buttercup winter hazel, Winter hazel

Witch Hazel Family (Hamamelidaceae)
Deciduous shrub
4'–6' h and w

Gardeners grow *C. pauciflora* for its scented, soft yellow flowers, which appear in small, dangling clusters in early spring before the shrub leafs out. It remains dainty throughout the rest of the gardening season with green leaves that unfurl with a bronzy tint and turn yellow in fall. Late frosts may kill flower buds. May be hard to find.

LANDSCAPE USE
Often branched to the ground, this fine-textured plant suits woodland gardens where it has maximum effect when planted in groups.

ORIGIN Asia

HARDINESS ZONES 6–8

LIGHT Bright to dappled light, where it's sheltered from high winds and harsh afternoon sun.

Corylopsis pauciflora

SOIL Moist, well-drained, acid soil.

GROWING If given the conditions recommended, *C. pauciflora* needs little care. Every few years, you may want to cut back the oldest stems after blooming to maintain the shrub's vigor and rounded, wide-branched form.

Corylopsis spicata ○

ko-ri-LOP-sis spi-KAH-ta

Spike winter hazel

Witch Hazel Family (Hamamelidaceae)
Deciduous shrub
6'–8' h × 6'–10' w

Spike winter hazel produces twisted branches, an open, horizontal habit, and 2", drooping clusters of light yellow flowers before the foliage appears.

LANDSCAPE USE
In the midsection of a mixed or shrub border, a delicate accent against evergreens or a dark brick wall.

ORIGIN Japan

HARDINESS ZONE 5–8

LIGHT See *C. pauciflora*.

SOIL See *C. pauciflora*.

GROWING Intolerant of drought. Water during dry spells and until established.

CORYLUS

Corylus avellana 'Contorta' ○

KO-ri-lus ah-vel-LA-na

Harry Lauder's walking stick

Filbert or Hazel Family (Corylaceae)
Deciduous shrub
8'–10' h and w

The bent and twisted shape of this popular shrub attracts buyers. Indeed, in fall after dropping its leaves, Harry Lauder's walking stick looks sculptural when used as an accent or focal point in a winter garden. At other times of year, it's not very interesting and requires more than a little maintenance to keep it looking its best. Japanese beetles consume the foliage until only the leaf skeletons remain.

The European native species, *C. avellana,* is a source of edible filberts, but Harry Lauder's walking stick rarely fruits. Both *C. avellana* and *C. maxima* 'Purpurea' (purple giant filbert) are popular landscape shrubs to 20' tall in England. The plant, which attracts birds, is also susceptible to blight. Most nurseries carry this cultivar and not the species.

LANDSCAPE USE
If you're looking for a way to spice up the winter landscape, particularly

Corylus avellana 'Contorta'

where soils are poor, this may be the right shrub or small tree for you.

ORIGIN Europe, Turkey

HARDINESS ZONES 5–8

LIGHT Full sun to partial shade.

SOIL Well-drained, acid to alkaline soil.

GROWING This cultivar is grafted onto the species, which is so vigorous that it may sprout from the base and eventually, if not kept in check by pruning all suckers, take over the plant. Careful top trimming accentuates the shrub's contortions, and you can use the prunings in flower arrangements.

COTINUS

Cotinus coggygria ○

ko-TIE-nus ko-GIG-gree-a

Smokebush, Smoketree

Cashew or Sumac Family
(Anacardiaceae)
Deciduous shrub or small tree
8'–15' h and w

Multi-stemmed smokebush makes a superb addition to mixed beds and borders, blending beautifully with roses, perennials, and ornamental grasses. In a Dover, Delaware, herb garden, I saw old-fashioned, pink garden roses growing against the lush, dark foliage of a purple-leafed smokebush — a breathtaking combination.

Smokebush grows best in full sun and well-drained soil but is otherwise adaptable. Maintenance is easiest if you grow these plants not only for their leaves that turn bright red, yellow, and purple in fall, but also for the fuzzy, 8", pinkish flower clusters that appear in early summer. Yet the actual flowers are tiny, chartreuse, and unobtrusive. What makes them showy are the long, tannish pink hairs on the flower stalks, which create a smoky effect lasting through early September, long after the flowers have faded.

These "smoke" puffs add drama to summer bouquets. The bark on young stems is a bloomy purple-brown, while old bark is thin, gray, and blocky. The fruit is not ornamental.

LANDSCAPE USE
Outstanding in mixed borders. Effective grouped in shrub borders or singly as an accent. Use purple-leafed cultivars as a backdrop for contrasting flowers or near plants with contrasting leaves. Try a purple cultivar with *Robinia pseudoacacia* 'Frisia', a black locust tree with bright yellow leaves. I've seen several green-leafed *Cotinus* cultivars by a driveway turnaround nearby. Their smoky pink puffs are so captivating that I forget all about the ugly driveway they frame.

ORIGIN From dry slopes and limestone-based open forests in Europe and Asia.

HARDINESS ZONES 5–8

LIGHT Full sun for best red foliage color.

SOIL Needs good drainage but adapts to most soil types, from sand to clay, and conditions; drought tolerant.

GROWING To grow *Cotinus* for flowers, prune right after blooming. If you prefer to grow purple *Cotinus* for intense leaf color and to manage its size, try pollarding it: First, let the shrub establish itself on site for a couple of years, then cut it back hard every year in early spring to the same point on the stem. With time, you'll see "fists" form, from which new shoots will emerge. You can also renew this shrub if it looks straggly by cutting one-third of the oldest and biggest stems to about 6" from the ground in late fall or early spring. New growth will occur below the cutback stems. Consistent renewal pruning encourages a more compact, mounded habit. Although generally a healthy plant, *Cotinus* is occasionally bothered by scale, rusts, leaf spot, or verticillium wilt.

CAUTION Skin rash possible upon contact.

Cotinus coggygria 'Royal Purple'

DESIGNER'S CHOICE

Cotinus coggygria 'Ancot' (Golden Spirit) A Dutch cultivar with bright yellow leaves through summer. 8' h × 6½' w.

C. coggygria 'Daydream' Floriferous with red-green new leaves and pink puffs. 8'–15' h and w.

C. coggygria 'Grace' This small tree, a hybrid between *C.* 'Velvet Cloak' and *C. obovatus,* produces 11"×14", deep pink floral puffs and young, purple-tinged leaves that turn from wine red to clear red-orange in fall. 20'–25' h and w.

C. coggygria 'Nordine' Hardiest purple cultivar with red-purple leaves in spring that turn green by late summer; showy, red fruit clusters in mid-summer; good drought tolerance. 8'–15' h and w. Zone 4.

C. coggygria 'Royal Purple' The dark red, spring leaves (to 3") mature to dark purple, holding that color in summer, except where summers are long and hot; puffs of 'Royal Purple' are fuzzy, dark rosy pink; fall color is scarlet. 8'–15' h and w.

C. coggygria 'Velvet Cloak' Blackish purple leaves with reddish purple fall color. 8'–15' h and w.

Cotinus obovatus ○

ko-TIE-nus o-bo-VAY-tus

American smoketree

Cashew or Sumac Family
(Anacardiaceae)
Deciduous large shrub or small tree
20'–30' h and w

For fabulous fall color, you can't do much better than this. The leaves, which are bluish green all summer, turn tints of red, orange, yellow, and red-purple in fall. It has attractive, gray, scaly bark. Flowers and fruit generally aren't showy.

LANDSCAPE USE
Like smokebush, smoketree may be grouped in shrub beds or borders.

ORIGIN   Limey soils of the south-central U.S.

HARDINESS ZONES   4–8

LIGHT   Smoketree is adaptable but grows best in full sun.

SOIL   Well-drained, limey to slightly acid soils.

GROWING   Smoketree is generally healthy, although it's sometimes given to wilt, rust, and leaf spot.

Cotinus obovatus

COTONEASTER

Cotoneaster apiculatus 🔺

ko-TOH-nee-as-ter a-pik-u-LA-tus

Cranberry cotoneaster

Rose Family (Rosaceae)
Deciduous shrub
2'–3' h x 3'–6' w

A dense, mounded plant with plenty of interest from pink, June blooms; big, red, cranberrylike fruits in August and September that may last through winter; and glossy, dark green leaves that turn bronzy red in fall.

LANDSCAPE USE
Useful medium-sized groundcover for erosion control on slopes. Congested branches may collect windblown debris and fallen leaves. Spread mulch around the shrub, since it won't smother weeds and the crowded branches make it hard to weed around it.

ORIGIN   China

HARDINESS ZONES   5–7

LIGHT   Full sun.

SOIL   See All About *Cotoneaster*. Somewhat salt tolerant.

GROWING   If necessary renew by hard pruning in early spring before bud break.

Cotoneaster dammeri 🔺

ko-TOH-nee-as-ter DAM-mer-I

Bearberry cotoneaster

Rose Family (Rosaceae)
Semi-evergreen to evergreen shrub
18"–36" h x 6' w

This flat, fine-textured shrub has dark green, lustrous, leathery leaves and purplish bronze fall color. White, fragrant flowers, ½" wide, are present

ALL ABOUT COTONEASTER

Whether you're looking for a 6" groundcover or a 10' screen, adaptable cotoneaster may meet your needs. This versatile landscape plant is easy to cultivate and includes many species and cultivars to meet different requirements. It features a widespread form, glossy leaves, white to pinkish flowers, and red to black berries. Use cotoneasters as groundcovers, for hedging, in foundation plantings, in masses, on banks, in rock garden and raised beds, or as a facer in front of tall leggy shrubs, depending upon species. Grow cotoneasters in full sun to partial shade, in rich, moist, well-drained, friable soils. However, they tolerate infertile soils, variable pH, drought, wind, and salt by species.

They are easiest to establish when transplanted from containers. Prune any time of year or see individual species for ideal timing. Redoing a bed, I recently pulled out two cotoneasters, no digging involved, and was amazed by the relative puniness of the root system

Cotoneaster species

compared with the size of the plants. This species may be troubled by canker, leaf spots, fireblight, scales, spider mites, or cotoneaster webworm. In general, it is not troubled by deer.

Cotoneaster dammeri

in spring; fruits turn red in late summer.

LANDSCAPE USE
Low, fast-growing groundcover. Tolerates windy sites.

ORIGIN   China

HARDINESS ZONES   5–7

LIGHT   Full sun for best fruiting.

SOIL   See All About *Cotoneaster*.

GROWING   Needs little pruning except for cutting back unruly shoots after blooming.

DESIGNER'S CHOICE
Cotoneaster dammeri 'Coral Beauty' (syn. 'Royal Beauty', 'Pink Beauty') Glossy green leaves; profuse fruiting, 2' h × 6' w.

C. 'Lowfast'   Fast-growing, hardy groundcover with profuse, shiny red berries. 12" h × 6'–10' w

C. × *suecicus* 'Skogholm'   White flowers, ¼" red berries, and reddish purple fall color make this an excellent fast-growing groundcover for difficult sites; less fruit than 'Coral Beauty'. 1'–3' h × 6'–8' w.

Cotoneaster divaricatus ☂

ko-TOH-nee-as-ter di-vay-ri-KA-tus

Spreading cotoneaster

Rose Family (Rosaceae)
Deciduous
5'–7' h × 6'–8' w

Shiny green, deciduous leaves on upright, arching branches turn radiant red and yellow in fall, lasting for a month or more. Clusters of small, white flowers in midsummer give way to bright, red, early fall berries that persist at least through November.

LANDSCAPE USE
Mixed border, low screen, tight hedge, or high foundation planting. Wind and salt tolerant.

ORIGIN   China

HARDINESS ZONES   (4) 5–7

LIGHT   Full sun.

SOIL   See All About *Cotoneaster*.

GROWING   To maintain a graceful shape, cut back selected branches to the base instead of shearing. For a hedge, prune stems after blooming back to dead flowers or forming fruit clusters (see *C. apiculatus* issues).

Cotoneaster horizontalis ☂

ko-TOH-nee-as-ter ho-ri-zon-TA-lis

Rockspray, Rock cotoneaster

Rose Family (Rosaceae)
Deciduous groundcover
2'–3' h × 5'–8' w

This slow- to medium-growing groundcover produces layers of horizontal, spreading, slightly arched branches with branchlets in a distinct herringbone pattern. Tiny, shiny green, deciduous leaves turn red-orange-purple in fall with persistent red fruits appearing in September.

LANDSCAPE USE
To show off the decorative branch pattern, train the branches to grow on or over a wall, or try it on a slope above a path so the branching is visible. Wind tolerant.

ORIGIN   China

HARDINESS ZONES   5–7

LIGHT   Full sun for best fruiting.

SOIL   See All About *Cotoneaster*. Also tolerates dry, salty, alkaline soils.

GROWING   If necessary, prune hard to renew in early spring before bud break.

DESIGNER'S CHOICE
Cotoneaster atropurpureus 'Variegatus' (syn. *C. horizontalis* 'Variegatus') Slow-growing accent plant with white-edge leaves that turn pinky red in fall; persistent red berries. 2'–3' h × 5'–8' w.

Cotoneaster horizontalis

Cotoneaster lucidus ○ › ○

ko-TOH-nee-as-ter LU-si-dus

Hedge cotoneaster

Rose Family (Rosaceae)
Deciduous shrub
6'–10' h and w

If you'd like to block the sight of your neighbor's pool from your patio, drought-tolerant hedge cotoneaster can do the job. Grow it for its glossy, dark green, 2" leaves during the growing season, and red fall color and purplish black berries that persist into winter.

LANDSCAPE USE
You can use this tall, screening shrub as an informal, unclipped hedge or as a sheared, formal hedge. Tolerates wind and salt.

ORIGIN   Siberia

HARDINESS ZONES   4–7

LIGHT   Full sun for best fruiting.

SOIL   See All About *Cotoneaster*.

GROWING   Cut back hard to renew when needed.

Cotoneaster lucidus

Cotoneaster multiflorus ○

ko-TOH-nee-as-ter mul-tee-FLO-rus

Many-flowered cotoneaster

Rose Family (Rosaceae)
Deciduous shrub
8'–12' h and w

Grow this big, bluish green shrub for its refined, bowlike branching; regular rounded shape; and showy clusters of white spring flowers. Bright red, berrylike pomes can also be decorative when fruit-set is heavy.

LANDSCAPE USE
Perfect for a large informal boundary or privacy hedge on a big lot. Or, plant one in a mixed border, where the spring blooms stand out; by summer, the dark foliage will set off cheery foreground perennials.

ORIGIN   Western China

HARDINESS ZONES   4–7

LIGHT   Full sun.

SOIL   Moist, well-drained; tolerates alkaline soils.

GROWING   See All About *Cotoneaster*. Less beset by pests and diseases than other species.

Cotoneaster nanshan ☙

(syn. *C. adpressus* var. *praecox*)

ko-TOH-nee-as-ter NAN-shan

Early cotoneaster

Rose Family (Rosaceae)
Deciduous shrub
2'–3' h x 6' w

This early, creeping cotoneaster's arched branches root where they touch the ground. The mounded, fine-textured, spreading plant is vigorous with shiny, deep green leaves and small, pinkish blooms followed by large, red berries. Very similar to *C. apiculatus,* but with waxy leaves and slightly larger berries.

LANDSCAPE USE
Makes an excellent hardy groundcover or foundation plant.

ORIGIN   Western China

HARDINESS ZONES   4–8

LIGHT   Full sun for best fruiting.

SOIL   See All About *Cotoneaster*.

GROWING   Prune back hard when needed in very early spring.

Cotoneaster salicifolius 'Repens' (syn. *C. salicifolius* 'Repandens') ☙

ko-TOH-nee-as-ter sa-li-si-FO-li-us

Spreading willow-leaf cotoneaster

Rose Family (Rosaceae)
Semi-evergreen to evergreen shrub
2' h x 6'–8' w

The narrow leaves of 'Repens' are shiny and dark green, making a handsome contrast for white flower clusters in summer. They are followed by ornamental, shiny, red fruits that may last through winter.

LANDSCAPE USE
The arching branches give this groundcover shrub a weeping effect,

Cotoneaster salicifolius 'Repens'

particularly when it grows over low walls and banks. Looks best when used in masses. Tolerates wind.

ORIGIN   China

HARDINESS ZONES   6–8

LIGHT   Full sun to partial shade.

SOIL   See All About *Cotoneaster.*

GROWING   Prune stray shoots when necessary after flowering.

DESIGNER'S CHOICE

Cotoneaster salicifolius 'Scarlet Leader' Slightly taller and wider than the species; disease-free foliage is purplish in winter; fast growing. 2'–3' h × 8'–10' w.

CRATAEGUS

Crataegus crus-galli var. inermis ○

kra-TEE-gus kruz-GAL-li in-ER-miss

Thornless cockspur hawthorn

Rose Family (Rosaceae)
Deciduous small flowering tree
15'–20' h and w

This charming but sturdy ornamental tree has many advantages: dark green, glossy, deciduous leaves that turn orange-red in fall; white, 3" flower clusters in spring followed by deep red, persistent, ½" fruits; and an attractive, rounded shape. The variety *inermis* is recommended because it is thornless; other species have sharp 2" thorns that are unsuitable for home landscapes because they can hurt you. The cultivar 'Cruzam' (Crusader) may be the same plant.

LANDSCAPE USE

A source of food and cover for wildlife; use for screening or at the back of a border.

ORIGIN   Quebec to the eastern and midwestern U.S.

HARDINESS ZONES   4–7

LIGHT   Full sun.

SOIL   Moist soil; tolerates drought once established; varying pH.

ALL ABOUT CRATAEGUS

Hawthorns include deciduous to semi-evergreen trees and shrubs. I have a love-hate relationship with hawthorn because it can look gorgeous or very, very bad. At its best, hawthorn attracts wildlife, and is suitable for barrier hedging, hedgerows, and specimens in coastal or exposed gardens. I adore Winter King hawthorn in the home landscape. Everything about it pleases me, from bark to leaves, flowers, fruits, and non-lethal thorns. Other species may also have pretty blooms and attract wildlife with their fruits, but bark may be discolored and leaves can look nasty, brown, or skeletonized by midsummer. Most species are prone to apple scab, a fungus that produces leaf spotting, which leads to defoliation and eventually to weakening the tree; fireblight, a potentially lethal bacterial disease of the Rose Family, spread by rain, wind, insects, and dirty pruning tools; and cedar-apple and cedar-hawthorn rusts, diseases where rust fungi split their time between hawthorn and juniper or eastern red cedar. Avoid planting hawthorns near junipers or red cedars, since that aggravates the situation. To deter rust fungi, you'd have to keep them at least 200 yards apart. That's impractical, because even if you have no junipers, your neighbor will. Washington and cockspur hawthorn are a bit resistant to cedar apple rust but still susceptible, while Winter King hawthorn is notable for its resistance to both rusts and fire blight.

Crataegus viridis

GROWING   It tolerates drought and urban pollution, but like many Rose Family members, it is susceptible to all sorts of pests and diseases, including blights, rusts, leaf spots, aphids, borers, leaf blotch miner, and cedar hawthorn rust, which damages the stems, fruits, and foliage.

Crataegus laevigata 'Crimson Cloud' ○

kra-TEE-gus le-vi-GAH-ta

'Crimson Cloud' English hawthorn

Rose Family (Rosaceae)
Deciduous small flowering tree
15'–20' h x 10'–20' w

Crimson Cloud's three to five, fine-textured, lobed, glossy green leaves make the perfect backdrop for its domed clusters of bright red, single flowers, each marked with a white star in the middle. In September and October, ½-inch, bright red fruits follow the mid-May blooms. Crimson Cloud is thornless with an upright, oval habit and casts light shade. This cultivar is somewhat resistant to leaf spot and blight.

LANDSCAPE USE

As a specimen or massed for screening or at the back of a shrub or mixed border.

ORIGIN   Europe and North Africa.

HARDINESS ZONES   4–7 (8)

LIGHT   Full sun to partial shade.

SOIL   Most well-drained soils.

GROWING   Tolerates some drought, urban pollution, poor drainage, and compacted soils. Resists the leaf spot diseases that beset double-flowered 'Paul's Scarlet', another popular cultivar.

Crataegus phaenopyrum O

kra-TEE-gus fay-no-PIE-rum

Washington hawthorn

Rose Family (Rosaceae)
Deciduous small flowering tree or multi-stemmed shrub
25'–30' h x 20'–25' w

On the one hand, Washington hawthorn is a four-season tree, featuring an oval crown, white flowers in spring, bright red fruits, burgundy autumn leaves, and brownish-gray peeling bark that exposes the orangey bark below. On the other hand, the flowers smell bad, and the tree is prone to recurring bouts of rust, including cedar hawthorn rust, and storm damage because of its skinny crotch angles.

LANDSCAPE USE
Because it tolerates salt and urban pollution, you can use it by the street. You can also plant it singly as a garden accent or in a border or cultivate it in groups as part of an informal hedge.

ORIGIN   U.S. South and Midwest.

HARDINESS ZONES   4–8

LIGHT   See *Crataegus laevigata* 'Crimson Cloud'.

SOIL   See *Crataegus laevigata* 'Crimson Cloud'.

GROWING   It grows better in cooler climates than in the South. Thorns up to 3" long on low branches may cause harm. To avoid injury, plant Princeton Sentry, a nearly thornless 30' h × 20' w cultivar.

Crataegus viridis 'Winter King' ▽ › O ✳

kra-TEE-gus VEE-ri-dis

'Winter King' green hawthorn

Rose Family (Rosaceae)
Deciduous small flowering tree
15'–25' h x 20'–30' w

As far as hawthorns go, this is one of the healthiest of the bunch, with a medium growth rate and a vase-shaped to rounded form. Its compact size, attractive shape, and constant four-season interest make this tree a sure bet for the home landscape.

In mid-May, it bears 2"-wide clusters of white, slightly smelly, ¾" flowers set against healthy, deep green leaves. The 2", green leaves are a glossy, deep green turning to chartreuse or a red-tinted yellow in fall. Peeling bark on the trunk and mature branches provide year-round interest; the brownish gray bark flakes off revealing the orange-brown bark underneath. The species name, *viridis,* is Latin for *green,* referring to the grayish green young branches. Young trees may have some thorns on inner branches of lower canopy. Mature trees are thornless. Clusters of large, shiny, red fruits up to ½" across persist into winter.

Crataegus viridis 'Winter King'

LANDSCAPE USE
Grouped by a wall and underplanted with low evergreens; in beds, borders, foundation plantings; a focal point, a small ornamental lawn tree near the house.

ORIGIN   U.S. South and Midwest.

HARDINESS ZONES   4–7

LIGHT   Full sun.

SOIL   An easy tree that prefers moist, well-drained loam; is pH adaptable but tolerates heat, drought, urban pollution, and compacted and infertile soils.

GROWING   When possible, transplant in spring. Absence of huge thorns makes tree easy to prune. Leaves are healthy and resistant to rust and scab, though rust may occur occasionally on young fruits. Birds and squirrels consume fruits in late winter.

CRYPTOMERIA

Cryptomeria japonica △ ✳

krip-toh-MAY-ree-a ja-PAH-ni-ka

Japanese cedar

Redwood or Bald Cypress Family (Taxodiaceae)
Evergreen conifer
50'–60' h x 20'–30' w

Grow this handsome, mid-sized evergreen conifer to add structure to your garden. It grows at a moderate pace, becoming a graceful, narrow, upright tree with a conical form, medium texture, and green to blue-green leaves. It has evergreen, awl-shaped, dark green to blue-green, shiny leaves set in spirals; foliage is bronzy in winter. The ornamental bark is thin and orange-brown, shredding in fine vertical strips. It has non-ornamental, light-green female and light-brown male flowers in early spring. Fruits are 1", red-brown, spiky cones.

Cryptomeria japonica 'Yoshino'

LANDSCAPE USE
Large-scale screening, specimen, borders, or groups where you can appreciate its uniformity of shape.

ORIGIN Moist mountainsides in Japan and China.

HARDINESS ZONES 6–8

LIGHT Full sun.

SOIL Deep, moist, fertile, light, acid soils rich in organic matter.

GROWING Needs a sheltered site that offers protection from harsh winds and other extremes of weather. If tree grows too big for its site, cut it back to 3', and it will resprout. Unprotected trees are subject to winter damage.

DESIGNER'S CHOICE
Cryptomeria japonica 'Yoshino' Fast growing with blue-green leaves; purplish bronze winter leaf color. 50'–60' h × 20'–30' w.

CUNNINGHAMI

Cunninghamia lanceolata △
kun-ning-HAM-ee-a lan-see-o-LA-ta
China fir

Redwood or Bald Cypress Family (Taxodiaceae)
Medium- to large-sized tree
30'–75' h × 10'–30' w

If you live in a warm climate, you can cultivate this single-trunk or multi-stemmed evergreen conifer for its interesting habit; stiff, linear leaves up to 3" long; and ornamental, grayish bark, which peels away to expose contrasting, reddish inner bark. Although the tree grows to 75', the pace is fairly slow. Trees are conical when young but open up with age. Dead needles stay on trees for years, which may give older China firs a scruffy look.

Cunninghamia lanceolata

LANDSCAPE USE
To protect it from wind damage, grow it in a border amidst or in front of other trees.

ORIGIN China

HARDINESS ZONES 7–9

LIGHT Sun to partial shade.

SOIL Prefers moist, well-drained soils, but tolerates heavy soils. Adapts to damp clay soils.

GROWING Prefers growing in moist regions with protection from harsh winds.

DESIGNER'S CHOICE
Cunninghamia lanceolata 'Glauca' Blue foliage, a wide upright habit; slow to medium growth rate; hardier than the species. 40–60' h × 20–30' w.

× CUPRESSOCYPARIS

× *Cupressocyparis leylandii* 0
ku-pres-so-si-PAH-ris lay-LAHN-dee-l
Leyland cypress

Redwood or Cypress Family (Cupressaceae)
Large evergreen conifer
50'–70' h × 12'–15' w

Fine-textured Leyland cypress grows 3' or more a year, making it an excellent choice for quick privacy. This speed, however, can be a drawback for small residential landscapes, which are quickly overwhelmed unless the tree is regularly pruned. The tree's narrow, conical to columnar habit suits it for traditional hedging. The downside is Leyland cypress's susceptibility to insects and diseases, which can weaken, disfigure, or kill it. It boasts flat, feathery sprays of green to blue-green scaly leaves and attractive, red-brown, scaly bark, but neither the flowers nor the fruit is ornamental. This plant is a rare hybrid between different genera (*Cupressus* and *Chamaecyparis*).

x Cupressocyparis leylandii

LANDSCAPE USE
Because it grows so quickly, it makes a good privacy hedge (trimmed or untrimmed) or to screen out ugly views; may also be used as a specimen. Grown a lot in the Southeast, where it's also produced as a Christmas tree.

ORIGIN   Garden origin

HARDINESS ZONES   6–10

LIGHT   Full sun to partial shade.

SOIL   Moist, light, rich, well-drained soils.

GROWING   For a pruned hedge, set plants out with 3' between them. Grow leaders until about 1' past the desired hedge height, then trim the tree tops to 6" below that height. Prune in July each year. It is easy to grow and tolerates salt spray. It has a relatively short lifespan (10–20 years), however, and is susceptible to many insects and diseases including bagworms, canker, spider mites on dry sites, and root rot on wet soils.

DESIGNER'S CHOICE
× *Cupressocyparis leylandii* 'Naylor's Blue' Blue-green leaves; more open habit and slower growing than species. 30'–50' h × 10'–15' w.

CYRILLA

Cyrilla racemiflora ○

si-RIL-la ra-si-mi-FLO-ra

Leatherwood, Swamp titi (TIE-tie)

Cyrilla Family (Cyrillaceae)
Deciduous, semi-evergreen, or evergreen shrub or small tree
10'–15' h and w

Cyrilla, a rounded, spreading tree, has multi-season interest. In the South, it produces glossy, narrow, deep green leaves that are evergreen; in the North, the leaves are deciduous, changing to scarlet in fall before dropping to expose the low, crooked trunk and twisted stems that give it winter character. Unusual, fragrant, white flower clusters appear May through July (depending upon the location) near twig tips below the current year's leafy growth. The tree attracts wildlife, including browsing deer and birds and small mammals searching for cover.

LANDSCAPE USE
Small garden specimen; outstanding grouped or massed in sun; mixed borders; wet woodland gardens.

ORIGIN   Southeastern U.S. swamps.

HARDINESS ZONES   (6) 7–10

LIGHT   Adapts to both sun and shade if soil conditions are right.

SOIL   Moist, acid soil high in organic matter.

Cyrilla racemiflora

GROWING   Can grow in wet, poorly drained soils; if desired, limb up and cut back suckers for a multi-stemmed small tree. Cyrilla is pretty but may be hard to find.

CYTISUS

Cytisus scoparius ○ ✳

SIT-i-sus sko-PAH-ree-us

Scotch broom, Common broom

Pea Family (Fabaceae)
Deciduous flowering shrub
5'–10' h × 5'–6' w

The disadvantages of this thicket-forming, rounded species outweigh its advantages as a garden plant. Grown as a four-season ornamental for its arched, upright green stems and showy, fragrant spring blooms that look like yellow pea flowers, Scotch broom produces seed that is viable up to 60 years. Seed spreads easily by wind, creatures, vehicles, and moving water. Instead of tempting brooms like soft yellow 'Moonlight', pink-flowered 'Pink Beauty', and 'Nova Scotia', a yellow-bloomer hardy to Zone 5, substitute a similarly carefree but less invasive shrub for poor, dry locations. Flowering quince, bayberry, smoketree, and gray dogwood are possibilities, or contact your Cooperative Extension for a shrub specific to your locale.

LANDSCAPE USE
Dry gardens and other difficult sites where other plants do not easily grow.

ORIGIN   Well-drained scrubland or heaths of Western Europe and the British Isles.

HARDINESS ZONES   (5) 6–8

LIGHT   Full sun.

SOIL   Well-drained soil; pH adaptable.

GROWING   Drought-tolerant. If you must grow this plant, cut it back as soon as flowers start to fade to avoid seed setting and scattering.

CAUTION Toxic to eat. Invasive tendency, particularly on dry, disturbed spots in much of the U.S. and parts of southern Canada, especially Nova Scotia, Prince Edward Island, and British Columbia and the nearby islands.

DAPHNE

Daphne × burkwoodii 'Carol Mackie' ○ › ◠

DAF-nee burk-WOOD-ee-i

'Carol Mackie' daphne

Thyme Family (Thymelaeaceae)
Semi-evergreen shrub
2'–3' h × 3'–4' w

Gardeners adore this rounded shrub for its intensely fragrant spring flowers, bright red berries, and neatly variegated leaves that brighten partly shaded spots. It forms a dense, twiggy mound that is wider than tall. The semi-evergreen, 1½", lancelike leaves have dark green centers banded by creamy edges. Clusters of light pink, heavily perfumed flowers in mid-spring sometimes rebloom in fall. 'Carol Mackie' daphne bears ornamental, red berries about ⅓" in diameter. The bark is not showy.

LANDSCAPE USE
Place 'Carol Mackie' daphne near doors, patios, or under windows to enjoy its spring scent. It's an attractive addition to entry gardens and shrub borders. Grow it in a lightly shaded woodland garden with delicate maidenhair ferns and astilbe or under the canopy of a lacy-leafed Japanese maple.

ORIGIN Garden origin, being a cross between *D. caucasica* and *D. cneorum*.

HARDINESS ZONES 4–7

LIGHT Full sun to partial shade.

SOIL A sunny spot in cool, dry, or very well-drained, somewhat fertile, alkaline soils.

Daphne x burkwoodii 'Carol Mackie'

Daphne odora 'Aureomarginata'

GROWING Needs perfect drainage, since too much moisture can be fatal. When absolutely necessary, prune 'Carol Mackie' daphne in late fall to early spring by cutting about one-third of the oldest, biggest stems to the ground to encourage new growth and a fuller appearance; otherwise, don't mess with or move this shrub. It has a short garden lifespan and may suddenly die. Twig blight, crown rot, and leaf spot are disease possibilities. It is hard to transplant.

CAUTION Do not eat this plant: Both berries and leaves are poisonous and potentially fatal. Leaf contact may irritate skin.

DESIGNER'S CHOICE

Daphne × burkwoodii 'Brimoon' ('Brigg's Moonlight') The opposite of 'Carol Mackie' with creamy yellow leaf centers and green margins. Grow in light shade. Less vigorous than species. 2'–3' h × 3'–4' w.

D. × burkwoodii 'Somerset' Strong grower with green foliage and pink flowers. 2'–3' h × 4'–5' w.

D. cneorum (rose daphne) A slow-growing evergreen groundcover with clusters of ½", rose-pink, perfumed flowers in spring. 'Alba' has

white flowers on a plant about 3" high. 'Eximia' has purplish red buds and bigger blooms and leaves. 'Ruby Glow' has strongly scented, dark rosy blooms. 1' h × 2' w or more.

D. mezereum (February daphne) This deciduous woodland shrub produces pinky-purple flowers on bare, old wood in late winter to early spring. Scarlet berries follow after the shrub has leafed out. Var. *album* has white flowers with yellow berries. With age, the shrub may appear leggy and rigid, so it's best grown in a border with other plants that can cover its bare base. 4' h × 3' w.

D. odora (fragrant daphne) This broad-leafed evergreen bears clusters of fragrant, pinky-purple, 1" flowers for several weeks in late winter. It's easy to transplant and adaptable to different kinds of soil. Grow in partial shade near doors, windows, patios, or decks where you can appreciate its fragrance and evergreen foliage. *D. f.* 'Alba' has white flowers. *D.* 'Aureomarginata' has yellow leaf edges and is hardier than the species. 3'–4' h and w. Zones 7–9.

DAVIDIA

Davidia involucrata △ › ○

da-VID-ee-a in-voh-lu-KRA-ta

Dove tree, Ghost tree, Handkerchief tree

Dogwood Family (Cornaceae)
Deciduous tree
20'–50' h x 20'–30' w

The mysterious common names for this tree evoke its blossom. Actually, the flower, a ¾" round head with visible, purple pollen stalks (anthers), looks insignificant on its own, but Nature gives this modest head a sure-fire way to focus the attention of pollinators: Two uneven white bracts, the larger measuring up to 8" long, surround it. During its 2-week spring bloom period, the tree looks like a flock of doves has nested in its branches, thus creating a ghostly presence in the landscape. In addition to flowers, this tree, which may be challenging to find at your local nursery, also has decorative peeling bark for year-round interest.

The 6" × 4½" leaves are heart shaped, bright green on top, and softly hairy underneath; the tree holds its foliage until hard frost;

Davidia involucrata

it has no significant fall color. The ornamental bark is orangey brown with vertical flaking. The striking flowers typically occur every other year, and you'll have to wait until the tree is roughly 10 years old for blooming to begin. The green fruits are 1" rounds, maturing in fall to reddish brown.

LANDSCAPE USE
Focal point or landscape specimen. I've seen it well planted along a quiet, shady, residential street in Swarthmore, Pennsylvania, where homeowners, along with the neighbors, can enjoy its beauty.

ORIGIN Moist Chinese mountain forests.

HARDINESS ZONES 6–8

LIGHT Full sun to partial shade. If you plant it in full sun, make sure to keep the soil moist at all times.

SOIL Moist, well-drained, acid to alkaline soils, high in organic matter.

GROWING Shape during winter dormancy. It's crucial to maintain soil moisture, so water dove tree during periods of drought. Generally free of pests and diseases. Best pruned young for a branchless trunk up to the point where you can enjoy the blooms from below.

DESIGNER'S CHOICE
Davidia involucrata var. *vilmoriniana* Smooth leaf bottoms. 20'–50' h × 20'–30' w. Zone 5.

DEUTZIA

Deutzia gracilis 'Nikko' ○ › ☘

DOOT-zee-a GRA-si-lis

'Nikko' slender deutzia

Hydrangea Family (Hydrangeaceae)
Deciduous shrub
2' h x 5' w

Many gardens with some sunshine and average garden soil can benefit from 'Nikko' deutzia. A selection by the U.S. National Arboretum, this adaptable shrub has 2 main seasons of interest. In spring, clusters of white flowers envelop the stems, and in fall, the foliage turns deep purplish red. Throughout summer, the shrub's relatively short branches are covered with lance-shaped leaves. Unlike larger deutzias, which look leggy over time, the stems are slim and slightly arched, giving the shrub a refined appearance.

The deciduous leaves are opposite, simple, and lancelike with serrated edges. Deep green during the growing season, they turn dark burgundy in fall. The bark is grayish brown with some peeling on old branches. Copious, elongated clusters of white, 5-petaled flowers, ¼" wide, bloom for about 2 weeks in mid-spring just after the leaves unfurl. Deutzia blooms on last season's growth. Flowers are lightly fragrant. Fruits are plain, brown capsules.

LANDSCAPE USE
Excellent plant for limited space, small gardens, and containers; handsome slow-growing groundcover of medium height. Outstanding little shrub for the front of mixed borders and perennial gardens, where it makes an attractive, deep green backdrop for short flowers.

ORIGIN Japan

HARDINESS ZONES 5–8

LIGHT Best flowering in full sun with plenty of water but tolerates partial shade. In the South, shade deutzia from the heat of the day.

SOIL Average garden soil is fine for deutzia, which adapts to may soil types and a wide range of pH.

GROWING This low-maintenance shrub flowers on old wood, so if you must prune it, do so right after flowering to preserve the next season's blooms.

DESIGNER'S CHOICE
Deutzia gracilis 'Duncan' (Chardonnay Pearls) Lime-hued foliage keeps the plant showy after the brief flowering

Deutzia x *hybrida* 'Magicien'

season. Buds look like pearls. 20"–
36" h × 36" w or more.

D. × *hybrida* 'Magicien' Big, pink
blooms with petals edged in white.
6'–8' h and w.

D. × *hybrida* 'Perle Rose' The cultivar
name means *pink pearl* in French and
refers to the buds, which look little
purple pearls. It bears rosy pink-and-
white flowers. 5'–6' h and w.

D. × *lemoinei* (Lemoine deutzia)
Profuse showy clusters of small
white flowers in late spring. 5'–8' h
and w. Zones (4) 5–8.

D. × 'Pink Minor' Dwarf with light
pink blooms. 2'–2½' h and w.

D. × *rosea* 'Carminea' Spring-
blooming, compact shrub with a
dense mound of arched, flexible
stems. 3'–4' h and w. Zones 4–8.

D. × *scabra* (fuzzy deutzia) Lanky,
arching shrub with long, scented,
snowy white to pale pink bloom
clusters in very late spring. 7'–10' h
× 4'–7' w.

DIERVILLA

Diervilla sessilifolia ⚘ ✳

deer-VIL-la ses-si-li-FOH-lee-a

Southern bush honeysuckle

Honeysuckle Family (Caprifoliaceae)
Deciduous shrub
4' h × 5' w

Although it may not be easy to find
southern bush honeysuckle at your
local nursery, it's worth discovering
for its fragrant, clustered, tubular,
yellow flowers, as well as for its
cream-striped, reddish-brown bark.
This rounded, deciduous shrub
spreads by suckers and has a medium
rate of growth. Neat and generally
healthy, it tolerates the difficult
situation of alkaline, dry shade.

Dark green, lance-shaped leaves
up to 6" long and 1"–3" wide have
serrated edges and are arranged in
an opposite pattern on the stems.
New growth is bronze, but fall color
is unreliable. Handsome, reddish
brown bark marked with creamy
vertical stripes covers the main
stems. Southern bush honeysuckle
bears fragrant, tubular, yellow flowers
in 2"–3" long clusters June through
August on new wood, depending
upon where you live. Fruits are
insignificant brown capsules.

LANDSCAPE USE

Site southern bush honeysuckle in
front of taller shrubs and small trees
in shrub borders and naturalized in
wild or woodland gardens. It can
grow in containers, harmonizing
with shrimp-, apricot-, and orange-
tinted flowers. Better for informal
landscapes where it will not need
much pruning.

ORIGIN Mountainsides and moist banks
of southeastern U.S.

HARDINESS ZONES 4–8

LIGHT Full sun to shade, although it
flowers best in full sun.

SOIL Tolerates most conditions, including
poor dry soils and cold windy sites but
prefers moist well-drained soil.

GROWING You can prune this easy
shrub, which flowers on new wood, in
early spring. Dig out suckers to control
the spread.

DESIGNER'S CHOICE

Diervilla lonicera 'Copper' (northern,
or dwarf, bush honeysuckle) Named
for its coppery new growth, this low,
mounded shrub produces yellow
flowers in midsummer and tolerates dry soils and full sun to partial
shade. The gray to brown bark is
peeling when mature. 2'–3' h and w.
Zones 3–7.

D. sessilifolia 'Butterfly' Erect clusters
of buttery blooms with bright green
leaves and a neatly branched habit.
Tolerates dry shade. New leaves are
bronze and fall color is purple to
wine red. 3'–5' h and w.

Diervilla lonicera

DIOSPYROS

Diospyros virginiana ○

di-OS-pi-ros vir-gin-ee-AY-na

Persimmon

Persimmon or Ebony Family
(Ebenaceae)
Deciduous tree
30'–50' h x 20'–35' w

Female persimmon trees produce edible, 1"–2" fruits in fall. Birds come for the fruit (and spread the seed), bees prefer the spring flowers, and butterflies use the tree as a larval plant. Grow as a landscape tree for its attractive rounded to oval crown; oblong, glossy leaves up to 5½" long with red fall color; and sweet yellowish orange round fruits. Trees bear persimmons as early as 10 years old, producing heavy seed crops in alternate years with lighter crops appearing in between. 'Early Golden', 'John Rick', and 'Miller' are productive cultivars with tasty fruit; 'Meader' is perhaps the hardiest.

LANDSCAPE USE
Lawn specimen, groups.

ORIGIN   Fields and woods of eastern U.S.

HARDINESS ZONES   5–9

LIGHT   Shade tolerant but prefers full sun.

SOIL   Prefers rich, deep, well-drained loam.

GROWING   Big trees are hard to transplant because of taproots.

Diospyros virginiana

Disanthus cercidifolius

DISANTHUS

Disanthus cercidifolius ○

di-SAN-thus ser-si-di-FOH-lee-us

Disanthus

Witch Hazel Family
(Hamamelidaceae)
Deciduous shrub
6'–10' h x 8'–10' w

Grow this little-known but lovely shrub for its outstanding fall color, which changes from burgundy and orange to luminous red as the season progresses; color is best in partial to full shade. The species name, *cercidifolius,* refers to the deciduous foliage, which resembles that of *Cercis* (eastern redbud). In summer, the wide, heart-shaped, 2"–4½" leaves are blue-green. Deep purple flowers appear in October but are not showy. Although large, disanthus looks delicate because of its fine twigs, slim horizontal branches, and the manner in which the leaves dangle from 1"–2" stems or petioles. A sheltered site is the key to happy disanthus — my first one died in 8 weeks from overexposure.

LANDSCAPE USE
Ideal for spacious woodland gardens and partly shaded shrub borders.

HARDINESS ZONES   5–8

LIGHT   Partial to full shade.

SOIL   Moist, acid soils high in organic matter.

GROWING   Needs wind protection and does not tolerate drought. Generally healthy and pest free.

ELEUTHEROCOCCUS

Eleutherococcus sieboldianus 'Variegatus' ⬡ ✳ (syn. *Acanthopanax sieboldianus*)

ell-oo-they-roh-KOK-kus see-bol-dee-AY-nus

Variegated five-leaf aralia

Aralia Family (Araliaceae)
Deciduous suckering shrub
4'–6' h and w

Dr. Richard L. Bitner, an instructor at Longwood Gardens, in Kennett Square, Pennsylvania, introduced me to this shrub, which I found so appealing that an 18" specimen now borders my house. I grow this thorny shrub for its cream-edged, long-stalked leaflets, which can enhance a planting of sun-loving grasses or brighten shady garden spots. The greenish-white flowers and black berries are not ornamental. The J.C. Raulston Arboretum in Raleigh, North Carolina, designated this shrub as a first-rate plant for the Southeast because it is deer proof and has no significant pests or diseases. Five-leaf aralia also tolerates both sun and shade, and moist to dry soils.

Its lovely, compound leaves are made up of 5–7, long-stalked, palmate leaflets about 1"–2" × 1"; the leaflets are a variegated bright green with irregular cream edges. The gray bark has spines below the buds. Neither the small, greenish-white flowers that bloom in late spring to early summer nor the black berries are ornamental.

LANDSCAPE USE
Thorny stems make five-leaf aralia an effective barrier between two properties; also good for hedges, groups, specimen, espalier, and difficult sites. This cultivar is less vigorous than the species.

ORIGIN   Eastern China

HARDINESS ZONES   (4) 5–8

LIGHT   Full sun to full shade.

SOIL   Tolerates most soil types and conditions, from clay to sand, from dry to moist, and from acid to alkaline pH. Also withstands drought and urban pollution.

GROWING   Though this shrub may sucker, you can shape it with occasional light pruning. Cut out dead wood in summer. Can be renewed with severe pruning.

CAUTION   Small spines below buds can scratch or pierce your skin.

DESIGNER'S CHOICE
Eleutherococcus senticosus (Siberian ginseng) Perennial used in herbal medicine to promote longevity and

Eleutherococcus sieboldianus 'Variegatus'

physical and mental performance. 2'–3' h × 2' w.

ENKIANTHUS

Enkianthus campanulatus 0 ✳
en-kee-AN-thus cam-pan-u-LAY-tus
Redvein enkianthus

Heath Family (Ericaceae)
Deciduous shrub or small tree
6'–10' h × 5'–8' w

You'll like enkianthus for its dense, hanging clusters of urnlike flowers and its rich red fall color on leaves that look whorled at the branch tips. This slow-growing, deciduous shrub, which blooms on old wood, has an interesting upright, yet tiered, form that opens toward the base as it matures.

Simple, alternate leaves, about 3" × 1", are bunched at stem ends; dark green in season, their fall color is often long lasting and outstanding in red, orange, and yellow. Fall color varies on shrubs raised from seed. Attractive, bright red young stems turn brownish with age. The ⅓"–½" flowers are held in hanging clusters near the branch tips. These cream-colored blooms have red veins and a reddish flush near the tip. Last spring, my enkianthus flowers persisted for weeks, starting out pale, then flushing deep rosy red as flowering progressed. The fruit capsules are not ornamental.

LANDSCAPE USE
Beds and borders, where you can group it with rhododendrons and azaleas, which require similar growing conditions; foundation plantings; near paths and doorways where you can see the delicate flowers.

ORIGIN   Japan

HARDINESS ZONES   5–8

Enkianthus campanulatus

Enkianthus perulatus

LIGHT   Full sun to partial shade.

SOIL   Moist, acid, well-drained soil.

GROWING   Enkianthus particularly needs moist, cool soil in the South where extreme heat and dry conditions can stress the plant, leaving it susceptible to spider mites. When necessary, cut out deadwood and trim untidy branches right after flowering to prevent removal of next year's blooms. Elsewhere it is not subject to particular pests or diseases, and it is somewhat deer resistant.

DESIGNER'S CHOICE
Enkianthus campanulatus 'Albiflorus' Unmarked, creamy white flowers on a vigorous plant. 6'–10' h × 5'–8' w.

E. campanulatus 'Red Bells' Red-veined creamy blooms with rich red tips and red to red-orange fall color. 6'–10' h × 5'–8' w.

E. campanulatus var. *sikokianus* Maroon buds, pinky-orange-veined, brick red blooms, and bright red stems in winter. 6'–10' h × 5'–8' w.

E. perulatus (white enkianthus) White pendulous flower clusters in late spring, red fall color; good, though rather rare, shrub for small land-scapes. 6' h and w. Zones 6–8.

ERICA

Erica carnea

ER-i-ka KAR-nee-a

Spring heath, Winter heath

Heath Family (Ericaceae)
Evergreen shrub
8"–15" h x 20" w or more

In the right conditions, this low, spreading shrub can add enduring color and fine texture to a garden. Spring heath forms a dense, finely textured cushion with a groundcover effect when massed. The whorled, needlelike, bright to dark evergreen leaves are up to ⅓" long; cultivars are available with lime, bronze, yellow, and light to dark green leaves. The bark is not ornamental. White, pink, purple, or red ¼" bell-like blooms are produced on one side of 1"–4"-long, terminal, leafy clusters in late winter and spring. The fruit capsules are not ornamental.

LANDSCAPE USE
Mass for groundcover; use specimens for low, spreading cushions in rock gardens along with heather (*Calluna vulgaris)* and dwarf mounded rhododendrons, such as *Rhododendron impeditum* (1' h × 2' w) or *R.* 'Scarlet Wonder Dwarf' (2' h × 3' w).

Erica carnea
'Springwood Pink'

ORIGIN   Heaths and moors of southern and central Europe.

HARDINESS ZONES   5–7

LIGHT   Full sun but tolerates some shade, especially in warmer climates.

SOIL   Prefers moist, well-drained, poor, acid soil high in organic matter but tolerates some alkalinity. In fertile garden soils, it grows loose and leggy.

GROWING   To maintain the appearance of a tight, informal cushion, prune each year after flowering by cutting back sections of leafy growth at different heights. Plants will not thrive in extremely hot sites.

DESIGNER'S CHOICE
Erica carnea 'Golden Starlet' Bright yellow leaves that turn lime in cool weather; bright white flowers from December to March; neat habit. 6" h × 16" w.

E. carnea 'King George' Blooms December to March with prolific crimson blooms on compact mound of deep green leaves. 6"–9" h × 18"–24" w.

E. carnea 'Springwood White' Vigorous groundcover with creamy buds and white blooms from October to January. 8"–10" h × 2' w.

E. carnea 'Springwood Pink' Pink flowers. 8"–10" h × 2' 2" w.

ERIOBOTRYA

Eriobotrya japonica

air-ee-oh-BOH-tree-a ja-PAH-ni-ka

Loquat, Japanese plum, Japanese medlar

Rose Family (Rosaceae)
Evergreen tree
20'–25' h and w

Loquats grow as ornamental trees as far north as the Carolinas; south of Jacksonville, Florida, and in California, the tree also produces small, sweet, yellow fruits fit for jellies and preserves. This short-trunked, rounded tree has a coarse landscape texture because of its stiff rough leaves, 10"–12" long and set in whorls at the branch ends. Leaves are shiny, dark green on top, with silvery or rusty fuzz on the bottom. In late fall, fragrant white flowers appear in clusters, followed by edible fruits in spring.

LANDSCAPE USE
Patio tree; potted on decks.

ORIGIN   China, Japan

HARDINESS ZONES   7–10

LIGHT   Full sun to partial shade.

SOIL   Well-drained soil; pH adaptable.

GROWING   Somewhat drought-tolerant once established, but regular watering boosts fruit yield. Fruiting trees attract bees and wasps. Troubled by diseases of the Rose Family, including canker, root rot, and fireblight, where humid. Shows invasive tendency in Hawaii.

EUCALYPTUS

Eucalyptus cinerea

u-ka-LIP-tus sin-a-REE-a

Argyle apple, Mealy stringy-bark, Silver dollar gum

Myrtle Family (Myrtaceae)
Broad-leaf evergreen tree
15'–40' h and w

If you want a striking, irregular, accent tree for a hot, dry garden, try fast-growing Argyle apple. Its young silvery blue leaves are round, while mature foliage is oval and light blue with pointy ends. The bark is rough, stringy, and reddish to ashy brown. If you like the smell (I don't — it makes me cough), cut some of the young aromatic stems to bring indoors to stick in wreaths and vases. For an abundance of cutting stems, prune tree to the ground (coppice) each year in early spring; it will grow into a 6', multi-stemmed shrub with round juvenile leaves that are easy to harvest.

LANDSCAPE USE

Ideal for dry, poor, salty, windy, coastal sites, windbreaks, and as a specimen. If you have a lot of property, plant a grove or two for dramatic effect.

ORIGIN Australia, on dry rocky infertile slopes.

HARDINESS ZONES (7) 8–10

LIGHT Full sun.

SOIL Well-drained soil; adaptable pH.

GROWING Thrives in hot, dry weather. Once established, Argyle apple is drought-tolerant. Although the top may not be cold hardy in Zone 7, it is root hardy and can come back from the ground. Deer-resistant.

EUONYMUS

Euonymus alatus ○ ✳

u-WAH-ni-mus a-LAY-tus

Burning bush

Bittersweet Family (Celastraceae)
Shrub or small tree
20' h and w

Burning bush is ubiquitous in foundation plantings throughout much of the United States. Valued for its fabulous, red fall color and tidy, rounded form, this slow-growing, reliable deciduous shrub can outgrow its site and multiply with neglect. Avoid it especially if you live near open fields, parks, or woodlands, since it can seed itself into these areas and overtake our native plants. Plant a different shrub with brilliant fall color, medium landscape texture, and tolerance of adverse conditions. Burning bush's appealing corky bark diminishes with age, as does its tidy habit. I saw one old burning bush that had spawned hundreds of seedlings in nearby beds and around its base.

Burning bush has opposite, simple, dark green leaves, 1"–3" long with serrated edges; the leaves are a brilliant, true red in fall for about 2 weeks. The shrub has green to brown stems with corky, protruding wings. The spring flowers are yellowish but not ornamental. Fall fruits are small, red capsules, eaten and spread by birds.

LANDSCAPE USE

Foundation plantings, planted close for boundary hedges, groups, and specimens as garden accents.

ORIGIN China and Japan.

HARDINESS ZONES 4–8 (9)

LIGHT Full sun to full shade, although fall color won't be as bright in shade.

SOIL Tolerates many soils except wet and excessively dry ones; adapts to either acid or alkaline pH.

GROWING Mulch the roots in dry areas, water during drought; survives severe pruning.

CAUTION Invasive potential in the Midwest and eastern U.S.; outcompetes native vegetation in woodlands, abandoned pastures, and scrublands. Banned from sale in some states. Good substitutes include high-bush blueberry (*Vaccinium corymbosum*) and species or cultivars of hydrangea, enkianthus, and fothergilla.

DESIGNER'S CHOICE

Euonymus alatus 'Compactus' Don't buy this overused cultivar sold at most nurseries; similar to species except in slower growth, smaller overall size and smaller wing size. 6'–8' h × 6'–10' w.

E. alatus 'Rudy Haag' If you must grow burning bush, try this almost seedless, slow-growing, densely mounded dwarf with excellent red fall color. 3' h × 3½' w. *E. a.* 'Odom' (Little Moses) is similarly small, with low fruit set.

Euonymus alatus

Euonymus fortunei ▱ ✳

u-WAH-ni-mus for-TOO-nee-I

Winter creeper, Creeping euonymus

Bittersweet Family (Celastraceae)
Evergreen shrub or clinging vine
6"–12" h × 6'–40' w

This popular, fast-growing evergreen causes big trouble in some landscapes, so think hard before planting it. A vining plant cultivated as a shrub, it tolerates heavy pruning. Grown as a woody vine, however, it can climb by aerial roots to a height of 70'. It has dark green, silver-veined evergreen leaves, 1"–3" long, and slightly warty and thin bark with trailing roots. The greenish white flowers are not ornamental. Pink to red capsules open to reveal orange-coated seeds, which are eaten and spread by birds and wild mammals. Instead of winter creeper, try native ground cover shrubs and vines, such as *Arctostaphylos uva-ursi*, *Leucothoe fontanesiana*, and *Parthenocissus quinquefolia*.

Trellised on a wall or chimney, or trained to grow up a tree trunk, winter creeper brings lush greenness to the home landscape's vertical dimension for a softening effect; it also makes a dense evergreen groundcover.

ORIGIN   China

HARDINESS ZONES   5–8

LIGHT   Full sun to full shade.

SOIL   Many soil types except wet ones; tolerates poor, acid to alkaline soils.

GROWING   Tolerates heavy pruning, which can stimulate vigorous growth of roots and stems. Susceptible to many pests and diseases, including euonymus scale, aphids, mildews, and anthracnose.

CAUTION   Invasive potential in eastern U.S., where it can outcompete native vegetation in untended areas when birds seed this plant into wild landscapes.

DESIGNER'S CHOICE

Euonymus fortunei 'Coloratus' Fast-growing groundcover with dark, shiny green leaves that turn reddish bronze in fall and winter. Horizontally grown plants flower sparsely or not at all; trellised plants make more blooms and seeds. 6"–12" h × 1'–3' w.

E. fortunei 'Emerald Gaiety' Neat and mounded with green-and-white variegated leaves tinted pink in fall and winter. 3' h × 5' w.

E. fortunei 'Interbolwi' (Blondy) Green-edged yellow foliage with yellow stems that redden in winter. Winter leaves flushed pinkish purple. 3' h and w.

E. fortunei 'Longwood' Low-spreading cultivar with small, dark leaves; good for small spaces; heat and cold tolerant. Full sun to partial shade. 6"–12" h × indefinite spread.

E. kiautschovicus 'Manhatttan' Shear this deciduous to evergreen shrub into a formal hedge or trim as a rounded specimen. 6'–8' h × 5' w.

EXOCHORDA

Exochorda 'The Bride' ○ ✳
(syn. *E.* × *macrantha* 'The Bride')

ek-so-KOR-da ma-KRAN-tha

'The Bride' pearlbush

Rose Family (Rosaceae)
Deciduous shrub
3'–4' h and w

For an easy, white-flowering shrub that blooms in spring, it's hard to beat 'The Bride' pearlbush. For the short time that it's in bloom, abundant, white flowers cover the shrub, making it look like a pure white bridal gown. The elongated clusters of pearl-like buds and bright white, 1½", single flowers look flashy for about 2½ weeks in spring, after which the shrub recedes into the background of the garden. Leaves are green with no fall color. In colder climates, grow *E. serratifolia* 'Northern Pearls'. 6'–8' h and w.

LANDSCAPE USE

'The Bride' has a compact, rounded habit and a medium landscape texture, making it suitable for facing down tall or leggy bushes in shrub or mixed borders, small yards, and simple low hedges.

***Exochorda* 'The Bride'**

ORIGIN   Hybrid origin

HARDINESS ZONES   5–8

LIGHT   Full sun to partial shade.

SOIL   Well-drained, acid soil.

GROWING   Can withstand both heat and drought. If the shrub suckers a bit and looks rangy with age, simply prune it back hard when dormant. When necessary, cut out deadwood and crossed or rubbing branches after blooming.

FAGUS

Fagus grandifolia ○ › ◠ ✳

FAY-gus gran-di-FOH-lee-a

American beech

Beech Family (Fagaceae)
Large deciduous tree
50'–80' h × 40'–70' w

When cultivated in full sun with unlimited space, this big, deciduous tree develops a short trunk and an even, rounded, spreading crown with branches that rise on top, stay level in the middle, and sweep the ground at the base. In a forest, it shoots up toward the light, developing a tall, oval crown. Trees in their native setting may produce suckers that give rise to other smaller beeches growing nearby. In winter, recognize beeches by their gorgeous, smooth, silvery bark and branches with paper-thin, translucent tan leaves catching the light.

The simple 2½"–5½"-long leaves are alternate, with featherlike, teeth-tipped veins. Medium green in summer, they turn a bronzy yellow in fall. American beech often holds its translucent tan (dead) leaves through winter. The smooth, silvery-gray bark is attractive year round; zigzag, brown twigs have distinctive light brown, pointed, cigar-shaped buds. The spring flowers are not ornamental. The tree bears edible nuts in spine-covered, triangular, woody husks in fall.

Fagus grandifolia

LANDSCAPE USE

Big shade tree for large lawns, magnificent specimen, naturalized areas.

ORIGIN   Eastern U.S.

HARDINESS ZONES   4–9

LIGHT   Full sun to partial shade.

SOIL   Moist, well-drained, and acid soil.

GROWING   Avoid compacting the soil around the tree, since beech has a widespread, shallow root system. Gorgeous on large estates but too big for most suburban lots. Better to limb up when young so thorough healing occurs. Beech is sensitive to environmental stresses such as drought, salt, and soil compaction. It may contract beech bark disease, seen as white scales on the tree bark; aphids may also be a problem.

Fagus sylvatica 0 › ◌ ✳

FAY-gus sil-VA-ti-ka

European beech

Beech Family (Fagaceae)
Large deciduous tree
50'–70' h × 35'–50' w

While the mature species makes a big, leafy, and majestic low-branched pyramid that only a Newport, Rhode Island, estate can accommodate, European beech comes in cultivars to suit gardens of any size. Our 1¼-acre lot houses my husband's beech collection, which now stands at 18 *F. sylvatica* cultivars. Many will grow too big for our property. We'll deal with that problem when it happens, since most beeches grow fast when young but slow with maturity. For the moment, we enjoy watching our beeches develop into shrubs or trees with varied fine- to medium-textured leaves and erect, twisted or weeping, broad or fastigiate, habits.

Alternate, simple, dark green, 4" × 2" leaves with undulating edges turn bronze in fall; some foliage persists through winter. The distinctive trunk has thin, smooth, light gray bark and a wide muscled and fluted base. The flowers are not ornamental; fruits are 2 triangular nuts in a spiky husk.

LANDSCAPE USE

Noble landscape tree for big lawns; wide-spreading shade tree; pruned hedges; grouped in naturalistic woodland gardens.

ORIGIN   Forests of Europe.

HARDINESS ZONES   5–7

LIGHT   Full to partial shade.

SOIL   Well-drained, acid to alkaline soils.

GROWING   Flexible-branched cultivars like 'Cuprea' lend themselves to shearing as hedges. Prune hedges each year some time between late summer and winter. Give your beeches a couple of years to become established before trimming. Do not plant too close to your house or to power lines, or you may be faced with awkward pruning.

DESIGNER'S CHOICE

Fagus sylvatica 'Aspleniifolia' (fernleaf beech) Deeply cut, fine-textured leaves with golden-brown fall color. 20'–50' h × 25'–50' w.

F. sylvatica 'Cuprea' (copper beech) Copper foliage. 50'–60' h × 40'–50' w.

Fagus sylvatica hedge

Fagus sylvatica 'Aspleniifolia'

F. sylvatica 'Dawyck' Fast growing, bright green column, great accent. 60' h × 10' w.

F. sylvatica 'Dawyck Gold' Slower growing than *S. sylvatica* 'Dawyck'; yellow foliage changes to light green, then yellow in fall; about 12' tall after a dozen years. 60' h × 10' w at maturity.

F. sylvatica 'Dawyck Purple' Dark purple leaves. 60' h × 10' w at maturity.

F. sylvatica 'Pendula' Green-leafed weeping beech with broad contorted curves. 50'–60' h × 60'–80' w.

F. sylvatica 'Purple Fountain' Narrow, purple beech with weeping limbs. 12' h × 3' w.

F. sylvatica 'Purpurea Pendula' Compact, weeping, purple cultivar fading to purplish green with mushroom-

Fagus sylvatica 'Dawyck Gold'

Fagus sylvatica 'Pendula'

shaped habit. 12' h × 10' w.

F. sylvatica 'Riversii' (Rivers purple beech) Dramatic blackish purple foliage all season when planted in full sun. 60' h and w.

F. sylvatica 'Rotundifolia' Glossy, round, dark green leaves, very slow growing, leafs out later than many beeches. Brown, fall foliage hangs on until spring. 15'–40' h × 10'–20' w.

F. sylvatica 'Tortuosa' Contorted branches on low, broad tree. 10'–15' h × 20'–30' w.

F. sylvatica 'Tricolor' Deep purplish green leaves with creamy pink to rosy pink irregular margins. Planting this in light or dappled shade keeps edges of leaves from scorching in hot sun. 40' h × 30' w.

FORSYTHIA

Forsythia
× *intermedia* ○ › ☙ ✳

for-SI-thi-a in-ter-MEE-dee-a

Forsythia

Olive Family (Oleaceae)
Deciduous flowering shrub
10' h × 14' w and more

Forsythia is a suburban landscape cliché. Grown for its bright yellow flowers, which appear before the leaves in spring, it's a fast-growing, multi-stemmed shrub that spreads by suckers into a huge, tangled mass filled with birds seeking cover. Spring is the big bang for this shrub and it delivers, unless it's been pruned into a short, after the buds have set, or a severe winter has killed the flower buds (leaf buds are hardy). In Zones 4 and 5, extreme cold can destroy flower buds before bloom. It is a stunning, deer-resistant accent in the April landscape when planted far enough away from the house so the shrub can assume its natural fountainlike form. Look for cultivars

with a neater habit or multi-season interest that suit the size of your property.

The alternate, simple, medium green leaves may turn purple in fall. The non-showy, young stems are tan with many lenticels. Yellow, 1½" flowers bloom on old stems before leaves appear. The fruit is not ornamental.

LANDSCAPE USE
Massed, grouped, or singly at a distance from the house; shrub borders. Smaller cultivars make a good unpruned, informal hedge marking a distant property line.

ORIGIN Hybrid origin

HARDINESS ZONES 5–8

LIGHT Full sun for best blooming.

SOIL Any good, well-drained garden soil. Tolerates drought and pollution once established.

GROWING Prune for looks and to reinvigorate by cutting out the oldest growth, or renew the shrub by cutting it to the ground. Best time to prune old stems is right after flowering before new buds are set. Pruning in winter or early spring sacrifices blooms, but you can force what you remove for early indoor blooms. Frequent pruning keeps it tidy, but gives it an ugly, thwarted, unnatural look.

DESIGNER'S CHOICE
Forsythia 'Arnold Dwarf' Groundcover forsythia with light yellow blooms that roots where stems touch the ground, making it great for massing on slopes. 3' h × 5' w. Zone 6.

F. × 'Courtasol' (Gold Tide) Nice, small, floriferous cultivar with brilliant yellow flowers, light green leaves, dark purplish fall color. Use as a groundcover. 2'–3' h × 4'–5' w.

F. × *intermedia* 'Fiesta' Gold flowers, cream to gold-centered green leaves, reddish stems for multi-season interest. 4'–6' h × 6'–8' w.

Forsythia x intermedia 'Fiesta'

F. × intermedia 'Princeton Gold' Prolific flowers are bright gold with orange throats; purple fall leaves. 8'–10' h × 6'–8' w.

F. × intermedia 'Spring Glory' Popular, fast-growing, old cultivar with abundant, large, light yellow blooms, early blooming. 10' h × 14' w.

F. ovata 'New Hampshire Gold' Bright gold flowers with purplish fall color. 8' h and w. Zone 3.

F. ovata 'Northern Gold' Golden flowers on upright, bud-hardy shrub. 7' h and w. Zone 3.

F. suspensa var. *sieboldii* (weeping forsythia) Yellow flowers on cascading stems that root where they touch the ground. Nice above a retaining wall; use to control erosion on banks.

F. 'Suwan Gold' Bright yellow leaves throughout the growing season. Grow in shade to partial shade. 4' h and w.

F. viridissima 'Bronxensis' A choice, slow-growing forsythia cultivar with interest from pretty, light yellow blooms (less showy than other selections) and green stems. Use for groundcover, containers, facing taller shrubs, hedging. 1' h × 3' w.

FOTHERGILLA

Fothergilla gardenii ○ › ⚘ ✳

fa-ther-GIL-la gar-DEE-nee-I

Dwarf fothergilla

Witch Hazel Family
(Hamamelidaceae)
Deciduous flowering shrub
3'–6' h x 3'–4' w

This terrific, multi-stemmed shrub produces creamy white flowers in spring and handsome leaves in summer and fall. It is fairly compact and spreading but easy to prune and control if that's your wish. What more can you ask of a hardworking landscape shrub?

The alternate, simple leaves are blue-green to dark green, changing to glowing orange, yellow, and red in fall. Depending upon the weather, fall color of the species may vary from year to year. Cultivars of *F. major* often show better fall color in warmer climates (Zones 7 and 8). Grayish brown bark and flexible stems dotted with lenticels; bark is not showy. The white, 2", faintly honey-scented bottlebrush blooms appear in spring before leaves. Fruits are not ornamental.

LANDSCAPE USE

Masses, groups, singly as an accent, shrub border, in high foundation plantings. I grow it massed under river birches, where it complements the tree's creamy pinkish, peeling bark.

ORIGIN Boggy soils in southeastern U.S.

HARDINESS ZONES 5–8

LIGHT Full sun to partial shade.

SOIL Moist, well-drained, acid soils.

GROWING You don't need to tinker with this carefree shrub. New shoots at the base keep it from looking leggy. My massed fothergilla formed a thicket that grew so tall it blocked a view of beautiful birch trunks. Last year I thinned the shrubs, cutting out tall stems, and this year they look better than ever.

DESIGNER'S CHOICE

Fothergilla gardenii 'Appalachia' Short and suckering; good, low, shrubby groundcover. 2' h × 4' w.

F. gardenii 'Blue Mist' Small and less thickly stemmed than the species. Widely sold but not my favorite plant. My neighbor planted one next to my massed species and it pales in comparison, lacking the species' great fall color. Summer color is a nice grayish blue-green. 3' h and w.

F. gardenii 'Mount Airy' Suckering cultivar with consistently outstanding red, yellow, and orange fall color and deep blue-green summer leaves. Performs well in both cold and warm climates. 6' h × 6'–8' w.

F. major Excellent, large, rounded shrub with outstanding fall color and abundant, white bottlebrush flowers in spring. 8' h × 10' w.

Fothergilla gardenii 'Mount Airy'

FRANGULA

Frangula alnus ○ ✳
(syn. Rhamnus frangula)

FRAN-gu-la ALL-nus

Glossy buckthorn, European alder, Alder buckthorn

Buckthorn Family (Rhamnaceae)
Deciduous shrub
10'–20' h x 6'–10' w

I learned about glossy buckthorn in a parking lot outside Boston before climbing a wooded drumlin for a landscape design class. The instructor pointed out an unkempt, upright, twiggy, shrub by the damp-edged lot and described its invasiveness. The shiny dark green leaves with wavy edges were attractive, and the few glossy black fruits on the plant in early fall had visual appeal. Then I looked around. Glossy buckthorn, which also grows as a small tree with an open spreading crown, flourished in the disturbed soil around the lot. Buckthorn's handsome leaves and red young fruits turn shiny black with age; flowers are inconspicuous.

Buckthorn is usually sold as tall narrow 'Columnaris' (syn. *F. alnus* 'Tallhedge') for hedging or 'Aspleniifolia' (fernleaf buckthorn) for fine landscape texture and a broad, rounded habit. 'Ron Williams' (Fine Line) combines columnar shape and ferny leaves in a 5'–7' h shrub with few fruits.

LANDSCAPE USE
Hedges, screens, transitional areas, and woodland gardens.

ORIGIN Open wet woods and meadows in Europe, W. Asia, N. Africa.

HARDINESS ZONES 2–7

LIGHT Full sun to shade.

SOIL Prefers moist, acid soil but grows under most conditions.

GROWING Sun-grown plants fruit more and may form thickets.

CAUTION Invasive tendencies in wetlands, forests, and disturbed areas of many regions of the U.S., including the Great Lakes, Mid-Atlantic, North Central, Northeast, and Southeast. For a shrubby habit and bird-attracting fruits, substitute chokeberry (*Aronia*), blueberry (*Vaccinium*), or witherod (*Viburnum nudum*) for buckthorn. For a tall, moisture-tolerant hedge, plant evergreen Atlantic white cedar (*Chamaecyparis thyoides*), or for a small deciduous tree, substitute serviceberry (*Amelanchier*).

FRANKLINIA

Franklinia alatamaha ○

frank-LI-nee-a a-la-ta-MA-ha

Franklinia

Tea Family (Theaceae)
Deciduous flowering multi-stemmed tree
10'–20' h x 15' w

History buffs and plant collectors love this small flowering tree or shrub, which botanist John Bartram found in southeastern Georgia in 1765 and named for his buddy Benjamin Franklin. Although a flood destroyed the plants at the original site, Bartram's tree flourished and is the source of franklinias sold today. We planted two franklinias when we moved to New Hampshire. We irrigated one enthusiastically and it died. We planted the other in well-drained acid garden soil of average fertility in a semi-exposed mixed border, where it still exists as a 3½' h × 2½' w multi-stemmed shrub. (Compare that to a shrubby 8-trunk 122-year-old franklinia at the Arnold Arboretum measuring 21' h × 53' h in 2005!) Last September, after 11 years, we celebrated its first blossom. The 3-inch-wide fragrant flowers have a simple allure — five, cupped, overlapping, white petals around a shaggy tuft of yellow stamens from late July to September. The glossy, dark green leaves have excellent red to orange and purple fall color.

LANDSCAPE USE
A great specimen and conversation piece in the garden. Also lovely naturalized in woodland gardens. Tucking it in a border as we did does it no justice. May be hard to find.

ORIGIN Georgia (U.S.)

HARDINESS ZONES 5–8

LIGHT Prefers partial shade but tolerates full sun and deeper shade.

SOIL Very well drained, acid soil high in

Franklinia alatamaha

organic matter. The ideal pH is 5 to 6.

GROWING Shelter from harsh winds; susceptible to phytophthora, a fungal disease, in heavy wet soils.

FRAXINUS

Fraxinus americana 'Autumn Applause' ◖

FRAK-si-nus ah-me-ri-KAN-ah

'Autumn Applause' white ash

Olive Family (Oleaceae)
Deciduous tree
40'-h x 25'-w

'Autumn Applause' has a smaller habit with an oval crown and denser branching than the species *(Fraxinus americana)* and excellent, lasting, deep-burgundy fall color. This cultivar is a clean, healthy, non-fruiting male. Choose this or one of the cultivars below and not the species to grow in the home landscape, as they will not produce abundant nuisance seedlings. By the way, because of its lightness, flexiblility, and strength, white ash is the standard wood for such sports gear as baseball bats, hockey sticks, and tennis racquets.

LANDSCAPE USE
A neat shade tree for medium to large sunny lawns.

ORIGIN The species comes from eastern North America.

HARDINESS ZONES 4–9

LIGHT Full sun.

SOIL Moist, deep, rich, well-drained soil; pH tolerant.

GROWING Tolerates salt, heat, and drought but subject to many pests and diseases including rust, anthracnose, borers, scales, ash dieback, and ash yellows.

DESIGNER'S CHOICE
Fraxinus americana 'Chicago Regal' Upright, symmetrical habit with dark green leaves that change to purple in fall, crack-resistant bark. Convenient, small size suits many residential

Fraxinus americana

landscapes. 30' h × 15' w.

F. americana 'Jeffnor' (Northern Blaze) Upright, oval form with purple fall color chosen for cold hardiness and ability to withstand winter damage and frost cracking. 50'–60' h × 25'–30' w.

Fraxinus excelsior 'Aurea' ○ ✳

FRAK-si-nus ek-SEL-see-or

Golden European ash, Yellow-twig ash

Olive Family (Oleaceae)
Deciduous tree
30' h and w

This tree is easy to grow — so easy that my husband and I planted a bareroot whip (basically, a rooted stem) 15 years ago in Delaware, dug it up, moved it in a pot to New Hampshire in December, kept it for months in a hotel room and garage, then planted it outdoors in spring. It flourished in spite of the unintentional abuse, and today it's about 20' tall with a round, symmetrical canopy and outstanding foliage, stems, and bark.

Yellow, early spring leaves turn shiny, dark green by late spring and bold yellow in autumn. Leaves are opposite and compound with 7–11 leaflets. The handsome bark is a yellow-tinged gray-brown; young stems are gleaming yellow with contrasting big, black, hairy buds. Neither the flowers nor the samaras are ornamental.

LANDSCAPE USE
Specimen, border, or group.

ORIGIN Moist banks and forests of Europe.

HARDINESS ZONES 5–7

LIGHT Full sun for best color.

SOIL Moist, well-drained soil but tolerates acid to alkaline soil and fertile to poor conditions.

GROWING Some ashes need their crowns thinned to prevent imbalance and breakage. Leaf spot, powdery mildew, and scales may be problems of stressed trees, but our tree remains healthy. Borers are a common and often serious problem in North America. If it weren't for the bright yellow leaves of this popular European tree, I'd suggest growing a native green ash instead.

Fraxinus excelsior 'Aurea'

Fraxinus excelsior 'Aureafolia' (Golden Desert) Golden leaves become greener through summer; small enough tree to grow below utility wires, in mixed borders, and as a garden accent. 15'–20' h and w.

Fraxinus pennsylvanica ○ 'Cimmzam' (Cimmaron)

FRAK-si-nus pen-sil-VAN-ih-kah

Cimmaron green ash

Olive Family (Oleaceae)
Deciduous tree
50' h x 30' w

Cimmaron green ash is seedless with an upright, oval to rounded form and thick, waxy green leaves that turn from dark maroon to brick red and then scarlet in fall. The trunk and branches are strong and resistant to storm damage. Although *F. pennsylvanica* will grow anywhere, grow seedless cultivars instead of the species. The species tolerates drought, salt, wet springs, infertile soils, pollution, and light shade but is susceptible to rust, borers, and scales, to name a few of its problems. Seedless cultivars look neater; they have improved disease resistance, more reliable fall color, and produce no annoying seedlings.

LANDSCAPE USE
Shade tree grown for fall color and adaptability. Its fast growth (about 3 feet a year in good soil) makes it well suited to new homes on bare lots.

ORIGIN Eastern North America (species).

HARDINESS ZONES 3–9

LIGHT Full sun.

SOIL Somewhat acid, well-drained to wet soils.

GROWING Avoid growing this salt-tolerant cultivar in compacted soils.

DESIGNER'S CHOICE

Fraxinus pennsylvanica 'Marshall Seedless' Much improved over the native North American species, with glossy, deep green leaves; good pest and disease resistance; yellow fall color; and a broad, oval habit. 50'–60' h × 40' w. Zones 4–7.

F. pennsylvanica 'Patmore' Extremely cold hardy, seedless tree with an even, oval to rounded form and shiny deep green leaves that turn yellow in fall. 40'–60' h × 35'–45' w. Zones 3–9.

F. pennsylvanica 'Summit' Grow it for fine, yellow fall color and even, oval crown; seedless. 45'–55' h × 25'–35' w. Zones 4–9.

GARDENIA

Gardenia jasminoides ○ (syn. G. augusta)

gar-DEE-nee-a jaz-min-OY-dees

Gardenia, Cape jasmine

Madder Family (Rubiaceae)
Evergreen shrub
4'–6' h x 4'–8' w

About 35 years ago, my high-school sweetheart gave me a gardenia corsage for his senior prom. I don't remember the color of my dress, but I remember the flowers! My date thrilled me with his gift, a sensuous juxtaposition of sight, smell, and touch that lived in the fridge for days afterwards.

Gardenia, a slow-growing, mounded shrub emblematic of the Deep South, grows best in Zones 8–10, but some varieties survive in the colder areas of Zone 7 (0° F). Notably, the cultivars 'Chuck Hayes' and 'Kleim's Hardy' are hardier than most and available in commerce. The shrub bears smooth, buttery-white, perfumed blooms against deep green, leathery leaves.

LANDSCAPE USE
Grow gardenias near doors, windows, and patios, in courtyards, shrub borders, and entry gardens — anywhere you can enjoy their sweet fragrance and lovely looks.

ORIGIN China

HARDINESS ZONES 7–10

LIGHT Partial shade.

SOIL Well-drained, fertile, nearly neutral to acid soil with plenty of organic matter and regular watering.

GROWING Apply a fertilizer for acid-loving plants after bloom and mulch around the base to keep roots cool. This terrific tropical is prone to whiteflies, sooty mold, scales, stem canker, and other troubles, so watch your plants carefully and treat problems as soon as they occur.

DESIGNER'S CHOICE

Gardenia jasminoides 'Chuck Hayes' Hardy to 0° F; semi-double ivory white flowers, profuse blooms in June, repeating sporadically from late August and September to frost. 5' h × 7' w.

G. jasminoides 'Kleim's Hardy' A dwarf with single, star-shaped, ivory flowers; tolerates full sun with some protection from intense heat. 2'–3' h and w. Hardy to 0° F.

Gardenia jasminoides 'Chuck Hayes'

GARRYA

Garrya elliptica ▽

GAYR-ree-a el-LIP-ti-ka

Silk tassel

Silk Tassel Family (Garryaceae)
Evergreen shrub or small tree
8'–20' h x 8'–15' w

Known for its decorative, 5"–10", yellowish to gray silk tassels, this broad-leaf evergreen grows dense and bushy but can be pruned into a small tree. The elegant tassels are pendant clusters of 10" male catkins that appear in winter. Short female catkins, followed by purplish persistent fruits, occur on separate female plants. The elliptical leaves are shiny, green, and leathery with gray undersides.

LANDSCAPE USE
West Coast sheltered shrub borders and woodland gardens.

ORIGIN West Coast of U.S.

HARDINESS ZONES (7) 8–10

LIGHT Partial shade but tolerates full sun to deep shade. Away from the coast, give *Garrya* afternoon shade.

SOIL Prefers well-drained, acid to alkaline soils, and light, loamy, or heavy soils.

GROWING It withstands some drought, salt, and air pollution. Needs moderate summer watering. Prune when dormant.

Garrya elliptica

CAUTION *Garrya* has medicinal properties. Ingesting the plant can be toxic.

DESIGNER'S CHOICE
Garrya elliptica 'James Roof' Has 10"–12"-long, showier catkins. 13' h and w.

GAULTHERIA

Gaultheria procumbens ☁

gall-THAY-ree-a pro-KUM-benz

Wintergreen, Checkerberry, Teaberry

Heath Family (Ericaceae)
Broad-leaf evergreen creeper
6" h x 2'–3' w

This slow-spreading, broad-leaf evergreen shrublet and groundcover not only has year-round interest, but also is the source of wintergreen oil, a popular flavoring in breath mints and chewing gum. Native Americans used wintergreen oil for medicinal properties. It contains methyl salicylates, an aspirin-like chemical with painkilling, fever-lowering, anti-rheumatic, and antiseptic characteristics. Wintergreen berries are edible fresh, cooked, or frozen, and its leaves are the source of mountain tea.

Dark green evergreen leaves are tinged deep red in cold weather. The flowers are pinkish white bells in little clusters of 2 or 3 in early to midsummer. From late summer to spring, birds, rodents, and people enjoy its bright red, round, edible berries. In winter, this low-grower is often invisible because of snow cover.

LANDSCAPE USE
Woodland groundcover.

ORIGIN Dry to boggy forests of North America and Eurasia.

HARDINESS ZONES 3–5 (6)

LIGHT Partial to full shade.

Gaultheria procumbens

SOIL Prefers sandy or peaty acidic soils high in organic matter.

GROWING If you supply the right growing conditions, the plant should thrive.

Gaultheria shallon ☁ ✳

gall-THAY-ree-a shal-LON

Salal

Heath Family (Ericaceae)
Broad-leaf evergreen shrub
1'–8' h x 5' w

Salal spreads so aggressively that it can form impenetrable evergreen thickets under conifers in soils both dryish and boggy. Ubiquitous in parts of the Northwest, it played an important role in the lives of early Native Americans, who used the juicy fruits, both fresh and dried, for nourishment and trading. Chewing leaves lessened their hunger pangs and whole branches flavored fish soups.

It produces sharp-pointed, glossy, evergreen, ovate, 4" leaves. In late spring and early summer, white to light pink, lily-of-the-valley-like blooms hang in open clusters; these blossoms are attractive to hummingbirds. In late summer to fall, the edible, black berries are useful to birds and for jam.

Gaultheria shallon

LANDSCAPE USE
Because of its adaptability and aggressive spread, salal makes an excellent groundcover for banks, under trees, and mass planted with rhododendrons and conifers; best in coastal habitats with abundant summer fog and rain.

ORIGIN   Coastal forests from northern California north to northwestern U.S. and British Columbia.

HARDINESS ZONES   6–8

LIGHT   Adaptable to sun, where it grows 1'–2' high, and shade, where height ranges from 4'–8'.

SOIL   Moist, acid, humusy soils.

GROWING   Easy once established. Control size by removing suckers; cut out dead wood. Mulch with leaves or compost annually to maintain the soil's rich humus content. It's not a good plant for small spaces since it spreads freely by suckers.

GAYLUSSACIA

Gaylussacia brachycera 🝙
gay-lu-SAY-chee-a bra-KIS-er-a

Box huckleberry

Heath Family (Ericaceae)
Dwarf evergreen shrub
6"–24" h x indefinite spread

This rare shrub creates big mats that can spread a mile. Leaves are small, dense, and glossy green. Stems have 3 sharp angles with a ridge at the base of each leaf. In late spring, erect pinkish to white flowers occur in clusters in the leaf axils, followed by bluish berries. The shrub forms colonies by spreading from underground roots. Few nurseries carry this singular plant, making it one for collectors. A colony in Pennsylvania over a mile long is estimated to be over 12,000 years old, making it a remnant of the last Ice Age and one of the oldest living plants.

LANDSCAPE USE
Groundcover for open sites or under taller ericaceous shrubs like mountain laurel or rhododendron; attracts nesting, roosting, and hungry birds.

ORIGIN   Eastern U.S. on wooded, north-facing slopes.

HARDINESS ZONES   5–7

LIGHT   Full sun to partial shade.

SOIL   Dry well-drained acid soil, tolerates poor sandy soils.

GROWING   Some scientists consider box huckleberry endangered. Do not collect it from the wild. Make sure when buying plants that they are nursery-propagated and not collected from the wild.

DESIGNER'S CHOICE
Gaylussacia baccata 'Black Huckleberry' A deciduous shrub of eastern North America similar to low-bush blueberry, but with rosy red flowers followed by edible fruits. Grows best in partial shade to sun, in acidic, well-drained soils. 3" h and w. Zone 6.

GENISTA

Genista tinctoria ◯ ✳
je-NEE-sta tink-TOH-ree-a

Dyer's greenweed, Dyer's broom, Common woadwaxen

Pea Family (Fabaceae)
Deciduous shrub
2'–3' h x 2'–3' w

Cheery yellow blooms peak in late spring or early summer but continue on and off for months. Like common broom (*Cytisus*), greenweed's bare stems are bright green, giving the shrub year-round interest. The shrub's rounded, upright, twiggy form and narrow, 2-inch-long, dark green leaves complement perennials in a mixed border, where it attracts bees and butterflies. You can make a natural yellow dye from the entire plant, particularly the flowers and new wood.

LANDSCAPE USE
Groundcover on exposed banks; shrub and mixed borders; dry gardens; cottage gardens.

ORIGIN   Europe, western Asia.

HARDINESS ZONES   4–7

LIGHT   Full sun.

SOIL   Well-drained, average to poor, dry soils; pH adaptable.

GROWING   Tolerates drought and wind. Nitrogen fixer. Trim lightly to shape in late winter or early spring but avoid cuts into old wood. No serious diseases, but aphids and scales may be problems.

CAUTION   All parts are poisonous. Invasive tendency in the eastern U.S. and around the Great Lakes.

DESIGNER'S CHOICE
Genista tinctoria 'Plena' Dwarf, with double, yellow flowers; excellent groundcover. 10" h and w.
G. tinctoria 'Royal Gold' Erect shrub with 3", cone-shaped, upright clusters of deep yellow flowers. 3' h and w.

GINKGO

Ginkgo biloba △ › ⌢

GINK-go by-LOH-ba

Ginkgo, Maidenhair tree

Deciduous conifer tree
Ginkgo Family (Ginkgoaceae)
50'–80' h × 40'–80' w

The ginkgo is a tree and a legend, its ancestors preceding the dinosaurs by millions of years. Considered the oldest living seed plant, ginkgo is a male or female conifer that can live 2,500 years or more. Although ginkgo's habit may vary, it tends to be pyramidal with a strong central leader when young. With great age, it may lose the leader and develop several upright trunks and a vast, spreading, irregular crown. To say ginkgoes are adaptable is an understatement, since some survived the fire and radiation of the Hiroshima atomic blast.

In herbal medicine, ginkgo leaves promote efficient blood circulation and memory retention. People eat the nuts pickled, for a dessert or vegetable, or use them medicinally as aids to digestion and bladder health.

Lovely light-green, fan-shaped leaves split into 2 lobes *(biloba).* The leaves resemble the fronds of maidenhair fern (thus the common name, maidenhair tree). Ginkgoes may have stunning, bright yellow fall color, but we grow the cultivar 'Princeton Sentry', which in our garden typically turns a disappointing yellowish green and, when ready, drops all its leaves overnight. Young trees have light brown bark; the bark on older trees has dark, vertical ridges and furrows. New stems are tan, thick, and fairly smooth, aging to gray with thread-like exfoliation. After 20 or more years, females produce green to brown ovules in stalked pairs, while males develop cylindrical green catkins on short shoots; the catkins contain live sperm. Females bear edible, fleshy, messy, pulp-covered seeds resembling pale apricots with a nasty smell; hence, female trees are seldom for sale, and cultivars don't produce seeds. (*Ginkgo* means silver apricot in Chinese.)

LANDSCAPE USE

If you can wait for it to grow, it makes a good shade tree for large lawns. Use ginkgo in groves, formal allées, and as a park or street tree.

ORIGIN   Valleys, forests, rocky banks of eastern China.

HARDINESS ZONES (3) 4–8

LIGHT   Full sun to partial shade.

SOIL   Prefers moist, well-drained, acid, deep, sandy loam, yet ginkgo in so adaptable is that it tolerates compacted infertile soils and a wide range of pH.

GROWING   Water during hot, dry periods until well established. Needs little or no pruning, but if you find it necessary, trim it in early spring. The tree grows slowly, requiring neither spraying nor mulching of its deep roots. It resists diseases and insect attacks and withstands heat, drought, snow, ice, salt, and air pollution. Female ginkgoes bear messy fruits that stink as they decay.

DESIGNER'S CHOICE

Ginkgo biloba 'Autumn Gold' Symmetrical conical habit when young; the crown of old trees is broader and more uneven; good yellow fall color; male, so no seeds. 50' h × 30'–40' w.

G. biloba 'Magyar' Seedless male with a narrow, pyramidal habit. 50'–60' h × 20'–30' w.

G. biloba 'Princeton Sentry' Seedless male with narrow columnar to pyramidal habit. Use like 'Magyar'. 50'–60' h × 20'–25' w.

Ginkgo biloba
'Princeton Sentry'

GLEDITSIA

Gleditsia triacanthos f. inermis ⚬ ✳

gle-DIT-see-a tri-a-KAN-thos i-NER-mis

Thornless honey locust

Cassia or Caesalpinia Family (Caesalpiniaceae)
Deciduous tree
60' h × 40' w

If creating areas of dappled shade is your gardening challenge, here's the answer: honey locust. Considered garden worthy for the pleasing filtered shade under its canopy, honey locust has an attractive, upright, open, rounded form. It withstands high winds and ice storms, thanks to its substantial roots. Although the species develops huge, pronged thorns on its trunk and lower branches, the thornless variety is safe to touch. Honey locust's trunk splits near the ground into several main stems but it can be pruned to one trunk. This fast-growing tree lives about 125 years; unlike many members of the pea family, it doesn't fix atmospheric nitrogen in the soil to feed the plant roots.

Gleditsia triacanthos

Many small leaflets comprise honey locust's 10" compound leaves. They cast dappled shade, which lets many kinds of plants grow below the canopy. Fall color ranges from chartreuse to golden yellow. It features brownish-red zigzag twigs. The bark on young trunks is smooth and greenish gray, while older bark is brownish gray and scaly. It blooms in May and June, but the yellow-green, fragrant flowers are not decorative. Bees make honey from the pollen, but it's the sweetness of the fleshy fruit pod that gives the tree its common name. When it is about 10 years old, it produces dark reddish-brown, twisted, 8" × 1" pods containing many hard seeds. Although these fruits ripen from September to October, they can stay on trees into winter. Many animals eat the pods, including deer, squirrels, crows, rabbits, and opossums, as well as goats and cattle. Thornless cultivars usually bear little fruit and are thus preferred in landscapes.

LANDSCAPE USE
Shade tree in residential lawns with plantings underneath, erosion control, windbreaks, and shelterbelts. Dramatic winter landscape silhouette.

ORIGIN   Native to the floodplains of the eastern, southern, and midwestern U.S.

HARDINESS ZONES   4–9

LIGHT   Full sun, so site in gaps, woodland edge, or open areas. Tolerates reflected heat. Shade can slow tree growth.

SOIL   Prefers moist, deep, fertile, well-drained neutral to alkaline soils if in full sun. In clay soils, it grows fast in sun or shade. Tolerates reflected heat, restricted root zones, urban pollution, some wounding and a wide range of pH, salt, drought, and infertile soils. Popular in the North for resisting de-icing salts once established.

GROWING   Honey locust is fast growing and easy to establish. In cold areas, transplant honey locust in spring. For the first year, keep the soil watered and protected from salt. Fall clean up is fairly easy because the leaflets are tiny and thornless trees rarely have fruit; the species, however, has fruit litter in late fall and winter. It may be attacked by leaf eaters like spider mites, moths, and honey locust plant bug. Rarely, canker kills the tree. Thorny stems can sucker from rootstock of some grafted cultivars and need immediate removal. Unmulched surface roots can cause mowing difficulty.

CAUTION   The species form of honey locust has 1½" spines on lower branches and trunk.

DESIGNER'S CHOICE
Gleditsia triacanthos 'Impcole' (Imperial)   Compact with denser, rounded crown, thornless. 30' h and w.

G. triacanthos 'Shademaster'   Fast growing and rather drought tolerant with straight trunk and symmetrical ascending branches; dark green leaves; thornless and mostly fruitless. May be less hardy. 45' h × 35' w.

G. triacanthos 'Skycole' (Skyline)   Upright pyramidal with dark green leaves turning golden yellow in fall, mostly thornless and fruitless. 50' h × 30'–35' w.

G. triacanthos 'Suncole' (Sunburst)   Rounded to pyramidal; new growth yellow changing to bright green; fruitless; susceptible to cankers and borers. 35' h × 30'–35' w. Zones 5–9.

GYMNOCLADUS

Gymnocladus dioica ○ ✳

jim-noh-KLA-dus dee-oh-EE-kus

Kentucky coffee tree

Cassia or Caesalpinia Family (Caesalpiniaceae)
60'–75' h × 40'–50' w

If you're looking for a different kind of lawn tree, consider Kentucky coffee tree. Not your average pretty tree with a straight trunk, dense rounded crown, and spreading branches, *Gymnocladus* stands medium tall with an interesting, expressive structural form. Its straight trunk, thick ascending branches, and chubby twigs covered with orange lenticels (raised pores) appear striking in winter. The tree is also handsome in summer when it's covered with large, compound, blue-green leaves and casts a desirable, light shade under which shade tolerant grasses and perennials can grow. Cabinetmakers use the wood. Native Americans drank root and bark infusions for constipation, and Kentucky settlers brewed a coffee substitute from roasted seeds.

The alternate, twice-compound leaves are 12"–36" × 24" with 1½" leaflets. Leaves are dark bluishgreen in summer; fall color varies from dull yellow green to yellow. In autumn, leaflets drop several weeks before the midribs. The attractive bark is coarse-textured, dark grayish brown, and deeply fissured with rough ridges. In late spring, female trees have whitish, fragrant flowers in branched clusters up to 1' long and 4" wide, while males produce similar clusters up to 4" long. Hard, red-brown, 3"–10"-long pods ripen in fall and persist through winter. Inside are brown seeds in sweet, sticky, brown pulp; females start fruiting at 4 to 8 years old.

LANDSCAPE USE
A fine shade tree in large lawns, since Kentucky coffee tree's big leaves with little leaflets create desirable filtered shade in summer.

ORIGIN Bottomlands (low-lying alluvial land near rivers) in the Midwest and eastern U.S.

HARDINESS ZONES 4–8

LIGHT Full sun.

SOIL Prefers deep, rich, moist, well-drained soil but is adaptable to many conditions including drought, salt, pollution, and acid and alkaline soils.

GROWING No special care. Females are messy, since leaves, midribs, and fruits drop at different times. Wood can be brittle. For lower maintenance, choose male trees that produce less litter. May send up suckers in unmowed areas.

CAUTION Leaves and seeds can be toxic if ingested raw.

Gymnocladus dioica

DESIGNER'S CHOICE
Gymnocladus dioica 'J. C. McDaniel' (Prairie Titan) Male cultivar. Most nurseries carry only the species, and even this might be hard to find. 60'–70' h × 30'–40' w.

HALESIA

Halesia carolina ○
(syn. *H. tetraptera*)

ha-LEE-see-a kar-oh-LINE-a

Carolina silverbell, Snowdrop tree

Silverbells Family (Styracaceae)
Small to medium deciduous flowering tree
25'–40' h × 20'–30' w

In mid- to late spring, there's no prettier sight than a young *Halesia* with pink-flushed white blooms planted with pale pink flowering rhododendrons. These multi-season trees, typically low branched and rounded in habit, may grow much bigger in the wild. Birds, including hummingbirds, like the flowers.

The 8" × 4", pointed, oval leaves have serrated edges and yellow fall color. The gray-brown bark has light and dark striations, turning blocked and scaly with age. Hanging flowers are white to pinkish, ¾" bells with long stalks, grouped along the stems. The four-winged fruit has a rounded, pearlike shape, changing from light green to light brown.

LANDSCAPE USE
Understory tree in woodland gardens, mixed borders, groups, specimen in shade garden.

ORIGIN Moist fertile woods, banks, and slopes in the southeastern U.S.

HARDINESS ZONES 5–8

LIGHT Sun to partial shade; tolerates shady sites.

SOIL Rich, moist, acid, well-drained soil high in organic matter; tolerates

occasional flooding; may turn yellow in alkaline soils.

GROWING Needs no special care after establishment.

DESIGNER'S CHOICE
Halesia carolina 'Wedding Bells' Profuse, bright white blooms larger than species before leaves, which are often shiny; rounded habit and more shrubby than species. 15' h × 10' w in 10 years.

H. diptera (two-winged silverbell) Rounded tree with abundant, 4-lobed, white, bell-shaped blooms and fruit with two wings; yellow fall color; attractive bark; rarer than *H. carolina*. 20'–30' h and w. Zones 5–8.

H. monticola (mountain silverbell) Oval to rounded crown with 1", larger white flowers and habit than *H. carolina*, yellow fall color, and decorative bark. 40'–60' h × 40'–50' w. Zones 5–8.

H. monticola f. *rosea* Pink flowers, fuzzier leaves; rare. 25'–35' h × 20'–30' w.

Halesia carolina

Hamamelis mollis

HAMAMELIS

Hamamelis × intermedia 'Pallida' ○ › ◡ ✳

ha-ma-MEL-is in-ter-MEE-dee-ah

Pallida hybrid witch hazel

Witch Hazel Family
(Hamamelidaceae)
Deciduous flowering shrub or small
tree
10'–20' h and w

On a bleak winter day, the sweet scent and pale yellow hue of 'Pallida' flowers hint of spring to come. At Wisley in England, I saw it grouped with deep-yellow-flowered *H. × intermedia* 'Arnold Promise' and dark reddish-copper *H. × intermedia* 'Diane'. 'Pallida' stood out for its lovely profuse blooms. It has ascending branches and can be pruned to form a small tree. Sub-zero cold may harm the buds.

The leaves are alternate, simple, and dull green, becoming yellow in fall. This shrub is often listed under *H. mollis* because its foliage has the softness of that species. The bark is smooth and gray. In later winter before most other flowering plants, red-purple cupped sepals envelop 4 pale yellow, straplike petals. Fruits are insignificant capsules.

LANDSCAPE USE
Shrub border, mixed border with other shrubs, small trees, and perennials.

ORIGIN Western and western central China.

HARDINESS ZONES (5) 6–8

LIGHT Full sun to partial shade.

SOIL Prefers moist, acid, well-drained soils but adaptable to poor soils.

GROWING Relatively carefree with tighter form in full sun, more open shape in partial shade. If grown in full sun, the foliage may attract Japanese beetles.

DESIGNER'S CHOICE
Hamamelis × intermedia 'Arnold Promise' (hybrid witch hazel) Fragrant gold blooms, long-lasting yellow to orangey red fall color. 10'–20' h × 10'–15' w. Zones 5–8.

H. × intermedia 'Diane' Fragrant russet flowers, orangey red fall color. 10'–20' h × 10'–15' w. Zones 5–8.

H. × intermedia 'Jelena' (syn. 'Copper Beauty') Fragrant copper blooms, orangey red fall color, wide habit. 10'–20' h and w. Zones 5–8.

H. × intermedia 'Primavera' Abundant, scented flowers, yellow at the tip and red at the base; good yellow fall color. 15' h and w.

H. vernalis Long-blooming flowers in yellow, orange, or red with reddish calyces and long-lasting yellow fall color. Native to the Midwest and South. 6'–12' h and w. Zones 4–8.

H. virginiana Sun to shade; shrub to small tree; yellow fragrant flowers in mid to late fall. Native to eastern North America. 20'–30' h and w. Zones 4–8.

Hamamelis x intermedia 'Diane'

Hamamelis virginiana

HEPTACODIUM

Heptacodium miconioides ⬭ ✳

hep-ta-KOH-dee-um mi-koh-nee-OY-deez

Seven-son flower

Honeysuckle Family (Caprifoliaceae)
Deciduous flowering shrub or small tree
10'–15' h x 10' w

Seven-son flower ranks high on my list of desirable shrubs. It looks pleasing four seasons a year, thanks to vertically shredding, pale tan and brown bark, and opposite simple leaves that open chartreuse in spring, then turn dark green. In late summer to early fall in the North, it produces white, fragrant flowers that attract butterflies. It features a whorled petal-like calyx that initially supports a developing flower bud then, when fruit forms, becomes showy and reddish. Even better, seven-son flower is easy to grow. Uneven in outline, my shrub, which I bought 5 years ago in a small pot, stands roughly 5' h × 3' w.

LANDSCAPE USE
Shrub border, specimen. New Hampshire landscape designer Jill Nooney uses *Heptacodiums* as transitional plants between wild and cultivated areas. She limbs them up to show off the bark, which peels off in long thin strips.

ORIGIN   China's mountains, about 2000 feet high.

HARDINESS ZONES   4–8

LIGHT   Prefers full sun, but adapts to partial shade.

SOIL   Well-drained, average garden soil.

GROWING   Irregular branching makes it look a bit unkempt; benefits from some light shaping.

Heptacodium miconioides

HIBISCUS

Hibiscus syriacus ◑ ✳

hi-BIS-kus si-RYE-a-kus

Rose of Sharon, Althaea, Hardy hibiscus

Mallow Family (Malvaceae)
Deciduous flowering shrub or small tree
12' h x 6'–10' w

To give your garden a hint of the tropics, plant rose of Sharon, an upright, oval shrub or small tree with large, exotic, funnel-shaped blooms. Its 2"–4", mid-green leaves are alternate and simple with 3 lobes and toothed edges. My husband wants to remove our rose of Sharon each spring because it leafs out so late (usually June) that he thinks it's dead. The bark is gray, not showy. In late summer, when most flowering shrubs have already bloomed, it bears 2"–4"-wide, trumpetlike flowers similar to hollyhock in white, pink, red, purple, or violet, sometimes with contrasting darker color at the throat. Most profuse flowering occurs after a long, hot summer. The fruit capsules are persistent but not ornamental. When they ripen and disperse, they can be annoying, creating seedlings everywhere; self-sowing cultivars do not come true.

LANDSCAPE USE
Blends beautifully into the back of shrub and mixed borders, where they disappear when not in bloom. Since they leaf out late and have one season of interest, they look best grouped with other plants where they are not the focus of a planting.

ORIGIN   Various habitats in China and India.

HARDINESS ZONES   5–8

LIGHT   Full sun.

SOIL   Prefers moist, fertile, well-drained soils high in organic matter but adapts to many soils and a range of pH.

GROWING   Plant container-grown specimens any time during the growing season and water deeply until established. Eliminate ripe seedheads and thus rampant self-sowing by shearing after flowering before the seeds can scatter or site plants in island beds where they can develop without interference. Mulch generously (about 4") in cold climates. Cut back in spring to shape the plant, remove winter-killed stems, and encourage plentiful big blooms. If you wish, you can train this shrub into a small tree (see page 119). Grows best in hot climates and microclimates. In the same family as Japanese beetle–bait hollyhocks, rose of Sharon also attracts these voracious little beasts.

CAUTION   Rose of Sharon can self-sow and become invasive in average garden soils and natural environments. If this happens in your area, plant the triploids (hybrids with few or no viable seedlings) 'Aphrodite', 'Diana', 'Helene', or 'Minerva'.

Hibiscus syriacus

DESIGNER'S CHOICE

Hibiscus syriacus 'Diana' Big, flat, bright white, prolific blooms stay open at night; dark green leaves; sterile, so seedlings aren't a problem; performs best in mild climates. I grow 'Diana' in the northernmost part of its range. Slow to establish here, it grows slowly but blooms reliably each year until frost. 12' h × 6'–10' w.

H. syriacus 'Freedom' Single and double, red flowers on one plant. 12' h × 6'–10' w.

H. syriacus 'Helene' Pink-tinged white flowers with dark maroon centers; sterile so seedlings aren't an issue. 12' h × 6'–10' w.

H. syriacus 'Marina' (Blue Satin) Single, blue blooms with dark red-purple throats. Look also for pale pink Blush Satin, dark pink 'Minrosa' (Rose Satin), and 'Floru' (Violet Satin) hibiscus. 5'–8' h × 5'–6' w.

H. syriacus 'Notwoodone' (Lavender Chiffon) Single flowers with lacy centers give ruffled effect. 5'–8' h × 5'–6' w.

H. syriacus 'Notwoodtwo' (White Chiffon) Single 4"–5" white blooms with lacy centers; more flowers and longer bloom period than 'Diana'; outstanding. 5'–8' h × 5'–6' w.

HIPPOPHAE

Hippophae rhamnoides ○ › ⌂

hip-POH-fye ram-NOY-deez

Sea buckthorn

Oleaster Family (Elaeagnaceae)
Deciduous shrub or small tree
10'–20' h × 10'–25' w

Good for hedging, this large thorny shrub or small tree with a rounded, symmetrical shape works well near both salty seas and dry, windy prairies. Long popular in Europe and Asia for its anti-inflammatory, regenerative, and other medicinal properties, sea buckthorn is also used in teas (leaves), jams (fruits), and face creams (seed oil).

The silvery gray, 1"–3"-long leaves are alternate, simple, narrow, lance shaped, and smooth edged, and grow on brown, coarse stems. Sea buckthorn fruits on the 2-year-old wood of female plants. The blooms are modest but the orange, oval fruits that ripen in September are showy and persist to April. Because of their acidic taste, birds at first forego the fruits, which are edible and high in protein and vitamins C and E. Sea buckthorn needs both male and female plants for fruit at a typical ratio of 1 male to 6 or 8 females.

LANDSCAPE USE
Seaside or prairie hedges, screens. Because the widespread roots fix nitrogen, mass plantings of sea buckthorn can help recover land and prevent future erosion.

ORIGIN Mountainous areas of Europe, Siberia, and China.

HARDINESS ZONES 3–7

LIGHT Full sun.

SOIL Prefers well-drained, sandy, organic loam with neutral pH, but tolerates more acid and alkaline conditions; also tolerates drought and salt.

GROWING For an effective windbreak, plant about 3'–4' apart. Prune crossed and too-long branches every year. Invasive potential on Canadian prairies, where widely planted.

DESIGNER'S CHOICE

Hippophae rhamnoides 'Sprite' Fruitless male with gray-green leaves and a dense, rounded form for low hedging and foundation plantings. 5' h × 4' w.

H. rhamnoides 'Leikora' Female with lush orange berries, pollinated by male 'Pollmix'.

HOLODISCUS

Holodiscus discolor ⌂

ho-lo-DIS-kus DIS-ko-lor

Ocean spray, Cream bush

Rose Family (Rosaceae)
Deciduous shrub
4'–8' h and w; up to twice as large on the coast

In late spring, creamy white, sweetly fragrant flowers form 5"–8"-long, foamy plumes that droop from arched branches. Grow in a sunny, well-drained site; partial shade encourages taller growth; use this vigorous deer-resistant shrub away from the house in shrub borders, since close-up, the scented clusters may smell of old newsprint.

LANDSCAPE USE
Mass on slopes and banks for erosion control; naturalize in lightly shaded woodland gardens; use in shrub and mixed beds and borders.

ORIGIN Dry woods of western North America.

HARDINESS ZONES 5–9

LIGHT Full sun to partial shade.

SOIL Moist, rich, well-drained soil with plenty of organic matter; tolerates poor dry soils.

GROWING Needs little pruning; just cut out. Grows best in the Pacific Northwest.

HOVENIA

Hovenia dulcis 0 ✳

ho-VEE nee a DUL sis

Japanese raisin tree

Buckthorn Family (Rhamnaceae)
Deciduous mid-sized tree
30'–35' h x 20'–25' w

If you're looking for a rugged, easy-to-maintain, moderate-growing shade tree that attracts wildlife to its edible fruit, try Japanese raisin tree. An upright tree with an oval crown and shiny green, heart-shaped and oval leaves, it produces creamy, scented flower clusters in midsummer, followed by edible, red fruit in September. Although young bark is fairly smooth, older bark is furrowed and exfoliates in strips that expose the darker bark underneath.

LANDSCAPE USE
Small shade tree for small suburban gardens, specimen in large gardens.

ORIGIN   China

HARDINESS ZONES   (5) 6–8

LIGHT   Sun to partial shade.

SOIL   With good drainage, it tolerates many soils and conditions.

GROWING   Cannot grow in wet soils. Mostly pest and disease free.

HYDRANGEA

Hydrangea anomala subsp. *petiolaris* ⏢

hy-DRAN-ja a-NAH-ma-la pe-ti-oh-LA-ris

Climbing hydrangea

Hydrangea Family (Hydrangeaceae)
Climbing deciduous vine or mounding shrub
30' h or more when grown as a vine, 4' h x about 16' w when grown as a shrub

This woody plant with fabulous, shaggy bark is versatile, growing as a mounded shrub on the ground or as a vine climbing high into a tree.

Climbing hydrangea sticks to surfaces by means of aerial roots. Grown as a vine, it can knock over weak wooden arbors with age or harm clapboard houses by trapping moisture against wooden walls. From the main stem, it produces small horizontal branches that give the plant added texture and dimension. It attracts bees, birds, and butterflies. Japanese hydrangea (*Schizophragma)* and the Southeastern native woodvamp (*Decumaria)* are similar vines.

It holds its medium-textured, gleaming, dark green foliage until late in the season. The showy reddish-brown, rough, peeling bark is visible in late fall and winter. White, fragrant, lacecap flowers up to 10" wide are comprised of an outer ring of showy white florets surrounding a delicate central cluster of fertile flowers in early summer. The fruit is not ornamental.

LANDSCAPE USE
Makes a lovely, mounded ground-cover in partly shaded places. Looks especially nice mounded at the base of a tree trunk, lamppost, or brick wall, then climbing up the surface of the support. Also makes an effective cover up for unsightly stumps in shade or woodland gardens.

ORIGIN   China and Japan.

HARDINESS ZONES   (4) 5–7

LIGHT   Full sun to shade.

SOIL   Moist, loose, fertile, well-drained soils of varying pH that are high in organic matter.

GROWING   Water moderately for best performance. Climbing hydrangea requires patience: it is slow to establish, particularly in dry or windy sites, and may take years to flower.

DESIGNER'S CHOICE
Hydrangea anomala subsp. *petiolaris* 'Firefly' Irregular yellow leaf margins fade to chartreuse in summer, slower growing than species; spectacular accent for shade. 'Miranda' is similar, with gold edges fading to cream. 30' h or more × 5' w grown as a vine; 4' h × about 16' w when grown as a shrub.

Hydrangea anomala **subsp.** *petiolaris*

ALL ABOUT HYDRANGEA

Hydrangeas, grown for showy blooms that vary from bumptious to refined clusters of cream, white, lime, pink, purple, blue, or bicolor flowers? Climbing and oakleaf hydrangea also have handsome reddish brown shredding bark for winter display, while oakleaf hydrangea ends the growing season with reddish purple fall color. Gorgeous grouped in beds and borders or grown in masses against an evergreen background, hydrangeas produce excellent cut flowers for fresh or dry arrangements. Except for adaptable panicle hydrangea, give these shrubs moist, well-drained, fertile soil high in organic matter in sun to partial shade and provide some protection from harsh winds. Leaf spot, powdery mildew, aphids, Japanese beetles, and slugs are among the problems you may sometimes encounter, but they generally stay attractive if grown in suitable conditions.

Hydrangea flowers occur in panicles (long conical clusters) or corymbs (flat to convex clusters.) Lacecaps are corymbs with flat tops, while hortensias, also known as mopheads, are corymbs with ball-like blooms. Each cluster has both fertile and sterile flowers. Sterile flowers are showy, drawing pollinators to the unremarkable fertile blooms at the center of lacecaps and in the interior of mopheads. Hydrangea cultivars with all-sterile flowers are extra splashy.

Caution. Hydrangeas are toxic if eaten, but poisoning rarely occurs, since they are not appealing as food.

change from green to white in summer, then tan in winter. The fruit is not ornamental.

LANDSCAPE USE They light up shady borders, woodland gardens, and perennial gardens, blending in discreetly when not in bloom. Showy cultivars like 'Annabelle' make good cut flowers and foundation plantings in Victorian or "grandmother" gardens.

ORIGIN Mountains and foothills in the eastern U.S.

HARDINESS ZONES 4–9

LIGHT Partial shade to full sun. In the North, plants can withstand full sun, but in the South, some afternoon shade is best.

SOIL See *Hydrangea anomala*.

GROWING Most gardeners grow cultivars of wild hydrangea, which they prune by cutting the old stems to the ground in late winter or spring before new growth begins. Without pruning, the species and cultivars look messy and produce smaller flowers.

DESIGNER'S CHOICE

Hydrangea arborescens 'Annabelle' 10"–14", rounded, flower heads packed with sterile blossoms; blooms on new wood so that buds can't be winterkilled as in some hydrangea species. Cut old stems to the ground in late winter or early spring. 'Annabelle' can flop under the weight of the heavy blooms for a lush, sensuous effect. If you prefer your shrubs to stand erect, you can stake stems to support the massive flower heads. Makes a striking low deciduous hedge. 4' h × 4' or more w. Zone 4.

H. arborescens 'Grandiflora' (snowhill or hills-of-snow hydrangea) White, 6"–8" balls of sterile flowers; smaller and earlier than 'Annabelle'. 4' h × 4' or more w.

Hydrangea arborescens ○ ➤ ☙ ✳

hy-DRAN-ja ar-bo-RES-senz

Smooth hydrangea, Wild hydrangea

Hydrangea Family (Hydrangeaceae)
Deciduous flowering shrub
3'–5' h and w

Even if your garden is shady and you live where winters are cold, you can still grow this hydrangea with good results. It grows fast, suckering and spreading with slim stems and no side branches. Its clustered green to white blooms and open habit give the

species an understated charm, while the popular cultivar 'Annabelle' will make you smile at its fulsome flower heads. Wild hydrangea's blossoms attract bees and butterflies and offer long-lasting floral interest in naturalistic woodland gardens when little else is blooming.

The dark green, up to 8" × 6" leaves are opposite, simple, and ovate. The bark is brownish and shredded. The blooms are 4"–6", flat-topped, lacy clusters comprised of flashy, 4–5-petal, sterile flowers encircling tiny, fertile flowers on new wood in early summer. These long-lasting flowers

Hydrangea arborescens 'Annabelle'

Hydrangea macrophylla ○ › ⌂

hy-DRAN-ja mak-roh-FIL-la

Big-leaf hydrangea, French hydrangea

Deciduous flowering shrub
Hydrangea Family (Hydrangeaceae)
3'–12' h and w, depending upon the cultivar

Take a summer drive on Cape Cod or any other seashore community along the East Coast, and you'll see a proliferation of fat, blue mopheads. These fast-growing, classic garden hydrangeas, suckering and unbranched, complement both traditional and contemporary landscapes, adding shades of pink and blue to beds, borders, and foundation plantings.

The big, dark green leaves are serrated. The tan stems occasionally peel or split. In the North, stems can die back in winter with new growth emerging from the roots. There are two flower types: Hortensias, or mopheads, are big heavy balls of showy, sterile flowers. Lacecaps are subtler in effect, being flat or domed discs of delicate fertile blooms ringed by showy, sterile flowers. Both types may have flower buds at the shoot tips and along the stems. Their color depends upon the amount of available aluminum in the soil. Acidity in the soil frees up the aluminum, leading to blue to deep purple flowers. Alkaline soils bind the aluminum ions so that they're not accessible to the roots, and here the flowers are shades of pink. The fruits are not ornamental. Excellent salt tolerance makes this a good choice for shady areas on the coast.

LANDSCAPE USE

Short cultivars make terrific salt-tolerant foundation plantings for beach houses. Use massed under trees that give dappled shade. Choose from dozens of cultivars: Blue-flowered forms look stunning next to sunny yellow or chartreuse-leafed shrubs, and cultivars with variegated leaves brighten woodland shrub beds and borders. These shrubs work well in the midst of perennial borders, where spring flowers mask hydrangea's coarse leaves until their summer blooms begin.

ORIGIN   Korea and Japan.

HARDINESS ZONES   6–9

LIGHT   Partial shade to full sun. Morning sun and afternoon shade is ideal; hydrangeas in hot climates can wilt in the heat of afternoon sun.

SOIL   See *Hydrangea anomala*. The soil's pH and the resulting accessibility of aluminum ions determine the flower hue (see above). For pink flowers, the soil pH should be from 6.0 to about 6.5 or above. Liming acid soils can raise their pH and produce pinker blooms. Using hard water and growing hydrangeas near concrete sidewalks and house foundations also increases the soil's pH. For blue flowers, the soil pH is usually acid (below 5.5). Sulfur, iron sulfate, leaf mold, and peat moss can all increase the soil's acidity over time in areas with alkaline soils. Ask your local nursery for a product to acidify the soil and follow the directions. Fertilize hydrangeas with acid-loving plant food as needed. You can also grow blue-flowered hydrangeas in containers or contained beds to control the soil composition. Choose pots about 2 to 4 inches wider and deeper than those in which they're growing at the nursery, and make sure they have big drainage holes.

GROWING   Big-leaf hydrangeas rarely need significant pruning except when stems die back in winter. Typically, blooms occur at the stem tips of the previous year's growth. If the top part of the stem is removed before the terminal bud breaks, then flowers will come from buds farther down the stem. If the whole plant dies to the ground, cut dead stems out and let the shrub regenerate from the base. In the North (Zone 5), cold winters and late freezes often kill off flower buds set the previous fall. If all the buds are cold-killed, your plant will miss one season's bloom. If some live flower buds remain at the bottom of the stem, you should still have flowers, even if you prune off the dead material. If you want to prune live stems, do that right after flowering, before the shrub sets new buds for the following year. Pruning after August 1 may cut off the next season's flower buds. Though generally healthy, aphids, mites, scales, leaf spot, rust, and powdery mildew may trouble this species.

DESIGNER'S CHOICE

Hydrangea macrophylla 'All Summer Beauty' Pink or blue mophead that blooms on new growth and is therefore hardier than most macrophyllas. 3'–5' h and w. Zone 5.

Hydrangea macrophylla
'Nikko Blue'

H. macrophylla 'Bailmer' (Endless Summer) Pink or blue mopheads for months on old and new wood. In my garden, this shrub is a winner planted near brilliant chartreuse *Robinia pseudoaccacia* 'Friisia' and *Cotinus* 'Royal Purple'. 3'–5' h and w. Zone (4) 5.

H. macrophylla 'Glowing Embers' (syn. *H. macrophylla* 'Forever Pink') Pink to blue mopheads begin in late June and continue into fall. 3' h and w.

H. macrophylla 'Maculata' (syn. *H. macrophylla* 'Variegata') Grown for its showy variegated leaves with irregular, white margins and gray to green centers; lacecap flowerheads with pink or blue fertile flowers surrounded by a ring of white infertile blooms. 3' h and w.

H. macrophylla 'Nikko Blue' Pink to blue mopheads, more blue in more acid soils; floriferous; said to be hardier than most, as some may flower on new growth; most common mophead form. 4'–6' h and w. Zone 5.

H. macrophylla 'Red Star' Red to purple-red lacecaps in alkaline soils; blue-violet in acid soils. Leaves have bright fall color. 4' h and w.

H. macrophylla 'Setsuka-yae' (syn. *H. macrophylla* 'Domotoi') Double

mophead flowers in pink or blue. 5'–6' h and w.

H. macrophylla 'Shamrock' Double pink lacecaps from July turn red and dark pink; violet on acid soils; a compact, long-blooming French hybrid, more refined than many cultivars. 3½'–5' h and w.

H. macrophylla 'Tokyo Delight' Lacecap with pink fertile flowers surrounded by white florets that age pink. Green leaves with reddish flush in fall. 5' h and w.

H. macrophylla 'Tovelit' (syn. 'Tovelil') Round, dwarf plant covered with mauve to rosy pink mopheads above narrow, dark green leaves; similar to 'Pia' and 'Glowing Embers'. 3' h and w.

H. serrata (syn. *H. macrophylla* var. *serrata*) (mountain hydrangea) Similar to *H. macrophylla* but hardier. 4'–5' h and w. Zone (5) 6.

H. serrata 'Blue Billow' Big, deep blue to pink lacecaps; foliage has excellent fall color. 3'–5' h × 3'–4' w.

H. serrata 'Blue Bird' Lacecap with dark blue, fertile flowers ringed by light blue, sterile florets; in high pH soils, pink florets ring blue fertile flowers. Coppery-red fall color. 3'–5' h and w.

H. serrata 'Golden Sunlight' New foliage is yellow, maturing to light green; lacecap with pale pink, fertile florets; showy outer florets are white, aging to deep purplish red. 3' h and w.

Hydrangea paniculata ○ › ☁ ✳

hy-DRAN-ja pa-ni-kew-LAH-ta

Panicle hydrangea

Hydrangea Family (Hydrangeaceae)
Deciduous flowering shrub or
small tree
8'–20' h and w

Gardeners grow this familiar hydrangea for its big, decorative blooms that appear from midsummer

to fall. It forms a fast-growing, upright, arching shrub that is frequently seen growing near the high foundations of Victorian homes.

The opposite, whorled, simple, dark green leaves have serrated edges; leaves are up to 6" h × 3" w. The grayish-brown bark has uneven furrows. Blossoms are elongated (6"–10"), branched clusters of showy, sterile, white florets on the outside, with small, fertile, inner flowers. The blooms turn rosy pink to purplish pink in fall. Cut for fresh or dried bouquets. Fruits are contained in a brown capsule and are not ornamental, but faded flowers add winter interest, especially in northern gardens.

LANDSCAPE USE

Small cultivars work well in foundation plantings or in the middle of mixed shrub and perennial beds. Larger cultivars make nice additions to shrub borders. You can also train large forms such as PeeGee or The Swan into small trees.

Hydrangea paniculata 'Limelight'

ORIGIN Eastern China and Japan.

HARDINESS ZONES 3–8

LIGHT Full sun to partial shade.

SOIL See *H. anomala*.

GROWING This relatively carefree shrub blooms on new wood. Judicious shaping in late winter or early spring before leaves appear can tame its untidy spreading habit. It tolerates urban pollution and a wide range of soils, although it is coarse in form and texture.

DESIGNER'S CHOICE

Hydrangea paniculata 'Barbara' (The Swan) 8"–12" flowerheads with white petals 5 times bigger than other panicle hydrangeas from mid-summer to fall. 8'–10' h × 8' w.

H. paniculata 'Bulk' (Quick Fire) Flowers open white in midsummer, about 4 weeks earlier than other cultivars, then quickly turn pink. Cut back by half in early spring for bigger blooms. 6'–8' h × 3'–5' w. Zones 4–9.

H. paniculata 'Compacta' Smaller version of PeeGee (see below). 6'–7' h and w.

H. paniculata 'Grandiflora' An old-fashioned cultivar known by its initials as P. G. hydrangea (PeeGee); characterized by white flowers that change to pink in fall. I like to cut and dry PeeGee's rose-tinted blooms, but its messy, suckering habit and tendency to layer itself where stems touch the ground drive me nuts. Gardeners who like tidier plants can buy PeeGee at many nurseries as a standard, grown with a single stem. 8'–25' h × 8'–20' w.

H. paniculata 'Kyushu' Upright shrub with sterile and fertile midsummer flowers; airy, white-pointed panicles set against shiny deep green foliage. Good for cutting. 6'–8' h and w.

H. paniculata 'Limelight' (syn. 'Zwijnenburg') Lime-green, 6"–12", erect blooms in mid-summer turn dark pink in fall. Flower heads look

good fresh or dried in bouquets. Although this shrub likes full sun, plants in the South will need some shade; not as hardy as the species. 6'–8' h and w. Zone 4.

H. paniculata 'Little Lamb' Dwarf with delicate flowers held above the leaves; smallest petals of any cultivar. 6' h × 8' w. Zone 4.

H. paniculata 'Pee Gee' See 'Grandiflora'.

H. paniculata 'Pee Wee' Dwarf version of PeeGee, with smaller leaves and blooms on a smaller plant. 4' h and w.

H. paniculata 'Pink Diamond' Cone-shaped, 12" × 8" white flowerheads turn pink early in the season; a selection of 'Unique'. 6'–8' h and w. Zone 4.

H. paniculata 'Tardiva' Late-blooming, large, open, lacy flower heads on heavy stems. 8'–15' h and w.

H. paniculata 'Unique' This Belgian selection blooms early with big, round, cone-shaped, white blooms that turn pink with cooler temperatures; plants found for sale may be variable. 6'–9' h and w. Zone 4.

H. paniculata 'White Moth' 14" flowerheads starting in midsummer and continuing into fall. White flowers turn green in September. 6' h and w. Zone 4.

Hydrangea paniculata 'Grandiflora'

Hydrangea paniculata 'Tardiva'

DRYING HYDRANGEA FLOWERS

I love collecting and drying PeeGee flowers for winter decorations. I dry them a couple different ways, always choosing flower clusters free from spotting or insect damage and gathering them at peak bloom or slightly before peak. I select older blooms flushed with pink, since that color will persist when dry.

Method 1. I cut PeeGee bouquets with stems long enough to fit into a clean, medium-sized vase. I put about an inch of water in the bottom of the vase, remove leaves from the stems, position the flowers, and set the arrangement in a dry room away from direct sunlight. As the water evaporates, the flowers dry in place without wilting.

Method 2. To air dry the traditional way, cut leaves off the stems and bind them together with a rubber band. Hang bunches upside down in a warm, dark, dry room with good air circulation until completely dried, usually a 2-week process.

Hydrangea quercifolia ○ › ⌂

hy-DRAN-ja kwer-si-FOH-lee-a

Oak-leaf hydrangea

Hydrangea Family (Hydrangeaceae)
Deciduous flowering shrub
6′–8′ h and w

What's not to like about this plant? From its big, handsome leaves with their spectacular burgundy to purple fall color to its glorious 8"–14" white to rosy pink flower panicles to its fine, cinnamon-colored exfoliating bark, oak-leaf hydrangea is an elegant native showstopper with a wide suckering habit. Yet, unlike other faster-growing hydrangeas in my Zone 5 garden, oak-leaf hydrangea taught me patience. It took several years for my oakleaf hydrangeas to

Hydrangea quercifolia 'Flemygea'

Hydrangea quercifolia 'Flemygea'

bloom and grow, but the wait was worthwhile and we now enjoy their bark, leaf, and flower displays.

Coarse, oak-shaped, deep green leaves have light, hairy undersides and outstanding deep red to purplish red fall color. Older stems have handsome, brown to reddish-brown, exfoliating bark. The pyramidal flower clusters, up to 12" long in creamy white, comprise both tiny fertile flowers and showy sterile flowers that frequently turn shades of pink with age. It blooms in summer on old wood. Fruits are not ornamental.

LANDSCAPE USE

Shrub borders, understory plant in woodland gardens, specimen or groups. Can also grow in a container.

ORIGIN   An understory plant in the woods and on stream banks of the southeastern U.S.

HARDINESS ZONES   5–9

LIGHT   Full sun (more so in the North) to heavy shade. When grown in full sun, my oakleaf hydrangeas attracted Japanese beetles; when I moved them next to a shady stonewall, the sun-loving beetles turned their attention to other plants.

SOIL   See *Hydrangea anomala.*

GROWING   Keep watered during a drought for best performance. Prune after flowering before the next year's buds are set; pruning after the end of July may remove the next year's blooms. Cut out dead wood. You can also trim back stems to renew or decrease the shrub in size.

DESIGNER'S CHOICE

Hydrangea quercifolia 'Alice'   10"–12" pyramidal white to pink flowers, wine-red fall color, more sun tolerance. 10′–12′ h and w.

H. quercifolia 'Flemygea' (Snow Queen) Dense 6"–8" upright flowers with deep reddish bronze fall color; similar to species, but flower panicles are larger, showier, and on more rigid, erect stems. 4′–5′ h × 5′–6′ w. Zone (4) 5.

H. quercifolia 'Pee Wee' Mounded dwarf with 4"–5" flowers. 'Little Honey' is a yellow-flowered form of 'Pee Wee'. 3′–4′ h × 3′–4′ or more w.

H. quercifolia 'Sike's Dwarf' Floriferous dwarf. 2′–3′ h × 4′ w.

H. quercifolia 'Snowflake' Stacked sepals form double droopy 12"–15" flower panicles, white to rosy and buff; burgundy fall foliage; incredibly beautiful shrub with long period of bloom; one of the best; not to be confused with the single 'Snow Queen'. 6′ h and w.

HYPERICUM

Hypericum 'Hidcote' ○

hy-PEE-ri-kum HID-kut

Hidcote St. Johnswort

St. John's Wort Family (Clusiaceae)
Evergreen or semi-evergreen
flowering shrub
2′–4′ h and w

Valued for its long season of bloom (May/June through September/October) and its handsome, dark blue-green opposite leaves, this charming shrub produces cheerful, 3", 5-petal, yellow flowers with long, tufted, gold stamens in the center. Although it grows best in the moist temperate climate of the Pacific Northwest, gardeners can grow it in other places including rock soils and in a crescent-shaped area from Texas to Virginia noted for its dark, rich clay soils.

LANDSCAPE USE

Looks attractive massed in beds, grown in the middle of a perennial border, or planted as a low hedge.

ORIGIN   Garden hybrid

HARDINESS ZONES   (5) 6–8

LIGHT   Full sun to partial shade.

SOIL   Well-drained, average garden soil.

Hypericum 'Hidcote'

GROWING Late winter or early spring pruning promotes heavier blooming. In cold climates, cut to the ground in early spring and treat like a perennial.

DESIGNER'S CHOICE

Hypericum calycinum (Aaron's beard) An aggressive evergreen to semi-evergreen species used as a groundcover. Excellent for growing beneath trees, erosion control, and rock gardens. Tolerates alkaline clay soils. 1–2' h × 2' w. Zones 5–8.

H. frondosum 'Sunburst' Native to the South, a deciduous shrub with bluish green leaves, red-brown exfoliating bark, and 1"–2" yellow flowers in summer. Grown for its long period of bloom, 'Sunburst', which blooms on new wood, is deer resistant, salt and drought tolerant, and pH adaptable. Plant it in full sun to partial shade and use it massed as a low-maintenance planting for a slope or mixed with other shrubs in a border. 2'–4' h and w. Zones 5–8.

H. kalmianum (Kalm St. Johnswort) Dense, evergreen, mounded shrub with linear leaves; covered with clusters of tufted yellow flowers in mid to late summer; native to Great Lakes area. 2'–3' h and w. Zones 4–7.

ILEX

Ilex aquifolium △

I-leks ah-kwi ГОН Icc·um

English holly

Holly Family (Aquifoliaceae)
Evergreen shrub or tree
12'–50' h × 8'–15' w

Slow-growing English holly produces gleaming, red berries in fall from a young age. This erect, pyramidal holly prefers a moderate, coastal climate in the U.S., but I grew two 'Argenteomarginata's in a tall, backyard, raised bed filled with 1'–2' of concrete rubble at the base in hot, humid, downtown Wilmington, Delaware. We still visit the trees when we return to the state, and they're thriving. English holly has medium texture in the landscape. Prunings with profuse, red berries and lovely leaves make excellent holiday decorations; some salt-tolerance makes it a good coastal planting.

Young leaves are shiny and evergreen with wavy, spiny margins; adult leaves, still glossy, have smooth edges. The bark is smooth and gray. It produces insignificant, cream flowers in spring. In the fall, the shrubs bear abundant bright red berries. Cultivars with orange or yellow berries are also available.

LANDSCAPE USE
Hedge, screen, or barrier because of the density of the branches and its sharp-tipped leaves

ORIGIN Beech and oak forests of Europe and western Asia.

HARDINESS ZONES 6–8

LIGHT Full sun to partial shade.

SOIL Moist, acid, very well-drained, organic soils. Prefers temperate coastal conditions. Declines in poorly drained clay soils and in soils with a high pH.

ALL ABOUT ILEX

If you value hollies for their spiny-leafed evergreen boughs or bright scarlet fruits, you're not alone. Yet this genus offers much more than the predictable combo of red and green. You can also find hollies with yellow, orange, and ivory berries and with variegated green-and-white or green-and-gold leaves. Most hollies need male and female plants for the ornamental fruits, but a few cultivars can set fruit without a pollinator. There's a holly to suit your style, climate, and growing conditions. For example, evergreen inkberry, with its smooth-edged, dark green leaves and black fruits; yaupon, another evergreen holly with scarlet fruits; and deciduous winterberry with its lavish red fruits are all great hollies for moist to wet soils in the eastern U.S. Watch out for aphids, leaf miners, and scale. Depending upon the species or cultivar, Ilex serves many landscape purposes from grand lawn specimens and low foundation plantings to naturalizing and formal or informal hedges and barriers. The berries, however, which can cause an upset stomach, are strictly for the birds.

Ilex x meserveae 'Blue Princess'

Ilex aquifolium
'Aurea Marginata'

GROWING   Needs male English holly for best pollination. Shear to shape; withstands severe trimming. Shelter English holly from extreme winds and high temperatures.

CAUTION   Invasive potential in the North-west, Southwest, and Mid-Atlantic regions.

DESIGNER'S CHOICE

Ilex aquifolium 'Argentea Marginata' Leaves have white to cream margins. 15'–20' h × 8'–12' w.

I. aquifolium 'Ferox Argentea' (hedgehog holly) Striking non-fruiting male cultivar; variegated, green-centered leaves with white spiny edges and white spines on the upper leaf surface. 15' h × 8'–10' w.

I. aquifolium 'Monvila' (Gold Coast) Compact male with yellow-edged, deep green, shiny, small leaves. 4'–6' h and w.

Ilex × aquipernyi 'San Jose' △

I-leks a-kwi-PER-nee-i
San Jose holly

Holly Family (Aquifoliaceae)
Small broad-leaf evergreen tree
8'–20' h × 4'–12' w

Grow this small female tree as an understory planting on your property or use it in formal gardens. You won't be disappointed. Like other hollies, it boasts glossy, evergreen foliage with spiny margins; a dense, compact form; and brilliant, big, red berries. 'Meschick' and 'San Jose' hollies show resistance to deer browsing. Culture is similar to other evergreen hollies. Use male blue hollies such as 'China Boy', 'Blue Prince', or 'Blue Stallion' to pollinate. 'San Jose', a hybrid of English and Perny hollies, has a compact, broad, upright form.

LANDSCAPE USE
Specimen.

ORIGIN   Garden hybrid

HARDINESS ZONES   6–8

LIGHT   Full sun to partial shade.

SOIL   Moist, acid, very well-drained, organic soils. Declines in poorly drained clay soils and in soils with a high pH.

GROWING   For abundant berry production, grow in full sun.

DESIGNER'S CHOICE

Ilex × aquipernyi 'Meschick' (Dragon Lady) Narrow, erect with very shiny foliage. 16'–20' h × 4'–6' w.

Ilex × attenuata 'Fosteri' △

I-lex at-te-new-AY-ta FOS-te-ri
Foster's holly, Foster #2

Holly Family (Aquifoliaceae)
Small evergreen tree
20'–30' h × 12' w

Frequently seen in the Southeast, Foster's holly is a thickly branched, small female tree, pyramidal in shape. It has handsome, small, shiny, spiny-edged, evergreen leaves and abundant, dark red berries up to .3" in diameter, which persist and give it prolonged winter interest. The showy female cultivar 'Savannah' grows bigger — up to 30' h × 25' w; big, radiant red berries cover the tree in winter and fall, and the leaves are shiny and light green. 'Big John' is a non-fruiting male. 'Sunny Foster's new leaves are gleaming yellow, turning green as they age. Female Fosters fruit without males.

LANDSCAPE USE
Its pyramidal shape makes it a good choice for a natural screen or grouping.

ORIGIN   Garden hybrid of American and Dahoon hollies.

HARDINESS ZONES   6–9

LIGHT   Best fruiting in full sun, but tolerates partial shade.

SOIL   Moist, well-drained, fertile, slightly acid soils. Leaves may yellow in alkaline soils.

GROWING   Spittlebugs may be a problem.

Ilex cornuta 'Burfordii' ○

I-leks kor-NU-ta bur-FOR-dee-i
Burford Chinese holly

Holly Family (Aquifoliaceae)
Evergreen shrub or small tree
8'–10' h (20' when grown as a small tree) × 5'–10' w

Burford hollies are popular in the South for formal hedging and informal screening. This vigorous Asian shrub, a form of Chinese holly, has a dense, rounded habit; glossy, evergreen leaves up to 4" long with spiny margins; and abundant, red berries all winter, even when no pollinators are present. Pollinators on this and similar cultivars may produce more berries. Many cultivars available.

LANDSCAPE USE
Formal hedging, informal screening.

ORIGIN   China, Korea

HARDINESS ZONES   7–9

LIGHT   Full sun to partial shade.

SOIL   A variety of soils, including acid, alkaline, dry, and wet conditions.

GROWING   Scales can trouble it.

Ilex cornuta 'Burfordii Nana'

Ilex cornuta 'Berries Jubilee' Rounded form. Produces abundant, vivid red fruits. No pollinator needed. 6'–10' h and w.

I. cornuta 'Burfordii Nana' (dwarf Burford holly) Looks good as a foundation plant or near the front of the shrub border. Growth may be more open in shady sites. No pollinator needed. 4'–7' h and w.

I. cornuta 'Willowleaf' Glistening leaves, bright dark red fruits with or without a pollinator; makes a good windbreak or barrier. 15' h and w.

Ilex crenata ○

I-leks kre-NAH-ta

Japanese holly

Holly Family (Aquifoliaceae)
Broad-leaf evergreen shrub or small tree
10'–12' h x 3'–5' w

Although Japanese holly, the species, is a big evergreen shrub or small tree, most gardeners grow it for its boxwoodlike cultivars with small, dark, evergreen leaves and dense, tight forms. A favorite cultivar is the ubiquitous 'Helleri', the small, rounded, slow-growing shrub found in foundation plantings throughout much of the country. It needs no pruning to keep its beautifully rounded, almost hemispherical shape. Yet, although it's sold in Zone 5 nurseries, it won't survive a harsh Zone 5 winter. We planted several in our southern New Hampshire garden near the seacoast, but none survived temperatures of –15°F with little snow cover.

The dark green, ½" × ¼"–½" leaves are alternate, simple, and evergreen. The non-ornamental bark is green when young, then gray-green with age. Insignificant flowers are whitish. Only female plants produce the non-showy, round, black berries (drupes) in fall that remain until spring. Many cultivars are available.

LANDSCAPE USE

It has the landscape versatility of boxwood, especially in Zones 6 and 7, where its pure and often geometrical form has a pleasant, stiff formality. Use in foundations, massed as a groundcover, and as a low hedge.

ORIGIN Asia

HARDINESS ZONES 6–8 (some cultivars hardy in Zone 5).

LIGHT Full sun to shade.

SOIL Moist, loose, well-drained, somewhat acid soils.

GROWING Shelter from winter winds and mulch the base, especially in the North. It requires little to no pruning to stay in shape. It may be afflicted by spider mites, nematodes, and black knot.

Ilex crenata 'Beehive' Mounding form with glossy, deep green leaves. 4' h × 5'–6' w.

I. crenata 'Convexa' Male with convex leaves. 9' h × 2' w. Zone 5.

I. crenata 'Geisha' Tiny, shiny leaves with yellow berries. 2½' h and w.

I. crenata 'Glory' Extremely cold-hardy male with glossy, deep green foliage. 5' h × 8' w. Zone 5.

I. crenata 'Green Lustre' Very hardy; shiny, dark geen leaves. 4' h × 6'–7' w. Zone 5.

I. crenata 'Helleri' Small mound growing eventually to about 4' h × 5' w. My 10-year-old plants were about 2' h × 3½' w when they died after an exceptionally cold winter. I wouldn't plant this cultivar in any Zone colder than 6.

I. crenata 'Northern Beauty' Birds eat the black fruits in fall; use it for a trimmed or untrimmed barrier hedge. 4' h × 4'–5' w.

I. crenata 'Sky Pencil' Tight, branching column with glossy, dark leaves. 6'–10' h × 1'–2' w.

Ilex crenata 'Helleri'

Ilex decidua 🐦 ✳

I-leks de-SID-u-a

Deciduous holly, Possumhaw

Holly Family (Aquifoliaceae)
Deciduous shrub or small tree
7'–20' h x 5'–15 ' w

Grow this upright, suckering shrub or small tree for red, orange, and yellow fall berries, which persist into winter or spring and attract cedar waxwings, quail, and other birds. As with winterberry *(I. verticillata),* best fruiting comes from planting both female and male plants, though some possumhaws can fruit without males. Berries and leaves, which turn yellow in fall, typically cluster on blunt thornlike spurs or short stems.

LANDSCAPE USE
Naturalizing, screening, informal hedging, massing at the edge of a large property for winter interest, especially in the South.

ORIGIN   Swamps, stream banks, and forest understories of the southeastern and central U.S.

HARDINESS ZONES   5–9

LIGHT   Full sun to partial shade; plants produce more berries in sun.

SOIL   Moist, acid, well-drained soil high in organic matter is ideal, but plants are pH adaptable and tolerant of both heavy, moist, compacted soils and dry soils once established.

GROWING   Use male possumhaw or male American holly *(Ilex opaca)* to pollinate. Shape the plant by trimming in early spring before growth starts. Thicket-forming when left alone. Pest- and disease-resistant, except for infrequent scales, leaf spots, and powdery mildew.

DESIGNER'S CHOICE
Ilex decidua 'Byer's Golden' Yellow berries. 7'–20' h × 5'–15' w.

I. decidua 'Red Escort' Male pollinator with dense branching. 7'–25' h × 5'–20' w.

I. decidua 'Sundance' Red fruit on a robust, twiggy shrub. 6' h and w.

I. decidua 'Warren's Red' Lavish red berry producer; very hardy; more upright than species. 7'–25' h × 5'–20' w.

Ilex glabra 0 › 🐦 ✳

I-leks GLA-bra

Inkberry

Holly Family (Aquifoliaceae)
Evergreen shrub
6'–8' h x 8'–10' w

Ilex glabra is a native broad-leaf evergreen that can form a mass when conditions are right. Deer resistant, this suckering shrub tolerates shade, damp soils, seaside living, and hard pruning and is easy to plant and grow.

Its glossy, deep green, evergreen leaves are up to 2" × ¾". The bark is a smooth green. Insignificant, creamy white flowers appear in spring. Depending on cultivar, berries can be a showy white or reddish purple turning black; berries, which appear in fall and last until mid-spring, are up to ⅓" wide.

LANDSCAPE USE
Take advantage of its spreading nature to fill slopes; use compact forms as foundation plantings. Use as a boxwood alternative in cities and problem sites.

ORIGIN   Swamps of eastern North America.

HARDINESS ZONES   5–9

LIGHT   Full sun to partial shade.

SOIL   Moist, acid soils.

GROWING   Site inkberry where it's protected from extreme winds and cold temperatures, since the foliage can burn in these conditions. It tends toward legginess and may experience occasional leaf spot.

Ilex glabra 'Nigra'

DESIGNER'S CHOICE
Ilex glabra 'Chamzin' (Nordic) Tight, rounded habit; very hardy, cut back to keep it from getting leggy; handsome, dark green leaves year round. 4' h and w. Zone (4) 5.

I. glabra 'Compacta' With pruning, prolific black berries through winter; twiggy, good for hedges and shrub borders; hardier than some cultivars. 4'–6' h × 2' w.

I. glabra 'Densa' Withstands moisture, shade, heat, drought, and severe pruning. 4'–10' h and w. Zone 4.

I. glabra 'Nigra' Bushy, with decent lower leaf retention; glossy, dark green leaves may turn purplish in winter; good cultivar for the South, according to a study by the University of Georgia's Professor Michael Dirr. 6'–8' h × 8'–10' w.

I. glabra 'Shamrock' Slow growing with small, shiny, deep green leaves, 1½" × ½"; holds lower leaves pretty well, making it good for foundation plantings and massing. 3'–5' h and w.

Ilex × meserveae ○ › △ ✳

I-leks me-SER-vee-i

Meserve hybrid holly, Blue holly

Holly Family (Aquifoliaceae)
Broad-leaf evergreen shrub to
small tree
6'–15' h and w

Because of its excellent cold hardiness
for a holly, this is one for northern
gardeners. Even in the north,
however, leaves can dry out and die
on plants exposed to harsh winter
winds. Blue hollies have rich, deep
green to blue-green foliage that
harmonizes with most garden
settings. I've seen a handsome,
informal hedge covering the legs
of a sunny deck, and a pair of plants
casually flanking the mudroom entry
of a heavily shaded suburban house;
the hollies thrived in both sites.
Female blue hollies need a pollinator.

LANDSCAPE USE
Meserve hollies make excellent
informal or sheared formal hedges,
thick screens, and spiny, densely
branched barriers.

ORIGIN Garden

Ilex x meserveae 'Blue Princess'

HARDINESS ZONES 5–6

LIGHT Thrives in sun or shade.

SOIL Moist, well-drained, average to
fertile, slightly acidic to slightly alkaline
soils.

GROWING Shelter from winter wind and
summer sun by avoiding western and
southern exposures. Water well in fall. In
the north, best grown in sites receiving
reliable snowfall.

Ilex x meserveae 'Blue Angel'

DESIGNER'S CHOICE
Ilex × meserveae 'Blue Girl' Hardy and
shrubby with bright red berries; use
'Blue Boy' or other blue holly for
pollinator. 6'–8' h × 3'–6' w.

I. × meserveae 'Blue Princess' Dark
blue-green leaves on purplish stems,
profuse red berries on hardiest
dense, bushy blue holly; use 'Blue
Prince' or other male blue holly for
pollinator. 8'–15' h × 6'–10' w.

I. × meserveae 'Mesan' (Blue
Stallion) Fast-growing male, lacking
leaf spines; long bloom season makes
it an effective blue holly pollinator;
hardier. 16' h × 12' w.

I. × meserveae 'Mesgolg' (Golden
Girl) Yellow berries; shiny, spiny,
blue-green leaves; purplish stems;
densely branched. 12' h and w.

I. × meserveae 'Mesid' (Blue Maid)
Fast-growing blue holly with big,
red berries. Use male blue hollies
for pollinators; hardier. 8'–15' h ×
6'–10' w.

I. × meserveae 'Mesog' (China Girl)
Mounding habit, brilliant red berries, small shiny green leaves tinged
blue; heat tolerant; use China Boy®
'Mesdob' or other male blue holly for
pollinator; hardier. 8'–10' h × 6'–8' w.

Ilex 'Nellie R. Stevens' △

I-leks

'Nellie R. Stevens' holly

Holly Family (Aquifoliaceae)
Small broad-leaf evergreen tree or
large shrub
15'–20' h x 10'–18' w

'Nellie R. Stevens' is an excellent
holly for the South because it grows
fast and tolerates heat and drought
once established. Although the
brilliant scarlet berries are big (⅓")
and plentiful, they're popular with
wildlife and don't last long. Use male
Chinese hollies (*I. cornuta*) or the
male 'Edward J. Stevens' to pollinate
for berry production.

LANDSCAPE USE
With its glossy, dark, evergreen
leaves and pyramidal shape, 'Nellie R.
Stevens' makes a handsome, southern
garden specimen or an effective windbreak or barrier plant because of its
multitude of tough, spiny leaves.

ORIGIN Garden origin

HARDINESS ZONES 6–9

LIGHT Full sun but tolerates partial shade.

SOIL Well drained acid soil with medium
to dry moisture levels.

GROWING Needs regular deep watering
until established; little or no pruning.

Key: ◖ Oval △ Pyramid ○ Rounded ▽ Vase ◠ Spreading ⋒ Weeping ⪜ Creeping/Suckering/Trailing ✳ Easy ■ 253

Ilex opaca △

I-leks o-PAY-ka

American holly

Holly Family (Aquifoliaceae)
Broad-leaf evergreen tree
30'–50' h x 20'–40' w

With time and proper growing conditions, American holly grows into a small to medium pyramidal tree with one or more trunks and branches to the ground. The leathery, evergreen leaves of the species are not as attractive as some of the cultivars. This holly can grow to 50' in its native Southeast, but it's usually smaller. Although salt, drought, somewhat wet sites, and air pollution won't bother it, wind can be a problem. Plant it in a somewhat protected spot for best results. American holly is seldom bothered by deer, but the red berries draw birds, especially spring robins, and are a larval food for Henry's elfin butterfly.

The 4" × 2" evergreen foliage is alternate and simple; on some cultivars it is a shiny, deep green. The non-showy bark is green in youth, then pale gray and lenticelled with age. Flowers are whitish. The species bears persistent, red, lackluster berries (drupes) up to ½" wide; cultivars may have brilliant showy fruits. Needs male *I. opaca* for fruit production.

LANDSCAPE USE
Cultivars are handsome in groups or alone; tall screen.

ORIGIN   Southeastern U.S.

HARDINESS ZONES   (5) 6–9

LIGHT   Full sun to partial shade.

SOIL   Moist, rich, well-drained, friable soils. Good drainage a must.

GROWING   Protect from wind. Best transplanted in early spring in the North. Plant a male within 100 feet of females for best fruit set. Tough once established,

withstanding drought, somewhat wet sites, and air pollution. Look out for scales, mites, holly leaf miner, powdery mildew; winter burn in exposed sites.

DESIGNER'S CHOICE

Ilex opaca 'Jersey Princess' Dense and pyramidal; glossy, dark green leaves; and matte-red, heavy fruit set. Use 'Jersey Knight' to pollinate. Both male and female retain dark green color through winter; one of the best cultivars. 15'–30' h × 8'–18' w.

I. opaca 'Judy Evans' Fine, shiny, deep green leaves, excellent cold hardiness, and vigorous growth. 25'–40' h × 15'–20' w.

I. opaca 'Maryland Dwarf' Nice in foundations plantings or low hedges with its sparse but persistent red berries that attract birds. 3' h × 3'–10' w.

I. opaca 'Miss Helen' Profuse, red berries ripen early and persist into winter; dense pyramidal shape. 15'–30' h × 10'–20' w.

I. opaca 'Old Heavy Berry' A top cultivar for vigor, rich red berry set, and excellent winter hardiness. 15'–30' h × 10'–20' w.

I. opaca 'Satyr Hill' Glossy, spiny, dark olive-green leaves; ⅜", vivid red berries all winter into spring, when they're eaten by birds. American Holly Society's Holly of the Year for 2003. 9' h and w at 10 years, slow growing to 40' h.

I. opaca 'Stewart's Silver Crown' Variegated foliage with cream edges and gray-green marbling. 25' h and w.

Ilex pedunculosa △

I-leks pe-dun-kew-LOH-sa

Longstalk holly

Holly Family (Aquifoliaceae)
Evergreen shrub to small tree
20'–30' h x 15'–20' w

Longstalk holly stands out for its cold hardiness and for its handsome,

wavy, green, spine-free leaves up to 3" long. The species name derives from the showy, red fruits that appear on long 1"–2" stalks in fall.

LANDSCAPE USE
Use as a specimen for its distinctive long-stalked one-quarter inch red berries and handsome shiny green leaves; plant a male with a couple of females for an impressive group or evergreen privacy planting. An under-utilized landscape plant, worth the hunt.

ORIGIN   China, Japan, Taiwan.

HARDINESS ZONES   5–8

LIGHT   Sun to partial shade.

SOIL   Moist, slightly acidic, and well-drained.

GROWING   Although it withstands both salt and air pollution, it doesn't like strong winds, which turn leaves yellowish green in exposed sites.

Ilex verticillata ⬥ ✳

I-leks ver-ti-sil-LAH-ta

Winterberry

Holly Family (Aquifoliaceae)
Deciduous shrub
6'–12' h and w

The first time I saw the brilliant, red berries of 'Winter Red' and 'Red Sprite' after leaf drop in the shrub border between our house and our neighbor's, they looked gorgeous. Each day I admired them through the window or when I wandered by — until Thanksgiving, that is, when my neighbor phoned to tell me that 19 wild turkeys were munching their way through our yard. I dashed to the window and there they were, feasting on my winter interest that was supposed to last till spring. Obviously, this shrub attracts birds and other wildlife!

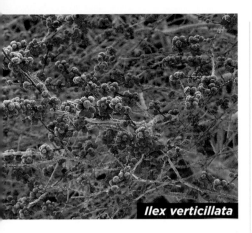
Ilex verticillata

The alternate, simple green leaves are usually without notable fall color but sometimes may be yellow to purple. Neither the dark-gray bark nor the small, white, cup-shaped flowers that bloom in early summer are showy, but pollinated females produce dazzling red berries along the stems.

LANDSCAPE USE
Informal hedge in naturalized wet areas, massed in beds and borders where the red berries shine after leaf drop; nice in woodland gardens, native gardens, at pond's edge; compact cultivars useful as foundation plantings. Winterberry fruits look terrific against tall ornamental grasses both in the fall when the grasses bloom, as well as in winter, when the fruits stand out against the pale buff hues of the grasses.

ORIGIN Swamps and low spots of the eastern U.S.

HARDINESS ZONES 3–9

LIGHT Full sun to partial shade, with heavier fruit set in full sun.

SOIL Moist, fertile, acid soils high in organic matter. They can grow with their roots in water.

GROWING As long as soils are moist and acid, winterberry is an easy shrub to grow. Depending upon its origin, it can grow slowly or with vigor: twiggy, suckering and spreading to form wide clumps.

DESIGNER'S CHOICE
Ilex verticillata 'Afterglow' Grown for its orangey-red fruits. 6' h and w. Zone 4.

I. verticillata 'Jim Dandy' Oval to rounded male; effective pollinator for many early female winterberries because of long bloom season. 6'–10' h and w. Zone 4.

I. verticillata 'Maryland Beauty' Shiny, big, deep red fruit; used for commerical cutting. 6' h and w. Zone 4.

I. verticillata 'Nana' (syn. *I. verticillata* 'Red Sprite') 'Jim Dandy' to pollinate, dense oval to rounded form. 'Nana' is an outstanding cultivar that can fit into most gardens, no matter what the size. I grow this cultivar and never cease to admire the size and abundance of the berries, which are eventually eaten by the birds. 3'–5' h and w. Zone 4.

I. verticillata 'Stoplight' Bold, long-lasting, shiny, dark red berries; its pollinator is 'Jim Dandy'. 8' h and w.

I. verticillata 'Winter Gold' Peach or gold-orange to gold berries; a sport of 'Winter Red'. 6'–9' h and w. Zone 4.

I. verticillata 'Winter Red' Upright female with shiny, dark green leaves; berries persist from late summer to late winter until birds eat the fruit. Stunning display against the snow. Pollinated by 'Southern Gentleman'. 6'–9' h × 6'–10' w. Zone 4.

HYBRID CHOICES
I. verticillata × *serrata* 'Harvest Red' Upright vase-shaped hybrid with profuse red berries from late summer through early winter. Pollinated by 'Apollo'. 8'–10' h × 4'–6' w. Zone 5.

I. verticillata × *serrata* 'Sparkleberry' Bright red berries from late summer to early fall; red new growth; yellow to purple fall color; hybrid pollinated by 'Apollo', which also pollinates 'Harvest Red' and 'Bonfire'. 8'–10' h and w. Zone 5.

Ilex vomitoria 🌿 ✳
I-leks vah-mi-TOH-ree-a

Yaupon holly

Holly Family (Aquifoliaceae)
Broad-leaf evergreen, multi-stemmed shrub or small tree for southeast
15'–20' h × 10'–15' w

Ilex verticillata 'Winter Gold'

Ilex vomitoria 'Bordeaux'

Fast-growing yaupon, a small-leafed, evergreen holly native to both sandy and swampy soils in the southeastern U.S., puts up with just about anything. It grows in sun and shade, seaside and inland, and tolerates both moisture and drought. With its small, bright red berries and its leathery, evergreen leaves, it offers food and shelter to birds and other wildlife. For the berries, which persist through winter, you need both male and female plants. Many cultivars.

LANDSCAPE USE
Use yaupon for naturalistic barriers, hedges, and screens.

ORIGIN Both sandy and swampy soils in the southeastern U.S.

HARDINESS ZONES 7–10

LIGHT Sun or shade.

SOIL Tolerates both moisture and drought.

GROWING Disease resistant.

CAUTION Eating leaves causes vomiting.

DESIGNER'S CHOICE
Ilex vomitoria 'Condeaux' (Bordeaux)
  Dark green leaves turn burgundy in winter. 3' h and w.
I. vomitoria 'Stoke's Dwarf' (syn. *I. vomitoria* 'Schillings' or 'Schilling's Dwarf') Small, mounded, male holly ideal for massing and foundations. 2'–3' h × 4' w.

ILLICIUM

Illicium floridanum △

Il-LI-see-um flo-ri-DA-num

Florida anise, Stink-bush

Illicium Family (Illiciaceae)
Broad-leaf evergreen shrub or small tree
10' h × 8' w

Florida stink-bush makes an attractive specimen in the shrub border, with year-round interest from its shiny, evergreen leaves. You can't remove this endangered species from the wild (as a rule of thumb, in fact, don't take *any* plants from the wild), but you can sometimes find it at native plant nurseries. Make sure these plants are nursery-propagated and not wild-collected. The name stink-bush comes from the malodorous, fishy-smelling, red or white flowers and glossy leaves, which smell like anise when crushed (its common name is Florida anise).

LANDSCAPE USE
Singly or grouped in shrub and mixed borders; informal naturalistic hedge for shade gardens.

ORIGIN Moist, steep valleys in Florida and Louisiana.

HARDINESS ZONES 7–10

LIGHT Shade to partial shade is best.

SOIL Moist, mulched soil.

GROWING Intolerant of drought; keep mulched and water during dry spells.

CAUTION Poisonous if eaten.

DESIGNER'S CHOICE
Illicium parviflorum Grown as a clipped formal hedge or used for low maintenance casual screening in the Southeast, yellow anise is a small conical broad-leaf evergreen tree or big shrub native to moist spots in Florida. The shiny, 4" × 2" leaves are fragrant when crushed, but unlike *I. verum*, the edible Asian spice, the endangered *I. parviflorum* is poisonous if consumed. 20' h × 15' w. Zones 8–10.

INDIGOFERA

Indigofera kirilowii ☁ ✳

in-di-GAH-fe-ra ki-ri-LOW-ee-I

Kirilow's indigo

Pea Family (Fabaceae)
Deciduous flowering shrub
2'–3' h and w

This highly adaptable Asian native has a low, suckering habit, making it suitable for an easy groundcover, particularly under taller deciduous shrubs in alkaline soils. Bright green leaves cover its dense twigs, and rosy pink, sweet-pea-like blooms appear in early summer. Although this indigo dies to the ground annually in cold-winter climates, it blooms on new wood and flowers every year. There's also a white-flowered form that's hardier than the species.

LANDSCAPE USE
Grow as a deciduous groundcover or in mixed borders as a buddleia-like cut-back perennial in Zone 5 and the cold part of Zone 6.

ORIGIN Asia

HARDINESS ZONES 5–7

LIGHT Full sun.

SOIL Moist, well drained, slightly acid to alkaline soils.

GROWING Drought tolerant for short periods but cannot bear high heat and humidity. To renew, prune to the ground in late winter or early spring.

Indigofera kirilowii

ITEA

Itea virginica ⚘

i-TEE-a vir-GIN-i-ka

Sweetspire

Escallonia Family (Escalloniaceae)
Deciduous flowering shrub
3'–8' h × 3'–12' w

Virginia sweetspire makes a bushy fountain of arching stems sometimes branched near the top. In late spring to early summer, tiny, white, sweet-scented flowers are arranged in up to 6"-long, narrow spires along the stems, giving them a droopy grace. The shrub suckers and can colonize a wide area, especially where soils are rich and moist.

The foliage consists of alternate, simple, green, 2"–4" × 1"–1½" leaves; they exhibit excellent fall color in burgundy, fluorescent crimson, yellow, and orange. Newer stems are green to purplish red; older stems are smooth and brown. Fruits are not showy.

LANDSCAPE USE
Massed in naturalized shrub borders or along the water's edge where its loose, arching, graceful form creates billows of showy flowers in late spring and early summer and its terrific fall color can paint the landscape.

ORIGIN   Swamps and pond edges of
   southeastern U.S.

HARDINESS ZONES   (5) 6–9

LIGHT   Full sun to partial shade.

SOIL   Rich, moist, well-drained soils;
   tolerates both acid and alkaline soils;
   tolerates periods of both flooding and
   drought.

GROWING   Needs infrequent pruning to
   eliminate weak or old wood. Snipping
   off flower shoots after blooming to
   new growth enhances the display of
   fresh foliage and fall color. There are
   some hardiness issues in Zone 5. I've

grown 'Henry's Garnet' at the sunny southeastern corner of my house for the last 7 years, and it's still a scraggly bunch of 2' stems.

DESIGNER'S CHOICE
Itea virginica 'Henry's Garnet' Reliable, wine-red fall color and showy, white flowers on a more compact plant than the species. 3'–4' h × 5'–7' w.

I. virginica 'Merlot' Compact twiggy shrub, denser than species, with fragrant flowers and orange to burgundy fall color. 3' h and w.

Itea virginica **'Henry's Garnet'**

Itea virginica **'Henry's Garnet'**

I. virginica 'Morton' (Scarlet Beauty) Chosen for its cold hardiness and scarlet fall color. 4'–5' h and w. Zone (4) 5.

I. virginica 'Saturnalia' Brilliant pink, yellow, red, and orange fall color. 3'–4' h × 4'–5' w.

I. virginica 'Sprich' (Little Henry) Small version of 'Henry's Garnet'. 3'–4' h × 4'–5' w.

JASMINUM

Jasminum nudiflorum ⚘ ✳

jaz-MY-num nu-dee-FLO-rum

Winter jasmine

Olive Family (Oleaceae)
Deciduous shrub
4' h × 10' w

The bare, bright green, young stems and yellow flowers of this mounding, spreading, deciduous shrub offer welcome relief from winter's dull hues. Winter jasmine blooms early, beginning in January and continuing through March. In summer, shiny, dark green leaves cover the long, trailing stems, which root where they touch the ground and create new plants. From these babies, fast-growing winter jasmine keeps mounding and spreading. It looks impressive grown in masses or tumbling over walls.

The glossy, dark green, opposite leaves are made up of three leaflets, each about ½"–1¼" long; they have no fall color. The four-angled stems are vivid green when new, then woody brown with age. Jasmine blooms on old wood before the leaves appear. The flowers are slim, yellow, tubular petals that flare into flat lobes at right angles to the tube. Fruits are black berries.

LANDSCAPE USE
Groundcover for banks, accent for retaining walls, massing.

Jasminum nudiflorum

ORIGIN   China

HARDINESS ZONES   6–9

LIGHT   Full sun to shade.

SOIL   Prefers moist, well-drained soils but adjusts to many conditions including drought and infertility.

GROWING   Very cold winters can destroy flower buds. Trim straggly plants to the crown every five years or so to renew them. Winter jasmine is easily transplanted and tends to be a very healthy plant. However, it is an aggressive spreader.

CAUTION   Entrenched plants may be hard to contain or eliminate.

JUGLANS

Juglans nigra ○ › ○

JUG-lanz NY-gra

Black walnut

Walnut Family (Juglandaceae)
Deciduous tree
50'–75' h and w

Black walnut is common in the East and Midwest, thanks to squirrels that plant the seeds and to people who farm the tree for its hardwood and edible nuts. When black walnut is raised for wood production, it is grown in competitive, forestlike conditions to encourage columnar trees with long trunks and short crowns. The heartwood, which is warp-, shrink-, and splinter-free, can touch the ground without rotting. Gun makers use it for strong, smooth stocks and railroad engineers use it for ties. On the other hand, cultivating black walnut for its fruit is best done in a sunny, open space, where the tree develops a short trunk that splits into upward-growing, widespread branches laden every couple of years with large nut crops. The heaviest fruiting begins when trees are about 30 years old. Black walnuts, enclosed in an outer, green husk and an inner, dark-brown shell, are good to eat but hard to shell. Abrasives made from ground walnut shells are used for blast-cleaning metals, alloys, and plastics without scratching and without mineral and metal contamination.

Black walnut tree bears alternate, deciduous, compound leaves up to 2' long, comprised of 15–23 lance-shaped 3½" × 1½" leaflets arranged featherlike along a midrib. The summer green turns to a yellowish color in fall. Dark blackish gray bark has diamond-shaped ridges surrounded by deep, irregular grooves. Like birch, black walnut produces spring flowers on male catkins and female spikes. Rounded, green, 2" fruits appear every 2–3 years, dropping just after the leaves and then turning black. Inside are sweet, oily, edible nuts in a ridged brown shell.

Juglans nigra

ALL ABOUT JUGLANS

Walnut trees produce tasty, high-protein nuts for baking, roasting, or eating raw. In addition to their edible hard-shelled fruits, they are grown for their powerful winter structure and distinctive, coarse-textured foliage that grows 1'–2' long in a featherlike pattern of leaflets along a midrib. To ward off competition from other plants, walnuts secrete juglone, a chemical toxic to many nearby plants. The juglone exudes from all parts of the tree, especially from the roots and nutshells (see Gardening with Black and White Walnut). Its deep taproots make walnuts difficult to transplant. These trees do not perform well in the heat and humidity of the Deep South, where the related pecans grow well, and they do not tolerate shade.

LANDSCAPE USE

Grow as a specimen in large lawns for its fruit and for shade. Plant away from the house because of litter from nuts and big fallen leaves. For nuts, plant two so that you get pollination.

ORIGIN   Eastern North America.

HARDINESS ZONES   4–9

LIGHT   Full sun to light shade.

SOIL   Prefers deep, fertile, moist, well-drained soils with neutral pH for maximum growth.

GROWING   See All About *Juglans*.

CAUTION: Wear gloves when collecting ripe black nuts off the ground, since they can stain the skin.

DESIGNER'S CHOICE

Juglans cinerea (butternut, white walnut)   Eastern North American native valued for sweet, oblong nuts and shade-bearing crown; pale, furniture-quality wood. Endangered species because of butternut canker, a fatal fungal disease; disappeared from the Carolinas; Wisconsin's large butternut population is under attack. The USDA Forest Service says proper pruning and tree care increases butternut survival in a cultivated landscape; healthy, well-maintained seedlings planted away from competing vegetation and in disease-free surroundings will probably survive. 40'–60' h × 30'–50' w. Zones 3–7.

Juglans regia ⚪

JUG-lanz REE-ja

English walnut, Persian walnut

Walnut Family (Juglandaceae)
Deciduous tree
40'–60' h and w

This Eurasian native produces the hard-shelled, edible walnuts you buy at the supermarket. Most of those nuts come from California, the center

GARDENING WITH BLACK AND WHITE WALNUTS

Don't despair if walnut trees are killing your plants. Here's how to help plants survive the terrors of juglone:

- Clean up debris immediately. These trees may shed a massive leaf or two intermittently throughout the growing season. Don't wait until fall foliage drops to pick them up. The more contact that tree parts have with the soil, the more they can affect what's growing nearby. Similarly, collect nuts as soon as they fall. The toxins in the husks increase as the nuts ripen.

- Make sure your soil contains plenty of organic matter to improve its health, aeration, and drainage. Microorganisms in compost, for example, may consume some of the leached juglone for energy, thus neutralizing it. Regularly adding a top layer of compost can increase your soil's organic matter, but resist the urge to use walnut debris as mulch until it has thoroughly decomposed in a hot compost pile.

- Learn which plants resist juglone. Avoid plants like apple trees, mountain laurels, rhododendrons, blueberries, and white birches that can die from its effects. For black walnut companions, try the following 20 ornamental trees and shrubs:

Trees	
American arborvitae	*Thuja occidentalis*
American holly	*Ilex opaca*
Carolina silverberry	*Halesia carolina*
Dogwood	*Cornus* species
Eastern redbud	*Cercis canadensis*
Golden raintree	*Koelreuteria paniculata*
Hawthorn	*Crataegus* species
Japanese maple	*Acer palmatum*
River birch	*Betula nigra*
Serviceberry	*Amelanchier* x *grandiflora*

Shrubs	
Blackhaw viburnum	*Viburnum prunifolium*
Daphne	*Daphne* species
Forsythia	*Forsythia* species
Juniper	*Juniperus* species
Lilac	*Syringa* species
Ninebark	*Physocarpus opulifolius*
Rose of Sharon	*Hibiscus syriacus*
Spicebush	*Lindera benzoin*
Wild hydrangea	*Hydrangea arborescens*
Witch hazel	*Hamamelis* species

of the American walnut industry. While *J. regia* is usually grown for its nuts, *J. nigra* is typically cultivated for its hard, close-grained wood.

LANDSCAPE USE
A wide-spreading shade tree and specimen for large lawns; edible nuts.

ORIGIN   Eurasia

HARDINESS ZONES   3–7

LIGHT   Full sun.

SOIL   Deep, rich, well-drained soil.

GROWING   Although self-fertile, this cultivar is more productive with one or more similar trees nearby to ecourage bigger crops.

Juniperus chinensis △ › ⌂

ju-NI-per-us chi-NEN-sis

Chinese juniper

Cypress Family (Cupressaceae)
Evergreen tree
50'–60' h x 15'–20' w

In nature, Chinese junipers tend to be narrow trees with blue-green, gray-green, or plain green leaves, either pressed and overlapping or awl shaped. At the nursery, you'll find cultivars of this plant but not the species itself.

LANDSCAPE USE
See individual cultivars below.

ORIGIN   China, Mongolia

HARDINESS ZONES   4–9, although this may vary with the cultivar.

LIGHT   See All About *Juniperus.*

SOIL   See All About *Juniperus.*

GROWING   See All About *Juniperus.*

DESIGNER'S CHOICE
Juniperus chinensis 'Angelica Blue' A horizontal, Pfitzer-type juniper with waxy blue leaves, dense branches. 5'–6' h × 20' w.

J. chinensis 'Blue Point' Dense, broad pyramid with bluish green leaves makes good lawn specimen or tall screen. 12' h × 8' w.

ALL ABOUT *JUNIPERUS*

Junipers remind me of a dinner that my husband, Bob, cooked for our two children and me a few years ago. He wanted to be a gourmet chef and decided to prepare beef with juniper berries, a traditional flavoring of gin. The kids refused to taste it, but I tried a bit, wanting to encourage his newfound interest. The berries imparted an odd flavor to the beef, not one I particularly enjoyed. Bob loved it. He ate the whole dish, including the flavoring berries. Within hours he was sick with violent cramping, which took days to pass.

Lesson: Junipers are for planting, not eating, unless you know what you're doing. Landscape junipers are tough and hardy. Depending upon the species and cultivar, they can be trees, shrubs, or woody groundcovers, and their color varies from green and bright blue to silvery and gold. Many withstand conditions such as drought, road salt, and air pollution. When I drive the Massachusetts Turnpike, the numerous Eastern red cedars (*Juniperus virginiana*) thriving on the parkway impress me with their resilience. Similarly, when I see a juniper pruned into cloud forms with foliage puffs at the branch tips, I marvel at how much one plant can suffer for looks' sake and still flourish.

The evergreen, prickly, aromatic leaves of juniper can be needles or scales, sometimes on the same plant. Young leaves are sometimes needlelike, while mature foliage is comprised of tightly overlapping scales. The bark usually sheds in flakes or thin strips.

Color is reddish brown to gray. Male and female flowers develop on separate plants. The fruit is a handsome, silver-coated, deep blue cone that resembles a berry.

Juniper's greatest advantage is its versatility in the landscape. If you have the right growing conditions, there's a juniper for you, from tall, dramatic sculptural accents to carpetlike groundcovers and mid-sized shrubs in yellow, bicolor, and silvery blue. Some make excellent rock garden plants, others are fine as foundation plantings or even in containers. On the other hand, Juniper will not tolerate competition from other plants. Susceptible to blights and cankers, it's also an alternate host for rusts affecting crabapples, hawthorns, and serviceberries (all members of the Rose Family). Problem insects include bagworms and sap-sucking red spider mites.

They prefer full sun; the shadier the site, the more open and unattractive the plant will look. They grow in acid to alkaline soils, but need light, moist, sandy, soil, though they tolerate dry clay. Soils must be well drained for juniper to thrive.

Junipers usually need no pruning, although you may want to cut back groundcovers and vigorous varieties for density or to keep them in check. Juniper also makes a successful, easily trimmed hedge. Most garden junipers are cultivars of the species on the following pages.

Juniperus chinensis 'Kaizuka'

J. chinensis 'Daub's Frosted' Ground-cover with blue-green leaves tipped in gold. Great contrast plant with dark evergreens. 15" h × 5' w.

J. chinensis 'Kaizuka' (syn. *J. torulosa*) (Hollywood juniper) Fast-growing, arty, twisted shape makes distinctive accent. 'Torulosa Variegata' has a similar form with creamy markings on the dark green foliage. 15' h × 10' w.

J. chinensis 'Keteleeri' Broad, pyramidal, light green tree; popular in the Midwest. 15'–20' h and w.

J. chinensis 'Robusta Green' Slow-growing, jagged columnar form with tufts of green foliage. Use for windbreak, screen, or accent. 16' h × 7' w.

J. chinensis 'San José' (San José juniper) Slow-growing ground cover, low border, or container plant. Blight prone. 2' h × 6' w.

J. chinensis var. *sargentii* (syn. *J. sargentii*) (Sargent juniper) Excellent, fast-growing, bluish green groundcover with blue cones and rising offshoots; resists juniper blight; low-maintenance; good for sunny slopes. 2' h × 9' w.

J. chinensis var. *sargentii* 'Viridis' Year-round, soft green color; a personal favorite. 18" h × 8'–10' w.

J. chinensis 'Sea Spray' Disease-resistant groundcover with bluish green leaves. 12"–16" h × 6' w.

J. chinensis 'Spartan' Fast-growing, green column for accent, screen, or windbreak. Bagworm and Kabatina-blight resistant. 15'–20' h × 3'–8' w. Zones 4–8.

Juniperus communis ⭘ › 🌿

ju-NI-per-us kom-MU-nis

Common juniper

Cypress Family (Cupressaceae)
Evergreen shrub or tree
Various dimensions

In the wild, common juniper can be anything from a flat or irregular shrub to a 5'–10' tree with an equal or greater spread. Leaves vary from blue- or gray-green to bronzy green in winter.

LANDSCAPE USE
See individual cultivars below.

ORIGIN Several continents, including eastern North America.

HARDINESS ZONES 3–7

LIGHT See All About *Juniperus*.

SOIL See All About *Juniperus*.

GROWING See All About *Juniperus*.

DESIGNER'S CHOICE

Juniperus communis 'Compressa' Very slow-growing, dwarf column with blue-green leaves, erect narrow habit. Use as accent in rock gardens, troughs, or in well-drained ornamental beds of miniature and dwarf conifers. 3'–5' h × 18" w.

J. communis var. *depressa* 'AmiDak' (Blueberry Delight) Deep green needles with silver-blue line on topside of the leaf. Bears profuse blueberry-like cones when male cultivars grow nearby. Use in sunny to partly shaded foundation plantings or as a groundcover. 15"–22" h × 4'–5' w. Zones 3–7.

J. communis 'Mondap' (Alpine Carpet) Dark bluish-green leaves and dense, prostrate habit, forming a carpetlike, low groundcover. Withstands extremes in temperature and humidity. 8" h × 36"–48" w. Zone 3.

J. communis 'Sentinel' (syn. *J. communis* 'Pencil Point') Slow growing with silvery blue, awl-shaped leaves. Outstanding garden accent or focal point; also striking grouped in beds and borders. 6'–12' h × 1'–2' w. Zones 3–7.

Juniperus conferta 🌿

ju-NI-per-us kon-FER-ta

Shore juniper

Evergreen shrub
Cypress Family (Cupressaceae)
1½' × h × 6'–9' w

This low, shrubby evergreen has overlapping, awl-shaped leaves with blue-green leaves in summer that change to bronzy green in winter.

ORIGIN Japan

HARDINESS ZONES (5) 6–9

LIGHT See All About *Juniperus*.

SOIL See All About *Juniperus*.

GROWING See All About *Juniperus*.

Juniperus conferta 'Blue Pacific' Rich blue-green, heat-tolerant ground-cover with trailing stems; looks good alone or in a mass. Better winter color than species. 12" h × 6'–7' w. Zones 5–9.

J. conferta 'Emerald Sea' This light greenish blue groundcover has short, erect, densely growing stems and thrives at the seacoast. Hardier than the species, it tolerates salt, cold, some shade, and heat but not drought; it makes an effective mass planting on banks or cascading over walls. Holds color better in winter than species. 12" or more h × 8' w. Zones 5–9.

J. conferta 'Silver Mist' (syn. 'Shiro Toshio') Salt-tolerant, blue-green needles have white bands, making the plant look bicolor. Leaves turn plum in winter. Try this on difficult sites. Tolerates some shade. 12" h × 6' w. Zones 5–9.

Juniperus horizontalis 🍃

ju-NI-per-us ho-ri-zon-TA-lis

Creeping juniper

Cypress Family (Cupressaceae)
Evergreen conifer
1'–2' h × 4'–8' w

Unlike some junipers, creeping juniper tolerates heat, drought, and salt. Juniper blight is a potential problem for this wide-spreading, soft-textured shrub with the purplish winter hue.

LANDSCAPE USE
See specific cultivars below.

ORIGIN North America on steep inland and coastal slopes.

HARDINESS ZONES (3) 4–9

LIGHT See All About *Juniperus*.

SOIL See All About *Juniperus*; unlike some junipers, creeping juniper tolerates heavy clay and somewhat alkaline soils.

GROWING See All About *Juniperus*.

Juniperus horizontalis 'Bar Harbor' This low, expansive, fast-growing groundcover is blue-green in summer, turning purplish in winter. Discovered on Mt. Desert Island in Maine, it can survive the cold climate, salty air, and thin rocky soil of coastal Maine as well as the heat and drought of the U.S. Southwest. 1' h × 8'–10' w.

J. horizontalis 'Blue Chip' This low, mounding, silvery-blue groundcover, which thrives in colder climates, develops plum tints in winter. Somewhat susceptible to juniper blight. 10"–12" h × 6'–8' w.

J. horizontalis 'Hughes' Silvery blue-green foliage on twisty stems gives this juniper a strong presence when planted near a boulder, by the street, on a bank for erosion control, or on a retaining wall where branches can droop over the edge.

J. horizontalis 'Limeglow' Vase-shaped, spreading shrub with soft vibrant chartreuse foliage that holds its color in the heat; turns burnt orange in winter. 1' h × 4' w.

J. horizontalis 'Monber' (Icee Blue) Forms a silvery-blue carpet with dense branching. 4"–6" h × 8' w.

J. horizontalis 'Prince of Wales' The foliage of this exceptionally hardy Canadian shrub, which originated in frigid Alberta, Canada, is blue green in summer and plum tinted in winter. The plant's center may open when mature. 4"–6" h × 4'–8' w.

J. horizontalis 'Wiltonii' (syn. *J. horizontalis* 'Blue Rug') (Blue Rug juniper) Silvery-blue groundcover with trailing branches that can also hide curbs, control erosion, or tumble over retaining walls; the most common cultivar; dependable in high-desert landscapes with extremely variable daily temperatures. 6" h × 6'–8' w.

J. horizontalis 'Youngstown' (also seen as 'Plumosa Compacta Youngstown'; Andorra juniper) This common groundcover juniper has bright green leaves that turn purplish in winter. It looks good in rock gardens and at the front of mixed or shrub borders. 12" h × 6' w.

Juniperus horizontalis 'Wiltonii'

Juniperus × pfitzeriana ◯ › ☙

ju-NI-per-us fit-zer-ee-AY-na

Pfitzer juniper

Cypress Family (Cupressaceae)
Evergreen shrub
5' h × 10' w

Adaptable and widely used, this hybrid, spreading juniper is equally at home in seaside and city gardens. Main stems rise at angles from the ground, while new shoots have droopy tips, giving the plant an attractive layered look.

LANDSCAPE USE
See individual cultivars below.

ORIGIN Garden origin

HARDINESS ZONES (3) 4–9

LIGHT Full sun is best. but tolerates partial shade.

SOIL See All About *Juniperus*.

GROWING See All About *Juniperus*.

DESIGNER'S CHOICE

J. × pfitzeriana 'Armstrongii' (syn. *J. chinensis* 'Armstrongii') Light green, lacy leaves on lightly arched stems; good for mass plantings, hedges, foundations. 4'–5' h and w.

J. × pfitzeriana 'Aurea' Shrub with grayish green leaves with yellow new growth; this form is effective as a sound barrier, hedge, or low-maintenance screen. 5' h × 10' w.

J. × pfitzeriana 'MonSan' (Gold Coast Improved) Brilliant yellow, lacy foliage on a compact shrub; makes a striking border or foundation accent. 3' h × 4' w.

J. × pfitzeriana 'Mint Julep' Versatile shrub with dark mint green leaves and fountain-like stems. 4'–6' h × 6'–8' w.

J. × pfitzeriana 'Old Gold' Lacy gold leaves on a refined spreading shrub. 2'–3' h × 4'–5' w.

Juniperus procumbens ☙

ju-NI-per-us pro-KUM-benz

Japanese garden juniper

Cypress Family (Cupressaceae)
Evergreen conifer
2' h × 12' w

Untroubled by limey, high pH soils, this species thrives in open, sunny spots, no matter how infertile. With time, it may develop a mounded center, especially when grown tight against large rocks or a wall. Juniper blight can sometimes be a problem with this species.

LANDSCAPE USE
Outstanding as a groundcover in dry, flat spaces, slopes, and rock gardens.

ORIGIN Mountains of southern Japan.

HARDINESS ZONES 4–9

LIGHT Full sun.

SOIL See All About *Juniperus;* tolerates alkaline, infertile soils.

GROWING See All About *Juniperus*.

DESIGNER'S CHOICE

Juniperus procumbens 'Nana' (dwarf Japanese garden juniper) A dwarf mounding groundcover with blue-green needled leaves that take on a plum tint in winter; starts out 4"–6" high, but gets taller as it mounds upon itself. 1'–2' h × 6' w.

Juniperus sabina ▽ › ☙

ju-NI-per-us sa-BEE-na

Savin juniper

Cypress Family (Cupressaceae)
Evergreen shrub
3'–6' h × 5'–10' w

A green to blue-green, broad, vase-like form with upright, horizontal branches gives this shrub a dramatic appearance in the landscape. Leaves are disagreeably smelly when smashed or broken.

LANDSCAPE USE
Tough enough to use as a hedge or driveway divider in cold climates; can be massed to form a backdrop for colorful flowers. See also specific cultivars below.

ORIGIN Asia, Siberia, central and southern Europe.

HARDINESS ZONES 4–7

LIGHT See All About *Juniperus*.

SOIL See All About *Juniperus*.

GROWING See All About *Juniperus*. Many cultivars have resistance to juniper blight.

DESIGNER'S CHOICE

Juniperus sabina 'Arcadia' Low stems look mounded when massed and used as a groundcover. Use singly or in groups in mixed borders or rock gardens where you can combine it with low-growing contrasting shrubs such as blue junipers, purple pygmy barberries, or the bright red berries of cotoneaster; blight resistant. 12"–18" h × 6'–8' w. Zone 3.

J. sabina 'Blue Forest' Silvery-blue leaves and vertical branch tips make this slowly creeping groundcover or rock garden juniper look like a tiny evergreen forest. Tolerates alkaline soils, heat, and drought; blight resistant. 1' h × 3' or more.

J. sabina 'Broadmoor' Rich green leaves; resistant to juniper blight; wind tolerant; good for filling open spaces in borders or to manage erosion on slopes. 2'–3' h × 6'–10' w.

J. sabina 'Buffalo' Feathery, vibrant green leaves; keeps green color in winter. Let it tumble over walls or containers or grow it massed as an airy groundcover. Resistant to juniper blight. 1' h × 8'–10' w. Zone 3.

J. sabina 'Monna' (Calgary Carpet) This tough, durable landscape plant combines well with taller shrubs. Suits sites exposed to heat and drought, such as concrete foundations with a southern exposure. 9" h × 10' w.

J. sabina 'Tamariscifolia' (syn. *J. sabina* var. *tamariscifolia*) Blue-green leaves on dense, horizontal, mounded branches. Outstanding groundcover for foundations and banks. Combines well with perennials and accent shrubs that have contrasting leaf colors and textures. 18"–30" h × 10' w.

Juniperus scopulorum △

ju-NI-per-us sko-pu-LO-rum

Rocky Mountain juniper

Cypress Family (Cupressaceae)
Evergreen tree
40' h × 15' w

This juniper forms a slow-growing pyramid with scented, blue-tinted, scaly leaves. Prefers cool, night temperatures in summer.

LANDSCAPE USE

Specimen in dry sunny conditions; privacy screening at the edge of a property.

Juniperus scopulorum
'Blue Arrow'

ORIGIN Western North America.

HARDINESS ZONES 3–7

LIGHT See All About *Juniperus.*

SOIL See All About *Juniperus;* alkaline soils; tolerates drought.

GROWING See All About *Juniperus.*

DESIGNER'S CHOICE

Juniperus scopulorum 'Blue Heaven' Blue-gray, scaly leaves on pyramidal shrub. Maintains blue foliage year-round. Use for specimen or in a screen or windbreak. 20' h × 5'–8' w.

J. scopulorum 'Gray Gleam' Silvery-gray leaves, no berries. Silvery appearance increases in cold weather. 15'–20' h × 4'–7' w.

J. scopulorum 'Moonglow' Pyramidal shape with dense, bluish-gray-green leaves; usually bears cones. 15'–20' h × 3'–8' w.

J. scopulorum 'Skyrocket' (syn. *J. virginiana* 'Skyrocket') Fast-growing, skinny, tight-branched columnar form with blue-gray leaves. Use for vertical interest; an impressive accent or focal point in a shrub border; mass for screening. 20' h × 3' w.

J. scopulorum 'Tolleson's Blue Weeping Juniper' Striking treelike specimen with arched, pendulous branches and gray-blue leaves; its languishing grace makes a big statement on a deck or patio. 20' h × 10' w.

J. scopulorum 'Wichita Blue' Slow-growing pyramidal form with silvery-blue leaves year round; blight prone. 15' h × 6' w.

Juniperus squamata △ › ◯ › ☙

ju-NI-per-us skwa-MA-ta

Singleseed juniper

Cypress Family (Cupressaceae)
Small evergreen tree
15' h × 5' w

This drought-tolerant plant is variable in shape but is often found as a small conical tree with needled blue-green or gray-green summer leaves tinged plum in winter. Cultivar forms range from trees to shrubs and low groundcovers.

LANDSCAPE USE

See specific cultivars below.

ORIGIN Asia

HARDINESS ZONES 4–8

LIGHT See All About *Juniperus;* specific cultivars below.

SOIL See All About *Juniperus;* specific cultivars below.

GROWING See All About *Juniperus.*

DESIGNER'S CHOICE

Juniperus squamata 'Blue Star' Slow-growing shrub with bright silvery blue leaves. Use as a garden accent or massed as a groundcover. Grows in full sun to light shade. Prefers northerly climates with cool, night temperatures to hot, humid areas. 2'–3' h × 3'–4' w.

J. squamata 'Holger' New, needled leaves are yellow in spring, turning silvery-blue-green later in the growing season. The contrast of the old and new leaves gives the plant a bicolor effect. Makes a striking accent or mass. 2'–6' h × 4'–6' w.

Juniperus squamata
'Blue Star'

Juniperus virginiana △

ju-NI-per-us vir-gin-ee-AH-na

Eastern red cedar, Pencil cedar

Cypress Family (Cupressaceae)
Evergreen tree
40'–50' h x 8'–20' w

Eastern red cedar looks like a cone on a short trunk. It attracts birds to its fruits, adapts to difficult conditions such as infertile and acid or alkaline soils, and establishes itself in deserted lots, fields, and pastures. Wood used for cedar posts and fencing.

LANDSCAPE USE
Screens, mass plantings, windbreaks, foundation plantings (set far enough away from building to allow for growth), difficult sites, natural open areas.

ORIGIN   Eastern North America.

HARDINESS ZONES   3–9

LIGHT   Full sun.

SOIL   See All About *Juniperus;* moist, well-drained soils; tolerates infertile and acid or alkaline soils; tolerates drought.

GROWING   See All About *Juniperus.*

DESIGNER'S CHOICE
Juniperus virginiana 'Emerald Sentinel' Dark green tree with narrow, pyramidal growth habit. Leaves are mostly scaly, overlapping, and keep their color in winter. 15'–20' h × 6'–8' w.

J. virginiana 'Hetzii' (syn. *J. chinensis* 'Hetzii', *J. chinensis* 'Hetzii Glauca', *J. virginiana* 'Hetz Glauca') Leaves have icy-blue cast; fountain form; makes dense screen; a cross between *J. chinensis* 'Pfitzeriana' and *J. virginiana* 'Glauca'. 8' h × 10' w.

J. virginiana 'Idyllwild' Dark green, pyramidal tree with dense, upright branches. Good for screens and hedges. 15' h × 5'–7' w.

J. virginiana 'Monbell' (Prairie Pillar) A column of short, dense branches covered with gray blue green foliage

Juniperus virginiana 'Grey Owl'

that holds its color in winter. A spectacular accent against a background of dark green leaves. 15'–20' h × 2'–3' w.

J. 'Grey Owl' Silvery leaves on a feathery, spreading shrub with attractive, frosted-blue cones in fall and winter; a cross between *J. chinensis* 'Pfitzeriana' and *J. virginiana* 'Glauca'. 3' h × 6' w.

KALMIA

Kalmia latifolia ○ › ○

KAL-mee-a lat-i-FOH-lee-a

Mountain laurel, Calico bush

Heath Family (Ericaceae)
Evergreen shrub
5'–15' h x 6'–15' w

Grown for its showy, late spring to early summer flowers and handsome evergreen leaves, this eastern U.S. native is an upright shrub or small tree with contorted stems and a twisted trunk. In sunny areas, the habit tends to be compact, but in some shade, the branching is looser. In nature, the flowers are pink to white, but many excellent cultivars exist, thanks in particular to plant

breeder Richard A. Jaynes, Ph.D. He co-owns Broken Arrow Nursery in Hamden, Connecticut, and is the author of *Kalmia: Mountain Laurel and Related Species* (Timber Press).

Shiny, dark green on top with raised mid-veins, the evergreen elliptical leaves of mountain laurel are 2"–5" long with sharp tips. The dark reddish-brown bark is slightly grooved; new twigs are green. Mountain laurel bears convex clusters of ¾"–1" wide, white to pink flowers with varying amounts of red markings at the branch tips; there is a decorative color contrast between the fat, inflated buds and the flowers. The state flower of Connecticut and Pennsylvania, *Kalmia* blooms in late spring to midsummer, depending upon the cultivar and location. Fruits are inconspicuous, brown capsules held in erect clusters.

LANDSCAPE USE
An outstanding native for naturalizing, growing in partly shaded borders, masses, foundations, and woodland transitions and openings.

ORIGIN   Rocky woods with filtered light in the eastern U.S.

HARDINESS ZONES   (4) 5–9

Kalmia latifolia

LIGHT Partial shade to full sun, with protection from winter winds. Jaynes says dappled sunlight is best; or, if grown in full sun, keep the plant away from heat-reflecting south or southwest walls. When grown in heavy shade, bright colors may lose their intensity, but plantings in the South need some shade.

SOIL Acid, well-drained soil. Avoid planting in wet or clay soils or soils with high pH. Jaynes offers the following *Kalmia* planting tips: "On heavy (clay) soils set the plant on the ground, surround it with well-drained soil (raised bed), and work in large amounts of coarse organic material such as aged pine bark."

GROWING Until established, keep soil moist but not wet, preferably watering deeply and less often instead of daily quick hits of the sprinkler. According to Jaynes, new *Kalmia* plantings need 2" of water weekly, and sprinklers usually apply about 1" of water per hour. Long term, Kalmia's shallow roots require shielding from extreme heat and too much fertilizer. Cover them with organic mulch such as wood chips or pine needles, and use a fertilizer for acid-loving plants at one-quarter strength. Since *Kalmia* makes next year's buds on this year's new growth, help the process by removing faded flowers right after blooming. Thus, instead of setting seed, the plant's energy goes into new growth and next year's flowers. The plant is intolerant of damp shade, which can lead to leaf spot. Foliage may burn when grown in open, exposed condition. May attract lacebugs.

DESIGNER'S CHOICE

Kalmia angustifolia (sheep laurel) Low shrub with bluish-green foliage and rosy pink blooms in June and July. 1'–3' h and w. Zones 3–7.

K. latifolia 'Carol' Low, rounded mound of wavy, glossy, dark green leaves covered with red buds opening to bright white flowers. 3'–4' h and w.

K. latifolia 'Elf' Dwarf with pink buds opening to pale pink to white blooms, small leaves. 3' h and w.

K. latifolia 'Heart of Fire' Deep red buds open to pink bordered by deep pink flowers. 5' h and w.

K. latifolia 'Little Linda' Red buds open to pink blooms on dwarf plant with shiny tiny leaves. 3' h and w.

K. latifolia 'Minuet' Dwarf with light pink buds opening to white-centered flowers with a white-edged maroon band and shiny narrow leaves. 3'–4' h × 3'–5' w.

K. latifolia 'Raspberry Glow' Burgundy buds open to raspberry-pink flowers; keeps color in shade. 4'–6' h and w.

K. latifolia 'Royal Dwarf' ('Pumila') Dark rosy pink flowers from June to July and again in late August and early September. 1'–3' h and w.

K. latifolia 'Sarah' Red buds open to deep pink flowers; long bloom period, good foliage and mounding habit; more sun tolerant than other varieties. 4'–8' h and w.

K. latifolia 'Snowdrift' White blooms with a central dab of red. 4' h and w.

K. latifolia 'Tiddlywinks' Dark pink buds with medium pink flowers. 2½'–3' h and w.

K. latifolia 'Tightwad Too' Light pink buds with darker pink tips enlarge without opening, staying full and colorful on the shrub for a month or more. 2½'–3' h and w.

Kalmia latifolia 'Little Linda'

Kalmia latifolia 'Raspberry Glow'

Kalmia latifolia 'Sarah'

Kalmia latifolia 'Tightwad Too'

KALOPANAX

Kalopanax septemlobus ○ ✳
(syn. *K. pictus*)

kal-oh-PAN-aks sep-tem-LOH-bus

Castor aralia

Aralia Family (Araliaceae)
Deciduous tree
40'–60' h and w

At first glance, castor aralia's glossy-lobed, 7"–12" leaves give it a tropical flair. (The deeply dissected lobes of var. *maximowiczii* look even more exotic). Adding to the coarse landscape texture is the heavy structure of trunk and branches. Grown as a single- or multi-trunk tree, it has an open, erect habit in youth, developing into a rounded tree with a dense, wide-spreading crown that creates dark shade underneath. Prickles fortify young trunks and stems. With age, the trunk blackens and develops deep grooves. The stems and shoots stay barbed. In summer, 1" flowers appear in huge, flattened, decorative clusters up to 2' wide held above the leaves. The nectar draws bees, making castor aralia a good honey plant. Bluish-black fruits follow in fall but are quickly eaten by birds. Fall color is yellow to red tinged, but not particularly ornamental. Castor aralia is hardy, robust, and easy to grow, but it may be difficult to find.

LANDSCAPE USE
In difficult sites or where you need dense shade on a hot open lawn.

ORIGIN Moist, temperate, East Asian woodlands.

HARDINESS ZONES 4–7

LIGHT Full sun to partial shade.

SOIL It thrives in moist, deep, rich, well-drained soils but tolerates dry and heavy soils and a wide range of pH.

GROWING Thrives with a little protection from the elements and in cool zones. No serious pests or diseases. Caution: Young

trunks, branches, and shoots are spiny. Profuse flower clusters up to 2' wide attract bees. Consider planting another tree if you have very young children.

KERRIA

Kerria japonica ○ › ⌂ ✳

KAYR-ree-a juh-PA-ni-ka

Japanese kerria

Rose Family (Rosaceae)
Deciduous shrub
4'–6' h × 6'–9' w

Kerria is an old-fashioned shrub, perfect for grouping in small Victorian-style shrub borders. It has an upright suckering habit with arching stems and a rounded form. The green, deciduous leaves turn variable to pleasant yellow in fall; they are simple and alternate with serrated edges. Vibrant green stems give the plant year-round interest. Spring flowers are bright yellow. Fruits are inconspicuous.

LANDSCAPE USE
Shrub borders, masses, understory planting, or drifts.

ORIGIN Mountain stream banks in Japan and China.

HARDINESS ZONES (4) 5–9

LIGHT Partial shade to shade.

Kerria japonica

Kerria japonica 'Albiflora'

Kerria japonica 'Picta'

SOIL Loamy, well-drained soil.

GROWING Can be renewal pruned as it starts to die out from center or gets leggy. Overfertilizing can decrease flowering and stimulate too much growth. May be affected by blights, cankers, and leaf spot. May suffer stem death in cold winters without snow cover.

DESIGNER'S CHOICE
Kerria japonica 'Albiflora' White, single flowers against lime-green foliage. 3'–5' h × 3½' w.

K. japonica 'Golden Guinea' Big yellow flowers set against bright green leaves and stems; densely branched. 6'–8' h × 5'–6' w.

K. japonica 'Picta' Variegated, grayish-green leaves with white edges; stands out in shady sites. 3'–5' h and w.

K. japonica 'Pleniflora' (syn. 'Flora Pleno') (double-flowering Japanese kerria) Bright green leaves on bright green stems; ball-shaped flowers in April and May make long-lasting cut flowers; flowers well in sun or shade, insignificant fall color. 4'–5' h × 4½' w.

Koelreuteria paniculata ○ › ◔ ✳

kohl-ru-TEE-ree-a pa-nik-u-LAH-ta

Golden raintree

Soapberry Family (Sapindaceae)
Deciduous tree
30'–40' h and w

If you're looking for a small, pretty, robust tree that tolerates a wide range of soils and conditions, then golden raintree may be right for you. It has an erect spreading habit, forming a rounded landscape shape. One hot, droughty summer day, I wandered down some streets in Manhattan's Greenwich Village and saw rows of them tricked out in vibrant yellow blooms against the dark brick and brownstone homes. The effect of these tough, small, street trees in bloom was memorable. If you grow this tree, however, you'll have to balance its considerable merits with its flaws, including nuisance seedlings to pull and messy twig and seed litter.

Compound, deciduous, 14"–18" leaves change from purplish to bright green in spring and then to a variable yellow in fall. The 7–15 toothed leaflets are each about 4" long. Older bark has light gray ridges with reddish-brown furrows, giving it an attractive, bicolor appearance. It bears big, fluffy, ½", yellow flowers in 18", conical, branched clusters at stem ends in mid- to late summer (late June to July), when few other trees are blooming. The fruits are inflated capsules that change from green or reddish green to tan.

LANDSCAPE USE

Specimen, patio tree, street tree, or difficult sites.

ORIGIN Dry, hot valleys in China and Korea.

HARDINESS ZONES 5–8

LIGHT Full sun.

SOIL Adapts to wide range of soils and conditions.

GROWING When necessary, prune this tree in winter to maintain its shape. Tolerates salt, heat, drought, wind, and urban pollution. Fallen twigs and seedpods can make a mess.

CAUTION: The tree has a tendency to self-sow or naturalize in the wilds of the eastern U.S. According to scientists at the University of Connecticut, this tree shows invasive tendencies in New England. In the mid-Atlantic, you may have to dig and dispose of abundant seedlings.

DESIGNER'S CHOICE

Koelreuteria paniculata 'Rose Lantern' Extended period of interest from yellow flower clusters in late summer, followed by good yellow fall color in October and rosy pink fruit capsules for another 5–6 weeks. 30'–40' h and w.

Koelreuteria paniculata

Kolkwitzia amabilis ▽ › 🝙 ✳

kohl-KWIT-see-a a-MA-bi-lis

Beautybush

Honeysuckle Family (Caprifoliaceae)
Deciduous shrub
6'–10' h x 6'–8' w

For a couple of weeks in late spring, beautybush will be the highlight of your garden. Its graceful stems droop under the weight of the pink flowers clustered along the length. The pinkness of the blooms stands out against the shrub's dark green, matte foliage. The habit is vase-shaped and spreading with stems growing up and arching over at the ends. This easy, old-fashioned shrub particularly suits outlying shrub borders around old houses, where it draws attention in bloom, then fades into the background for the rest of the season.

The 1½"–3" long leaves are dark, flat green above and lighter below; they are opposite, simple, and egg-shaped leaves with pointy tips. Old stems have interesting, light brown bark with up and down cracks that sheds with age. Young twigs start out thin and fuzzy but grow smooth over time. In May to June, beautybush produces flaring, pink, ½"–1", tubular, bell-shaped flowers in profuse, showy clusters along the stems. Fruits, which are inconspicuous, hairy seed capsules, last into winter.

LANDSCAPE USE

Because of legginess, plant beautybush in outlying shrub beds and borders or in masses. You can also use it singly as a specimen with the knowledge that it will only be ornamentally effective for two weeks.

ORIGIN Dry slopes and ravines of central China.

HARDINESS ZONES (4) 5–8

Kolkwitzia amabilis 'Pink Cloud'

LIGHT Full sun

SOIL Thrives in dry, sandy soils; tolerates wide range of pH

GROWING Easy to transplant. You don't have to prune. In order to control size, however, remove old stems right after blooming. Shrubs have a rough winter form, and old shrubs show unattractive bare legs.

DESIGNER'S CHOICE

Kolkwitzia amabilis 'Pink Cloud'
Bright pink flowers that are larger and more prolific than species. 10' h and w.

LABURNUM

Laburnum × *watereri* 'Vossii' (syn. *L. vossii*) ❶ › ○

la-BUR-num wa-TE-re-ri

Golden chain tree

Pea Family (Fabaceae)
Deciduous flowering tree
12'–15' h x 9'–12' w

In mid- to late spring, golden chain tree looks bewitching, its branches clothed with sunshine yellow, pealike blooms in 10"–20" cascading clusters. It has light blue-green leaves with no significant fall color. In Europe, 'Vossii' is the cultivar of choice for its 2' long flower chains and denser

habit. In the U.S., it grows best in parts of the East and the Pacific Northwest. Longwood Gardens has an arched walk with golden chain tree trained over the top and sides. In spite of its lovely spring bloom and attractive compound leaves, I wouldn't choose this tree for most small home landscapes, which would benefit more from plants with multi-season appeal.

LANDSCAPE USE
Site golden chain tree as a short-season specimen at the back of a mixed border underplanted with mid- to late-blooming spring bulbs, where it will be a backdrop for other plants later in the season; or train it over an arbor for shade.

ORIGIN Garden hybrid

HARDINESS ZONES 5–7

LIGHT Full sun to partial shade.

SOIL Moist, well-drained soils. Although it tolerates a wide range of conditions, including alkaline soils, avoid planting on waterlogged sites.

GROWING Twig blight can affect this tree, as well as leaf spot, aphids, and mites.

CAUTION The entire tree is poisonous if any part of it is ingested.

Laburnum x watereri

Lagerstroemia indica ○

la-ger-STROH-mee-a IN-di-ka

Crape myrtle

Loosetrife Family (Lythraceae)
Deciduous medium to large flowering shrub or small tree
Usually 8'–25' h x 6'–20' w, but possibly 18'–40' h

Most crape myrtles are handsome, small, multi-trunk trees with four seasons of interest. The tree's rounded crown displays the showy bark of the supporting trunks. In summer, flowers appear at the tips of the arching to erect branches and last for months. Many cultivars exist, from tiny to large and from heat lovers to those with increased cold hardiness. Dr. Donald Egolf of the U.S. National Arboretum has created many hybrids that are root hardy to Zone 6 with excellent mildew and leaf spot resistance, depending upon the cultivar. Choose the right crape myrtle for your particular site, purpose, and climate.

Leaves are simple, smooth, 1"–3" long, with bronze new growth, dark green mature leaves, and red to yellow and orange fall color. The gray outer bark exfoliates to reveal mottled cinnamon, brownish beige, and greenish inner bark. Elongated 8" clusters of white, red, pink, purple, or lavender flowers develop at branch tips and last 2–3 months. The fruits are brown, persistent capsules.

LANDSCAPE USE
Looks terrific massed or in groups, where you can appreciate the gorgeous bark exposed by its multi-stemmed barelegged habit topped by a rounded crown. Also makes an attractive lawn specimen, especially when mature, since older plants have not only the year-round bark display but also a handsome architectural

form. Small bushy cultivars work well massed or as an informal hedge. Dwarfs make good plants for foundations, massing, border specimens, and containers or hanging baskets.

ORIGIN Southeast Asia; many of the best are of hybrid origin.

HARDINESS ZONE 7–9

LIGHT Full sun.

SOIL Moist, well-drained soils; drought tolerant once established; prefers heavy loam with pH of 5.0–6.5.

GROWING Planting in full sun helps avoid powdery mildew. Remove suckers to maintain tree forms; cut out dead and crossed branches; deadheading promotes a second flush of bloom in late summer on plants that flower before mid-July. Cutting live branches larger than a pencil width can create ugly sprays of new floppy growth. To grow crape myrtle as a shorter shrub, you can cut the whole plant to 6" above ground in early spring before growth begins. May be attacked by aphids and Japanese beetles, as well as sooty mold, leaf spot, canker, and powdery mildew.

DESIGNER'S CHOICE

DWARF SHRUBS (UNDER 5′ H)

Note: Dwarfs are not disease resistant and may need to be sprayed with fungicide.

Lagerstroemia indica 'Delta Blush' Pink blooms, floriferous, low-mounded form. 2′ h × 4′ w.

L. indica 'New Orleans' Purple flowers, shiny leaves, short spreading habit, good for hanging baskets. 3′ h × 5′ w.

L. 'Pocomoke' Deep rose pink in mid- or late summer until frost; dense, mounded form; mildew resistant; excellent container plant; from U.S. National Arboretum (USNA release). 1½′ h × 3′ w.

MEDIUM SHRUBS (5′ TO 10′ H)

L. indica 'Acoma' Small, gray-green foliage and white flowers, grayish-brown exfoliating bark, USNA; mildew resistant. 10′ h × 11′ w.

L. indica 'Caddo' Bright pink flowers, orangey brown bark, with high leaf spot and mildew resistance, USNA. 8′ h and w.

L. indica 'Hopi' Medium pink flowers, terrific beige exfoliating bark, orangey red to deep red fall color, rounded habit, high mildew resistance, USNA. 8′ h × 10′ w.

L. 'Tonto' Fuchsia red flowers, erect rounded form, cream to taupe bark, maroon fall color, resistant to mildew and leaf spot, USNA. 8′ h and w.

LARGE SHRUBS/SMALL TREES (10′ TO 20′ H)

L. indica 'Apalachee' Fragrant pale lavender flowers, very resistant to mildew and leaf spot. Dense growth, upright form, outstanding exfoliating cinnamon bark, persistent seedheads, USNA. 12′–20′ h × 8′–15′ w.

L. indica 'Comanche' Coral pink flowers, excellent bark, very resistant to mildew and leaf spot, USNA. 12′ h and w.

L. indica 'Lipan' Lavender flowers, lovely near-white bark, orange-russet fall color, very resistant to mildew, USNA. 13′–20′ h × 8′–15′ w.

L. indica 'Osage' Bright pink flowers with outstanding deep-orange peeling bark and superb mildew resistance, rounded to pendulous habit, USNA. 12′ h × 10′ w.

L. indica 'Sioux' Vivid pink, with excellent gray-brown bark, reddish purple fall color, and high resistance to mildew and leaf spot, USNA. 13′–20′ h × 8′–15′ w.

L. indica 'Tuskegee' Deep pink blooms, excellent creamy beige and gray exfoliating bark, orange fall color, with high resistance to powdery mildew and leaf spot, USNA. 15′ h × 18′ w.

TREES (MORE THAN 20′ H)

L. indica 'Fantasy' White flowers, outstanding reddish-orange bark, with

Lagerstroemia indica **'Hopi'**

high resistance to powdery mildew and leaf spot; cultivar of *L. fauriei*. 40′–50′ h × 30′–40′ w.

L. indica 'Miami' Dark pink blooms, excellent chestnut brown and tan bark, high mildew resistance, rounded habit, USNA. 20′–25′ h × 15′–20′ w.

L. indica 'Townhouse' White flowers, great mahogany reddish bark, high mildew resistance, cultivar of *L. fauriei*. 20′ h and w.

L. 'Natchez' White blooms all summer, yellow fall color, with handsome reddish brown and cream bark. Excellent mildew and aphid resistance, top performer in the Southeast. 35′–50′ h × 20′–35′ w after 30 years.

Razzle Dazzle series These five dwarf crape myrtles are ideal for container growing, shrub and perennial borders, low hedges, and foundation plantings. They bear red, pink, or white flowers summer to fall and are hardy in Zones 6–9. Ruby Dazzle ('GMAD IV') has particular appeal because of its pink blooms, shiny bronze-red leaves, small size (2′–3′ h and w), drought tolerance, and excellent resistance to powdery mildew and other diseases. Cherry Dazzle ('GMAD I') has cherry red flowers, good fall color, drought tolerance and mildew resistance. (3′–4′ h × 4′ w).

LARIX

Larix decidua △

LAR-iks de-SID-u-a

European larch

Pine Family (Pinaceae)
Deciduous conifer
70'–75' h x 25'–30' w

The larches I see near my New Hampshire home confirm for me this tree's landscape value. Although the light green foliage on their horizontal to down-sweeping limbs and hanging branchlets makes them appear graceful in spring and summer, it's in fall that they steal the scene. Each autumn, these northern conifers turn long-lasting buttery gold before shedding their needlelike leaves. This fast-growing larch has a tall straight trunk and pyramidal form.

The foliage consists of soft, fine, light green, 1" needles that turn a lovely gold in fall. Bark is scaly gray when young, then fissured with maturity, exposing red-brown inner bark. The ½" female flowers are scaly, egg-shaped, and red to yellow, sitting upright on the stem; males are smaller and yellow, projecting down from the bottom of the shoot. Fruits are brown cones. Similar to Eastern larch, only larger, hardier, more tolerant of dry soils, faster growing, and with somewhat larger cones.

LANDSCAPE USE
Sculptural specimen in large lawns or public spaces.

ORIGIN   Mountains of Europe.

HARDINESS ZONES   (3) 4–6

LIGHT   Full sun.

SOIL   Moist to wet, acid soils.

GROWING   Lower branches are often shaded out with age. Early spring spraying helps control pests. They are susceptible to canker, rust, larch sawfly, aphids, and larch case-bearer. They are intolerant of urban pollution and too big for many residential landscapes though small cultivars exist.

DESIGNER'S CHOICE
Larix decidua 'Pendula' Weeping branches on erect trunk. Elegant specimen. 10'–15' h × 6'–10' w.

Larix kaempferi △

LAR-iks KEMP-fer-i

Japanese larch

Pine Family (Pinaceae)
Deciduous conifer
70'–100' h x 25'–40' w

Japanese larch resembles European larch but has vibrant bluish-green summer foliage; rich, golden fall color; and waxy, reddish-brown winter shoots. It also fares slightly better farther south. The most ornamental larch for large American landscapes, it's too big for most yards, so choose smaller cultivars instead.

LANDSCAPE USE
Specimen in large lawns.

ORIGIN   Mountains of Japan.

HARDINESS ZONES   4–7

LIGHT   Full sun.

SOIL   Moist, well-drained, acid soils.

GROWING   See *Larix decidua*.

DESIGNER'S CHOICE
Larix kaempferi 'Diana' Weeping branches and twisted leaves. 17' h × 5' w.

Larix decidua 'Pendula'

Larix

L. kaempferi 'Nana' Rounded form with needles; perfect for rock or alpine gardens. 3'–4' h × 3'–4' w.

L. kaempferi 'Pendula' Soft, weeping form, like an upside-down mop head; slow growing; usually grafted for height; would add romantic character to a cottage garden. Variable in size; often seen about 4'–6' h × 3'–5' w.

Pseudolarix amabilis (syn. *P. kaempferi*) (golden larch) Slow growing, pyramidal, rather rare, deciduous conifer; turns gleaming yellow before dropping leaves in fall; from Eastern Asia. 40'–70' h × 20'–40' w. Zones 5–7.

Larix laricina △

LAR-iks la-ri-SI-na

Tamarack, Eastern larch

Pine Family (Pinaceae)
Deciduous conifer
40'–75' h × 15'–25' w

This native of northern North America thrives in full sun, cold temperatures, and moist, well-drained, acid to boggy peaty soils. Unless you live where these conditions prevail, it's better to choose a different larch for your landscape. It has bluish-green needles with yellow fall color. Though tamarack hates pollution, it tolerates salt and works well on the coast of northern New England and Canada.

LANDSCAPE USE
Keep this tree for its rugged habit and yellow fall color where it grows wild. Better yet, grow dwarf cultivars in conifer beds and borders, though they may be hard to find.

ORIGIN Peat lands of North America.

HARDINESS ZONES 2–5

LIGHT Full sun.

SOIL Moist, well-drained, acid to boggy peaty soils.

GROWING See *Larix decidua.*

DESIGNER'S CHOICE
Larix laricina 'Lanarck' Green globe with yellow fall color. 4' h and w.

L. laricina 'Newport Beauty' Little blue-green ball with crowded stems; charming with low, cushion-form perennials or as a standard with taller flowers. 2' h and w.

LEUCOTHOE

Leucothoe fontanesiana (syn. *L. catesbaei*) 🏠 › 🏡

le-KOH-tho-ay fon-ta-nay-see-AN-a

Drooping leucothoe

Heath Family (Ericaceae)
Broad-leaf evergreen shrub
3'–6' h and w

I liked the arching elegance of drooping leucothoe's stems, and when I saw it growing in Massachusetts or Pennsylvania, it turned me on. But when I grew it at home, I wasn't as impressed — until the spring after a harsh winter with little snow cover, that is. I'd grown 'Rainbow', a variegated cultivar that's not as vigorous as the species, in a shrub border for about 7 years. I guess I can thank that cold winter and no snow for destroying much of my leucothoe's top growth so that the shrub renewed itself from the base. For the first time ever, it was lush, compact (about 2½' h × 4' w), graceful, and flourishing.

Leucothoe's foliage is alternate and simple; pointed, 2½", shiny, dark green leaves have reddish new growth. The bark on some new stems is bright red; on others it is green to brown. Urn-shaped, white flowers are arranged in showy, 2"–3", droopy clusters along the stem in the leaf axils. The fruits are not ornamental.

LANDSCAPE USE
Low hedges; makes an elegant transition into woodland when planted as an edging or massed; woodland gardens; shady entry gardens.

ORIGIN Mountains of southeastern U.S.

HARDINESS ZONES 5–8

LIGHT Partial shade.

SOIL Moist, cool, well-drained, acid soil.

GROWING Plant shallow, protected from winter winds, and far enough back from paths and edges to avoid having to destroy its naturally graceful habit by pruning. Prune lightly in spring after flowering, removing only weak, dead, or damaged stems at ground level. Mulch lightly. To renew old tattered plants, cut to the base in spring. Fertilize when necessary with acid-loving-plant food

Leucothoe fontanesiana

Leucothoe fontanesiana 'Rainbow'

just before growth begins in spring or right after flowering, keeping the fertilizer at the drip line and not directly on the surface roots. Leucothoe is subject to windburn and can look worn with age.

DESIGNER'S CHOICE

Leucothoe axillaris (coast leucothoe) Similar to but more compact than drooping leucothoe and with fewer flowers per inflorescence. 2'–4' h × 3'–6' w. Zones 5–8.

L. fontanesiana 'Nana' (syn. *L. fontanesiana* 'Compacta') Shorter than species. 2' h × 3'–5' w.

L. fontanesiana 'Rainbow' (syn. *L. fontanesiana* 'Girard's Rainbow') Green leaves speckled with cream, pink, and reddish bronze; reddish stems; looks ratty in my Zone 5 garden. 3'–5' h and w.

L. 'Zeblid' (Scarletta) New growth tinted red, reddish bronze in winter. 3'–6' h and w.

LIGUSTRUM

Ligustrum species ◐ › ◠ ✳

li-GUS-trum

Privet

Olive Family (*Oleaceae*)
Deciduous, semi-evergreen, and evergreen shrubs and trees
8'–15' h and w, depending upon species; cultivars may be smaller

I was tempted to skip the privets because I think they are boring, pervasive, and invasive in many American landscapes. Homeowners grow this immensely popular shrub for its dark green leaves; white, scented flowers; fast growth; and dense branching, which makes it ideal for hedging. The strong-scented flower clusters appear in late spring, followed by copious fruits devoured by birds, which spread the seed far and wide. Privet's vigor and tolerance of pollution and drought enhance its weedy tendencies. Popular species that are troublesome in different regions of the country include Amur privet (*L. amurense*); Japanese privet (*L. japonicum*), glossy privet (*L. lucidum*), border privet (*L. obtusifolium*), Chinese privet (*L. sinense*), and common privet (*L. vulgare*).

LANDSCAPE USE
Formal hedges, screens, shrub borders. Rather than choosing this weedy, overused plant, select something else, such as Mohican viburnum, yew, holly, or European beech.

ORIGIN Most privets are Asian, though some come from Europe, North Africa, and Australia.

HARDINESS ZONES 3–10, depending upon the species.

LIGHT Full sun to partial shade.

SOIL Well drained.

GROWING Prune privet right after flowering. Susceptible to leaf spot, root rot, blights, powdery mildew, aphids, mites, scales, and Japanese beetles.

CAUTION Before buying privet, check with your local Cooperative Extension Service to see which species are invasive in your region.

LINDERA

Lindera benzoin ○

lin-DAY-ra BEN-zo-in

Spicebush

Laurel Family (Lauraceae)
Deciduous flowering shrub
6'–12' h and w

This open, rounded, slow-growing shrub adds immeasurable beauty to our native woodlands with the subtle delicacy of its small, yellow, spring blooms, which appear before the leaves, and its stunning, butter-yellow fall color. In summer, spicebush may look ordinary, but squash a leaf in your fist and enjoy its piquant scent. You'll understand how spicebush earned its common name.

The pointed, bright green, alternate, simple, 3"–5" × 2" leaves turn yellow in fall. The bark is grayish brown with

Lindera benzoin

white lenticels; new stems are greenish brown and also smell spicy when cut. The small yellow flowers are grouped in leaf axils before the leaves appear in spring. Red, oval, pepper-scented berries mature in fall and may persist after leaves fall.

LANDSCAPE USE
Plant with deciduous azaleas in the understory of woodland gardens, shrub borders, woodland's edge.

ORIGIN Moist woods and streamsides of Eastern U.S.

HARDINESS ZONES (4) 5–9

LIGHT Full sun to partial shade.

SOIL Moist, well drained soil.

GROWING Nothing special. If sited properly, grows without problems.

LIQUIDAMBAR

Liquidambar styraciflua ◐ › △

li-kwi-DAM-bar sty-ra-si-FLU-a

Sweet gum

Witch Hazel Family
(Hamamelidaceae)
Large deciduous tree
60'–75' h x 40'–60' w

Grow this big tree for its spectacular fall color, which varies from scarlet to purple and yellow. Its habit is straight and tall with a single trunk and oval or pyramidal crown that becomes rounded with age. Wildlife visits this tree, which can tolerate both flooding and drought once established.

The alternate, simple leaves are a handsome, shiny, dark green. Starlike with 5–7 pointed lobes and 4"–7" wide, they are similar to some maples, except maple's leaves are opposite on the stems. The bark is grayish brown with ridges and furrows. The spring flowers are not ornamental. Long-lasting fruits in the form of gumballs — hard, brown, spiky, 1"–1½" spheres — hang on long stems and mature in fall.

LANDSCAPE USE
A shade tree for large lawns, border plantings, but use the fruitless 'Rotundiloba' if you plant to grow it in the lawn near the house.

ORIGIN Eastern U.S. coastal plane in moist stream valleys.

HARDINESS ZONES 5–9

LIGHT Full sun.

SOIL Moist, deep, fertile, somewhat acid soils.

GROWING Nothing special, except for planting with ample space for root growth. Plan on cleaning up the gumballs over a period of months as they drop from the branches. Water regularly and mulch generously until established. The strong roots can break concrete.

CAUTION A fine tree, but keep fruiting plants away from driveways where you can trip on the balls. Avoid planting within 10 feet of sidewalks since the vigorous roots can tilt or crack them.

DESIGNER'S CHOICE
Liquidambar styraciflua 'Festival' Peach to red autumn color, more columnar and less cold hardy than species; better for Zones 8 and 9. 60' h × 20' w. Zones 7–9.

Liquidambar styraciflua

L. styraciflua 'Gumball' Dense and shrubby with leaves to the ground, wine-red fall color; height depends on whether the globelike head has been grafted on a trunk to make a taller plant. 5'–15' h and w.

L. styraciflua 'Moraine' Fast growing; oval upright habit; most cold-hardy cultivar. 60' h × 40' w.

L. styraciflua 'Rotundiloba' Fruitless cultivar that saves on cleanup time; rounded leaf lobes, purple fall color. 50'–75' h × 35'–50' w.

LIRIODENDRON

Liriodendron tulipifera △ ✳

lee-ree-oh-DEN-dron tu-li-PIF-er-a

Tulip tree, Tulip poplar

Magnolia Family (Magnoliaceae)
Large deciduous tree
70'–100' h x 35'–50' w

When we lived in Delaware, a wild tulip tree grew like crazy near the top of our driveway. How I loved that tree! Since the road was higher than our house, I could see the tree's crown without craning my neck when I drove up the hill towards home. The 2 best times of year, of course, were spring and fall. For several weeks in late spring, the tree produced lovely yellow, green, and orange "tulip flowers" that delighted me. In fall, the leaves turned as yellow as summer squash. And it had such a towering, grand, upright habit, pyramidal and symmetrical! The tree is really too big for most home landscapes, however, and it's not a city tree, especially in its warmer range where it grows largest.

The leaves are alternate, simple, and measure 5"–8" × 4"–8"; medium green, they have 4–6 almost rectangular lobes; in fall they turn showy yellow. The bark is gray, marked with white, furrowed, sapsucker holes evident on mature trees. In late spring, the tree

Liriodendron tulipifera

produces 2½", tuliplike flowers with yellow to chartreuse petals and orange at the base of the cup. Trees usually don't bloom until they're at least 15 years old, and the upright flowers are easy to miss because they're at the branch tips, high in the canopy of the tree. The conical, persistent, green to brown fruits are not ornamental.

LANDSCAPE USE
Shade, specimen, grouped in a field. I worked with a couple that had recently bought a house with a newly planted tulip tree in the moist backyard. The husband and wife wanted to remove the tree because it was little and not doing much, but I suggested they wait. Soon the tree will shade their hot, sunny, second-story deck and give them an annual show — in spring they'll have flowers, in summer bees will buzz the leaves, and in fall the tree will turn gold.

ORIGIN Bottomlands of eastern U.S.

HARDINESS ZONES 5–9

LIGHT Full sun.

SOIL Moist, deep, somewhat acid to neutral soils.

GROWING Transplant in spring. Avoid planting in hot, dry locations. Wind, ice, and snow can tear brittle limbs off these tall vulnerable trees. It may also be afflicted with leaf spot, scales, aphids, and sooty mold.

LONICERA

Lonicera fragrantissima ○ ✳

luh-NI-se-ra fray-gran-TIS-si-ma

Winter honeysuckle, Fragrant honeysuckle

Honeysuckle Family (Caprifoliaceae)
Deciduous flowering shrub
6'–10' h and w

Folks grow this rounded to uneven, bluish green shrub for the sweet, fruity, lemony scent of its cream-white flowers. Buds open over a long time. In the South, bloom starts as early as January; in the North, it starts in early spring. Flowers attract hummingbirds; berries draw songbirds.

LANDSCAPE USE
Informal hedge, screen, and containers.

ORIGIN China

HARDINESS ZONES (4) 5–8

LIGHT Full sun to partial shade.

SOIL Average garden soil. Adapts to high and low pH and to medium-wet to dry conditions.

GROWING Prune right after flowering to shape and control. Renew overgrown shrubs by cutting to the ground. No serious pests or diseases.

CAUTION Look out for seedlings. Escaped cultivation in the southeastern United States, including Alabama, Tennessee, and Virginia. Avoid planting the following extremely invasive shrub honeysuckles: amur (*L. maackii*), Morrow's (*L. morrowii*), tartarian (*L. tartarica*), Bell's (*L. × bella*), and European fly (*L. xylosteum*). Numerous birds eat their abundant seeds, spreading these adaptable shrubs far and wide.

DESIGNER'S CHOICE
Lonicera 'Freedom' (syn. *L. korolkowii* 'Freedom') (freedom honeysuckle) Unscented, pink-tinged white flowers still attract bees and birds; resistant to Russian honeysuckle aphids. 6'–9' h and w. Zone 4.

L. maximowiczii var. *sachalinensis* (Sakhalin honeysuckle) Deep red blooms; red fruits; bright yellow fall color. 9' h and w. Zones 3–6.

L. standishii (Standish's honeysuckle) Similar in ornamental value, size, and hardiness to winter honeysuckle. 6'–10' h and w.

LOROPETALUM

Loropetalum chinense ○ › ▽

loh-roh-PET-a-lum chi-NENS

Loropetalum, Fringe flower

Witch Hazel Family (Hamamelidaceae)
Evergreen to semi-evergreen shrub or small tree
8'–15' h and w

Southerners delight in this fine-textured, fast-growing shrub for its fragrant white, pink, or deep rose flowers, its evergreen leaves, and its attractive layered growth habit. Blooms, which resemble those of witch hazel with straplike petals, open from late winter to early spring and occasionally thereafter.

LANDSCAPE USE
Formal and informal hedges, screening, woodland gardens, containers, groundcover. Prune tall forms into specimen trees or espaliers.

ORIGIN Japan, China

HARDINESS ZONES (7) 8–9

LIGHT Full sun to partial shade; best blooming in full sun.

SOIL Moist, well-drained soil, high in organic matter.

GROWING Water when young; drought tolerant once established. Good for shearing.

DESIGNER'S CHOICE
Loropetalum chinense f. *rubrum* 'Blush' Shocking pink flowers in clusters of 5–10; bronzy red new growth on compact shrub. 6' h × 4'–5' h.

L. chinense f. *rubrum* 'Burgundy' Shocking pink blooms in clusters of 4–7; reddish purple new foliage; older leaves dark reddish purple to dark olive. Very showy. 6'–10' h and w.

L. chinense 'Ruby' Small, ruby red leaves; pink flowers; nice foundation plant. 3'–5' h and w.

L. chinense 'Snow Muffin' White-flowered groundcover with small, dark green leaves. 2' h × 2' or more w.

MAACKIA

Maackia amurensis ○ ✳

MAK-ee-a a-mu-REN-sis

Amur maackia

Pea Family (Fabaceae)
Small deciduous tree
20'–30' h and w

I found this tree balled-and-burlapped at a big New England wholesale nursery one summer. It gets its appeal from its dark green, compound leaves that look silvery in spring; green stems and twigs; and glossy, coppery-brown bark that will

Maackia amurensis var. buergeri

exfoliate on old branches over time. It bears erect clusters of fragrant, white flowers in early summer, but may not bloom well each year. Abundant seedpods can be messy, so not necessarily a good lawn tree. Amur maackia fixes nitrogen, absorbing this vital plant nutrient from the atmosphere and making it available to the roots. This tree is problem free and easy to grow, and tolerates tough sites, drought, and poor fertility. May be hard to find.

LANDSCAPE USE
Specimen; small shade tree.

ORIGIN Manchuria

HARDINESS ZONES 4–7

LIGHT Full sun.

SOIL Well-drained, acid to alkaline soils.

GROWING No serious problems; no significant pruning except for the occasional unruly shoot and crossed, dead, or diseased branches.

MACLURA

Maclura pomifera ○ ✳

mak-LU-ra po-MI-fe-ra

Osage orange, Osage apple, Hedge apple

Mulberry Family (Moraceae)
Medium-sized deciduous tree
20'–40' h and w

Okay, this may not be the prettiest tree in the book but it has its uses, including fat, fall fruit for a game of catch. If you're looking for a green fence or fast-growing barrier planting, then this may be the plant for you. Osage orange has a short trunk and rounded crown with dense, thorny branches that droop near the ground. Moreover, it grows just about anywhere, from acid to alkaline and from wet to poor, droughty soils, as long as it gets enough sun. Male and female trees exist, but it's the latter that produce the curious fruits, which make a mess when they drop in the fall. Unless you find the fruits appealing, buy a male for less mess or look for a nearly thornless, fruitless cultivar, such as 'White Shield' or 'Wichita'. Otherwise, plant male and female trees for pollination. Keep the tree at your property's edge and away from the house, as sharp ½"–1" spines in leaf axils can draw blood and heavy 4"–6" fruits may clobber you in autumn when you're walking by. Native Americans made archery bows from the wood, giving the tree its other common name, bodark or *bois d'arc* (French for bow wood).

LANDSCAPE USE
Green fence or fast-growing barrier.

ORIGIN South-central U.S.

HARDINESS ZONES 4–9

LIGHT Full sun.

SOIL Acid to alkaline soils and wet to infertile, dry soils.

GROWING No significant pruning, except for the occasional unruly shoot and crossed, dead, or diseased branches.

CAUTION Dermatitis may result from contact with milky sap in the stems and fruit.

Maclura pomifera

MAGNOLIA

Magnolia acuminata △ › ○ ✳

mag-NO-lee-a a-kew-mi-NAH-ta

Cucumber tree

Magnolia Family (Magnoliaceae)
Large deciduous tree
50'–75' h and w

Although you may not want to grow this jumbo species in your garden, one of its smaller cultivars may suit your space. This native species is handsome in the landscape, having a straight trunk and pyramidal habit when young and a more rounded form when older. Cucumber tree looks good underplanted with groundcovers such as bigroot geranium *(G. macrorrhizum)* or 'Green Sheen' pachysandra.

The alternate, simple, dark green leaves are deciduous, 5"–10" long and oval with smooth edges and a pointed tip. The grayish brown bark is soft and flaky; the reddish brown twigs are fragrant when crushed. The greenish yellow, late spring flowers of the species are not ornamental, but popular yellow cultivars have excellent, fragrant flowers in mid-spring. The immature fruit looks like a green cucumber; when ripe in fall, the fruit is red, bumpy, and cylindrical with bright red seeds.

LANDSCAPE USE

The species is too big for most home landscapes, but cultivars and hybrids make suitable shade or specimen trees. Not a city tree because it is sensitive to air pollution. The fruit of the species attracts birds.

ORIGIN   Cool moist mountain valleys and woodland edges in the eastern U.S.

HARDINESS ZONES   4–8

LIGHT   Full sun to partial shade.

SOIL   Moist, loose, well-drained, slightly acid soils with plenty of organic matter; tolerates some alkalinity.

Magnolia denudata

GROWING   Once planted, don't move this tree, because its shallow network of surface roots doesn't like to be disturbed. If you live where soils are extremely alkaline, you can put sulfur on the soil in spring to make it more acid or apply acidic mulch such as pine needles or shredded bark.

DESIGNER'S CHOICE

Magnolia × *brooklynensis* 'Yellow Bird' (syn. M. 'Yellow Bird') Upright, fast-growing, pyramidal tree with 3" yellow blooms for 2 to 3 weeks in late spring. 40' h × 25' w.

M. 'Butterflies' Profuse quantity of true yellow, 5", fragrant flowers that bloom before leaves are fully open; blossoms sometimes killed by late frosts; hybrid with *M. denudata*. My 'Butterflies' grew very fast for several years, producing copious blooms, but after a late spring snowstorm the top of the crown with its slightly angled leader broke off. Now we're training a new leader perpendicular to the ground. 30' h and w. Zones 5–9.

M. 'Elizabeth' Gorgeous, pale primrose yellow, fragrant flowers on a vigorous tree that blooms when young; blooms about a week later than 'Butterflies' in late April and May while leaves are opening; hybrid with *M. denudata*; cold hardy. 40'–50' h × 20'–25' w.

Magnolia 'Elizabeth'

ALL ABOUT MAGNOLIA

Beauty and decay dance an endless tango in the garden. What's more poignant than watching magnolia petals unfold soft, smooth, and pure as a baby's cheek, then rot in a late spring frost? I love everything about these trees: the seduction of their scented white, pink, purple, or yellow flowers; their gaudy red or orange seeds; and their ancient mystique, told through fossils that prove their existence almost 60 million years ago. Give magnolias the right conditions — a sheltered spot with moist, acid, humsy soil, in sun to partial shade — and these deciduous or evergreen flowering shrubs and trees will bring beauty, shade, and wildlife to your yard.

Magnolia x *soulangeana*

Magnolia 'Daybreak' 0

mag-NO-lee-a

'Daybreak' magnolia

Magnolia Family (Magnoliaceae)
Deciduous small flowering tree
18–30 ' h x 4'–12' w

With its tight, columnar form, Daybreak magnolia is perfect for growing in small spots, narrow side yards, or along urban boundaries. It grows at a slow to medium rate, producing extremely fragrant, 8"–10", vivid pink, saucer-shaped flowers in late spring, thus avoiding frost injury.

LANDSCAPE USE
Small sites such as narrow side yards or along urban boundaries.

ORIGIN   Garden hybrid

HARDINESS ZONES   5–8

LIGHT   Full sun to partial shade.

SOIL   Moist, well drained, humusy, acid to neutral soils.

GROWING   Look out for scale, leaf miners.

Magnolia denudata △ ✳

mag-NO-lee-a de-nu-DA-ta

Yulan magnolia

Magnolia Family (Magnoliaceae)
Medium-sized deciduous flowering tree
30'–40' h and w

Even without its flowers, this handsome magnolia would be a fine-looking tree with its erect, compact form and big, deep green foliage about 5" long and half as wide. The white flowers are about 5" wide and fragrant, and the rich red, cylindrical fruits are roughly 5" long.

LANDSCAPE USE
Lovely specimen with a multi-stemmed form and attractive leaves and flowers. Good for shading a patio or in a lawn.

ORIGIN   China

HARDINESS ZONES   5–8

LIGHT   Full sun to partial shade.

SOIL   Moist, rich, humusy soil.

GROWING   Late frost can kill the early flowers; needs wind protection in Zone 5.

Magnolia grandiflora △ ✳

mag-NO-lee-a gran-di-FLO-ra

Southern magnolia

Magnolia Family (Magnoliaceae)
Medium to large evergreen flowering tree
60'–90' h x 30'–50' w

If you were to ask me what I remember about touring colleges with my daughter, I'd say walking onto Emory University's campus in suburban Atlanta in June. Southern magnolias lined the roadway, their flowers exuding a rich, lemony-sweet perfume. Peak bloom had passed, but still the trees stopped foot traffic with their heady splendor.

Handsome year round with their pyramidal form that branches to the ground, southern magnolias have alternate, simple leaves that are evergreen, leathery, and a glossy dark green. On many plants, the leaf undersides look rusty red because of a dense covering of red-brown hairs. The gray-brown bark is thin when young, scaly when mature. In early summer (May and June), the trees bear intensely fragrant, white, cup-shaped blooms up to 12" wide. The green to red, 5", aggregate fruits are cylindrical with red seeds.

LANDSCAPE USE

Excellent plant for screening, shade, formal gardens, and specimens.

ORIGIN   Southeastern U.S.

HARDINESS ZONES   7–9

LIGHT   Full sun to partial shade.

SOIL   Moist, rich, well-drained, acid soils with plenty of organic matter.

GROWING   Plant new trees in spring and protect from harsh winds and too much sun in the northern part of its range. It may get some leaf spot, and it's hard to grow anything else under its low, crowded branches.

DESIGNER'S CHOICE

Magolia grandiflora 'Bracken's Brown Beauty' Small, many-branched tree with glossy, dark green leaves that have brown hairy bottoms, popular in the Southeast but also fairly cold hardy. I can vouch for the hardiness, since we planted a 4' specimen one October before a winter when temperatures dropped to −15°F. In December, my husband erected a low burlap screen around the plant, which lost all its leaves. The following May we transplanted it to another spot, where it grew new leaves and thrives. 30'–50' h × 15'–30' w.

M. grandiflora 'D. D. Blanchard' Pyramidal form with glossy, dark green leaves with orangey-brown undersides. 50' h × 25'–35' w.

M. grandiflora 'Edith Bogue' Relatively

Magnolia grandiflora 'D. D. Blanchard'

cold hardy with 8"-wide, fragrant, creamy blooms. 30' h × 15' w. Zones 6–9.

M. grandiflora 'Little Gem' Dwarf southern magnolia with smaller leaves and white, cup-shaped flowers. Blooms in early and late summer in full sun. Good for small yards. 20'–25' h × 10'–15' w.

M. grandiflora 'MGTIG' (Greenback) Densely branched, conical tree with glossy leaves and cup-shaped, fragrant blooms; heat and drought tolerant. 25'–40' h × 10'–15' w.

M. grandiflora 'TMGH' (Alta) Tight columnar form good for screening on narrow urban sites. Leaves have rust-hued bottoms. 40' h × 15' w.

Magnolia liliiflora 'Nigra' ○

mag-NO-lee-a li-li-i-FLO-ra

Nigra lily magnolia

Magnolia Family (Magnoliaceae)
Deciduous flowering shrub
6'–10' h × 4'–8' w

In cold winter climates, this small deciduous magnolia is worth growing for its 4" goblet-shaped flowers that are purple outside and pink inside in mid-spring. Its diminutive size, compared with many magnolias, makes it suitable for small yards. You can also grow 'The Little Girl Hybrids' as small trees.

LANDSCAPE USE

Because lily magnolia may look shabby as the season progresses, it works well as a specimen or as an accent in shrub borders, mixed with later-blooming ornamental plants.

ORIGIN   China (species)

HARDINESS ZONES   5–8

LIGHT   Full sun to partial shade.

SOIL   Moist, well-drained, humusy, acid to neutral soils.

GROWING   Needs wind protection; mulch with compost in spring.

DESIGNER'S CHOICE

M. 'Galaxy' (*M. liliiflora* 'Nigra' × *M. sprengeri* 'Diva') Abundant 6" pink flowers, conical habit, and yellow-bronze fall leaf color. USNA, 25' h × 12' w. Zone (4) 5.

'The Little Girl Hybrids' (*M. liliiflora* 'Nigra' × *M. stellata* and *M. stellata* 'Rosea') Bloom later than *M. stellata*. Because of this, they can sometimes escape frost injury. Later in the season, some of these 8 hybrids may become susceptible to mildew. 15'–20' h × 12'–15' w. Zones 4–6.

M. 'Ann': 4", dark purplish red blooms before leaves; open habit; 8'–10' h and w. *M.* 'Betty': Flowers are dark purplish red outside, white inside, with reddish new foliage; 10'–15' h × 12' w.

Magnolia 'Galaxy'

Magnolia 'Ann'

Magnolia × loebneri 'Leonard Messel' △ ✳

mag-NO-lee-a LOHB-ne-ri

Leonard Messel magnolia

Magnolia Family (Magnoliaceae)
Deciduous small flowering tree
20' h x 25' w

Slow-growing Leonard Messel magnolia is garden worthy for its small size, healthy foliage, and decorative, late spring flowers. The deep purplish pink buds open to fragrant, 2-toned flowers with 12–15 straplike petals, pale pink inside and dark purplish pink outside.

LANDSCAPE USE
Grow it as a small tree or big multi-stemmed shrub. I have a young one in full sun in a shrub border, where it bloomed the first spring after planting.

ORIGIN Garden origin; chance hybrid.

HARDINESS ZONES (4) 5–9

Magnolia x loebneri
'Leonard Messel'

LIGHT Full sun to partial shade.

SOIL Moist, well-drained, fertile, humusy soil high in organic matter. Doesn't tolerate extremely wet or dry soil.

GROWING Occasional mildew. Doesn't tolerate urban pollution.

DESIGNER'S CHOICE

Magnolia × loebneri 'Ballerina' White, very scented flowers with 30 petals, tinted pink in the middle. 15'–20' h × 15' w.

M. × loebneri 'Merrill' Abundant 3", white flowers in mid-spring; fast-growing, thrives in the heat of the Southeast and the cold of the North. 20'–25' h × 25'–30' w. Zones (3) 4–8.

Magnolia macrophylla △

mag-NO-lee-a mak-ro-FIL-la

Big-leaf magnolia

Magnolia Family (Magnoliaceae)
Medium-sized deciduous
flowering tree
30'–40' h x 12'–15' w

This native of the southeastern U.S. is not your typical magnolia. Its tropical-looking leaves (light green with whitish undersides) are the biggest of any native tree, measuring up to 32" long. Its off-white, fragrant flowers are 10"–14" wide. Its ultra-coarse texture makes it hard, but not impossible, to use in most home landscapes. Thanks to my friend Neil Jorgensen, who gave us a *macrophylla* seedling, I now have an 8' specimen growing in the partly shaded, protected understory of a pin oak *(Quercus palustris)* and two bald cypresses *(Taxodium distichum).* The soil is moist, acid, and well drained, and the magnolia is flourishing. Though my little tree has an open habit, those grown in full sun would be denser and more pyramidal.

LANDSCAPE USE
Lawn or woody border specimen for dramatic textural effect; especially striking when the silver-bottomed leaves flap in a breeze.

ORIGIN Fertile wooded steep valleys of southeastern U.S.

HARDINESS ZONES 5–8

LIGHT Full sun to partial shade.

SOIL Acid, moist, well-drained soil with plenty of organic matter. Doesn't tolerate wet or dry soil extremes.

GROWING Rarely troubled by pests or diseases. Takes seedlings at least 10 years to flower. Protect from strong winds, which can shred the large leaves. Doesn't tolerate urban pollution.

Magnolia × soulangeana ◐ › ◌

mag-NO-lee-a su-lan-ji-AY-na

Saucer magnolia

Magnolia Family (Magnoliaceae)
Small deciduous flowering tree
or large shrub
20'–30' h and w

This old-fashioned favorite appears in the front yard of many farmhouses and suburban homes. Flowers usually appear before the leaves open in spring. Even very young trees produce the sweetly fragrant flowers, which are flushed rosy purple on the outside and white to pale pink inside. It has a handsome, densely branched, oval habit. Old trees have one or more short, gray trunks with an irregular to rounded crown and spreading low-lying branches, which make viewing the flowers a snap. The winter effect is coarse but not unattractive. A late cold snap can kill the frost-sensitive blooms, browning them in hours. This is a hybrid species (*M. denudata* × *M. liliiflora*).

LANDSCAPE USE
Deer-resistant specimen in the lawn or a spring accent for shrub border.

Magnolia x *soulangeana*

ORIGIN Garden

HARDINESS ZONES 4–9

LIGHT Full sun.

SOIL Moist, well-drained, slightly acid soil.

GROWING When planted in the lawn, keep the tree lightly mulched so that you don't disturb the fleshy surface roots.

DESIGNER'S CHOICE

Magnolia × *soulangeana* 'Alexandrina' Flowers are deeper purple on the outside than species, and white inside. 20'–25' h and w.

M. × *soulangeana* 'Lennei' Wide, shrubby plant with dark green leaves and flowers flushed deep purplish-magenta outside, white inside. Blooms later than species; not as hardy as species. 15'–20' h and w. Zone 5.

M. × *soulangeana* 'Lennei Alba' Ivory blooms, not as hardy as species. 15'–20' h and w. Zone 5.

Magnolia stellata ⓞ › ○

mag-NO-lee-a stel-LA-ta

Star magnolia

Magnolia Family (Magnoliaceae) Deciduous flowering shrub or small low-branched, multi-stemmed tree 15'–20' h x 10'–15' w

Star magnolias flower when very small and young. The white or pink blooms appear before the leaves, brightening the spring landscape with their light hue and fragrance. Although their flowering season is short, these trees look good all summer, thanks to their compact, oval, shrubby form and smooth, deep green leaves. Whether you live North or South, this versatile landscape plant is a worthy garden choice.

The dark green, alternate, simple leaves measure 2"–4" × 1"–2"; for the most part, the foliage stays whole and undamaged through the growing season. The smooth bark on the trunks is gray. Fuzzy buds open to delicately scented, white to pink, 3"–4"-wide and up to 2"-long flowers with 12–18 straplike tepals; cultivars may have many more. Fruits are bumpy, greenish, irregular, 2" clusters with scarlet seeds that ripen in fall; they are not particularly ornamental.

LANDSCAPE USE
Specimen for large and small yards, grouped in a woodland area in dappled shade, near a deck or patio, or large foundation plantings.

ORIGIN Mountain woods of Japan.

HARDINESS ZONES 4–8

LIGHT Full sun to partial shade; better flowering in full sun.

SOIL Moist, rich, well-drained, acid soils high in organic material; adaptable.

GROWING Star magnolias need little care. If you must prune, do so immediately after flowering so you don't cut off next year's buds. Necessary pruning jobs include removal of dead or damaged wood. Blooms early enough in spring that frost can injure the flowers. Breakage from heavy snow and ice may injure the soft wood.

DESIGNER'S CHOICE

Magnolia stellata 'Centennial' Conical plant with open flowers made of 28–32 white tepals tinted pink on the outside; one of the best cultivars. 25' h × 20' w.

M. stellata 'Royal Star' Pink buds, fragrant white blooms with 25–30 tepals. 15' h × 20' w.

M. stellata 'Waterlily' Later blooming cultivar with deep pink buds opening to big, white, fragrant flowers, about 30 tepals. 15'–20' h × 10'–15' w.

Magnolia stellata 'Centennial'

Magnolia stellata 'Waterlily'

Key: ⓞ Oval △ Pyramid ○ Rounded ▽ Vase ◌ Spreading 🌿 Weeping 🌲 Creeping/Suckering/Trailing ✳ Easy ■ 281

Magnolia tripetala ○ › ◯

mag-NO-lee-a try-PET-a-la

Umbrella magnolia

Magnolia Family (Magnoliaceae)
Deciduous multi-trunk flowering tree
15'–30' h and w

The umbrella magnolia is good for magnolia enthusiasts and native plant collectors. In late spring, when its leaves unfold, it bears creamy white, 5"-wide blooms with 6–9 tepals and a nasty scent. The medium green leaves are shiny and big — up to 2' long — and set near the branch tips. Trees typically have more than one trunk. My friend Neil Jorgensen gave me several *tripetala* seedlings, now 6 years old. They're uneven in habit but both the few flowers we've seen and the pinkish seedpods filled with red seeds are attractive. *Tripetala* is similar to *macrophylla,* only shorter, less hardy, and with smaller flowers that bloom earlier and have an unpleasant scent.

LANDSCAPE USE
Specimen for its coarse-textured 2' leaves. Grow away from windows and doors so the stinky flowers aren't a nuisance.

ORIGIN Southeastern U.S.

HARDINESS ZONES 5–8

LIGHT Full sun to partial shade.

SOIL Moist, well-drained, acid soil high in organic matter.

GROWING Low drought tolerance; needs plenty of moisture.

Magnolia virginiana △

mag-NO-lee-a vir-ji-nee-AY-na

Sweet bay, Sweet bay magnolia

Magnolia Family (Magnoliaceae)
Evergreen to deciduous flowering shrub or tree
12'–60' h x 12'–30' w

Sweet bay magnolia is the right choice for gardens with moist to wet, acid soils. It grows in the North as a deciduous shrub or multi-stemmed, small tree, 10'–20' high. In the South, it tends to grow into an evergreen tree with an upright, pyramidal form up to 60' high. It is a larval host for tiger swallowtail butterflies, and both game birds and songbirds eat the fruit.

The beautiful, glossy, dark green foliage is alternate and simple, with grayish undersides; about 4" × 2", the leaves are evergreen in the South and deciduous in the North, depending upon how far north you live. The tree has greenish stems and smooth, gray bark. It flowers on and off from late spring to late summer with creamy white, saucer-shaped, 2"–3" blooms that have a lemony fragrance. The ornamental, conical fruits contain clustered, red seeds in fall.

LANDSCAPE USE
Plant this handsome tree near streams, ponds, and the woodland's edge. It also looks attractive in a shrub border or as a lawn specimen or patio tree.

ORIGIN Swampy sites in southeastern U.S.

HARDINESS ZONES 5–9

LIGHT Full sun to partial shade.

SOIL Moist to wet acid soils. In alkaline soils an iron deficiency can yellow the leaves.

GROWING Shelter from winter winds in the North.

DESIGNER'S CHOICE
Magnolia virginiana var. *australis* Shrubby in Zone 5, with silver leaf bottoms; excellent cultivar in the South, where it is a tall evergreen tree with flowers more strongly scented than the species. 10'–60' h and w.

M. virginiana 'Henry Hicks' Stays evergreen into Zone 5. 12'–60' h × 10'–30' w.

M. virginiana 'Jim Wilson' (Moonglow) Cup-shaped, creamy white, fragrant flowers on an upright, multi-stemmed, semi-evergreen tree. Has survived −33°F without injury. 35' h × 18' w.

MAHONIA

Mahonia aquifolium ○ › ☁

ma-HO-nee-a a-kwi-FO-lee-um

Oregon grape holly

Barberry Family (Berberidaceae)
Broad-leaf evergreen shrub
3'–6' h and w

Oregon grape holly makes a superb evergreen barrier hedge, especially in the moist moderate Pacific Northwest, its native climate. It has dense, prickly leaves like holly and a suckering habit. Added interest comes from lightly fragrant clusters of yellow, spring flowers; silvery-coated, dark blue berries; bronze new growth; and purplish leaves in fall and winter. The bark is grayish brown.

LANDSCAPE USE
Good for hedging, shrub borders with other acid-loving plants, low screens and barriers, naturalistic gardens, and Japanese gardens.

ORIGIN Conifer forests of coastal Pacific Northwest.

HARDINESS ZONES 5–8

LIGHT Partial shade.

SOIL Moist, acid, well-drained soils.

GROWING Shelter from winter sun and wind, and summer's extreme heat and drought. It is deer and drought resistant. It may be afflicted with leaf spot, leaf scorch, and aphids.

DESIGNER'S CHOICE
Mahonia aquifolium 'Compacta' (syn. 'Compactum') Similar to, but smaller than, species. Use masses in entry gardens and foundations, under trees, in shrub borders. 2'–3' h × 3'–4' w.

Mahonia japonica

M. japonica (syn. *M. bealei*) (leather-leaf mahonia) Rigid, dull, dark blue-green leaves; fragrant yellow flowers in elongated terminal clusters in spring, light blue berries in summer. 5'–10' h × 4'–5' w. Zones 6–9.

M. repens (creeping mahonia) Evergreen creeper, native to Northwestern U.S., with yellow flower clusters followed by sour, edible, dark blue berries, covered with a whitish bloom; handsome ground cover. Grow like *M. aquifolium*. 9"–15" h × 1½'–3' w.

MALUS

Malus species and hybrids ○

MA-lus

Flowering crabapple, Apple

Rose Family (Rosaceae)
Small, flowering deciduous tree
5'–25' h × 6'–25' w

Walking around my neighborhood in summer, I'm struck by the fact that my most and least favorite plants are crabapples. My favorite is a 6' tree with healthy green leaves, single white flowers, and a rounded crown that holds its bright red pomes all winter long. The bigger, badder crabs look fried in July. By August each year, I want to wield an axe and relieve these trees of their ugly, half-dead lives.

Why do I care about crabapples?

Their allure comes from lovely spring flowers matched by few other trees and colorful fall fruits attracting bunches of birds. Summer leaves may be green, purple, or reddish green. In winter, the bare trees show off the striking form that can develop with age. Some crabs have fall color or particularly handsome bark, while others are hardy to Zone 2, making them treasured assets for cold-climate gardeners. But buyers beware! These seemingly perfect ornamental trees are related to finicky roses and are susceptible to some of their pests and diseases, plus some problems all their own. For healthy crabapples, always plant disease-resistant cultivars and keep in mind the cultural requirements of the genus when planting and maintaining your trees.

The green, purple, or bronze-tinged foliage is simple, alternate, and deciduous. The scaly bark is a glossy, grayish brown. In spring, crabapple bears white, pink, or red single or double blooms, sometimes fragrant. Some crabapples are annual flowering, while others produce flowers more abundantly every other year. The red, yellow, or orange pomes are 2" or less in diameter.

LANDSCAPE USE
Foundations, groups, lawn specimen, or accent.

ORIGIN A variety of habitats in North America, Europe, and Asia, and hundreds of garden origin.

HARDINESS ZONES 2–8, depending on species and cultivars; 4–7 more typical.

LIGHT Full sun is best.

SOIL Moist, well-drained, acid soils.

GROWING Use debris-free pruners and loppers when working on crabapples to keep from spreading disease from plant to plant. When you know disease is present, clean blades with a disinfectant wipe after each cut. At the end of each pruning session, lubricate blades and wipe with a soft, dry rag. Keep tool blades sharp, as dull blades make rough cuts that slow healing and lead to infections. If your tree becomes diseased, do not mulch the damaged leaves. Instead, collect them right away and deposit them in the trash. Prune branches by early June to avoid removing next year's bloom; cut out suckers from understock, and thin the middle branches to let in air and light. These trees are pollution tolerant but susceptible to many pests and diseases, including apple scab, cedar apple rust, fireblight, Japanese beetles, and borers. Asian species are more pest- and disease-resistant than North American species. Hundreds of ornamental cultivars exist with varying degrees of pest and disease resistance.

DESIGNER'S CHOICE

Malus 'Adams' Rounded habit; deep red buds; single, medium-pink flowers; shiny red, medium-sized fruits last through winter; red-tinged dark green leaves. Disease resistant but susceptible to Japanese beetles. 25' h and w. Zones 4–8.

M. 'Adirondack' Columnar and slow growing, red buds, single white flowers, long-lasting orangey red (½") fruits; very disease resistant. 18' h × 11' w. Zones 4–7.

M. 'Callaway' Pink buds; white flowers; big, edible, persistent, maroon fruits; disease resistant. One of the best for southern gardens. 15'–25' h and w.

M. 'Cardinal' Bright red flowers and shiny red leaves; small, dark red fruits; decent disease resistance. 15'–20' h and w. Zones 5–7.

M. 'Donald Wyman' Pink buds; white flowers; shiny red, medium-sized, persistent fruits; upright to rounded shape; shiny dark green leaves; mostly disease resistant. 20' h × 25' w. Zones 4–7.

Malus 'Donald Wyman' (left); 'Prairiefire' (right)

M. floribunda (Japanese flowering crabapple) Dark pink buds, fragrant pink flowers fading to white, small yellow-and-red fruits, Japanese beetle resistant. 20' h × 25' w. Zone 5.

M. 'Fox Fire' Pink buds, white flowers, gold-blushed-red medium fruits, spreading form, very disease resistant. 15' h and w.

M. hupehensis (tea crabapple) Pink buds; large, pinkish white flowers; handsome vase-shaped habit; yellow to red. Small, persistent fruits; resists scab and Japanese beetles but susceptible to fireblight. 20'–25' h and w. Zones 4–8.

M. 'Louisa' Weeping habit good for softening effect, red buds, pink flowers, gold medium fruits, deep shiny green leaves; resists most diseases and Japanese beetles but scab susceptible. 15' h and w. Zones 4–7.

M. 'Jewelcole' (Red Jewel) Showy, white flowers, followed by lots of little red fruits on tree with an oval to rounded crown and decent pest and disease resistance. 12'–15' h × 10'–12' w.

M. 'Prairiefire' Late-blooming, red flowers; maroon, cone-shaped, persistent fruits; retains leaves well in summer; handsome, shiny, deep red bark with big lenticels; disease resistant. 15'–20' h × 20' w. Zones 4–7.

M. 'Professor Sprenger' Pink buds; prolific white flowers; medium, vivid orange, persistent fruits; upright oval crown; excellent disease and pest resistance. 20' h and w. Zones 4–8.

M. 'Purple Prince' Red buds, profuse red blooms, blue-tinged purple fruit, purple leaves fading to purplish green, attractive cherry-like bark; disease resistant. 20' h and w. Zones 4–7.

M. Round Table Series (dwarf flowering crabapples, disease and pest resistant) Use as a specimen or arrange several symmetrically in a formal garden 8'–10' h × 8' w. Zones 4–7. 'Camzam' (Camelot): red buds, fuchsia pink on white flowers, medium burgundy fruits, rounded form, burgundy-tinged dark green leaves; disease resistant; 10' h × 8' w. 'Guinzam' (Guinevere): mauve buds; white blooms; persistent, bright red, medium-sized fruit; and burgundy-tinged, dark green, glossy leaves; rounded form; disease resistant; 8'–10' h × 10' w. 'Lanzam' (Lancelot): red buds, white flowers; persistent gold medium fruits; upright form with dense oval crown; gold fall color; very scab resistant. There are several others in this series. 8'–10' h × 8' w.

M. 'Sutyzam' (Sugar Tyme) Light pink buds open to fragrant white flowers followed in fall by shiny red pomes that last into winter; upright branches; oval crown; very disease resistant. 15'–18' h × 12'–15' w.

M. toringo 'Tina' (syn. *M. sargentii* 'Tina') (Tina Sargent crabapple) Dark pink buds; fragrant, single, white flowers; small, profuse, persistent, red fruits eaten by birds by early winter; low, horizontal, dwarf habit; highly disease resistant. 4'–6' h × 6'–8' w. Zones 4–7.

M. transitoria 'Schmidtcutleaf' (Golden Raindrops) Pink buds; abundant, starry, white flowers; small, gold fruits; fine-textured, deeply cut foliage on vase-shaped tree; disease resistant and may resist Japanese beetles. 20'–25' h × 15'–20' w.

M. × *zumi* 'Calocarpa' Red buds, white single flowers. Birds like the red, persistent fruits. Shiny, dark green leaves with orange and yellow fall color, densely branched rounded habit; may be susceptible to fireblight, scab, and powdery mildew. 15'–25' h × 10'–25' w. Zones 4–8.

Malus domestica 'Lanzam'

Metasequoia glyptostroboides △ ✳

me-ta-se-KWOY-a glip-to-stro-BOY-deez

Dawn redwood

Bald Cypress Family (Taxodiaceae)
Deciduous conifer
70′–120′ h x 25′ w

From a distance, the foliage of dawn redwood is so fine that it looks like a soft blur. But that's all that's soft about this soaring, fast-growing, architectural tree with a strong central leader that narrows as it rises high in the sky. Reddish-brown bark peels in long strips from its powerfully buttressed trunk, and the low-branched crown has an elongated conical shape. Fossils show that dawn redwood, once known to the dinosaurs, has been around for 100 million years.

The deciduous, opposite, flat and linear, bright light green leaves turn orange- to ruddy-bronze in fall. The ornamental, red-brown bark is fibrous, peeling vertically. Neither the clustered flowers nor the cones are ornamental.

LANDSCAPE USE
Elegant in groups, arresting specimen; because of its large size, it works best on large properties.

ORIGIN   Moist soils in southwestern China.

HARDINESS ZONES   5–8

LIGHT   Full sun.

SOIL   Deep, moist to wet, slightly acid soils.

GROWING   Easily transplanted, rarely needs pruning. Grows late in the season and early frost may injure it; leaves may attract Japanese beetles.

DESIGNER'S CHOICE
Metasequoia glyptostroboides 'Goldrush' (syn. *M. glyptostroboides* 'Ogon') Bright gold to chartreuse leaves,

Metasequoia glyptostroboides 'Goldrush'

particularly when foliage is young. Tree is slower growing than species and ultimately shorter. I flipped for this tree a few years ago at the Variegated Plant Nursery in Connecticut. Mine is 2′ high and looking good. 15′ h × 6′ w at 10 years.

M. glyptostroboides 'Jack Frost' Variegated cultivar. New branchlets have whitish tips in spring fading to light green in summer. Ultimately smaller than species. 15′ h × 6′ w at 10 years.

Microbiota decussata ⌂ ✳

my-kro-bi-OH-ta de-kus-SA-ta

Siberian cypress, Russian arborvitae

Cypress Family (Cupressaceae)
Evergreen shrub
1½′ h x 6′ w

This evergreen shrub has year-round interest because of its bright, evergreen leaves that turn purplish bronze in winter. Similar appearance to, and sometimes confused with, junipers, but tolerates part shade.

The foliage is set in flattened, arborvitae-like sprays. Found in 1921 in the mountains above the tree line near Vladivostok, Russia.

LANDSCAPE USE
Excellent groundcover; works well on slopes and in rock gardens.

ORIGIN   High in the mountains of Siberia.

HARDINESS ZONES   2–7 (extremely hardy).

LIGHT   Full sun to partial shade, as long as the climate is fairly cool.

SOIL   Moist and very well-drained soil.

GROWING   Mostly pest and disease free. Needs little to no pruning. Does not tolerate heat and heavy soils. Vigorous spreading grass can become a weed issue, as this plant is not very dense.

Microbiota decussata

MORUS

Morus rubra ○ ✳

MO-rus RU-bra

Red mulberry

Mulberry Family (Moraceae)
Deciduous fruit tree
35-50' h x 40' w

You don't know messy till you've grown this one. As a little kid in Webster Groves, Missouri, I adored the mulberry tree in my backyard. I ate the dark bluish purple, summer fruit that dropped on the ground and helped pick berries for pie. Our mulberry grew near the driveway, not a good site for a fast-growing untidy native tree. The sweet, blackberry-like fruit, popular with birds and squirrels, stained the cement. I had to take off my shoes at the door to keep from tracking smashed berries into the house. Still, the tree's rounded crown with stout branches and coarse lobed leaves in different shapes and sizes sheltered my friends and me from summer heat. The foliage turns yellow in fall.

LANDSCAPE USE
The question with red mulberry is not should you plant it (since you may not find one at your local garden center), but should you keep it if you have one growing wild on your property. I say, yes, preserve it if it's healthy: for shade, for the wildlife it attracts, and for its delicious fruits, which make excellent pies and jams. But make sure the tree is far enough from paths and driveways to keep them clean.

ORIGIN   Sheltered woods and valleys in the eastern U.S. and southern Ontario, where it is endangered.

HARDINESS ZONES   5–9

LIGHT   Full sun.

SOIL   Moist, well drained soils; drought resistant and adaptable.

GROWING   Tolerates city life; survives flooded roots for one growing season. Watch out for borers. Red mulberry may produce male and female flowers on the same tree, so a separate pollinator isn't always necessary.

CAUTION   White mulberry (*M. alba*), an Asian tree introduced in colonial times as food for silkworms, is invasive throughout the country; it hybridizes with red mulberry and may be spreading fatal root disease to the native red population, which is vanishing from its central range.

MYRICA

Myrica pensylvanica ○ › 🍂 ✳

MEER-i-ka pen-sil-VAN-i-ka

Bayberry

Bayberry Family (Myricaceae)
Deciduous to semi-evergreen suckering shrub
2'–10' h x 5'–10' or more w

At the shore, bayberry grows just a couple feet tall but it can colonize a big stretch on dunes. Inland, I've seen it grow near ponds and marshes, where it reaches 5'–6' tall. Try a free-growing, naturalistic planting

Myrica pensylvanica

with ornamental grasses and easy perennials like *Eupatorium rugosum* 'Chocolate' and *Sedum* 'Autumn Joy.' The waxy, whitish berries are useful in crafts such as bayberry candlemaking and dried flower arranging.

The alternate, simple, deciduous to semi-evergreen foliage is aromatic and glossy, up to 4" long. The smooth bark is grayish brown. Non-ornamental male and female catkins appear before leaves in early spring. Female shrubs have waxy, round fruits in short-stalked clusters that persist from late summer through spring; these berries are icy bluish to grayish white.

LANDSCAPE USE
Excellent for naturalistic, wild, and coastal gardens, where its spreading root system can help prevent erosion. Planted in a mass, it makes a good groundcover for sunny sites with poor soil and harsh growing conditions.

ORIGIN   Coast of eastern North America.

HARDINESS ZONES   5–8

LIGHT   Full sun to partial shade.

SOIL   Well-drained, acid soil. Being a coastal plant, *Myrica* thrives on poor, sandy, acid soils and tolerates salt and wind.

GROWING   Do not plant in soils with high pH, because plants will suffer chlorosis. Since fruiting occurs only on female plants, make sure you have plants of both genders. A ratio of one male for five females should be sufficient. Consider buying named males ('Myriman') and females ('Myda') to guarantee fruiting.

DESIGNER'S CHOICE
Myrica pensylvanica 'Morton' (Silver Sprite) Grow this cultivar for a more controlled-looking bayberry, which becomes a dense mass after several years. 5' h × 7' w.

Nandina domestica ○ › ☁ ✳

nan-DEE-na doh-MES-ti-ka

Heavenly bamboo

Barberry Family (Berberidaceae)
Broad-leaf evergreen shrub
6'–8' h x 3' w

Although this heavenly shrub is not a real bamboo, it certainly has Asian elegance and flair. Fine canes arc gracefully under the weight of white flower or red berry clusters held above the foliage. *Nandina's* compound leaves, each up to 2' long, also bend lightly on the stems. Copper to bronze new leaves turn blue-green in summer, changing for fall and winter to red or reddish green. Once established, *Nandina* is a moderate grower that can endure for more than a century. Dwarf forms of this four-season plant are especially popular in the South, where (unfortunately) this plant is most invasive. Its narrow habit is a design bonus because it won't outgrow its location.

The compound, semi-evergreen to evergreen leaves are up to 2' × 1', made up of 2 or 3 pairs of compound, lancelike leaflets. New growth is coppery bronze. Summer color is blue-green, changing to red or reddish green in fall and winter. The old bark is brown; the leaf stems wrap around the canes. Starry white, ½" flowers open from pink-tinged buds. Flowers occur in late spring to early summer in upright, branched clusters at the stem tips. Round, bright red berries, ⅓" wide, appear in fall. The huge berry clusters, which last through winter, can bow the canes with their weight.

LANDSCAPE USE

A great accent or massing shrub for woodland gardens, Asian-influenced

Nandina domestica 'Harbor Dwarf'

gardens, patio plantings, and narrow spaces. Use it in a courtyard or flanking a tight gateway. Use it for informal hedging or massed in a border with mid-size to short ornamental grasses.

ORIGIN   East Asia

HARDINESS ZONES   6–9

LIGHT   Full sun to partial shade. Flowers are more profuse in full sun, but the shrub also blooms in shade.

SOIL   Likes moist, rich, well-drained garden soils but can adapt to a wide range of soils and landscape conditions.

GROWING   Establish *Nandina's* root system by keeping it well watered for the first season, after which you can lessen the amount of water it receives. Once fully established, *Nandina* is drought tolerant. Before spring growth starts, apply a general-purpose fertilizer. To avoid legginess on older plants, cut out some of the oldest canes annually. It's also drought tolerant, relatively trouble free, and may be deer resistant. You may see a rare spot of powdery mildew on its leaves. May need a protected site in Zone 6.

CAUTION   Avoid planting *Nandina* in southeastern gardens from Texas to Virginia, where it can be weedy and invasive. Berries may be toxic to cats and grazing animals.

DESIGNER'S CHOICE

Nandina domestica 'Fire Power' Dense, even habit with light green leaves in

summer turning spectacular scarlet in autumn and winter. Use it in borders, foundation plantings, and masses. 2½' h × 3' w.

N. domestica 'Harbor Dwarf' Dense, mounding, suckering groundcover or border specimen, with bronzy to purplish red color in fall and winter. Well proportioned and refined. 2' h × 3' w.

N. domestica 'Moon Bay' Smaller, light green leaves becoming red to reddish green in fall; fine texture; thick mounding habit. Grow massed in beds and borders. 2½' h × 3' w.

N. domestica 'Monum' (Plum Passion) Narrow leaflets are deep purplish red when new, turning dark green in summer and reddish purple in autumn and winter. For color drama, grow it with golden variegated euonymus (*Euonymus japonica* 'Aureo Marginata') or a yellow grass such as *Hakonechloa macra* 'Aureola'. 4–5' h × 3' w.

N. domestica 'Wood's Dwarf' Slow-growing, evergreen groundcover with healthy foliage and a vivid scarlet hue in winter. 2' h and w.

Nandina domestica 'Fire Power'

Nerium oleander ▢ ✳

NEE-ree-um oh-lee-AN-der

Oleander

Dogbane Family (Apocynaceae)
Broad-leaf evergreen shrub or
small tree
2'–20' h x 2'–20' w, depending
upon cultivar

The first time I saw this tough shrub, it was massed along a highway near downtown San Diego. This dense planting with narrow, leathery leaves up to 10" long looked fresh and appealing. Soon I noticed oleander everwhere. Its showy, terminal clusters of pink, red, purple, white, or pale yellow flowers were fragrant and lovely. Flowering peaks in summer to fall, but blooms occur sporadically all year.

LANDSCAPE USE
Screening, hedges, shrub border, containers, massing. Very popular on the Gulf Coast, where it survives drought, pollution, and salt spray.

ORIGIN   Eastern Mediterranean

HARDINESS ZONES   8–11

LIGHT   Full sun to partial shade.

SOIL   Moist, average, well-drained soil; pH tolerant.

GROWING   When not actively growing, let soil dry between waterings; reduce water if leaves start to yellow. Avoid legginess by pruning the tips of young stems for more branching in late winter. Turn shrub into a small tree by keeping a few open, robust stems and cutting out suckers from the base. You can also use suckers to start new plants. No significant diseases or pests, though occasionally bothered by leaf spot, mealybugs, and caterpillars. In cool climates, bring potted oleander indoors as a houseplant after temperatures drop below 20°F. Reduce water and keep in a cool, bright room.

CAUTION   Do not plant in home landscapes with young children; all parts are poisonous. Smoke from burning shrubs is toxic. Wear gloves when handling, since contact with sap may cause allergic reactions.

DESIGNER'S CHOICE
(hundreds of cultivars available)
Nerium oleander 'Calypso'   Purplish red, single flowers on a robust, hardy shrub. 10'–20' h × 10'–15' w.

N. oleander 'Hardy Double Yellow' Pale yellow flowers. 5'–6' h and w. Hardy to warm areas of Zone 7.

N. oleander 'Hardy Pink'   Dark pink buds open to medium pink, single flowers. 5'–6' h and w. Root hardy to warm parts of Zone 7.

N. oleander 'Petite Pink'   Dwarf with single, light pink blooms to grow in protected spots; this and other dwarfs tend to be less hardy than species. With pruning, 3'–4' h and w.

N. oleander 'Soeur Agnes' (syn. 'Sister Agnes', 'White Oleander')   Tough and hardy with big, white, single blooms. 10'–12' h × 10' w.

N. oleander 'Variegatum'   Green leaves edged in white to cream; double, purplish pink blooms. 10'–20' h × 10'–15' w.

NYSSA

Nyssa sylvatica △ › ▢

NIS-sa sil-VAT-i-ka

Sour gum, Black tupelo

Dogwood Family (Cornaceae)
Deciduous tree
30'–50' h x 20'–30' w

Tupelo is an outstanding, native garden tree, a true beauty grown for its lustrous, deep green summer leaves that change to brilliant orangey red in fall. This medium-sized tree grows upright with a strong central leader and a pyramidal shape. Tupelo has fine branches set at right

Nyssa sylvatica

angles to the trunk. I find its refined, horizontal pattern of slender pagoda-like limbs particularly appealing in winter when I look out my office window at a 15'–20' specimen.

Its handsome, glossy leaves measure up to 5" × 2". They're simple, deciduous, deep green, and somewhat oval in shape with burgundy-tinted new growth. The foliage has outstanding fall color ranging from yellow and purple to brilliant orange and red. The gray bark is scaly and, on old branches, chunky. It bears small, non-ornamental, light green flowers. Its long, oval, blue-black fruits are eaten by birds and wildlife. Fruits are edible but sour, hence the common name.

LANDSCAPE USE
Shade tree and lawn specimen; near a pond's edge, singly or in groups. Naturalized areas, or areas subject to periodic flooding.

ORIGIN   From old fields to mountainous ridges and swamps in eastern North America.

HARDINESS ZONES 5–9

LIGHT Full sun to partial shade.

SOIL Moist, deep, acid to neutral soils; intolerant of high pH soils.

GROWING Because it has a strong taproot, a large specimen is difficult to transplant, and for that reason, big tupelos may be hard to find at nurseries and garden centers. Plant small trees only, either balled-and-burlapped or in containers, making sure that there are no girdling roots that could damage the bark and eventually kill the tree. Spring planting is best. Give the plant plenty of water until established. Once settled, it can withstand some dryness. Tupelo is generally a healthy tree when well sited and slow growing. Because it branches to the ground, you may want to prune it up to make room underneath. Possibility of leaf spots, cankers, scales, and leaf miners.

DESIGNER'S CHOICE

Nyssa sylvatica 'NXSXF' (Forum) Faster growth rate than typical seedlings. Selected for dense, glossy, dark green leaves through summer, turning bright red with yellow-streaked veins in fall; dominant central leader. 17' h × 8' w at 9 years old.

OSMANTHUS

Osmanthus heterophyllus ○

oz-MAN-thus het-uh-RAH-fil-lus

False holly, Holly tea olive, Holly osmanthus

Olive Family (Oleaceae)
Broad-leaf evergreen shrub
8'–15' h × 10'–18' w

Osmanthus leaves resemble those of another broadleaf evergreen, holly, thus its common name, false holly. It grows slowly into a medium-textured, rounded shrub crowded with spiny leaves and woody stems, creating an opaque, impassable barrier. This is the hardiest *Osmanthus* species. Grow it where you can enjoy

the scent of the fall-blooming flowers. False holly's evergreen leaves are shiny, dark green on top, tinged yellow below, and tough like hide. Young (juvenile) leaves are edged with spiny teeth, while adult foliage is oval with smooth edges and a pointed tip. Leaves are opposite, simple, and measure up to 2½" × 1½". The smooth, light brown bark has tiny lenticels where gaseous exchanges occur. In mid- to late fall, the white 4-petal blooms clustered in the leaf axils of female plants exude an intense fragrance. Rare, inconspicuous, bluish black, one-seeded fruits take a year to mature after blooming.

LANDSCAPE USE

Year-round hedges, barriers, borders, and screens.

ORIGIN Japan

HARDINESS ZONES 6–9

LIGHT Full sun to partial shade. A little shade in the Southeast may keep foliage from fading.

SOIL Prefers moist, rich, well-drained, acid soils but is tolerant of alkaline soils.

GROWING *Osmanthus* takes severe pruning, renewing itself from old wood. You can prune *Osmanthus* into an attractive informal hedge by clipping long shoots back to lateral or side growths within the shrub in May or you can rejuvenate it by drastic pruning in April. It is relatively disease and pest free.

CAUTION The hard, spiky leaves of the cultivar 'Sasaba' can be treacherous to touch, so keep young children away from them.

DESIGNER'S CHOICE

Osmanthus heterophyllus 'Goshiki' *Goshiki* means "five colors" in Japanese and refers to its multi-colored leaves. New growth has pink and bronze tints, and mature foliage has yellow, green, and cream variegation. It brightens shady garden spots

and makes an outstanding accent in partial shade against a dark evergreen backdrop. Variegated plants may bleach in the strong sunlight of hot climates and may be less cold hardy than species. 5'–8' h × 4'–10' w or more.

O. heterophyllus 'Gulftide' Hardy with shiny, spiny, bent leaves. 8'–15' h × 10'–18' w.

O. heterophyllus 'Purpureus' Very hardy with dark purple to purple-tinged young foliage that's darkest in full sun. 10' h × 12' w.

O. heterophyllus 'Sasaba' Next to beach rose (*Rosa rugosa* 'Rubra'), the ultimate barrier with weaponlike, rigid, shiny leaves, deeply cut, and tipped with spines. Slow growing with an open, upright habit with profuse, fragrant flowers. Prefers partial shade. 5'–10' h × 4' w.

O. heterophyllus 'Variegatus' Leaves have green centers and uneven, creamy edges. Useful, since it grows slowly and won't discolor in full sun. 5' h × 4' w.

O. × burkwoodii Dense, drought-tolerant, rounded mound of shiny, deep green leaves; fragrant, white flowers in spring. 6'–10' h and w.

***Osmanthus heterophyllus* 'Sasaba'**

O. delavayi Fragrant spring flowers; 1", shiny, dark green, oval-toothed leaves. 6'–10' h and w. Zones 7–10.

O. × fortunei (Fortune's osmanthus) Hybrid between *O. heterophyllus* and *O. fragrans*. Opaque rounded shrub with 2"–4", tapering, oval leaves. Young leaves have spiny-toothed edges; adult leaf margins are smooth. 15'–20' h and w. Zones 7–10.

O. fragrans (sweet olive, tea olive) Powerfully fragrant, long-lived shrub or small tree. Blooms autumn through early spring and infrequently in summer. Use as an espalier or plant in a container and, where marginally hardy, bring indoors when cold. Continually flowering var. *semperflorens* is hardiest, but 'Nanjing's Beauty' and orange-flowered f. *aurantiacus* are also hardy in Zone 7. 20' h × 8'–20' w. Zones (7) 8–10 depending upon the cultivar or variety.

OSTRYA

Ostrya virginiana △ ‣ ○

OS-tree-a ver-gin-ee-AY-na

Hop hornbeam, American hop hornbeam, Ironwood, Hardhack

Filbert or Hazel Family (Corylaceae)
Deciduous tree
25'–50' h and w

Many of us take this eastern North American native for granted, rarely saving it when clearing home sites, yet it's great for naturalizing. Fast growing when young, it's a small- to medium-sized understory tree with a muscled trunk and rounded crown with spreading branches. Ironwood, its other common name, describes the exceptionally hard wood of its trunk and branches, which withstand winter storms without damage; the wood is used for tool handles. Ironwood's nuts feed wildlife

Ostrya virginiana

including squirrels, wild turkeys, pheasants, grouse, purple finches, and downy woodpeckers. Mature trees are small and grow slowly. They're good in groups and in dry locations.

The medium green, simple, deciduous, oval leaves are birchlike with pointed tips and twice-serrated margins; they are arranged in an alternating pattern. Foliage turns yellow to yellowy brown in fall. The gray, scaly, rough bark sometimes sheds in vertical pieces. It produces male catkins in sets of 3 at the twig tips. A leafy, 1"–2", hoplike, cream to brown, structure encloses a nutlet. These nutlets are attached to short stems in midsummer (South) to fall (North) and remain on the tree through winter. Trees start fruiting after 25 years. May be hard to find.

LANDSCAPE USE
Plant it in lawns, woodland gardens, and naturalized areas; grow it for interesting bark and fruit with hybrid flowering dogwoods, witch hazel, beautyberry, and American holly.

ORIGIN Dry woodlands and slopes of eastern North America.

HARDINESS ZONES 4–9

LIGHT Full sun to shade.

SOIL Loamy, well-drained, slightly acid soils. Once established, lives in dry, shady soils.

GROWING Hard to transplant because of taproot, so plant when small. The tree is relatively free from pests and diseases. It is intolerant of salt and air pollution, however, and sometimes hard to transplant and establish.

OXYDENDRUM

Oxydendrum arboreum △

ok-see-DEN-drum ar-BOH-ree-um

Sourwood, Sorrel tree, Lily-of-the-valley tree

Heath Family (Ericaceae)
Deciduous tree
20'–30' h × 10'–20' w, larger in the wild

Beautiful year round, the sourwood in our backyard reminds me of Molly, my teenage daughter. Elongated, flower clusters flip at the tips like her ponytail, and the bright fall foliage looks as enchanting as a party dress worn once a year for a special occasion. Sourwood's habit looks girlish too — narrow and pyramidal with a slender trunk, trim branches, and slim, red or olive-green twigs. This tree (like my child!) is a beauty.

Alternate, simple, deciduous leaves, 3"–8" long and smooth, glossy green on top, change to crimson, purple, and yellow in autumn. They exhibit the best color in full sun. Sour-tasting leaves have been used as a tonic and diuretic. The grayish brown bark is smooth when young, becoming plated and grooved with age. Drooping, 10" clusters of white, bell-like, fragrant flower spikes appear in early to midsummer, held above the leaves. Flowers resemble lily-of-the-valley. It flowers profusely in full sun, drawing bees and butterflies. Sourwood honey is a southern delicacy. After flowering, decorative chartreuse capsules, enjoyed by birds, extend the season of interest. By leaf drop, the long-lasting fruit clusters have turned brown, making a subtle but definitely decorative statement on the bare tree.

LANDSCAPE USE

A fabulous, slow-growing specimen in lawns or against a dark evergreen border, massed in large landscapes, in naturalistic plantings, and along woodland edges.

Oxydendrum arboreum

Oxydendrum arboreum

ORIGIN   Moist, well-drained woodlands in the eastern U.S.

HARDINESS ZONES   5–9

LIGHT   Full sun to partial shade.

SOIL   Moist, well-drained, acid soils. Thrives in gravelly soils and tolerates some dryness once established.

GROWING   Transplant from a container into deep, fertile, well-drained, acid soil, and maintain constant moisture until established. It is intolerant of pollution and hard to transplant.

PAEONIA

Paeonia suffruticosa ○

pee-O-nee-a suf-fru-ti-CO-sa

Tree peony

Peony Family (Paeoniaceae)
Deciduous flowering shrub
3'–6' h and w

A visit to the peony garden at the H. F. du Pont Winterthur Museum in Delaware inspired my husband and me to plant a tree peony grouping toward the front of our viburnum garden. These slow-growing, woody peonies took four years to establish themselves as floriferous shrubs, but they finally hit their stride, providing a glorious display of crimson, pink, and white for several weeks. They also looked fine afterwards, thanks to their handsome, deep-cut leaves that take on a reddish tint in fall. Tree peonies can be expensive, especially when you choose named cultivars from a specialist catalog. We bought ours — identified

only by pink, red, and white — at local nurseries. The grouping is now the early June focal point of the bed.

The alternate, compound, deeply cut, coarse-textured foliage is an attractive, dull green to bluish green throughout the growing season. The non-ornamental bark is brownish. Single, semi-double, or double flowers in white, green, pinks, purples, yellow, orange, and rosy reds appear for a couple of weeks in late spring or early summer, depending on your climate. Often fragrant, they are big and flashy: about 10" in diameter. Single flowers can look like dinner plates with central bosses of yellow stamens, while double blooms resemble giant cabbage roses. The fruits are not ornamental.

LANDSCAPE USE

Tree peonies are excellent additions to shrub and mixed beds and borders. You can use them individually, but in groups they make a spectacular late-spring garden accent.

ORIGIN   Mountains of northwestern China.

HARDINESS ZONES   4–8

LIGHT   Full sun to partial shade (the shade is a must in the South).

SOIL   Fertile, well-drained loam preferred, but ordinary garden soil will do. Neutral to slightly alkaline; abundant organic matter.

GROWING   Before planting, choose a site protected from glaring midday sun and harsh winds. Set tree peonies about 3'–4' apart with the crown about 6" below the soil line to encourage the graft to develop its own roots. Where the climate is dry and hot, mulch the plants to help preserve moisture and cool the soil. Tree peonies don't need pruning, except for getting rid of dead branches and basal suckers from the herbaceous–peony rootstock. If you don't like saggy stems, you may want to stake branches that are heavy with blooms and remove wilting flowers. Plants may be hard to transplant, and may be susceptible to *Botrytis* blight and verticillium wilt.

DESIGNER'S CHOICE

Paeonia suffruticosa 'Border Charm' Dwarf with single, nodding, yellow blooms; dark blue-green leaves. Great size for perennial gardens. 2' h and w.

P. suffruticosa 'Hana-kisoi' Cherry pink, semi-double blooms with deep ink blotches around central yellow boss. 4'–5' h × 3'–4' w.

P. suffruticosa 'High Noon' Double, yellow flower splotched with crimson around large central boss of gold stamens. 3'–5' h × 3'–4' w.

P. suffruticosa 'Kamada-nishiki' Deep purple, semi-double blossoms. 3'–5' h × 3'–4' w.

P. suffruticosa 'Rimpo' Very deep purple semi-double early blooms. 4'–5' h × 3'–4' w.

Paeonia suffruticosa 'High Noon'

PARROTIA

Parrotia persica 0 › ◌

par-ROH-tee-a PER-si-ka

Persian parrotia, Persian ironwood

Witch Hazel Family (Hamamelidaceae)
Small to medium deciduous tree or large shrub
20'–40' h × 15'–30' w

Parrotia may not be easy to find, but it's worth the search. In youth, it has a low-branched, oval habit with ascending branches. With age, the branches grow more horizontal and the medium-textured, short-trunked tree develops a rounded form.

Alternate, simple leaves up to 5" × 2½" are purplish in spring, then medium, shiny green. The outstanding fall color is yellow, orange, and red. The bark provides year-round interest with its outer layer that reveals a mottled gray, green, and brownish layer underneath. Before the leaves in spring, the red to yellow anthers of the flowers give branches a ruddy cast. The tan capsules of the fruits are not ornamental.

LANDSCAPE USE

Plant parrotia where you can see its bark close-up. I have one next to a lawn path that I'm developing in our backyard. Parrotia would also shine in entry gardens and courtyards.

ORIGIN   Forests of the Caucasus and northern Iran.

HARDINESS ZONES   5–8

LIGHT   Full sun to partial shade.

SOIL   Moist, well-drained slightly acid to neutral soils. Tolerates some alkalinity.

GROWING   Be patient. I've had this tree for several years (it's about 5' high now) and it hasn't started to exfoliate. Persian parrotia is virtually pest and disease resistant and tolerates urban conditions.

Parrotia persica

DESIGNER'S CHOICE

Parrotia persica 'Pendula' (Kew form) Rounded specimen with wide, spreading, drooping branches; gorgeous, graceful, sculptural, and rare. 5'–8' h × 10'–12' w.

P. persica 'Vanessa' Grow for its striking skinny habit; ideal four-season tree for a tight space or vertical accent. 25' h × 5' w.

PAULOWNIA

Paulownia tomentosa ○ ✳

paw-LO-nee-a toh-men-TOH-sa

Princess tree, Empress tree, Royal paulownia

Figwort Family (Scrophulariaceae)
Large flowering deciduous tree
30'–60' h x 20'–30' w

Where I live in Zone 5, empress tree dies to the ground each fall and comes back from its roots in the spring. Grown this way, it develops a shrubby habit with stems up to 20' tall in a season. Farther South, empress tree is a coarse-textured, fast-growing, weak-wooded tree, so adaptable that it can outcompete native species in their own habitat and naturalize in the Southeast.

The dark green foliage is alternate and simple, hairy above and below; up to 12" × 10", it is lobed or oval to heart shaped. When coppiced, it features leaves up to 2' wide. The grayish-brown bark is rough to smooth. Light purple, trumpetlike, fragrant flowers, 2" long, appear in upright, elongated, 16" clusters before the tree leafs out in spring. Because it blooms on old wood, plants that die to the ground in colder climates won't bloom. Brown, woody, seed-containing capsules are non-ornamental; the opened capsules stay on the tree in winter, creating lots of litter. Soft, lightweight Paulownia wood resists rot and warping, making it valuable for furniture, plywood, boat building, and home construction. The wood has many uses in Japan, and the American Paulownia Association promotes the forestry cropping of this plant.

LANDSCAPE USE

Tough and adaptable, coppiced trees make dramatic, tropical-looking garden accents. Coppicing (cutting back) young wood prevents empress tree from flowering and setting seed. Coppiced trees are fun to use in hot-colored tropical beds with castor bean *(Ricinus)*, crocosmia, kniphofia, and canna.

ORIGIN Mountains of China.

HARDINESS ZONES 5–9

LIGHT Full sun to partial shade.

SOIL Prefers moist, fertile, acid soils but tolerates drought, salt spray, urban pollution, and soil infertility.

GROWING It seems like *Paulownia* thrives almost anywhere, including a public park downriver from a 1,455-acre chemical plant and hazardous-waste treatment facility in Deepwater, New Jersey. Uncoppiced, it's a big mess in fall when seedpods and big leaves drop to the ground. Consistently coppiced, it makes a worthy garden accent. Depending upon the size of the other plants in the bed, you may need to cut back coppiced *Paulownia* at least once during the summer to keep it in scale with your overall planting design.

CAUTION Invasive in the Southeast and much of the mid-Atlantic by seeds spreading on wind and water and by root sprouts and suckering. Poses an ecological threat to some native species. Non-invasive in the coldest states, where it dies to the ground.

Paulownia tomentosa

PHELLODENDRON

Phellodendron amurense ○ ✳

fel-lo-DEN-dron a-mew-RENS

Amur corktree

Rue Family (Rutaceae)
Deciduous tree
30'–45' h and w

Amur corktree has a broad, picturesque habit that makes it a good shade tree, plus medium height, glossy compound leaves, and nice corky bark. Females of the species can self-sow and thus act like a weed. Non-fruiting male selections such as 'RNI 4551' (Shademaster), 'Macho', and 'His Majesty' don't produce the untidy fruits and seedlings under the canopy but they still pollinate females and contribute to the spread of the species.

LANDSCAPE USE
Wide-spreading lawn specimen planted for shade and appealing form.

ORIGIN Along streams in mountains of eastern Asia.

HARDINESS ZONES 4–7

LIGHT Full sun.

SOIL Prefers moist, rich, well-drained soils, where it bears abundant seeds; also grows in clay to sand and is pH adaptable.

GROWING No serious pests or diseases. Tolerates drought.

CAUTION Invasive potential in suburbs and disturbed forest edges.

Phellodendron amurense

PHILADELPHUS

Philadelphus coronarius ○ ✳

fi-la-DEL-fus co-ro-NAY-ree-us

Sweet mock orange

Hydrangea Family (Hydrangeaceae)
Deciduous flowering shrub
8'–12' h and w

For a couple of weeks in late spring, this old-fashioned, super-fragrant shrub is at its blooming best. Showy, white, single (4-petal) or double flowers cover it, saturating the air with their intensely sweet scent. For the rest of the growing season, this tough, hardy, carefree shrub looks like a gawky wallflower, its awkward leggy shape and ordinary, opposite leaves condemning it to live tucked away mercifully unnoticed in shrub beds and borders. If you crave mock orange's fragrance on a prettier shrub, grow a *Philadelphus* hybrid, especially one with interesting leaves. Although many species and hybrids exist, those described below are easy to buy at local nurseries and online.

LANDSCAPE USE
Shrub and mixed borders; in entry or back door gardens or along paths underplanted with shorter shrubs or tall perennials that hide its base in and, especially, out of bloom.

ORIGIN Gravelly slopes in southern Europe.

HARDINESS ZONES 4–8

LIGHT Full sun to partial shade.

SOIL Moist, well-drained, organic soil but adapts to almost any soil.

GROWING When shabby, prune to renew.

DESIGNER'S CHOICE
Philadelphus coronarius 'Aureus'
Leaves open bright yellow and fade to lime green by midsummer; intensely fragrant white, single flowers. 8' h and w.

P. 'Buckley's Quill' Compact hybrid with clusters of frilly, white, scented

Philadelphus coronarius **'Aureus'**

bloom, each with 30 pointed petals. 5' h × 4' w.

P. 'Innocence' Possibly the strongest perfume of all mock oranges; single white flowers and variegated cream-and-green leaves. 8' h and w.

P. lewisii 'Blizzard' Profuse clusters of single, white-scented flowers for a prolonged period of bloom (up to 4 weeks). 4'–5' h × 3' w. Zone 3.

P. lewisii 'Cheyenne' Perfumed white flowers up to 2" wide; selected at the USDA Field Station in Cheyenne, Wyoming; great for high plains and Western intermountain region. 7' h × 6' w, Zones 3–8 up to 8,000'.

P. 'Miniature Snowflake' Profuse, clustered, double, white blooms and disease-resistant leaves on a dwarf plant; a sport of 'Minnesota Snowflake'. 2'–4' h × 1'–2' w.

P. 'Minnesota Snowflake' Arching shrub with 2", double, white blooms; extra hardy. 6'–8' h × 5'–6' w. Zone 3.

P. 'Natchez' Abundant 1½", slightly fragrant, single, white blossoms cover a broad, well-branched shrub. Prone to leaf spot in poor, dry soils. 6'–8' h × 5'–6' w.

P. 'Polar Star' 2½", semi-double, white flowers. 10' h and w. Zones 5–8.

PHOTINIA

Photinia × fraseri ⓞ

foh-TIN-ee-a FRAY-zer-I

Fraser photinia, Redtip

Rose Family (Rosaceae)
Evergreen shrub or tree
10'–20' h x 5'–10' w

Southerners know this shrub well because of its shiny, green, leathery leaves to 6" long with bright red new growth; it has a bushy habit and easy, vigorous growth, making it a popular hedge plant. Grown as a small tree, redtip has grayish brown bark that becomes flaky with age. From late spring to summer it bears showy, 6-inch, flattish clusters of rank-smelling white flowers and occasional, red fall fruits.

LANDSCAPE USE
Redtip hedges are a time-honored custom in Southern gardens, to the point of overuse.

ORIGIN Garden origin

HARDINESS ZONES 6–9

LIGHT Full sun to partial shade.

SOIL Sandy to clay soils; average moist to dry soil; neutral to acid pH.

GROWING For best results, give redtip good drainage and sufficient air circulation. Cutting back the shrub in summer will produce new red shoots in fall. Redtip tolerates extensive pruning but, like other Rose Family members, is not without problems, including scales, leaf spots, mildew, and fireblight. Leaf spot can kill redtip. Avoid crowding it or planting it in cool, humid areas; spray weekly with fungicide if you see spots or lesions on either leaf surface.

CAUTION Abundant pollen can worsen allergies.

DESIGNER'S CHOICE
Photinia × fraseri 'Cassini' (Pink Marble) Stable, green and white variegation; deep pink new growth. 10' h × 5' w.

PHYSOCARPUS

Physocarpus opulifolius ⓞ › 🌿 ✳

fi-so-CAR-pus o-pew-li-FOH-lee-us

Ninebark

Rose Family (Rosaceae)
Deciduous flowering shrub
5'–10' h x 6'–10' w

Extremely hardy, ninebark thrives in many situations, including drought and variable soil pH. Consider planting one or more in a shrub border at your property line, where ninebark's coarse texture will not overwhelm the rest of the garden.

Ninebark's dull green leaves are single, alternate, and 3-lobed; some cultivars have colorful leaves (see Designer's Choice). Older stems peel heavily in long tan strips, revealing the reddish brown inner bark. Two-inch clusters of pinkish white flowers appear in late spring, followed by smooth, reddish fruits in fall.

LANDSCAPE USE
Boundary hedges, screens, shrub borders, and groups.

ORIGIN By streams and rocky slopes in eastern North America.

HARDINESS ZONES 3–7

LIGHT Full sun to partial shade.

SOIL Average garden soils but very adaptable.

GROWING If the shrub looks straggly, prune it to the ground before new growth begins in early spring. This plant is tough and relatively trouble free.

DESIGNER'S CHOICE
Physocarpus opulifolius 'Dart's Gold' Rounded form, yellow leaves, white flowers, reddish brown bark; best color in full sun. 4'–5' h and w.

P. opulifolius 'Mindia' (Coppertina) Exceptional coppery-orange spring leaves mature to red. Wow! — color accent. 8'–10' h and w.

P. opulifolius 'Monlo' (Diabolo) (syn. 'Diabolo') Deep purple leaves, pinkish white flowers in early to midsummer; best in full sun; upright, arching habit. Foliage holds color through the summer in the North and Midwest. 8'–10' h and w.

P. opulifolius 'Nugget' Globe with yellow new growth turning lime-green in summer; similar to 'Dart's Gold', but denser and better. 6' h and w. Zone 3–8.

P. opulifolius 'Seward' (Summer Wine) Finely textured, deep wine-red leaves, and pinkish flowers in midsummer, and compact branching. 4'–6' h × 5'–6' w. Zones 3–8.

Photinia x fraseri

Physocarpus opulifolius 'Dart's Gold'

PICEA

Picea abies △

pi-SEE-a A-beez

Norway spruce

Pine Family (Pinaceae)
Evergreen conifer
40'–60' h × 25'–35' w

In the Northeast and Midwest, Norway spruce doesn't stand out in a crowd. In fact, we see so many in New England that we tend to take these big evergreens that dominate numerous front yards for granted. They're reliable, fast growing, and well suited for privacy screens on large properties. Pyramidal Norway spruce brings stability to mixed conifer screens, where it creates a dense, dark background for showier trees.

Norway spruce bears stiff, needled, evergreen leaves up to 1" long with pointed tips; foliage is deep green. The grayish brown bark is cracked and scaly. It produces non-ornamental male and female flowers on the same tree. Cylindrical cones up to 6" long change from green or purplish to brown.

LANDSCAPE USE

Although the species is too big for many residential lots, it provides a fast-growing windbreak or shade in big landscapes. See Designer's Choice for cultivars suitable for average residential landscapes.

ORIGIN   Forests of northern and central Europe.

HARDINESS ZONES   3–7

LIGHT   Full sun.

SOIL   Prefers moist, well-drained, acid soils but will also grow in average to heavy garden soils.

GROWING   Easy to transplant, Norway spruces do best in cold climates. In order to give the lower spruce branches the sun and space they need to develop, don't plant shrubs or flowers touching your spruce. Spruces usually don't need much pruning because of their naturally stiff, formal shape. For denser leaves, prune in spring when new growth is supple and before young needles open out. For major pruning, cut to a bud, a lateral branch, or the trunk whenever you have time for the job. In general, spruces are susceptible to a variety of pests and diseases including aphids, bagworms, spider mites, budworms, scales, rusts, canker, and root rots.

DESIGNER'S CHOICE

Many desirable cultivars are available, including:

Picea abies 'Elegans' (knight's dwarf spruce) Dense conical dwarf that's good for small sunny gardens; as with most dwarf cultivars, the light lime-green buds in spring are attractive. 4'–5' h × 3'–5' w.

P. abies 'Little Gem' Dwarf globe; hot summer days can burn plants, so a site with midday shade in hot climates is helpful. 2' h and w.

P. abies 'Nidiformis' (bird's nest spruce) Densely branched, flattened, spreading globe with a slight depression

Picea abies 'Nidiformis'

on top. Although sold as a little shrub, this spruce grows rather large. The 15-year old 'Nidiformis' in my neighbor's yard is about 3' h × 5' w. 2'–5' h × 2'–6' w.

P. abies f. 'Pendula' (syn. 'Pendula') (weeping Norway spruce) Branches weep skirtlike to the ground, striking and sculptural year round, a common focal point in front yard shrub beds and entry gardens; several cultivars fall within this group, the most common in this country being 'Reflexa'. 20'–25' h × 10'–14' w. Zone 4.

ALL ABOUT **PICEA**

These forest trees grow best in cool climates. Some species bear highly decorative, male and female, red to purple cones. Species with dense conical growth habits and sturdy branches are perfect for Christmas trees (except for the sharp needles!) or stringing with outdoor lights. Spruces have short, sharp-tipped, 4-sided needles that loop around the stem. They are set singly, not bunched like pines. Large trees are excellent for shelter belts, while dwarf or slow-

growing cultivars make striking additions to conifer beds and borders and grow well in containers. Watch out for signs of white pine weevil infestations, which you can recognize by the dieback of leaders. Cut off droopy leaders as soon as you see them and before they reach the first ring of branches; set the diseased material in a trashcan straight away, before it touches the ground, then pick a strong stem at the top of the first branch whorl and train it to a stake as the new leader.

Picea engelmannii △

pi-SEE-a en-gul-MAN-nee-i

Engelmann spruce

Pine Family (Pinaceae)
Evergreen tree
40'–100' h x 10'–15' w

Narrow, conical tree with downward branching. Wind and cold tolerant; garden height, 40'–50'. 'Glauca' is similar, with dependably matte, grayish blue-green foliage. Food source for birds and small mammals; wood used for musical instruments and aircraft parts.

LANDSCAPE USE
Screening, windbreaks; group several to emphasize their cylindrical growth.

ORIGIN High elevations in western North America with short cool summers and long cold winters.

HARDINESS ZONES 3–5

LIGHT Full sun to light shade.

SOIL Acid, well-drained soil high in organic matter.

GROWING Spruce beetles can be troublesome; loss of leaf color is an early symptom.

Picea glauca △

pi-SEE-a GLAW-ka

White spruce

Pine Family (Pinaceae)
Evergreen conifer
40'–60' h x 10'–20' w

White spruce is distinguished by deer resistance and salt, drought, and heat tolerance. Dense in youth but more open with age, it has a slim, conical outline. It's easy to grow in the Great Plains and northern New England.

LANDSCAPE USE
Hedges, windbreaks, and seaside plantings.

ORIGIN Northern U.S. and Canada.

HARDINESS ZONES 2–6

LIGHT Full sun.

SOIL Moist, well-drained soil; tolerates wetter sites than *P. abies* or *P. pungens*.

GROWING If spruce spider mites turn needles yellow and bronze use a strong jet of water from a garden hose to dislodge them before trying other controls. Bagworms, adelgids, and root rot can also occur on this species.

DESIGNER'S CHOICE
Picea glauca 'Conica' (dwarf Alberta spruce) Dense, slow-growing, bright green cone; overused but not well used in the landscape; good formal specimen. Several cultivars are similar to 'Conica' including 'Jean's Dilly' with slower growth and shorter needles; 'Pixie', which is smaller and denser; and 'Conica Golden' with light green, new spring leaves turning yellow by early summer. 6'–12' h × 3'–6' w. Zone 4.

Picea omorika △

pi-SEE-a o-mo-REE-ka

Serbian spruce

Pine Family (Pinaceae)
Evergreen conifer
50'–60' h x 10'–20' w

Grow this tree for its bolt-upright, narrow, conical form and flipped-up branches with shiny-topped green needles.

LANDSCAPE USE
Grown as a single lawn specimen, an old skinny Serbian spruce looks like a missile ready to launch. Graceful planted in small groups.

ORIGIN The Balkans

HARDINESS ZONES (3) 4–7

LIGHT Full sun to partial shade.

SOIL Prefers somewhat moist, well drained soil; tolerates both acid and alkaline, clay and sandy soils, and some drought.

GROWING Shield from strong winds and winter sun, which can damage needles.

White pine weevils may kill shoot tips, resulting in a bushy shape.

DESIGNER'S CHOICE
Picea omorika 'Pendula' (weeping Serbian spruce) Striking narrow tree with droopy, twisted branches. Up to 50' h × 20' w.

Picea orientalis △ ✳

pi-SEE-a o-ree-en-TAL-is

Oriental spruce

Pine Family (Pinaceae)
Evergreen conifer
50'–70' h x 20'–30' w

Oriental spruce is a medium to large, slow-growing, evergreen conifer. Its slim, conical shape features upswept branches with hanging branchlets. This outstanding tree is a personal favorite because I like stroking the needled branch tips, which feel silky compared to other spruces. We grow little 'Nigra Compacta' and 'Bergman's Gem', which are easy to fit into Northeastern or Midwestern residential landscapes. We also grow 'Skylands' because we like it, though it may one day be too big for its site.

Picea orientalis 'Skylands'

The blunt-tipped, pliable, short needles of Oriental spruce are rich, lustrous green and up to ½" long. The bark is gray on top and red-brown below with flaking ridges and furrows. It bears cylindrical, red males and purple-tinged green females in spring. The 2"–4" purple cones turn brown when ripe.

LANDSCAPE USE
Mixed tree and shrub borders, landscape specimens. If you want a sizeable evergreen and have room for only one, why not plant (in my view) the loveliest one you can find?

ORIGIN Mountain forests of the Caucasus and northern Asia Minor.

HARDINESS ZONES 4–7

LIGHT Full sun to partial shade.

SOIL Prefers moist, well-drained soils but can live on rocky infertile soils.

GROWING Plant in a sheltered spot away from winter's strong winds; slow growing. See *P. abies*.

DESIGNER'S CHOICE
Picea orientalis 'Aureospicata' Creamy yellow new growth turns deep green by early summer; full sun for best color. 50'–70' h × 20'–30' w.

P. orientalis 'Bergman's Gem' Dense, dwarf, dark green, flattened globe. 3' h and w.

P. orientalis 'Nana' Dwarf. 3' h and w.

P. orientalis 'Nigra Compacta' Dense, dwarf, very dark green cone, eventually wider than high. 3' h and w.

P. orientalis 'Skylands' (syn. 'Aurea Compacta') I like yellow trees, and this yellow-needled broad pyramidal spruce is particularly fine in the north. May burn in hot sun in warmer climates; the small one in our border grows protected from harsh winds and glaring afternoon sun. 5'–10' h × 4'–7' w.

Picea pungens △

pi-SEE-a PUN-jenz

Colorado spruce

Pine Family (Pinaceae)
Evergreen conifer
40'–60' h × 10'–20' w

About 8 years ago, we planted an evergreen screen to block the view of condominiums in our backyard. The screen includes bright silvery blue 'Hoopsii', a beacon among dark companion Norway spruces and Alaska cedar. Although 'Hoopsii' sometimes makes an interesting accent when the border is in shade, it looks jarring to me in brilliant sunlight. I learned the hard way that large light blue spruces are more appropriate to the arid western landscape than to my lush New England garden. However, dwarf and compact cultivars work well in many landscapes because their impact, though striking, is smaller and easier to balance with the rest of the design.

Colorado spruce's blue-green, sharp, rigid needles measure up to 1¼" long. The gray bark has reddish brown scales. The tree produces male and female flowers on same tree and 2"–4" brown cones in fall.

LANDSCAPE USE
Screens, windbreaks, and groups.

ORIGIN Stream banks and crags of western U.S.

HARDINESS ZONES 3–7

LIGHT Full sun.

SOIL Moist, well-drained, fertile soils.

GROWING Tolerates dry winds; an adaptable, drought-tolerant tree especially good in the western U.S.

DESIGNER'S CHOICE
Picea pungens 'Fat Albert' Broad, pyramidal, blue-green tree; a perfect cone; slow growing. 15' h × 12' w.

P. pungens f. *glauca* (Colorado blue spruce) Tiered, upturned, blue-needled branches. 40'–60' h × 10'–20' w.

P. pungens 'Glauca Globosa' Flattened blue ball. 3'–5' h × 5'–6' w.

P. pungens 'Hoopsii' Light silvery blue on fast-growing, upright, pyramidal tree; perhaps the bluest cultivar. 30'–50' h × 10'–20' w.

P. pungens 'Iseli Foxtail' Narrow pyramid with very bright light blue, twisted needles tufted at the branch tips; use as informal accent. 10'–15' h × 7'–8' w.

P. pungens 'Montgomery' Powder blue needles on slow-growing dwarf that's broader than tall with age. 6' h × 5' w.

P. pungens 'Thomsen' This rigid, green to silvery blue pyramid is branched to the ground in youth but opens with age. 40'–60' h × 20'–30' w.

Picea pungens

Pieris floribunda ○

pi-AYR-is flo-ri-BUN-da

Mountain pieris, Mountain andromeda

Heath Family (Ericaceae)
Broad-leaf evergreen shrub
3'–5' h x 3'–8' w

Mountain pieris is a garden-worthy, compact, rounded shrub with fine-textured, broad-leaf evergreen leaves. White, fragrant flowers resembling lily-of-the-valley appear in spring in upright clusters, contrasting with dark, leathery, evergreen leaves up to 4" long.

LANDSCAPE USE
Foundations, masses, naturalistic areas, and mixed borders.

ORIGIN   Southeastern U.S.

HARDINESS ZONES   4–6

LIGHT   Prefers partial shade, but tolerates full sun.

SOIL   Prefers moist, well-drained, humusy, acid soils but tolerates some soil alkalinity.

GROWING   Grows slowly. Free of the lace bugs that trouble Japanese pieris. Prune in spring right after blooming, eliminating winter-damaged and over-long stems that ruin the plant's bushy, rounded looks. Renew healthy shrubs infrequently by cutting almost to the ground. Grows best when not exposed to drying winter sun and winds. Prone to stem rots in soils with poor drainage. Can be difficult to transplant and establish.

DESIGNER'S CHOICE
Pieris 'Brouwer's Beauty' (syn. *P. floribunda* 'Brouwer's Beauty') Hybrid between *P. floribunda* and *P. japonica*. Winter interest comes from droopy trusses of red buds opening in spring to profuse, dangling clusters of white, urn-shaped flowers, all set against dark green leaves and yellow-green new growth. 5'–6' h × 6' w. Zone 5.

Pieris floribunda

Pieris japonica 'Dorothy Wyckoff'

Pieris japonica ◐ › ○

pi-AYR-is ja-PAH-ni-ka

Japanese pieris

Heath Family (Ericaceae)
Broad-leaf evergreen shrub
6'–12' h and w

This slow-growing, upright, rounded shrub has shiny, green leaves and red to purplish new growth; pendulous clusters of white, urn-shaped blooms in spring.

LANDSCAPE USE
See *P. floribunda.*

ORIGIN   Japan

HARDINESS ZONES   5–7

LIGHT   See *P. floribunda.*

SOIL   See *P. floribunda.*

CARE   For best results, choose a protected site with excellent drainage and afternoon shade. Susceptible to lace bugs, especially in the eastern U.S.

DESIGNER'S CHOICE
Pieris japonica 'Cavatine' A slow-growing dwarf hybrid with upright, fragrant, white flower clusters in spring. 3' h and w.

P. japonica 'Dorothy Wyckoff' Rosy winter buds open to light pink spring flowers; considered one of the nicer cultivars. 6'–8' h × 4'–6' w.

P. japonica 'Mountain Fire' Bright red new growth; very popular. 9'–12' h × 6'–8' w.

P. japonica 'Prelude' Spreading, rounded dwarf, with pink new growth and long droopy clusters of pink buds opening to white flowers. 1'–2' h × 2'–3' w.

Pinus bungeana ○

PI-nus bun-jee-AH-na

Lacebark pine

Pine Family (Pinaceae)
Evergreen conifer
30'–50' h × 25'–30' w

Slow-growing, lacebark pine deserves a place in your garden because of its showy bark and picturesque form, which is even more striking with age. Rounded and multi-stemmed in youth, it becomes flatter, wider, and more open at maturity. All pine needles come bundled in groups of 2–5, and those of lacebark are grouped in 3s.

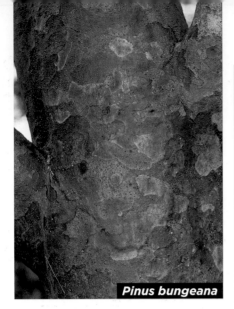

Pinus bungeana

Leaves are stiff and sharply pointed, up to 3" long. The flaking and mottled bark is a glorious patchwork of cream, reddish brown, gray, and green. In early summer, yellow male and green female flowers develop on the same tree. The tree produces egglike, brownish cones about 2¼" long.

LANDSCAPE USE

Site it so that you can see the bark, removing lowest branches if necessary. Plant it along a path or above a pond as a specimen in an Oriental-style garden.

ORIGIN   Mountainsides in China.

HARDINESS ZONES   5–7

LIGHT   Full sun.

SOIL   Moist, well-drained soils.

GROWING   Lacebark pine's relatively slow growth rate keeps it garden sized for years. See All About *Pinus*.

Pinus cembra △ › ◌

PI-nus SEM-bra

Swiss stone pine

Pine Family (Pinaceae)
Evergreen conifer
30′ h x 10′–20′ w

Because of its columnar or narrow conical shape, slow-growing Swiss stone pine is an excellent choice for small lots. It transplants well and adapts to harsh conditions, including salt spray and severe winds. Bark is reddish to grayish brown and scaly; blue-green needles occur in bundles of five; and cones on old trees draw wildlife to their edible seeds.

LANDSCAPE USE

Under power lines, lawn specimen on exposed or coastal sites, mixed conifer borders, planted for privacy and wind protection in front of taller evergreens.

ORIGIN   Mountains in central Europe.

HARDINESS ZONES   3–7

LIGHT   Full sun.

SOIL   Moist, well-drained soils.

GROWING   Nothing too serious. Resists pine blister rust. One source of edible pine nuts.

DESIGNER'S CHOICE

Pinus cembra 'Blue Mound' Very slow-growing, silvery blue dwarf, mounded when young and a small tight cone at maturity. Good for rock gardens, dwarf conifer beds, and the front of shrub borders. 3′ h × 2′ w.

P. cembra 'Klein' (Silver Whispers) Ascending branches of white-striped, dark green needles; compact symmetrical form; bluish violet cones. Choice, but may be hard to find. 12′ h × 6′ w.

ALL ABOUT PINUS

Pine trees and shrubs originate in forests throughout the northern hemisphere. Unlike spruce, pine leaves occur in bundles of 2 to 5 needles, depending upon the species. Ornamental bark sometimes adds to the tree's desirability. Pines aren't picky as to soil. Give them a patch of well-drained soil in full sun and they're off. Large trees are excellent for shelter belts, while dwarf or slow-growing cultivars make striking additions to rock gardens and conifer beds and borders, and they also grow well in containers. Watch out for signs of white pine weevil infestations, which you can recognize by the dieback of leaders. Cut off droopy leaders as soon as you see them and before they reach the first ring of branches; set the diseased material in a trashcan straight away before it touches the ground. Then pick a strong stem at the top of the first branch whorl and train it to a stake as the new leader. Pruning pines requires "candling" to control new growth. (Candles are the pliable shoots on the branch tips in spring.) To do this, take your thumb and forefinger and twist off a piece of each candle in late spring before the soft needles stiffen and spread out. For major pruning, cut just above a bud, a lateral branch, or the trunk whenever you have time for the job. (For more on candling and pruning, see pages 103–118.) In general, pines are susceptible to various pests and diseases, including aphids, borers, beetles, moths, miners, scales, weevils, root rot, dieback, rusts, and tip blights. Fall needle drop on the interior of pines, however, is natural and nothing to worry about.

Pinus mugo 'Aurea'

Pinus densiflora ○ › 🖾

PI-nus den-si-FLO-ra

Japanese red pine

Pine Family (Pinaceae)
Evergreen conifer
40'–60' h and w

Japanese red pine is a terrific slow-growing tree for home landscapes with broad, horizontal limbs and needles bunched in 2s. Its irregular, twisted trunk gives it an arty look, and its handsome bark consists of flaky, orange plates. Mature trees may be flat-topped, and are quite variable. Ice and snow may break branches.

LANDSCAPE USE
Comely year-round specimen with ornamental bark and form.

ORIGIN Hills of China, Korea, Russia, and Japan.

HARDINESS ZONES 3–7

LIGHT Full sun.

SOIL Well-drained slightly acid to neutral soil.

GROWING Needles may yellow in winter. Intolerant of salt spray and salty soils so keep away from coastal plantings and streets and sidewalks coated with salt in winter.

DESIGNER'S CHOICE
Pinus densiflora 'Jane Kluis' Flat-topped, globose dwarf with dense, stiff, green needles. 4' h × 6' w. Zone 5.

P. densiflora 'Oculus-Draconis' (Dragon's Eye) A broad, irregular shrub with variegated needles, which have two yellow bands and look like a dragon's eye seen from above; leaves may burn from winter sun in the Midwest. 25' h × 15' w.

P. densiflora 'Umbraculifera' (Tany-osho pine) Multi-trunk, shrubby, slow-growing, globose or flat-topped dwarf with attractive cinnamon bark. 12'–20' h × 18' w. Zone 4.

P. densiflora 'Umbraculifera Compacta' Many trunks and a flattened,

Pinus densiflora **'Oculus-Draconis'**

umbrella-like crown with dense shrubby branches. 4' h × 6' w. Zone 5.

Pinus flexilis △ › ○

PI-nus FLEK-si-lis

Limber pine

Pine Family (Pinaceae)
Evergreen conifer
30'–50' h × 15'–35' w

This North American native comes from high in the Rocky Mountains but survives well in the East and Midwest. It features pleasing, deep blue-green needles year round.

LANDSCAPE USE
Good tree for screening out ugly views because of its pyramidal shape and dense branching when young; older trees develop more character as they grow, becoming open with a flat or rounded top.

ORIGIN Rocky Mountains of U.S.

HARDINESS ZONES 4–7

LIGHT Full sun to partial shade.

SOIL Moist, well-drained soils.

GROWING Survives, indeed thrives, in harsh growing conditions but is

vulnerable to white pine blister rust if alternate hosts of gooseberries or currants are nearby.

DESIGNER'S CHOICE
Pinus flexilis 'Vanderwolf's Pyramid' Broad, upright, pyramidal form with ascending branches and attractive, blue-green, twisted leaves. 20'–25' h × 10'–15' w.

Pinus flexilis **'Vander-wolf's Pyramid'**

Pinus mugo ○ › ◌

PI-nus MEW-go

Swiss mountain pine, Mugo pine

Pine Family (Pinaceae)
Evergreen conifer
5'–25' h and w

Mugo pines are useful in Northern landscapes. Shrubby habit, dense growth, rigid deep green needles bundled in 2s, and an abundance of miniature, dwarf, and intermediate-size cultivars assure their popularity among landscapers and homeowners. Many mugo pines start out small but can grow very big, despite what the nursery label says, so choose your cultivars carefully.

LANDSCAPE USE
Depending upon the cultivar, you can use mugos in foundation plantings, in masses, in conifer beds, or as elements in formal and informal gardens.

ORIGIN   Mountains of central Europe.

HARDINESS ZONES   2–7 (some cultivars, such as 'Slowmound', may be less hardy).

Pinus mugo 'Valley Cushion'

LIGHT   Full sun to partial shade.

SOIL   Deep, moist, well-drained, acid to limey soils.

GROWING   Intolerant of drought. Susceptible to pine pests and diseases including scales, sawflies, shoot tip moths, adelgids, and particularly pine needle scale.

DESIGNER'S CHOICE
Pinus mugo 'Big Tuna' Upright, oval growth. 10'–12' h × 6'–7' w.

P. mugo 'Mops' This miniature conifer has been a favorite of mine for its rich, dark color and crowded, hemispherical growth since I saw it in the entry garden of Blue Sterling Nursery in New Jersey. 3' h and w.

P. mugo subsp. *mugo* (syn. var. *mughus*) Broad upright form, ubiquitous but varies in size depending upon the source. 6'–8' h × 8'–10' w.

P. mugo var. *pumilio* (Pumilio Group) Low, prostrate, slow-growing. 3' h × 8'–10' w.

Pinus nigra △ › ◌

PI-nus NI-gra

Austrian pine, European black pine

Pine Family (Pinaceae)
Evergreen conifer
40'–100' h × 20'–25' w

A conifer, Austrian pine is a pyramidal tree with a top that flattens with age; its needles are bunched in 2s. You'll often find this tough species planted in cities for its fast growth and cold-, ice-, wind-, and pollution-tolerance, or by lakes and oceans, where it tolerates salt spray and dry, sandy, infertile soils. Garden height is about 40'.

LANDSCAPE USE
Windbreaks, screens, roadside plantings, Christmas trees; naturalize for wildlife habitat.

ORIGIN   Europe, the Balkans, North Africa; most U.S. trees of Austrian origin.

HARDINESS ZONES   5–8

LIGHT   Full sun.

SOIL   Adaptable to most soils, including clay; light, dry, sandy soils; and fill. Tolerates alkalinity, but prefers acidic soils.

GROWING   May be damaged by needle and tip blights, particularly in the East, where you should avoid using it.

Pinus parviflora △ › ◌

PI-nus par-vi-FLO-ra

Japanese white pine

Pine Family (Pinaceae)
Evergreen conifer
50' h × 35' w

This slow-growing tree's habit, familiar to bonsai enthusiasts, wins admiration for its vast, picturesque trunk and flared, bluish-green, short needles bunched in tufts of 5; it also has distinctive, cracked, scaly bark.

LANDSCAPE USE
A striking specimen, particularly in Japanese-style gardens, small landscapes, and coastal landscapes.

ORIGIN   Mountains and rocky slopes of Japan and Korea.

HARDINESS ZONES   4–7

LIGHT   Full sun to partial shade.

SOIL   Well-drained soil; salt tolerant.

GROWING   Intolerant of wet feet. Drought tolerant once established.

DESIGNER'S CHOICE
Pinus parviflora 'Adcock's Dwarf' Broad, upright habit with short, blue-green needles clustered at the branch tips. 3'–5' h and w.

P. parviflora 'Glauca' (Glauca Group) Silver Japanese white pine, blue leaves tufted on branch ends of a very slow-growing, irregular tree. 10'–40' h × 7'–40' w. Zone 5.

Pinus parviflora 'Glauca'

Pinus resinosa △

PI-nus re-zi-NO-sa

Red pine, Norway pine

Pine Family (Pinaceae)
Evergreen conifer
50'–75' h x 40' w

This upright, 2-needled pine loves cold weather. It offers year-round interest with its excellent, scaly, warm orange-red to reddish-brown bark and evergreen leaves. I often walk by a wild exposed grove near my house, and its raw charm always draws me. For small-space gardens, see if your nursery carries dwarf selections such as purple-coned 'Don Smith' and ball-shaped 'Quinobequin' or 'Morel'. Cultivars may be hard to find.

LANDSCAPE USE

Beautiful bark makes this tree worth saving if it grows on your property. Plant red pine in groups on difficult rocky exposed sites.

ORIGIN   Northeastern U.S., northern Midwest, Southern Canada.

HARDINESS ZONES   2–5

LIGHT   Full sun.

SOIL   Poor, acid, gravelly soil; short-lived on clay soils.

GROWING   Look out for red pine scale, salt damage (does not tolerate salt, so keep away from roads where salt is used in winter), and alkaline soils, which can cause yellowing of leaves due to chlorosis, a chlorophyll deficiency.

Pinus strobus △ › ◯

PI-nus STRO-bus

Eastern white pine, White pine

Pine Family (Pinaceae)
Evergreen conifer
50'–75' h x 30'–40' w

In the right conditions, this fast-growing, 5-needled pine can live hundreds of years. When young, Eastern white pine is full and pyramidal with smooth, thin bark and attractive fine-textured, flexible, blue-green needles that soften its looks. With age, the top can flatten, ascending to horizontal branches that expand. The bark develops deep ridges and furrows, and the tree develops a pleasingly rough, open, asymmetrical habit.

LANDSCAPE USE

Large landscapes, sheared hedge; small cultivars are valuable for home landscapes in beds, boundaries, and foundations.

ORIGIN   Eastern North America.

HARDINESS ZONES   3–7

LIGHT   Full sun.

SOIL   Tolerant of many soil types, from rocky ridges to wet bogs.

GROWING   Easy to transplant. White pine blister rust, a fungal disease, may prevent widespread planting of white pines in cool, moist areas of the West. The disease exists in the Northeast but has a much lower incidence. Wind, ice, and heavy snow may break branches; may winter burn in coldest climates.

DESIGNER'S CHOICE

Pinus strobus 'Blue Shag' Slow-growing, globose dwarf for foundations, shrub borders. 4'–6' h × 5'–7' w.

P. strobus 'Fastigiata' Narrow and upright with ascending branches. 60'–70' h × 25'–30' w. Zone 4.

P. strobus 'Radiata' (syn. *P. strobus* 'Nana') Slow-growing, mounding, rounded dwarf. 5'–7' h and w. Zone 4.

P. strobus 'Soft Touch' Densely branched cushion of fine, twisted, blue-green needles. 2'–3' h × 3'–4' w.

Pinus strobus 'Pendula'   Pinus strobus

Pinus sylvestris △ › ◠

PI-nus sil-VES-tris

Scots pine, Scotch pine

Pine Family (Pinaceae)
Evergreen conifer
30'–90' h x 20'–35'

With its broad, irregular, pyramidal form and blue-green needles bunched in 2s, fast-growing Scots pine looks like a Christmas tree when young. With age, it develops a rounded top and longer bole as high branches shade out lower ones. Many trees may develop twisted trunks and copious branches with weak branch connections to the trunk; branches can break at the crotches during windstorms.

LANDSCAPE USE
Attractive specimen when young; plant in tree and shrub borders; use as erosion control; grow as Christmas tree.

ORIGIN Most widespread pine in the world, originating throughout most of Europe and Asia.

HARDINESS ZONES 2–7 (8)

LIGHT Full sun.

SOIL Well-drained; grows well on sandy or gravelly soils and hillsides.

GROWING Tolerates drought and infertile soils, but the stress of growing in very poor locations makes this tree subject to pests and diseases, including moths, weevils, sawflies, spittlebugs, canker, and rust.

DESIGNER'S CHOICE
'Aurea' Chartreuse foliage in summer but bright, stunning gold in winter; broad, upright habit. I've grown a couple of these for years, and they are a delight to behold against the snow and a dark green Norway spruce. They grow more slowly than the species. 30' h × 15'–20' w.

'Beuvronensis' Wide, densely branched, ball-shaped shrub; slow growing, to about 3'–6' h and w.

Pinus thunbergii △ › ◠

PI-nus thun-ber-jee-i

Japanese black pine

Pine Family (Pinaceae)
Evergreen conifer
20'–50' h x 20'–25' w

Japanese black pine is valued for the contrast between its dark green foliage and its silvery candles in spring. Old trees are quite picturesque, with scaly, flaking, grayish bark. Harsh growing conditions suit 2-needled Japanese black pine just fine.

LANDSCAPE USE
Thrives in exposed windy or polluted sites and on sandy, salty soils, making it an excellent choice for the seacoast. Drought tolerant.

ORIGIN Coastal lowlands of Japan and S. Korea.

HARDINESS ZONES (5) 6–8

LIGHT Full sun.

SOIL Well-drained soil.

GROWING Cut back the candles or silvery new shoots by half to shape the tree. Needles can winter burn at coldest temperatures.

DESIGNER'S CHOICE
Pinus thunbergii 'Thunderhead' (syn. 'Angelica's Thunderhead') White candles and blackish green needles;

Pinus thunbergii **'Thunderhead'**

mounding, spreading dwarf with a crooked, sculptural form. 8'–10' h and w.

PINE WILT DISEASE

Some non-native pines, such as Japanese black pine (*P. thunbergii*), Scotch pine (*P. sylvestris*), and Austrian pine (*P. nigra*) are susceptible to pine wilt disease. Nematodes cause this fatal disease, which beetles spread to the needles. Once weakened, blue-stain fungus infects the tree, leading to its death. The USDA Forest Service suggests these steps to manage the disease, which has no cure:

- Don't plant exotic (non-native) pines where the mean summer temperature is warmer than 68°F.
- Keep susceptible landscape pines well watered, especially during dry spells.
- If you see signs of this disease on your property, get rid of infested pines to curb the damage and protect other vulnerable trees.

PITTOSPORUM

Pittosporum tobira ○ › ◯

pit-toh-SPOH-rum toh-BEE-ra

Japanese mock orange

Pittosporum Family (Pittosporaceae)
Broad-leaf evergreen shrub or
small tree
6'–30' h x 5'–10' w

This handsome shrub produces glossy, rich green leaves about 3" long and leathery to the touch. Leaf tips are blunt and round, and their edges curve down. Clusters of sweetly fragrant, creamy white flowers appear from late spring to early summer, becoming yellow with age. Yellowish to brownish, round seed capsules contain big, showy, sticky, red-orange seeds. Shrubs tend to be rounded in habit and branched to the ground. Limbed up as a single or multistemmed tree, Japanese mock orange has a globular to rounded and spreading crown.

LANDSCAPE USE
Dense, handsome specimen; screen; informal or formal hedge (shearing destroys flower buds); can be container grown in cooler areas and brought indoors in winter; leafy stems cut as filler for flower arrangements.

ORIGIN China, Japan, Korea.

HARDINESS ZONES 8–10

LIGHT Full sun to partial shade.

SOIL Moist, fertile, well-drained soil with a slightly acid to neutral pH. Salt tolerant.

GROWING No serious pests or diseases in good conditions, but subject to root rot in wet soils.

DESIGNER'S CHOICE
Pittosporum tobira 'Wheeler's Dwarf' Small form for containers and small gardens. 3' h × 4' w. Zones 9–10.

Platanus x *hispanica* 'Columbia'

PLATANUS

Platanus × *hispanica* △ › ◯
(syn. *P.* × *a*)

PLA-ta-nus hi-SPAN-ik-ah

London plane tree, Buttonwood

Sycamore Family (Platanaceae)
Large deciduous tree
50'–80' h x 50'–70' w

London plane trees look elegant lining the sides of long drives, where their stunning mottled bark is on display. The outer bark flakes in patches revealing an inner surface of cream, brown, and light olive green. Because the persistent, dangling, 1", ball-shaped sycamore fruits can make a mess when they drop and the vigorous shallow roots can raise a path or sidewalk, it's best to plant this big tree in a naturalized area or large lawn away from the house. A cross of *occidentalis* and *orientalis,* being less susceptible to anthracnose disease than the former, which should not be planted in areas prone to this disease; plant only cultivars showing such resistance.

LANDSCAPE USE
Lawn specimen, shade tree, nice for lining gravel drives.

ORIGIN Garden hybrid

HARDINESS ZONES 5–8

LIGHT Full sun.

SOIL Prefers moist, well-drained soils; tolerates a wide variety of soils, including dry and wet compacted ones; pH adaptable.

GROWING Tolerates urban pollution and salt spray. Prone to winter damage (such as frost cracking of bark in the Midwest or breakage from ice and heavy snow) and multiple insects and diseases, including mildew and cankerstain. Widely available; resists but is not immune to the anthracnose plaguing sycamore in the eastern U. S. Lace bugs may eat the leaves, but canker stain can kill it.

DESIGNER'S CHOICE
Platanus × *hispanica* 'Bloodgood' This attractive tree starts out pyramidal but becomes rounded and spreading with age. Though prone to many pests and diseases, it is fairly resistant to anthracnose; can take severe pruning. 50'–80' h × 50'–70' w

P. × *hispanica* 'Yarwood' Handsome tree with symmetrical, pyramidal crown; resists anthracnose and is more resistant to powdery mildew than 'Bloodgood'; tolerates smog, pollution, and other urban stresses; starts exfoliating when young. 30'–50' h × 30' w. Zone 6.

P. × *hispanica* 'Liberty' Pyramidal, fast-growing tree that resists eastern strains of anthracnose, mildew, heat, and drought. 50' h × 40'–45' w.

Platycladus orientalis △
(syn. *Thuja orientalis*)

pla-tee-CLAH-dus oh-ree-en-TAH-lis

Oriental arborvitae

Cypress Family (Cupressaceae)
Evergreen shrub
20'–30' h x 12'–15' w

Like American arborvitae (*Thuja occidentalis*), sturdy *Platycladus* appears frequently in American gardens. It grows as a bushy, cone-shaped, multistemmed shrub; with pruning, it forms a neat, single-stemmed, pyramidal tree. Foliage appears in flat, vertical sprays. Ideal conifer for southern and southwestern gardens. Popular, low-maintenance cemetery planting.

LANDSCAPE USE
Screens, hedges, and windbreaks; ideal for dry sites and low-maintenance landscapes.

ORIGIN   China, Iran

HARDINESS ZONES   6–9

LIGHT   Full sun to partial shade.

SOIL   Average, well-drained garden soil; pH adaptable; drought tolerant once established.

GROWING   Thrives in milder climates

Platycladus orientalis **'Semperaurea'**

than American arborvitae. Its fragile twigs and branches break readily when covered with ice or snow.

DESIGNER'S CHOICE
Platycladus orientalis 'Bakeri' Bright green leaves on a columnar to pyramidal tree. 25' h × 20' w.

P. orientalis 'Elegantissima' Easy-to-find, cone-shaped cultivar with scaly, overlapping yellow leaves in spring; chartreuse in summer; bronzy in winter. 15' h × 10' w.

P. orientalis 'Sunkist' Dwarf, with gold-tipped foliage. 2' h and w.

Podocarpus chinensis ○
(syn. *P. macrophyllus var. maki,* 'Maki')

poh-doh-KAR-pus chi-NEN-sis

Shrubby Japanese yew, Yew pine

Podocarp Family (Podocarpaceae)
Evergreen shrub
8'–10' h x 3'–4' w

Valued in Southern gardens for its dense, upright form and very dark green, leathery, needlelike, 2"–3" leaves, which are arranged in spirals. Male plants produce yellowy cones resembling catkins. Females produce showy, red-purple, ½" long, fleshy fruits in fall. Though this showy berrylike stem is edible, the attached green seed is not. Slow-growing.

LANDSCAPE USE
Screen, specimen, hedge; foundation plantings, especially in coastal areas, where it tolerates salt spray; cut flower arrangements; indoor plant in cold climates; bonsai.

ORIGIN   Japan, China

HARDINESS ZONES   (7) 8–10

LIGHT   Full sun to partial shade.

SOIL   Prefers moist, fertile, slightly acidic, well-drained soil but tolerates average, well-drained garden soils.

GROWING   Hedges or foundation plants need regular shearing for size and uniformity. Resists pests and diseases, though you may see occasional fungal disease and scales, especially on indoor plants; tolerates heat and humidity.

CAUTION   Do not eat shrubby Japanese yew; it is particularly toxic to pets.

Populus tremuloides △

POP-u-lus trem-u-LOY-deez

Quaking aspen

Willow Family (Salicaceae)
Deciduous tree
40'–60' h x 15'–30' w

A grove of quaking aspen looks attractive at the sunny edge of a woodland, especially in fall when they are yellow. During the growing season, the leaves rustle and quiver at the slightest breeze. This small- to mid-size suckering tree is undemanding, which is probably why it has the widest native range of any tree in North America.

LANDSCAPE USE
Plant a group of quaking aspen against a background of tall dark green conifers for a naturalistic screen. The dark backdrop shows to advantage the quivering movement of the leaves and accentuates the contrast in fall, when the aspens turn shimmering yellow. They cast wonderfully dappled shade, perfect for underplanting with ornamental native shrubs and wildflowers or perennials.

ORIGIN   Much of North America, from the Atlantic to the Pacific coasts.

HARDINESS ZONES   1–7

LIGHT   Full sun.

SOIL   Adaptable to most growing conditions, including wet soils and soils with a pH between 5.5 to 8.0, but prefers rich, moist, limey, well-drained loam.

Populus tremuloides

GROWING Place quaking aspens far from your septic system, since they colonize areas by aggressive root suckering. Trees are short-lived because of weak wood and susceptibility to pests and diseases. Aspens attract songbirds, deer, elk, and ruffled grouse, which eat the male buds in winter. Intolerant of shade. Depends on fire for survival, since seeds only germinate in full sun, which is typically after a burn. Even though native, may be invasive in some areas. Although many species of aspen exist, many, including white poplar (*P. alba*), Lombardy poplar (*P. nigra*), and Eastern cottonwood (*P. deltoides*), are not suitable for home landscapes because they are messy, weak-wooded trees, prone to disease and early death.

DESIGNER'S CHOICE

Populus tremula 'Erecta' (columnar European aspen) Tall, narrow habit; deep green foliage with silver bottoms; more canker-resistant that many columnar poplars. Good screen. 40' h × 10' w. Zones 2–5.

P. canescens 'Tower' Narrow, pyramidal form with excellent hardiness and resistance to stem cankers; seedless. 50' h × 10' w. Zone 3.

Potentilla fruticosa ○ ✳

po-ten-TIL-la fru-ti-CO-sa

Shrubby cinquefoil

Rose Family (Rosaceae)
Deciduous flowering shrub
1'–4' h × 2'–4' w

This hardy, disease-resistant little shrub brings long-lasting color to cold-climate shrub borders, foundations, and perennial beds. Although the flowers of the species are yellow, cultivars with single or double flowers abound in hues ranging from white and pink to red and orange.

The grayish green to deep green foliage is alternate and compound with 3 to 7 linear leaflets; fall color is not ornamental. The shredding, brown bark doesn't show up enough to be decorative. In June, it produces 5-petal, bright yellow, wide-open, 1¼" flowers with a central boss of golden stamens, with continuing flowers through summer. The brown fruits are not ornamental.

LANDSCAPE USE

Groundcover, shrub border, perennial garden, foundation, or facer for taller plantings.

ORIGIN Boggy soils across the U.S.

HARDINESS ZONES 2–6

LIGHT Full sun; light shade in the heat of the day keeps blossoms from fading; tolerates cold.

SOIL Well-drained, moist, fertile, garden soils. It tolerates drought, flooding, and heavy, poor, rocky, slightly alkaline soils.

GROWING Cut out old stems in late winter or early spring to keep it compact or prune back to the ground. It is pest-, deer-, and disease-resistant. It looks gangly and awkward with age unless pruned to keep compact.

DESIGNER'S CHOICE

These are some of the 100-plus cultivars you can buy.

Potentilla fruticosa 'Abbotswood' Pure white, single flowers; bluish green leaves; spreading habit. 2'–3' h and w.

P. fruticosa 'Dakota Sunspot' Deep gold blooms from spring to frost on spreading shrub with bright green leaves. 3' h × 3'–4' w.

P. fruticosa 'Goldfinger' Big, intense yellow flowers on mounding shrub with dark green foliage. 3'–4' h × 4' w.

P. fruticosa 'Goldstar' (syn. 'Goldstern') Prolific 2" gold blooms on mildew-resistant, relatively heat-tolerant, dense shrub. 2'–3' h × 3' w.

P. fruticosa 'Medicine Wheel Mountain' (syn. 'Yellow Gem') Bright yellow single flowers with ruffled petals, gray-green foliage, low spreading habit. 1'–2' h × 2'–4' w.

P. fruticosa 'Monsidh' (Frosty) Single white flowers. 1'–3' h and w.

P. fruticosa 'Pink Beauty' (Lovely Pink) Abundant pink blooms that may fade with hot nights; bushy compact habit. 2' h and w.

P. fruticosa 'Primrose Beauty' Profuse soft yellow blooms on shrub with lovely silvery leaves. 3' h × 4' w.

P. fruticosa 'Sunset' (syn. 'Red Sunset') Orange flowers fading to yellow in summer's heat; partial sun. 2'–3' h and w.

P. fruticosa 'UMan' (Mango Tango) Bicolor red and orange flowers over a yellow base; mounded form. 2' h and w.

Potentilla fruticosa

PRUNUS

Prunus caroliniana ○ ✳

PRU-nus ca-ro-li-nee-A-na

Carolina cherry laurel

Rose Family (Rosaceae)
Evergreen shrub or small tree
20'–40' h x 15'–20' w

Carolina cherry laurel bears handsome, glossy, dark evergreen leaves year round, with yellow to bronze-tinged new growth. Elongated, 3" clusters of fragrant, white flowers appear in early spring. The flowers attract butterflies, and the small, blackberry-like fruits ripen in fall and appeal to birds, which drop seeds far and wide.

LANDSCAPE USE

Because it tolerates severe pruning, Carolina cherry laurel works well in screens and formal or informal hedges.

ORIGIN   Southeastern U.S. lowlands.

HARDINESS ZONES   7–10

LIGHT   Full sun to partial shade.

SOIL   Moist, well-drained soils.

GROWING   Tolerates severe pruning; handsome but you'll need to weed out the numerous seedlings if you let it go to seed. Does not tolerate wet soils.

CAUTION   Toxic leaves, stems, and seeds can kill humans and livestock, though they smell of maraschino cherries.

DESIGNER'S CHOICE

Prunus caroliniana 'Monus' (Bright 'N Tight)   Tightly branched shrub makes a good formal hedge and also works in shrub and mixed borders. 10' h x 8' w.

Prunus cerasifera ○ › ○

PRU-nus ser-ah-SIF-er-a

Flowering plum, Purple-leaf plum

Rose Family (Rosaceae)
Deciduous flowering tree
15'–30' h x 15'–25' w

With all the splendid, small, flowering trees available, I wouldn't choose this one because it's overused. Flowering plum's pretty pink or white flowers are harbingers of spring, and the purple leaves or striking forms of some cultivars can sometimes be effective in the landscape. Although some cherry trees have gorgeous bark, this isn't one of them.

Flowering plum, which lives about 20 years, has alternate, simple, deciduous, green leaves that are 2" long with serrated edges and pointy tips. The red-brown to gray bark is smooth with raised horizontal pores for gaseous exchanges; old bark has low ridges and furrows. It produces light pink to white, single flowers before the leaves unfold and edible, 1", reddish fruits. Similar to purpleleaf sand cherry (*P. × cistena*), but larger and more upright.

LANDSCAPE USE

Species not in use; use cultivars as specimens and accents.

ORIGIN   Western Asia on woody slopes.

HARDINESS ZONES   (4) 5–8

LIGHT   Full sun for best bloom; purple-leafed cultivars color up best in full sun.

SOIL   Prefers deep, moist, well-drained, acid soil but can tolerate slightly alkaline soils. It is drought tolerant.

ALL ABOUT *PRUNUS*

Cherry's popularity as an ornamental landscape tree comes from its showy red, white, or pink blooms, which range from the exquisite little pink-centered white flowers of 'Hally Jolivette' to the big bumptious blooms of deep pink 'Kanzan'. A few have great bark, others flashy foliage, and some have habits of exceptional grace. Although I don't like growing trees with such a short period of interest, by incorporating plum or cherry into a mixed planting, you can achieve longer interest and thus more usefulness in the landscape.

On the flip side, they are often short lived and prone to many pests and diseases. Most ornamental cherries have one short season of interest: spring. And some look downright weird and ugly, especially without leaves, thanks to the awkward proportions created by high grafts joining fast-growing, thick-trunk rootstocks to slender-branched scions or implants. Note that some plants are grafted because you can't make them any other way. Grafting may produce a bigger flowering tree in less time than one grown from cuttings. Grafting can also fortify weaker trees or shrubs, giving them cold hardiness, tolerance to different soil types, and resistance to pest and diseases. The point is to examine each tree you buy not just for healthy roots and foliage but also for the harmony of its overall form. Trees grown on their own roots or grafted near the ground usually look more natural and well-proportioned than trees with high, clearly visible grafts.

Prunus x yedoensis

GROWING Best transplanted in spring. Prune after blooming. Like many Rose Family members, short-lived *Prunus* is prone to many pests and diseases, including caterpillars, aphids, borers, scale, mites, leaf hoppers, canker, crown gall, fireblight, leaf spot, powdery mildew, and more. Where I live, Japanese beetles congregate on ornamental cherry trees.

DESIGNER'S CHOICE

Prunus cerasifera 'Krauter's Vesuvius' Light pink flowers before dark purple leaves appear on the upright oval crown; similar to 'Thundercloud'. 20'–30' h × 15'–20' w.

P. cerasifera 'Newport' Ubiquitous cultivar with pale pinkish white blooms; leaves open bronzy purple and mature to dull dark purple; dull purple fruits. 20' h × 15' w. Zone 4.

P. cerasifera 'Thundercloud' Pale pink flowers before dark purple leaves and small red fruits. 20' h and w.

Prunus × cistena ○

PRU-nus sis-TAY-na

Purple-leaf sand cherry

Rose Family (Rosaceae)
Deciduous flowering shrub
6'–10' h × 5'–8' w

Purpleleaf sand cherry, an upright, open, multi-stemmed shrub or single-trunk, small tree, grows best in cold climates and tolerates coastal conditions. In spring, bowl-shaped, pale pink blooms with deep pink centers open after the red-purple leaves unfurl, and the little blackish purple fruits that follow attract wildlife. Both summer and fall foliage is purple. Rather fine and pretty.

LANDSCAPE USE
Colorful leaves give this shrub extended interest in beds and borders, or use for hedging since it tolerates severe pruning.

ORIGIN Garden origin

HARDINESS ZONES 3–8

LIGHT See *P. cerasifera*.

SOIL Moist, well-drained, somewhat fertile soil, but tolerates poor soils and drought.

GROWING See *P. cerasifera*.

DESIGNER'S CHOICE

Prunus maritima (beach plum) Salt-tolerant, suckering, native shrub with white, single and semi-double flowers before the green foliage; round, bluish-black fruits in late summer make outstanding jelly and preserves; needs sandy, rocky soil. 4' h × 10' w. Zones 3–7.

Prunus 'Hally Jolivette' ○ ✳

PRU-nus

'Hally Jolivette' flowering cherry

Rose Family (Rosaceae)
Deciduous flowering shrub or small tree
12'–15' h and w

I grow just one flowering cherry, and that's 'Hally Jolivette', an irresistibly refined, shrubby hybrid with year-round interest from flowers, fall color, and habit. My plant is small, about 2' × 3', and has been in the ground for 2 years. Even at that young age, pink buds open to showy clusters of white to pale pink, double flowers with deep pink centers, which flourish for almost 3 weeks in spring. In summer, the plant has fine-textured, shiny, green leaves that turn yellow and persist in fall. The winter habit is twiggy, delicate, and rounded, thanks to the many flexible stems that comprise the plant. Trained to a single trunk, 'Hally Jolivette' has a fairly even rounded crown. A cross

Prunus x cistena

Prunus 'Hally Jolivette'

of *P. subhirtella* and *P. × yedoensis*. Longer lived and longer bloom than many cherries.

LANDSCAPE USE
Perfect as a big shrub or little specimen tree in a small garden. Grow in the ground or in a container underplanted with spring bulbs. In large gardens, plant a group against a conifer hedge to accentuate their fine forms.

ORIGIN   Garden origin

HARDINESS ZONES   (5) 6–7

LIGHT   Full sun.

SOIL   Well-drained soil. Tolerates acid to alkaline soils of clay, loam, and sand.

GROWING   Drought tolerant, deer resistant, more pest and disease resistant than most other flowering cherries.

DESIGNER'S CHOICE
Prunus glandulosa (flowering almond) Attractive shrub with single or double white or pink blooms; fine stems give it a delicate appearance in flower. Cut back hard for more blooms and when shrub looks unkempt; drought-tolerant. Possible substitute for viburnums afflicted with leaf beetles. 5' h × 4' w. Zones 4–8.

P. tomentosa (Nanking cherry) Wind-tolerant, wide shrub with pink buds, white single flowers, and sour red fruits suitable for jams, jellies, and birds. You can prune this shrub as a small tree. 8' h and w. Zone 2.

P. virginiana (chokecherry) Adaptable, upright tree or shrub native to much of the U.S. and southern Canada; in late spring, white flowers appear in bottlebrush clusters; the bitter fruits are eaten by birds or used for jams and jellies. 'Shubert' (purpleleaf chokecherry) has foliage that opens green, aging to deep purple. Tent caterpillars are serious pests. 3'–20' h × 3'–15' w. Zone 2.

Prunus laurocerasus ○
PRU-nus lo-ro-se-RA-sus
Cherry laurel, English laurel

Rose Family (Rosaceae)
Evergreen flowering shrub or small tree
10'–20' h × 8' w

Cherry laurel bears excellent, glossy, 6", dark green leaves year round. Clusters of perfumed blooms appear in spring, followed by black fruits that attract wildlife.

LANDSCAPE USE
A good formal hedge; even better as an informal hedge or screen with a naturalistic form; mass in groups.

ORIGIN   Eastern Europe and southwest Asia.

HARDINESS ZONES   6–8

LIGHT   Prefers partial to full shade but will also grow in full sun.

SOIL   Prefers moist, very well-drained, organic soils but will also grow in salty conditions.

GROWING   Insects may feed on its glossy leaves.

DESIGNER'S CHOICE
Prunus laurocerasus 'Nana' Small version of the species; use for low hedging, edging, or facing down large leggy shrubs. 6'–8' h and w.

P. laurocerasus 'Otto Luyken' Dwarf with 4" leaves and abundant blooms. 3' h × 6' w.

P. laurocerasus 'Zabeliana' Fast-growing, densely branched dwarf with willowlike leaves; hardier than most other cherry laurels; can be used like a groundcover in shade. 4' h × 8' w.

P. laurocerasus 'Schipkaensis' Hardiest cherry laurel, with long, shiny green leaves. 10' h × 7' w. Zone 5.

Prunus 'Okame' ▽
(syn. *Prunus × incam* 'Okame')
PRU-nus
'Okame' cherry

Rose Family (Rosaceae)
Deciduous flowering large shrub or small tree
15'–30' h × 20'–30' w

This medium-textured, hybrid vase-shaped cherry grows well in the South, but it can survive both hot and cold weather. Its attractive, shiny, red-brown bark gives it year-round interest. It produces deep pink buds followed by graceful dangling bell-like clusters of fragrant, medium

***Prunus laurocerasus* 'Otto Luyken'**

Prunus 'Okame'

pink blooms for a long period in spring; red to orange fall color adds to its appeal. Very pretty. A cross of *P. campanulata* and *P. incisa*.

LANDSCAPE USE
Lovely garden specimen, underplanted with early spring bulbs; grow in containers; plant near decks where you can enjoy the tree's scent and its changes through the season.

ORIGIN Garden origin

HARDINESS ZONES 6–8

LIGHT Full sun to partial shade.

SOIL Well-drained to heavy soils.

GROWING No serious problems. Canker worm chews up the leaves. Borers attack weak or wounded trees.

DESIGNER'S CHOICE
Prunus 'Dream Catcher' This 'Okame' seedling bears copious, medium pink, single flowers with dark pink centers in early spring; upright, vase-shaped tree; yellow-orange fall color; pest-tolerant. 25' h × 15' w.

P. 'First Lady' 'Okame' selection from U.S. National Arboretum with upright columnar habit; shiny, dark green, relatively disease-resistant leaves; deep pink, single blossoms in spring. Grows best in full sun and well drained soil. 25' h × 14' w.

Prunus maackii ○

PRU-nus MAK-ee-i

Amur chokecherry, Amur cherry

Rose Family (Rosaceae)
Deciduous flowering tree
25' h x 20' w

This fast-growing, small, oval tree is worth growing for its lustrous, copper-red bark streaked with whitish, horizontal lenticels. Abundant, showy, white bottlebrush flowers appear in spring, followed by little black fruits that are eaten by birds.

LANDSCAPE USE
Specimen with year-round interest, groups, under power lines.

ORIGIN Korea, Manchuria, Siberia.

HARDINESS ZONES 2–6

LIGHT Full sun.

SOIL Moist, fertile, well-drained soil.

GROWING May be short-lived due to girdling roots or damage from weak branch attachments, but tougher than many cherries.

Prunus pendula 'Pendula Rosea' ⋒

(syn. *P.* × *subhirtella* 'Pendula')

PRU-nus PEN-du-la

Weeping Higan cherry, Japanese flowering cherry, Oriental cherry

Rose Family (Rosaceae)
Deciduous flowering tree
25' h and w

This elegant cherry — truly pretty in pink — grows fast and big, and boasts a graceful winter silhouette. The clustered, single, pink flowers bloom in early spring before the tree leafs out, creating a fall of pink in the landscape. In fall the leaves may turn yellow. It bears oval, red fruits that mature to lustrous black. This cultivar is still often listed under *subhirtella*.

LANDSCAPE USE
Graceful specimen.

ORIGIN Japan

HARDINESS ZONES 5–8

LIGHT Full sun.

SOIL Well-drained soil.

GROWING See *P. cerasifera*. As beautiful as this tree can be, it can also be homely: weeping cherries grafted about 5' high on a thick, fast-growing rootstock can turn

Prunus pendula

a refined tree into an unnatural umbrella. Picture a ballerina with a tiny torso and sinuous arms topping the massive trunk and legs of a he-man bodybuilder and you get the point. To avoid this visual imbalance and eliminate the eye-level seam between the robust rootstock and the scion, buy a weeping Higan cherry grown on its own roots or grafted low near the soil surface.

DESIGNER'S CHOICE

Prunus × subhirtella 'Autumnalis' Semi-double, light pink blooms on an upright tree. 'Autumnalis Rosea' has dark pink flowers. 40' h and w. Zone 4.

P. × subhirtella 'Pendula Plena Rosea' (syn. *P. pendula* 'Yae-beni-shidare') (weeping double pink cherry) Weeping habit, pink double blooms. 12' h and w.

Prunus sargentii ○

PRU-nus sar-JEN-tee-i

Sargent cherry

Rose Family (Rosaceae)
Deciduous flowering tree
35' h and w

Slow-growing Sargent cherry has more going for it than springtime blooms of showy, single, pink flowers up to 1½" wide. Bronzy to reddish new

Prunus 'Accolade'

growth may emerge with the flowers; shiny, red-tinged bark with horizontal lenticels gives year-round interest; showy red and orange fall color tints the simple, dark green, deciduous leaves. Although the fruit is not flashy, it attracts birds. One of the best of the hardier cherries for the north.

LANDSCAPE USE
Often used as a lawn specimen and ornamental shade tree, it may look better grouped in the landscape or at the woodland's edge.

ORIGIN   Japan

HARDINESS ZONES   4–7

LIGHT   Full sun to part shade.

SOIL   See *P. cerasifera*.

GROWING   Plants in this genus may be short lived because of vulnerability to insects and diseases; Sargent cherry, however, is less problem-prone than many other cherries. Since it's often grown from seed, plants may have variable shapes.

DESIGNER'S CHOICE

Prunus 'Accolade'   Vigorous hybrid of *P. sargentii × P. subhirtella* with hanging clusters of semi-double pink blooms in spring and a rounded, spreading form. 30' h × 25' w.

P. sargentii 'Columnaris'   Pink, single flowers on upright tree with glossy, reddish-brown bark; emerging leaves have a reddish tinge; orange to red fall color; early leaf drop. 30' h × 15' w.

Prunus serrulata ○

PRU-nus ser-ru-LAH-ta

Japanese flowering cherry, Oriental cherry

Rose Family (Rosaceae)
Deciduous small flowering tree
25' h and w

Oriental cherries are notable for lavish, pink, single to double flowers that hang in clusters for about 2 weeks in spring, followed by small red cherries; their smooth, shiny, reddish brown

Prunus serrulata 'Kanzan'

to gray bark with raised horizontal lenticels is distinctive year round. New growth is bronze to reddish, followed in fall by lovely bronze to subdued red color. These trees are often grafted high on the trunk, making a fat ugly bulge at eye level with a bunch of branches emerging on the same plane.

LANDSCAPE USE
Best in groups against a dark green background.

ORIGIN   Japan, China, Korea.

HARDINESS ZONES   5–6

LIGHT   Full sun.

SOIL   Well-drained.

GROWING   Susceptibility to pests and diseases usually cuts short the life of this tree.

DESIGNER'S CHOICE

Prunus serrulata 'Amanogawa'   Columnar habit, with pink, scented, single to semi-double blooms and bronzy fall color. 20' h × 6' w.

P. serrulata 'Kanzan' (syn. *P. serrulata* 'Kwanzan' or 'Sekiyama')   Vase-shaped crown; flashy, bluish-pink, double blossoms clustered along stem in early spring; sterile (non-fruiting) cultivar. Perhaps most popular of doubles. 25'–30' h and w.

P. serrulata 'Shirotae' (syn. *P. serrulata* 'Mt. Fuji')   Broad crown, pink buds, double white flowers; may grow on acid, alkaline, or dry soils. 15' h × 20' w.

Prunus × *yedoensis* ○

PRU-nus ye-doh-EN-sis

Yoshino flowering cherry, Yoshino cherry

Rose Family (Rosaceae)
Deciduous flowering tree
30'–35' h and w

In spring, when you visit Washington, D.C., for the cherry blossoms, this tree and *P.* 'Kanzan' (*P. serrulata* 'Kwanzan') are what you'll see. Yoshino cherry flowers open light pink and fade to white; the foliage turns yellow to orange in fall.

LANDSCAPE USE
Garden accent; tree and shrub borders.

ORIGIN   Garden origin

HARDINESS ZONES   (5) 6–8

LIGHT   See *P. cerasifera.*

SOIL   See *P. cerasifera.*

GROWING   See *P. cerasifera.*

DESIGNER'S CHOICE
Prunus × *yedoensis* 'Afterglow' Pink, fragrant flowers; adaptable to different soils and in full sun to partial shade. 25' h and w.

Prunus x *yedoensis*

Prunus × *yedoensis* 'Akebono' (syn. *P.* × *yedoensis* 'Daybreak') Fragrant, semi-double, soft pink flowers in spring; yellow fall color; rounded spreading form. 25' h and w.

P. × *yedoensis* 'Shidare Yoshino' Spreading weeper covered in spring with white to very light pink flowers, followed by black fruits; yellow fall color. 20' h × 30' w.

P. × *yedoensis* 'Snow Fountains' (*P.* 'Snofozam') (syn. 'White Fountains') Semi-weeping with white flowers before the leaves; yellow and orange fall color. 6'–12' h and w.

PSEUDOTSUGA

Pseudotsuga menziesii △

su-doh-SU-ga men-ZEE-zee-i

Douglas fir

Pine Family (Pinaceae)
Evergreen conifer
40'–75' h × 12'–20' w

Dignified in the landscape, this fast-growing conifer has a tall, straight trunk and a narrow, conical, symmetrical crown. Branches on young trees are horizontal to

Pseudotsuga menziesii

ascending. Older trees are more open with top branches reaching upward while lower branches exhibit a graceful droop.

The linear 1" to 1½" aromatic leaves in gray-green, blue-green, or glossy green are evergreen and spiral around the stem. The bark is fairly smooth on young trees, but becomes a handsome red-brown, ridged and fissured, on older trees. The flowers are not ornamental, but the odd 4", reddish-brown, shaggy cones offer their own interest with their 3-pointed bracts set between scales.

LANDSCAPE USE
Its tall, narrow habit makes it particularly effective in groups on large properties; also a fine specimen tree, screen, Christmas tree.

ORIGIN   Coast and Rocky Mountains of the western North America.

HARDINESS ZONES   4–6

LIGHT   Full sun.

SOIL   Moist, well-drained soils.

GROWING   Likes a humid environment such as the Pacific Northwest. It suffers in strong wind, drought, and extreme heat, and may be affected by canker.

PTEROSTYRAX

Pterostyrax hispida ◯ ✳

tay-ro-STY-raks HIS-pi-da

Epaulette tree

Styrax Family (Styracaceae)
Deciduous flowering shrub or
small tree
20'–30' h and w

This plant is worth growing for its
fragrant, creamy-white flowers,
which hang in 9" × 4" wisteria-like
bunches from the leaf axils in late
spring or early summer, and its
showy, downy seedpods, which last
into winter. Epaulette tree starts
blooming when it's about 8' tall. It's
hard to find, but healthy and easy to
grow.

LANDSCAPE USE
Shrub border, woodland garden,
container.

ORIGIN Mountain woods of Japan and
China.

HARDINESS ZONES (4) 5–8

LIGHT Full sun to partial shade; blooms
its best in a hot site in full sun.

SOIL Deep, moist, acid soils.

GROWING Shelter from harsh winds in
the North and prune in winter. Young
plants may suffer damage in severe
winters.

Pterostyrax hispida

PUNICA

Punica granatum ◯

POO-ni-ka gra-NAY-tum

Pomegranate

Loosestrife Family (Lythraceae)
Deciduous flowering shrub; small
tree with pruning
6'–15' h × 6'–12' w

This dense, arching, sometimes
spiny shrub looks charming, with its
flamboyant trumpet- or carnation-
shaped flowers in red, orange, cream,
and apricot, followed in some cultivars
by 2"–3" berries filled with juicy, edible
seeds. For fruits, grow full-size plants.
Dwarfs produce no, or very small,
berries. Long-blooming, double-
flowered cultivars are sterile; single-
flowered shrubs are better for fruits.

LANDSCAPE USE
Containers, espalier; small specimen
tree; use dwarfs as edging or in mixed
borders; hedges. For low hedge, grow
miniatures 2' apart; for a colorful
fruiting hedge, leave about 5' between
full-size plants.

ORIGIN Iran, N. India, in dry, limely soil.

HARDINESS ZONES (7) 8–10

LIGHT Full sun to partial shade.

SOIL Chalky to acid, well-drained soils.

GROWING Drought-tolerant once
established. Good for a hot, semi-arid
climate, but best fruiting occurs with
some moisture.

DESIGNER'S CHOICE
Punica granatum 'Chico' Dwarf with
nearly nonstop, double, orangey red
blooms that resemble carnations; no
fruits. 2' h and w.

P. granatum 'Nana' Dense dwarf with
orangey red, 1", single trumpets
practically year round, but mostly
spring and summer; pink fruit 2"
across. 3' h and w.

P. granatum 'Emperor' Slow-growing
dome with good cold tolerance and
1½", brownish purple fruits. 3' h × 4' w.

PYRACANTHA

Pyracantha coccinea ⬬

pie-ra-KAN-tha kok-SIN-ee-a

Firethorn

Rose Family (Rosaceae)
Broad-leaf evergreen to semi-
evergreen shrub
10'–15' h and w

On a winter trip to England, I saw a
breathtaking *Pyracantha* with brilliant
orange fruit sprawling in front of a
golden-tan Cotswold stone cottage.
Pyracantha grows at a medium rate
into an upright, spreading shrub with
rigid thorny stems. Yet when I grew it
in Wilmington, Delaware (Zone 6), it
looked awful. So, if you try this showy
shrub, choose it for hardiness, disease
resistance, and site size.

The alternate, simple foliage has a
serrated edge; it is glossy dark green
on top, paler and hairy below; in
winter it's bronzy. Exposed plantings
may experience foliar burn, turning
the leaves brown. Bark is smooth and
ruddy with lenticels. It produces small,
single, white flowers with an unpleasant
scent. These are held in dense, flattish
clusters in late spring. Showy, gleaming
orange-red, clustered, berrylike fruits
appear from late summer through
winter. Adored by cedar waxwings; the
thorny stems also offer shelter to birds.

LANDSCAPE USE
Espalier on a brick or stone wall;
barrier plantings; against a wall of
an entry courtyard, where its bright
fruits provide winter interest.

ORIGIN Southeastern Europe to China.

HARDINESS ZONES (5) 6–9

LIGHT Full sun to partial shade.

SOIL Well-drained soil with a pH of 6 to
6.5; does well in dry soils.

GROWING Plant disease-resistant
cultivars and choose compact forms for
small areas, since hard pruning reduces
the next year's blooms. If shoots die off

Pyracantha coccinea

from fireblight, remove the sick stem and throw it in the trash, not the compost pile, then clean your pruner with bleach to prevent disease transmission. Like other Rose Family plants, firethorn is prone to many pests and diseases, with fireblight and scab the most serious. Hard to transplant; site properly when planting.

CAUTION Sharp spines may cause an allergic reaction; wear thick gloves when pruning or handling.

DESIGNER'S CHOICE

Pyracantha 'Apache' Resistant to scab and fireblight; long-lasting red fruits, shiny green leaves; smaller size makes an effective short hedge without pruning. 5' h × 6' w.

P. 'Fiery Cascade' Disease-resistant, persistent fruits change from orange in August to red in October. 8' h × 9' w.

P. 'Mohave' Resistant to scab and fireblight; profuse flowers and orange-scarlet berries not eaten by birds. 12' h × 16' w.

P. 'Teton' Semi-evergreen, resistant to scab and fireblight, orange berries, more erect than most firethorns, vigorous. 12'–16' h × 9' w.

PYRUS

Pyrus calleryana △ ✳

PIE-rus kal-le-ree-AY-na

Ornamental pear, Callery pear

Rose Family (Rosaceae)
Deciduous flowering tree
20'–40' h × 20'–30' w

My New Hampshire friend Margaret loved her 'Bradford' callery pear,

which lived in a front-yard foundation planting. Unaware of its ultimate size, Margaret watched as her little tree grew fast and tall, obscuring her home's second floor. Still she loved it, saying it was the first tree in her yard to leaf out in spring, it buzzed with bees for 2 weeks in May when white blooms covered its crown, and it didn't drop its pretty, reddish purple fall leaves until early December. Margaret's pear was just 14 years old when, in the midst of a Halloween nor'easter, she heard a crack and looked outside to see that half the tree had split off, not unusual in the eastern U.S., where callery pears are problematical. Although some new cultivars have better branching than the ubiquitous, weak, sterile-fruiting 'Bradfords', they set viable seed by cross-pollinating with the latter. As a result, 'Bradford' callery pears are escaping from gardens and overrunning disturbed open areas and wet and dry natural areas throughout the East.

The simple, alternate, toothed, dark green foliage is glossy above with fine reddish purple fall color. The ridged bark is gray-brown. The white, single flowers are ⅛" wide and appear in clusters. Fruits are not ornamental.

LANDSCAPE USE
Frequently used (overused) as a front-lawn specimen or focal point.

ORIGIN Woods and stream banks in central and southern China.

HARDINESS ZONES 5–8

LIGHT Full sun.

SOIL Most garden soils; tolerates some drought, occasional wet soils, and pollution.

GROWING Transplant or prune from late winter to early spring. It produces occasional thorns. Some cultivars are susceptible to fireblight, especially in the South. Dense, upright limbs, such as those of 'Bradford', result in narrow-

angled branch crotches, which may cause trees to break apart before maturity. Choose cultivars with wider branching.

CAUTION Thorny! In the East, this tree is invading disturbed and natural habitats.

DESIGNER'S CHOICE

Pyrus calleryana 'Aristocrat' Highly ornamental, better than 'Bradford'; forms a stronger central trunk; has an upright, pyramidal branching in youth, developing a broad open oval with age; less subject to wind breakage. 25'–40' h × 20'–30' w.

P. calleryana 'Bradford' A fast-growing tree with 3" clusters of white flowers and orangey red fall color; very narrow, weak crotches prone to split when tree is about 20 years old. Avoid this one. 50' h × 40' w (about 15' high in 10 years).

P. calleryana 'Chanticleer' (syn. *P. calleryana* 'Cleveland Select', 'Stonehill', 'Glen's Form', and 'Select') Dense, pyramidal habit; thornless, with even branching; reddish new growth, reddish-purple fall color; profuse flowering; fast growing. Preferable to 'Bradford'. 35' h × 16' w.

P. betulaefolia 'Pizazz' (syn. *P. betulaefolia* 'Pzazz') Ruffled leaf margins, improved branching. 35' h × 25' w. Zones 5–7.

Pyrus calleryana 'Bradford'

Quercus acutissima △ › ◯ ✳

KWAYR-kus ak-you-TIS-si-ma

Sawtooth oak

Beech Family (Fagaceae)
Deciduous tree
40'–60' h and w

This is a fine shade tree for large lawns because of its spreading habit and abundance of shiny, dark green, chestnutlike leaves.

LANDSCAPE USE
Shade tree for large lawns.

ORIGIN   Woods of Asia.

HARDINESS ZONES   (5) 6–9

LIGHT   See All About *Quercus*.

SOIL   Prefers well-drained, acid soil but adjusts to more alkaline conditions.

GROWING   Prolific acorn production.

CAUTION   Occasionally invasive in Maryland, South Carolina, Tennessee, and Virginia.

Quercus acutissima

Quercus alba △ › ◯

KWAYR-kus AL-ba

White oak

Beech Family (Fagaceae)
Deciduous tree
50'–80' h x 60'–80' w

The residents of Connecticut, Illinois, and Maryland recognized a grand tree when they made white oak their state tree. It has a large, rounded, uneven canopy with glossy, almost blue-green leaves that turn

Quercus alba

purplish red in fall. With great age, its limbs crook downward, creating a coarse yet powerful outline against the sky. The massive structure of a mature white oak is grand to behold. If you're building a house and have a straight-growing white oak on the property, it's usually worth saving. This tree is drought tolerant and disease resistant, and few oak troubles inflict lasting injury. Numerous wild creatures eat the acorns and seek the shelter of white oak, while woodworkers make furniture from its sturdy heartwood. White oaks are too big for most homes, but because they grow slowly, you may want to grow one in a large lawn or wild area on your property.

The dark bluish green, deciduous, 4"–8" leaves have 5–9 rounded lobes and long-lasting, purplish red fall color. The tree may hold its dead leaves into winter. The light gray bark is fissured. Male catkins make a mess in May. The fruits are 1" acorns with warty cups. White oak may hybridize with both native and introduced oak species.

LANDSCAPE USE
Great specimen tree for large lawns without overhead utility wires.

ORIGIN   Hardwood forests of eastern North America.

HARDINESS ZONES   4–9

LIGHT   Full sun to partial shade.

SOIL   Prefers moist, fertile, well-drained soils. Cannot tolerate compacted soils.

GROWING   Plant in spring only and know where you want it to grow, since white oak is hard to transplant because of its long taproot. Avoid doing construction around the tree, because it cannot tolerate compacted soils. If your child plants an acorn, give the tree that results plenty of growing space. By the time her great-grandkids come to call, it can spread 2 or 3 times the width of an old suburban house. Weakened trees are susceptible to many of the oak pests and diseases listed. See All About *Quercus*.

ALL ABOUT QUERCUS

To me, oaks are sublime. Some survive for hundreds of years with vast trunks and sheltering branches bent and outspread with age. Oak's deep anchoring taproot stabilizes the tree, which symbolizes strength, long life, and steadfastness in many cultures. Six U.S. states and one Canadian province list oak as their official tree, and Congress named it the official U.S. national tree in 2004.

Oak leaves are simple and alternate on the branches; many have pointed or rounded lobes. Oaks crossbreed freely in the wild, so a particular tree may be hard to identify. In spring, oaks have male and female flowers on the same tree. Sure, oaks can be messy, shedding catkins, acorns, and leaves that annoy many homeowners, but they are manna from heaven to the wildlife eating their mast, or acorns, gathered on the ground and finding cover in their trunks, limbs, and foliage. They are ideal shade trees for large lawns and naturalized spaces.

There are two main groups of oaks. The red or black oak group has leaves with sharp, bristle-tipped divisions; trees in this group are easier to transplant because of their more fibrous roots. They bear acorns every 1 to 2 years. On the other hand, trees in the white oak group produce acorns every year and foliage with smooth, rounded lobes. Trees in this group have a deeper taproot and can therefore be challenging to transplant.

Oaks prefer full sun to partial shade; full sun is best for evergreens. Plant them in moist, rich, deep, well-drained soil; they prefer acid soil but most tolerate some alkalinity.

Probably the most reliable way to cultivate an oak is by planting acorns directly into well-drained soil. If you prefer starting oaks in containers, choose deep ones and transplant trees by the time they're 2 or 3 years old. Many species are hard to find in nurseries. If you buy balled-and-burlapped oaks from retail outlets, water and fertilize them for several years until they are well established. Plant acorns, seedlings, and balled-and-burlapped trees in spring. Depending upon the species, oaks may have a slow, medium, or fast growth rate. Most need plenty of space and sunlight to develop the characteristic widespread, weathered architecture of trunk and limbs.

Although generally tough and persistent, oaks may be troubled by powdery mildew, canker, leaf spot, leaf scorch, rust, root rot, twig blights, and anthracnose. *Phytopthora ramorum,* the sudden oak death pathogen, may also be a problem, particularly for white and chestnut oaks, according to early findings from several USDA research projects. Some oaks, including red, black, pin, shumard, and live oak, are vulnerable to oak wilt, mainly in the Midwest and Texas. Oaks in the white group are more tolerant of this disease. To prevent this fatal disease, which progresses from crumpling foliage to wilted brown-edged leaves into the inner tree, prune only when dormant or in mid- to late summer. Gypsy moths and various galls, scales, caterpillars, weevils, leaf miners, mites, and borers can also bother oaks, which tend to survive most problems. If you have questions, check with an arborist about pruning and preserving the tree.

For a fascinating study of oaks, check out *Oaks of North America* by Howard A. Miller and Samuel H. Lamb (see Appendix).

Quercus bicolor △ › ○

KWAYR-kus BI-co-lor

Swamp white oak

Beech Family (Fagaceae)
Deciduous tree
50'–60' h and w

Designated one of 1999's "Great Plants for the Great Plains" by the Nebraska Nursery and Landscape Association, this long-lived, rounded tree has saggy lower branches covered with 4"–8" × 2"–4", shiny, deciduous leaves with rounded lobes. Foliage is dark green above and whitish below with yellow to red fall color. The dark brown bark is peeling with deep grooves. Its 1" paired acorns are gleaming brown and attract wildlife.

LANDSCAPE USE
If you have the space, grow swamp white oak as a shade-giving lawn specimen.

ORIGIN   Floodplains of eastern North America.

HARDINESS ZONES   (3) 4–8

LIGHT   Full sun to partial shade; will not thrive in dark shade or polluted cities.

SOIL   Prefers swampy, acid soils, although it can withstand drier soils.

GROWING   Unlike white oak, swamp white oak is relatively easy to transplant because it lacks a deep taproot. While not as majestic as the white oak, it is slightly hardier.

Quercus bicolor

Quercus coccinea △ › ○

KWAYR-kus kok-SIN-ee-a

Scarlet oak

Beech Family (Fagaceae)
Deciduous tree
75' h × 50' w

Valued for its vivid red fall color, this fine oak is worth saving when you build a house or do construction on your lot. Early on, scarlet oak takes on a pyramidal shape similar to pin oak, growing more rounded in its prime. With great age, it develops an uneven and expansive crown.

Scarlet oak has simple, deciduous, glossy green leaves, set in an alternating pattern on the stem. The leaf lobes are pinnate, or featherlike, in arrangement. The leaves, which turn an intense red in fall and color up later than many oaks, stay on the tree into winter. Leaves cluster mostly at the twig tips. Young trees have grayish brown bark, but the bark on older trees turns gray-black and acquires uneven ridges. Male catkins and female spikes occur in spring at the same time the foliage unfurls. Every 2 years, it produces acorns up to 1" long and wide, sometimes paired, with a deep, close, shiny cap.

LANDSCAPE USE
Shade tree, lawn specimen. When possible, scarlet oak is worth saving during construction.

ORIGIN   Sandy acid soils in eastern and central U.S.

HARDINESS ZONES   4–7

LIGHT   Full sun.

SOIL   Prefers dry, sandy, acid soil.

GROWING   Less likely to develop iron chlorosis in high pH soils than pin oak. It's hard to transplant and can be messy in fall when acorns ripen.

Quercus coccinea

Quercus imbricaria △ › ○

KWAYR-kus im-bri-KA-ree-a

Shingle oak, Laurel oak

Beech Family (Fagaceae)
Deciduous tree
35'–65' h × 35'–70' w

Grown for its handsome, glossy, rich green leaves, laurel oak is a mid-sized tree that's equally at home in the city or the country. The 6" × 1½" deciduous leaves resemble laurel but turn bronze to russet in autumn. Young trees hold their leaves through winter. Male catkins are yellow; dark brown, ⅝" acorns occur every 2 to 4 years, creating less debris than many oak species. Shingle oaks are used for manufacturing shingles.

LANDSCAPE USE
See All About *Quercus*.

ORIGIN   Woods of central and eastern U.S.

HARDINESS ZONES   5–7

LIGHT   Full sun.

SOIL   Prefers moist, well-drained soils but tolerates dry soils and urban pollution.

GROWING   Slow to medium growth rate.

Quercus imbricaria

Quercus macrocarpa △ › ◯

KWAYR-kus mak-ro-KAR-pa

Bur oak, Mossy cup oak

Beech Family (Fagaceae)
Deciduous tree
70'–80' h and w

Although you'd probably grow bur oak for its adaptability, I like it for the acorns, which look like they have mullet haircuts. The acorns are big — up to 1½" long — and mostly covered with tight, bumpy caps edged in long, curly fringe. The fruits ripen every year from late summer through fall. At maturity, slow-growing bur oak has an interesting form with a big trunk and heavy, up-reaching limbs like arms stretching up to heaven. Its big leaves are up to 1' long, giving the tree a coarse texture in the landscape. The foliage has numerous small lobes decreasing in size toward the tip. Fall color is yellowish brown and nothing special.

LANDSCAPE USE
See All About *Quercus*.

ORIGIN   Central and eastern North America.

HARDINESS ZONES   3–8

LIGHT   Full sun.

SOIL   Tolerates most types of soils — wet or dry, acid or alkaline; withstands urban pollution.

GROWING   Can be a challenge to establish.

Quercus montana △ › ◯
(syn. Q. prinus)

KWAYR-kus mon-TAN-a

Chestnut oak, Rock oak, Mountain chestnut oak

Beech Family (Fagaceae)
Deciduous tree
60'–70' h x 60'–70' w

Although young trees appear low-branched and pyramidal, mature trees have rounded to irregular crowns with stunning, charcoal gray, bold-textured bark that contrasts high rough ridges with deep V-shaped furrows. Leaves are shiny green, pointed ovals with shallow lobes. Acorns attract wildlife.

LANDSCAPE USE
Attractive shade tree.

ORIGIN   On dry ridges and shallow wooded soils in the eastern U.S.

HARDINESS ZONES   4–8

LIGHT   Full sun.

SOIL   Moist to dry, well-drained, acid soil; intolerant of wet feet.

GROWING   Easy to transplant. See All About *Quercus* for pests and diseases.

Quercus muehlenbergii ◯

KWAYR-kus mu-len-BER-gee-i

Chinkapin oak, Yellow chestnut oak

Beech Family (Fagaceae)
Deciduous tree
40'–70' h x 50'–80' w

This adaptable native produces chestnutlike leaves with red to yellowish brown fall color and small-capped little acorns less than an inch in length that ripen each fall. Rough, flaky, gray bark covers the straight trunk of this mid-sized tree, which tends to be wider than tall with age. In youth, it grows at a medium rate, but it slows with age. Folks sometimes confuse the young tree with 9' tall, dwarf chinkapin oak (*Q. prinoides*) or with chestnut oak (*Q. montana*). The main difference between dwarf chinkapins and chestnut oaks is foliage, which on the former has pointed lobes and on the latter, rounded.

LANDSCAPE USE
Makes a healthy and attractive ornamental shade tree for lawns.

ORIGIN   Central and eastern North America, on alkaline limestone rock.

HARDINESS ZONES   4–7

LIGHT   Full sun.

SOIL   Tolerates soils from alkaline and acid to dry, clay, moist, wet, and loamy, but prefers limestone or alkaline soils.

GROWING   Can withstand environmental conditions such as moderate drought and urban pollution.

Quercus nigra ◯ ✳

KWAYR-kus NI-gra

Water oak, Possum oak, Spotted oak

Beech Family (Fagaceae)
Deciduous tree
50'–80' h x 30'–50' w

You can recognize water oak, a common tree in landscapes of the Southeast, by its even, rounded canopy and overall pleasing shape. Its dull bluish green leaves with bristle-tipped edges look like spatulas, wider toward the tip than the base. Leaves on saplings are often long and skinny. Although the water oak is deciduous, leaf drop in the South can come so late that the tree appears almost evergreen. Young trees have smooth, brown bark, which turns rough, ridged, and dark gray with maturity. Acorns attract wildlife.

LANDSCAPE USE

Used in southern landscapes as a shade tree or grouped in groves on large, moist properties. It grows fast and provides quick shade for new homes, but its lifespan can be as short as 60 years.

ORIGIN From stream banks to forest bottomlands in the southeastern U.S. and Coastal Plain.

HARDINESS ZONES 6–9 (10)

LIGHT Full sun.

SOIL Moist, well-drained loam to wet, silty clay soils, but tolerates most conditions, including drier locations and heavy compaction.

GROWING Intolerant of air pollution; subject to mistletoe parasite.

Quercus palustris △ ✳

KWAYR-kus pa-LUS-tris

Pin oak, Swamp oak

Beech Family (Fagaceae)
Deciduous tree
60′–70′ h x 30′–50′ w

A pin oak separates our land from that of our next-door neighbors'. Despite its annual leaf drop and occasional (every couple of years) drop of acorns, our pin oak is a desirable, attractive, mid-sized, symmetrical tree that we saved during the construction of our house. This fast-growing tree looks pyramidal with top limbs reaching upward, middle limbs growing horizontally, and the widespread bottom limbs drooping gracefully. It's no surprise that it thrives in our neighborhood, an area of wetlands and glacial till near Great Bay, an inlet of the Atlantic Ocean carved out millions of years ago by the glaciers. From the East to the Midwest, pin oaks occur naturally on such sites.

Pin oak produces 3"–6" leaves, shiny dark green on top, light green below, with 5–9 deeply cut lobes with a U-shaped space between each. Its fall color, which ranges from scarlet red to brown, is inconsistent. (Ours is typically warm golden brown.) The smooth, dark-grayish-brown bark acquires shallow fissures with age. Male flowers on catkins and female flowers on spikes appear when the leaves unfurl. The ½" acorns have short, flattish caps.

LANDSCAPE USE

Handsome shade tree for big lawns.

ORIGIN Wet woods of eastern U.S. and southeastern Canada.

HARDINESS ZONES 4–8

LIGHT Full sun.

SOIL Prefers moist, acid, well-drained soils, but tolerates swampy conditions and clay soils if not compacted. Beware of chlorosis (seen as light green leaves with dark green veins), a result of iron deficiency on soils with a high pH.

GROWING Pin oaks transplant well because of their fibrous roots, which are more developed on older trees. Trees are rather messy, but the leaves of my pin oak tend to stay near where they fall,

Quercus palustris

unlike my maples and beeches, whose leaves blow into my neighbors' yard.

DESIGNER'S CHOICE

Quercus palustris 'Pringreen' (Green Pillar) A fastigiate (narrow columnar) form with maroon fall color; an alternative for narrow city gardens or for its striking architectural shape. May also be sold as Emerald Pillar. 50′–60′ h × 12′–15′ w.

Quercus phellos △ › ○

KWAYR-kus FEI -los

Willow oak

Beech Family (Fagaceae)
Deciduous tree
40′–75′ h x 30′–60′ w

In the lower Mid-Atlantic states and in the South, willow oak is a popular street and lawn tree because of its handsome pyramidal to rounded habit, dense shady canopy, relatively fine texture, good health, and red to bronze fall color. This oak produces skinny, willowlike leaves up to 5½" long and an inch or less wide and small acorns up to ½" long. With age, the smooth, young bark develops deep, uneven grooves.

LANDSCAPE USE

Shade-giving lawn specimen or a street tree away from utility wires.

ORIGIN Native to moist and wet soils of the eastern U.S. as far north New Jersey and Pennsylvania.

HARDINESS ZONES 5–9

LIGHT Full sun.

SOIL Prefers moist, acid soils but can adjust to many situations.

GROWING In the South, willow oak grows fast (up to 2′ per year): in the North, it is slower growing. For hardiness, plant oaks from northern seed sources in its northern range. Its fibrous root system allows willow oak to establish more readily than many oak species, but twiggy branches are a trimming chore.

Quercus phellos

Quercus robur △ ▷ ◌

KWAYR-kus RO-bur

English oak, Truffle oak

Beech Family (Fagaceae)
Deciduous tree
60'–80' h x 50'–70' w

Although English oak is too big for the typical home landscape, some cultivars are worth growing in your garden. In Europe, these towering oaks can live more than 700 years and reach 120' high and more than half as wide. In gardens, it grows much smaller. The canopy is rounded and the trunk is short. Make sure you have ample space if you decide to grow the species.

The dark green, 5" × 3" leaves are similar to those of white oak and are attached to twigs by very short stems; the leaves turn brown in fall. The furrowed bark is a dark grayish brown. Male catkins and female spikes appear at the same time as the leaves in spring. The curious 1" acorns are shaped like extended ovals with a cap covering the acorn's top third. A stem, or peduncle up to 4 inches long attaches clusters of 2–3 acorns to the twigs.

LANDSCAPE USE

Good for large landscapes such as private estates and parks. Some cultivars work well in garden settings.

ORIGIN   Forests of Europe, western Asia, and northern Africa.

HARDINESS ZONES   5–8

LIGHT   Full sun.

SOIL   Prefers well-drained acid to alkaline soils.

GROWING   Withstands drought, urban pollution, and a limited root area. Although susceptible to many oak diseases, mildew is a frequent but not life-threatening complication.

CAUTION   May show invasive tendency in the State of Washington.

DESIGNER'S CHOICE

Quercus robur 'Asjes' ('Rosehill') Mildew-resistant tree with narrow, oval form; lustrous, bluish green leaves in summer turn yellow to yellow-brown in fall; likely hybrid with *Q. bicolor*. 60' h × 20' w.

Q. robur 'DTR 105' ('Attention') Mildew-resistant fastigiate cultivar. 60' h × 15' w.

Q. robur 'Concordia' (golden-leaved English oak) Slow-growing cultivar with foliage that opens yellow but may turn green during the summer. I have two young 'Concordias'. One retains its vibrant bright yellow hue and the other turns lime green. Site in partial shade to avoid leaf scorch. 60' h × 50' w.

Q. robur 'Fastigiata' (Skyrocket) Dense fastigiate habit with mildew resistance. 45' h × 15' w.

Quercus robur **'Fastigiata'**

Q. robus 'Michround' (Westminster Globe) Round, spreading, well-branched head on nice, mid-size shade tree; thrives in northern zones; use alone in small landscapes or grouped in larger ones. 45' h and w.

Q. robus 'Pyramich' (Skymaster) Mildew-resistant foliage on narrow to pyramidal tree with good main leader and branch angles. 60' h × 25'–30' w.

Quercus rubra ◌ ✳

(syn. Q. borealis, Q. rubra var. borealis)

KWAYR-kus RU-bra

Northern red oak

Beech Family (Fagaceae)
Deciduous tree
60'–90' h x 50'–70' w

This fast-growing oak, which adds about 2' in height per year, may be the state tree of New Jersey, but its range extends from southeastern Canada through much of the eastern U.S. Red oak develops a tall, straight

Quercus rubra

trunk and rounded crown with erect, widespread limbs.

Shiny, green leaves up to 8" × 6" turn different shades of red in autumn. The foliage has 7–11 lobes, each with a bristle at the tip. The bark is smooth when young, then deeply furrowed and brownish black with age. It produces male catkins and female spikes in the leaf axils. Acorns about 1" long with flattish cups occur alone or in clusters of 2–5.

LANDSCAPE USE
Specimen or shade tree for big lawns.

ORIGIN   Forests of eastern North America and the Appalachians.

HARDINESS ZONES   3–8

LIGHT   Full sun.

SOIL   Well-drained, dry, acid soils.

GROWING   Tolerates city living; easy to transplant; long lived; needs large space to thrive, as with pin oak, risk of chlorosis in high pH soils.

DESIGNER'S CHOICE
Quercus rubra 'Aurea' Bright yellow to chartreuse spring color turns green over time. 60'–70' h × 50' w.

Quercus shumardii △ › ◯

KWAYR-kus shu-MAR-dee-i
Shumard oak

Beech Family (Fagaceae)
Deciduous tree
40'–80' h x 40'–60' w; much bigger in the wild

This handsome oak is a versatile plant with leathery, green leaves and gray-brown ridged and furrowed bark. The foliage has a showy bronze to deep red fall color. Shumard oak is drought tolerant but you can also find it in wet soils.

LANDSCAPE USE
Specimen shade tree with rapid growth for large lawns.

ORIGIN   Southeastern and central U.S.

HARDINESS ZONES   5–9

LIGHT   See All About *Quercus*.

SOIL   See All About *Quercus*.

GROWING   Compared with many other oaks, chlorosis isn't a problem on alkaline soils. Shumard oak withstands salt, air pollution, and soil compaction. Abundant fruits make this a messy tree; easily transplanted.

Quercus velutina △ › ◯

KWAYR-kus ve-loo-TEE-na
Black oak

Beech Family (Fagaceae)
Deciduous tree
50'–60' (90' in very old age) h x 40' w

Grow black oak for its leaves, which open red, age to shiny green, and have a reddish brown fall color. Hairs on leaf bottoms rub off easily. The habit is pyramidal in youth to irregular and spreading with age. The blackish bark is deeply ridged and furrowed. *Velutina* (which means *velvety*), refers to the tree's fuzzy buds. Black oak can live up to 200 years. Birds, deer, and rodents eat the acorns.

LANDSCAPE USE
If you have black oak on your property, keep it as a mid-size shade tree.

ORIGIN   Eastern and central U.S., south-western Ontario in high, dry places, such as upland deciduous forests and transitional areas.

HARDINESS ZONES   3–9

LIGHT   Full sun.

SOIL   Moist, well-drained, acid soils; tolerates salt, wind, poor soils, and drought.

GROWING   Transplant when small because of tap root. Challenging to establish.. If one grows on your land, let it be. Performs best in the Midwest.

Quercus virginiana ◯

KWAYR-kus vir-gin-ee-AY-na
Live oak

Beech Family (Fagaceae)
Evergreen tree
40'–80' h x 60'–100' w

Live oak is irresistible for its grand picturesque presence and historical connotations. Draped with shaggy Spanish moss, they often flank entry roads of old plantations in the Deep South. Old specimens may have trunks more than 6' in diameter and widespread shallow roots. The vast, rounded crown has lower branches that dip to the ground, twisting up

Quercus virginiana

at the ends. The tree holds its shiny leaves until spring, when last season's foliage drops and new leaves reappear within weeks.

LANDSCAPE USE
See All About *Quercus*. Not for small properties.

ORIGIN   Moist soils in southeastern U.S.

HARDINESS ZONES   (7) 8–10

LIGHT   See All About *Quercus*.

SOIL   See All About *Quercus*; grows in moist compacted clay soils.

GROWING   See All About *Quercus*; good coastal tree because of salt tolerance.

RHAMNUS

Rhamnus cathartica 🌿 ✳

RAHM-nus ka-TAR-tee-ka

Common buckthorn, Hart's thorn, Waythorn, Rhineberry

Buckthorn Family (Rhamnaceae)
Deciduous shrub or small tree
20'–25' h x 15'–20' w

Buckthorn grows just about anywhere that birds drop its seeds. Depending upon how you prune it, buckthorn forms either a wide, suckering, rounded to irregular shrub or a low-branched, little tree. Twigs often have a sharp thorn at the tips. Although young bark is smooth and reddish brown, old plants have dark gray, blocky bark. The lustrous black fruits are small, profuse, showy, and consumed by birds.

LANDSCAPE USE
Typically planted for screens, hedgerows, and hedges.

ORIGIN   Europe, western and northern Asia.

HARDINESS ZONES   3–7

LIGHT   Full sun.

SOIL   Average to poor soils.

GROWING   This weedy, thicket-forming plant tolerates drought, pollution, and heavy pruning. Aphids, mildew, and leaf spots bother it.

CAUTION   Common buckthorn and glossy buckthorn (*Frangula alnus*) are considered invasive in wetlands, forests, and disturbed areas throughout most of the U.S. and parts of Canada. Sales are banned in Connecticut, Massachusetts, and New Hampshire. Instead of planting buckthorn for a wildlife-friendly shrub, substitute chokeberry (*Aronia*), blueberry (*Vaccinium*), or nannyberry (*Viburnum lentago*). If you want to grow buckthorn as a small deciduous tree, substitute Osage orange (*Maclura pomifera*), Cornelian cherry dogwood (*Cornus mas*), or another dogwood tree.

RHODODENDRON

Rhododendron species
▽ ◯ ◯ 🌿

ro-doh-DEN-dron

Rhododendron and azalea

Heath Family (Ericaceae)
Evergreen, semi-evergreen, and deciduous flowering shrubs or trees
3'–30' h and w

All types of *Rhododendron* have garden interest. In addition to lovely, sometimes fragrant flowers, evergreen rhododendrons and azaleas have foliage with year-round appeal, including red to mahogany winter color and interesting texture, which can be smooth and glossy or fuzzy with silver or bronzy hairs. Some deciduous azaleas produce leaves with excellent fall color. By choosing several species and hybrids, you can extend the rhododendron flowering period from early spring to late summer, depending on each plant's species or parentage. Another benefit of the genus is diversity of form, ranging from rock garden dwarfs to giant, treelike, background plants.

Rhododendrons and azaleas have alternate, simple leaves, which may be broad-leaf evergreen, semi-evergreen, or deciduous, depending upon the plant's species or parentage. Their bark is not ornamental. The white, pink, red, orange, peach,

ALL ABOUT RHODODENDRON

Rhododendrons have an almost magical garden presence in New England and the Pacific Northwest, where they grow best. "Evergreen rhododendrons add texture to the landscape not just in summer but particularly in winter," says Wayne Mezitt, chairman of Weston Nurseries in Hopkinton, Massachusetts, where many excellent rhododendron hybrids originate. "They're not stone and not conifers, but they have some substance and solidity to them and create structure in the garden." Summer-blooming deciduous azaleas have a different landscape value, believes Mezitt. "They're very hardy, they bloom when many woody shrubs have finished blooming, and some have excellent fall color."
The genus *Rhododendron* includes rhododendrons and both evergreen and deciduous azaleas, but knowing which is which can be tough. The American Rhododendron Society describes rhododendron leaves as more leathery than azaleas, which have thinner, more pliable foliage. Evergreen azaleas produce two sets of leaves, one in spring in conjunction with flowering and another thicker, smaller group in summer. Summer leaves stay on evergreens through winter, while deciduous azaleas drop foliage in fall. While buds at the stem tips of evergreens generate shoots and blooms, similar buds on deciduous types yield flowers alone.

yellow, blue, lavender, or purple flowers are usually funnel-shaped and arranged in small to large clusters. Most rhododendrons and azaleas flower for 2 weeks each year, although white-flowered *R. maximum, R. prunifolium, R. viscosum,* and *R.* 'Weston's Lemon Drop' bloom for 3 weeks, and Encore Azaleas flower twice a year, in spring and again in midsummer. Their fruits are not ornamental.

LANDSCAPE USE

These plants grow beautifully at the edge of the woods, where they receive enough sunlight for maximal blooms. Plant them in masses or groups to enhance the effect. Rhododendrons and azaleas look stunning in woodland gardens and shrub borders. Small varieties may sometimes work in foundation plantings, but make sure the soil is acidic enough for them to thrive.

ORIGIN   Mostly eastern U.S. and Asia, with many hybrids of garden origin.

HARDINESS ZONES   3–8, depending upon species.

LIGHT   Full sun to partial shade, depending upon the variety. Most do fine in partial shade.

SOIL   Light, moist, acid, well-drained, and well-aerated soils, high in acidic organic matter such as pine needles or composted oak leaves. Rhododendrons and azaleas prefer a pH of 5.5.

GROWING   Rhododendrons are shallow rooted, so make sure you plant them high, not buried deep below the soil surface. Water them regularly until they are established and use coarse organic mulch, such as chipped or shredded bark, around the base. Immediately after blooming, you can deadhead large-leaf plants by breaking off the truss or flower cluster. The plant will look neater, won't expend its energy setting seed, and will thus encourage heavier

flowering the following year. I usually don't have time to deadhead my large-leafed rhododendrons, however, and they still bloom beautifully the next spring. Don't bother deadheading small-flowered plants. Feed rhododendrons in later winter or early spring with a fertilizer made for acid-loving plants, following the package directions for rhododendrons and azaleas.

Many rhododendrons are too big for their sites. Choose plants according to their mature size and light requirements, so they won't obscure your windows without drastic pruning. Test the soil if you see new foliage turning yellow. Rhododendrons in foundation plantings may lack sufficient iron because the soil pH is high from limey mortar in the soil. Do a soil test and make the necessary adjustments to correct the imbalance.

DESIGNER'S CHOICE

More than 1000 species, hybrids, and cultivars exist, so choosing the right rhododendron or azalea for your site can be confusing. Using the categories of the American Rhododendron Society (ARS), I suggest several varieties to get you started. For a better knowledge of the genus, check the detailed and fascinating ARS

website, www.rhododendron.org.

LARGE-LEAFED RHODODENDRONS

These typically grow big. Most are hardy with flowers clusters and large, non-scaly, evergreen leaves. Large-leaf rhododendrons include the tough, tall, iron-clad cultivars of *R. catawbiense,* which produce flowers in tints of red, pink, white, and lilac purple. Another group, grown for leaves and blooms, are 'Yak' cultivars and hybrids from *R. degronianum* ssp. *yakushimanum.* Their new leaves may look silver to orangey on top because of colored hairs that disappear by late summer. Rust-colored hairs form a long-lasting, feltlike coat on the leaf bottoms for year-round effect. The Finnish hybrids from *R. brachycarpum* var. *tigerstedtii* tend to be very hardy, small, and wide.

R. 'Janet Blair'   Dexter hybrid, bred by C.O. Dexter of Sandwich, Massachusetts (Dexter hybrids are big, dense, well-branched shrubs with outstanding flowers); midseason bloomer with ball-shaped cluster of pale pink, lightly fragrant blooms with greenish-bronze flare on upper lobe; sun to shade. 6'–8' h and w. Zone 5.

R. 'Ken Janeck'   Cultivar of *yakushimanum;* midseason bloomer with big

Rhododendron 'Dora Amateis'

Rhododendron 'Scintillation'

trusses of 13–17 pale pink blooms that age to white; silvery flower buds give winter interest; thick tan fuzz on leaf bottoms; flourishes in much of the Midwest and Northeast; sun to shade. 3' h × 6' w. Zone 5.

R. maximum (rosebay rhododendron) Purplish pink to white flowers; big, leathery leaves tend to sag in winter; fast-growing, open shrub or small tree; excellent for naturalizing; partial to full shade; thicket-forming native of the eastern U.S. 5'–12' h and w. Zone 4 (some cultivars may be slightly hardier).

R. 'Scintillation' Dexter hybrid; mid-season bloomer with ball-shaped trusses of 11–15 pink flowers with small bronze flare; heat resistant. 5' h and w. Zone 5.

SMALL-LEAFED, OR EARLY, RHODODENDRONS

These tend to be low-growing, evergreen shrubs that bloom in early spring. Many have little leaves with scaly bottoms. Some Weston hybrids, developed by the Mezitt family at Weston Nurseries in Hopkinton, Massachusetts, are sun tolerant with aromatic leaves.

R. 'Dora Amateis' Clusters of 6–8, lightly fragrant, white flowers with greenish spotting in the throat; leaf bronze in full sun, prefers some shade; early midseason. Best in partial shade. 3' h × 6' w. Zone 5.

R. 'Ginny Gee' Compact habit; small, terminal clusters of wavy-lobed, white blooms with pink at the inner and outer edges; early spring bloomer. Prefers filtered light. Heat and drought resistant. ARS Superior Plant award. 2' h × 3' w. Zone 6.

R. mucronulatum (Manchurian azalea) Purplish pink flowers on an erect open deciduous shrub; early blooming; good fall color. 'Cornell Pink' has big, clear pink blooms. 4'–8' h and w. Zone 4.

R. 'Olga Mezitt' Dome-shaped clusters of bright pink flowers with rusty-speckled throats; bright green, aromatic leaves turn shiny mahogany in winter; blooms early midseason. Plant in full sun for best growth and shear young plants annually. Weston hybrid. 5'–8' h × 5'–8' w. Zones 4–8.

P. J. M. Group Showy, lavender-pink flowers, early bloomer; compact when young but grows big in shade or when unsheared; leaves turn dark mahogany in winter. Best in full sun. Weston hybrid. 4'–8' h and w. Zones 4–8.

Rhododendron mucronulatum 'Cornell Pink'

R. 'Weston's Aglo' (syn. *R.* 'Aglo') Ball-shaped trusses of funnel-shaped, pink flowers, blooms early mid-season; scented leaves turn deep bronze in winter; fast-growing plant, mounded when young but taller when mature. Plant in full sun for best growth and shear young plants annually. 3'–7' h and w. Zones 4–8.

R. 'Weston's Pink Diamond' Double, true pink flowers on a semi-evergreen plant with outstanding fall color. Wayne Mezitt says it's the earliest blooming rhododendron at Weston Nurseries, one to two weeks earlier than PJM. 8' h and w. Zone 5.

DECIDUOUS AZALEAS

These upright-growing shrubs bloom mostly in June, though some of the newer Weston hybrids flower in summer up to the beginning of August.

R. 'Gibraltar' Ball-shaped trusses of 10–12, frilly, orange flowers on an upright shrub. A Knap Hill hybrid bred at Anthony Waterer's Knap Hill Nursery in Surrey, England; these hybrids are known for their yellow, orange, red, pink, or cream flowers. 5' h and w. Zones 5 7.

Rhododendron 'Olga Mezitt'

R. Northern Lights Series Flowers are showy; some cultivars fragrant. All cultivar names include the word *lights*, and there are many cultivars, including light pink 'Pink Lights', 'White Lights', 'Golden Lights', and 'Northern Hi-Lights', with bicolor creamy white and bright yellow blooms, red fall color, and some mildew resistance. Bred at the University of Minnesota. 4'–8' h and w. Zones (2) 3.

R. *schlippenbachii* (royal azalea) Trusses of 3–6, funnel-shaped, pink flowers, early midseason; shrub or small tree; good fall color in sun; native to China and Korea. 4'–15' h and w. Zones 5–8.

Rhododendron schlippenbachii

EASTERN NORTH AMERICA NATIVES

R. *arborescens* (sweet azalea, smooth azalea) White, perfumed, funnel-shaped flowers with reddish style and stamens, blooms late to very late; part shade, red fall color, needs moist soil; native to stream banks of eastern North America. 5'–20' h and w. Zones 4–7.

R. *atlanticum* (dwarf azalea, coast azalea) Fragrant pale pink to white flowers, midseason; deciduous, spreading habit; native to pine barrens of eastern North America, sun to shade. 3' h and w. Zones 5–8.

R. *austrinum* (orange azalea, Florida flame azalea) Yellow to orange, funnel-shaped, fragrant flowers in big clusters on a medium-sized, twiggy shrub, early midseason; partial shade and moist-well drained soils with some drought tolerance; eastern North America. 5'–12' h and w. Zones 6–9.

R. *calendulaceum* (flame azalea) Big, flashy flowers in orange, red, and yellow, midseason or later; occasional light yellow fall color; shade to partial shade; used to breed Exbury hybrids, eastern North America. 5'–8' h and w. Zones (4) 5–8.

R. *canescens* (hoary azalea, Florida pinxter azalea) Lightly fragrant, pale to deep pink flowers, rarely white, with stamen twice the length of the sticky floral tube, blooms early midseason; slow-growing tall shrub or small tree; eastern North America. 5'–15' h × 5'–6' w. Zones 6–9.

R. *periclymenoides* (pinxterbloom azalea) Funnel-shaped, slightly fragrant, pink flowers similar to R. *canescens,* blooms midspring as leaves expand; eastern North America. 4'–6' h × 8'–10' w. Zones (4) 5–8.

R. *prinophyllum* (syn. R. *roseum*) (roseshell azalea) Terminal clusters of 5–9, pink, tubular, clove-scented flowers, midseason; slow growing; brilliant scarlet fall color; New England native; parent of the Northern Lights Series of hardy azaleas. 6' h and w. Zone (3) 4–8.

R. *prunifolium* (plumleaf azalea) Orange to red tubular flowers in late summer; needs afternoon shade. 8'–12' h × 6'–8' w. Zone 6.

R. *vaseyi* (pink shell azalea) Graceful pink to white clustered blossoms before leaves, blooms early midseason; red fall color; upright spreading shrub, eastern North America. 5'–10' h and w. Zones 5–8.

Rhododendron calendulaceum

Rhododendron prunifolium

R. vaseyi 'White Find' Fragrant white flowers with yellow spots. 4'–6' h and w. Zone 5.

R. viscosum (swamp azalea) White to light pink, fragrant flowers with sticky tubes and greenish stamens, very late blooming; eastern North America. 8' h and w. Zones 4–8.

EVERGREEN AZALEAS

R. 'Delaware Valley White' White flowers in early midseason; open spreading habit; *mucronatum* hybrid. 3' h × 4' w. Zones (5) 6–8.

R. 'Hino Crimson' Glowing crimson red flowers, early midseason to midseason bloom; dark green leaves turning deep red in cold weather; Kurume hybrid from the southernmost island of Japan. 2'–4' h and w. Zone 7.

R. kaempferi (torch azalea) Upright, semi-evergreen shrub with trusses of 2–4 flowers in shades of red, blooms midseason; from Japan. 10' h × 5' w. Zones (5) 6–9.

R. kiusianum var. *kiusianum* (Kyushu azalea) Funnel-shaped flowers in pink, purple, or white, midseason; from Japan; semi-evergreen shrub that grows best in full sun. 4' h and w. Zones (5) 6–9.

R. 'Stewartstonian' Clusters of two, bright red flowers on a mid- to late-blooming dense shrub with glossy green leaves that turn wine red in winter. Gable hybrid bred by Joseph Gable of Stewartstown, Pennsylvania; notable for cold hardiness and drought and heat tolerance. 5' h and w. Zones 5–8.

R. yedoense var. *poukhanense* (Korean azalea) Rose pink to pale lilac purple clustered flowers bloom early midseason; deciduous in cold climates. 3'–6' h × 4'–6' w. Zones 5–8.

ENCORE AZALEA COLLECTION

A relatively new group of evergreen, compact hybrids hardy in Zones 7–9

***Rhododendron* 'Delaware Valley White'**

that flower in spring and again in midsummer or fall. Foliage is green in summer and purple in winter. Plants prefer northern or eastern exposure with morning sun and afternoon shade. Dozens of cultivars, including pink 'Conlef' (Autumn Cheer) (3' h × 3½' w); *R.* 'Conled' (Autumn Coral), light orange-pink with fuchsia center and a prolific bloomer (2½' h × 3' w); white 'Robler' (Autumn Moonlight) (5' h × 4' w)); and purple 'Conlec' (Autumn Royalty), an ARS Rhododendron of the Year (4' h × 4½' w).

RHODOTYPOS

Rhodotypos scandens ○ ✳

ro-doh-TEE-pos SKAN-denz

Black jetbead

Rose Family (Rosaceae)
Deciduous flowering shrub
4'–6' h × 4'–8' w

At first glance, straggly, suckering black jetbead won't attract much attention. But if you plant it where most other plants won't grow, it will do the job. The 1½", 4-petal blooms and glossy, beadlike fruits that appear in clusters of 3 and 4 aren't showy; nor is the fall color, which ranges from light yellow to yellowish green.

LANDSCAPE USE

As a shrub border away from your house for summer screening; give it room to sucker and spread.

ORIGIN Japan and central China.

HARDINESS ZONES 4–8

LIGHT Full sun to full shade.

SOIL Any pH; moist or dry soils.

GROWING Fast growing; tolerates pollution and is pest and disease resistant.

CAUTION Potentially invasive in Delaware, Illinois, Massachusetts, Michigan, New York, Virginia, and Wisconsin. In questionable areas,

---

EXTENDING THE FLOWERING SEASON WITH RHODIES

With a little planning, you can extend your rhododendron flowering season from early spring to midsummer, suggests Wayne Mezitt of Weston Nurseries. *R. mucronulatum* 'Cornell Pink' starts flowering in early April in Mezitt's Zone 6 Massachusetts garden, followed by double-pink 'Weston's Pink Diamond' in mid-April, and lavender-pink *R.* 'PJM' the last week of the month. Large-leafed 'Ken Janeck' and 'Scintillation' take you through the month of May, followed by *R. maximum* the first three weeks in June. Bicolor 'Ribbon Candy', a deciduous pink-and-white-striped fragrant azalea with burgundy fall leaves, blooms at the end of June, while *R. prunifolium* and *R.* 'Weston's Lemon Drop' display orange and yellow blooms, respectively, for the first three weeks of July. Soft pink, sweetly fragrant 'Pennsylvania' starts blooming the third week of July and its leaves turn coppery yellow in fall.

ROSA ○ ○ ⌂

ALL ABOUT ROSA

The reason for growing these prickly plants, of course, is all about flowers. Blooms may be as small as a dime or as big as a fat peach and come in most hues but blue and black. Once-blooming roses usually flower profusely in early summer; repeat bloomers flower less but for a longer time. Roses come in a wide range of hardiness (Zones 2–9, depending upon the particular species or cultivar), as well as in a variety of sizes, from 6″ to 12″ micro-minis to the 15′ tall and wide, tangled, multiflora rose I saw at my friend Susan's country house in upstate New York.

Some time back, we hired Jason, a teenage neighbor, to rid our garden of roses. I'd grown some modern shrub and once-blooming old varieties and found myself too busy to keep up with their demands. Although my roses were vigorous, some got blackspot in summer and all but one attracted Japanese beetles that ate the leaves and mated in the flowers. So why am I writing about roses now? I never give up. Many roses are being developed and tested for landscape use. For instance, I've heard so many good stories from clients and fellow garden writers about Knock Out roses that I'm trying some myself. Moreover, my favorite rose, *R. glauca,* has brought me nothing but joy for the last 10 years.

What follows are a few tough roses that solve some specific landscape problems. I've chosen a tiny sampling of this vast genus, mostly easy-to-grow shrubs that do well in many areas of the country. Roses — elegant high-maintenance hybrid teas, romantic climbers, sweet miniatures, divinely fragrant old garden roses, and more — deserve a book of their own. To learn about the multitude of roses you can grow and the ins and outs of growing them, I suggest joining the American Rose Society. You'll find the address in the Appendix.

Roses can be high-maintenance plants requiring regular feeding, spraying for insects and diseases, and pruning. Problems include black spot, powdery mildew, rust and rose rosette; apply fungicide regularly in humid climates.

Test soil before planting roses and every three years afterwards to check on soil pH and nutrient levels. Work 2″ to 4″ of organic matter, such as well-rotted compost or manure, into rose beds before planting. Organic matter contains nutrients and improves drainage and soil texture. Give roses an extra boost with commercial rose food according to package directions. Maintain an acid to neutral pH from 5.5 to 7.0 by adding lime or sulfur to the soil.

When needed, prune roses during dormancy with sharp, disinfected clippers to remove deadwood, promote growth, and improve the form. Get rid of inward-growing canes, making pruning cuts at a 45° angle ¼″ above an out-facing bud or cane for good air circulation. On grafted roses, cut off all suckers originating below the bud union (the swelling on the main stem where the grafted bud joins the rootstock; see page 146). Planting the bud union 2″–4″ below the soil surface helps reduce suckering from the understock.

In cold climates, before the soil freezes but after killing frost, prune hybrid tea roses, floribundas, and grandifloras back to roughly 3′ tall, clearing away all cut stems and dropped leaves. Tie the cane tips together and pile a foot of mulch at the base of the tied branches. If you have rodents, use soil or compost instead, as this provides a less attractive home for them. After lifting climbing roses off their support, set them on the ground and cover with a few inches of soil.

Deadhead faded flowers to promote more flowering. Water from below in the morning, keeping the ground mulched to retain moisture. Read up on roses and consult your Cooperative Extension service before you buy them.

Rosa 'Radrazz'

Rosa species

DESIGNER'S CHOICE

A small sampling of roses:

Rosa banksiae 'Lutea' (Lady Banks yellow rose) Light yellow, double flowers in late spring on long, thornless, arching canes suited for rambling on sunny slopes and walls or training to a support; evergreen leaves in warmest areas of range; semi-evergreen in coolest spots. As shrub, 12' h × 6'–12' w; as climber, 20' h × 6'–12' w. Zones 8–10.

R. glauca (syn. *R. rubrifolia*) (red leaf rose) Upright and arching, with red-tinged, prickled canes and plum-gray leaves, singular among rose species. Single, bright pink flowers with white centers and a crown of primrose yellow stamens are scattered on the shrub in early summer, followed by scarlet, oval hips. Well-suited for hedging, woodland planting, and shrub borders. Grows in full sun to partial shade; prefers moist, fertile, well-drained soils with plenty of organic matter, but tolerates drought once established. 4'–6' h × 2'–5' w. Zones 2–7.

R. 'Radrazz' (Knock Out) An ever-blooming, very popular shrub rose grown for its 5–11 petal, 3½", cherry red flowers. Once established, low-maintenance 'Knock Out', a 2000 All-America Rose Selection winner, tolerates heat, drought, cold, humidity, and a half-day of shade.

Rosa 'William Baffin'

Its compact habit, mild tea rose fragrance, orangey red hips, and burgundy-violet fall foliage lend themselves to mass plantings and mixed borders of shrubs and flowers. Grow in full sun to partial shade, in moist, well-drained to dry soil. The tough, glossy, dark green leaves may resist both disease and Japanese beetle attacks. Doesn't need deadheading to bud and bloom again. In addition to red Knock Out, light-pink, semi-double Blushing Knock Out, medium-pink Pink Knock Out, and cerise Double Knock Out are all available. 3' h and w. Zones (4) 5–7.

R. rugosa 'Rubra' (beach rose) A hardy rose with 3", single, mauve flowers; edible, showy, 1", red hips; and prickly, suckering stems. Shape this bush into a dense spiky hedge or use as a barrier or for erosion control; it tolerates harsh seaside conditions including salt, poor sandy soils, wind, and even some shade. Prefers full sun and well-drained acid soil; tolerates drought and a wide range of pH. Invasive in Connecticut, New Jersey, New York, Rhode Island, and Washington. 'Alba', the white form, is equally tough and has 3½"–4" blooms. 'Rubra' is 4'–6' h × 6' w. Zones 2–7.

Explorer Series An excellent group of more than 20, super-hardy, vigorous Canadian hybrids resistant to pests and diseases, with mostly pink or red, semi-double blooms. Examples include 'David Thompson', a *rugosa* hybrid with fragrant, medium-red blooms reliably recurrent from June until hard frost and little scarlet hips into winter; hardy to Zone 2; 'Jens Munk', a vigorous *rugosa* hybrid, with medium pink, double blooms and showy, yellow stamens; compact

Rosa glauca

WHEN BEAUTY IS ONLY SURFACE DEEP

Invasive *R. multiflora* has spread amok throughout the U.S., except for deserts, Rocky Mountains, and southeastern Coastal Plain. That beachside regular, *R. rugosa*, has escaped gardens and naturalized in Washington and along parts of the East Coast (where it's considered invasive) and the central and upper Midwest. Some other species roses have escaped from gardens into the wild. The National Park Service link, *www.nps.gov/plants/alien/list/a.htm*, lists several other rose species and the states where they are problematical.

size 3'–4' h × 4'–6' w; tolerates shade and poor soils. It is a good choice for low hedging, ground covering, and woodland planting; medium red 'Henry Kelsey', medium-red 'John Cabot', and deep pink 'William Baffin' have long arching canes that you can train to trellises or grow as wide shrubs about 8' h × 6' w. Resistant (not immune) to black spot, powdery mildew, rust and rose rosette; apply fungicide regularly in humid climates.

ROSMARINUS

Rosmarinus officinalis ○ ✳

ros-ma-RI-nus of-fi-si-NAL-is

Rosemary

Mint Family (Lamiaceae)
Evergreen shrub
2'–6' h and w

In hot, dry climates, rosemary belongs not only in herb gardens but also in shrub borders and perennial beds. Its gray-green, linear leaves, which are fragrant year round,

Rosmarinus officinalis

can enhance both xeriscape and Mediterranean-style gardens with warm summers and dry mild winters. You can buy upright or prostrate cultivars of this deer-resistant plant. White, pink, and light or dark purplish-blue flowers cluster in the leaf axils from fall to spring. Harvest branch tips for crafts and cooking whenever you like.

LANDSCAPE USE

Herb gardens, shrub and perennial borders, xeriscape and Mediterranean-style gardens, excellent in containers.

ORIGIN   Sharply drained soils around the Mediterranean Sea.

HARDINESS ZONES   (7) 8–10

LIGHT   Full sun.

SOIL   Neutral to alkaline, light gravelly soil with low to average moisture and sharp drainage. Established plants have good drought tolerance.

GROWING   If you prefer a more formal look, you can prune rosemary into a short hedge or cut back individual stems to keep plants from straggling. Leave 2'–3' between grouped plants. Or, train into a ball-shaped topiary standard. In the North, grow in containers and overwinter indoors. May get root rot in wet, poorly drained conditions, or powdery mildew in humid conditions.

DESIGNER'S CHOICE

Rosmarinus officinalis 'Arp' The hardiest cultivar. 2'–5' h and w. Zone 7.

R. officinalis 'Lockwood de Forest' Creeping form with dense leaves, profuse light blue flowers, excellent trailing groundcover for rocks, walls, and steep slopes. 2' h × 6'–8' w.

R. officinalis 'Majorca Pink' Lavender-pink blooms; grows erect. 3'–4' h × 2' w.

R. officinalis 'Tuscan Blue' Broader leaves, big lavender-blue flowers, and a stiff, upright habit good for hedging. 4'–6' h × 4'–5' w.

Rubus cockburnianus 'Wyego' ☁ ✳

ROO-bus co-bur-nee-AY-nus

Golden Vale white-stemmed bramble

Rose Family (Rosaceae)
Deciduous suckering shrub
3'–4' h and w

'Wyego' has gleaming yellow spring leaves that green up as summer progresses and an arching habit. Like its relative, the raspberry, white-stemmed bramble is prickly and spreads by suckers. One winter in England, I saw an inspired, wide-open pondside planting where gardeners contrasted an otherworldly mass of white-stemmed brambles with a large group of red-twig dogwood (*Cornus sericea* 'Isanti') and a smaller planting of yellow-twig dogwood (*C. sericea* 'Budd's Yellow'). Wow.

LANDSCAPE USE

Winter interest, impenetrable hedge.

ORIGIN   North and central China.

HARDINESS ZONES   6–8

LIGHT   Full sun for best leaf color.

SOIL   Prefers light, well-drained, sandy soil of moderate fertility; adaptable to most soils.

GROWING   After flowering, prune back to out-facing buds or young stems; renew by pruning one-fourth of old canes to the base. Watch out for gray mold (botrytis).

CAUTION   Grow prickly, white-stemmed bramble in large spaces and check for invasiveness with your local cooperative extension. Hard to find.

Salix alba 'Chermesina' ○
(syn. *S. alba britzensis*)

SAY-liks AL-ba

Coral bark willow, White willow

Willow Family (Salicaceae)
Deciduous shrub or small tree
40' h and 30' w

Grown for its ornamental, scarlet winter bark, coral bark willow grows best in moist loam. Usually coppiced and maintained as a shrub in order to obtain the young, bright orangey red winter stems. Old stems turn yellowish brown.

LANDSCAPE USE
Focal point in a winter garden; grouped or massed by ponds; use uncoppiced full-size plants for shade trees or windbreaks.

ORIGIN   Species from Europe, North Africa, Central Asia; this clone originated in Germany.

HARDINESS ZONES   2–8

LIGHT   See All About *Salix*.

SOIL   See All About *Salix*.

GROWING   Since older stems are duller in hue, prune this male willow clone back hard every year or two in early spring to keep it producing young shoots with vivid coral red bark.

Salix alba 'Chermesina'

ALL ABOUT SALIX

Willows can be trees, shrubs, or woody groundcovers. They grow in moist or wet soils throughout North America. The leaves are usually narrow, like lances. Male and female flowers are catkins that occur on separate trees. The catkins, especially on soft and fuzzy pussy willows, may contribute to the plant's decorative value because they appear before or while the leaves unfold. All of the willows I describe below possess ornamental qualities. Willows contain a compound called salicin, similar to the active ingredient in current-day painkillers, and Native Americans used willow for this purpose.

Willows prefer deep, moist, fertile loam but many tolerate poor soils. They prefer moderately alkaline soil, although fairly adaptable. Most are fast growing and short lived. Problems besetting willows include aphids, caterpillars, leaf beetles, sawflies, anthracnose, scab, and rust. Because their suckering roots can create thick stands and interfere with water-management systems, keep them far from sewers, septic systems, and water supplies. Their weak brittle wood causes twigs and branches to break in winter, storms, and wind. Thus, you may need to prune willows with regularity to keep them neat and their ornamental qualities intact. Tree willows can be cut back to the same point each year (pollarded) to keep in bounds and shapely; shrub willows can be cut back to the ground (stooled or coppiced) each spring (see pages 103–118 for further information on these pruning techniques). I'll discuss tree and shrub willows separately, though some belong in both groups (for example, coral bark willow, a tree that is usually grown as a shrub). Shrubs appear under Designer's Choice.

CAUTION   Can be invasive in some areas.

DESIGNER'S CHOICE
Salix alba subsp. *vitellina* (golden willow)   Bright yellow winter stems. 40' h × 30' w.

Salix babylonica 'Crispa' ⊚
(syn. *S. babylonica* 'Annularis')

SAY-liks ba-bi-LAH-ni-ka

'Crispa' weeping willow, Weeping willow

Willow Family (Salicaceae)
Deciduous tree
40' h x 30'–40' w

Although the flowing rounded habit of Crispa weeping willow offers year-round interest, it is particularly delightful in summer because of its narrow, curly, green leaves that twist into tight coils. Cut stems make a terrific addition to summer flower arrangements, or you can display them in a vase on their own.

LANDSCAPE USE
Graceful specimen in moist to wet soil; grouped and coppiced in moist to wet shrub borders for a 5'–6'-high planting.

ORIGIN   Northern China

HARDINESS ZONES   6–9

LIGHT   See All About *Salix*.

SOIL   See All About *Salix*.

GROWING   See All About *Salix*.

DESIGNER'S CHOICE
S. babylonica var. *pekinensis* 'Tortuosa' (syn. *S. babylonica* 'Tortuosa', *S. matsudana* 'Tortuosa') (corkscrew willow, contorted willow, dragon claw willow)   Wide oval tree with upright,

gnarly, green stems and branches; bright green, twisted leaves with yellow fall color; great for moist sites. Hybrid *S.* 'Erythroflexuosa' (syn. *S.* 'Golden Curls') is similar in all ways except for bright gold winter bark. 30'–40' h × 20'–25' w. Zones (4) 5–9.

Salix × *sepulcralis* 'Chrysocoma' 🔊
(syn. *S. alba* 'Tristis', *S. alba vitellina pendula*, *S. chrysocoma*, *S. vitellina* 'Pendula')

SAY-liks se-pul-KRA-lis

Golden weeping willow, Niobe weeping willow

Willow Family (Salicaceae)
Deciduous tree
40'–50' h and w

Weeping willows are trees of imagination and romance. They offer year-round interest, thanks to their graceful, weeping habit with drooping yellow branches in winter; bright green, dangling summer leaves; and yellow fall color. Leaves are skinny, bright green, and about 5" long, while flowers are 2" catkins appearing with foliage in spring. In autumn, the leaves turn yellow before dropping. Winter interest comes from the tree's bare golden stems. Golden willow grows fast, about 10' per year. This is the weeping willow commonly found in gardens.

LANDSCAPE USE
Looks best planted by a pond, where the surface can reflect its flowing form.

ORIGIN Garden hybrid

HARDINESS ZONES 4–9

LIGHT See All About *Salix*.

SOIL Needs moist planting site for healthy growth.

GROWING See All About *Salix*.

CAUTION Invasive tendencies in Connecticut, District of Columbia, Illinois, North Carolina, New York, Oregon, Washington, and West Virginia, according to the National Park Service's Plant Conservation Alliance.

DESIGNER'S CHOICE
Salix caprea 'Kilmarnock' (syn. *S. caprea pendula*) (weeping goat or pussy willow) This native of Europe and Asia has big, silky catkins in early spring. Sometimes grafted on a standard, it makes a nice border accent or small-space specimen. This species does not require a particularly moist to wet site. A male clone, similar to the often-found female clone 'Weeping Sally', which is less effective for flowers. 5'–6' h × 5'–8' w. Zones 4–8.

S. cinerea 'Tricolor' (variegated gray willow) Shrubby willow with dull green leaves marbled with pink-and-cream variegation; grows about 2' per year in both marshy and drier conditions. Use for screening, or sheared and informal unpruned hedges. Can be invasive in some areras. 7'–15' h and w. Zones 2–7.

S. discolor (pussy willow) Native to wet spots in the eastern U.S. Grown for the gray male 1" catkins born in mid- to late spring on bare, dark brown branches; prone to canker so no good for gardens, but useful for pond and stream bank stabilizaton; may be present in wet, wild depressions on your land. 10'–15' h × 8'–10' w. Zones 2–7.

S. elaeagnos 'Angustifolia' (syn. *S. elaeagnos lavandulifolia*, *S. elaeagnos rosmarinifolia*, *S. rosmarinifolia* (rosemary willow) Grow for its linear 8" rosemary-like leaves that are deep, shiny green above and felted white below; yellow fall color; keep the shrub in shape with hard pruning. Very attractive fine texture and moderate drought tolerance. 5'–10' h and w. Zones 4–7.

Salix elaeagnos 'Angustifolia'

S. 'Flame' Multi-stemmed willow with orangey red stems in summer and winter; bright yellow fall color against the flame red stems; compact oval crown with upturned branch tips; prefers ample moisture but pH adaptable. To keep it in shape, prune lightly by removing selected branches. 15'–20' h × 10'–15' w. Zones 3–7.

S. gracilistyla 'Melanostachys' (black pussy willow) Grow for showy deep brown to black catkins contrasting with orange pollen-bearing stalks that show up against spring snows; excellent slow-growing shrub for erosion control on banks or small spaces with moist, fertile soil; control habit by selectively pruning stems. 5'–10' h × 6' w. Zones 5–8.

S. integra 'Hakuro-nishiki' (dappled willow, variegated willow) Four seasons of interest: pink and white young leaves are dappled with green, mature leaves are white-streaked gray-green, red winter stems, and pendant catkins in early spring. Plant against dark evergreen background and prune in late winter or early spring to encourage colorful shoot and foliage display. 5'–10' h × 3'–10' w. Zones 4–8.

S. 'Prairie Cascade' No catkins; a fast-growing, weeping shade tree with yellow stems; 3"–5", glossy, green leaves; introduced from Morden, Manitoba. Too big for most home landscapes, but good for large properties with ponds or low lands. 35' h and w. Zones 3–5.

S. purpurea 'Nana' (dwarf arctic willow, purple osier willow) Finely branched multi-stemmed compact shrub with tiny, bluegreen leaves and mounded shape; yellow-green autumn leaves; maroon new growth; adaptable and moderately drought tolerant; prunes easily for a refined formal look. 3'–6' h and w. Zones 4–6.

Salix integra 'Hakuro-nishiki'

Salix purpurea 'Nana'

SAMBUCUS

Sambucus canadensis ⚘ ✳

sam-BOO-kus kan-a-DEN-sis

Elderberry, American elder

Viburnum Family (Caprifoliaceae)
Deciduous flowering shrub
10'–15' h and w

Although this tough American native has a coarse landscape texture, it is effective when planted in a mass. It is valued for its jumbo, flat-topped, flower clusters that appear in June (later than its European relative) and its huge, shiny, black berry clusters from July through September that attract numerous bees, butterflies, and at least 50 types of birds. Although the raw fruits taste bad and contain poisonous compounds in small amounts, the cooked fruits taste better.

The featherlike foliage is opposite and comprised of 1' leaves with 5–9, green leaflets that smell rank when crushed. The bark is corky with warty lenticels. Elderberry produces huge, compound clusters of tiny, white flowers in June and July. The glossy, blue-black fruits are high in vitamin C and are cooked to make jams, jellies, and wine.

LANDSCAPE USE
Naturalistic borders with grasses and coneflowers, edible borders, and wildlife gardens; grow plants with interesting foliage as specimens.

ORIGIN Banks, roadsides, and edge of woodlands in eastern North America.

HARDINESS ZONES (3) 4–9

LIGHT Full sun to partial shade.

SOIL Prefers fertile, moist, well-drained soil but adapts to most conditions.

GROWING Cut back hard in early spring to promote more compact growth and discourage legginess. It is mostly free of pests and diseases. It possibly, though rarely, is affected by powdery mildew.

Growth can be straggly and suckering.

CAUTION The stems and leaves are poisonous for humans and livestock to eat. Eating raw fruit can also upset your stomach.

DESIGNER'S CHOICE
Sambucus canadensis 'Aurea' Red berries and lime-yellow leaves, tolerates wet soils, grows fast. Cut back hard in early spring to produce an abundance of fresh golden leaves. 8'–10' h × 8'–12' w.

S. canadensis 'Laciniata' Deeply cut, lacy leaves. 8' h and w.

S. canadensis 'Maxima' Massive flower heads 15"–18" wide. 8'–10' h and w.

S. canadensis 'York' Most abundant and biggest berries of cultivated elderberries; plant more than one cultivar to improve fruit set. 10'–12' h × 8'–12' w.

Sambucus nigra ○ ✳

sam-BOO-kus NI-gra

European black elderberry

Viburnum Family (Caprifoliaceae)
Deciduous flowering shrub or small tree
15'–30' h × 15' w

European black elderberry produces attractive spring flowers, followed by blackish fruits in summer to fall.

LANDSCAPE USE
See *S. canadensis.*

ORIGIN Woods and hedgerows of Europe, north Africa, and western Asia.

HARDINESS ZONES 4–7

LIGHT See *S. canadensis.*

SOIL See *S. canadensis.*

GROWING This shrub can grow tree-size unless you cut it back hard in early spring. By pruning, you can keep growth dense and in check.

CAUTION The stems and leaves are poisonous for humans and livestock to eat. Eating raw fruit can also upset your stomach.

Sassafras albidum

LANDSCAPE USE
Perfect tree for woodland gardens and transitional plantings at forest edges.

ORIGIN Forests and thickets in Eastern North America.

HARDINESS ZONES 5–9

LIGHT Full sun to partial shade.

SOIL Moist, acid, well-drained loam; also grows well in sandy or rocky soils.

GROWING Hard to establish when dug from the wild because of taproot. Try container-grown trees and transplant them in early spring.

CAUTION Root oil can cause illness and abortion and has been shown to cause cancer in mice, so is now banned by the FDA. Do not ingest. (Root beer is safe because it uses artificial spices.)

SCIADOPITYS

Sciadopitys verticillata △
(syn. *Podocarpus verticilolatus*)

sigh-a-DAH-pi-teez ver-ti-sil-LAH-ta

Umbrella pine, Japanese umbrella pine

Umbrella Pine Family (Sciadopityaceae; formerly Taxodiaceae)
Small to mid-sized evergreen conifer
20'–40' h x 15'–20' w

At first glance, young umbrella pines look like little plastic Christmas trees. They grow slowly, forming a dense, single- or multi-trunk, pyramidal tree of shiny evergreen needles year round. As these long-lived trees mature, their conical form opens up so the habit is less dense. The Japanese make boats from the spicily fragrant, water-resistant wood.

The foliage appears in terminal whorls of about 25, rich green, glossy, 2"–5" needles; small scaly leaves appear around shoots below the whorls. The cultivar 'Winter Green' stays green and shiny through winter, but at least in my Zone 5 garden the species remains just as perfect. The bark is orangey brown and shredding. Clustered male and solitary female flowers exist on the same plant. Fruits are 2"–4", brown, scaly cones when ripe. This conifer is the only species in this genus and has no close relatives; it has been found in fossils dating back 230 million years.

LANDSCAPE USE
Umbrella pine's unusual glossy leaves make a grand statement in the garden. Use as a landscape specimen or a striking addition to mixed conifer borders.

ORIGIN Mountains of Japan.

HARDINESS ZONES 5–7

LIGHT Full sun.

SOIL Moist, fertile, well-drained acid soils.

GROWING Plant where protected from winter winds. Umbrella pine is susceptible to wind damage in winter. Intolerant of drought and pollution.

Sciadopitys verticillata

Skimmia japonica ○ ✳

SKIM-me-a ja-PAH-ni-ka

Japanese skimmia

Rue Family (Rutaceae)
Small evergreen shrub
2'–5' h x 3'–6' w

Enjoy this slow-growing, compact shrub every month of the year. Evergreen leaves compete with the plant's handsome flowers and fruits for your attention. The alternate, simple, shiny, leathery, dark green leaves are fragrant when bruised. The bark is not ornamental. In April and May, it produces creamy white flowers in thick, upright clusters. Both male and female plants are needed to produce fruits, which are clusters of shiny, bright red berries in winter.

LANDSCAPE USE
An attractive, high, woody ground-cover or low hedge in woodland gardens with rhododendrons, camellias, and glossy *Pachysandra* 'Green Sheen'. Cultivars may be hard to find.

ORIGIN Woodlands of Japan.

HARDINESS ZONES 7–9

LIGHT Partial shade.

SOIL Moist, well-drained, acid or alkaline soils.

GROWING Prune to shape after flowering; best in the moderate summer temperatures of the Pacific Northwest. May be afflicted with spider mites.

CAUTION Do not eat any plant parts, including the red berries. In small amounts, they can cause upset stomach; they're poisonous in large amounts and can cause abortions or cardiac arrest.

DESIGNER'S CHOICE
Skimmia japonica subsp. *reevesiana*
Self-pollinating dwarf with male and female blooms. Only one plant needed for red berries in fall and winter. 2' h × 2'–3' w.

Skimmia japonica

S. japonica 'Rubella' Male skimmia with dark pink to red winter buds opening to fragrant flowers in late spring; yellow and green variegated leaves.

Sophora japonica ⌒ ✳
(syn. *Styphnolobium japonicum*)

so-FOR-ah ja-PAH-ni-ka

Chinese scholar tree, Japanese pagoda tree

Pea Family (Papilionaceae; formerly Fabaceae)
Deciduous tree
40'–60' h and w

This tree works well in cities because it tolerates heat, drought, and polluted urban conditions. It stands out in the landscape because it's one of the few trees with showy blooms in mid- to late summer and bright olive-green shoots visible in winter. Although litter from flowers, fruits, and leaves may be a nuisance, the tree is valuable for its stately habit and the delicate shade it provides during the growing season.

The alternate, 10" leaves are featherlike and glossy, with up to 17 leaflets; they have little fall color. On older trees, the light grayish-brown bark has interlacing curved ridges; young shoots and stems are bright olive green with raised tan lenticels. These green stems and shoots provide winter interest in the landscape. The cream to greenish white, pealike

blossoms are lightly scented; they appear in 1' clusters in mid- to late summer. Green pods aging to yellow and then brown resemble fine, beaded ropes up to 8" long.

LANDSCAPE USE
Excellent for shading large lawns, since grass grows under its lightly shaded canopy.

ORIGIN   China's mountain valleys and woods.

HARDINESS ZONES   5–8

LIGHT   Full sun.

SOIL   Moist, rich, well-drained soils.

GROWING   Transplant in spring. It may take about 10 years for the tree to bloom. It is prone to winter injury when young; canker make be worsened by extreme cold.

DESIGNER'S CHOICE
Sophora japonica 'Fleright' (Princeton Upright) Compact oval crown with upright branches and better pest and disease resistance than species. 40' h × 30' w. Zones 6–8.

S. japonica 'Pendula' Beautiful weeping tree with elegant drooping branches and colorful, olive-green stems in winter; blooms infrequently. 15'–25' h and w.

Sophora japonica

S. japonica 'Regent' Faster growing, earlier blooming, with straight trunk and more uniform crown with better leaves, flowers, and leafhopper resistance. 45' h × 35' w.

Sorbus alnifolia ⃝ ✳

SOR-bus al-ni-FOH-lee-a

Korean mountain ash

Rose Family (Rosaceae)
Deciduous tree
40' h x 25' w

Each fall I look forward to seeing the brilliant, long-lasting, fall color on our Korean mountain ash. This tree thrives in partial shade and well-drained, acid soil. It has grown pretty fast; after 10 years in the backyard it stands about 20' h × 10' w.

The dark green, 2"–4" foliage is alternate and simple, turning brilliant orange to scarlet in fall. The smooth, dark brown bark is lightly furrowed. In mid-spring to early summer, it produces 5-petal, white flowers in dense, flat-topped clusters held above the leaves. Persistent, shiny, orangey red berries ripen in September and October.

LANDSCAPE USE
For lawns, a fine shade tree with multi-season interest; lovely specimen.

ORIGIN   Forests of Asia.

HARDINESS ZONES   4–8

LIGHT   Full sun to partial shade.

SOIL   Well-drained, acid soil.

GROWING   Easily transplanted and grown in cool climates without heavy air pollution; prune during winter dormancy. Korean mountain ash is more resistant to pests and diseases than other *Sorbus* species, but it is intolerant of urban pollution.

Sorbus americana 'Dwarfcrown' (Red Cascade) (American mountain ash) A compact, showy cultivar of the native North American species; features white flower clusters, bright red fruits, and orangey yellow fall color. 30' h × 20' w. Zone 3.

S. aucuparia 'Michred' (Cardinal Royal) (European mountain ash, Rowan) An improvement over the species, this vigorous tree, often seen in nurseries, has an oval crown; dark green, pinnate leaves with silvery undersides turning yellow to red in fall; white, clustered flowers in May; and bright red berry clusters in August and September (instead of the bright orangey red fruit of the species). Would be much more desirable were it not for susceptibility to fireblight, sunscald, and borers. 20'–30' h × 15–20' w. Zone 3.

Sorbus alnifolia

SPIRAEA

Spiraea species ○ ◐ ✳

spy-REE-a

Spirea, Bridal wreath

Rose Family (Rosaceae)
Deciduous flowering shrub
½'–8' h × 1'–8' w, depending upon the selection

This popular and reliable flowering shrub fills several functions in the landscape. Low-growing selections (under 2' tall), like *S. japonica* 'Golden Elf' and 'Walbuma' (Magic Carpet), work well as groundcovers; mid-sized plants (3'–5' tall), such as *S. × cineria* 'Grefsheim' or *S. japonica* 'Goldmound', look good in borders and as foundation plantings; while large forms (5'–9'), such as *S. nipponica* 'Snowmound', *S. prunifolia*, and *S. × vanhouttei* 'Renaissance', make informal hedges and additions to shrub borders. Some spireas have colorful leaves or attractive fall color, both of which extend the plant's relatively short season of interest.

Alternate, simple leaves range in hue from lime to dark green; leaves of some species turn scarlet in fall. Abundant terminal clusters of tiny, 5-lobed flowers in pink, white, or yellow appear in spring or summer. Neither the bark nor the fruit is ornamental.

LANDSCAPE USE

Depending upon the size, use as a mounding groundcover, for an accent, in shrub groups or borders, in foundation plantings, or as an informal hedge. Many species and cultivars exist (see Designer's Choice for some examples).

ORIGIN North America, Asia, Europe.

HARDINESS ZONES 4–8, depending upon the species or cultivar.

LIGHT Full sun.

SOIL Prefers moist, rich, well-drained soil but adapts to a variety of conditions.

GROWING Prune spring bloomers, which set their buds on old wood, right after flowering to allow new stems and buds to form. Prune the faded flowering stems back by one third to a new bud or shoot. Cut back some stems to the ground for fresh basal growth. Prune summer-blooming varieties early the following spring. Spirea is susceptible to fireblight, powdery mildew, aphids, and scales.

CAUTION *Spirea japonica* has invasive tendencies in the Mid-Atlantic and southeastern U.S. Before buying, check with your Cooperative Extension to make sure the plant is not invasive in your area.

DESIGNER'S CHOICE

Spiraea × cinerea 'Gretsheim' (First Snow) (Garland spirea) Weeping shrub with fine, cascading leaves and mounding form; white flowers in April before leaves. 4'–6' h and w. Zones 4–7.

S. japonica (syn. *S. × bumalda*) 'Anthony Waterer' Magenta pink flowers in big, flat-topped clusters in early summer; new foliage is reddish purple; fall foliage is also reddish purple; overused. 3'–5' h × 3'–6' w. Zones 4–9.

Spiraea japonica 'Anthony Waterer'

S. japonica 'Dolchica' Slim mounded stems with flashy, purplish-pink flower clusters in summer. Leaves are deeply dissected with purplish-red new growth. Similar to 'Crispa'. 3' h × 4' w. Zones 4–9.

S. japonica 'Flaming Mound' Red new growth turns orange then yellow in summer; bronzed purple in fall. Deep pink clustered flowers on little, rounded shrubs. 1'–2' h and w.

S. japonica 'Genpei' (syn. *S. japonica* 'Shibori' and *S. japonica* 'Shirobana') Mounded shrub with flat flower clusters ranging in color from pink to white to deep pink within clusters and from cluster to cluster. 3' h and w. Zones 4–9.

S. japonica 'Golden Elf' Pink blooms and yellow leaves create a fine-textured mass, edging, groundcover, or accent in rock and perennial gardens. 6"–8" h × 18"–24" w. Zones 4–9.

S. japonica 'Goldflame' Bright red new foliage turns yellow, then bronzy green; crimson blooms in midsummer; reddish bronze fall color. Look for the improved cultivar 'Firelight'. 2'–3' h × 3'–4' w. Zones 3–8.

S. japonica 'Lemon Princess' Improved version of 'Goldmound', with brighter gold-green foliage that stays yellow longer in heat; pink, 6" wide flower clusters attract butterflies. 2'–3' h and w.

S. japonica 'Limemound' (syn. 'Monhub') Spring growth is russet-tinged yellow aging to lime on a dense, rounded shrub; light pink blooms; orangey red fall leaves on red stems. Nice with red-leafed shrub and perennials. 3' h × 4' w. Zones 3–9.

S. japonica 'Little Princess' Rounded form with summer-blooming, rosy pink flowers. 3' h × 6' w. Zones 4–9.

S. japonica 'Neon Flash' Hot pink flowers on dense, rounded plant; foliage opens red-purple, fades to green, then turns burgundy in fall. 3' h and w.

S. japonica 'Walbuma' (Magic Carpet) Three-season dwarf with red-tipped gold leaves and red new growth, deep long-lasting pinkish purple flowers in early spring, and red-brown fall leaf color. Good filler in the perennial border or massed as groundcover. 12"–18" h × 2' w. Zones 4–9.

S. nipponica 'Snowmound' Snow-white flower clusters on shrub with arching stems; pollution tolerant. 3'–5' h and w. Zones 4–8.

S. prunifolia 'Plena' (bridal wreath spiraea) Old-fashioned shrub with arching stems and double, white flowers in late spring. Rangier and less pretty than *S. nipponica* 'Snowmound'. 8' h and w.

S. × *vanhouttei* 'Renaissance' Fast-growing, fountainlike, arching stems covered with clusters of bright white blooms in mid- to late spring; orangey red fall leaf color. Terrific for informal hedges, shrub borders, and specimens; improved disease resistance over *S.* × *vanhouttei*. 5' h × 6' h. Zones 3–7.

STEPHANANDRA

Stephanandra incisa 'Crispa' 🪴 ✳

ste-fa-NAN-dra in-SEE-za

Cut-leaf stephanandra

Rose Family (Rosaceae)
Deciduous shrub
1'–3' h × 3'–6' w

This shrub doesn't shout its presence, but I like it anyway. I grow it as an arching groundcover in the partial shade of a red maple, but Long Island's Farmingdale University has a terrific *Stephanandra* planting by a wooden bench in the midst of

Stephanandra incisa 'Crispa'

a somewhat shady shrub border. Zigzag stems make a massive, layered mound, about 4' h × 6' w, especially interesting in winter. Those interesting zigzag branches are leaf and litter catchers, however. Leaves turn bronze to green in spring, then red-orange in fall.

LANDSCAPE USE
Large ground cover for foundations and slopes, shrub border, erosion control.

ORIGIN Edging woods in eastern Asia.

HARDINESS ZONES (4) 5–7 (8)

LIGHT Full sun to partial shade.

SOIL Moist, well-drained, acid soils with plenty of organic matter.

GROWING No major pests or diseases. Shrub spreads by suckers and by rooting where branches contact moist earth. May have considerable stem injury in severe winters. This cultivar is shorter than the species.

STEWARTIA

Stewartia pseudocamellia ⊙ › △

stu-WAR-tee-a su-doh-ka-MEEL-lee-a

Japanese stewartia

Tea Family (Theaceae)
Deciduous flowering tree
20'–40' h x 15'–20' w

For glorious fall color and lovely summer flowers, stewartia can't be beat. The leaves of this relatively small, flowering tree turn rich, warm hues in fall. Young stewartias are narrow and columnar, but with maturity, the crown becomes more oval. Bob and I grow stewartia as a specimen on our front lawn instead of the typical flowering cherry. Once July rolls around in my neighborhood, ornamental cherries and flowering plums are Japanese beetle bait. On the other hand, summer for stewartia means flowers, not beetles. Stewartia is a four-season plant, with orangey-gold to deep ruby red fall foliage and peeling, colorful bark. Fall color varies some from tree to tree. A stewartia we bought from a local nursery is not as colorful as one

Stewartia pseudocamellia

Stewartia pseudocamellia

we received from a friend, reminding me that the best way to ensure good fall color is to see how a tree colors up before taking it home.

Stewartia's foliage is alternate and simple; the 4" × 2½", dark green leaves are tapered and toothed. In fall, they take on an orange to deep red color. The ornamental bark is reddish brown, peeling to expose a pink, cream, and gray inner bark, particularly on older trees. The trunk is smooth and muscled, with skinlike creases. In midsummer (June or July), stewartia produces 2½" white, camellia-like blossoms in the leaf joints by 1s and 2s in rapid sequence. Flowers have 5 petals and a central boss of bright yellow stamens. The fruit capsules are not ornamental.

LANDSCAPE USE

Front-yard specimen; near decks, patios, and windows where you can see the bark; along lightly shaded paths in woodland gardens; in the understory below large trees.

ORIGIN Mountainous forests of Japan.

HARDINESS ZONES 5–8

LIGHT Full sun in cooler climates to partial shade.

SOIL Moist, fertile, well-drained, organic soils.

GROWING Transplant when young.

This is a trouble-free four-season plant, though old plants may be difficult to establish and it will not tolerate drought or the heat of southern gardens.

DESIGNER'S CHOICE

Stewartia monadelpha (tall stewartia) Grow for its stunning, cinnamon-colored, flaking bark. This heat-tolerant tree produces little white blooms up to 1½" wide in June. Best choice for southern gardens. 25'–35' h × 20'–25' w. Zones 6–8.

S. pseudocamellia 'Ballet' Bigger (3"–4") blooms and a more graceful and spreading form. 15' h × 12' w in ten years.

S. pseudocamellia Koreana Group (syn. *S. koreana*) (Korean stewartia) Wide-open, white flowers with showy yellow stamens in midsummer; excellent red fall color on some plants; smooth trunk with flaking ornamental bark in gray, orangey pink, and brown. Very similar to species. 20'–40' h × 15'–20' w. Zones 5–8.

STYRAX

Styrax japonicus ⊙ ✳

STY-raks ja-PAH-ni-kum

Japanese snowbell

Styrax Family (Styracaceae)
Deciduous tree
20'–30' h and w

Japanese snowbell offers year-round interest. In late spring, this lovely, low-branched, spreading tree

Styrax japonicus 'Pink Chimes'

Styrax japonicus

produces clusters of white bells that hang below the leaves, making it perfect for planting next to a patio or bench where you can sit and look up into the branches. Not only can you look into the 5-petal, lightly fragrant flowers from below, you can also appreciate the delicate texture created by its graceful leaves and smooth, attractive bark, which cracks with age, showing orangey inner bark. The tree casts light to dappled shade.

The alternate, simple leaves are 1"–4" ovals with pointed tips and fine teeth along the sides; fall color is not particularly ornamental. The smooth bark is deep gray-brown with orangey brown, interlacing crevices. The lightly scented, white, ¾", bell-like blossoms droop in clusters below the branches. The fruits, or drupes, are not ornamental.

LANDSCAPE USE
Specimen, especially near patios or walkways, where you can see the flowers hanging under the branches; lovely addition to shrub borders.

ORIGIN Sunny, moist soils in Japan and China.

HARDINESS ZONES (5) 6–8

LIGHT Full sun to partial shade.

SOIL Rich, moist, acid, well-drained soils with plenty of organic matter.

GROWING Give plants extra water during dry spells, especially those planted in full

sun and hot climates.

DESIGNER'S CHOICE
Styrax japonicus Benibana Group Light pink blooms from an early age; seed forms, so plants may be variable among individuals. 10' h × 8' w.

S. japonicus 'Issai' Faster growing than species; rare. 20'–30' h and w.

S. japonicus 'Kusan' Globular, early-flowering small tree; rare. 11' h and w.

S. japonicus 'Pink Chimes' (syn. 'Roseus') Shrubby little tree with dangling, soft pink flowers. 10'–25' h × 7'–15' w.

Styrax obassia △ › ○

STY-raks oh-BAHS-see-a

Fragrant styrax

Styrax Family (Styracaceae)
Deciduous tree
20'–30' h × 15'–25' w

This handsome Asian tree has big, dark green leaves up to 8" × 6". In late spring, fragrant, white flowers droop in graceful, elongated clusters. The bark is thin, so be particularly careful when mowing around it since sharp blades can injure the trunk. To protect it, lay a mulch or groundcover bed around the trunk or place fragrant styrax in a tree and shrub border. May be hardier than *S. japonicus* and flower earlier.

LANDSCAPE USE
Lovely flowering specimen, especially when seen from below the canopy; near patios, entrances, grouped in woodland gardens.

ORIGIN Woods of China, Japan, Korea.

HARDINESS ZONES 5–8

LIGHT Full sun.

SOIL Moist soil.

GROWING Plant young trees, as large ones are hard to establish.

Styrax obassia

SYMPHORICARPOS

Symphoricarpos orbiculatus ⚘ ✳

sim-foh-ri-KAR-pos or-bi-q-LAY-tus

Coralberry, Indian currant

Honeysuckle Family (Caprifoliaceae)
Deciduous shrub
3'–5' h x 4'–8' w

This deciduous shrub produces showy, pink-white, bell-shaped blooms in summer (June to July). Bright coral to purplish red berries ripen in autumn and persist through winter. Fruits attract birds, and you can snip stems for indoor decorations. Coralberry forms dense thickets in nature; not a plant for small properties.

LANDSCAPE USE
Plant this fast-growing shrub on open hillsides for erosion control, or as a groundcover on open sites where it can spread.

ORIGIN Eastern U.S.

HARDINESS ZONES 2–7

LIGHT Full sun to partial shade.

SOIL Prefers well-drained, moist soils of average fertility but tolerates drought and a wide range of soils.

GROWING If you want to restrict its growth, you'll have to pull up suckers when they appear. Can get mildew.

CAUTION Berries can cause upset stomach when eaten, particularly by children.

Symphoricarpos albus (snowberry) Twiggy, suckering shrub with light pink blooms; white berries from September to November and even into winter; native to Canada and the U.S. 6' h and w. Zones 3–7.

S. × *chenaultii* 'Hancock' Low, mounding groundcover with small, blue-green leaves, pink flowers and berries that are rose-pink on one side and whitish on the other. 2'–3' h × 6'–10' w. Zone 5.

Symphoricarpos albus

S. × *doorenbosii* 'Magic Berry' Profuse pink berries on a shade-tolerant shrub. 5' h and w. Zones 3–7.

SYMPLOCOS

Symplocos paniculata ⚘ ✳

sim-PLOH-kos pa-nik-u-LAH-ta

Sapphire berry, Asiatic sweet-leaf

Symplocos Family (Symplocaceae)
Deciduous shrub or small tree
15' h and w

This low-maintenance, slow-growing shrub has few requirements. Plant 2 or more sapphire berry shrubs for best fruiting and flowering. Bears clusters of scented, star-shaped white blooms in late spring and early summer, followed by abundant, bright blue oval berries in late summer to early fall; berries very attractive to birds. Sapphire berry has dark green leaves and medium texture.

LANDSCAPE USE
Grow sapphire berry as a naturalistic screen between properties or in the shrub border, where it can blend with other plants when neither blooming nor fruiting.

ORIGIN East Asian and Himalayan woodlands.

HARDINESS ZONES 4–8

LIGHT Full sun to partial shade.

SOIL Well-drained soil.

GROWING Plant can self-sow, creating seedlings that need removal. Blooms on previous year's growth; prune right after flowering to avoid removing next year's flower buds.

SYRINGA

Syringa reticulata ◐ › ○

si-RING-a re-tik-u-LA-ta

Japanese tree lilac

Olive Family (Oleaceae)
Deciduous small flowering tree
20'–30' h x 15'–20' w

Japanese tree lilac makes a lovely accent in a shrub border. You can buy it as a single-stem or multi-trunk tree. It has an attractive, rounded open form, but the scented white flowers it bears in early summer are its showiest feature.

The opposite, simple, dark green leaves are oval with pointed tips; they have no strong fall color (usually yellowish brown). The season of interest is extended beyond the 2-week flowering period by the attractive, reddish brown young bark with white horizontal lenticels, similar to cherry. In spring, creamy white flowers are arranged in erect

Syringa microphylla 'Superba'

showy and airy-looking clusters, up to 12" × 10"; the flowers are aromatic (similar to privet). Fruits are capsules and attract birds, particularly cardinals, chickadees, and finches.

LANDSCAPE USE
Borders, patio beds, and groups, or as a specimen; use it to soften the corner of a building but make sure it's planted far enough from the structure to accommodate its mature growth.

ORIGIN China

HARDINESS ZONES 3–7

LIGHT Full sun to partial shade.

SOIL Well-drained, acid soils.

GROWING Tree lilacs are easy to transplant and grow in cool climates. Plants tolerate urban pollution and are generally pest free.

DESIGNER'S CHOICE
S. reticulata 'Golden Eclipse' A cultivar with variegated leaves that are green in the center and bright yellow around the edges; creamy white flowers. 18'–24' h × 8'–14' w.

S. reticulata 'Ivory Silk' Smaller and more refined than the species; flowers when young; heavy bloomer. 20' h × 15' w.

S. pekinensis 'Morton' (China Snow) (Peking lilac) A four-season plant with creamy white, fragrant flowers in mid-June; amber, exfoliating

Syringa reticulata 'Ivory Silk'

bark; semi-glossy, dark green leaves. Drought, salt, and pollution tolerance make this a good choice for urban street plantings and town-house gardens. Similar to Japanese tree lilac, but with finer twigs, smaller leaves, and flaky bark; it is also less hardy and less common than tree lilac. I planted two whips of this lilac a few years back. They're now about 3½' high, and though they haven't flowered yet, the bark alone makes them worth planting. 25' h × 20' w at 20 years. Zones 5–7.

Syringa vulgaris ▽ › ⌂

si-RING-a vul-GAY-ris

Common lilac

Olive Family (Oleaceae)
Deciduous shrub sometimes pruned to a more treelike form
12'–15' h × 10'–12' w

The sight of a plain old common lilac in bloom thrills me. That's why I grow one at the back of a shrub border separating my house from my neighbors. It lives in the back not only for its height, but also because powdery mildew turns the leaves a sickly gray by midsummer. In front of the house, I grow late-blooming mildew-resistant lilacs, *S. patula* 'Miss Kim' and *S.* × *prestoniae* 'James Macfarlane' to extend the lilac-growing season into June. Both the icy-pale purplish-blue blooms of 'Miss Kim' and the pink flowers of 'James Macfarlane' harmonize with a low underplanting of Crimson Pygmy barberry (*Berberis thunbergii* 'Crimson Pygmy'), which I hack back each year to keep from blooming and spreading. In fall, the barberry

ALL ABOUT SYRINGA

Lilac, with its fragrant flower clusters in white, pale yellow, pink, purple, bicolor, or traditional lilac blue, evokes the past but looks to the future. Because of shrub lilac's popularity, new hybrids and cultivars keep appearing. Some, like white 'Betsy Ross' and lilac-blue 'Old Glory' resist diseases common in lilac's warmer range. Others like pink 'Bailbelle' (Tinkerbelle), lilac 'Bailsugar' (Sugar Plum Fairy), reblooming light-pink 'Baildust' (Fairy Dust), and light pink *S.* × *prestoniae* 'Minuet' are compact. Lilac tree developments include primrose yellow flowers (*S. pekinensis* 'Zhang Zhiming' (Beijing Gold); *S. p.* 'Sundak' (Copper Curls), with peeling bark like a river birch; and *S. p.* 'DTR 124' (Summer Charm), which has creamy blooms, fine-textured leaves, yellow fall color, and some disease resistance.

complements the reliably deep purple leaves of 'Miss Kim'.

The opposite, simple, wide, dark green leaves are heart-shaped with smooth margins; several variegated and gold-leafed cultivars exist but are hard to find and less appealing than many green-leafed varieties. As stems age, they become dark brownish gray, twisted and peeling. Coarse textured year-round, common lilacs bear conical clusters of single or double, fragrant, tubular flowers in magenta, purple, blue, lilac, pink, white, pale yellow, and bicolor. Fruits are not ornamental but are attractive to birds.

LANDSCAPE USE

Shrub borders, informal hedges, screens, or groups. Many nineteenth-century farmers planted a lilac below a window of their house so they could breathe in the scent. In New England, you can still see gnarly lilacs blooming on the east, west, or south side of farmhouses. If you're planting lilac in front of your house or where many people pass by, plant a mildew resistant lilac such as *S. meyeri* 'Palibin' or *S. × prestoniae* 'James Macfarlane'.

ORIGIN Well-drained soils in Europe, typically with limestone or similar substrate.

HARDINESS ZONES (2) 3–6 (7)

LIGHT Full sun to partial shade, although best flowering and bushiest growth is in full sun.

SOIL Well-drained, preferably limey loam with plenty of organic matter but tolerates most as long as well drained.

GROWING Prefers cooler climates. Plant so that air can circulate around the shrub to reduce mildew. Pruning is necessary to maintain attractive form and abundant blooms. First, remove stems that look sick or dead, then take off the oldest unproductive canes, skinny suckers, and wild twiggy growth.

Keep the biggest stems for the shrub's framework but cut out one-quarter of the remaining old stems. Remove all but the strongest suckers. Repeat this process each year just after bloom to keep your lilac blooming its best. Every few years, sprinkle about a cup of limestone around the base of each lilac if grown on acid soils. Lilacs prefer low fertility, and if fertilizing, do so just after bloom. *S. vulgaris* has one season of interest, spring, and is generally pest free or pest tolerant. It may be susceptible to frost damage, and pests and diseases such as lilac scales and borers and lilac bacterial blight. Powdery mildew is common and ugly but will not hurt the plant.

DESIGNER'S CHOICE

A few of the hundreds available:

Syringa vulgaris 'Alba' White, single flowers in fragrant clusters. 12'–15' h × 10'–12' w.

S. vulgaris 'Edith Cavell' Double white. 8'–12' h and w.

S. vulgaris 'Krasavitsa Moskvy' (syn. Beauty of Moscow) Pink-lilac buds open to double-flowered, white blooms, tinged pale lavender. 8'–12' h and w.

S. vulgaris 'Marie Frances' Single, pink. 8'–12' h and w.

S. vulgaris 'Monge' Single, dark purple flowers. 8'–12' h and w.

S. vulgaris 'Primrose' (syn. 'Yellow Wonder') Single, creamy yellow-green buds open to light yellow blooms. 8'–12' h and w.

S. vulgaris 'Sensation' Single, deep purple buds opening to purple with white edge. 8'–12' h and w.

S. vulgaris 'Wedgwood Blue' Single, blue flowers with lilac-pink buds in pendant clusters. 8'–12' h and w.

S. vulgaris 'Marie Frances' Single, pink. 8'–12' h and w.

Syringa vulgaris **'Sensation'**

Syringa meyeri **'Palibin'**

OTHER SHRUB SPECIES AND HYBRIDS

Syringa 'Bailbelle' (Tinkerbelle) Wine-red buds become clusters of deep pink, single flowers with a spicy scent. 5'–6' h × 4'–5' w. Zones 3–8.

S. meyeri 'Palibin' Rounded shrub with fragrant, 4", violet purple flower clusters in May; long-lasting bronzy red fall color. 4'–6' h × 6'–8' w. Zones 3–8.

S. microphylla 'Superba' Small-leaved, dense shrub blooms twice with deep pink, fragrant, single flowers. 6' h × 10'–12' w. Zones 4–9.

S. 'Miss Canada' (syn. *S.* × *prestoniae* 'Miss Canada') A very late bloomer with reddish buds and deep pink blooms. 6'–12' h and w.

S. patula 'Miss Kim' (syn. *S. microphylla* 'Miss Kim') Rounded shrub with light icy-bluish-purple flowers and long-lasting, dark purplish red fall color; late-blooming with healthy foliage. 6'–9' h and w. Zones 3–8.

S. × *prestoniae* 'James Macfarlane' Upright form with pink, single flowers in large, fragrant clusters; light green leaves; late-blooming with healthy foliage. 10' h × 8' w.

Syringa patula 'Miss Kim'

Tamarix ramosissima ⌒

TAM-a-riks ra-mo-SIS-si-ma

Salt cedar, Five-stamen tamarisk

Tamarisk Family (Tamaricaceae)
Deciduous shrub
5'–15' h and w

Tamarisk is a fast-growing open shrub notable for its fine-textured, gray-green leaves; arching, reddish shoots; and feathery sprays of pink flowers that bloom in summer. Cultivars like 'Pink Cascade', with lush pink plumes, and 'Summer Glow', with silvery leaves and rosy pink flowers, are widely available.

LANDSCAPE USE
Erosion control, borders.

ORIGIN Southern Europe, Northern Africa, Asia in salty soils.

HARDINESS ZONES 2–8

LIGHT Full sun.

SOIL Average to dry.

GROWING No serious pests or diseases. Salt and wind tolerant. Tamarisk blooms on new growth. For a denser, more attractive habit and better flowering, cut to the ground before spring growth begins.

CAUTION Tamarisks, including *T. aphylla*, *T. chinensis*, *T. gallica*, *T. parviflora*, *T. tetranda* and *T. ramosissima*, show invasive tendencies, especially in warm areas. *T. ramosissima* is spreading into untended areas in the West, Southeast, Southwest, and parts of the central U.S. Instead of tamarisk, substitute elderberry (*Sambucus*), California lilac or New Jersey tea (*Ceanothus*), possumhaw (*Ilex decidua*), sumac (*Rhus*), or yucca. Before using this plant, check with your local Cooperative Extension to see if it is invasive in your area.

Taxodium distichum △ ✳

tak-SO-dee-um DIS-ti-kum

Bald cypress

Bald Cypress Family (Taxodiaceae)
Large deciduous conifer
50'–80' h × 20'–30' w

Bald cypresses grow fast and easily in moist, acid, well-drained soils. Their straight, tapering trunks are buttressed at the base, giving them a powerful, soaring perspective. Young trees have thin, conical crowns, but the branching of mature specimens tends to be flatter, wider, and more uneven; trees provide light shade. The knees, or protrusions, developed by old trees in wet soils are woody projections from a widespread network of roots. Their function is not certain, but they may bring oxygen to underwater roots or hold up the tree in shifting soils. The deeper the water, the taller the knees may grow, with some growing 6' high.

The ½"-long, needled, soft, deciduous leaves are light bright green, turning gold to russet-brown in fall. In my garden, bald cypress and rose of Sharon are among the last woodies to leaf out in spring and

Taxodium distichum

Taxodium distichum

to drop their leaves in fall. Needled bald cypress leaves have a featherlike arrangement on deciduous stems, while leaves on persistent stems appear spiraled. The bark is fibrous and reddish brown when young, then becoming scaly gray with age; it has both deciduous and persistent stems. Neither the flowers nor the bark is ornamental.

LANDSCAPE USE
Lawn specimen, grouped on moist to wet sites. I grow them surrounded by giant butterbur (*Petasites japonicus* 'Giganteus') for a contrast of textures and a primeval look.

ORIGIN   Swamps and wetlands of southeastern U.S.

HARDINESS ZONES   5–10

LIGHT   Full sun to partial shade.

SOIL   Rich, acid, moist to wet soils; tolerates wind, compacted soils, and some drought.

GROWING   Relatively carefree when planted in the right spot. Be aware that cypress knees, which emerge in wet soils, can trip unknowing visitors to your property. Trees may be afflicted with spider mites and twig blight.

DESIGNER'S CHOICE
Taxodium distichum 'Mickelson' (Shawnee Brave) Forms a tall, thin cone; narrower and hardier than the species. 70' h × 15'–20' w. Zone 4.

TAXUS

Taxus species △ ✳

TAK-sus

Yew

Yew Family (Taxaceae)
Evergreen shrub or tree
3'–60' h × 4'–25' w

A client wanted to replace an overgrown, shady foundation planting with something clean and formal. We decided on two cultivars of slow-growing Japanese yew, a fine-textured, dark evergreen. We chose it for shade and pH tolerance and because the variety of available cultivars makes it easy to find both small and columnar forms that minimize pruning and maintenance. Also, yew's dark green color and uniform texture focus attention on her house while harmonizing with the wooded surroundings. Japanese yew thrives in sun or shade and looks good in both formal and informal

designs. Yews come in most shapes and sizes from a big, pyramidal tree (*T. cuspidata* 'Capitata') to a short, wide shrub (*T.* × *media* 'Taunton') to a dense groundcover (*T. cuspidata* 'Monloo' [Emerald Spreader]). *T.* × *media* is a hardy cross between English yew (*T. baccata*) and Japanese yew (*T. cuspidata*).

Year round, flat, linear leaves up to 1" long are a lustrous dark green with yellow-green on the undersides; after pruning, they can re-grow on old wood. Yews have attractive, peeling, reddish-brown bark. If you grow yew as a tree, you can limb it up to expose the bark. (For information about limbing up, see page 121.) The flowers are not ornamental. Female plants produce edible, showy, fleshy, red arils surrounding poisonous seeds; male and female plants are necessary for fruit production. Although these evergreens produce berries, they are not conifers.

LANDSCAPE USE
Foundations, shrub borders, specimen, hedges, screens, topiary, and specimen tree; spreading cultivars make excellent groundcovers.

ORIGIN   Japan

HARDINESS ZONES   4–7

LIGHT   Full sun to shade.

SOIL   Well-drained, moist, fertile soil is ideal, but yew can tolerate some drought and urban pollution once established. Yews may not survive in wet soil, which causes their roots to rot.

GROWING   Keep yews compact by pinching or shearing new shoots. If you prune your yews once a year, do so in early summer, after yew's two growth spurts in early and late spring. Yews withstand drastic pruning for shape and thickness because they can re-grow on old wood. In addition to being very attractive to deer, it is also susceptible to mealybugs, mites, scales, and black vine weevil. Plant with a northern or eastern exposure to protect leaves from turning brown from winter sun.

CAUTION In some eastern parts of the U.S., Japanese yew (*T. cuspidata*) may escape into wild areas. Candy to deer, but toxic to people and some animals.

DESIGNER'S CHOICE

Taxus baccata 'Repandens' (creeping English yew) wide spreading habit with branches that arc downwards at tips; excellent groundcover or low hedge for sun or shade; edge with perennials if desired. Keep plants from windy areas. Set plants 3' apart for dense coverage 2'–3' h × 12'–15' w. Zone 5.

T. cuspidata 'Capitata' (pyramidal Japanese yew) An upright, pyramidal tree or shrub with one to several trunks. 10'–25' h and w.

T. cuspidata 'Monloo' (Emerald Spreader) Similar character to creeping English yew but Emerald Spreader is shorter, hardier, and more densely branched. 30" h × 8'–10' w.

T. cuspidata 'Nana Aurescens' (golden dwarf Japanese yew) Golden needles light up the dark, very slow growing. 1' h × 3' w.

Taxus cuspidata 'Dwarf Bright Gold'

T. × *media* 'Brownii' Good for hedging; 6'–8' h × 10' w.

T. × *media* 'Geers' (Margarita) Lime green foliage that retains good color; 4'–5' h × 6'–7' w.

T. × *media* 'Hicksii' (Hicks yew) Columnar form; 10'–12' h × 3'–6' w.

T. × *media* 'Nigra' Rich deep green needles, spreading formal globular habit; 3'–4' h × 6'–8' w.

T. × *media* 'Sentinalis' Tall, narrow, densely branched column; use more than one for rhythmic accents in large perennial gardens. Similar to 'Beanpole', 'Fastigiata' (Captain), 'Flushing', 'Viridis', and others. 10' h × 2' w.

T. × *media* 'Taunton' (Taunton yew) Resists winter burn, tolerates summer heat; a super plant; 3'–4' h × 5'–6' w.

TEUCRIUM

Teucrium chamaedrys ○ ✳

TU-kree-um ka-MEE-dris

Wall germander

Mint Family (Lamiaceae)
Low evergreen shrub with woody branches and non-woody tips
18" h × 12" w

Shear this woody herb once a year to make a dense, low, evergreen hedge suitable for formal knot gardens. Wall germander also makes an appealing dark groundcover or edging. It thrives in heat and gravelly, infertile soils. It has shiny, evergreen leaves year round, and in summer (August), pink flower spikes attract bees.

LANDSCAPE USE
Hedge, groundcover, or edging.

ORIGIN Limestone outcrops in Mediterranean region; western Asia.

HARDINESS ZONES 6–9

LIGHT Full sun.

SOIL Well-drained soil.

GROWING To keep it dense, shear it once a year. Space hedging plants about 6" apart.

Teucrium chamaedrys

THUJA

Thuja occidentalis ○

THU-ja ok-si-den-TAL-is

Eastern arborvitae, White cedar

Cypress Family (Cupressaceae)
Evergreen coniferous tree or shrub
40' h × 10'–15' w

Tall and skinny by nature, arborvitae is popular for privacy screens and garden focal points. Almost columnar, it grows slowly (about 8"–12" per year), forming a thin, dense pyramid of leaves when young. I don't like the species, which is horribly overused in the landscape and over time looks dull and shabby.

Evergreen, scalelike, yellow-green, shiny leaves are aromatic and arranged in level sprays. Some cultivars maintain this yellow-green color year round, but some species and cultivars become bronzed in winter. The ruddy brown bark shreds in vertical strips. The flowers and tiny cones are not ornamental; males and females occur on the same plant.

LANDSCAPE USE
Hedges, screens, windbreaks, and accents.

ORIGIN   Moist woods and mountain
slopes of eastern North America.

HARDINESS ZONES   3–7, depending
upon the cultivar.

LIGHT   Full sun.

SOIL   Moist, rich, well-drained soil.
Unlike yews, arborvitaes can tolerate
moist to swampy soils.

GROWING   Early summer is the ideal time
to shear arborvitae, which can produce
new growth on old wood. If you need to
remove whole branches, you can do that at
any time. Although this plant grows best
in colder climates, some tall forms split
under the weight of snow and ice. Deer
love this plant. It may also be attacked by
bagworms and red spider mites.

DESIGNER'S CHOICE

Thuja occidentalis 'DeGroot's Spire'
Twisted, fanlike foliage on skinny
cone, good specimen. 10' h × 2'–3' w.
Zone 4.

T. occidentalis 'Golden Globe' Golden
foliage on globular plant, doesn't
burn in full sun. 4' h and w.

T. occidentalis 'Hetz Midget' Dense
globe needs no pruning. 3'–4' h and w.

T. occidentalis 'Holmstrup' Stays
green through winter. 10' h × 3'–4' w.
Zone 4.

T. occidentalis 'Mr Bowling Ball' (Bob-
ozam, syn. 'Linesville') Versatile,
sage-green dwarf sphere that needs
no pruning. 3' h and w. Zone 5.

T. occidentalis 'Nigra' Popular cultivar
in the Northeast, retains dark green

Thuja occidentalis 'Sunkist'

Thuja occidentalis
'Yellow Ribbon'

color all winter. 10'–30' h × 10'–12' w.

T. occidentalis 'Rheingold' Gold leaves
turn copper in winter, good for low
hedging or accent; larger with age.
4'–5' h and w.

T. occidentalis 'Smaragd' (emerald
arborvitae, emerald green arborvitae) Green winter color, fine texture, slow growing, good for hedges;
tolerates partial shade. 10'–15' h ×
3'–4' w. Zone 4.

T. occidentalis 'Techny' Nice hedge
plant with wide base when young;
dark green year round. 10'–15' h ×
6'–8' w.

T. occidentalis 'Teddy' Blue-green
globe takes on bronzy tint in winter.
1' h × 2' w.

Thuja plicata △

THU-ya pli-KAY-ta

Western red cedar, Giant arborvitae

Cypress Family (Cupressaceae)
Evergreen conifer
50'–70' h x 15'–25' w

This western North American native is
larger, faster growing (up to 2' per
year), more shade tolerant, and generally healthier than its eastern counterpart, but less hardy in cold climates.
Sturdy and attractive, it resists the
pests (including deer) that bother

T. occidentalis and stays in better shape
during harsh winters because its
narrow, pyramidal form has a single
trunk. Although it can grow twice as
big in the wild, you can keep its
growth in check by regular pruning.
Its leaves are a glossy, rich green year
round. Use it instead of hemlock
where woolly adelgid is a problem.

LANDSCAPE USE
See *T. occidentalis*.

ORIGIN   Western North America.

HARDINESS ZONES   5–7

LIGHT   Full sun to partial shade.

SOIL   Moist, rich, well-drained soil;
tolerates boggy sites.

GROWING   Habit is looser in shade.
Early summer is the ideal time to shear
arborvitae, which can produce new
growth on old wood. If you need to
remove whole branches, you can do that
at any time. They may be attacked by
bagworms and red spider mites.

DESIGNER'S CHOICE

Thuja plicata 'Atrovirens' Vigorous,
uniform growth; good for hedges
and specimens. 30' h × 12' w.

T. plicata 'Green Giant' Fast growing,
up to 5' per year; drought tolerant,
carefree; terrific tree for tall hedges
and privacy screens. Leyland cypress
alternative. 50'–75' h × 12'–20' w.

T. plicata 'Grovpli' (Spring Grove)
Tight, pyramidal habit with dark,
shiny leaves; fast-growing hedge or
screen. 18'–24' h × 3'–6' w. Zone 4.

T. plicata. 'Zebrina' Green-and-gold-
splashed leaves, rounded to pyramidal. 30' h × 12' w.

THUJOPSIS

Thujopsis dolobrata △ ✱

thu-OP-sis doh-loh-BRAH-ta

Hiba false arborvitae

Cypress Family (Cupressaceae)
Evergreen conifer
15'–45' h x 6'–15' w

Thujopsis dolobrata 'Nana'

Thujopsis looks a lot like arborvitae but better. It features prominent, flat sprays of glossy evergreen foliage on a dense, pyramidal tree. The leaves are scaly, bright green on top and white on the bottom. They overlap, forming flat, cordlike sprigs that give the tree an intriguing complex surface with a strong interplay of dark and light. The bark is reddish and shredding. Both flowers and fruits are small and not ornamental. Much less common than arborvitae in the U.S.

LANDSCAPE USE
Screens, shrub borders, and openings in woodland gardens.

ORIGIN Woods of Japan.

HARDINESS ZONES 6–9

LIGHT Full sun.

SOIL Moist, well-drained soils high in organic matter.

GROWING Plant away from the harsh winds of winter; tolerates light pruning.

DESIGNER'S CHOICE
Thujopsis dolobrata 'Nana' Attractive small shrub. 3' h and w.

T. dolobrata 'Variegata' Irregular white variegation. 20'–30' h × 12' w.

TILIA

Tilia cordata △ › ○ ✳
TIL-ee-a kor-DAH-ta

Little-leaf linden

Linden Family (Tiliaceae)
Medium to large deciduous tree
45'–70' h × 25'–45' w

If you're seeking a formal-looking, medium-growing shade tree, then little-leaf linden, with its handsome, symmetrical habit, may be just right for you. Pyramidal when young, it becomes rounded with age. It's easy to grow and needs little pruning, making it a good choice for novice gardeners. It is versatile in the landscape and adapts to many growing conditions.

Its alternate, simple, 3" leaves are a glossy, dark green, rounded and tapering to a point, with toothed margins and a heart-shaped leaf base. The grayish brown bark is ridged. In midsummer, it produces clusters of fragrant, yellow flowers with long, green, leafy bracts, followed by interesting clusters of dangling, round nutlets in late summer. Flowers attract bees. An excellent linden species.

LANDSCAPE USE
Specimen in lawns, shade tree, tall deciduous hedging; widespread use as street tree.

ORIGIN Limey soils in Europe and western Asia.

HARDINESS ZONES 4–7

LIGHT Full sun to partial shade.

SOIL Moist, well-drained soil, preferably with neutral to alkaline pH but adaptable to acid soils, pollution, and tough conditions. Does not tolerate poor drainage.

GROWING Prune off basal suckers. It may attract Japanese beetles. It may also be attacked by aphids and other leaf-eating pests, as well as sooty mold, anthracnose, and powdery mildew, but pests and diseases are generally not serious.

DESIGNER'S CHOICE
Tilia cordata 'Greenspire' Straight trunk, faster growing than species, with narrower branch angles, which may be injured by ice and heavy snow. A very popular cultivar. 40'–50' h × 30' w.

Tilia cordata

AMERICAN LINDEN

American linden, or basswood (*Tilia americana*) is native to moist forests of eastern North America. A medium to large deciduous tree (60'–80' h × 50' w), it has a tall straight trunk, which makes a handsome foil for the large, coarse-textured, 8" × 6" leaves. The tree, known as American lime in England, bears fragrant, early summer blooms that attract bees. This linden also appeals to numerous pests, which eat the leaves until they're almost gone. Because of its size, this species is best suited to large properties and public parks. European little-leaf linden is a more refined and attractive landscape alternative to its native counterpart.

T. cordata 'Ronald' (Norlin) Fast growing, resists sunscald and leaf galls, developed for northern plains. 35'–45' h × 30' w. Zones 3–7.

T. cordata 'Baileyi' (Shamrock) Faster growing than 'Greenspire', with sturdier branching and a more open crown. 40'–50' h × 30' w.

T. mongolica 'Harvest Gold' Very hardy and upright, exfoliating bark; the deeply cut leaves, which are unlike those of other lindens, are shiny, disease free, and aphid resistant with consistent gold fall color; 30'–40' h × 25'–35' w. Zone 2.

T. tomentosa 'Sterling' (syn. 'Sterling Silver') (Sterling Silver linden) Even habit, glossy deep green leaves with silvery bottoms; tolerates heat and drought, resists Japanese beetles and gypsy moths. 45' h × 35' w.

Tilia tomentosa 'Sterling'

TSUGA

Tsuga canadensis △

SU-ga kan-a-DEN-sis

Eastern hemlock, Canadian hemlock

Pine Family (Pinaceae)
Evergreen conifer
30'–60' h x 15'–30' w

All around me in New Hampshire, I see native hemlock woods, especially on stark, shady, north-facing slopes where nothing seems to grow on the forest floor. Grown in the open, hemlocks have fine-textured foliage, a wide pyramidal habit, and branches that droop with age. Although its many handsome cultivars make it an ideal landscape plant for New England, I no longer recommend the species to folks where I live in Rockingham County. Present in the county since 2001, the voracious hemlock woolly adelgid insect can destroy a tree in 3 to 4 years. *T. caroliniana* is also prone to wooly adelgid, while the native western U.S. hemlocks, *T. heterophylla* and *T. mertensiana,* are not. Certified arborists can treat diseased hemlocks with insecticidal soap, horticultural oil, or other chemical products with good results if you take immediate action (see page 137).

Eastern hemlocks have ½", dark green, flattened needles with 2 white bands underneath. The bark is grayish brown, ridged, and scaly. Flowers are not ornamental, but the tree bears numerous little cones.

LANDSCAPE USE
Excellent for fine-textured hedging, screening, and naturalizing in open to wooded areas; some of the cultivars make exceptional sculptural specimens.

ORIGIN Woods of eastern North America.

HARDINESS ZONES 3–7

LIGHT Full sun to partial shade; tolerates full shade.

SOIL Moist, well-drained soil.

GROWING Ideally, plant hemlocks in a cool, sheltered spot away from heat and drying winds; prune hedges in spring. Hemlock woolly adelgid, a Japanese sap-sucker that deposits cottony white egg sacs at the base of hemlock needles, feeds on young branches. These insects threaten the survival of this native tree in much of New England, the Mid-Atlantic, and southeastern U.S.

DESIGNER'S CHOICE
A sampling of available cultivars:

Tsuga canadensis 'Bennett' Vase-shaped dwarf with central dip. 2'–5' h × 4'–6' w.

T. canadensis 'Cole's Prostrate' (syn. *T. canadensis* 'Cole') Prostrate dwarf conifer with exposed center wood; grows best in cool, partially shaded locations; groundcover. 1' h × 3' w after 10 years. Zone 4.

T. canadensis 'Hussii' Dwarf, upright, irregular, and slow growing. 12' h × 6' w.

T. canadensis 'Moon Frost' Dwarf globe with white new shoots for a frosty look, tinted pink in winter. 3' h and w. Zone 4.

T. canadensis 'Pendula' (syn. 'Sargentii') (Sargent's weeping hemlock) Variable dimensions due to training; low spreading, elegant, slow-growing form. Often a collective grouping of

Tsuga canadensis 'Cole's Prostrate'

Tsuga canadensis **'Pendula'**

weeping forms. 10'–15' h × 30' w.

T. canadensis 'Westonigra' Exceptional dark green foliage; use as backdrop for colorful shrubs and perennials. 40'–60' h × 15'–30' w. Zone 4.

T. caroliniana (Carolina hemlock) Grows fast in youth with graceful, dense, irregular form; shorter needles and height than *T. canadensis* and more pollution tolerant; golden brown fall cones; southeastern U.S. native susceptible to hemlock woolly adelgid. Grow in moist, cool, well-drained soils in partial shade. 25'–60' h × 20'–25' w. Zones 4–7.

T. heterophylla (western hemlock) Native to coast of western North America, likes shady to partly shady site with moist atmosphere and plenty of water; grows best in the Northwest; resists woolly adelgid. 70'–150' h × 20'–30' w. Zones 6–8.

T. mertensiana (mountain hemlock) Native to western Northern America, slow growing, bluish gray-green needles, resists woolly adelgid. Avoid planting in the East, where it doesn't do well. In cultivation, drooping branches look attractive draped over rocks in a rock garden or in containers. 30'–50' h × 20' w. Zones 5–6.

HEMLOCK WOOLLY ADELGID

Eastern and Carolina hemlocks are versatile, shade-tolerant native conifers with numerous outstanding cultivars. Yet the hemlock woolly adelgid, a tiny Asian insect, is destroying their usefulness for low-maintenance home landscapes by feeding on and killing hemlocks in as little as a year. These sap-suckers deposit woolly, white egg sacs at the base of needles. They have spread throughout the eastern U.S. from Maine to Georgia and west to Tennessee, but pose little threat to western hemlock species. The Pennsylvania Department of Conservation and Natural Resources proposes the following steps to preserve susceptible hemlocks on your property.

- Drench the leaves and twigs of affected, single, ornamental trees less than 30' tall with horticultural oil or insecticidal soap in spring or early summer when crawling insects are present, or in autumn when the adults break their summer dormancy.
- Water hemlocks well, applying 1" of water during dry spells around the dripline.
- Avoid tilling or disturbing the root zone of hemlocks.
- Because birds can spread the insects, keep birdfeeders away from your hemlocks.
- If the infestation is heavy, cut down and burn the affected trees to limit the spread to other trees.
- Avoid stressing trees by changing the grade of the land or changing the water runoff pattern.
- Do not fertilize infested trees with nitrogen, which vastly increases adelgid populations. Instead, wait until you've treated the tree and destroyed the adelgids, then fertilize with a balanced plant food.
- Keep lime and herbicides at least 10' from the dripline of hemlocks.

ULMUS

Ulmus americana ▽

UL-mus a-may-ri-KA-na

American elm

Elm Family (Ulmaceae)
Deciduous tree
80' h × 60' w

American elm is a majestic tree with a spreading form. Until 1930, American elms, with their towering vase-shaped habit and huge arced limbs, shaded the lawns and lined the streets of U.S. cities and towns. In 1930, however, Dutch elm disease appeared in Ohio, killing many elms.

To date, many more elms in this country, especially in the Northeast and Midwest, have succumbed. Only the desert Southwest appears safe from the rampant fungus. If you're willing to take a chance on elms, grow newer, disease-resistant cultivars, or cultivate an elm of a different species.

American elm produces simple, dark green leaves up to 6" long with pointed tips, serrated edges, and yellow fall color. The dark gray bark is layered and scaly.

LANDSCAPE USE

Shade tree, lawn specimen, and large public plantings.

ORIGIN North American bottomlands from the East Coast to the Rockies.

HARDINESS ZONES 3–9

LIGHT Full sun.

SOIL Moist, well-drained, fertile soil.

GROWING American elms are susceptible to many diseases including Dutch elm disease (DED). Plant only DED-resistant varieties and take action at the first sign of wilting or browning leaves. If you have an American elm, baby it. Hire a professional tree-care company to prune and fertilize the tree below ground once a year, or check with your Cooperative Extension service to find out the safest and best way to fertilize it. An arborist can cut away dead branches that could harbor disease-carrying beetles. When necessary, deliver moisture with a soaker hose placed just beyond the tree's drip line at the branches' farthest reach. Avoid wounding the tree with a lawnmower or cutting into the roots of the tree. In addition to Dutch elm disease, it may attract leaf spot and cankers and pests such as beetles, borers, and aphids. It may also be susceptible to storm damage.

DESIGNER'S CHOICE

Ulmus americana 'New Harmony' Introduced by the U.S. National Arboretum, this DED-resistant cultivar has a vase shape and yellow fall color. It prefers moist, well-drained soils and tolerates poor soils and air pollution. 50'–70' h and w. Zones 5–7.

U. americana 'Princeton' This fast-grower with a straight trunk and vase-shaped habit likes fertile well-drained soil. Highly resistant to Dutch elm disease, it has yellow fall color and makes a striking lawn specimen and shade tree. 60'–70' h × 30'–40' w. Zones 3–9.

U. americana 'Valley Forge' This introduction from the U.S. National Arboretum is the most DED-resistant American elm. A vase-shaped tree, it has yellow fall color and prefers fertile, well-drained soils. 50'–70' h × 60'–70' w. Zones 5–7.

U. 'Camperdownii' (syn. *U. glabra* 'Camperdownii') (Camperdown elm) Small, wide, weeping landscape tree with rounded top and twisted branches that can droop to the ground. 15' h × 30' w. Zones 4–6.

U. × 'Cathedral' Broad, vase-shaped hybrid resistant to DED and verticillium wilt; low susceptibility to black leaf spot. 45' h × 50' w. Zones 4–7.

U. × 'Morton' (Accolade) Vase-shaped hybrid that looks like American elm but is resistant to DED and elm leaf beetle; yellow fall color. 70' h × 45' w. Zones 4–7.

Ulmus parvifolia ○ ✳

UL-mus par-vi-FOH-lee-a

Chinese or lacebark elm

Elm Family (Ulmaceae)
Deciduous tree
50' h and w

For year-round interest, the mottled bark of lacebark elm is hard to beat. Irregular plates of gray, green, and orange bark peel off to expose reddish orange inner bark. Sometimes the trunk looks muscular and fluted. The shady, round canopy with its spreading branches and small, dark green leaves offers relief on a hot summer afternoon.

Ulmus americana 'Princeton'

Ulmus 'Camperdownii'

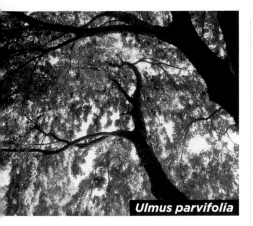
Ulmus parvifolia

The leaves are pointed ovals, about 2½" long with serrated edges. Shiny dark green on top, they develop red, yellow, or purple fall color. The gray, green, and orange bark sheds in puzzlelike patterns.

LANDSCAPE USE
Shade, lawn specimen, and allées.

ORIGIN   Rocky sites in China, Japan, and Korea.

HARDINESS ZONES   4–9

LIGHT   Full sun.

SOIL   Moist, well-drained, fertile soil.

GROWING   This tough, attractive, fast-growing, medium-sized tree is resistant to DED, Japanese and elm-leaf beetles, and urban pollution. It may suffer winter storm damage.

CAUTION   Potentially invasive in the District of Columbia, North Carolina, Nebraska, New Jersey, Virginia, and Wisconsin.

DESIGNER'S CHOICE
Ulmus parvifolia 'Emerald Isle' (Athena) (syn. 'Emer I') Thick, rounded crown of shiny, blackish-green leaves on a trunk with multihued, exfoliating bark in gray, green, and orange. DED resistant. 40' h × 50' w. Zones 5–9.
U. parvifolia 'Emerald Vase' (Allee) (syn. 'Emer II') Vase-shaped habit with deep green leaves that turn yellow to blushing pink in fall. Multicolor bark starts shedding when young. Disease resistant. 75' h × 55' w. Zones 5–9.

VACCINIUM

Vaccinium angustifolium 🝘

vak-SIN-ee-um an-gus-ti-FOH-lee-um

Low-bush blueberry

Heath Family (Ericaceae)
Deciduous shrub
1'–2' h × 2' w

This little, three-season shrub grows wild in New England, forming a thick groundcover and offering bell-shaped, white spring flowers; sweet, edible, summer fruit; and red fall color. The tiny, frosty-blue fruits are sweet, meaty, and delectable beyond description. I prefer them for baking and eating to the fruits of highbush blueberry, which tend to be more watery.

LANDSCAPE USE
Groundcover, edging for a shrub border, edible landscapes, naturalized areas.

ORIGIN   Northeastern U.S.

HARDINESS ZONES   2–5

LIGHT   Full sun.

SOIL   Moist, well-drained, sandy, acid soils with a pH between 4.5 and 5.5 and high in organic matter.

Vaccinium angustifolium

GROWING   Add organic matter by mulching the root zone.

DESIGNER'S CHOICE
Vaccinium angustifolium 'Burgundy' Fruits reliably; turns wine red in fall. 1' h × 3' w. Zone 3.

Vaccinium corymbosum ○

vak-SIN-ee-um kor-im-BOH-sum

High-bush blueberry

Heath Family (Ericaceae)
Deciduous shrub
5'–12' h and w

I love how the bare burgundy stems of blueberry bushes color the winter landscape near my home, creating red ribbons and rectangles against the snow. These slow-growing eastern natives make outstanding four-season plants, ideal for the shrub border. They feature small, white spring blooms, scrumptious blueberries in summer (which attract birds), rich red fall color, and red or yellow winter stems. Blueberries are twiggy, with many stems and a rounded or uneven shape. Although the species is lovely, you can grow cultivars to extend the berry-producing season and vary the size and taste of the fruit. Although some blueberries are self-pollinating, your shrubs will do best if you grow a few varieties within 100 feet of each other for easier cross-pollination by bees.

High-bush blueberry bears alternate, simple, deciduous leaves, elliptical and shiny dark green that changes to reds, oranges, and yellows in fall. The old bark is grayish brown; new wood is red or yellow, depending upon which blueberry you grow. Clusters of hanging, bell-shaped, white or sometimes pale pink blooms are attractive but not flashy. The blueberries are up to ½" across, consumed by people and animals.

Fruits ripen from mid- to late spring in the South, mid- to late summer farther North. Ivy, our 6-year old Corgi, harvests all fruits low on the bushes, leaving the high berries for our family and the birds.

LANDSCAPE USE
Shrub borders, low spots, edging for ponds and bog gardens, groups and masses, and hedgerows; a fine native substitute for invasive burning bush (*Euonymus alata* 'Compacta').

ORIGIN   Swamps and lowlands in North America.

HARDINESS ZONES   3–7

LIGHT   Full sun to partial shade — but the more sun the more berries.

SOIL   Moist, acid, well-drained soils rich in organic matter; soil pH should be 4.0–5.0; tolerates wet feet (roots).

GROWING   Plant at least two types for best pollination. Set high-bush blueberries about 3' apart for informal hedgerows; 4'–5' apart for accessible and most fruit. Keep roots moist throughout the growing season. If you like, use fertilizer for acid-loving plants or organic fertilizer such as cottonseed meal and blood meal. Do not overfertilize. As plants age, prune out weak, short, dead, damaged, and unproductive wood in winter or early spring in favor of brightly colored wood. Eliminate scraggly shoots at the base.

DESIGNER'S CHOICE
Vaccinium corymbosum 'Bluecrop' Big, plentiful, high-quality fruit; disease resistant, somewhat drought resistant; midseason fruit. 4'–6' h and w.

V. corymbosum 'Bluejay' Fast-growing shrub with plentiful, firm, mid-sized berries; yellow-orange fall color, yellow winter stems; early mid-season fruit. 6'–7' h and w. Zones 4–7.

V. corymbosum 'Blueridge' A vigorous, low-chill, Southern high-bush blueberry with firm, light blue fruit; resists stem blight, early mid-season fruit. 5'–10' h and w. Zones 3–8.

V. corymbosum 'Friendship' Abundant mid-sized berries on compact plant with bright red fall color; *V. corymbosum* × *V. angustifolium* hybrid; extremely hardy. 2'–3' h × 3' w.

V. corymbosum '1613-A' (Hardyblue) Vigorous shrub with big yields of sweet, dark blue, medium-sized fruits in midseason; excellent yellow-orange fall color; dark red winter stems; good in the Northwest, tolerates heavy clay soils, adaptable. About 6'–8' h and w. Zones 4–7.

V. corymbosum 'Late Blue' Medium to large, firm, dark blue, somewhat tart fruits into September. 6' h and w.

V. corymbosum 'Northcountry' Blazing red fall color. 2' h and w.

V. corymbosum 'Northland' Half-high high-bush (*V. corymbosum* × *V. angustifolium*); small dark blueberries; brilliant orange fall color; bright yellow winter wood; early fruit. 2'–4' h × 2'–5' w.

V. corymbosum 'Northsky' Small, frosted blue fruits; glossy red fall foliage. 18" h × 24" w.

V. corymbosum 'Patriot' Big, sweet, flattened fruit; disease resistant, adaptable to many soils; early fruit. 6' h and w.

V. corymbosum 'Tophat' Profuse blooms, abundant small light blue berries, self-pollinating; brilliant red fall color; needs some shade in

Vaccinium corymbosum

Zones 5–7; good for woodland edging, mixed perennial beds, containers, and bonsai. 1'–2' h × 2'–3' w.

V. corymbosum 'Toro' Slow-growing ornamental shrub with clusters of bright pink to white blooms against bronzy spring leaves; followed by tight, hefty clusters of firm, big, blue berries in summer and brilliant red fall foliage; USDA release; does well in the Pacific Northwest; midseason fruit. 4'–6' h and w. Zones 4–7.

VIBURNUM

Viburnum acerifolium 🍂

vi-BUR-num a-se-ri-FOH-lee-um

Maple-leaf viburnum

Honeysuckle Family (Adoxaceae, formerly Caprifoliaceae)
Deciduous flowering shrub
4'–6' h × 4 w

Maple-leaf viburnum bears rounded, 3", white, terminal flower clusters on new wood in late spring to early summer. The 3"–4" long, toothed, dark green leaves have 3 lobes and fuzzy bottoms and leaf stems. Clusters of purplish black fruit are set against red to purple fall leaves and attract wildlife. It spreads by suckers, forming open thickets of erect woody stems under trees. Known for shade tolerance, maple-leaf viburnum is ideal for naturalizing in shady woods beneath maples, pines, and birches.

LANDSCAPE USE
To use maple-leaf viburnum effectively, grow it in a naturalistic setting.

ORIGIN   Native to well-drained woods and slopes of the eastern U.S.

HARDINESS ZONES   (3) 4–8

LIGHT   Grows best in partial to deep shade.

SOIL   Moist, well-drained, acidic soil high in organic matter.

GROWING If wild clumps pre-exist on wooded building land, they're worth saving. Move them to an area with similar growing conditions. Ask for plants grown from seed or cuttings, since grafted plants may have suckering rootstocks. Viburnum leaf beetle may damage this species.

Viburnum × bodnantense 'Dawn' ○

vi-BUR-num bod-nan-TENSE

'Dawn' Bodnant viburnum

Honeysuckle Family (Adoxaceae, formerly Caprifoliaceae)
Deciduous flowering shrub
10' h x 6' w

This viburnum is valued for its pink, fragrant flowers in late winter or early spring. Wandering around the Royal Horticultural Society's Wisley Garden in England one January, I smelled a powerful sweet scent, which I followed to the pretty pink blooms of an unimpressive, upright shrub labeled *Viburnum × bodnantense* 'Dawn'. Cut stems in early spring to bring indoors for forcing into bloom.

LANDSCAPE USE
Plant in a bed or border near a door, window, well-used path, since the shrub is not handsome enough to stand alone as a specimen.

ORIGIN Garden origin

HARDINESS ZONES 5–9

LIGHT Full sun to partial shade.

SOIL Moist, well-drained, rich soil.

Viburnum x bodnantense 'Dawn'

LEAF BEETLE VULNERABILITY

The viburnum leaf beetle came from Europe and preys on arrowwood viburnums (*V. dentatum*), European cranberrybush viburnum (*V. opulus*), and American cranberrybush viburnum (*V. trilobum*). Also vulnerable are maple-leaf viburnum (*V. acerifolium*), wayfaring tree viburnum (*V. lantana*), southern blackhaw (*V. rufidulum*), and Sargent viburnum (*V. sargentii*). This is a partial listing of affected plants and treatment options. For the latest on viburnum leaf beetle, go to www.hort.cornell.edu/vlb.

The pest is active in parts of northern New England, Pennsylvania, New York, Ohio, Ontario, British Columbia, and the Maritimes. It skeletonizes the foliage of affected trees and shrubs and can kill them within three years. Check twigs in early spring for overwintering eggs — you'll see rows of tiny dark bumps on new tan or greenish twigs — and again study young leaves for small holes. Immediately prune out affected stems and dispose of them in the trash, not the compost pile. Do not plant susceptible species and cultivars in you live in an affected area.

Viburnums such as leather-leaf viburnum (*V. rhytidophyllum*), with thick or fuzzy leaves, are not affected as much by leaf beetles as those with thin leaves.

GROWING To keep 'Dawn' looking neat and attractive, cut out the oldest, least productive stems and any floppy branches that have rooted themselves at the base. This hybrid viburnum resists viburnum leaf beetle.

Viburnum × burkwoodii ○ ✳

vi-BUR-num burk-WOOD-ee-i

Burkwood viburnum

Honeysuckle Family (Adoxaceae, formerly Caprifoliaceae)
Deciduous to semi-evergreen shrub
6'–10' h and w

Grow this shrub for its clusters of clove-scented, pink buds that turn into white spring flowers; spicily fragrant, semi-evergreen foliage; and orange-red to burgundy fall color.

LANDSCAPE USE
See All About *Viburnum*.

ORIGIN Garden origin

HARDINESS ZONES 5–8

LIGHT See All About *Viburnum*.

SOIL Moist, deep, rich, and well-drained soil.

GROWING Prune like *V. × bodnantense*. This easy-growing hybrid viburnum is moderately resistant to viburnum leaf beetle.

DESIGNER'S CHOICE
Viburnum × burkwoodii 'Conoy' Dark pink buds open creamy white; small, dark green, glossy leaves, which are evergreen with a maroon winter tint in Zones 7–8; slightly hanging, clustered, bright red fruit persists from late summer into fall; pest and disease resistant; drought tolerant; use as a compact specimen, for informal hedging, or in containers; U.S. National Arboretum release. 5' h x 7' w. Zone (5) 6–8.

ALL ABOUT VIBURNUM

Grown for flowers, fruits, and leaves, viburnums satisfy the sensualist in me. I smell the white, cream, or pink clustered flowers in spring or summer (some good, some bad) and watch the butterflies they attract. I study their forms: upright to sprawling; twiggy and open to dense; rounded, oval, and spreading shrubs or small trees ranging from 3'–30' tall. Leaves beg to be touched — some lustrous deep green, others a coarse, hairy, leathery, dull green. Prominent clusters of berries in shiny red, pink, yellow, blue, or black — food for birds and sometimes people — usually follow and sometimes persist into winter. Impressive fall foliage on some deciduous species turns bright to wine red and purple. In winter, birds seek cover in the bare, twiggy branches. Who can fault me for growing about 20 viburnums and wanting to try more?

Viburnum plicatum 'Mariesii'

The opposite, simple, green foliage is shiny to dull and hairy (above and/or below), sometimes lobed; the edges are usually serrated but sometimes smooth. The leaves of some species turn red to purple in fall; there are both evergreen and deciduous plants. Bark is usually grayish brown. The white, cream, or pink blooms develop in flattened, hemispherical, or snowball-shaped clusters; some are fragrant. In fall, plants are covered with showy fruit clusters in fiery reds and yellows, glowing blue, and shiny black; some have decorative red stems that look flower-like and last long after birds have consumed the fruits.

Use viburnums for informal hedging, in shrub beds and borders and native plant landscapes, as specimen plants or as background. You can naturalize or use them in groups or in masses. Plant fragrant viburnums near roads and paths, where you can smell them when you pass by.

Most of the species mentioned here come from woodlands in eastern North America, Asia, Europe, and Northern Africa. They are hardy in Zones 2–9, depending on the species. They may be grown in full sun to shade, but most thrive in full sun to partial shade but adapt to partial shade. They prefer well-drained, moist, moderately fertile, slightly acid soils (6.0–7.0), but most adapt to many soils and conditions.

Plant two or more viburnums to guarantee cross-pollination and improve fruit set of plants grown for fruiting interest. Cut out dead or damaged wood in early spring. To control the spread of some species, you can remove suckers and layered stems (stems that root where they touch the ground) at any time. Composted leaves or other organic materials make good mulch for viburnums. The viburnum leaf beetle came from Europe and preys on some viburnums. (See Leaf Beetle Vulnerability, on page 357.) Also, aphids may harm snowball viburnums and European cranberrybush viburnum (V. opulus); nematodes, leaf spot, and powdery mildew may affect plants in close, shady sites.

V. × burkwoodii 'Mohawk' Profuse, deep red buds (showy for weeks) open to waxy white blooms blushed pink and intense clove scent; bright reddish-orange fall color; resists powdery mildew and bacterial leaf spot; background for perennial bed, specimen, shrub border; from the U.S. National Arboretum. 8' h × 10' w. Zones 5–8.

Viburnum carlesii ○ ✳

vi-BUR-num kar-LEE-zee-i

Korean spice viburnum

Honeysuckle Family (Adoxaceae, formerly Caprifoliaceae)
Deciduous shrub
4'–8' h and w

Each May I drive through the picturesque town of Newfields, New Hampshire, just to inhale the potent scent of Korean spice viburnum through my open car windows. The overwhelming fragrance of this slow-growing viburnum, with its clusters of waxy, pale pink blooms that fade to white, perfumes the late spring air far from the shrub border where it grows. In fall, the bright red berry clusters of late summer turn black, and the fuzzy, dull green leaves change to burgundy. The plant has a rounded, somewhat irregular form, and attracts birds and butterflies.

LANDSCAPE USE
See All About *Viburnum*.

ORIGIN   Korea, Japan

HARDINESS ZONES   4–8

LIGHT   See All About *Viburnum*.

SOIL   See All About *Viburnum*.

GROWING   See All About *Viburnum*. The species, cultivars, and hybrids all resist viburnum leaf beetle.

DESIGNER'S CHOICE
Viburnum × carlcephalum 'Cayuga' Hybrid with *V. carlesii*; compact shrub with slightly wavy, dark green

leaves turning orangey red in fall; profuse pink buds open to waxy, white, fragrant, long-lasting, snowball flowers; adaptable to many soils, resists leaf spot and powdery mildew. From U.S. National Arboretum. 5'–7' h and w. Zones (5) 6–8.

V. carlesii 'Compactum' Dwarf with the attributes of the species. 2½'–4' h and w.

V. carlesii 'Juddii' (syn. *Viburnum juddii*) (Judd viburnum) Upright, rounded viburnum with dark bluish green to grayish green leaves that resist bacterial leaf spot and turn red-purple in fall; medium-texture leaves; in early to mid-spring, pink buds open to rounded clusters of fragrant, white semi-snowball flowers, but in my opinion, the floral scent can't compare with the heavy, spicy fragrance of *V. carlesii*, which is one of its parents. 6–8' h and w. Zones (4) 5–8.

Viburnum carlesii

Viburnum carlesii 'Compactum'

Viburnum dentatum ⟳ › 🌱 ✳

vi-BUR-num den-TAY-tum

Arrowwood viburnum

Honeysuckle Family (Adoxaceae, formerly Caprifoliaceae)
Deciduous shrub
6'–10' h x 6'–20' w

This rounded, arching, suckering, and layering shrub makes a tough, effective, fast-growing screen with leaves from top to bottom, especially where space is no consideration. In May and June, it bears profuse, cream-white, flat flower clusters. In fall, leaves turn red to yellow and purple and it produces bluish black fruits that attract birds and other wildlife.

LANDSCAPE USE
Good for naturalizing, shrub borders, and informal hedges.

ORIGIN Eastern U.S.

HARDINESS ZONES 3–8

LIGHT Full sun to shade.

SOIL Adapts to most soils.

GROWING Adapts to city conditions. Prune right after blooming because it flowers on old wood. Highly susceptible to viburnum leaf beetle, so choose alternate species where this pest is prevalent.

DESIGNER'S CHOICE
Viburnum dentatum 'Christom' (Blue Muffin) Dense dwarf with blue fruit. 4' h x 4'–6' w.

V. dentatum 'Morton' (Northern Burgundy) Upright to vase-shaped shrub with shiny deep green foliage that turns wine red in autumn. Birds devour the inky blue fall fruits. 10'–12' h x 6'–8' w.

V. dentatum 'Patzam' (Pathfinder) Upright shape; glossy, dark green leaves; no pruning necessary to maintain shape. 5'–6' h x 3'–4' w.

V. dentatum 'Ralph Senior' (Autumn Jazz) Upright form with good fall color; attracts butterflies, birds, wildlife. 6'–10' h x 8'–12' w

V. dentatum 'Synnestvedt' (Chicago Lustre) Wide, rounded, twiggy shrub with thin arching stems that layer and spread; ideal for bird cover and nesting. 6'–8' h x 8'–10' w.

Viburnum dilatatum ○

vi-BUR-num di-la-TAY-tum

Linden viburnum

Honeysuckle Family (Adoxaceae, formerly Caprifoliaceae)
Deciduous shrub
8'–10' h and w

Linden viburnum has a medium texture and rounded form. In mid-spring, little creamy white flowers form flat, 4"–6" clusters. In fall, it turns yellow to orangey red and produces flattened clusters of red berries that shrivel in frost and persist into winter. May grow better in warmer states but doesn't thrive in my Zone 5b garden where other viburnums flourish.

LANDSCAPE USE
See All About *Viburnum*.

ORIGIN Japan

HARDINESS ZONES (5) 6–8

LIGHT See All About *Viburnum*.

SOIL Adapts to many kinds of soil.

GROWING See All About *Viburnum*. Moderately resists the viburnum leaf beetle.

CAUTION Invasive tendencies of the species observed in some parts of the Northeast and Midwest; use a non-invasive species in these areas.

DESIGNER'S CHOICE
Viburnum dilatatum 'Erie' Pest and disease resistant; red fruits turn coral in cold weather. A U.S. National Arboretum release. 6½' h x 11' w.

V. 'Iroquois' Grow for its massive fruit set, which weighs down the branches; bigger fruit and broader habit than 'Erie'; better for screening. A U.S. National Arboretum release. 10' h x 10'–12' w.

Viburnum dilatatum 'Erie'

V. 'Oneida' Hybrid with lavish, flat, white flower clusters in May, followed by a profusion of small, shiny, persistent, deep red berries. 8'–10' h and w.

Viburnum 'Eskimo' ○ ✳

vi-BUR-num

'Eskimo' viburnum

Honeysuckle Family (Adoxaceae, formerly Caprifoliaceae)
Semi-evergreen shrub
4'–5' h and w

Years ago I bought this shrub, a U.S. National Arboretum release, at my local nursery on name alone, assuming a plant named Eskimo would certainly make it through a southern New Hampshire winter. No way. This little viburnum lasted awhile but looked worse every year until a winter with –15°F temperatures killed it for good. The moral here is to do what I say and not what I do — always research the hardiness of the plants you buy if you want them to flourish.

In the right conditions, this little viburnum is a charmer. Eskimo viburnum bears 3"–4" snowballs of small white flowers in spring, preceding red fruits that blacken in fall. The thick, lustrous, semi-evergreen leaves have an orangey red autumn hue and resist bacterial leaf spot.

LANDSCAPE USE
See All About *Viburnum.*

ORIGIN   Garden origin

HARDINESS ZONES   6–8

LIGHT   See All About *Viburnum.*

SOIL   See All About *Viburnum.*

GROWING   See All About *Viburnum.*

DESIGNER'S CHOICE

Viburnum 'Chippewa' Semi-evergreen, dense shrub with shiny, deep green leaves that become red to dark maroon in late fall; creamy white blooms in May; persistent, deep red, lustrous fruits. Plant with 'Huron' for best fruiting. 8' h × 9' w.

V. 'Huron' Semi-evergreen, dense shrub with dull, dark green foliage that turns purple-red in late fall; creamy white blooms in May; persistent, deep red, lustrous fruits. Fruits heavily when planted with 'Chippewa'. 8' h × 9' w.

Viburnum lantana 'Mohican' ○ ✳

vi-BUR-num lan-TAN-a

Mohican wayfaring tree

Honeysuckle Family (Adoxaceae, formerly Caprifoliaceae)
Deciduous shrub
9' h × 7'–9' w

Mohican viburnum is truly a desirable plant. In my garden, its dense, oval form is taller than it is wide and needs no pruning to maintain its impressive shape. It holds its blackish green, thick, glossy leaves well into November and is resistant to bacterial leaf spot. In fact, I write this entry November 12, and my Mohican shows no sign of impending winter. In spring, the creamy clustered flowers are evident but not particularly showy. Similarly,

Viburnum nudum 'Winterthur'

the summer fruit display may be orangey red and lasting in some areas, but not in my garden. U.S. National Arboretum release.

LANDSCAPE USE
Its height, symmetry, and denseness make it perfect for medium to tall deciduous hedging and screening.

ORIGIN   Europe and Asia.

HARDINESS ZONES   4–8

LIGHT   Full sun.

SOIL   Dry, somewhat acid to chalky soils.

GROWING   Thrives in the North. Susceptible to the viburnum leaf beetle.

CAUTION   Invasive tendencies of the species observed in parts of the Northeast and Midwest, particularly Illinois and Wisconsin.

Viburnum nudum 'Winterthur' ○ ✳

vi-BUR-num NU-dum

'Winterthur' smooth witherod viburnum

Honeysuckle Family (Adoxaceae, formerly Caprifoliaceae)
Deciduous shrub
10'–15' h × 5'–6' w

This handsome, upright, rounded shrub has lots going for it — except fragrance. In fact, the flowers stink. When massed, you can smell them far away. The large, cream-colored flower clusters appear in June. Leaves are a deep shiny green with excellent red fall color. Summer fruit clusters change from white to pink to blue. Leaves are glossier and habit more compact than the species. A top choice landscape shrub in areas where beetles aren't an issue. Species *cassinoides* (sometimes seen listed as a variety of *nudum*) is similar, but slightly smaller and from a more northern area so more hardy (Zones 3–8). The latter is moderately resistant to the viburnum leaf beetle, so it is a substitute for *nudum* where the beetles are prevalent.

LANDSCAPE USE
Singly or grouped in shrub borders or boundary hedges away from the house.

ORIGIN   Species from wet areas and understories in eastern N. America.

HARDINESS ZONES   5–9

LIGHT   See All About *Viburnum*. Tolerates part shade to shade.

SOIL   See All About *Viburnum*. Tolerates boggy sites.

GROWING   See All About *Viburnum*. Highly susceptible to viburnum leaf beetle, so plant other choices in areas where this insect is present.

Viburnum opulus ○ ✳

vi-BUR-num OH-pu-lus

European cranberrybush, Guelder rose

Honeysuckle Family (Adoxaceae, formerly Caprifoliaceae)
Deciduous shrub
8'–12' h x 10'–15' w

European cranberrybush viburnum is common in the northern half of the United States. Attributes include 3"–5", lacecap, white flower clusters in late May followed by showy, pendulous, ¼", bright red fruit clusters in fall; fruits are attractive to birds. The dark green, maple-like three-lobed foliage of *V. opulus* may have red and purple fall color.

LANDSCAPE USE
See All About *Viburnum*.

ORIGIN   Europe, North Africa, Asia.

HARDINESS ZONES   3–8

LIGHT   See All About *Viburnum*.

SOIL   Moist, rich, well-drained soil; adaptable; tolerates wet feet.

GROWING   May become infested with aphids, which cause twisted and distorted growth, detracting from the ornamental effect. Viburnum leaf beetles devour this species.

CAUTION   Invasive tendencies in the upper Midwest.

DESIGNER'S CHOICE
Viburnum opulus 'Compactum' Similar to the species but half the size. 4'–5' h × 4'–6' w.

V. opulus 'Nanum' Rounded dwarf that tolerates wet or clay soils; neither flowers nor fruits, so use for background foliage or border filler. 2' h × 2'–3' w.

V. opulus 'Roseum' (European snowball) Showy, snowball-like flower clusters; traditional in the South for borders and screening. 10' h and w.

V. opulus 'Xanthocarpum' Golden yellow fruits from early fall into winter. 4'–6' h × 5'–6' w.

Viburnum plicatum 'Shasta' ○ ✳

(syn. V. *plicatum* f. tomento-sum 'Shasta')

vi-BUR-num pli-KAY-tum

Shasta doublefile viburnum

Honeysuckle Family (Adoxaceae, formerly Caprifoliaceae)
Deciduous shrub
6' h x 10'–12'

Viburnum plicatum 'Mariesii'

I love Shasta viburnum. Its gorgeous, symmetrical shape is wide and rounded, giving it a graceful look even when bare. In spring, it is covered with clusters of non-fragrant, white, lacecap blooms; these showy, sterile flowers surround a group of tiny, white, fertile flowers and occur all along the wide-spreading stems, accentuating their tiered, horizontal growth. Birds quickly eat the showy, brilliant red fruits that change to black if they're on the plant long enough. But not to worry — the rounded clusters of stalks that supported the berries retain their vibrant red hue, giving the shrub an extra 4–6 weeks of showy summer color. Shasta's leaves are deep green and turn an attractive dark red in fall. A U.S. National Arboretum introduction.

LANDSCAPE USE
Perfect specimen, but works equally well in groups or hedges.

ORIGIN   Japan, China

HARDINESS ZONES   (5) 6–8

LIGHT   See All About *Viburnum*.

SOIL   See All About *Viburnum*.

GROWING   See All About *Viburnum*. Resistant to vibrunum leaf beetle.

DESIGNER'S CHOICE
Viburnum plicatum 'Mariesii' (syn. *V. plicatum* f. *tomentosum*) Horizontal, layered branching; rounded form;

white lacecap flowers in spring; fine deep red fruits; maroon fall color. 6'–8' h × 8'–10' w.

V. plicatum 'Newzam' (Newport) Dwarf with showy, white flowers and burgundy fall color; rarely fruits. 4'–5' h × 5'–6' w.

V. plicatum 'Pink Beauty' Flowers open white blushed with pink but age to deeper pink. 5' h × 8' w.

V. plicatum 'Popcorn' Lavish white flower balls. 7' h × 6' w.

V. plicatum 'Rosace' (syn. 'Kern's Pink', 'Pink Sensation') Pink ball-shaped blooms. 15' h × 8' w.

V. plicatum 'Shoshoni' Compact size makes attractive compact hedge. A U.S. National Arboretum introduction. 5'–6' h and w.

V. plicatum 'Summer Snowflake' Compact with abundant lacecap flowers that may bloom intermittently through summer; reddish-purple fall color. 6' h and w.

Viburnum prunifolium ○ ✳

vi-BUR-num pru-ni-FOH-lee-um

Blackhaw

Honeysuckle Family (Adoxaceae, formerly Caprifoliaceae)
Deciduous shrub or small tree
12'–15' h x 8'–12' w

Although blackhaw may sucker in wet soils, with some shaping it makes an attractive addition to the garden. It's ideal for difficult spots, since it tolerates both wet and dry sites in full sun or shade. In the wild, you often find it growing at the forest's edge in partial shade. Red leaf stems contrast with small, glossy, green leaves, which usually turn lovely purplish red in fall. It develops showy, white flower clusters in spring. The clustered, edible fruits ripen black in September. Blackhaw is so sturdy that Swarthmore College

Viburnum prunifolim

uses it by a parking lot. I planted mine in the shade of a tall pin oak; it has grown slowly into a small, twiggy, horizontally branched tree.

LANDSCAPE USE
See All About *Viburnum*.

ORIGIN Eastern U.S.

HARDINESS ZONES 3–9

LIGHT Adapts to both full sun and shade.

SOIL Adapts to both wet and dry sites.

GROWING See All About *Viburnum*. Moderately resistant to viburnum leaf beetle.

DESIGNER'S CHOICE
Viburnum prunifolium 'Ovazam' (Ovation) Tight, columnar form with creamy white flowers and blue-black fruits. Use for tough deciduous hedge. 8'–10' h × 4' w.

Viburnum × rhytidophylloides 'Alleghany' ○ ✳

vi-BUR-num rye-ti-di-fil-LOY-deez

Lantanaphyllum viburnum

Honeysuckle Family (Adoxaceae, formerly Caprifoliaceae)
Deciduous to semi-evergreen shrub
6'–8' h and w

This U.S. National Arboretum release, a hybrid with leather-leaf viburnum, is a four-season plant with very dark green, leathery, persistent leaves; plentiful clusters of cream-colored, fertile flowers in late spring; and

brilliant red berries in fall that ripen to blue black and attract birds. It is noted for its vigor, globelike habit, and resistance to bacterial leaf spot.

LANDSCAPE USE
Combine it with other broad-leafed evergreens in shrub borders or in a mass.

ORIGIN Garden origin

HARDINESS ZONES 5–8

LIGHT Adapts to sun or shade.

SOIL Moist, well-drained soil.

GROWING Protect from wind. Moderately resistant to viburnum leaf beetle.

DESIGNER'S CHOICE
Viburnum rhytidophyllum (leatherleaf viburnum) Chinese broadleaf evergreen, coarse texture with hairy leaves and stems; 4"–8" cream-colored smelly fertile flower clusters in spring; fruit clusters with red (immature) and black (mature) oval berries devoured by birds; trouble-free shrub useful for massed background plantings. It resists the viburnum leaf beetle. I planted one too close to the front of a shrub border, where its ugly winter appearance is all too evident. 15' h and w.

Viburnum rufidulum ○

vi-BUR-num roo-FID-uh-lum

Southern blackhaw, Rusty blackhaw

Honeysuckle Family (Adoxaceae, formerly Caprifoliaceae)
Deciduous shrub to small tree
10'–20' h and w

The foliage on this attractive shrub or small tree is bright green and shiny on top with rust-colored hairs on leaf buds, stems, and bottoms; it has reddish purple fall color. The white, flat-topped flower clusters and oval white to blue-black edible fruits are larger than their northern counterparts.

LANDSCAPE USE

See All About *Viburnum*.

ORIGIN Dry woods in the southeastern U.S.

HARDINESS ZONES 5–9

LIGHT Sun or shade, where it looks more delicate.

SOIL Well-drained soil; tolerates drought and dry shade.

GROWING See All About *Viburnum*. Susceptible to viburnum leaf beetle.

DESIGNER'S CHOICE

Viburnum rufidulum 'Royal Guard' Compact shrub with erect, narrow form; wine-red fall color. 8'–15' h × 6'–10' w.

Viburnum x *rhytidophylloides* 'Alleghany'

Viburnum sargentii ○ ✳

vi-BUR-num sar-GEN-tee-i

Sargent viburnum

Honeysuckle Family (Adoxaceae; formerly Caprifoliaceae)
Upright deciduous shrub
12'–15' h and w

This coarse, rounded shrub has maplelike foliage that opens bronze, then may turn red to yellow in fall. It bears abundant, showy, white, flattened flower clusters.

LANDSCAPE USE

See All About *Viburnum*.

ORIGIN Species is from eastern Siberia, northeast Asia.

HARDINESS ZONES 3–7

LIGHT Full sun to partial shade.

SOIL Moist, well-drained soils.

GROWING See All About *Viburnum*. To avoid weak stems, don't overfertilize. Species is susceptible to viburnum leaf beetle.

DESIGNER'S CHOICE

Viburnum sargentii 'Onondaga' Upright shrub with leaves that open deep maroon, remain tinged with maroon in summer, then turn to wine-red in fall. Large, white, sterile flowers around an inner circle of purple buds open to pinkish fertile flowers; it produces little fruit. A U.S. National Arboretum introduction. 6'–8' h and w.

V. sargentii 'Susquehanna' A big, spreading shrub with showy, sterile, and fertile white flower clusters; abundant, bright red fruits in late summer persisting into winter; corky bark; big, maplelike foliage coarser in texture than 'Onondaga'. U.S. National Arboretum introduction. 10' h and w.

Viburnum setigerum ○ ✳

vi-BUR-num se-TI-je-rum

Tea viburnum

Honeysuckle Family (Adoxaceae, formerly Caprifoliaceae)
Deciduous shrub
10' h × 6' w

I love tea viburnum for its odd, top-heavy look. Shaped like a distorted umbrella, this tall, upright Chinese shrub grows leggy fast. Specifically, the leaves, flowers, and fruits occur mostly in the top one-third to half of the shrub, while the bottom part

Viburnum setigerum

consists of long, bare, woody legs. Tea viburnum produces dark green leaves, white clustered blooms, and wondrous, droopy clusters of fat (½"), shiny red fruits in late summer. If the habit bothers you, face down the legs with small shrubs such as 2' h × 3' w *V. opulus* 'Nanum' or 4'–5' h × 5'–6' w *V. plicatum* 'Newport'.

LANDSCAPE USE

See All About *Viburnum*.

ORIGIN China

HARDINESS ZONE 5–7

LIGHT See All About *Viburnum*.

SOIL See All About *Viburnum*.

GROWING See All About *Viburnum*.

Viburnum sieboldii 'Seneca' ○ ✳

vi-BUR-num see-BOHL-dee-i

'Seneca' siebold viburnum

Honeysuckle Family (Adoxaceae, formerly Caprifoliaceae)
Deciduous shrub or small tree
15'–20' h x 10'–12' w

'Seneca' viburnum is valuable for its persistent, firm, red fruit clusters produced above the leaves and lasting far longer than the brilliant, 2-week show of the species. The red fruits, which eventually turn black, make a handsome display in late summer and fall and are not eaten by birds. Profuse, showy, 3"–6", creamy white flower clusters precede the fruit. A U.S. National Arboretum introduction.

LANDSCAPE USE
Irregular multi-trunk form adds interest to shrub borders, masses, and patio plantings.

ORIGIN   Japan
HARDINESS ZONES   4–8
LIGHT   See All About *Viburnum*.
SOIL   See All About *Viburnum*.
GROWING   See All About *Viburnum*.
   Resistant to viburnum leaf beetle.

Viburnum trilobum ○
(syn. *V. opulus var. americanum, V. opulus subsp. trilobum*)

vi-BUR-num OP-yoo-lus a-mer-ih-KAY-num

American cranberrybush

Honeysuckle Family (Adoxaceae, formerly Caprifoliaceae)
Deciduous shrub
8'–12' h and w

An American native, similar to *V. opulus* but more resistant to aphids. Birds love the fruits. Unlike European cranberrybush, American cranberrybush has edible fruits

that make good jelly. Considered endangered or rare in some Midwest states.

LANDSCAPE USE
See All About *Viburnum*.
ORIGIN   Northern U.S., southern Canada
HARDINESS ZONES   3–7
LIGHT   See All About *Viburnum*.
SOIL   See All About *Viburnum*.
GROWING   Native variety resists aphids. Viburnum leaf beetles devour this species.

DESIGNER'S CHOICE
Viburnum trilobum 'Alfredo' Compact, rounded form with edible, red fruits, orangey-red fall color. 5'–6' h and w.

V. trilobum 'Compactum' Dwarf with scarlet fruits persisting into winter; so-so fall color; good aphid resistance. 5'–6' h and w.

V. trilobum 'Hahs' Grown for larger and good-quality fruits. 6'–8' h and w.

V. trilobum 'Wentworth' Abundant, late-ripening, scarlet fruits of high quality for eating; fine red fall color. 10'–12' h and w.

VITEX

Vitex agnus-castus ○ ✳

VI-teks AG-nus-KAS-tus

Chaste tree, Monk's pepper, Hemp tree

Verbena Family (Verbenaceae)
Large shrub or small multi-trunk tree
6'–20' h and w

The strange common names of *Vitex* are derived from its edible, peppery berries, traditionally used to reduce sex drive when ingested. *Vitex* leaves look like those of marijuana, thus hemp tree, its third common name. Chaste tree varies in size from a 6' cutback shrub in New England to a small, 20', flowering tree with knotty bark in the South. It has erect branches and twigs with handlike compound leaves and fingerlike, gray-

green, aromatic, 4" leaflets. Buddleia-like purple flower spikes, which attract hummingbirds and butterflies, appear on the tree on new wood in late spring and continue intermittently until fall.

LANDSCAPE USE
Works well in shrub and mixed borders; small trees make nice specimens.

ORIGIN   Southern Europe and Asia
HARDINESS ZONES   (6) 7–8 (9) (or grow as a herbaceous perennial in Zones 5 and 6).
LIGHT   Full sun to partial shade.
SOIL   Prefers moist, somewhat fertile, well-drained soil but tolerates heat, drought, salt, and many types of soil.
GROWING   Easily cultivated.

DESIGNER'S CHOICE
Vitex agnus-castus 'Blushing Spires' Pale pink flowers in late summer. 8'–12' h and w.

V. agnus-castus 'Shoal Creek' 12"–18" blue-violet flower spikes; resists leaf spot. 6'–20' h and w.

V. agnus-castus 'Silver Spire' White flowers. 6'–20' h and w.

Vitex agnus-castus

Weigela florida ○ ✳

why-GEE-la FLO-ri-da

Old-fashioned weigela

Honeysuckle Family (Caprifoliaceae)
Deciduous shrub
6'–8' h × 6'–10' w

Old-fashioned weigela reminds me of my mom, Libby Bass. She liked gilded antiques and shrubs like weigela with an opulent, yet traditional air. In bloom, weigela looks lavish with its rosy pink, tubular flowers clothing long, sometimes arching branches for 2 weeks in late spring. There, of course, was the problem. Two weeks of interest isn't much. Sure, an odd flower opened after peak, but basically it was done — no flashy leaves, no fall color, no sexy fruit, and no gorgeous bark. Mom would have adored today's weigelas. Refined flowers, snazzy leaves, and extended and reliable bloom (a good thing in St. Louis, where I grew up) characterize some of the cultivars.

Opposite, simple, green leaves up to 4" long with tiny-toothed edges offer no fall color; cultivars may have purple, yellow, or variegated leaves. The grayish-brown, flaky bark is not ornamental. Flashy, 5-petal, pink trumpets appear along branches for 2 weeks in May and June, and infrequently thereafter; some cultivars are fragrant and are available in shades of pink, white, red, yellow, peach, and lavender. Hummingbirds are drawn to the tubular flowers, especially those in shades of red and pink. Fruits are non-ornamental capsules. Weigelas including 'Midnight Wine' and 'Ruby Queen' may leaf out late. Folks phone me each year in mid spring asking about the dead shrub in the border. I tell them to check the base for new growth and to give the shrub two

more weeks. By then, shrubs are fully leafed out.

LANDSCAPE USE

Mixed borders, shrub borders, foundation plantings, background shrub for perennials, container planting, screens. Cultivars with interesting foliage make good bed and border accents.

ORIGIN East Asia

HARDINESS ZONES (4) 5–8

LIGHT Full sun (a must for purple-leafed cultivars).

SOIL Well-drained, average garden soil.

GROWING Easily transplanted. As with most shrubs, keep weigela well watered after planting. Apply a general-purpose fertilizer before spring growth begins. When necessary, shape the shrub right after flowering, since weigela blooms on the previous season's wood. You can also prune in winter when you see the shrub's structure, but you'll sacrifice some flowers. Prune off old stems where strong new shoots break out on the branches. Some winter dieback may occur.

DESIGNER'S CHOICE

Weigela florida 'Alexandra' (Wine & Roses) Deep purplish-burgundy leaves, deep pink flowers. Grow in full sun for best leaf color. Pinch lightly after blooming for a second flower crop and better leaf color. 5' h and w.

W. florida 'Elvera' (Midnight Wine)

Weigela florida 'Variegata'

Mounding form and metallic, dark burgundy leaves look good with silvery perennials. Small, pink flowers appear in spring. Grow this weigela for its leaves. 18"–24" h × 24"–30" w.

W. florida 'Verweig' (Monet, My Monet) Variegated dwarf with green, cream, and pink leaves; mass in borders like a perennial; pink spring flowers. Needs partial shade in the South. 10"–18" h × 24" w. Zone 4.

W. florida 'Polka' Big, two-toned, pink blooms with yellow throats and thick, dark green leaves. Blooms from June to September. 3'–4' h × 4'–6' w.

W. florida 'Sunny Princess' Variegated leaves with narrow yellow edges and bright pink flowers. 4'–5' h and w. Zone 4.

W. 'Briant Rubidor' (syn. 'Rubidor', 'Rubigold', 'Olympiade') Deep red blooms, bright yellow leaves. Great border accent. Grow this cultivar in partial shade in the South to prevent leaf burn. Similar to 'Olympiade' (Briant Rubidor). 5' h and w.

W. 'Courtalor' (Carnaval) (syn. *W. florida* 'Carnaval') White, pink, and dark pink to red blooms; big, thick, azalea-like, long blooming flowers; no fruit. 4' h and w. Zone 4.

W. 'Minuet' (syn. *W. florida* 'Minuet') Fragrant flowers are lavender pink inside, redder outside. Green leaves tinged red harmonize with blooms, which last for 3–6 weeks. 3' h × 5' or less. Zone 4.

W. 'Red Prince' Fade-resistant, dark red flowers have extended period of bloom. One of the best reds. 5'–6' h and w. Zone 4.

W. subsessilis 'Canary' Yellow spring flowers on erect, rounded shrub with arched stems. 4'–5' h and w. Zone 4.

W. 'White Knight' Pale pink buds open to white flowers with a long period of bloom. Dark green leaves. 5'–6' h and w. Zone 4.

XANTHORHIZA

Xanthorhiza simplicissima 🌿 ✳

zan-tho-RIY-za sim-pli-SIS-si-ma

Yellowroot

Buttercup Family (Ranunculaceae)
Deciduous groundcover shrub
2'–3' h × 5' w or wider

Grow this thicket-forming shrub for long-lasting, mostly purple fall color and spreading habit. At Mt. Cuba, a Wilmington, Delaware, non-profit organization focusing on plants native to the Piedmont region, it is used as a groundcover in the woodland garden where it makes an effective bright green mass under a canopy of shade trees. The scraped roots are vivid yellow.

The summer foliage is bright green, finely cut, and up to 12" long. Comprised of 3–5 leaflets, leaves are bunched at the ends of the 2', upright, woody shoots that emerge from the roots. Fall color ranges from claret to yellow and orange. Leaf drop occurs later than that of most woody plants. The bark is pale tan on the outside, yellow on the inside. Roots are also yellow, giving the plant its common name. Native Americans used the plant, which has astringent and anti-inflammatory properties, in teas and tonics to alleviate sores and ulcers and as a yellow dye. It bears elongated, drooping clusters of insignificant, small, five-petaled, dark brownish red flowers in spring, followed by tiny brown fruits.

LANDSCAPE USE

A groundcover under deciduous trees, near ponds and streams, in wild or woodland gardens.

ORIGIN   Stream banks and moist woods of the eastern U.S.

HARDINESS ZONES   3–9

LIGHT   Partial shade to shade.

SOIL   Likes moist, well-drained soils but tolerates both heavy and drier soils

GROWING   As long as the soil is average to moist and the pH is not too high, yellowroot will thrive and make a fast-growing, dense groundcover. In fact, yellowroot's spreading character can become invasive when it's grown close to other plants. It needs space to spread or a contained area in which to grow. (Longwood Gardens, in Kennett Square, Pennsylvania, grows it around a tree in a bed curbed in concrete.) Dry, inhospitable soil may slow its movement.

CAUTION   The roots have been used medicinally, but may be toxic when consumed in large doses.

YUCCA

Yucca filamentosa ○ ✳

YUK-ka fil-a-men-TOH-sa

Adam's needle

Century Plant Family (Agavaceae)
Evergreen shrub
3' h × 4' w; 6' high in flower

Filaments or curly white fibers edge new leaves of this evergreen shrub, which many gardeners treat as a flowering perennial. The stiff, swordlike foliage emerges from one place, similar to a rose unfurling its petals, and forms a spiky dome that's sometimes formidable to behold. This is a tough, durable, architectural, xeriscape plant with an exotic structure that limits its usefulness in some gardens. The other limiting factor is that once established, yucca can last forever, defeating your efforts to dispense with it. Yucca is a matter of taste: Gertrude Jekyll (1843–1932), the grand dame of early twentieth-century English garden design, used *Yucca gloriosa*, a similar but less hardy species, in the Grey Garden of her home in Surrey, England.

Foliage is dark green, rigid, and sharp tipped, measuring up to 3' long and 1" wide. It produces branched,

Xanthorhiza simplicissima

Yucca filamentosa

elongated clusters of bending, 2", bell-shaped, creamy flowers that rise 6' or higher from the center of the leaf rosette. Its evening fragrance attracts nighttime pollinators.

LANDSCAPE USE
Southwestern gardens, Mediterranean gardens, low-water gardens, accent in beds and borders, and massed for dramatic effect; a conversation piece (like prickly pear in a New England garden). Also combines well with sleek contemporary architecture. Great for large containers in warm climates.

ORIGIN   East coast of U.S. from New Jersey to Florida.

HARDINESS ZONES   5–(9) 10

LIGHT   Full sun.

SOIL   Average to dry garden soil; tolerates drought, and hot, dry, sandy soils.

GROWING   Avoid wet rich soils. After flowering and fruiting, the rosette dies but is quickly replaced by new plants from side buds at the old plant's base. If you decide to move or discard the plant, you may find that you can't. Even the tiniest root remaining in the ground will start new plants.

CAUTION   To avoid sharp tips injuring skin or eyes, use care when working around these plants.

DESIGNER'S CHOICE
Yucca filamentosa 'Bright Edge' Leaves have wide, yellow edges. 3' h × 4' w.

Y. filamentosa 'Color Guard' Bold, creamy yellow-centered leaves take on a coral tint in winter. 2'–3' h × 3' w.

Y. filamentosa 'Ivory Tower' Abundant, ivory blooms tinted green that face outward rather than droop. 3'–4' h and w.

Y. filamentosa 'Variegata' White-edged, blue-green leaves with creamy white flowers on 6' spikes. 3'–4' h and w.

Y. flaccida (weak-leaf yucca) Softer leaves and shorter flower spikes than *Y. filamentosa*. 3' h and w. Zones 6–9.

Y. flaccida 'Golden Sword' Yellow-centered leaves with green edges and creamy blooms. 3' h × 5' w.

Y. glauca (soapweed) Evergreen prairie native with narrow, white-edged, gray-green, 2'-long leaves that form a 3'–4' dome; 4' spikes of 3", green-tinged white flowers in midsummer. 2' h × 3' w. Zones 4–8.

Y. gloriosa 'Variegata' Stiff, blue-green leaves edged in creamy yellow have soft leaf points that will not penetrate skin. 4' h × 3' w. Zone 7.

ZELKOVA

Zelkova serrata ▽

zel-KOH-va ser-RAY-ta

Japanese zelkova, Sawtooth zelkova

Elm Family (Ulmaceae)
Deciduous tree
80' h × 60' w

This tree has popped up all over the place. A popular substitute for American elm along streets and in corporate office parks, it shares American elm's familiar, neat, vase shape and arched, up-reaching limbs. Yet *Zelkova* shows much better resistance to Dutch elm disease than its American counterpart.

The simple, dark green foliage is deciduous, up to 5" long and 2" wide, with a pointed tip and serrated edge; it has yellow to orange fall color. The gray bark is smooth, peeling with age.

LANDSCAPE USE
Shade tree, lawn specimen, good street tree when planted away from utility lines, large public plantings.

ORIGIN   Moist soils and stream banks of eastern Asia.

HARDINESS ZONES   5–8

LIGHT   Full sun.

SOIL   Moist, well-drained soil.

GROWING   Plant in spring only. Treat your zelkova well, because this member of the Elm Family can succumb to some of the same pests and diseases of American elm when stressed. For best results, treat it like an elm. Hire a professional tree-care company to prune and to fertilize the tree below ground once a year or check with your Cooperative Extension about the safest and best way to fertilize it yourself. An arborist can cut away dead branches that could harbor any disease-carrying insects. When necessary, deliver moisture with soaker hose placed just beyond the tree's drip line at the branches' farthest reach. Avoid wounding the tree with a lawnmower or

Zelkova serrata

Planning Chart

For your convenience, we designed this planning chart to lead you to trees and shrubs that fit your fancy and suit your surroundings. Use the chart as an adjunct to the encyclopedia, which contains more and different information. Note that some woody plants in the chart may be bad for your area. If you like their ornamental qualities, look up their entries in the encyclopedia to find other landscape choices and suggestions. Shapes are approximate and somewhat subjective; they may vary by variety and age. For example, the creeping/suckering/trailing symbol could represent a low groundcover and a tall shrub that widens over time through vigorous suckers. On the other hand, the spreading symbol represents plants that grow wide, usually with horizontal branching. White oaks and kousa dogwoods, for example, may change in shape from pyramidal to rounded to broad and spreading with age (The mature shape is to the right of the symbol, ›. Popular decorative features include bark, stems, flowers, fruit, fall color, and form for winter or year-round interest. "Attracts" wildlife refers to trees and shrubs that feed and shelter songbirds, hummingbirds, and/or butterflies.

Latin Name	Pg#	Zone	Light	Soil	Foliage	Type	Shape	bark/ stems	flowers	fruits	form	fall color	attracts wildlife
Abelia													
× *grandiflora*	156	6–9	○◐	◈	D	S	○		✔			✔	✔
Abeliophyllum													
distichum	156	(4) 5–9	○	◈	D	S	○		✔				
Abies													
balsamea 'Nana'	157	3–7	○	◈	E	S	○						✔
concolor	157	3–/	○◐	◈◇	E	T	△						✔
fraseri	157	4–7	○	◈	E	T	△						
koreana	158	5–6 (7)	○	◈	E	T	△		✔				
lasiocarpa 'Arizonica Compacta'	158	(4) 5–6	○◐	◈	E	S	△						
nordmanniana 'Golden Spreader'	158	4–7	○◐	◈	E	T	◠ › △						
Acer													
buergerianum	158	5–8	○◐	◈◇	D	T	◊ › ○	✔				✔	
campestre	159	(4) 5–8	○◐	◈	D	T	○					✔	
capillipes	159	5–7	○◐	◈	D	T	○	✔		✔		✔	
circinatum	160	6–9	○◐●	◈	D	T S	◠ › ▨		✔	✔		✔	✔
griseum	160	5–7	○◐	◈	D	T	◊ › ▽	✔				✔	
japonicum	161	5–7	○◐	◈	D	T	○ › ◠		✔			✔	
mandschuricum	161	4–7	○◐	◈	D	T	▽ › ◠					✔	
negundo	162	3–8	○◐	◆◈◇	D	T	○						✔
palmatum	162	6–8	○◐	◈	D	T	○ › ⊚	✔			✔	✔	
pensylvanicum	163	3–7	◐●	◈	D	T S	○	✔				✔	✔
platanoides	164	3–7	○◐	◈	D	T	○ › ◠		✔			✔	
pseudoplatanus	164	4–7	○◐	◈	D	T	◊ › ○	✔					
pseudosieboldianum	164	4–7	○◐	◈	D	T	○		✔			✔	
rubrum	165	3–9	○◐	◆◈	D	T	△ › ○		✔	✔		✔	✔
saccharinum	166	3–9	○	◆◈	D	T	◊ › ○						✔
saccharum	166	3–8	○◐	◈	D	T	◊ › ○	✔				✔	✔
shirasawanum 'Aureum'	167	5–7	◐	◈	D	T	○ › ◠		✔	✔		✔	
tataricum subsp. *ginnala*	167	3–7	○◐	◈◇	D	T	○		✔	✔		✔	
triflorum	168	(4) 5–7	○◐	◈◇	D	T	○ › ◠	✔			✔	✔	
'White Tigress'	168	4–7	○◐	◆◈	D	T	○	✔				✔	

Light ○ Full Sun ◐ Part Shade ● Full Shade **Type** T Tree S Shrub
Soil ◆ Wet ◈ Moist/Well Drained ◇ Dry **Foliage** D Deciduous E Evergreen

								Special Features					
Latin Name	Pg#	Zone	Light	Soil	Foliage	Type	Shape	bark/stems	flowers	fruits	form	fall color	attracts wildlife
Aesculus													
× carnea 'Briotii'	168	(4) 5–7 (8)	○◑	◇	D	T	○		✔				✔
parviflora	169	4–8	○◑	◇	D	S	≏		✔			✔	✔
pavia	170	4–8 (9)	○◑	◇	D	T	○		✔				✔
Amelanchier													
species	170	(3) 4–8 (9)	○◑	◆◇	D	T S	0 › ○	✔	✔	✔		✔	✔
Andromeda													
polifolia	171	2–6	○◑	◆	E	S	○ › ≏		✔				
Aralia													
elata	172	(3) 4–8	○◑	◇	D	T S	○ › ≏		✔		✔		✔
Arbutus													
menziesii	172	(5) 7–9	○	◇◇	E	T	○	✔	✔	✔	✔		✔
Arctostaphylos													
uva-ursi	173	2–6	○◑	◇◇	E	S	≏		✔	✔		✔	✔
Aronia													
arbutifolia	174	4–9	○◑	◆◇	D	S	≏		✔	✔		✔	✔
Asimina													
triloba	174	5–9	○◑	◆◇	D	T	○ › ≏		✔	✔		✔	✔
Aucuba													
japonica	175	7–10	◑●	◇◇	E	S	○			✔	✔		
Baccharis													
halimifolia	175	5–9	○◑	◆◇◇	D E	T S	▽		✔				✔
Berberis													
× gladwynensis 'William Penn'	176	5–7 (8)	○◑	◇◇	E	S	○		✔	✔			
julianae	176	(5) 6–8	○◑	◇◇	D E	S	○		✔	✔		✔	✔
koreana	177	3–7	○	◇◇	D	S	○		✔	✔		✔	
× mentorensis	177	5–7	○◑	◇◇	E	S	○		✔	✔		✔	
thunbergii	178	4–7	○◑	◇	D	S	○		✔	✔		✔	✔
verruculosa	178	6–9	○◑	◇◇	E	S	○		✔	✔			
Betula													
lenta	178	3–8	○◑	◆◇◇	D	T	△ › ○	✔	✔			✔	✔
nigra	179	4–9	○◑	◆◇	D	T	△	✔	✔			✔	✔
papyrifera	180	2–6	○	◇◇	D	T	△	✔				✔	✔
pendula	181	4–7	○	◇◇	D	T	△ › 🔄	✔				✔	✔
populifolia	181	3–7	○	◆◇◇	D	T	△	✔	✔			✔	✔
utilis var. jacquemontii	182	4–7	○◑	◇	D	T	△	✔				✔	
Buddleja													
alternifolia	182	5–9	○◑	◇◇	D	S	○ › 🔄		✔				✔
davidii	183	5–10	○	◇◇	D E	S	○		✔				✔
Buxus													
microphylla	185	5–9	○◑●	◇◇	E	S	○				✔		
sempervirens	185	6–8	○◑●	◇◇	E	T S	○				✔		
Callicarpa													
dichotoma	186	(5) 6–8	○◑	◇	D	S	○		✔	✔		✔	✔
Calluna													
vulgaris	187	4–6	○	◇	E	S	≏		✔				✔
Calocedrus													
decurrens	188	5–8	○◑	◇◇	E	T	0	✔					✔

Key: 0 Oval △ Pyramid ○ Rounded ▽ Vase ○ Spreading 🔄 Weeping ≏ Creeping/Suckering/Trailing ✳ Easy ■ 371

Latin Name	Pg#	Zone	Light	Soil	Foliage	Type	Shape	Special Features					
								bark/stems	flowers	fruits	form	fall color	attracts wildlife
Calycanthus													
floridus	188	5–9	○◑	◇	D	S	○ › ☁		✔			✔	
Camellia													
japonica	189	(6) 7–9	◑	◇	E	T S	△		✔		✔		
sasanqua	190	(6) 7–9	◑	◇	E	T S	△ › ○		✔		✔		
sinensis	190	6–9	◑	◇	E	T S	○		✔				
Caragana													
arborescens	190	2–7	○	◇ ◇	D	T S	0		✔				✔
Carpinus													
betulus	191	(4) 5–7	○◑	◇	D	T	○				✔	✔	✔
caroliniana	192	3–9	○◑●	◆◇	D	T	○					✔	✔
Carya													
ovata	192	(4) 5–8	○◑	◇	D	T	0	✔		✔		✔	✔
Caryopteris													
× clandonensis	193	6–9	○◑	◇ ◇	D	S	○		✔				✔
Castanea													
mollissima	194	4–8	○	◇	D	T	○			✔		✔	✔
Catalpa													
bignonioides	194	5–9	○◑	◇	D	T	⌒		✔				✔
Ceanothus													
species	195	8–10	○	◇ ◇	D E	T S	⌒		✔				✔
Cedrus													
deodara	196	7–9	○	◇ ◇	E	T	△	✔		✔	✔		
libani	196	(5) 6–9	○	◇ ◇	E	T	△				✔		
Celtis													
occidentalis	197	3–9	○	◆◇ ◇	D	T	⌒	✔					✔
Cephalanthus													
occidentalis	197	5–9	○◑	◆◇	D	S	○		✔				✔
Cephalotaxus													
harringtonii	198	6–9	○◑●	◇ ◇	E	T S	⌒	✔					
Cercidiphyllum													
japonicum	198	4–8	○	◇	D	T	△ › ○	✔	✔		✔	✔	
Cercis													
canadensis	199	5–9	○◑	◇	D	T	▽ › ○		✔	✔	✔	✔	✔
Chaenomeles													
speciosa	200	4–8	○◑	◇ ◇	D	S	○ › ⌒		✔	✔			
Chamaecyparis													
lawsoniana	201	(5) 6–7	○◑	◇	E	T	△						
nootkatensis	201	(4) 5–7	○◑	◇	E	T	△				✔		
obtusa	202	5–8	○◑	◇	E	T	△				✔		
pisifera	202	(4) 5–8	○	◇	E	T	△				✔		
thyoides	203	4–8	○	◆◇	E	T S	0 › △		✔		✔		
Chimonanthus													
praecox	203	7–9	○◑	◇	D	S	⌒		✔				
Chionanthus													
virginicus	204	(4) 5–9	○◑	◆◇	D	T	○ › ⌒		✔				✔
Cladrastis													
kentukea	204	4–8	○	◇	D	T	▽ › ○		✔		✔	✔	✔

Light ○ Full Sun ◑ Part Shade ● Full Shade **Type** T Tree S Shrub
Soil ◆ Wet ◇ Moist/Well Drained ◇ Dry **Foliage** D Deciduous E Evergreen

Latin Name	Pg#	Zone	Light	Soil	Foliage	Type	Shape	bark/stems	flowers	fruits	form	fall color	attracts wildlife
Clerodendrum													
trichotomum	205	(6) 7–10	○	◈	D	T S	creeping		✔	✔			
Clethra													
alnifolia	205	4–9	○◐	◆◈	D	S	0 › creeping		✔			✔	✔
barbinervis	206	(5) 6–8	◐	◆◈	D	T S	○	✔	✔		✔	✔	
Comptonia													
peregrina	207	2–5 (6)	○◐	◈◇	D	S	○ › creeping						✔
Cornus													
alba	207	3–7	○◐	◆◈◇	D	S	○ › creeping	✔					✔
alternifolia	208	(3) 4–7	○◐	◈	D	T S	spreading		✔	✔	✔	✔	✔
canadensis	208	3–6	◐●	◈	D	S	creeping		✔	✔		✔	✔
florida	209	5–9	○◐	◈	D	T	○ › spreading		✔	✔		✔	✔
kousa	210	5–8	○◐	◈	D	T	vase › spreading	✔	✔	✔		✔	✔
mas	211	5–7	○◐	◈	D	T S	0 › spreading	✔	✔	✔		✔	✔
sericea	211	3–7	○◐	◆◈	D	S	○ › creeping	✔	✔	✔		✔	✔
Corylopsis													
pauciflora	212	6–8	◐	◈	D	S	○		✔				
spicata	212	5–8	◐	◈	D	S	spreading		✔				
Corylus													
avellana 'Contorta'	212	5–8	○◐	◈	D	S	○		✔		✔		✔
Cotinus													
coggygria	213	5–8	○	◈◇	D	T S	○		✔			✔	
obovatus	214	4–8	○	◈◇	D	T S	○	✔	✔			✔	
Cotoneaster													
apiculatus	214	5–7	○	◈	D	S	creeping		✔	✔			✔
dammeri	214	5–7	○	◈	D E	S	creeping		✔	✔			✔
divaricatus	215	(4) 5–7	○	◈	D	S	creeping		✔	✔			✔
horizontalis	215	5–7	○	◈	D	S	creeping			✔	✔		✔
lucidus	216	4–7	○	◈	D	S	0 › ○			✔			✔
multiflorus	216	4–7	○	◈	D	S	○		✔	✔	✔		
nanshan	216	4–8	○	◈	D	S	creeping		✔	✔			✔
salicifolius 'Repens'	216	6–8	○◐	◈	D E	S	creeping		✔	✔			✔
Crataegus													
crus-galli var. inermis	217	4–7	○	◈	D	T	○		✔	✔		✔	✔
laevigata 'Crimson Cloud'	217	4–7 (8)	○◐	◈	D	T	0		✔	✔			✔
phaenopyrum	218	4–8	○	◈	D	T S	0	✔	✔	✔		✔	✔
viridis 'Winter King'	218	4–7	○	◈	D	T	vase › ○	✔	✔	✔		✔	✔
Cryptomeria													
japonica	218	6–8	○	◈	E	T	△	✔			✔		
Cunninghamia													
lanceolata	219	7–9	○◐	◆◈	E	T	△	✔			✔		
× Cupressocyparis													
leylandii	219	6–10	○◐	◈	E	T	0	✔					
Cyrilla													
racemiflora	220	(6) 7–10	○◐	◆◈	D E	T S	○		✔		✔	✔	✔
Cytisus													
scoparius	220	(5) 6–8	○	◈	D	S	spreading	✔	✔				
Daphne													
x burkwoodii 'Carol Mackie'	221	4–7	○◐	◆◇	D E	S	○ › ○		✔				

Key: 0 Oval △ Pyramid ○ Rounded ▽ Vase ◡ Spreading Weeping Creeping/Suckering/Trailing ✳ Easy ■ 373

Latin Name	Pg#	Zone	Light	Soil	Foliage	Type	Shape	bark/stems	flowers	fruits	form	fall color	attracts wildlife
Davidia													
involucrata	222	6–8	○ ◑	◇	D	T	△ › ○	✔	✔				
Deutzia													
gracilis 'Nikko'	222	5–8	○ ◑	◇	D	S	○ › ⌂		✔		✔	✔	
Diervilla													
sessilifolia	223	4–8	○ ◑	◇ ◇	D	S	⌂	✔	✔				✔
Diospyros													
virginiana	224	5–9	○ ◑	◇ ◇	D	T	○	✔		✔		✔	✔
Disanthus													
cercidifolius	224	5–8	◑ ●	◇	D	S	⌒					✔	
Eleutherococcus													
sieboldianus 'Variegatus'	224	(4) 5–8	○ ◑ ●	◇ ◇	D	S	⌂						
Enkianthus													
campanulatus	225	5–8	○ ◑	◇	D	T S	0		✔			✔	
Erica													
carnea	226	5–7	○ ◑	◇	E	S	⌂		✔				✔
Eriobotrya													
japonica	226	7–10	○ ◑	◇	E	T	○		✔	✔			✔
Eucalyptus													
cinerea	226	(7) 8–10	○	◇	E	T	⌒						
Euonymus													
alatus	227	4–8 (9)	○ ◑ ●	◇	D	T S	○	✔				✔	✔
fortunei	227	5–8	○ ◑ ●	◇	E	S	⌂						✔
Exochorda													
× macrantha 'The Bride'	228	5–8	○ ◑	◇	D	S	○		✔				
Fagus													
grandifolia	228	4–9	○ ◑	◇	D	T	0 › ⌒	✔			✔	✔	✔
sylvatica	229	5–7	◑ ●	◇			0 › ⌒				✔	✔	✔
Forsythia													
× intermedia	230	5–8	○	◇	D	S	○ › ⌂		✔		✔	✔	
Fothergilla													
gardenii	231	5–8	○ ◑	◇	D	S	○ › ⌂		✔			✔	✔
Frangula													
alnus	232	2–7	○ ◑ ●	◆ ◇	D	S	⌒						✔
Franklinia													
alatamaha	232	5–8	○ ◑ ●	◇	D	T S	○		✔			✔	
Fraxinus													
americana 'Autumn Applause'	233	4–9	○	◇	D	T	0					✔	✔
excelsior 'Aurea'	233	5–7	○	◇	D	T	○	✔				✔	✔
pennsylvanica 'Cimmzam' (Cimmaron)	234	3–9	○	◇	D	T	○					✔	✔
Gardenia													
jasminoides	234	7–10	◑	◇	E	S	○		✔				
Garrya													
elliptica	235	(7) 8–10	○ ◑ ●	◇ ◇	E	T S	▽		✔				✔
Gaultheria													
procumbens	235	3–5 (6)	◑	◇	E	S	⌂		✔	✔			✔
shallon	235	6–8	○ ◑ ●	◇	E	S	⌂		✔	✔			✔
Gaylussacia													
brachycera	236	5–7	○ ◑	◇ ◇	E	S	⌂		✔				✔

Light ○ Full Sun ◑ Part Shade ● Full Shade **Type** **T** Tree **S** Shrub

Soil ◆ Wet ◇ Moist/Well Drained ◇ Dry **Foliage** **D** Deciduous **E** Evergreen

Latin Name	Pg#	Zone	Light	Soil	Foliage	Type	Shape	bark/stems	flowers	fruits	form	fall color	attracts wildlife
Genista													
tinctoria	236	4–7	○	◇ ◇	D	S	⌒	✔	✔				✔
Ginkgo													
biloba	237	(3) 4–8	○ ◐	◇ ◇	D	T	△ › ⌒			✔		✔	
Gleditsia													
triacanthos f. *inermis*	237	4–9	○	◆ ◇ ◇	D	T	○					✔	✔
Gymnocladus													
dioica	238	4–8	○	◆ ◇	D	T	O	✔		✔	✔	✔	
Halesia													
carolina	239	5–8	○ ◐	◇	D	T	○	✔	✔	✔		✔	✔
Hamamelis													
× *intermedia* 'Pallida'	240	(5) 6–8	○ ◐	◆ ◇	D	T S	○ › ⌒		✔			✔	
Heptacodium													
miconioides	241	4–8	○ ◐	◇	D	T S	⌒	✔	✔	✔		✔	✔
Hibiscus													
syriacus	241	5–8	○	◇ ◇	D	T S	O		✔				✔
Hippophae													
rhamnoides	242	3–7	○	◇ ◇	D	T S	○ › ⌂			✔			✔
Holodiscus													
discolor	242	5–9	○ ◐	◇ ◇	D	S	⌂		✔				✔
Hovenia													
dulcis	243	(5) 6–8	○ ◐	◇ ◇	D	T	O	✔	✔	✔			✔
Hydrangea													
anomala subsp. *petiolaris*	243	(4) 5–7	○ ◐ ●	◇	D	S	⌂	✔	✔				✔
arborescens	244	4–9	○ ◐ ●	◇	D	S	○ › ⌂		✔				✔
macrophylla	245	6–9	○ ◐	◇	D	S	○ › ⌂		✔				
paniculata	246	3–8	○ ◐	◇	D	T S	○ › ⌂		✔				
quercifolia	248	5–9	○ ◐ ●	◇	D	S	○ › ⌂	✔	✔			✔	✔
Hypericum													
'Hidcote'	248	(5) 6–8	○ ◐	◇ ◇	E	S	○		✔				✔
Ilex													
aquifolium	249	6–8	○ ◐	◇	E	T S	△			✔	✔		✔
× *aquipernyi* 'San Jose'	250	6–8	○ ◐	◇	E	T	△			✔	✔		✔
× *attenuata* 'Fosteri'	250	6–9	○ ◐	◇	E	T	△			✔	✔		✔
cornuta 'Burfordii'	250	7–9	○ ◐	◆ ◇	E	T S	○			✔			✔
crenata	251	6–8	○ ◐	◇	E	T S	○				✔		✔
decidua	252	5–9	○ ◐	◆ ◇	D	T S	⌂			✔			✔
glabra	252	5–9	○ ◐	◆ ◇ ◇	E	S	O › ⌂						✔
× *meserveae*	253	5–6	○ ◐ ●	◇	E	T S	○ › △			✔	✔		✔
'Nellie R. Stevens'	253	6–9	○ ◐	◇ ◇	E	T S	△			✔			✔
opaca	254	(5) 6–9	○ ◐	◆ ◇	E	T	△			✔	✔		✔
pedunculosa	254	5–8	○ ◐	◇	E	T S	△			✔			✔
verticillata	254	3–9	○ ◐	◆ ◇	D	S	⌂			✔			✔
vomitoria	255	7–10	○ ◐ ●	◆ ◇ ◇	E	T S	⌂			✔			✔
Illicium													
floridanum	256	7–10	◐ ●	◆ ◇	E	T S	△		✔				✔
Indigofera													
kirilowii	256	5–7	○	◇	D	S	⌂		✔				

Key: O Oval △ Pyramid ○ Rounded ▽ Vase ⌒ Spreading 🌳 Weeping ⌂ Creeping/Suckering/Trailing ✳ Easy ■ 375

Latin Name	Pg#	Zone	Light	Soil	Foliage	Type	Shape	bark/stems	flowers	fruits	form	fall color	attracts wildlife
Itea													
virginica	257	(5) 6–9	○ ◐	◆ ◇	D	S	(shrub)		✔			✔	✔
Jasminum													
nudiflorum	257	6–9	○ ◐ ●	◇	D	S	(shrub)	✔	✔	✔			
Juglans													
nigra	258	4–9	○	◇	D	T	○ › ○			✔			✔
regia	259	3–7	○	◇	D	T	○			✔			✔
Juniperus													
chinensis	260	4–9	○	◇ ◇	E	T S	△ › (shrub)			✔	✔		✔
communis	261	3–7	○	◇ ◇	E	T S	○ › (shrub)			✔	✔		✔
conferta	261	(5) 6–9	○	◇ ◇	E	S	(shrub)			✔			✔
horizontalis	262	(3) 4–9	○	◇ ◇	E	S	(shrub)						✔
× pfitzeriana	263	(3) 4–9	○ ◐	◇ ◇	E	S	○ › (shrub)						✔
procumbens	263	4–9	○	◇ ◇	E	S	(shrub)				✔		✔
sabina	263	4–7	○	◇ ◇	E	S	▽ › (shrub)						✔
scopulorum	264	3–7	○	◇ ◇	E	T	△				✔		✔
squamata	264	4–8	○	◇	E	T S	△ › ○ › (shrub)			✔			✔
virginiana	265	3–9	○	◇ ◇	E	T	△			✔			✔
Kalmia													
latifolia	265	(4) 5–9	○ ◐	◇	E	T S	○ › ○		✔				✔
Kalopanax													
septemlobus	267	4–7	○ ◐	◇	D	T	○		✔				✔
Kerria													
japonica	267	(4) 5–9	◐ ●	◇ ◇	D	S	○ › (shrub)	✔	✔			✔	
Koelreuteria													
paniculata	268	5–8	○	◇ ◇	D	T	○ › ○		✔			✔	
Kolkwitzia													
amabilis	268	(4) 5–8	○	◇ ◇	D	S	▽ › (shrub)		✔				✔
Laburnum													
× watereri	269	5–7	○ ◐	◇	D	T	○ › ○		✔				
Lagerstroemia													
indica	269	7–9	○ ◐ ●	◇	D	T S	○	✔	✔			✔	✔
Larix													
decidua	271	(3) 4–6	○	◆ ◇	D	T	△	✔	✔			✔	
kaempferi	271	4–7	○	◇	D	T	△					✔	
laricina	272	2–5	○	◆ ◇	D	T	△					✔	✔
Leucothoe													
fontanesiana	272	5–8	◐	◇	E	S	○ › (shrub)		✔				
Ligustrum													
species	273	3–10	○ ◐	◇	D E	T S	○ › ○		✔				✔
Lindera													
benzoin	273	(4) 5–9	○ ◐	◆ ◇	D	S	○		✔	✔		✔	✔
Liquidambar													
styraciflua	274	5–9	○	◆ ◇	D	T	○ › △			✔		✔	✔
Liriodendron													
tulipifera	274	5–9	○	◇	D	T	△		✔		✔	✔	✔
Lonicera													
fragrantissima	275	(4) 5–8	○ ◐	◇	D	S	○		✔				✔

Light ○ Full Sun ◐ Part Shade ● Full Shade **Type** T Tree S Shrub
Soil ◆ Wet ◈ Moist/Well Drained ◇ Dry **Foliage** D Deciduous E Evergreen

Latin Name	Pg#	Zone	Light	Soil	Foliage	Type	Shape	Special Features					
								bark/stems	flowers	fruits	form	fall color	attracts wildlife
Loropetalum													
chinense	275	(7) 8–9	○ ◑	◆ ◇	E	T S	○ › ▽		✔				
Maackia													
amurensis	276	4–7	○	◇	D	T	○	✔	✔				
Maclura													
pomifera	276	4–9	○	◆ ◇ ◇	D	T	○			✔		✔	✔
Magnolia													
acuminata	277	4–8	○ ◑	◇	D	T	△ › ○		✔	✔			✔
'Daybreak'	278	5–8	○ ◑	◇	D	T	0		✔	✔	✔		
denudata	278	5–8	○ ◑	◇	D	T	△		✔	✔			✔
grandiflora	278	7–9	○ ◑	◇	E	T	△		✔	✔		✔	✔
liliiflora 'Nigra'	279	5–8	○ ◑	◇	D	S	○		✔				✔
× loebneri 'Leonard Messel'	280	(4) 5–9	○ ◑	◇	D	T	△		✔				
macrophylla	280	5–8	○ ◑	◇	D	T	△		✔	✔			✔
× soulangeana	280	4–9	○	◇	D	T S	0 › ◠	✔	✔				
stellata	281	4–8	○ ◑	◇	D	T S	0 › ○		✔				✔
tripetala	282	5–8	○ ◑	◇	D	T	○ › ◠		✔	✔			✔
virginiana	282	5–9	○ ◑	◆ ◇	D E	T S	△	✔		✔			✔
Mahonia													
aquifolium	282	5–8	◑ ●	◇ ◇	E	S	○ › ⬢		✔	✔			✔
Malus													
species and hybrids	283	2–8	○	◇	D	T	○	✔	✔	✔		✔	✔
Metasequoia													
glyptostroboides	285	5–8	○	◆ ◇	D	T	△	✔			✔	✔	
Microbiota													
decussata	285	2–7	○ ◑	◇	E	S	⬢					✔	
Morus													
rubra	286	5–9	○	◇	D	T	○			✔		✔	✔
Myrica													
pensylvanica	286	5–8	○ ◑	◇	D E	S	○ › ⬢			✔			✔
Nandina													
domestica	287	6–9	○ ◑	◇ ◇	D E	S	○ › ⬢		✔	✔		✔	✔
Nerium													
oleander	288	8–11	○ ◑	◆ ◇	E	S T	◠		✔				
Nyssa													
sylvatica	288	5–9	○ ◑	◆ ◇	D	T	△ › ◠				✔	✔	✔
Osmanthus													
heterophyllus	289	6–9	○ ◑	◇ ◇	E	S	○		✔				
Ostrya													
virginiana	290	4–9	○ ◑ ●	◇ ◇	D	T	△ › ○	✔		✔			✔
Oxydendrum													
arboreum	290	5–9	○ ◑	◇	D	T	△		✔	✔		✔	✔
Paeonia													
suffruticosa	291	4–8	○ ◑	◇	D	S	○		✔			✔	
Parrotia													
persica	292	5–8	○ ◑	◇ ◇	D	T S	0 › ◠	✔	✔		✔	✔	
Paulownia													
tomentosa	293	5–9	○ ◑	◇	D	T	○		✔				

Key: 0 Oval △ Pyramid ○ Rounded ▽ Vase ◠ Spreading ⌂ Weeping ⬢ Creeping/Suckering/Trailing ✳ Easy ■ 377

Latin Name	Pg#	Zone	Light	Soil	Foliage	Type	Shape	Special Features bark/stems	flowers	fruits	form	fall color	attracts wildlife
Phellodendron													
amurense	293	4–7	○	◈ ◇	D	T	⌒				✔	✔	✔
Philadelphus													
coronarius	294	4–8	○ ◑	◈	D	S	○		✔				✔
Photinia													
× fraseri	295	6–9	○ ◑	◈ ◇	E	T S	0	✔	✔				
Physocarpus													
opulifolius	295	3–7	○ ◑	◆ ◈ ◇	D	S	○ › ⌂	✔	✔	✔			✔
Picea													
abies	296	3–7	○	◈	E	T	△					✔	✔
engelmannii	297	3–5	○ ◑	◈	E	T	△						✔
glauca	297	2–6	○	◈	E	T	△				✔		
omorika	297	(3) 4–7	○ ◑	◈	E	T	△				✔		
orientalis	297	4–7	○ ◑	◈ ◇	E	T	△		✔		✔		
pungens	298	3–7	○	◈ ◇	E	T	△						✔
Pieris													
floribunda	299	4–6	○ ◑	◈	E	S	○		✔				
japonica	299	5–7	○ ◑	◈	E	S	0 › ○		✔				
Pinus													
bungeana	299	5–7	○	◈	E	T	○	✔			✔		✔
cembra	300	3–7	○	◈	E	T	△ › ⌒				✔		✔
densiflora	301	3–7	○	◈	E	T	⌒ › ⌘	✔			✔		✔
flexilis	301	4–7	○ ◑	◈ ◇	E	T	△ › ⌒				✔		✔
mugo	302	2–7	○ ◑	◈	E	T S	○ › ⌒				✔		✔
nigra	302	5–8	○	◆ ◈ ◇	E	T	△ › ⌒						✔
parviflora	302	4–7	○ ◑	◈	E	T	△ › ⌒	✔			✔		✔
resinosa	303	2–5	○	◈ ◇	E	T	△	✔					✔
strobus	303	3–7	○	◈	E	T	△ › ⌒				✔		✔
sylvestris	304	2–7 (8)	○	◈ ◇	E	T	△ › ⌒						✔
thunbergii	304	(5) 6–8	○	◈ ◇	E	T	△ › ⌒	✔			✔		✔
Pittosporum													
tobira	305	8–10	○ ◑	◆ ◈	E	T S	○ › ⌒		✔	✔			
Platanus													
× hispanica	305	5–8	○	◆ ◈	D	T	△ › ○	✔					
Platycladus													
orientalis	306	6–9	○ ◑	◈	E	S	△				✔		
Podocarpus													
chinensis	306	(7) 8–10	○ ◑	◆ ◈	E	S	0			✔			
Populus													
tremuloides	306	1–7	○	◆ ◈	D	T	△					✔	✔
Potentilla													
fruticosa	307	2–6	○	◆ ◈ ◇	D	S	○		✔				
Prunus													
caroliniana	308	7–10	○ ◑	◈	E	T S	0	✔	✔				✔
cerasifera	308	(4) 5–8	○	◈	D	T	0 › ○		✔	✔			✔
× cistena	309	3–8	○	◈	D	S	○		✔	✔			✔
'Hally Jolivette'	309	(5) 6–7	○	◈	D	T S	○		✔		✔	✔	
laurocerasus	310	6–8	○ ◑ ●	◈	E	T S	⌒		✔	✔			✔

Light ○ Full Sun ◑ Part Shade ● Full Shade **Type** T Tree S Shrub
Soil ◆ Wet ◈ Moist/Well Drained ◇ Dry **Foliage** D Deciduous E Evergreen

Latin Name	Pg#	Zone	Light	Soil	Foliage	Type	Shape	Special Features: bark/stems	flowers	fruits	form	fall color	attracts wildlife
'Okame'	310	6–8	○ ◑	◇	D	T S	▽	✔	✔			✔	
maackii	311	2–6	○	◆ ◇	D	T	○	✔	✔				✔
pendula 'Pendula Rosea'	311	5–8	○	◇	D	T	🙟(weeping)		✔	✔	✔	✔	✔
sargentii	312	4–7	○ ◑	◇	D	T	○	✔	✔	✔		✔	✔
serrulata	312	5–6	○	◇	D	T	○		✔			✔	✔
× yedoensis	313	(5) 6–8	○	◇	D	T	○		✔			✔	✔
Pseudotsuga													
menziesii	313	4–6	○	◇	E	T	△	✔		✔	✔		✔
Pterostyrax													
hispida	314	(4) 5–8	○ ◑	◇	D	T S	⌒	✔	✔	✔			
Punica													
granatum	314	(7) 8–10	○ ◑	◇	D	T S	○		✔	✔			✔
Pyracantha													
coccinea	314	(5) 6–9	○ ◑	◆ ◇	E	S	creeping		✔	✔			✔
Pyrus													
calleryana	315	5–8	○	◇	D	T	△		✔		✔	✔	✔
Quercus													
acutissima	316	(5) 6–9	○ ◑	◇	D	T	△ › ⌒			✔		✔	✔
alba	316	4–9	○ ◑	◇	D	T	△ › ⌒			✔	✔	✔	✔
bicolor	318	(3) 4–8	○ ◑	◆ ◇	D	T	△ › ○			✔		✔	✔
coccinea	318	4–7	○	◇ ◇	D	T	△ › ⌒			✔		✔	✔
imbricaria	318	5–7	○	◇ ◇	D	T	△ › ⌒			✔			✔
macrocarpa	319	3–8	○	◆ ◇ ◇	D	T	△ › ⌒			✔	✔	✔	✔
montana	319	4–8	○	◆ ◇ ◇	D	T	△ › ○						✔
muehlenbergii	319	4–7	○	◆ ◇ ◇	D	T	○			✔		✔	✔
nigra	319	6–9 (10)	○	◇ ◇	D	T	○						✔
palustris	320	4–8	○	◆ ◇	D	T	△			✔	✔		✔
phellos	320	5–9	○	◆ ◇	D	T	△ › ○			✔		✔	✔
robur	321	5–8	○	◇	D	T	△ › ⌒			✔			✔
rubra	321	3–8	○	◇	D	T	○			✔		✔	✔
shumardii	322	5–9	○ ◑	◆ ◇	D	T	△ › ⌒			✔		✔	✔
velutina	322	3–9	○	◆ ◇	D	T	△ › ○					✔	✔
virginiana	322	(7)8–10	○ ◑	◇	E	T	⌒			✔	✔		✔
Rhamnus													
cathartica	323	3–7	○	◇ ◇	D	T S	creeping						✔
Rhododendron													
species	323	3–8	○ ◑	◇	D E	S	▽○⌒creeping		✔			✔	✔
Rhodotypos													
scandens	327	4–8	○ ◑ ●	◇ ◇	D	S	⌒		✔	✔			
Rhus													
species	328	3–9	○ ◑	◇ ◇	D E	T S	creeping			✔		✔	✔
Ribes													
sanguineum	329	6–8	○	◇ ◇	D	S	⌒		✔	✔			✔
Robinia													
pseudoacacia 'Frisia'	329	4–8	○	◇	D	T	0		✔				✔
Rosa													
banksiae 'Lutea' (Lady Banks yellow rose)	331						⌒		✔	✔			✔
glauca	331	2–7	○ ◑	◇ ◇	D	S	⌒		✔	✔			✔

Key: 0 Oval △ Pyramid ○ Rounded ▽ Vase ⌒ Spreading 🙟 Weeping creeping Creeping/Suckering/Trailing ✳ Easy ■ 379

								Special Features					
Latin Name	Pg#	Zone	Light	Soil	Foliage	Type	Shape	bark/stems	flowers	fruits	form	fall color	attracts wildlife
'Radrazz' (Knock Out)	331	(4) 5–7	○ ◑	◇ ◇	D	S	○		✔	✔		✔	✔
rugosa 'Rubra'	331	2–7	○	◇	D	S	⌂		✔	✔			✔
Explorer series	331	(2) 3–9	○	◇	D	S	⌂		✔	✔			✔
Rosmarinus													
officinalis	332	(7) 8–10	○	◇ ◇	E	S	○		✔				✔
Rubus													
cockburnianus 'Wyego'	332	6–8	○ ◑	◇	D	T	⌂	✔	✔				✔
Salix													
alba 'Chermesina'	333	2–8	○ ◑	◆ ◇	D	T S	○	✔				✔	✔
babylonica 'Crispa'	333	6–9	○ ◑	◆ ◇	D	T	⌖				✔		✔
× sepulcralis 'Chrysocoma'	334	4–9	○ ◑	◆ ◇	D	T	⌖	✔			✔	✔	✔
Sambucus													
canadensis	335	(3) 4–9	○ ◑	◆ ◇	D	S	⌂		✔	✔			✔
nigra	335	4–7	○ ◑	◆ ◇	D	T S	○		✔	✔			✔
racemosa	336	4–9	○ ◑	◇	D	S	○		✔	✔			✔
Santolina													
chamaecyparissus	336	7–9	○	◇	E	S	○		✔				✔
Sarcococca													
hookeriana var. humilis	337	(6) 7–9	◑ ●	◇	E	S	⌂		✔				
Sassafras													
albidum	337	5–9	○ ◑	◇	D	T	△ › ⌂	✔				✔	✔
Sciadopitys													
verticillata	338	5–7	○	◇	E	T	△	✔			✔		
Skimmia													
japonica	338	7–9	◑	◇ ◇	E	S	○		✔	✔			✔
Sophora													
japonica	339	5–8	○	◆ ◇	D	T	◠	✔	✔	✔			
Sorbus													
alnifolia	339	4–8	○ ◑	◇	D	S	0		✔	✔		✔	✔
Spiraea													
species	340	4–8	○	◇	D	S	○ ◠		✔			✔	✔
Stephanandra													
incisa 'Crispa'	341	(4) 5–7 (8)	○ ◑	◇	D	S	⌂		✔			✔	
Stewartia													
pseudocamellia	342	5–8	○ ◑	◇	D	T	0 › △	✔	✔			✔	
Styrax													
japonicus	342	(5) 6–8	○ ◑	◇	D	T	○		✔				✔
obassia	343	5–8	○	◇	D	T	△ › ○		✔				
Symphoricarpos													
orbiculatus	344	2–7	○ ◑	◇	D	S	⌂		✔	✔			✔
Symplocos													
paniculata	344	4–8	○ ◑	◇	D	T S	⌂		✔	✔			✔
Syringa													
reticulata	345	3–7	○ ◑	◇	D	T	0 › ○	✔	✔				✔
vulgaris	345	(2) 3–6 (7)	○ ◑	◇	D	S	▽ › ⌂		✔				✔
Tamarix													
ramosissima	347	2–8	○	◇ ◇	D	S	◠		✔				
Taxodium													
distichum	347	5–10	○ ◑	◆ ◇	D	T	△	✔			✔	✔	

Light ○ Full Sun ◑ Part Shade ● Full Shade **Type** T Tree S Shrub
Soil ◆ Wet ◇ Moist/Well Drained ◇ Dry **Foliage** D Deciduous E Evergreen

Latin Name	Pg#	Zone	Light	Soil	Foliage	Type	Shape	bark/ stems	flowers	fruits	form	fall color	attracts wildlife
Taxus													
species	348	4–7	○◑●	◇◇	E	T S	△	✔		✔	✔		✔
Teucrium													
chamaedrys	349	6–9	○◑	◇◇	E	S	○		✔				✔
Thuja													
occidentalis	349	3–7	○◑	◆◇◇	E	T	0	✔			✔		✔
plicata	350	5–7	○◑	◆◇	E	T	△				✔		✔
Thujopsis													
dolobrata	350	6–9	○	◇	E	T	△	✔			✔		
Tilia													
cordata	351	4–7	○◑	◇	D	T	△ › ○		✔		✔		
Tsuga													
canadensis	352	3–7	○◑●	◇	E	T	△						✔
Ulmus													
americana	353	3–9	○	◇	D	T	▽					✔	✔
parvifolia	353	4–9	○	◇	D	T	○	✔			✔	✔	✔
Vaccinium													
angustifolium	355	2–5	○◑	◇	D	S	≋		✔	✔		✔	✔
corymbosum	355	3–7	○◑	◆◇	D	S	○	✔	✔	✔		✔	✔
Viburnum													
acerifolium	356	(3) 4–8	◑●	◇	D		≋		✔	✔		✔	✔
× bodnantense 'Dawn'	357	5–9	○◑	◇	D	S	0		✔	✔		✔	✔
× burkwoodii	357	5–8	○◑	◇	D E	S	○		✔	✔		✔	✔
carlesii	358	4–8	○◑	◇	D	S	○		✔	✔		✔	✔
dentatum	359	3–8	○◑	◇◇	D	S	○ › ≋		✔	✔		✔	✔
dilatatum	359	(5) 6–8	○◑	◆◇◇	D	S	○		✔	✔		✔	✔
'Eskimo'	360	6–8	○◑	◇	E	S	○		✔	✔		✔	✔
lantana 'Mohican'	360	4–8	○	◇	D	S	0		✔	✔	✔		✔
nudum 'Winterthur'	360	5–9	○◑	◇	D	S	○		✔	✔		✔	✔
opulus	361	3–8	○◑	◆◇	D	S	○		✔	✔		✔	✔
plicatum 'Shasta'	362	(5) 6–8	○◑	◇	D	S	⌒		✔	✔		✔	✔
prunifolium	362	3–9	○◑●	◆◇◇	D	T S	⌒		✔	✔		✔	✔
× rhytidophylloides 'Alleghany'	362	5–8	○◑●	◇	D E	S	○		✔	✔	✔		✔
rufidulum	362	5–9	○◑●	◇◇	D	T S	○		✔	✔		✔	✔
sargentii	363	3–7	○◑	◇	D	S	○		✔	✔		✔	✔
setigerum	363	5–7	○◑●	◇	D	S	○		✔	✔		✔	✔
sieboldii 'Seneca'	364	4–8	○◑	◇	D	T S	⌒		✔	✔			✔
trilobum	364	3–7	○◑	◇	D	S	○		✔	✔		✔	✔
Vitex													
agnus-castus	364	(6) 7–8 (9)	○◑	◇◇	D E	T S	⌒		✔	✔			✔
Weigela													
florida	365	(4) 5–8	○	◇	D	S	○		✔				✔
Xanthorhiza													
simplicissima	366	3–9	◑●	◇	D	S	≋					✔	✔
Yucca													
filamentosa	366	5–9 (10)	○	◇◇	E	S	○		✔		✔		✔
Zelkova													
serrata	367	5–8	○	◇	D	T	▽	✔			✔	✔	
Zenobia													
pulverulenta	368	5–9	○◑	◇	D E	S	⌒		✔			✔	

Key: 0 Oval △ Pyramid ○ Rounded ▽ Vase ⌒ Spreading Weeping ≋ Creeping/Suckering/Trailing ✳ Easy ■ 381

USDA Hardiness Zone Map

The United States Department of Agriculture (USDA) created this map to give gardeners a helpful tool for selecting and cultivating plants. The map divides North America into 11 zones based on each area's average minimum winter temperature. Zone 1 is the coldest and Zone 11 the warmest. Recently, the zones were further divided into "a" and "b", with "a" being the colder portion. To locate your zone, refer to the map here, or for the most up-to-date information, visit the National Arbor Day Foundation's Web site: *www.arborday.org/media/zones.cfm.*

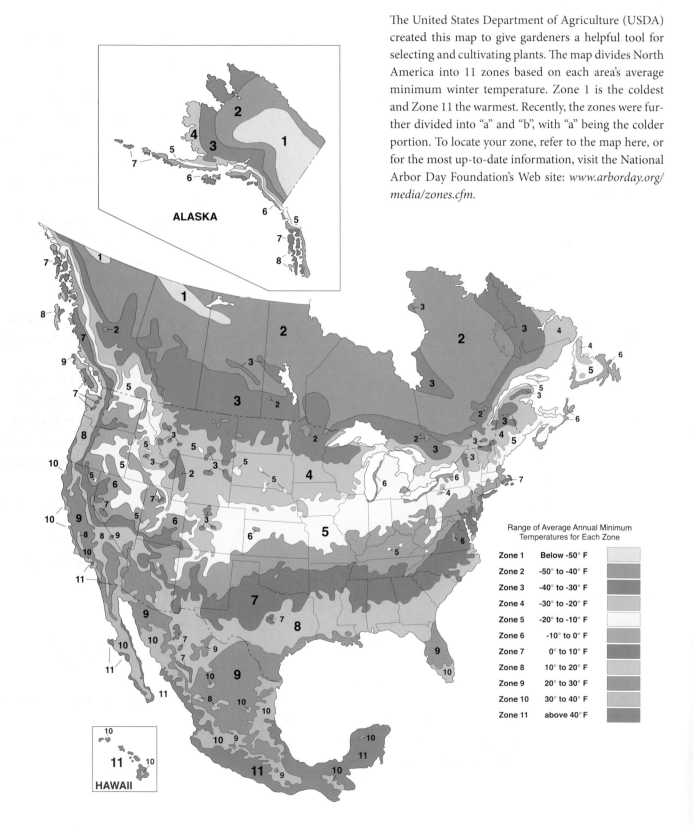

ALASKA

HAWAII

Range of Average Annual Minimum Temperatures for Each Zone

Zone 1	Below -50° F
Zone 2	-50° to -40° F
Zone 3	-40° to -30° F
Zone 4	-30° to -20° F
Zone 5	-20° to -10° F
Zone 6	-10° to 0° F
Zone 7	0° to 10° F
Zone 8	10° to 20° F
Zone 9	20° to 30° F
Zone 10	30° to 40° F
Zone 11	above 40° F

Resources

Nomenclature

We derived the scientific names in this book from *List of Names of Woody Plants (Naamlijst Van Houtige Gewassen)*, International Standard, European Nurserystock Association's European Plant Names Working Group 2005-2010, M.H.A. Hoffman, Applied Plant Research, Boskoop, The Netherlands, 2005. See *www.internationalplantnames.com*

Invasives

For information about invasives in your area:

The WeedUS Database, a listing of plants invading natural areas in the U.S., including Hawaii: *www.nps.gov/plants/alien/list/a.htm*

Weed Science Society of America: *www.wssa.net*

Tree Care

International Society of Arboriculture maintains an excellent tree care Web site: *www.treesaregood.com*

Techno Tree Biology Dictionary contains a wealth of tree information compiled by John A. Keslick Jr., and including articles by Dr. Alex L. Shigo: www.treedictionary.com

Tree Care Industry Association lists accredited tree care companies and offers tree care and health information online at *www.natlarb.com*

TreeGator: *www.watersavers.com/docs/ yardandgarden_specpro.shtml*

Databases

Missouri Botanical Garden's Kemper Center for Home Gardening: For Plant Information resource page: *www.gardeninghelp.org*

Ohio State's Plant Facts factsheet dictionary and database: *http://plantfacts.osu.edu/web*

Tree Selector for urban and suburban sites: For USDA hardiness zones 2–7 and 8–11; helps you develop a tree list by using your soil, site, and desired plant attributes; from Rutgers University, the University of Florida, and the USDA Forest Service Northeast Region: *http://orb. at.ufl.edu/TREES/index.html*

The University of Connecticut Database of Trees, Shrubs and Vines: *www.hort.uconn.edu/plants*

USDA Forest Service and the University of Florida: For 680 tree fact sheets, including range, size, and potential pests and diseases: *http://hort.ufl.edu/trees*

USDA Natural Resources Conservation Service Plants Database: *http://plants.usda.gov*

UI Plants: A database on woody landscape plants for the Midwest from the University of Illinois at Urbana-Champaign: *http://woodyplants.nres.uiuc.edu*

Other Web sites of Interest

Arbor Day Foundation guide to identifying, planting, growing, and pruning common landscape trees, plus a hardiness zone locator: *www.arborday.org*

Cooperative Extension Service offices: For the office nearest you, go to *www.csrees.usda.gov/Extension/ index.html*. State-by-state Web sites provide science-based practices and information to use in your home and garden, including information on controlling specific pests and diseases.

Cornell Gardening Resources: *www.gardening.cornell.edu*

Garden Club of America: *www.gcamerica.org*

National Garden Clubs, Inc.: *www.gardenclub.org*

National Gardening Association: *www.garden.org*

New England Wildflower Society: *www.newfs.org*

Northern Nut Growers Association: *www.northernnutgrowers.org*

Sustainable Trees and Shrubs, URI Cooperative Extension: *http://131.128.91.217/maynard_susplants/html_ spl2000/index.htm*

Virginia Tech/Virginia Cooperative Extension: *www.ext. vt.edu/resources*

Reading List

de Beaulieu, Antoine le Hardy. *An Illustrated Guide to Maples,* English translation (Timber Press, 2003)

Bitner, Richard L. *Conifers for Gardens: An Illustrated Encyclopedia* (Timber Press, 2007)

Brickell, Christopher, and Judith D. Zuk, editors. *The American Horticultural Society A–Z Encyclopedia of Garden Plants* (DK Publishing, 1997)

Church, Thomas D. *Gardens are for People,* 3rd edition (University of California Press, 1995)

Cullina, William. *Native Trees, Shrubs, and Vines* (Houghton Mifflin, 2002)

Dirr, Michael A. *Manual of Woody Landscape Plants,* 5th edition (Stipes Publishing, 1975; revised 1998)

Gerhold, Henry D., Norman L. Lacasse, Willet N. Wandell, editors. *Landscape Tree Factsheets,* 3rd edition (Pennsylvania State University Press, 2001)

Jaynes, Richard A. *Kalmia: Mountain Laurel and Related Species,* 3rd edition (Timber Press, 1997)

Krüssmann, Gerd, with Hans-Dieter Warda, editor. *Manual of Cultivated Conifers,* 2nd revised edition (Timber Press, 1991)

Lancaster, Roy. *Travels in China: A Plantsman's Paradise* (Antique Collectors' Club Ltd, 1989)

Miller, Howard A., and Samuel H. Lamb. *Oaks of North America* (Naturegraph Publishers, 1984)

Nelson, William R. *Planting Design: A Manual of Theory and Practice,* 2nd edition (Stipes Publishing, 1985)

Shigo, Alex L. *Modern Arboriculture: A Systems Approach to the Care of Trees and Their Associates* (Shigo and Trees, Associates, 1991)

Shigo, Alex L. *Tree Basics: What Every Person Needs to Know about Trees* (Shigo and Trees, Associates, 1996)

Shigo, Alex L. *Tree Pruning: A Worldwide Photo Guide* (Shigo and Trees, Associates, 1989)

Vaucher, Hugues. *Tree Bark: A Color Guide,* English translation (Timber Press, 2003)

Some Gardens to Visit

For public gardens and displays of shrubs and trees in your area, check out the website of the American Public Gardens Association (formerly American Association of Botanical Gardens & Arboreta): *www.publicgardens.org*

Among the many sites to visit are the following:

Arnold Arboretum, Jamaica Plain, MA: *www.arboretum.harvard.edu*

Chanticleer Garden, Wayne, PA: *www.chanticleergarden.org*

Ladew Topiary Gardens, Monkton, MD: *www.ladewgardens.com*

Longwood Gardens, Kennett Square, PA (for magnificent specimens, including those started in the 18th century arboretum of Quaker farmers, Joshua and Samuel Peirce): *www.longwoodgardens.org*

Montreal Botanic Garden, Montreal, Quebec, Canada: *www2.ville.montreal.qc.ca/jardin/en/menu.htm*

Morris Arboretum, Swarthmore, PA: *www.business-services.upenn.edu/arboretum*

Morton Arboretum, Lisle, IL: *www.mortonarb.org*

Tower Hill Botanic Garden, Boylston, MA (for trees and shrubs that grow well in New England): *www.towerhillbg.org*

VanDusen Botanical Garden, Vancouver, British Columbia, Canada: *www.city.vancouver.bc.ca/parks/parks/vandusen/website*

Plant Societies

American Boxwood Society: *www.boxwoodsociety.org*

American Camellia Society: *www.camellias-acs.com*

American Conifer Society: *www.conifersociety.org*

American Forests: *www.americanforests.org*

American Hibiscus Society: *http://americanhibiscus.org*

American Horticultural Society: *www.ahs.org/index.htm*

American Hydrangea Society: *www.americanhydrangeasociety.org*

American Rhododendron Society: *www.rhododendron.org*

American Rose Society: *www.ars.org*

Azalea Society of America, Inc.: *www.azaleas.org*

Canadian Rose Society: *www.mirror.org/groups/crs*

Garden Conservancy: *www.gardenconservancy.org*

Gardenia Society of America: P.O. Box 879, Atwater, CA 95301

Heather Society: *www.users.zetnet.co.uk/heather*

Holly Society of America, Inc.: *www.hollysocam.org*

International Clematis Society: *www.clematisinternational.com*

International Lilac Society, Inc.: *http://lilacs.freeservers.com*

International Oak Society: *www.saintmarys.edu/~rjensen/ios.html*

International Oleander Society: *http://oleander.org*

International Ornamental Crabapple Society: *www.malus.net*

North American Heather Society: *www.northamericanheathersociety.org*

North American Rock Garden Society: *www.nargs.org*

The Magnolia Society: *www.magnoliasociety.org*

Glossary

Alternate. Leaves staggered in two lines on either side of an axis or stem instead of paired. (Paired leaves are known as opposite.)

Aril. Fleshy cover that envelops a seed; often brightly colored. For example, the showy red aril around a yew seed is edible, but the seed itself is poisonous.

Berm. A mound or bank of soil or sand built for improved drainage, as an insulating barrier, or to form a landscape screen.

Bract. A leaflike structure that grows beneath a flower (or cluster of flowers). Its form is different from that of the plant's leaves, and can be mistaken for flower petals. Flowering dogwood is a good example of a tree with prominent bracts.

Calyx. Husklike cover that envelopes a developing bud or a flower. Leaflike divisions of the calyx are known as *sepals*.

Compost. Decomposed organic debris, including animal manure and decaying vegetation such as dead leaves, grass clippings, wood chips, and twigs. The composting process is the action of tiny life forms (microbes) feeding upon these organic molecules in the presence of air. This microbial action generates heat, which destroys vulnerable disease-causing organisms in the pile. Compost must reach a minimum temperature of 131°F and stay that hot for at least 3 days.

Compound leaves. Leaves, such as those on walnut, that have several divisions or leaflets.

Conk. The hard, flat, reproductive body of a wood-decay fungus, projecting beyond the bark of tree trunks, branches, or stumps.

Cooperative Extension. The Cooperative Extension system is a nationwide educational outreach between the U.S. Department of Agriculture and land grant colleges and universities. To find an office near you, check *www.csrees.usda.gov/Extension*.

Deadhead. Detach faded flowers or flower clusters from the stem for neat appearance. When practiced before seeds form on plants that bloom on old wood, it may encourage them to direct their energy into next year's buds.

Deciduous. Trees and shrubs that drop their leaves in autumn at the end of the growing season.

Dormant. State of biological rest when plants are not in active growth but may again become active.

Drupe. Fleshy, one-seeded fruit such as olive, cherry, and elderberry, which spontaneously open to release their seeds when ripe.

Inoculum. The spores or tissues of a pathogen that can trigger disease in a plant.

Leader. Main growing stem of a single-trunk tree; usually the tallest, most vigorous shoot at the center of the plant.

Opposite. Two even lines of leaves forming pairs of leaves along a stem. *See also* Alternate.

Pathogen. Disease- or injury-producing agent such as a virus, bacterium, or other microorganism.

Pome. Type of fleshy fruit such as pear or apple with seed chambers and a thick outer layer.

Sepal. A modified leaf or green part in a flower's outer layer (calyx), which protects the flower in bud.

Simple leaves. Leaves, such as those on a lilac, which are in one unsubdivided piece. *See also* Compound leaves.

Spore. Small, often one-celled, reproductive body produced by bacteria and fungi; similar to seed in flowering plants.

Sport. Odd or atypical growth on a plant that differs from the rest of the plant, such as a variegated shoot on an otherwise green-leafed shrub.

Tepal. A segment of the outer parts of a flower like magnolia, undifferentiated from the other parts by shape or color.

Truss. A cluster of flowers, as in rhododendrons.

Whip. An unbranched tree seedling or shoot about 1½ to 3 feet high, bred for planting out.

Author's Acknowledgments

This book represents an intricate collaboration that evolved from a 2002 conversation in Seattle with my editor and friend, Gwen Steege. Without her guidance, encouragement, and steady hand, this book would not exist. Pam Art, president of Storey Publishing, and Deborah Balmuth, editorial director, also believed in this book's potential and gave it their unstinting support. I thank Cindy McFarland for designing a book that is both beautiful and accessible; Liseann Karandisecky for producing this book; and Kevin Metcalfe, who prepared text and photos for the printer.

A book is often as good as its pre-publication readers, and mine were superb. Leonard Perry, Ph.D., extension professor in the Department of Plant and Soil Science at the University of Vermont, provided detailed comments on content and nomenclature that enriched the encyclopedia. Kevin T. Smith, Ph.D., plant physiologist and project leader for the USDA Forest Service, offered insights into tree science and helped me explain it to the layman.

I am indebted to arborist Jeff Ott of Northeast Shade Tree in Portsmouth, NH, for inviting me to his tree biology workshops, where I met Kevin and the late Alex Shigo, former chief scientist of the Forest Service. Alex, deemed the father of modern arboriculture, saw the universe in a tree. He, Kevin, and participating arborists helped me see for myself some basics of tree biology.

I thank Ron Yaple of Race Mountain Tree Services Inc. for modeling proper planting technique and Tchukki Andersen of the Tree Care Industry Association for providing a sample pruning specification form. Dr. Richard Bitner, Tim Woods, and Danielle Smith were generous with answers to my questions.

Photographer Karen Bussolini's perfectionism paid off in the beautiful images filling this book. Many came from the garden of my friends Neil Jorgensen and Martha Petersen, landscape designers whose garden is for me an amazing synthesis of practicality, personal taste, and a profound respect for the natural environment. Many thanks to Lynne Barnes, Debbie and Neil Martin, and Linda and Bill Schuler; I drew on their gardens as examples in this book. Kirk Brown's home landscape and Chanticleer Garden stand out in my mind for creativity, color, and flow in the use of woody plants.

I thank my walking buddies — Debbie Martin, Nora Funk, and Margaret Felton in New Hampshire, and Carolyn Schmidt in Tennessee — for keeping me grounded while my thoughts were in the trees; Margo Woodacre in Delaware and Winnie Hohlt in New Hampshire offered continuous encouragement.

My family strengthens me. My husband, Bob O'Sullivan, an ardent beech collector, knows that hauling and digging are the way to my heart. My children, Nich Cope and Molly O'Sullivan, and my niece Laura Fineberg give me my writing voice. My parents, Morris and Libby Bass, sister Barbara Fineberg, and dearest Louise Parker introduced me to beauty, whimsy, and awe. Without these extraordinary folks, I have no stories to tell.

Photographer's Acknowledgments

Thanks to Penny O'Sullivan and our editor, Gwen Steege, for inviting me to join them in this exploration of trees, which sent me to new places and challenged me to see familiar ones through new eyes.

I am very grateful to those garden professionals who generously offered their time, insight, suggestions, identifications, friendship, and access to gardens, most notably Jonathan Wright and Bill Thomas at Chanticleer Garden, Brad Roeller at The Institute of Ecosystem Studies, John Trexler and Michael Arnum at Tower Hill Botanic Garden, Karl Lauby, Melinda Manning, Lynden Miller and the horticultural staff at New York Botanical Garden, Dr. Allan Armitage, Natalia Hamill, Kirk Brown, Colleen Belk at Barton Springs Nursery, Madalene Hill and Gwen Barclay, Wayne Mezitt at Weston Nurseries, Patricia Evans at Longwood Gardens, staff at Brookside Gardens, Melodie Leach at Riverbanks Zoo and Garden, Martha Petersen, Neil Jorgensen, Duncan and Julia Brine, Carole Ottesen, Nancy Wong at VanDusen Botanical Garden, Mark Weathington at The Norfolk Botanical Garden, Tom Brinda at The Lewis Ginter Botanical Garden, Ann and Mike Johnson at Summer Hill Nursery, Inta Krombolz, Scott Rothenberger, Claire Sawyers and Rhoda Maurer at The Scott Arboretum, Harold Sweetman at The Jenkins Arboretum and Dorthe Hviid at The Berkshire Botanical Garden. Thanks also to Dr. Richard Iversen at Farmingdale University, The Kent Greenhouse, David Ellis at *The American Gardener*, Nancy Dubrule at Natureworks, Andrew Durbridge, Jan Axel at Delphinium Design, Joanne Kostecky, Betsy Manning, Brian Minter, Wilbur & King, Kathleen Nelson, Lorraine Ballato, Dick Jaynes at Broken Arrow Nursery, Bob McCartney at Woodlanders Nursery, Larry Weaner. Ken Twombly of the Twombly Nursery and horticulturist Christine Froehlich-Sanguedolce have earned special thanks for their patient modeling and good advice.

Thanks also to the many friends and private garden owners who welcomed me, sometimes for days on end, especially Liz and Doug Berry, Kirk and Sara Brown, Vince Dooley, Nora

Funk, Darlene Huntington, Philip Jenkins, Joan Larned, Dr. Nicholas Nickou and Carol Hanby, Jenny Reed, Barry Remley, Missy Stevens, Linda and Marty Wasserstein, Betsy Williams, Thyrza Whittemore, Adrian and Margaret Selby; and to my husband, John Scofield, and son, Jackson Scofield, for being so good-natured about my long hours in the garden and days away from home and frequent requests to model, hold branches out of the way, and aim reflectors. I can only convey the beauty of all I've seen through these photographs. Page references for specific images are as follows:

Afton Villa, LA, 11, 322

Andrew Durbridge, Garden Designer, NY, 167

Arbor Services of Connecticut, 101

Berkshire Botanical Garden, MA, 354 (left)

Betsy Manning Garden Design, CT, 45, 206 (right)

Brookside Gardens, MD, 56, 196 (top right)

Chanticleer Garden, PA, 3, 32, 69 (right), 111, 112, 120 (bottom right), 147 (top right), 199 (top), 219 (top), 229 (top right), 256 (bottom), 258 (right), 277 (top), 278, 281 (top), 284 (top), 312 (bottom), 320

Classic Courtyards, WA, 25

Delphinium Design, NY, 169

Dickson DeMarche Landscape Architects, CT, 68 (right), 132

Duncan Brine/Horticultural Design, NY, 199 (bottom left), 335 (bottom)

Farmingdale University, NY, 8, 129, 238, 301 (top left)

"Gardens," TX, 115 (top)

Institute of Ecosystem Studies, NY, 165, 229 (bottom right), 237

Inta Krombolz, PA, v, 152–53, 208 check this last

Jenkins Arboretum, PA, 175

Jennifer Myers, TX, 5 (top)

Joanne Kostecky Garden Design, PA, 321 (bottom right)

Johnsen Landscapes and Pools, NY, 249 (top)

Kathleen Nelson Perennials, CT, 231 (top)

Ken Mark Co. Landscaping, CT, 12

Kirk R. Brown, PA, 9, 13, 27, 43, 298, 310, 345 (left)

Lewis Ginter Botanical Garden, VA, 280

Longwood Gardens, PA, 26, 148 (bottom right), 182 (right)

Lynden B. Miller Garden Design, NY, 7 (bottom), 47, 51 (top), 92

Martha Petersen, MLD/Neil Jorgensen, ME, 2, 4, 15, 16, 24, 30, 42, 74–75, 81, 82 (bottom), 96 (top left and right), 100, 122, 134

Nancy Webber/Ground Xero, TX, 28

Nasami Farm, MA, 76

New York Botanical Garden, NY, 14, 33 (middle), 34 (right), 35 (left), 82 (top), 171 (top and bottom), 174, 182 (left), 200 (left), 264 (left), 288, 313

Norfolk Botanical Garden, VA, 189, 194 (top left), 256 (top)

Penelope O'Sullivan, NH, 233 (bottom)

Pepsico/Russell Page, NY, 179

Philip Johnson, Architect, CT, 121

Rice Creek Gardens, MN, 262

Richard Bergmann, AIA, ASLA, CT, 115 (bottom), 191 (bottom)

River Banks Zoo and Garden, SC, 332

Scott Arboretum, PA, 265 (top)

Scott Rothenberger Garden Designer, PA, 23, 187 (left), 246 (right), 261 (right)

Sharon Mann/Designs of Mann, CT, 40

Summer Hill Nursery, CT, ii, 95, 207 (right), 271 (middle), 343 (bottom)

Sundial Herb Garden, CT, 6 (bottom), 49 (top)

Swamp Fox Garden Design, CT, 331

Sydney Eddison, CT, 7 (top), 239 (right), 309 (right), 311 (bottom)

Tower Hill Botanic Garden, MA, 5 (bottom), 141 (bottom right), 147 (bottom left), 160 (bottom right), 180 (right), 249 (bottom), 285 (bottom), 317

Tramontano + Rowe Landscape Architects, CT, 49 (bottom)

Twombly Nursery, CT, 1, 66 (top left), 143, 181, 342 (bottom left)

Van Dusen Botanical Garden, BC, 34 (left), 196 (bottom right), 202

Ward's Nursery, MA, 77

Wesley Rouse/Pine Meadow Inc., CT, 44, 66 (top right), 370–71

Weston Nurseries, MA, 20

Wilbur & King Nurseries, CT, 83 (top)

INDEX

Page numbers in **bold** indiate tables; those in *italic* indicate photos.

cranberry bush viburnum.. *See Viburnum opulus*; *Viburnum trilobum*

crapc myrtlc (*Lagerstroemia indica*), *53*, **53**, 71, **71**, **108**, 134, **147**, 269–70, *270*

Crataegus species, 217
 diseases, 217, 218
 juglone resistance, **259**
 wildlife and, **73**

Crataegus crus-galli var. *inermis* (thornless cockspur hawthorn), 217
 'Cruzam' (Crusader), 217

Crataegus laevigata
 'Crimson Cloud', 217–18
 'Paul's Scarlet', 218

Crataegus phaenopyrum (Washington hawthorn), 217, 218

Crataegus viridis (hawthorn), **71**, *73*, **73**, **117**, 135, *217*
 disease resistance, 135, 217, 218
 hedges, **117**
 pollution resistance, **147**
 'Winter King', **71**, *73*, **117**, 217, 218, *218*

Cryptomeria japonica (Japanese cedar), **57**, *58*, 218–19
 'Yoshino', 219, *219*

Cunninghamia lanceolata (China fir), 219, *219*

× *Cupressocyparis leylandii* (Leyland cypress), 219–20, *220*
 'Naylor's Blue', 220

Cupressus sempervirens (Italian cypress), *25*

currant. *See Ribes*

cutting down trees, 143, *143*

cypress. *See Chamaecyparis*; *Microbiota*; *Taxodium*; × *Cupressocyparis leylandii*; *Cupressus sempervirens*

Cyrilla racemiflora (leatherwood), 220, *220*

Cytisus scoparius (Scotch broom), 220–21
 'Moonlight', 220
 'Nova Scotia', 220
 'Pink Beauty', 220

D

damage to plants
 chemicals, 145
 construction equipment, 128, 143, 144–45, *144*
 prevention, 144–45, 148–50, *148–49*
 storms, 148–50, *148–49*, 166
 suckers, 146, *146*
 See also environmental concerns

Daphne species, **107**, **141**, **259**

Daphne × *burkwoodii*, **57**
 'Brimoon' (Brigg's Moonlight), 221
 'Carol Mackie', 221, *221*
 'Somerset', 221

Daphne cneorum (rose daphne), 221

Daphne mezereum (February daphne), 221

Daphne odora (fragrant daphne), 221
 'Aureomarginata', *221*

dappled shade. *See* light shade

Davidia involucrata (dove tree), *63*, **63**, *85*, 222, *222*

deadheading, 109, 266, 324, 330

dead nettle, spotted (*Lamium maculatum*), *96*

deciduous plants, 154
 groundcovers, 169, 171, 214, 216, 222, 243, 256, 257, 307, 328, 340, 341, 344, 355, 366
 hedge plants, **116**, 156, 159, 167, 176, 183, 186, 191–92, 216, 218, 227, 228, 229, 230, 232, 242, 255, 269–70, 295, 310, 323, 340, 351, 358
 pruning, 111–12, *111–12*, **113**, 162, 177, 182–83, 184, 187
 pruning times, 106, 156, 163, 167, 187
 shade created by, 42–43, *42–43*
 silhouettes, *66–67*, 67, **67**, 154
 texture, 58, 59, **59**, *96*
 wet soils, **35**, 192, 197, 206–08, 223, 231, 232, 239, 255, 257, 271, 274–75, 282, 306, 318, 320, 332, 333–35, 347, 356, 362, 366, 368
 wind damage, 149
 See also foliage

decks, shading, 43–44, *43–44*

deer
 plant damage, 140
 resistant plants, *141*, **141**, *225*, *250*, *254*, 280, 282, 336, 350

defoliation, 170

depth of mulch, 97

depth of planting, 84, *84–88*, 85–88, *90*

designer's choice encyclopedia listings, 155

design principles, 4–17
 accents, 6, 49, *49*, *66–69*, 67–69, **67**, **69**
 balance, 5, *5*, 19, *27*
 color, 9, *9*
 direction and movement, 46–49, *46–49*
 focal points, 6, *6*, 48, *66–69*, 67–69, **67**, **69**
 form, 7, *7*, 10, *25*
 formal designs, 16, 19
 hardscape, 19, **22–23**, 29, *29*
 house style, 16–17, *16–17*, 19, 22, **22**
 informal designs, 16, 19, 27, *81*
 line, 7, *7*
 mulch and, 94–95, *95*
 regional character, 10–15, *10–12*, *14–15*, **20**, 30–39, *33*, **35–36**, **38–39**
 repetition, 4, *4*, 58
 safety, *21*
 scale, 6, *6*, 28
 sequence, 4
 silhouettes, *66–69*, 67–69, **67**, **69**, 154

texture, 8, *8*, 47, *58–59*, *58–59*, **58–59**, 59, **59**, *96*

unity, 4

views, *21*, 49, *49*, 143

woodland design, 30–31, 81–82, *81–82*

See also planning gardens; privacy solutions

Deutzia gracilis (slender deutzia), **61**, **107**, **116**
 'Duncan', 222–23
 'Nikko', *27*, *106*, 222–23

Deutzia × *hybrida*
 'Magicien', 223, *223*
 'Perle Rose', 223

Deutzia × *lemoinei* (Lemoine deutzia), 223

Deutzia × 'Pink Minor', 223

Deutzia × *rosea* 'Carminea', 223

Deutzia × *scabra* (fuzzy deutzia), 223

devil's walking stick (*Aralia spinosa*), 172

Diervilla lonicera, *223*
 'Copper', 223

Diervilla sessilifolia (Southern bush honeysuckle), 223
 'Butterfly', 223

Diospyros virginiana (persimmon), **39**, **73**, 224, *224*
 'Early Golden', 224
 'John Rick', 224
 'Meader', 224
 'Miller', 224

direction, 46–49, *46–49*

Disanthus cercidifolius, *55*, 224, *224*

diseases, 131–36, *133–36*
 foliage, 133, 170, 317
 fungi, 133–35, 209, 217, 304, 353
 inspecting for, 132
 preventing, 105, 131–32, *132*, 133–36, 209, 300, 304
 resistance, 27, 131, 135
 stressors for plants and, 128, 132, 134, 138, 139, 148–51, *148–49*, *151*, 209
 sudden oak death, 317
 treating, 127, 128, 133–36, 259
 See also damage; pests

dogs, 142

dogwood. *See Cornus*

dormancy, pruning during, 106, 108, **108**

dove tree (*Davidia involucrata*), *63*, **63**, *85*, 222, *222*

downy mildew, 134, *134*

downy serviceberry (*Amelanchier arborea*), **35**

drainage, 34
 construction and, 144

drastic renewal pruning, *112*, 176

drought, 150
 See also drought-tolerant plants; dry soils

drought-tolerant plants
 broad-leaf evergreen shrub, 282

Mezitt, Wayne, 323, 327
mice, 142
Microbiota decussata (Siberian cypress), *23*, *57*, **57**, 285, *285*
microclimates, 13, 41
　　See also energy savings
mildews, 134, *134*
Miller, Howard A., 317
mock orange. *See Philadelphus*; *Pittosporum tobira*
Modern Arboriculture (Shigo), 105
mold, sooty mold, 135, *135*
money
　　choosing plants, 77, 79
　　maintaining gardens, 28, *28*
Morus species (mulberry), **39**, **111**
Morus rubra (red mulberry), 286
mountain ash. *See Sorbus*
mountain laurel (*Kalmia latifolia*), **33**, **61**, *109*, **116**, **130**, **141**, 259, 265–66, *265–66*
movement, 46–49, *46–49*
mulberry (*Morus* species), **39**, **111**, 286
mulch, 82, *82*, 94–97, *95–97*
　　advantages of, 94–95
　　amounts, 97
　　damage prevention by, 145, 149
　　diseases helped by, 127
　　groundcovers as, *96*
　　maintaining, 97
　　timing, 97
multi-trunk tree pruning, *119*
mycorrhizae, 127–28
Myrica pensylvanica (bayberry), *35*, **36**, **38**, **117**, **141**, 176, 286, *286*
　　'Morton' (Silver Sprite), 286

N

names of plants, scientific, 154
Nandina domestica (heavenly bamboo), **108**
　　'Fire Power', *106*, 287, *287*
　　'Harbor Dwarf', 287, *287*
　　'Monum' (Plum Passion), 287
　　'Moon Bay', 287
　　'Wood's Dwarf', 287
nanking cherry (*Prunus tomentosa*), **117**, 301
native plants. *See* wild plants; woodland
naturalistic designs. *See* informal gardens; regional character; woodland
neighborhood, garden design and, 16–17
Nerium oleander (oleander), **38**, **141**, 288
　　'Calypso', 288
　　'Hardy Double Yellow', 288
　　'Hardy Pink', 288
　　'Petite Pink', 288
　　'Soeur Agnes' (Sister Agnes), 288
　　'Variegatum', 288
nettle. *See* dead nettle

New England, 10, 298
　　See also Northeast
New Jersey tea (*Ceanothus americanus*), 195
ninebark (*Physocarpus opulifolius*), **36**, *37*, **54**, **113**, **259**, 295, *295*
Nooney, Jill, 241
Northeast, climate, 10, *11*, 16
NPK ratios, 129
numbers of plants, 27
nurseries
　　balled-and-burlapped plants, 84, *84*, 317
　　choosing plants, 77–79, *77–78*, 131
　　container plants, 83, *83*
　　wild plant, 85
Nyssa sylvatica (sour gum; black tupelo), *34*, **35**, **130**, *131*, **147**, 288–89, *288*
　　'NXSXF' (Forum), 289

O

oak. *See Quercus*
oak wilt, 317
ocean. *See* marine climate
ocean spray (*Holodiscus discolor*), 242
oils, horticultural, 137, 138
old plantings, 28–29, *29*, 31, *31*
oleander (*Nerium oleander*), **38**, **141**, 288
on-line plant catalogs, 78
orange (*Citrus* species)
　　espaliers, **126**
　　See also Maclura pomifera; *Philadelphus*; *Poncirus trifoliata*
Oregon grape holly (*Mahonia aquifolium*), 58, **61**, **116**
organic fertilizers, 127, 128, 129
osage orange (*Maclura pomifera*), **111**, **117**, *276*, *276*
Osmanthus species
　　× *burkwoodii*, 289
　　× *fortunei*, 290
Osmanthus delavayi, 290
Osmanthus fragrans (sweet olive), **116**, 290
Osmanthus heterophyllus (false holly), *57*, **57**, **116**, 289–90
　　'Goshiki', 289
　　'Gulftide', 289
　　'Purpureus', 289
　　'Sasaba', 289, *289*
　　'Variegatus', 289
Ostrya virginiana (hop hornbeam), 290, *290*
Ott, Jeff, 128, 129
Oxydendrum arboreum (sourwood), **63**, **65**, *108*, **108**, 122, *130*, **130**, **141**, 290–91, *291*
ozone pollution, 146, **147**

P

pachysandra 'Green Sheen', 277, 339
Pacific Northwest

climate, *10*, 11
　　plants best in, 158, 202, 248, 282, 313, 323
Paeonia suffruticosa (tree peony), **61**, 291–92
　　'Border Charm', 292
　　'Hana-kisoi', 292
　　'High Noon', 292, *292*
　　'Kamada-nishiki', 292
　　'Rimpo', 292
Parrotia persica (Persian parrotia), **53**, 292, *292*
　　'Pendula' (Kew form), 292
　　'Vanessa', 292
partial shade, 32, *32*, **33**
Paulownia tomentosa (empress tree), **59**, **114**, 293, *293*
pawpaw (*Asimina triloba*), 174–75, *175*
peach (*Prunus* species), pruning, **107**
pearlbush (*Exochorda* × *macrantha*), **107**, 228, *228*
pear, ornamental, **107**, 315, *315*
pea shrub (*Caragana arborescens*), **36**, *37*, **38**, **141**, 190–91, *191*
pecan (*Carya* species), pruning, **111**
PeeGee hydrangeas, 114, 247, *247*
peony, tree (*Paeonia suffruticosa*), **61**, 291–92, *292*
persimmon (*Diospyros virginiana*), **39**, **73**, 224, *224*
personal choices
　　planning gardens, 3, **20**, **22–23**
　　plant choices, 23, 27, 28
pests
　　insects, 136–39, *136*, *138–39*, 352, 353, 357
　　prevention, 136, **137**, *138–39*, 140, *140*, **141**, 142, *142*, 330, 353
　　resistant plants, 27, 131, *141*, **141**, 173, 176, 211, 250, 254
　　treatment, 136–39, **141**, 142, *142*, 352
　　wildlife as, 140–42, *140*, **141**, *142*
　　See also damage; diseases
Petasites japonicus 'Giganteus' (giant butterbur), 172, 348
Petersen, Martha, 170, 180
pets, **22**
Phellodendron amurense (amur corktree), *53*, **147**, 293–94, *294*
Philadelphus species (mock orange hybrids)
　　'Buckley's Quill', 294
　　'Innocence', 294
　　'Miniature snowflake', 294
　　'Minnesota snowflake', 294
　　'Natchez', 294
　　'Polar Star', 294
Philadelphus coronarius (sweet mock orange), **38**, **61**, **107**, **126**, 294
　　'Aureus', 294, *294*
　　espaliers, **126**
　　salt tolerance, 38

rot
    canker, 133
    heart rot, 133
    phytophthora root rot, 134–35, *135*
rounded plants, 19
Rubus cockburnianus 'Wyego' (Golden Vale white-stemmed bramble), 332
rust fungi, 217

S

safety, **21**
    tree removal for, 143
    See also damage
St. Johnswort. *See Hypericum*
salal (*Gaultheria shallon*), 235–36, *236*
Salix species (willow), **111**, 139, 333
    'Flame', 334
    pollution intolerance, **147**
    'Prairie Cascade', 335
Salix alba (coral bark willow), **35**, **114**, 333
    'Britzensis' (red willow), 53
    'Chermesina', 333, *333*
    subspecies *vitellina*, 333
Salix babylonica (weeping willow), **35**, **67**, 333–34
    'Crispa', 333
    var. *pekinensis* 'Erythroflexuosa' ('Golden Curls' corkscrew willow), 333–34
    var. *pekinensis* 'Tortuosa' (corkscrew willow), 333–34
Salix caprea 'Kilmarnock', 334
Salix caprea pendula, 334
Salix cinerea 'Tricolor', 334
Salix discolor (pussy willow), 334
Salix elaeagnos 'Angustifolia', 334, *334*
Salix gracilistyla 'Melanostachys' (black pussy willow), 334
Salix integra 'Hakuro-nishiki' (dappled willow), **54**, 334, 335
Salix purpurea 'Nana', 335, *335*
Salix rosmarinifolia (rosemary willow), 334, *334*
Salix × sepulcralis 'Chrysocoma' (Golden weeping willow), 334
salt cedar (*Tamarix ramosissima*), 347
salt-tolerant plants, 38, **38–39**
    deciduous shrubs, 176, 206, 215, 286, 347
    deciduous trees, 164, 233, 305
    evergreen shrubs, 235, 249, 260, 262, 288, 306
    evergreen trees, 227, 254, 260, 297, 300, 302, 304
Sambucus species (elderberry), **35**, **73**, **108**
Sambucus canadensis (American elderberry), 335
    'Aurea', 335
    'Lacinata', *72*, *108*, 335

'Maxima', 335
    'York', 335
Sambucus nigra (European black elderberry), 335–36
    'Aureomarginata', 336
    'Eva' (Black Lace), **54**, 336
    'Gerda' (Black Beauty), 336
    'Guincho Purple', 336
    'Madonna', 336
    'Pulverulenta', 336, *336*
Sambucus racemosa (European red elderberry), 336
    'Goldenlocks', 336
    'Sutherland Gold', 336
sand cherry, purple-leaf (*Prunus × cistena*), *82*, 309, *309*
Santolina chamaecyparissus (lavender cotton), **117**, 336, *336*
sapphire berry (*Symplocos paniculata*), **65**, 344
Sarcococca hookeriana var. *humilis* (sweet box), 337, *337*
Sarcococca ruscifolia (fragrant sarcococca), *33*, 336
Sarracenia purpurea (purple pitcher plant), 171
Sassafras albidum (sassafras), *85*, 337–38, *337–38*
scale, 6, *6*, *28*, 138, *138*
Sciadopitys verticillata (umbrella pine), **58**, 338, *338*
scientific plant names, 154
screen plants, 26, 45, *45*, *48*
    broad-leaf evergreen shrubs, 189–90, 253, 288, 305
    decidous shrubs, 167, 174, 176, 184, 189, 191, 215, 232, 242, 273, 295, 310, 323, 327, 334, 344
    deciduous trees, 160, 167, 191, 217, 242, 273, 310, 323, 344
    evergreen shrubs, 249–50, 263, 273, 306, 308, 348, 349
    evergreen trees, 158, 202, 220, 249–50, 264, 273, 297, 298, 302, 308, 313, 348, 349, 351
    See also privacy solutions
sea buckthorn (*Hippophae rhamnoides*), 38, **117**, 242
seasonal interest, 26, *26*
    See also bark; deciduous plants; flowering trees and shrubs; foliage color; four-season plants; fruiting plants; time
sequence, 4
service areas, 19, **21**, 23
serviceberry. *See Amelanchier*
setbacks, 80
seven-son flower (*Heptacodium miconioides*), **53**, **71**, *120*, **120**, 241, *241*

shadblow. *See Amelanchier × grandiflora*
shade, 9, 32, *32–33*, **33**, 42–44, *42–44*
    espaliers, 123
    full shade, 32, **33**
    hedges for, **117**
    light shade, 32, **33**
    partial shade, 32, *32*, **33**
    plants to create, 25, 26, *28*, 42–44, *42–44*, 143, 164, 165, 166, 168, 169, 194, 197, 198, 205, 229, 234, 237–39, 243, 259–60, 267, 269, 275, 276, 277–82, 294
    woodlands, 30
    See also shade (plants that grow well in); sun
shade (plants that grow well in), 26, *33*, **33**, 143
    deciduous shrubs, 223, 245, 291, 341, 366, 368
    deciduous trees, 174, 209
    evergreen shrubs, 190, 198, 256, 265, 272, 337
    evergreen trees, 158, 353
shapes of plants
    encyclopedia symbols, 154
    See also form
sharpening tools, 104, *104*
Shigo, Alex L., 5, 105, 133
show-off plants. *See* four-season plants
shrubs
    buyer checklist, **79**
    pruning, 112–14, *112*, **113–14**, *114*
    pruning as trees, *119*, *120*, **120**
    trees differentiated from, 5, *5*
    See also deciduous plants; evergreens; flowering trees and shrubs; fruiting plants
Siberian pea shrub (*Caragana arborescens*), **36**, *37*, **38**, **141**, 190–91, *191*
silhouettes, *66–69*, *67–69*, **67**, **69**, 154
silk tassel (*Garya elliptica*), 235, *235*
silverbell (*Halesia carolina*), **63**, 239, *239*
single-stem tree pruning, 119
Sinocalycanthus chinensis (Chinese sweetshrub), 189
sites
    changes in, 3
    choosing plants for, 80–83, 131–32
    corner lots, 48
    maintaining, **21**, 26–27, 75
    old plantings, 28–29, *29*, 31, *31*
    pets, **22**
    plan drawing, 3, 18–19
    play areas, *21*, **22**
    private areas, 19, *21*, **21**
    public areas, 19, **21**, 29, *29*
    regional characteristics, 1, 10–15, *10–12*, *14–15*, **20**
    service areas, 19, **21**, 23

T

tamarack (*Larix laricina*), **35**, 171, 272
tamarisk (*Tamarix ramosissima*), 347
Tamarix ramosissima (salt cedar; tamarisk),
  347
    'Pink Cascade', 347
    'Summer Glow', 347
Taxodium distichum (bald cypress), 8, *34*, **35**,
    39, **67**, 347–48, *347–48*
    'Mickelson', 348
    See also pond cypress
Taxus species (yew), **33**, **47**, **58**
    common, 69, **69**
    'Dwarf Bright Gold', *58*
    espaliers, **126**
    hedges, **116**
    Taunton yew, 31
    topiary, **69**
    windbreaks, 40
Taxus baccata (English yew), 348
    'Repens', 349
Taxus cuspidata (Japanese yew), 348, 349
    'Capitata', 348, 349
    'Dwarf Bright Gold', *349*
    'Monloo', 348, 349
    'Nana Aurescens', 349
Taxus × media, 348
    'Brownii', 349
    'Geeta' (Margarita), 349
    'Hicksii' (Hicks yew), 349
    'Nigra', 349
    'Sentinalis', 349
    'Taunton', 348, 349
tea (*Camellia sinensis*), 190
tent caterpillars, 139, *139*
Teucrium chamaedrys (wall germander), **38**,
    117, 349, *349*
texture, 8, *8*, 47, 58–59, *58–59*, **58–59**, 59, **59**,
    96
Thalictrum aquilegifolium (meadow rue),
    174
three-part cuts, 105, *105*
Thuja species (arborvitae), **33**, **39**
    hedges, *115*, **116**, **117**, 349
    pollution resistance, **147**
    screen plants, 45, 349
    soil preferences, **117**
    windbreaks, 40, 41, 45, 349
Thuja occidentalis (eastern arborvitae), **35**,
    259, 349–50
    'DeGroot's Spire', 350
    'Golden Globe', 350
    'Hetz Midget', 350
    'Holmstrup', 350
    'Mr Bowling Ball' (Bobozam; Linesville),
      350
    'Nigra', 350

'Rheingold', 350
'Smaragd' (emerald arborvitae), *45*, *115*,
  350
'Sunkist', *39*, *350*
'Techny', 350
Techny Gold, **57**
'Teddy', 350
'Yellow Ribbon', *117*, *350*
Thuja orientalis (oriental arborvitae), 306, *306*
Thuja plicata (western red cedar), 350
    'Atrovirens', 350
    'Green Giant', 350
    'Grovpli' (Spring Grove), 350
    'Zebrina', 350
Thujopsis dolobrata (Hiba false arborvitae),
    350–51
    'Nana', 351, *351*
    'Variegata', 351
Tiarella cordifolia (foam flower), 170
tiered cordons, *124–25*
Tilia species (linden; basswood), leaf scorch,
    151
Tilia americana (basswood), 351
Tilia cordata (little-leaf linden), **36**, 81, **111**,
    147, 351–52, *351*
    'Baileyi' (Shamrock), 352
    'Greenspire', 351
    'Ronald' (Nordin), 352
Tilia mongolica, 'Harvest Gold', 352
Tilia tomentosa, 'Sterling', 352, *352*
time
    phasing, 29
    plant choices and, 3–4, 28, 80
    See also maintenance
tint, 9
tools
    choosing, 104
    cleaning, 132
    plant damage by, 145
    pruning, 104, *104*
topiary, 69, *69*, **69**, 185–86, 348
topping trees, 105
Tortuosa beech, 122, 127
training. *See* pruning
transitions
    garden to house, 19, **20**, *22*, *25*, 31, 40–41,
      40–41, *80*, *115*
    garden to wild plants, 12–13, *12*, 30–31,
      181, 182, 206, 207, 211, 241, 265, 272,
      291, 306, 312, 324, 338
trees
    buyer checklist, **79**
    life spans, 3
    removing, 143, *143*
    shrubs differentiated from, 5, *5*
    See also flowering trees and shrubs; fruiting
      plants

tree wells, 144–45, *145*
triads of colors, 9
Trillium grandiflorum (large-flowered tril-
    lium), 170
trillium, large-flowered (*Trillium grandiflo-
    rum*), 170
trimming
    roots, 88, *88*
    See also pruning
trunk flare, 84, 85, 87
trunks of trees
    evaluating tree health, **79**, 308
    mesh protection, *142*
    sculptural qualities, *68*
    sunscald, 150–51, 159
    See also bark
Tsuga species (hemlock), **33**
    designing with, 31
    soil requirements, **130**
Tsuga canadensis (eastern hemlock), **57**,
    352–53
    'Bennett', 352
    'Cole's Prostrate', 352, *352*
    'Hussii', 352
    'Moon Frost', 352
    'Pendula' (Sargentii), 352–53, *353*
    pests, 352
    'Westonigra', 353
Tsuga caroliniana (Carolina hemlock), 352,
    353
Tsuga heterophylla (western hemlock), 352,
    353
Tsuga mertensiana (mountain hemlock), 352,
    353
tulip tree (*Liriodendron tulipifera*), 26, 62, 135,
    274–75, *275*
tupelo (*Nyssa sylvatica*), *34*, **35**, **130**, *131*, **147**,
    288–89, *288*
tying up trees, 148

U

Ulmus species (elm)
    'Camperdownii', 354, *354*
    pruning, **111**
Ulmus americana (American elm), **147**,
    353–54
    diseases, 353
    'New Harmony', 354
    'Princeton', 354, *354*
    'Valley Forge', 354
Ulmus glabra, 'Camperdownii', 354, *354*
Ulmus parvifolia (Chinese elm), **36**, 355–56,
    356
    'Emerald Isle', 355
    'Emerald Vase', 355
umbrella pine (*Sciadopitys verticillata*), **58**,
    338, *338*

METRIC CONVERSIONS

For those of you using metric measurements, here are some basic conversion formulas:

Multiply inches x 2.54 to get centimeters
Multiply feet x .305 to get meters
Multiply yards x .9144 to get meters

Several Internet sites offer quick-and-easy conversions:

www.onlineconversion.com
www.worldwidemetric.com/Measurements